ANDBOOK OF WORK AND ORGANIZATIONAL PSYCHOLOGY

Volume 2: Work Psychology

15

'06

HANDBOOK OF WORK AND ORGANIZATIONAL PSYCHOLOGY

(Second Edition)
Volume 2: Work Psychology

Edited by

Pieter J.D. Drenth

Vrije Universiteit,
Amsterdam,
The Netherlands

Henk Thierry

Tilburg University,
The Netherlands

Charles J. de Wolff

Catholic University,
Nijmegen,
The Netherlands

Psychology Press
a member of the Taylor & Francis group

Psychology Press Ltd
27 Church Road
Hove
East Sussex, BN3 2FA, UK

British Library Cataloguing in Publication Data
A catalogue record for this title is available from the British Library

Volume 2
ISBN 0–86377–522–5 (Hbk)
ISBN 0–86377–523–3 (Pbk)

Cover illustration by Clive Goodyer
Cover design by Rachael Adams
Typeset by Mendip Communications Ltd, Frome, Somerset
Printed and bound in the United Kingdom by Redwood Books Ltd,
Trowbridge, Wilts, UK

Contents

Contributors to Volume 2

Jacques T. Allegro, Universiteit Leiden, Faculteit Sociale Wetenschappen, Wassenaarseweg 52, 2333 AK Leiden, The Netherlands.

Johannes Gerrit Boerlijst, Rupperink 4, 7491 GR Delden, The Netherlands.

Bram P. Buunk, Universiteit Groningen, Faculteit Psychologische, Pedagogische, Sociologische Wetenschappen, Grote Kruisstraat 2/1, 9712 TS Groningen, The Netherlands.

Pieter J.D. Drenth, Vrije Universiteit, Faculteit Psychologie en Pedagogiek, Van der Boechorststraat 1, 1081 BT Amsterdam, The Netherlands.

Arne Evers, Universiteit van Amsterdam, Faculteit Psychologie, Roetersstraat 15, 1018 WB Amsterdam, The Netherlands.

Henk van der Flier, Vrije Universiteit, Faculteit Psychologie en Pedagogiek, Van der Boechorststraat 1, 1081 BT Amsterdam, The Netherlands.

David Fryer, Department of Psychology, University of Stirling, Stirling FK94 4LA, UK.

Beate van der Heijden, Universiteit Twente, Faculteit Technologie en Management, Postbus 217, 7500 AE Enschede, The Netherlands.

Patrick T.W. Hudson, Universiteit Leiden, Faculteit Sociale Wetenschappen, Wassenaarseweg 52, Postbus 9555, 2300 RB Leiden, The Netherlands.

Ben Jansen, ATOS, Beleidsadries en-onderzoek BV, Gelderland plein 75d, 1082 LV Amsterdam, The Netherlands.

Jan de Jonge, Katholieke Universiteit Nijmegen, Faculteit Sociale Wetenschappen, Postbus 9104, 6500 HE Nijmegen, The Netherlands.

Theo F. Meijman, Universiteit Groningen, Faculteit Psychologische, Pedagogische, Sociologische Wetenschappen, Grote Kruisstraat 2/1, 9712 TS Groningen, The Netherlands.

Gijsbertus Mulder, Universiteit Groningen, Faculteit Psychologische, Pedagogische, Sociologische Wetenschappen, Grote Kruisstraat 2/1, 9712 TS Groningen, The Netherlands.

Joep M.A. Munnichs, Katholieke Universiteit Nijmegen, Montessorilaan 3, 6525 HR Nijmegen, The Netherlands.

Theo Poiesz, Katholieke Universiteit Brabant, Faculteit Sociale Wetenschappen, Warandalaan 2, 5037 AB Tilburg, The Netherlands.

Andries F. Sanders, Vrije Universiteit, Faculteit Psychologie en Pedagogiek, Van der Boechorststraat 1, 1081 BT Amsterdam, The Netherlands.

Henk Thierry, Katholieke Universiteit Brabant, Faculteit Sociale Wetenschappen, Postbus 90153, 5000 LE Tilburg, The Netherlands.

Theo J. Veerman, ASTRI, Sationsweg 26, 2312 AV Leiden, The Netherlands.

Willem A. Wagenaar, Universiteit Leiden, Faculteit Sociale Wetenschappen, Wassenaarseweg 52, 2333 AK Leiden, The Netherlands.

Charles J. de Wolff, Gomarius Messtraat 19, Alverna, 6603 CS Wychen, The Netherlands.

Jan F. Ybema, Vrije Universiteit, Faculteit Psychologie en Pedagogiek, Van der Boechorststraat 1, 1081 BT Amsterdam, The Netherlands.

Harry L.G. Zanders, Katholieke Universiteit Brabant, Faculteit Sociale Wetenschappen, Postbus 90153, 5000 LE Tilburg, The Netherlands.

1

Introduction

Pieter J.D. Drenth

As was indicated in the general introduction given in Volume 1 each of the following three volumes has its own accent. The emphasis of this first volume is on the micro-world of the worker and his or her task. It comprises the many chapters from the classical tradition of work psychology, including human factors psychology or, as it is sometimes called, ergonomics. The history of "work psychology" goes back about a hundred years. In fact, it was the main area of research of the first pioneers in applied industrial psychology, such as Münsterberg, Viteles, Weimar, Lahy and others. Numerous studies have been carried out since the early beginning, and each year hundreds of articles and books have contributed to a substantial body of knowledge and a well established tradition in this particular area.

This is not to say that no new issues have emerged and that no new studies are or can be undertaken. As an example the more recent interest in welfare, health and safety in work organizations can be mentioned. New and stricter laws and regulations on health and safety conditions at the workplace have stimulated work and organization psychologists in many countries to (re)study their causes and conditions, to provide training and to develop measurement devices in the field of occupational health and welfare. Subjects like safety, occupational stress, workload and sickness absence, therefore, are given a predominant place in this volume. Likewise, specific attention will be given to problems in work organizations and the labour market which have received a lot of attention of the work psychologists lately and which will continue to do so in the near future. One can think of issues related to work and aging, the problems of ethnic diversity and the consequences of the loss of work and unemployment.

Meijman and Mulder open this volume with a chapter on psychological aspects of workload. In their contribution they develop a conceptual outline of the psychological study of workload in which two traditions are combined; the study of mental load and the study of physical load. In the former the emphasis is on the effects of the nature and level of information load on task performance, and the latter focuses on the effects of energetical and biomechanical processes on task performance and health.

In the third chapter Sanders illustrates how ergonomics distinguishes itself from work and organizational psychology in general, in having different roots (psychonomics, work physiology and engineering as opposed to psychometrics, personality and social psychology) on the one hand, but that it is an indispensable chapter in work and organizational psychology on the other.

Too often human factors are disregarded in the design of machines, tools and work systems, which causes (sometimes serious) errors and accidents. Further integration of the ergonomic tradition in work psychology will certainly lead to an enrichment of this domain of psychology.

In a chapter on industrial safety Wagenaar shows that this is not simply determined by the use of safe equipment, and is not merely the corollary of low accident statistics. Whilst accidents usually occur on the shop floor, this is not the only level at which they must be prevented. Safety is the consequence of a good safety policy, and practicably effective measures to this end should be initiated at the management level. Information about the effectiveness of such measures is only gained on the shop floor, however, where indications of latent faults become discernible. Safety is therefore the responsibility of every employee in the organization.

During recent decades an increasing desire, or even need, for far-reaching changes in the arrangement of working hours has arisen. This concerns not so much shorter hours—the source of much social conflict in the past—but rather different timetabling and greater flexibility. The question concerns not so much the employee's health (the traditional argument), but rather his or her need for free time and a changing work ethos. Thierry and Jansen provide an overview of the various different working arrangements, such as flexible hours, intensive working weeks, part-time work and temporary contracts, as well as different types of shift work. Both actual arrangements and the results of research into their effects are considered.

Allegro and Veerman provide an approach to sickness absence and long-term inability to work from a social-scientific perspective. In this respect, avoidable absenteeism—in which there is no direct and unambiguous question of unfitness for work—is of especial interest.

Although abseenteeism itself is easy to measure, it is a complex phenomenon which encompasses many factors at different levels: the narrow (personal circumstances), the intermediate (workplace circumstances and social factors) and the broad (legislation and social protection). Authors offer an explanatory framework of thinking, which also has practical relevance in terms of a possible preventive, threshold-raising and curative policy.

Buunk, De Jonge, Ybema and De Wolff highlight a long-recognized problem: the negative effects of the work situation upon health. Only during the past few decades has the term "health" been expanded to encompass mental health, and the influence of the psychosocial aspects of the working environment begun to be considered. The principal idea in this respect is stress. Given how central work is in many people's lives, the circumstances of and events at their work have the potential to create strongly negative emotions. The perspective offered in this chapter is socio-psychological, emphasizing the social factors involved in the development and processing of negative emotions which may arise from stress at work.

In the next three chapters three specific groups of employees are described who have deserved greater attention from psychologists recently. The first of these is the older worker, which is given attention in a contribution by Boerlijst, Munnichs and Van der Heijden. Older employees are a vulnerable group where prejudice associates with falling productivity, inflexibility and health problems. Using the literature and their own research, the authors discuss whether these and other widely held opinions about older workers are justified, whether any other—positive—qualities counteract them, and in what ways the mobility and employment of older employees can be encouraged. In this respect, the importance of social support from leaders and colleagues is pointed out. The need for more longitudinal career research is also underlined.

In the next chapter Fryer provides an analysis of the psychological consequences of a phenomenon which has unfortunately become much more common in recent years: unemployment. The literature on this subject specifies a large number of physical and psychological complaints, including anxiety, depression, passivity, isolation, and a loss of self-esteem and hope, as well as various health problems. The author considers the extent to which empirical findings support these supposed consequences. His critical analysis shows that unemployment is indeed the cause of many of the psychological changes cited, although there are great differences between individuals as regards their experiences of and the consequences of unemployment.

Evers and Van der Flier discuss the position of a third specific group in work organizations: foreign workers, often including large numbers of refugees, immigrants and ethnic minorities. The position of this category on the labour market in most Western countries is quite unfavourable: high unemployment, low level of education and training, high turnover, and specific cultural and attitudinal traditions that hinder an easy and smooth integration in the local work culture. Authors give a comprehensive overview of the various problems related to the proper assessment of the capacities and skills of these "allochthonous" workers, and try to indicate ways to achieve an optimal balance between economic efficacy and a fair treatment of this vulnerable category of personnel.

The last two chapters in this volume deal with two domains that are somewhat distinct from, but at the same time conceptually closely linked to work psychology. The first deals with human economic behaviour. Poiesz convincingly shows that economic psychology is to be distinguished from economics. Both focus upon economic phenomena; however, the psychologist does so considering individual behaviour as their determi-

nant, whereas the economist considers an "aggregated" level: economic phenomena and processes on a large scale. In this contribution, it is shown that—with their different perspectives—organizational and economic psychologists are clearly complementary.

In Chapter 12 Zanders pays attention to a movement that is strongly based on work psychological insights, namely the attempt to describe and to evaluate large and complex systems, such as modern companies, in terms of social and human indicators. Traditionally these descriptions and evaluations were made using economic models. During the 1960s and 1970s, however, a demand arose for more than simple economic information. This was the beginning of the development of social indicator systems. A variety of models and parameters, built upon insights from social work psychology, were developed. Zanders provides an overview of the nature and evaluative possibilities of such systems, and the way they have been applied in social policy making.

Together the 12 chapters in this volume try to present a comprehensive overview of the relevant issues and achievements in the domain of work psychology; a domain with a long and established tradition, but in which also novel and new-sprung issues are raised and are being studied.

2

Psychological Aspects of Workload

Theo F. Meijman and Gijsbertus Mulder

1 INTRODUCTION

Working activities are always productive in more than one respect. Concrete or imaginary objects are converted into a product as a result of working activities and in performing the activities people are altered. The outcome may be positive, i.e. the task has been completed successfully and people have developed their skills or have found satisfaction through working activities. However, the outcome of work may also fail to meet the standards specified in the work assignment or a person's state may take a turn for the worse in performing the task. Positive outcomes are not likely to be associated with the term "load", although meeting task demands is always taxing and requires effort, for demands are made on the abilities and on the willingness to dedicate these abilities to the task. Thus, exposure to task demands does not necessarily have to be conceived of as a predominantly negative process, although it usually is. The term workload tends to be associated with decrements in performance or willingness to perform, or with the risk of impair-

ment of the well-being and health of the task operator. We will adhere to this convention.

The study of mental load focuses traditionally on decrements in performance due to changes in the nature and level of the information load of a specific task (Gopher & Donchin, 1986). In the study of physical load the emphasis is much more on the energetical and biomechanical processes in task performance, and their effects on health and well-being (Rohmert, 1983). In this chapter we shall present an outline of a conceptual framework of the work psychological study of workload that includes both aspects. Thereto a scheme is being developed which will be called the "effort-recovery" model. It is rooted in the classical frame of thought of exercise physiology and elaborates its prevailing concepts on the basis of insights from work psychology and occupational medicine.

2 THE CLASSICAL MODEL

2.1 Load and capacity

The classical frame of thought for the study of workload stems from exercise physiology. In The

Netherlands it is referred to as the "load-capacity" model (Burger, 1959; Bonjer, 1965; Ettema, 1973). In this model, load refers to a threatening disruption of the balance of certain physiological systems due to task performance or environmental influences. According to Ettema (1967) this threat will induce physiological responses which can be viewed as compensation mechanisms. He gives the example of a raised energy output needed to shift a heavy object. To be able to meet this demand, a raised energy uptake and transport are needed to keep the energy in the body at the required level. One of the physiological responses that does just that is an accelerated heart rate, as it enables the organism through compensation to maintain the threatened energy balance.

The load-capacity model distinguishes several concepts that in a modified or unmodified form are of interest to the work psychological study of workload. It concerns the concepts' external load or objective task demands, functional load and effort, capacity, and maximum capacity. External load comprises all external factors that stem from the task contents, task organization and work conditions, and give rise to responses of the organism. The effort expended by the organism to maintain the balance disturbed by a concrete external factor can be inferred from the responses of the physiological systems that are affected by that factor and play a role in the compensation mechanisms. These responses are referred to as functional load. They provide information on the exercise or effort that is needed to perform the task. Their nature and intensity depend on the person's capacity, which can be expressed as the percentage of maximum capacity. The latter is understood to mean (Zielhuis, 1967; Ettema, 1973) the maximum external load which, with a given work form, an individual is able to cope with or can endure during a certain period of time, which is still followed by full recovery. As both entities, i.e. external load and maximum capacity, are expressed in the same units, the percentage of maximum capacity can be represented by a ratio. As long as the percentage is more than zero the person is expending effort, which will show in changes in the relevant functional load parameters. With a percentage below one, the person remains within the limits of his own competence

and no negative effects need to occur. For then the external load does not exceed the maximum capacity. However, if the percentage exceeds the value one, a situation of overload will arise with the risk of negative effects. A similar situation may arise, if a certain exercise or level of effort has to be maintained for longer than an acceptable period of time. Thus, negative effects depend on the relationship between the external load and maximum capacity, and on the time during which the effort is exerted. Less well-trained people are, also depending on their age, unable or unwilling to cycle at 70% of their maximum capacity on a bicycle ergometer for much more than 15 minutes (Astrand & Rodahl, 1986). Van der Sluis and Dirken (1970) calculated that, in the energetical model, a percentage of maximum capacity of about 33% during an 8.5 hour working day is acceptable to industrial workers.

In the sixties Kalsbeek (1967) and Ettema (1967) applied this conceptual framework, which was originally constructed for energetical load, to the study of mental load. The latter focuses primarily on the demands made on the human information processing system. External load should be expressed in units relevant to this specific form of load, such as the number of signals per time unit that has to be reacted to, or the number of decisions needed to arrive at the proper solution for a certain task in relation to the available time. Functional load could be inferred from the changes in the functional systems that in one way or another are related to the mental processes of interest. On the basis of such indicators statements could be made about the mental effort needed to perform a particular information processing task. In their study Kalsbeek and Ettema used a classical indicator, i.e. the variability of the heart rhythm. Since the end of the last century this entity has played a role in the psychophysiological study of mental processes (Meijman et al., 1989). In the eighties Mulder (G. Mulder, 1980) and Mulder (L. Mulder, 1988) refined this measure and developed it into a standard indicator in the study of mental effort.

2.2 Elaborations of the classical model

The classical "load-capacity" conceptual framework has been criticized and supplemented at various points from the perspective of occupational medicine as well as work psychology. Meijman and O'Hanlon (1983), Kuiper (1985), Kompier (1988) and Van Dijk et al. (1990) commented on the classical conceptual framework and proposed changes for various parts. The objections mainly pertain to the static character of the model and its too little relevance to the practice of occupational medicine. We will discuss a number of these objections, because they are relevant to the work psychological conceptual framework for the study of workload that will be developed below.

2.2.1 The controversial concept of maximum capacity

The strength of the classical model is its quantitative character. However, in practice this is also its weakness. This can best be illustrated by a discussion of the concept of maximum capacity. Maximum capacity is a normative concept which in the classical model is operationalized in a specific way, i.e. the maximum external load which is still followed by complete recovery. Thus strictly defined, maximum capacity can be calculated on the conditions that the external load can be determined quantitatively and the quantified relationship is known between the functional load indicator studied and the load process of interest. In addition, the situations of maximum effort and complete recovery must be identifiable. This ideal is approximated in the energetical model, because it allows the load process to be measured directly by means of changes in the oxygen uptake. In practice the load process can be measured indirectly by means of changes in the heart rate, provided that its relationship is known with the individual's oxygen uptake in a standardized test for the determination of the maximum capacity, e.g. a test on the bicycle ergometer. If the latter proves impossible, more or less insurmountable difficulties will arise as a consequence of which we have to make use of all kinds of indirect parameters. For all other forms of load, including biomechanical load and information load, it has as yet not been possible to determine, even by approximation, the maximum capacity of an individual in consistency with the definition from the classical load-capacity model. In practice the

concept of maximum capacity has therefore mainly a heuristic value.

2.2.2 A static model

In the classical model the individual is regarded as a physiologically actively responding organism. In all other respects the individual appears to be a rather passive receiver and an easy target of external factors, irrespective of his work style, motives and attitudes. Thus, the classical model falls short of an illusion, viz. that the maximum capacity in a strict sense is in fact determinable. The classical model did recognize this. Kalsbeek & Ettema (1964) remarked that apart from the level of external load, the functional load is determined by numerous other factors with the willingness to actually expend the required effort being of major importance. According to Ettema (1967), it is not the maximum capacity but the willingness to spend capacity or the "Leistungsbereitschaft" (Graf, 1954; Lehmann, 1962) which is commonly determined. The energetical model allows for a reasonably adequate determination of whether someone has done his utmost by means of the measured oxygen uptake in relation to the observed heart rate. But then again, this is more or less the only model that allows such determination.

2.2.3 Work potential, work procedure and decision latitude

In an attempt to meet the above-mentioned problems, Meijman and O'Hanlon (1983) introduced the concept of work potential, therewith recognizing the fact that outside the energetical model the concept of maximum capacity has very little formal meaning. Its use had, therefore, better be restricted to this model. In addition, a concept like work potential does do better justice to the dynamic facets of the interaction between the working human and the demands work makes on him. The question is not so much whether someone is able to cope with certain demands, but rather whether someone is able to expend the effort at any given moment to meet these demands and with what intensity someone is willing to do so. Work potential seems here the more appropriate term.

In the interaction between person and demands

the adopted work procedure is important as it determines what abilities are deployed and the way in which this is done (Sperandio, 1972; Hacker, 1973; Bainbridge, 1974). It in turn determines the character of the load and its ensuing effects. That is to say, the adopted work procedure is a necessary link between the demands that are made and the abilities the working person has to mobilize at any moment to meet the demands. In the classical load-capacity model this was hardly taken into account. By now, partly because of work psychological considerations (Hacker, 1978), the load-capacity model has been adapted as to this aspect in the work physiology literature (Rohmert, 1983, 1984).

Endorsement of the importance of the work procedure raises the question as to what extent the task assignment and the work situation allow the operator to regulate the job demands and to adjust the work procedure when he/she considers this necessary. As said above, the classical model hardly takes such varieties into account, although in practice they are the rule rather than the exception. Hence, the study of workload in real task situations requires information on this matter (Van Dijk et al., 1990). In particular the study of work stress has pointed to the importance of decision latitude in work situations. Its effective use is not only important to the quality and level of the performance to be made (Fisher, 1986; Frese, 1987), it is also an essential link in the etiology of health and well-being problems ensuing from workload (Karasek & Theorell, 1990; Johnson & Johansson, 1991).

2.2.4   The relevance to health
In its original form the classical conceptual framework failed to work out the role of workload in the etiology of health and well-being problems. Kompier (1988) and Meijman (1988), among others, elaborated it into a cumulative process model of workload-related health outcomes. The core idea of this model is that the momentaneous compensation responses (functional load phenomena) can develop into negative load effects under the influence of continued exposure to work demands and insufficient recovery. Such load effects show initially as detriments to well-being and perceived health and in the long run even as manifest losses of function, health impairment or illness.

3   THE EFFORT-RECOVERY MODEL

The conceptual framework presented in this section gives an elaboration of the load-capacity model in which the above-mentioned comments are incorporated.

The work psychological study of workload is based on the premise that people will always try to interfere actively in their work situation and environment when confronted with certain demands. To avoid passive exposure, they always adopt a certain work procedure. What procedure will be adopted, depends on: (1) the character and the level of the demands, (2) the decision latitude the situation allows, (3) the level of knowledge and skills, and the willingness to meet the demands and to exercise control, and (4) the current psychophysiological state of the task operator. At a mental level the work procedure is controlled by a plan of action or strategy. Such a strategy may differ for the same work assignment, not only between persons but also within a person from situation to situation (Matern, 1984; Hacker, 1986). Figure 2.1 presents a scheme which summarizes these various aspects and which may serve as a conceptual framework for the work psychological study of workload. The scheme is an elaboration of a framework that was presented earlier (Meijman, 1988, 1989).

The scheme distinguishes three determinants: (1) the actual level of the task demands and the environmental factors, summarized in the scheme under the term "work demands", (2) the actual mobilization of work abilities and effort, summarized in the scheme under the term "work potential", and (3) decision latitude. Together these three factors determine the work procedure, which in turn results in two kinds of outcome: the product and the short-term physiological and psychological reactions. The product is the tangible result of work activities. It is always evaluated in some way or another by standards and regulations that are implicitly or explicitly included in the original work assignment. As has been argued in the discussion of the classical load-capacity model (see section 2.1), the short-term physiological and psychological reactions can be seen as adaptive

FIGURE 2.1

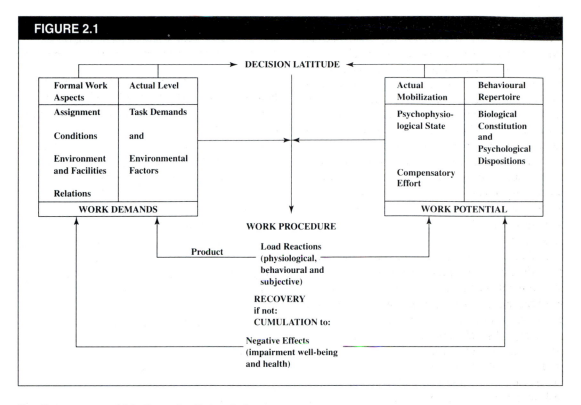

The effort-recovery model (further explanation see text).

responses. In the practice of the study of workload, the short-term reactions include all the responses at a physiological, behavioural and subjective level that can be related to the load process. These reactions are in principle reversible. When the exposure to load ceases, the respective psycho-biological systems will stabilize again at a specific baseline level within a certain period of time. This process is called recovery. In the practice of load research, the baseline level is assessed by means of measurements in a situation in which no special demands are made on the operator. It is then assumed that the operator has recovered completely from possible previous loads and that no demands are currently made on the systems under study.

Destabilization during the load process of the psycho-biological systems concerned involves changes in the psychophysiological state of the operator. These changes induce feedback to the actual mobilization of abilities and thereby to the effort to be made. Under the influence of behavioural changes in reaction to load, also fluctuations

in the character and the actual level of task demands and environmental factors may occur. Hence, the scheme in Figure 2.1 shows feedback to occur from the short-term reactions to the actual level of the task load. Section 4.2.2 will give some relevant examples.

A still functional adaptation response to a single and moderate load can develop through continued exposure and insufficient recovery into negative load effects, which may persist for a longer period of time or may even become irreversible. An (extremely) high momentaneous load can have similar effects. So the (negative) load effects are related to less transitory or even permanent symptoms that manifest themselves as a consequence of continued exposure to one or more load factors as more structural, negative changes of physiological or psychological functions. They bring about changes in the biological constitution and in the psychological dispositions. Thus, feedback takes place to work potential. In Figure 2.1 feedback is also shown to occur from the load effects to the work demands block. At first sight, this seems an unlikely relationship. However, load effects developed as a result of previous workloads, may in turn be conditional to the acceptability or "bearableness" of certain work aspects. This is very clearly illustrated in the situation in which an impairment has developed, which leads to functional limitations, which in turn results in a handicap in certain work situations. Thus, a back injury due to heavy physical work may render a person unsuitable for work on a forklift truck because of its mechanic vibrations affecting the back (Bongers & Boshuizen, 1990; Verbeek, 1991). Other examples are chronic stress complaints or depressive complaints due to mentally demanding work (Schellart et al., 1989, 1990), which make people less suitable to work under a high production pressure or without socio-emotional contacts and support.

In the next section we will discuss the various determinants and effects separately while also paying attention to the various forms of feedback presented in Figure 2.1.

4   WORK DEMANDS

4.1. Formal aspects of the work situation

The following formal aspects of the work situation are distinguished: work assignment, work conditions, work environment and facilities, and work relations.

The work assignment specifies the result of the work activities as well as the standards the result should meet. However, the specifications are often vague and the standards will often become clear only after the task has been completed. This vagueness may in itself function as a stress factor of the work situation. The work conditions concern the agreements regarding the assignment. The most important are the remuneration and the various time aspects, like production times, length of a working day, break schedules and the (ir)regularity in work-rest schedules. Remunerative aspects play a key role in regulating the work activities and the appreciation of their results (Thierry & de Jong, 1991; see also Volume 3, Chapter 8 and Volume 4, Chapter 12 of this Handbook) and therewith in the willingness to

spend capacity on the work task and to exert the required effort. The study of the temporal aspects of a work task provides the foundation for workload research. For this study can be used to determine the duration and intensity of the exposure to various load factors, as well as the periods of time between different kinds of exposures and the opportunities for recovery. The work environment and facilities concern the available aids and tools as well as aspects of the design of the workplace, the physical and chemical factors in the work situation, hygiene, canteens, etc. Work relations involve social and organizational aspects, such as hierarchical relationships, contacts with colleagues, etc.

4.2   Task demands and environmental factors

Task demands are the manifestations of the above-mentioned aspects in a concrete situation. They can be formulated as formal work aspects: "such and such has to be done", "within such and such a time", etc. At the same time task demands have to be considered from the perspective of the demand they make on the work abilities and their mobilization. Each study of workload sets out to determine the task demands for which various methods of task analysis are available (Karg & Staehle, 1982; Drury et al., 1987; Landau & Rohmert, 1989; Algera, 1991; Van Ouwerkerk et al., 1994).

Task demands are always met in a specific environment. Partly the environmental factors are stucturally determined by the formal aspects of the work situation, e.g. the physical-chemical factors inherent to the production process concerned. For another part they are coincidental, like the temperature of today, the burst of noise outside, someone having a bee in his bonnet, etc. Load research should also establish the character and level of these environmental factors. Ergonomics and industrial hygiene have thereto developed methods appropriate for workplace analysis (Klinkhamer, 1979; Schuffel, 1989; Van der Heide & Kragt, 1989; Voskamp, 1994).

4.2.1   Some complications

Classical theories in work psychology assumed that there is a one to one relationship between work demands and abilities or mental functions needed to meet these demands. As early as 1928 Baumgarten discussed the naivety of this theory. She argued that because of compensation mechanisms people may meet the same demands in completely different ways with similar results, without resorting to the same skills and mental processes. The relationship between the demands and abilities depends on the work procedure followed. This has at least two important consequences for the practice of the psychological study of workload. First, a task taxonomy based on basic abilities (Fleishman & Quaintance, 1984) is of limited value when it has not been established whether the abilities in question are indeed involved in the task performance, as different abilities may be involved in different working procedures with the same results. Second, the complication in the relationship between demands and abilities poses a methodological problem (Bainbridge, 1974). It concerns the distinction between external load and functional load. This distinction may be important from an analytical point of view, but in practice it may be hard to maintain. Thus, it is quite common to define mental load in terms of a specific information processing mode: the attention-demanding or controlled mode (see also section 5.2). The mental task load could then be determined on the basis of the time during which, in the task performance, demands are made on this particular processing mode (Mulder, 1980). As a consequence it is impossible to determine load independent of the way the task is performed and the mental processes involved in the performance. This poses a special problem which can probably best be illustrated by an example taken from Gopher & Donchin (1986). Under normal conditions, most of us are able to walk a 1-foot-wide plank that is placed just above the floor. However, if the plank is suspended between two houses at 50 feet, the same task will require much more effort and may even be impossible. The load decreases if we do not have to walk the plank between the houses upright but try to reach the other side of the street on all fours. For someone who has had too much to drink, the task will be impossible to perform even if the plank is laid on the floor. In short, the context in which a specific demand is made, makes a lot of

difference to the question of load in work psychology. So, load is a relative notion, in which the external load and the capacity to meet the ensuing demands can hardly be defined independent of one another.

4.2.2   Fluctuation of work demands

One of the practical consequences of the above-mentioned is that the task demands and environmental factors cannot be regarded as static factors in the study of workload. Fluctuations in the demands may be coincidental. A catch in the production process may occur occasionally, or today it is warmer than yesterday. Such influences are usually regarded as "error-variance". There is no objection to that if it indeed concerns coincidental fluctuations. However, it becomes objectionable if fluctuations in the task demands and the environmental factors are related to changes in the state of the operator that result from the work activities themselves. This will be illustrated by some examples. The design of office furniture may meet anthropometrical standards. However, fatigue developed in the course of the task performance makes people change their posture behind the word processor, thus disturbing the optimal ergonomical proportions. As a consequence all kinds of load effects can develop which may manifest themselves among other things as backpain and headache. Another example is taken from industrial toxicology. The uptake of dust particles through the bronchial tubes depends, among other things, on the frequency and depth of breathing. Changes in breathing, e.g. due to physical exertion, also result in changes in the uptake of dust particles even if repeated environmental monitoring measures the same concentrations in the work room. Industrial toxicology distinguishes, therefore, between environmental exposure and intake versus internal exposure and uptake, or the concentration of a substance as measured in a room versus the levels of uptake and circulation in the body (Zielhuis & Henderson, 1986). Behavioral factors, connected among other things with differences in working procedures between people, play a vital role in the relationship between environmental exposure and intake (Van Dijk et al., 1988). Ulenbelt (1991) showed that the uptake of lead dust with the same environmental concentrations in the work room may differ considerably between people depending on person-related and task-related differences in working procedures and related hygienic work behaviour.

5 WORK POTENTIAL

5.1 Introduction

The demands people are confronted with at work may stem from very different sources. They have in common that they always activate the adaptive systems of the organism. Relevant to the present discussion are those adaptive systems that play a role in the mental functioning or the information processing in a broad sense. This does not merely include perception and cognition, but also the emotional, motivational and psychomotor aspects of information processing. Two kinds of adaptive systems are important, i.e. the computational and the energetical processes in information processing (Mulder, 1979, 1986; Sanders, 1981 and 1983; Hockey, 1993; Revelle, 1993). Computational processes pertain to the storage of information and the operations executed on it. They include processes that receive input information, transform it and process it further. Energetical processes play a role in making and keeping computational processes available, given the individual's current mental and physical state. They pertain to the intensity of information processing and to its emotional and motivational control. That is to say, knowledge of computational processes is needed to answer the question whether someone is able to cope with a certain task, or has the competence to do so. Capacity and attention are central notions in the concept of competence. To answer the question about the willingness to perform requires knowledge of energetical processes. Central to willingness are notions like effort and the costs at which an effort is made.

5.2 Computational processes

The information that reaches us through the senses is subjected to a series of operations before it results in a specific, overt or covert reaction. Theories on the architecture of the system in which these processes take place, distinguish three kinds of memories, i.e. the sensoric memory, the long-term memory and the working memory (see for overviews Kyllonen & Alluisi, 1987; Cowan, 1988). Information enters the sensoric memory. This is a very short-term memory, that retains the information in a more or less sensory form for a few seconds. This raw information is then identified, coded and processed further in the working memory of which the main feature is its limited capacity. In discussions on the working memory, the notion of attention plays a key role (see section 5.2.2). In the long-term memory knowledge is stored in a sort of dormant form.

Research into the electric and magnetic activities of the brain and the cerebral blood flow during information processing tasks showed it to be possible to identify the brain mechanisms that are mobilized during the performance of computational processes (Mulder et al., 1989; Wijers, 1989; Kosslyn & Koenig, 1992; Posner & Raichle, 1994). A considerable number of these computational processes are not accessible to consciousness. They are fast and automatic. They cannot be made measurable by subjective methods, and only partly so by behavioural methods through reaction time research. In contrast, computational processes that appeal to the working memory are slower and partly accessible through self-reports.

5.2.1 Long-term memory

The long-term memory comprises two forms of knowledge: declarative and procedural knowledge (Anderson, 1993). Declarative knowledge comprises the "what" of our knowledge. In a network with knowledge elements as nodes, this knowledge is stored in an organized way (Tulving, 1991). The declarative memory has a hierarchical structure and its central representation form is directed at concepts and schemes (Rumelhart & Ortony, 1977). They reflect the contents of the statement or the general meaning of an occurrence rather than the surface structure of the original message. On the basis of concepts and schemes it is possible to draw inferences that were not part of the original message or occurrence.

Procedural knowledge comprises the "how" of our knowledge. We know how to ride a bicycle, how to comb our hair, etc. Most of the time this knowledge is hard to explain to others. Habituation and other forms of conditioning are examples of procedural learning. Procedural knowledge can best be represented in terms of "if-then" or "condition-action" rules. The entire set of such rules for a certain task is referred to as a production-system. The if-part of the production does not need to be task-specific but may comprise a general aspect. In such a case a general rule or action programme has been developed that can be applied in different situations. There are indications that the declarative memory and the procedural memory make use of different brain mechanisms (Squire, 1987) and that the declarative memory develops later in the ontogeny than the procedural memory.

5.2.2 Working memory

All information that is subjected to momentary cognitive processes is part of the working memory. Working memory is the locus of attention-demanding operations, like (1) selecting information that needs attention, (2) scanning the current contents of the working memory itself, (3) retaining relevant information in working memory for a short period of time, and (4) searching for information in the declarative memory.

The central notion with regard to working memory is attention. Its meaning is best illustrated by two metaphors: the metaphor of the search light (Cowan, 1988, 1993) and the metaphor of the resource (Navon & Gopher, 1979; Wickens, 1991 and 1994). The former describes attention as some sort of light beam with the thing we are currently conscious of at its focus. Everything within the light beam is processed, whether we want it or not, and everything outside the light beam is not processed. The search light metaphor emphasizes the indivisibility of attention, while the resource metaphor emphasizes its divisibility. Performing mental tasks involves various mental operations, such as perceiving, repeating the information perceived and interpreted thus to avoid loss from working memory, selecting and programming movements, etc. Performing all these activities requires certain resources. Because the capacity of these resources is limited, the resource metaphor explains the failure to perform simultaneously two or more tasks that appeal to the same resources.

However, if there is sufficient reserve capacity, two or more tasks can be combined successfully. According to some theoretical models, each processing stage can fall back on a general, limited-capacity resource (Moray, 1967; Kahneman, 1973). Only then the term reserve capacity is aptly used (Kantowitz, 1987). Other models assume that each stage or cluster of stages has command over its own resource which is basically not interchangeable with the resource of a different stage or cluster of stages (Navon & Gopher, 1980; Gopher, 1986). Finally, there are also hierarchical models (Sanders, 1981, 1983; Mulder, 1986) which assume that in addition to stage-specific resources there is also a general, non-stage-specific resource.

At all of these points the theory is still being developed; therefore its main value is at present of a heuristic nature. It is, however, generally accepted that information in the working memory may assume two codes, i.e. acoustic or spatial (Wickens, 1987). These codes seem to involve two subsystems that hardly interfere with one another. New spatial information interferes with present spatial information and the same applies to acoustic information. Furthermore, if nothing is done with it, information in the working memory declines rapidly.

5.2.3 Processing modalities

The distinction between automatized and controlled cognitive processes, which dates as far back as 1890 (James, 1890), has had a considerable influence on the development of the theory on mental load. The seventies showed a revival of this distinction (Shiffrin & Schneider, 1977). Controlled processes comprise a sequence of nodes in the long-term memory which is temporarily activated in working memory. This occurs under the influence of a central executive system which directs the attention and has a limited capacity. In principle only one such sequence can be activated at a time. In sum, controlled cognitive processes require attention, they are relatively slow, flexible, (consciously) controlled by the person, and serial.

An automatized process can be seen as a more or less permanent sequence of closely integrated associative links in the long-term memory that becomes active only in response to a specific input configuration. Practice under consistent conditions leads to automatization and renders the task increasingly independent of the limited-capacity systems of working memory. Dominant features of the automatized processes are: (1) the high speed and the limited variability of the activity, (2) the stimulus-specific character of the activity, (3) the uncontrollability of the process, once the process has been started, it is hard to slow it down or stop it, and (4) the decreased cognitive effort.

5.2.4   Cognitive processing levels

Work tasks differ as to the level in which they appeal to the attention-demanding operations in working memory and make use of knowledge from the declarative memory and the procedural memory. That is to say, they differ in the degree of mental effort that has to be spent in the task performance. In this respect work tasks can be classified into three broad categories of processing levels: skill-based, rule-based, and knowledge-based (Hacker, 1973; Rasmussen, 1987).

The processing level is called rule-based when the task performance is chiefly based on the application of general rules or relatively uniform action programmes in otherwise varying situations. It mainly employs knowledge from the procedural memory. Tasks performed at this level require some, but not excessive, mental effort. If a concrete stimulus situation usually yields the same response, the process can be automatized. Such automatization is the result of a mostly long-term learning process under consistent conditions. The task performance is then called "skill-based". In such cases, the various parts of the task performance require little to no mental effort. In contrast, tasks performed at a "knowledge-based" level appeal strongly to the knowledge in the declarative memory and to the attention-demanding (controlled) processes in working memory. Such tasks cannot be performed without expending mental effort.

The level of processing is determined by the variability of the work task in the situation concerned. This is characterized by three features (Matern, 1984; de Vries-Griever, 1989): (1) the stability of the working situation, (2) the number of task elements, and (3) the complexity of the relationships between the various task elements. The first feature pertains to the variability of the work assignment and the performance conditions. The second feature concerns the number of subtasks or elements of the task assignment concerned. The third characteristic involves the relationships between the various task elements. Important questions in this respect are: Is the order of the relationships always fixed, thereby guiding the course of action in the work situation, or, do their mutual relationships differ from situation to situation according to relatively complicated, and possibly unpredictable patterns? Tasks that have little stable assignments and comprise many different task elements with complex mutual relationships will require a "knowledge-based" level of processing. In such cases procedural knowledge will be hard to acquire and the operator will have to make a sustained appeal to the declarative knowledge and attention-demanding operations in working memory. The same applies to new situations or to tasks that are difficult to learn. In general, a "rule-based" level of processing is possible when a task consists of a limited number of elements with little complicated and relatively stable, mutual relationships. Stable situations in which the task elements have a fixed relationship and are more or less automatized or can be performed "absent-mindedly" generally allow for a "skill-based" level of processing.

5.2.5   Changing processing levels

The same work task is not always performed at the same processing level. This depends on: (1) the available time, (2) the level of the task demands, (3) the changes in the situational context, and (4) the psychophysiological state of the operator.

It should be noted that people often get satisfaction from performing tasks at a "knowledge-based" level. This is most evident in people who in order to relax solve complicated puzzles, chess problems, and so on. So, exerting mental effort in itself does not necessarily have to lead to negative effects. The risk becomes manifest only if the task demands exceed or threaten to exceed the capacity of the required computational processes. For then there is a conflict between the task load and the processing capacity. Whether this will occur in real task situations depends very much on the

2. PSYCHOLOGICAL ASPECTS OF WORKLOAD   15

relationship between the time needed for a proper task performance on a "knowledge-based" level and the available time. This relationship is affected by the task demands, as higher demands tend to require more processing time. It is also likely to be affected by changes in the performance conditions, e.g. noise during tasks that require a relatively high level of concentration. The relationship may also change when in addition to the main task, secondary tasks require the operator's attention. And finally, the relationship may be affected by changes in the state of the operator him/herself, as a consequence of which the actual level of performance capacity and/or willingness to perform may be lowered.

In general, it can be said that changes in the work procedure will occur when the task load and the processing capacity are or threaten to be in conflict. These changes come down to the operator trying to switch to a different level of cognitive processing: from "knowledge-based" to "rule-based" or to "skill-based" (Hacker, 1973). Thus the operator will try to keep the mental effort needed to perform the task within limits and still reach an acceptable performance (Welford, 1978). The possibility of making such a switch and its effectivity depend on control over the stringency of the task demands and the standards regarding the quality and the quantity of the product, in particular the temporal aspects. That is to say, having and exercising control is of overriding importance in the protection against mental (over) load, which the operator can get at his disposal by changing to another work procedure.

Various studies may illustrate the above-mentioned aspects. The first example pertains to a switch in processing levels during the performance of the same task in relation to fluctuations in the task load. Coeterier (1971) and Sperandio (1972) investigated the work procedures of air traffic controllers subjected to fluctuations in the number of airplanes to guide down. With a relatively low number of planes, they made them approach in complicated patterns thus to get each plane down in the most efficient way. While doing so the air traffic controllers deployed flexible, "knowledge-based" strategies. This requires a relatively high level of mental effort and is possible only with not too high a workload so that

each plane can be given individual attention. When asked in Coeterier's study, the air traffic controllers remarked that this was the most satisfying work procedure. With an increasing number of planes the work procedures changed. The air traffic controller switched to a procedure that treated all planes in a uniform pattern: "park in pancakes, have them fly in circles and get them in one after another". In this way the treatment of individual planes requires less attention because it meets an uniform rule. The work procedure has obtained a "rule-based" character. It protects the air traffic controller against overload, but it is little flexible towards individual planes and is perceived as less satisfying. Quite interestingly, Sperandio found also that less experienced air traffic controllers switch to "rule-based" strategies with a lower number of planes than their more experienced colleagues.

The study of fatigue provides other examples of such shifts in relation to changes in the state of the operator. In the course of a working day, with an objectively constant task load, crane drivers (Wendrich, 1973) are changing from a quite complicated, but flexible work procedure to a less complex and uniform procedure which makes a lesser appeal to attention-demanding information processing. Rasmussen & Jensen (1974) observed that fatigue made maintenance personnel change their search strategies for failures from complex and attention-demanding decision processes that could lead more quickly to a solution to work procedures that involve a sequence of successive and often mutually redundant, simple yes–no decisions. Holding (1983) described a similar phenomenon in a series of laboratory studies. The test tasks in these studies consisted of locating and repairing failures in an electrical circuit. To this end the subjects could apply alternative work procedures that differed in effort and expectable success. The more effortful work procedure resulted in a faster success. In separate sessions the subjects were made familiar with these alternative work procedures. The study showed that the subjects, under physical as well as mental fatigue conditions, both brought about by special pretreatments, preferred the work procedure that required less effort to the one that required more effort.

5.3 Energetical processes

5.3.1 Introduction

In the preceding section it has been argued that tasks require mental effort when in order to perform the task the operator has to appeal to the attention-demanding processes in working memory and to knowledge from declarative memory. In general, this will be the case when the operator does not have the required computational processes available, in situations that are new or hard to learn, and when the time is lacking to develop them. However, it may also involve relatively normal situations in which the operator lacks the necessary procedural knowledge or in which the current capacity of working memory is exceeded. The latter depends among other things on the psychophysiological state of the operator which may vary for a variety of reasons, e.g. because of psycho-biological factors such as circadian rhythms, or previous task loads with a subsequent deterioration of the work capacity and the willingness to perform (fatigue). These variations in the operator's state are closely linked to energetical processes.

5.3.2 Actual state and required state

Under some conditions, like fatigue or over-excitement, it takes more effort to concentrate or to divide attention between various task elements or to solve a difficult problem, etc. In such cases the state of the information-processing system is less than optimal for the performance of a certain task. That is to say, the computational processes vary as to their availability relative to the actual state of the information processing system. Therefore a distinction has to be made between the actual state of the information processing system and the required state or the state that is conditional to an optimal task performance (Hockey, 1984, 1986b).

The actual state varies because of a number of factors that are partly structurally given and partly situationally determined. Structurally given variations in the actual state are the result of circadian rhythms of numerous (psycho-)biological systems and differences between people in their physical states and psychological dispositions. The latter aspects can also vary within the individual over a longer period of time. Situational variations are determined predominantly by effects of previous activities and the experienced loads. Important factors in this respect are the length of the previous working time and the character of the tasks performed during that time, the load effects due to performance conditions, the time and quality of previous recovery, medicines and/or drug (ab)use, lack of sleep, and so on.

For the study of workload it is essential to find out whether, and if so to what degree, the actual state of the operator deviates from the required state. Both the searchlight and the resource metaphor include the notion that the operator's state affects the width of the searchlight and the available capacity, respectively. Thus, the width of the searchlight decreases as the arousal level increases, and vice versa. The resource metaphor assumes that the total capacity depends strongly on the level of arousal (Kahneman, 1973). Too high an arousal level, often caused by emotions, may lead to a decreased capacity.

5.3.3 Compensatory effort

The human information processing system disposes of various energetical mechanisms that play a role in making available the computational processes necessary for an adequate task performance (Hockey et al., 1986). They can be related to at least three aspects of information processing. The "arousal" mechanism would bring the input-related computational processes in a proper state, while the "activation" mechanism would do the same with the output-related computational processes. A third mechanism, the "effort-mechanism", is activated when the task demands attention and/or the actual state of the operator deviates from the required state (Pribram & McGuinness, 1975).

Tasks require mental effort when they appeal to central, attention-demanding processes in the working memory and to declarative knowledge. Tasks require compensatory effort when the actual state of the operator deviates strongly from the state needed for an optimal task performance. In both cases the effort mechanism is activated (Mulder, 1986). This self-regulatory activity can be observed by means of central as well peripheral physiological processes. If a task requires effort, which generally implies that it has to be performed at a knowledge-based level, and if cognitive control is possible, the so-called "effortful coping" will occur (Lundberg & Frankenhaeuser, 1980; Frankenhaeuser & Lundberg, 1985). This process is characterized by an elevated activity of the autonomous nervous system, in particular of the beta-sympathetic subsystem. This shows in, among other things, an accelerated heart rate, a raised systolic blood pressure, dilation of the pupils, and secretion of catecholamines, in particular adrenaline. As long as control is possible, thereby preventing the task demands from exceeding the possibilities of self-regulation, the effort will remain within acceptable limits. Effort expenditure will then be accompanied by positive affects. However, when the level of load becomes too high, as a consequence of which the mental task demands (threaten to) exceed the possibilities of self-regulation and the operator has trouble with mobilizing adequately the adaptive systems, a characteristic response can be observed that has a negative emotional charge and which is known as a tension response or a stress reaction. On the basis of findings from the Groningen study among city bus drivers (Meijman, 1989, 1991) this distinction will be elaborated on.

5.3.4 Changes in effort during real tasks

On two days (dayshift, 08.30–17.00 hours) 27 city bus drivers perform their normal task, i.e. both days they drive the same bus over the same trajectory. These two days, however, differ as to the number of passengers the bus drivers have to transport and the obstacles they are confronted with during the performance of their task. In other words, the level of the actual workload differs per day and per individual driver. Indices for the objective task load are: the number of passengers transported, and the time the driver has between arriving at the terminus and the start of his next ride. Both variables were measured while the drivers were working. In addition, various responses of the drivers were measured periodically while they were working. After each working hour the blood pressure was taken and the drivers scored their perceived work effort over the preceding hour on a rating scale (Zijlstra & Meijman, 1989). Before lunch and at the end of the working day urine samples were collected over the respect-ive preceding periods of about three and a half hours of working. These samples were analyzed as to the excretion rate of adrenaline and noradrena-line in urine. Immediately after the morning and afternoon working time the drivers also filled out a scale measuring fatigue, i.e. the SEB (Meijman, 1991), and the Groninger Adjective Checklist (Thayer, 1978, 1989; Dutch version Hellinga, 1985) regarding feelings of activation and tension. For each measure the difference scores were calculated between the two days. The correlations (rpm) between these difference scores are summarized in Figure 2.2, which differentiates between the morning and afternoon working periods.

The picture that emerges in the morning is that the various physiological measures are hardly related to the objective task load measures and the perceived effort score, while the physiological measures are interrelated and also correlate with the subjective measures at the end of the morning working period. The latter correlations are positive with feelings of activation and negative with feelings of tension. This seems to point to an "effortful coping" syndrome. At a subjective level this reflects in feelings of activation but not in feelings of fatigue and tension.

In the afternoon, when the drivers have already worked for half a day, a completely different picture emerges. The task load measures show a stronger interrelationship than in the morning. Both task load measures are related to the perceived work effort, with $r = + .46$ and $r = - .64$ respectively. The level of the latter correlation might indicate that the perceived effort score is mainly determined by the extent to which the driver fails to keep to his time schedule (time pressure). There is no direct relationship between the physiological responses during work and the objective task load. However, in contrast to the morning period, there is a relationship between the perceived effort score and the physiological responses during work. Thus, when a driver perceives of his task load as being more strenuous, the excretion rate of adrenaline and the systolic blood pressure are both elevated. This is consistent with the appraisal theories (Lazarus, 1966, 1991), which state that the subjective evaluation of situational factors is essential to the occurrence of

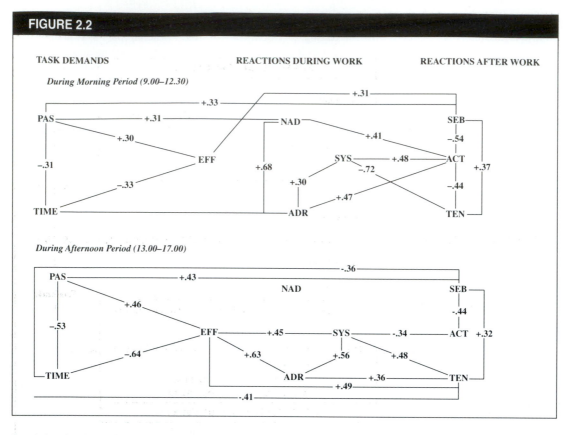

Correlations (rpm) of task demands, reactions during work and reactions after work. Computations on difference scores (working day A minus working day B) of 27 bus drivers. Only correlations .30 reported.
PAS = number of passengers; TIME = minutes of spare time between successive rides; EFF = perceived effort; NAD = excretion rate noradrenaline; ADR = excretion rate of adrenaline; SYS = systolic blood pressure; SEB = fatigue; ACT = activation; TEN = tension

tension reactions. The occurrence of these reactions in the afternoon may be inferred from the correlations between the physiological measures and the feelings of activation and tension immediately after the end of the working period. For, in contrast to the morning period, the elevated physiological reactions during the afternoon period do not relate to feelings of activation, but rather to feelings of tension. The "effortful coping" syndrome, as observed in the morning period, appears to be no longer present in the afternoon. This might be caused by the state of the operator being sub-optimal due to the work effort expended in the morning.

The above-mentioned findings illustrate an important insight into the meaning of physiological indicators in the work psychological study of load. Thus, it appears that, dependent on the psychophysiological state of the person and the duration of the load, the rise in adrenaline can either be related to the active mobilization of work capacities to meet the demands of the task situation, or may turn into a stress reaction with concomitant feelings of tension. Frankenhaeuser (1979) refers to these phenomena by "effort without distress", earlier called "effortful coping", and "effort with distress" respectively.

5.4 Computational and energetical processes: an integration
5.4.1 Self-regulation
People are able to regulate their activities efficiently. This self-regulation concerns both computational processes and energetical processes. These processes are schematically represented in Figure 2.3. The figure more or less

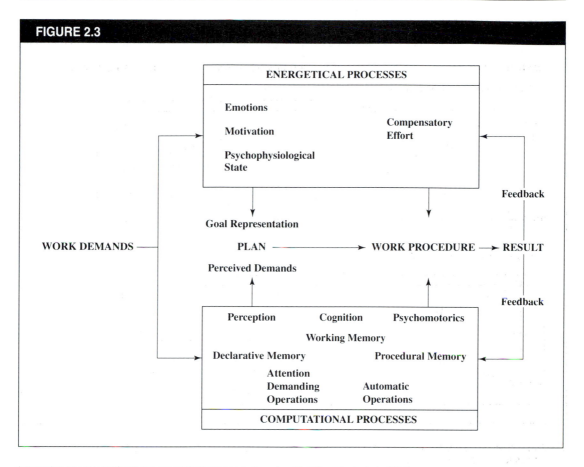

FIGURE 2.3

Integration of computational and energetical processes (based on Van Ouwerkerk et al., 1994).

summarizes the discussion so far of the various aspects of the processing capacity, and it is a more detailed elaboration of the effort-recovery model discussed earlier.

The work assignment specifies the goal of the activities. This goal has to be realized under certain working conditions. The result of the activities has to meet certain standards and temporal restraints. The stringency of such standards and restraints determines the level of decision latitude. Together, these factors determine the work demands on which the input into the system is based. The work demands are evaluated by the operator in terms of personal cognitions, experiences, skills, emotions and motivations. These evaluations yield a plan of action, in which at a mental level the specified goal and the demands are represented as an internal goal and perceived task demands, respectively. These representations

control the work procedure, which can be adjusted to possible changes in the computational and energetical processes due to performance. Such changes are effected on the basis of feedback from the result. The feedback is twofold. The realized product, or its different stages, are being compared to the representation of the work assignment and work conditions. And, the load effects, which develop during the performance, bring about changes with regard to both computational processes and energetics.

Feedback from the result to the computational system is conditional to explicit and implicit learning. In this way the meta-knowledge about our capacities to perform tasks is enhanced. Feedback to the energetical system can be related to the development of motivation and to the occurrence of positive and negative affects during the performance. In this context, the theory of

Carver and Scheier (1990) is important. According to this theory, during the performance continual comparisons are being made between the desired speed for obtaining a goal consistent with an intrapersonal standard and the actual speed with which the goal is obtained. If the actual speed is higher than the desired speed, positive affects would arise, while a lower actual speed would give rise to negative affects. The latter will occur if the time needed to perform a task or a task element would (threaten to) exceed the available time. They will also occur when the operator has to perform a task or a task element which exceeds the current capacity of the computational system and the time and/or possibilities to find solutions are lacking. In this respect, the occurrence of disturbances or interruptions in the work process is of great importance (Leitner et al., 1987), because with specified standards and times they can seriously slow down or even prevent the goal from being obtained.

5.4.2 Mental efficiency

With a given work assignment and under the present work conditions, self-regulation usually aims to maintain the required level of performance against an acceptable effort expenditure (Welford, 1953, 1978; Bainbridge, 1978). This efficiency point of view is of great relevance to the study of workload. As far as can be gathered, Dodge (1913) seems to have introduced this point of view in the study of task performance. Thorndike (1914) applies it in his discussion of the classical German study on mental fatigue. He pointed out that people are able to maintain the same level of performance by investing additional effort, even under extreme conditions like sleep deprivation or after hours of gruelling work. In contrast, they may fail to perform under conditions in which such failure is not expected. According to Thorndike, the question in the study of mental load and fatigue does not so much pertain to people's abilities to deliver a certain effort, but rather to their willingness to do so, and at what costs. In his opinion, the latter could best be measured by means of physiological arousal- and activation-measures. Although it seems an obvious thing to do, the efficiency point of view has been little applied in the study of mental load. Relevant

empirical studies were described by Tent (1962), Heemstra (1988) and Paas and Van Merrienboer (1993). The principle will be illustrated by some results from our own study (Meijman et al., 1989).

Eighteen city bus drivers perform a visual memory search task under different conditions of prior workload. The efficiency of information processing in the task is defined as the relation between the performance and the effort expenditure it requires. Figure 2.4 presents the results. The test is always performed at 12.30 hours. At that time, the drivers in the morning shift have worked for eight hours, in the day shift for four hours, and in the late shift they are about to start working. As a fourth condition, the drivers are studied during their day off.

The test involves recognizing a character, one of a set of four characters that has been memorized in advance, which is displayed on a screen surrounded by three characters that were not included in the memory set. The entire task consisted of 40 trials, 20 of which contained a character from the memory set and 20 that did not. Performance is measured by response latency in recognizing the character from the memory set. Effort is measured by the heart rate variability, the so-called 0.10 Hz component (G. Mulder, 1980; L. Mulder, 1988). This physiological measure is one of the standard indicators in the study of mental load (see also section 2.1). It is based on the phenomenon that the variability of the heart rate interbeat interval times is relatively low when a person is involved in an attention-demanding information processing mode and in that sense is expending mental effort.

It appears that on their day off performance is delivered (reaction time 620 milliseconds and 8% wrong responses) against a certain amount of effort (standardized 0.10 Hz: 35). Just before the start of the late shift, the drivers deliver more or less the same performance as on their day off (reaction time 585 milliseconds and 9% wrong responses) against an equal amount of effort compared with the day off (standardized 0.10 Hz: 30). So, under both conditions the mental task is performed equally efficient. After four hours working in the day shift, the efficiency of the information processing drops considerably. For, although the drivers invest the same effort

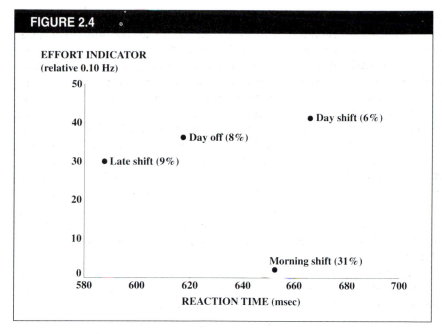

FIGURE 2.4

EFFORT INDICATOR
(relative 0.10 Hz)

Efficiency (reaction time by effort) in a visual memory search task; 18 bus drivers; differentiated to conditions of workload (for further explanation see text).

(standardized 0.10 Hz: 41) as on their day off or before the late shift, their performance is (statistically significantly) worse, i.e. 665 milliseconds with 6% wrong responses. Quite remarkably, after eight hours morning shift and after four hours day shift the levels of performance are virtually the same, but under the former condition it seems to take the drivers less effort while the percentage of wrong responses is considerably higher, i.e. 31%. The drivers seem to have adopted a different strategy that allows them to maintain the reaction time but not the quality of the reaction. Such a shift in strategy, that shows in changes in the efficiency of information processing, is characteristic of the phenomenon called mental fatigue. It may be assumed that mental fatigue will occur after working for eight hours in the morning shift, which often involves sleep deprivation.

5.4.3 Mental fatigue

The problem of fatigue as a work psychological issue does not so much concern the lack of competence, but rather the decision regarding its availability (Meijman, 1991). To allocate attention to a task and proceed to action is predominantly the outcome of strategic decisions. What the outcome will be depends on the person's appreciation of his current psychophysiological state in relation to the character and level of the demands the task and the task situation make on it. Several options are open to the person when to his judgement his actual state and the demands made on it are or threaten to be at conflict (Hockey, 1986a, 1986b). The person can (re)interpret the demands so that the (threatening) conflict is solved or at least becomes less serious. As a result he may not comply with the task assignment or he may comply with the assignment in a way that matches the appreciation of his actual state by following a less strenuous strategy or by not making an optimal effort. The bus drivers appeared to do just that when performing the visual memory search task after eight hours working in the morning shift. As a second option, the person can adjust his actual state in the direction of the required state by investing compensatory effort. Fatigue pertains to the decision regarding these options and the way in which this decision is acted upon. Looked at in this way, fatigue points to a distinct programme of action or strategy, i.e. not to adopt or having to adopt the above-mentioned, second option. The extent to which this programme is in fact realized depends above all on the personal interpretation or redefinition of the task assignment. At the same time, this also depends on the extent to which the performance to be delivered has been standardized and is as such compulsory or is considered to be so. For this determines whether, and if so to what degree, self-regulatory mechanisms are deployed to minimize the discrepancies between the actual state and the state an adequate task performance requires, that is to say, whether compensatory effort is invested or the necessary attention is devoted to a task. According to Bartlett (1953), the characteristic psychological feature of fatigue, i.e. the feeling of "aversion", or as Thorndike (1914) describes it "the intolerance of any effort", is associated with this process of self-regulation in real task activities.

6   DECISION LATITUDE

6.1   Objective and subjective decision latitude

The choice of a specific processing strategy and work procedure depends primarily on the possibilities of control which the situation allows. Therefore, and because of its great interest to the study of workload, decision latitude has been included as a distinct determinant in the effort-recovery scheme (Figure 2.1), although it is to an important part included in formal work aspects like assignment, conditions, facilities and relations.

It should be noted that, although decision latitude may objectively be included in the task assignment and work situation, the operator has to perceive it as such for him/her to utilize it. That is to say, that the utilization of decision latitude depends on the operator's abilities and his/her actual mobilization. If the operator fails to recognize the opportunity he/she objectively has, it is hard to take it. And even while being aware of the opportunity for exercising control, he/she may currently lack the required skills or willingness to do so.

It is important to note that subjective decision latitude is restricted as a consequence of the load itself. Thus, the Cambridge studies (Bartlett, 1943) showed that operators—pilots in a simulator in which very long flights were simulated—when tired not only persist in applying inefficient or even wrong strategies but also restrict their visual field and fail to notice signals from the periphery. As a consequence, they no longer utilize the decision latitude they objectively have.

6.2   Decision latitude and effort

The study of work stress has shown the great importance of having decision latitude (Karasek, 1979; Karasek & Theorell, 1990). Work situations with little decision latitude are particularly stressful because, among other things, they do not allow shifts in task performance strategies or hamper such shifts. We already pointed to the significance of such shifts in manipulating the load. The significance for the operator of having control over his work procedure is illustrated by the following laboratory experiment (Zijlstra et al., 1990).

This experiment aimed to investigate the relationships between, on the one hand, the task load in combination with the operator's state of fatigue and him having control over the task situation, and on the other hand, the effort the task requires. The task to be performed is a visual memory search task. Characters have to be memorized and subsequently recognized when displayed on a screen between other characters. Sixteen subjects, male students, performed the task in an imposed pace of work, i.e. they were unable to determine the work pace themselves. Another group of 16 students performed the task in a self-determined or free pace of work. All subjects were examined on two different days, at four o'clock in the afternoon. On one day the subjects were manipulated and worn out prior to the experimental session. For six hours they had to perform mentally demanding exams, which were repeatedly corrected and marked by the test supervisor. On the other day they could spend the time prior to the session as they liked, as long as they abstained from heavy, physical and mental activities. During the experimental session the task was performed twice, with varying task loads, i.e. with the two character sets containing either one or four characters. After the performance of each task, the subjects scored the amount of effort expended on the task on a standardized rating scale, the RSME (Meijman & Zijlstra, 1989; Zijlstra, 1993). The entire task consisted of 40 trials, 20 of which contained a character from the memory set and 20 did not.

In Figure 2.5 the mean reaction time of the correct answers is plotted against the mean effort score. In addition, it differentiates between the two levels of task load, i.e. one or four characters, and between the condition "worn out" (the black symbols in the figure) and the condition "not worn out" (the open symbols in the figure). The results of the tests with an "imposed pace of work" and with a "free pace of work" are presented next to each other.

First, it appears that a low task load (one character) requires hardly more effort than a higher task load (four characters) if the subjects are allowed to determine their own pace of work. Under the "free pace of work" condition, the differences between the effort scores for the four tasks are not statistically significant. This is not the case if the subjects have to work in an imposed pace of work. Then the increased task load is evaluated as (statistically significantly) more effortful as appears from the differences in scores between the four character trials and the one character trials. Second, fatigue appears to have little effect on the effort when the subjects are allowed to determine their own pace of work, especially with a low task load. For no statistically significant difference was found between the perceived effort scores in the "worn out" condition versus the "not worn out" condition. With a higher task load and a free pace of work, however, there seems to be a difference, though not statistically significant, between the two fatigue conditions.

With an imposed pace of work the outcome is completely different, with fatigue clearly playing a role. In both task load conditions, the perceived effort scores for the task are (statistically significantly) higher under the "worn out" condition as compared to the "not worn out" condition. Finally, in the imposed pace of work condition, subjects appear to react more quickly than in a free pace of work condition. However, in the first condition they make a lot more mistakes (70% correct answers) than in the second condition (95% correct answers). So, it is inapt to say that a higher

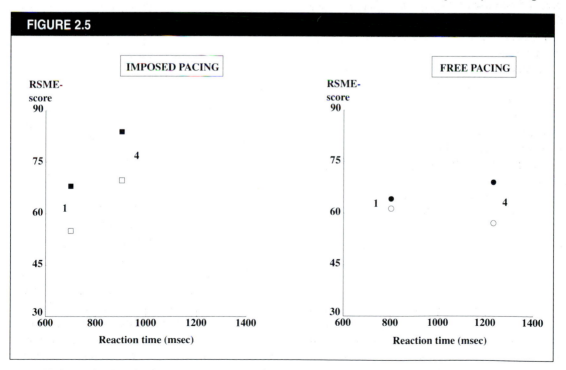

FIGURE 2.5

Efficiency (reaction time by effort) in a visual memory search task; differentiated to memory load (one or four characters), pretreatment (open symbols = "not worn out" pretreatment; closed symbols = "worn out" pretreatment).
Figure left: 16 students working in paced condition; figure right: 16 students working in unpaced condition.

level of effort expenditure will always result in an overall better performance.

The outcome of this experiment shows that making an effort is very much a dynamic process, depending on the task load in combination with the operator's state and the amount of active control he has over the relationship between his performance and the effort to be expended.

6.3   Mental load and stress; the impact of decision latitude

As long as control is possible, thereby preventing the task demands from exceeding the possibilities of self-regulation, the effort will remain within limits acceptable to the individual and will not necessarily elicit a tension reaction (see also section 5.3.4). So, mental load and stress are related. In both cases the adaptive systems are activated. However, mental load does not necessarily have to lead to stress. This happens only when the operator has no or insufficient possibilities for adequate coping and is incapable of developing these possibilities on short notice, while he/she cannot withdraw from the task, or only on pain of sanctions. Under such conditions the load may turn into a threat because the operator is forced to expend an amount of effort which is almost or entirely beyond her/his ability and which he/she is neither emotionally nor motivationally willing to expend. Being confronted with such a situation or just anticipating it, generates the typical reaction pattern with specific physiological and emotional components, which may be characterized as a tension or stress reaction.

So, essential to the occurrence or non-occurrence of such a reaction is the possibility of control (Fisher, 1986; Furda & Meijman, 1992). If there is no or insufficient possibility during the exertion of a mental effort, a physiological mechanism is activated, which Selye (1956) described as the classical stress reaction. Characteristic of this mechanism is an increased secretion of the hormone cortisol next to the secretion of catecholamines, in particular adrenaline. The latter hormone is also secreted as part of the sympatic activity that is characteristic of expending mental effort with the possibility of control.

7   NEGATIVE EFFECTS AND HEALTH CONSEQUENCES

7.1   Introduction

Expending effort yields the short-term reactions mentioned in Figure 2.1. These reactions involve responses of the organism's adaptive mechanisms that are already observable during the load period. In principle these responses are measured as changes in the physiological and psychological processes concerned with respect to a baseline value. At a physiological level, they may involve an increased secretion of a specific hormone that plays a role in activating the organism, like adrenaline. At a mental level, they may involve changes in mood or motivation. Such reactions are in principle reversible. This takes a certain amount of time in which no or little use is made of the systems concerned. This process of reversion is called recovery. The significance of recovery, in which time is the crucial variable, was very early recognized in the work psychological study of load. Both its founders, Mosso (1894) and Kraepelin (Rivers & Kraepelin, 1896), devoted attention to it. In theories on decrements in well-being and health due to mental workload and workstress, the concept of recovery takes a prominent place, because the (im)possibility to recover is essential to short-term load reactions turning into negative load effects. As was said in section 3, the load effects are related to the negative symptoms that may manifest themselves in the long run due to prolonged exposure to one or more load factors without sufficient time for recovery. They manifest themselves as more structural, negative changes in physiological and/or psychological functions and possibly as impairment, disorder or illness.

7.2   Cumulation and effects on well-being and health

Daily work usually involves loads which measured at a certain moment do not necessarily exceed a minimum level of harmfulness. However, because they recur daily and consequently function as a continued and therefore uncontrollable source of tension, loads may in the long run have negative effects. As was said earlier, for this to happen depends primarily on the opportunities for recovery between successive periods of exposure. If the opportunities for recovery after the exposure period are both quantitatively and qualitatively sufficient, the physiological and psychological processes activated while expending the daily work effort will stabilize at a baseline value. However, if these systems are again activated subsequent to insufficient recovery, the organism, which is still in a sub-optimal state, will have to make additional, compensatory effort. This will show in an increased intensity of the load reactions, which in turn will make higher demands, both quantitative and qualitative, on the recovery. Thus, a cumulative process may be started yielding negative load effects such as feelings of prolonged fatigue, complaints about chronic tension and sleep deprivation, and other psychosomatic complaints. Under unchanged conditions, these symptoms may develop into manifest health problems. Such a process has been described in various theories (Kagan & Levi, 1974; Frese et al., 1978; Gardell, 1980).

The question whether an elevated risk of psychosomatic complaints and illnesses may be caused by an increase in the intensity and duration of effects due to mental and emotional workloads, can empirically be answered only by a longitudinal study over a succession of years. Besides longitudinal studies (Johnson et al., 1991), transversal studies involving large-scale, epidemiological research by means of questionnaires (Caplan et al., 1975) indicate psychosocial workload factors and health indicators to be related. It should be noted that the relationships involve mainly indicators that in some way or another provide information on a high work pressure (House et al., 1986), possibly in combination with a low work autonomy or decision latitude (Karasek, 1979; Karasek et al., 1981). But the reported relationships tend to be low. This is not merely due to methodological weaknesses of the studies concerned (Kasl, 1978, 1986; Lazarus et al., 1985; House, 1987), but in particular to the multicausality of health problems (Frese, 1985). However, as yet much is still in the dark regarding the mechanisms underlying these relationships found in epidemiological studies. Animal experiments suggest

that a chronic (over)activation of the neuro-endocrine systems due to prolonged exposure to threatening and hence uncontrollable events play an important role (Henry et al., 1981; Bohus et al., 1987). (Work)stress research among humans also indicates that continued exposure over a succession of years to sources of tension, as in the work situation, may cause chronically elevated levels of adrenaline and noradrenaline, and of corticosteroids (Knardahl & Ursin, 1985; Levine, 1986; Frankenhaeuser, 1989). As a consequence, changes may occur in the regulation of the organ systems affected by these substances, e.g. catecholamines affect the cardiovascular system, in particular the regulation of blood pressure (Sterling & Eyer, 1981; Majewski & Rand, 1986; Marmot & Theorell, 1988; Dienstbier, 1989). A prolonged confrontation with stressors which are more or less beyond control, can lead to the development of decrements in the normal functioning of parts of the immune system which may persist over longer periods of time (Ballieux & Heijnen, 1988; Brosschot, 1991; Kaplan, 1991). Chronically elevated levels of corticosteroids are assumed to play a role in this development. Although these decrements have not as yet been shown to have a direct relationship with an increased susceptibility to colds and other infectious diseases, their role in situations of an already elevated susceptibility should be taken into account (Cohen & Williamson, 1991).

7.3 After effects of work pressure

In thinking about the development of negative load effects consequent to prolonged activation of neuroendocrine systems, it is of major interest that the secretion of a certain hormone as a response to workload does not stop immediately after the exposure.

Such after effects or "spillover" were found after periods of working excessive overtime (Rissler, 1977, 1979). Frankenhaeuser (1980) calls it "slow unwinding" when the hormone levels elevated in the course of the task performance drop to their baseline levels only several hours after the end of the performance. Our own field study among driving examiners under three work conditions confirmed this effect (Meijman et al., 1992). The work conditions differed as to the number of exams to be held during a working day from 08.00–16.00 hours, i.e. nine, ten or eleven exams, respectively. The duration of the exams did not differ between conditions. In other words, in this field study the level of work pressure or work intensity was manipulated systematically. On a "9-exams" day, a light working day, the examiners were directly productive, i.e. holding exams for 75% of their working day. In the "10-exams" condition, a normal working day, productivity amounted to 80%, and in the "11-exams" condition, an intensified day, it amounted to 86%. In the last condition, the examiners did not have a moment to spare between successive exams versus about five minutes on a "9-exams" day and two minutes on a "10-exams" day.

On these working days and after work, in the evening, the excretion levels of adrenaline (in nanograms per minute: Ng/min) in urine were determined. The same was done on a Sunday, when the examiners had a day off. Figure 2.6 presents the pattern of adrenaline excretion levels.

Adrenaline excretion levels are found to be higher on the working days than on the day off. Strikingly, on the working days the levels are the same for the three conditions. However, at the end of an intensive working day, at 16.00 hours, the adrenaline excretion level is (statistically significantly) higher than on the two other working days. Furthermore, and this is of great interest, after an intensive working day this increased level persists throughout the evening. Apparently, the organism remains activated for quite some time after a period of intensive load, even if it is not exposed to any special loads during the period of recovery. This condition of increased activation caused the examiners to be troubled by sleep complaints, in particular falling asleep, during the nights after the intensified working days. The following morning they reported increased feelings of tension. This study serves to illustrate the mechanism which may lead to the development of a state of prolonged neuroendocrine activation which eventually may lead to complaints.

7.4   Load effects and health

In a series of transversal field studies among city bus drivers (Mulders et al., 1982, 1988) indications were found of a relationship between workload-related elevated hormonal levels and health status. Epidemiological analyses (Kompier, 1988) showed this occupational group to be at an elevated health risk attributable to a combination of a high work pressure and insufficient recovery. As was argued above, prolonged disruption of the complementary relationship between load and recovery could start a process of increasing dysfunctioning. The field studies aimed to find out whether an apparently decreased resistance, measured by frequency of absenteeism, also manifest itself in an elevated hormonal reactivity in the normal work situation. Therefore, the drivers were examined both on working days and on days off. During the days off, no differences in the adrenaline excretion levels in urine were found between drivers with a high frequency (five times or more) of short sick leave in the year prior to the study and drivers of the same age and sex who had been absent only once or less. Both groups showed an elevated level of adrenaline on working days as compared to days off. However, on working days the excretion levels of the group with a relatively high absenteeism were considerably higher than the levels of drivers with a low absenteeism.

Absenteeism, however, is a complex measure, which cannot simply be used as an indicator of general health. That is why a series of new studies were started to investigate the relationship between the level of perceived health measured by a standard Dutch questionnaire (the VOEG; Dirken, 1969) and the reactivity in adrenaline under a normal workload. The adrenaline excretion levels on a normal working day and on a day off of 168 men from a wide variety of occupational backgrounds were compared. They had filled out the VOEG a few weeks prior to the physiological examination. The subjects were divided by their VOEG-scores and age. Figure 2.7 presents the results (Meijman et al., 1990).

As can be seen in Figure 2.7, all groups show an elevated excretion level on the working day as compared to the day off. However, in the older age groups, people with many perceived health complaints show a significantly higher excretion level than people with little to no complaints. On the day off, no difference was found between the two groups. So, it does not involve a habitual difference in general activation of the hormonal system,

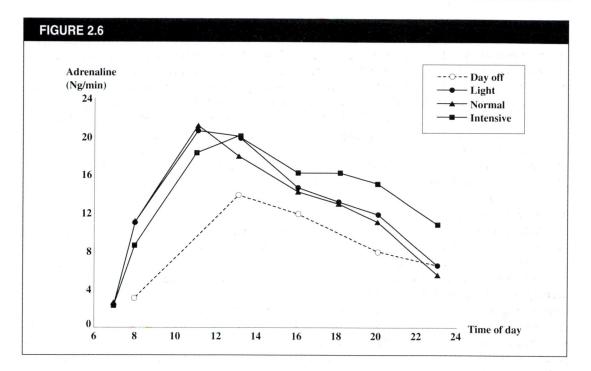

FIGURE 2.6

Excretion rate of adrenaline, in urine, during working days (light: five-minute breaks; normal: two-minute breaks; intensive: no breaks) and a day off. 27 driving examiners.

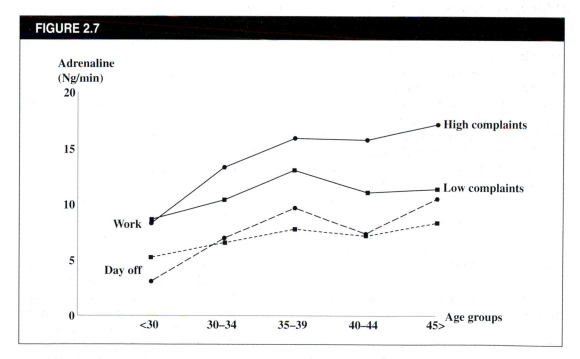

FIGURE 2.7

Excretion rate of adrenaline, in urine, during a normal working day and a day off (both between 900 and 1230).
Data of 168 men, from various occupations, differentiated to age (<30 N=36; 30–34 N=53; 35–39 N=36; 40–44 N=25; 45 > N=18) and to level of psychosomatic complaints. 102 subjects "low complaints", 66 subjects "high complaints".

but a difference in reactivity to the daily workload. This difference in hormonal reactivity is related to perceived health and occurs especially at an advanced age, i.e. after the age of 35 when most people have been exposed to daily workloads for over 15 years.

8   SOME CONCLUDING REMARKS

The work psychological study of workload concerns the changes in structure and regulation of work activities under influence of the demands made in the work situation. It comprises the study of changes in performance as well as the study of changes in the willingness to expend effort and of the costs involved. These changes are studied in functional relationship with the character and the level of the loads the worker is exposed to in the actual work situation. The demands that are thus made on the processing capacity are met by the mobilization of resources and therefore required activation of psycho-biological adaptive systems. This process of expending effort causes changes in the systems concerned, which can be observed as reversible load reactions. Under the condition of sufficient recovery, they stabilize at a baseline level within a short period of time after the end of the load period. Sustained load and insufficient recovery may lead to negative load effects which may persist for longer periods of time or may even be irreversible, which shows in a loss of function, impairment or illness.

The effort-recovery relationship—given the demand to expend a certain minimum effort—is pivotal to the work psychological study of workload. For, in case of no or insufficient recovery, the effort process may obtain a cumulative character in the course of a working day and in the course of a succession of working days. This process determines the costs in terms of decrements in work capacities and in the long run in well-being and health. In the final analysis, the study of workload does not concern the question whether a person is able to cope with a specific level of task demands but the short-term and long-term costs involved in

coping with loads in actual work situations. This has to be investigated from the perspective of the cycle of effort and recovery.

REFERENCES

Algera, J.A. (Eds.) (1991). *Analyse van arbeid vanuit verschillende perspectieven* (Approaches to task analysis). Amsterdam/Lisse: Swets & Zeitlinger.

Anderson, J.R. (1993). *Rules of the mind*. Hillsdale, NJ: Lawrence Erlbaum Associates.

Astrand, P.O., & Rodahl, K. (1986). *Textbook of work physiology: Physiological basis of exercise*. New York: McGraw-Hill.

Bainbridge, L. (1974). Problems in the assessment of mental load. *Le Travail Humain, 37*, 279–302.

Bainbridge, L. (1978). Forgotten alternatives in skill and workload. *Ergonomics, 21*, 169–185.

Ballieux, R.E., & Heijnen, C.J. (1988). Stress and the immune system. In D. Hellhammer, I. Florin, & H. Weiner (Eds.), *Neurobiological approaches to human disease*. Toronto: Hans Huber Verlag.

Bartlett, F.C. (1943). Fatigue following highly skilled work. *Proceedings of the Royal Society, 131*, 247–257.

Bartlett, F.C. (1953). Psychological criteria of fatigue. In W.F. Floyd, & A.T. Welford (Eds.), *Symposium on fatigue*. London: H.K. Lewis.

Baumgarten, F. (1928). *Die Berufseignungsprüfungen*. München/Berlin: Oldenbourg.

Bohus, B., Benus, R.F., Fokkema, D.S., Koolhaas, J.M., Nyakas, C., van Oortmerssen, G.A., Prins, A.J.A., de Ruiter, A.J.H., Scheurink, A.J.W., & Steffens, A.B. (1987). Neuroendocrine states and behavioral and physiological stress responses. In E.R. de Kloet, V.M. Wiegand, & D. de Wied (Eds.), *Progress in brain research, 72*, 57–70.

Bongers, P.M., & Boshuizen, H.C. (1990). *Back disorders and whole-body vibration at work*. Dissertation, University of Amsterdam.

Bonjer, F.H. (rap.) (1965). *Fysiologische methoden voor het vaststellen van belasting en belastbaarheid* (Physiological methods for the study of workload). Assen: van Gorcum/CargoTNO.

Brosschot, J.F. (1991). *Stress, perceived control and immune response in man*. Utrecht: ISOR; Dissertation, University of Utrecht.

Burger, G.C.E. (1959). De betekenis van kwantitatieve meting en functionele beoordeling van arbeidsbelasting en belastbaarheid voor de practische bedrijfsarts (The measurement of workload and capacity in occupational health practice). *Tijdschrift voor Sociale Geneeskunde, 37*, 377–387.

Caplan, R.D., Cobb, S., French, J.R.P. Jr., Harrison, R. van, & Pinneau, S.R. Jr. (1975). *Job demands and worker health*. Washington DC: NIOSH.

Carver, C.S., & Scheier, M.F. (1990). Origins and functions of positive and negative affect. A control-process view. *Psychological Review, 97,* 19–35.

Coeterier, J. (1971). Individual strategies in ATC freedom and choice. *Ergonomics, 14,* 579–584.

Cohen, S., & Williamson, G.M. (1991). Stress and infectious diseases in humans. *Psychological Bulletin, 109,* 5–24.

Cowan, N. (1988). Evolving conceptions of memory storage, selective attention and their mutual constraints within the human information-processing system. *Psychological Bulletin, 102,* 163–191.

Cowan, N. (1993). Activation, attention and short-term memory. *Memory and Cognition, 21*(2), 162–167.

Dienstbier, R.A. (1989). Arousal and physiological toughness: implications for mental and physical health. *Psychological Review, 96,* 84–100.

Dijk, F.J.H. van, Meijman, T.F., & Ulenbelt, P. (1988). Towards a dynamic model of exposure, susceptibility and effect. In W.R.F. Notten, R.F.M. Herber, W.J. Hunter, A.C. Monster, & R.L. Zielhuis (Eds.), *Health surveillance of individual workers exposed to chemical agents.* International Archives of Occupational and Environmental Health, Supplement. Berlin/Heidelberg: Springer Verlag.

Dijk, F.J.H. van, Dormolen, M., Kompier, M.A.J., & Meijman, T.F. (1990). Herwaardering model belasting-belastbaarheid (The load-capacity model revisited). *Tijdschrift voor Sociale Gezondheidszorg, 68,* 3–10.

Dirken, J. (1969). *Arbeid en stress* (Work and stress). Groningen: Wolthers-Noordhoff.

Dodge, R. (1913). Mental work: A study in psychodynamics. *Psychological Review, 20,* 1–43.

Drury, C.G., Paramore, B., van Cott, H., Grey, S., & Corlett, E.N. (1987). Task analysis. In G. Salvendy (Ed.), *Handbook of human factors.* New York/Chichester, UK: Wiley & Sons.

Ettema, J.H. (1967). *Arbeidsfysiologische aspecten van mentale belasting* (Physiological aspects of mental load). Assen: van Gorcum.

Ettema, J.H. (1973). Het model belasting en belastbaarheid (The load-capacity model). *Tijdschrift voor Sociale Geneeskunde, 51,* 44–54.

Fisher, S. (1986). *Stress and strategy.* Hove, UK: Lawrence Erlbaum Associates Ltd.

Fleishman, E.A., & Quantaince, M.K. (1984). *Taxonomies of human performance.* Orlando, New York: Academic Press.

Frankenhaeuser, M. (1979). Psychoneuroendocrine approaches to the study of emotion as related to stress and coping. In H.E. Howe, & R.A. Dienstbier (Eds.), *Nebraska symposium on motivation, 1978.* Lincoln: University of Nebraska Press.

Frankenhaeuser, M. (1980). Psychobiological aspects of life stress. In S. Levine, & H. Ursin (Eds.), *Coping and health.* New York: Plenum Press.

Frankenhaeuser, M. (1989). A biopsychosocial approach to work life issues. *Journal of International Health Services, 19,* 747–758.

Frankenhaeuser, M., & Lundberg, U. (1985). Sympathetic-adrenal and pituitary-adrenal response to challenge. In P. Pichot, P. Berner, R. Wolf, & K. Thau (Eds.), *Psychiatry, Vol. II.* New York, USA/London, UK: Plenum Press.

Frese, M. (1985). Stress at work and psychosomatic complaints: a causal interpretation. *Journal of Applied Psychology, 70,* 314–328.

Frese, M. (1987). A concept of control: implications for stress and performance in human-computer interaction. In G. Salvendy, S.L. Sauter, & J.J. Hurrell (Eds.), *Social, ergonomic and stress aspects of work with computers.* Amsterdam, The Netherlands/Oxford, UK: Elsevier Science Publishers.

Frese, M., Greif, S., & Semmer, N. (1978). *Industrielle psychopathologie.* Bern: Hans Huber Verlag.

Furda, J., & Meijman, T.F. (1992). Druk en dreiging, sturing van stress (Demands and threat: The impact of control). In J. Winnubst, & M. Schabracq (Eds.), *Handboek arbeid-en gezondheids psychologie.* Utrecht: Lemma.

Gardell, B. (1980). Psychosocial aspects of industrial production methods. In L. Levi (Ed.), *Society, stress and disease, Vol. IV: Working life.* London: Oxford University Press.

Gopher, D. (1986). In defence of resources: on structures, energies, pools and the allocation of attention. In G.R.J. Hockey, A.W.K. Gaillard, & M.G.H. Coles (Eds.), *Energetics and human information processing.* Dordrecht: Martinus Nijhoff Publishers.

Gopher, D., & Donchin, E. (1986). Workload: An examination of the concept. In K.R. Boff, L. Kaufmann, & J.P. Thomas (Eds.), *Handbook of perception and human performance, Vol. II: Cognitive processes and performance.* New York/Chichester: Wiley & Sons.

Graf, O. (1954). Der Begriff der Leistungsbereitschaft. *Zentralblatt Arbeitwissenschaft, 8,* 141–144.

Hacker, W. (1973–1978). *Allgemeine Arbeits und Ingenieurspsychologie.* Berlin: VEB Deutscher Verlag Wissenschaft.

Hacker, W. (1986). *Arbeitspsychologie.* Bern: Huber.

Heemstra, M.L. (1988). *Efficiency of human information processing. A model of cognitive energetics.* Dissertation, Free University, Amsterdam.

Heide, H. van der, & Kragt, H. (1989). Quick scan ergonomie. *Maandblad Arbeidsomstandigheden, 65,* 25–29.

Hellinga, P. (1985). *De constructie van de groninger adjectief checklist, de GACL* (The construction of the Groningen Adjective Checklist). Groningen: Heijmans Bulletin, HB-85-771-Ex.

Henry, J.P., Ely, D.L., & Stephens, P.M. (1981). Medical ethology in relation to occupational health. In L. Levi (Ed.), *Society, stress and disease, Vol IV: Working life.* London: Oxford University Press.

Hockey, G.R.J. (1984). Varieties of attentional state: The effects of environment. In R. Parasuraman, & D.R. Davies (Eds.), *Varieties of attention*. New York: Academic Press, Inc.

Hockey, G.R.J. (1986a). Changes in operator efficiency as a function of environmental stress, fatigue and circadian rhythms. In K.R. Boff, L. Kaufmann, & J.P. Thomas (Eds.), *Handbook of perception and human performance, Vol. II: Cognitive processes and performance*. New York/Chichester: Wiley & Sons.

Hockey, G.R.J. (1986b). A state control theory of adaptation to stress and individual differences in stress management. In G.R.J. Hockey, A.W.K. Gaillard, & M.G.H. Coles (Eds.), *Energetics and human information processing*. Dordrecht: Martinus Nijhoff Publishers.

Hockey, G.R.J. (1993). Cognitive-energetical control mechanisms in the management of work demands and psychological health. In A. Baddeley, & L. Weiskrantz (Eds.), *Attention: Selection, awareness and control. A tribute to Donald Broadbent*. Oxford: Clarendon Press.

Hockey, G.R.J., Gaillard, A.W.K., & Coles, M.G.H. (Eds.) (1986). *Energetics and human information processing*. Dordrecht: Martinus Nijhoff Publishers.

Holding, D.H. (1983). Fatigue. In G.R.J. Hockey (Ed.), *Stress and fatigue in human performance*. New York/Chichester: Wiley & Sons.

House, J.S. (1987). Chronic stress and chronic disease in life and work: Conceptual and methodological issues. *Work and Stress, 1*, 129–134.

House, J.S., Strecher, V., Metzner, H.L., & Robbins, C.A. (1986). Occupational stress and health among men and women in the Tecumseh community health study. *Journal of Health and Social Behavior, 27*, 62–77.

James, W. (1890). *The principles of psychology*. New York: Holt.

Johnson, J.V., & Johansson, G. (Eds.) (1991). *The psychosocial work environment: Work organization, democratization and health*. Amityville, NY: Baywood Publishing Co.

Johnson, J.V., Hall, E.M., Stewart, W., Fredlund, P., & Theorell, T. (1991). Combined exposure to adverse work organization factors and cardiovascular disease: Towards a lifecourse perspective. In L.D. Fechter (Ed.), *Proceedings of the 4th International Conference on the Combined Effects of Environmental Factors*. Baltimore: John Hopkins University School of Hygiene and Public Health.

Kagan, A.R., & Levi, L. (1974). Health and environment-psychosocial stimuli: A review. *Social Science and Medicine, 10*, 225–241.

Kahneman, D. (1973). *Attention and effort*. Englewood Cliffs NJ: Prentice Hall.

Kalsbeek, J.W.H. (1967). *Mentale belasting: Theoretische en experimentele exploraties ter ontwikkeling van een meetmethode* (Mental load: A theory and measurement method). Assen: van Gorcum/CargoTNO.

Kalsbeek, J.W.H., & Ettema, J.H. (1964). Physiological and psychological evaluation of distraction stress. *Proceedings of the 2nd International Ergonomics Congress*, Dortmund.

Kantowitz, B.H. (1987). Mental workload. In P.A. Hancock (Ed.), *Human factors psychology*. Amsterdam, The Netherlands/Oxford: Elsevier Science Publishers.

Kaplan, H.B. (1991). Social psychology of the immune system: A conceptual framework and review of the literature. *Social Science and Medicine, 33*, 909–923.

Karasek, R.A. (1979). Job demands, job decision latitude, and mental strain: implications for job redesign. *Administrative Science Quarterly, 24*, 285–307.

Karasek, R.A., Baker, D., Marxer, F., Ahlbom, A., & Theorell, T. (1981). Job decision latitude, job demands, and cardiovascular disease. *American Journal of Public Health, 71*, 694–705.

Karasek, R.A., & Theorell, T. (1990). *Healthy work: Stress, productivity and the reconstruction of working life*. New York: Basic Books.

Karg, P.W., & Staehle, W.H. (1982). *Analyse der Arbeitssituation: Verfahren und Instrumente*. Freiburg i/B: Rudolf Haufe Verlag.

Kasl, S.V. (1978). Epidemiological contributions to the study of workstress. In C.L. Cooper, & R. Payne (Eds.), *Stress at work*. Chichester: John Wiley & Sons.

Kasl, S.V. (1986). Stress and disease in the workplace: a methodological commentary on the accumulated evidence. In M.F. Cataldo, & T.J. Coates (Eds.), *Health and industry, a behavioral medicine approach*. Chichester: John Wiley & Sons.

Klinkhamer, H.A.W. (1979). *Beoordelingslijst ergonomie* (Ergonomics checklist). Deventer: Kluwer/NIVE.

Knardahl, S., & Ursin, H. (1985). Sustained activation and the pathophysiology of hypertension and coronary heart disease. In J.F. Orlebeke, G. Mulder, & L. van Doornen (Eds.), *Psychophysiology of cardiovascular control*. New York/London: Plenum Press.

Kompier, M.A.J. (1988). *Arbeid en gezondheid van stadsbuschauffeurs* (Work and health of city bus drivers). Delft: Eburon; Dissertation, University of Groningen.

Kosslyn, S.M., & Koenig, O. (1992). *Wet mind: The new cognitive neuroscience*. New York/Oxford: The Free Press.

Kuiper, J.P. (1985). Vertoont het belastingsmodel ideologische trekken? (Ideological aspects of the load-capacity model). *Tijds. Soc. Gezondhz., 63*, 579–580.

Kyllonen, P.C., & Alluisi, E.A. (1987). Learning and forgetting facts and skills. In G. Salvendy (Ed.), *Handbook of human factors*. New York/Chichester: Wiley & Sons

Landau, K., & Rohmert, W. (1989). *Recent developments in job analysis*. London: Taylor & Francis.

Lazarus, R. (1966). *Psychological stress and the coping process*. New York: McGraw-Hill.

Lazarus, R.S. (1991). *Emotion and adaptation*. New York/Oxford: Oxford University Press.

Lazarus, R.S., DeLongis, A., Folkman, S., & Gruen, R. (1985). Stress and adaptational outcomes: The problem of confounded measures. *American Psychologist, 40*, 770–779.

Lehmann, G. (1962). *Praktische Arbeitsphysiologie, 2 Aufl.* Stuttgart: Georg Thieme Verlag.

Leitner, K., Volpert, W., Greiner, B., Weber, W.G., & Hennes, K. (1987). *Analyse psychischer Belastung in der Arbeit*. Köln: Verlag TüV Rheinland.

Levine, P. (1986). Stress. In M.G.H. Coles, E. Donchin, & S.W. Porges (Eds.), *Psychophysiology: Systems, processes and applications*. Amsterdam, The Netherlands/Oxford: Elsevier Science Publishers.

Lundberg, U., & Frankenhaeuser, M. (1980). Pituitary-adrenal and sympathetic-adrenal correlates of distress and effort. *Journal of Psychosomatic Research, 24*, 125–130.

Majewski, H., & Rand, M. (1986). A possible role of epinephrine in the development of hypertension. *Medical Research Review, 6*, 467–486.

Marmot, M., & Theorell, T. (1988). Social class and cardiovascular disease: the contribution of work. *International Journal of Health Services, 18*, 659–673.

Matern, B. (1984). *Psychologische Arbeitsanalyse*. Berlin/Heidelberg: Springer Verlag.

Meijman, T.F. (1988). Belasting en herstel, een begrippenkader voor het arbeidspsychologisch onderzoek van werkbelasting (Load and recovery: A conceptual frame for the study of workload). In B.G. Deelman, & G. Mulder (Eds.), *Nederlands psychologisch onderzoek, deel 3*. Lisse: Swets & Zeitlinger.

Meijman, T.F. (Eds.) (1989). *Mentale belasting en werkstress, een arbeidspsychologische invalshoek* (Mental load and workstress: A work psychology approach). Assen: van Gorcum.

Meijman, T.F. (1991). *Over vermoeidheid, arbeidspsychologische studies naar de beleving van belastingseffecten* (On fatigue: The perception of workload effects). Studiecentrum Arbeid en Gezondheid University of Amsterdam; Dissertation University of Groningen.

Meijman, T.F., & O'Hanlon, J. F. (1983). Arbeidsbelasting, een inleidend overzicht van psychologische theorieën en meetmethoden (Workload: An introduction into psychological theories). In P.J.D. Drenth, Hk. Thierry, P.J. Willems, & C.J. de Wolff (Eds.), *Handboek arbeids en organisatiepsychologie*. Deventer: van Loghum Slaterus.

Meijman, T.F., Ouwerkerk, R. van, Mulder, L.J.M., & Vries-Griever, A.H.G. de (1989). Hartslagvariabiliteit, het onderzoek van mentale efficiëntie (Heart rate variability: The study of mental efficiency). In T.F.

Meijman (Ed.), *Mentale belasting en werkstress, een arbeidspsychologische invalshoek*. Assen: van Gorcum.

Meijman, T.F., Mulders, H.P.G., Kompier, M.A.J., & Dormolen, M. van (1990). Individual differences in adrenaline/noradrenaline reactivity and self-perceived health status. *Zeitschrift zur Gesammte Hygiene, 36*, 413–414.

Meijman, T.F., Mulder, G., Dormolen, M. van, & Cremer, R. (1992). Workload of driving examiners: A psychophysiological field study. In H. Kragt (Ed.), *Enhancing industrial performance*. London: Taylor & Francis.

Moray, N. (1967). Where is capacity limited? A survey and a model. In A.F. Sanders (Ed.), *Attention and performance, Vol. 1*. Amsterdam: North Holland Publishing Co.

Mosso, A. (1894). *La fatigue intellectuelle et physique*. Paris: Felix Alcan.

Mulder, G. (1979). Mental load, mental effort and attention. In N. Moray (Ed.), *Mental workload: Its theory and measurement*. New York: Plenum Press.

Mulder, G. (1980). *The heart of mental effort*. Dissertation, University of Groningen.

Mulder, G. (1986). The concept and measurement of mental effort. In G.R.J. Hockey, A.W.K. Gaillard, & M.G.H. Coles (Eds.), *Energetics and human information processing*. Dordrecht: Martinus Nijhoff Publishers.

Mulder, G., Wijers, A.A., Smid, H.G.O.M., Brookhuis, K.A., & Mulder, L.J.M. (1989). Individual differences in computational mechanisms: A psychophysiological analysis. In R. Kanfer, P.L. Ackerman & R. Cudeck (Eds.), *Abilities, motivation and methodology*. Hillsdale, NJ: Erlbaum.

Mulder, L.J.M. (1988). *Assessment of cardiovascular reactivity by means of spectral analysis*. Dissertation, University of Groningen.

Mulders, H.P.G., Meijman, T.F., O'Hanlon, J.F., & Mulder, G. (1982). Differential psychophysiological reactions of city busdrivers to workload. *Ergonomics, 25*, 1003–1011.

Mulders, H.P.G., Meijman, T.F., Kompier, M.A.J., Broersen, J.P.J., Westerink, B., & O'Hanlon, J.F. (1988). Occupational stress in city busdrivers. In J.A. Rothengatter, & R.A. de Bruin (Eds.), *Road user behavior, theory and research*. Assen: van Gorcum.

Navon, D., & Gopher, D. (1979). On the economy of the human information processing system. *Psychological review, 84*, 214–255.

Navon, D., & Gopher, D. (1980). Task difficulty, resources and dual task performances. In R.S. Nickerson (Ed.), *Attention and performance, Vol. 8*. Hillsdale, NJ: Lawrence Erlbaum.

Ouwerkerk R. van, Meijman, T.F., & Mulder, G. (1994). *De analyse van arbeidstaken op cognitieve en emotionele eisen* (The analysis of tasks: Cognitive and emotional demands). Utrecht: Lemma.

Paas, F.G.W.C., & Merrienboer, J.J.G van (1993). The

efficiency of instructional conditions: An approach to combine mental effort and performance measures. *Human Factors*, *35*, 737–743.

Posner, M.I., & Raichle, M.E. (1994). *Images of mind.* New York: Scientific American Library.

Pribram, K.H., & McGuinness, D. (1975). Arousal, activation and effort in the control of attention. *Psychological Review*, *82*, 116–149.

Rasmussen, J., & Jensen, A. (1974). Mental procedures in real-life tasks, a case study of electronic trouble shooting. *Ergonomics*, *17*, 293–307.

Rasmussen, J. (1987). The definition of human error and a taxonomy for technical system design. In J. Rasmussen, K. Duncan, & J. Leplat (Eds.), *New technology and human error.* New York/Chichester: Wiley & Sons.

Revelle, W. (1993). Individual differences in personality and motivation: "non-cognitive" determinants of cognitive performance. In A. Baddeley, & L. Weiskrantz (Eds.), *Attention: Selection, awareness and control. A tribute to Donald Broadbent.* Oxford: Clarendon Press.

Rissler, A. (1977). Stress reactions at work and after work during a period of quantitative overload. *Ergonomics*, *20*, 13–16.

Rissler, A. (1979). A psychobiological approach to quality of working life: Costs of adjustment to quantitative overload. In R.G. Sell, & P. Shipley (Eds.), *Satisfaction in work design: Ergonomics and other approaches.* London: Taylor & Francis.

Rivers, W.H.R., & Kraepelin, E. (1896). Uber Ermüdung und Erholung. *Psychologische Arbeiten*, *1*, 627–678.

Rohmert, W. (1983). Formen menschlicher Arbeit. In W. Rohmert, & J. Rutenfranz (Eds.). *Praktische Arbeitsphysiologie.* Stuttgart, Germany/New York: Georg Thieme Verlag.

Rohmert, W. (1984). Das Belastungs-Beanspruchungs Konzept, *Zeitschrift der Arbeitswissenschaften*, *38*, 193–200.

Rumelhart, D.E., & Ortony, A. (1977). *The representation in memory.* San Diego, CA: University of California, Center for Human Information Processing.

Sanders, A.F. (1981). Stress and human performance: A working model and some applications. In G. Salvendy, & M.J. Smith (Eds.), *Machine pacing and occupational stress.* London: Taylor & Francis.

Sanders, A.F. (1983). Towards a model of stress and human performance. *Acta Psychologica*, *53*, 61–97.

Schellart, A.J.M., Deynen, W., van, & Koten, J.W. (1989, 1990). Beroep en ziekte in de WAO, I, II en III (Occupation and diseases of disabled people). *Tijdschrift voor Verzekerings Geneeskunde*, *27*, 166–172, en *28*, 6–10 en 39–42.

Schuffel, H. (1989). *Richtlijnen ten behoeve van werkplek-ergonomie* (Prescriptions for the design of workplaces). Den Haag: Ministry of Social Affairs SoZaWe/DGA, rapport S59.

Selye, H. (1956). *Stress of life.* New York: McGraw-Hill.

Shiffrin, R.M., & Schneider, W. (1977). Controlled and automatic information processing: II. Perceptual learning, automatic attending and a general theory. *Psychological Review*, *84*, 127–190.

Sluis, H. van der, & Dirken, J.M. (1970). *Dagelijks energieverbruik van de Nederlandse industriearbeider: methoden ter bepaling en normen* (Daily energy use of the Dutch industrial worker). Leiden/Groningen: Ned. Instituut voor Preventieve Geneeskunde TNO/Wolthers-Noordhoff.

Sperandio, J.-C. (1972). Charge de travail et régulation des procèssus operatoires. *Le Travail Humain*, *35*, 85–98.

Squire, L.R. (1987). *Memory and brain.* New York/Oxford: Oxford University Press.

Sterling, P., & Eyer, J. (1981). Biological basis of stress related mortality. *Social Science and Medicine*, 15E, 3–42.

Tent, L. (1962). Untersuchungen zur Erfassung des Verhältnisses von Anspannung und Leistung bei vorwiegend psychisch beanspruchenden Tätigkeiten. *Archives zur Gesammte Psychologie*, *115*, 106–172.

Thayer, R. (1978). Factor analytic and reliability studies of the activation-deactivation adjective checklist. *Psychological Reports*, *42*, 747–756.

Thayer, R.E. (1989). *The biopsychology of mood and arousal.* New York/Oxford: Oxford University Press.

Thierry, Hk., & Jong, J.R. de (1991). Arbeidsanalyse ten behoeve van beloning (Function analysis for remuneration). In J.A. Algera (Ed.), *Analyse van arbeid vanuit verschillende perspectieven.* Amsterdam/Lisse: Swets & Zeitlinger.

Thorndike, E.L. (1914). *Educational psychology, Vol. III: Mental work and fatigue and individual differences and their causes.* New York: Teachers College Columbia University.

Tulving, E. (1991). Concepts of human memory. In L. Squire, G. Lynch, N.M. Weinberger, & J.L. McGaugh (Eds.), *Memory: Organization and locus of change* (pp. 3–32). New York: Oxford University Press.

Ulenbelt, P. (1991). *Omgaan met blootstelling aan chemische stoffen: grenswaarden, hygiënisch gedrag en regelmogelijkheden* (Coping with the exposure to chemical substances at work). Amsterdam: Studiecentrum Arbeid en Gezondheid University of Amsterdam; Dissertation University of Amsterdam.

Verbeek, J.H.A.M. (1991). *Arbeidsongeschiktheid op grond van rugklachten en andere aandoeningen van het bewegingsapparaat* (Disability due to low back pains). Amsterdam: Studiecentrum Arbeid en Gezondheid University of Amsterdam; Dissertation University of Amsterdam.

Voskamp, P. (Ed.) (1994). *Handboek ergonomie. De stand van de ergonomie in de ARBO wet* (Handbook of ergonomics). Alphen a/d Rijn: Samson BedrijfsInformatie.

Vries-Griever, A.H.G. de (1989). De methode van psychologische arbeidsanalyse (Psychological analysis of tasks). In T.F. Meijman (Ed.), *Mentale belasting en werkstress, een arbeidspsychologische invalshoek*. Assen: van Gorcum.

Welford, A.T. (1953). The psychologist's problem in measuring fatigue. In W.F. Floyd, & A.T. Welford (Eds.), *Symposium on fatigue*. London: K. K. Lewis.

Welford, A.T. (1978). Mental workload as a function of demand, capacity, strategy and skill. *Ergonomics, 21*, 151–167.

Wendrich, P. (1973). Methodische Probleme bei der Anwendung von Algoritmen zur Strukturanalyse von Arbeitstätigkeiten bei Belastungsuntersuchungen. In W. Hacker, W. Quaas, H. Raum, & H.J. Schultz (Eds.), *Psychologische Arbeitsuntersuchung*. Berlin: VEB Deuts Verlag Wissens.

Wickens, C.D. (1984). Processing resources in attention. In R. Parasuraman, & D.R. Davies (Eds.), *Varieties of attention*. Orlando: Academic Press.

Wickens, C.D. (1987). Information processing, decision making and cognition. In G. Salvendy (Ed.), *Handbook of human factors*. New York/Chichester: Wiley & Sons.

Wickens, C.D. (1991). Processing resources and attention. In D.L. Damos (Ed.), *Multiple-task performance*. London: Taylor & Francis.

Wickens, C.D. (1992). *Engineering psychology and human performance (2nd ed.)*. New York: Harper-Collins Publishers Inc.

Wijers, A.A. (1989). *Selective visual attention: an elektrophysiological approach*. Dissertation, University of Groningen.

Zielhuis, R.L. (1967). Theoretisch denkraam voor hygiënisch beleid, I, II en III (Theoretical framework for occupational health research). *Tijdschrift voor Sociale Geneeskunde, 45*, 345–352, 392–397, 427–423.

Zielhuis, R.L., & Henderson, P.Th. (1986). Definitions of monitoring activities and their relevance for the practice of occupational health. *International Archives of Occupational and Environmental Health, 57*, 249–257.

Zijlstra, F.R.H. (1993). *Efficiency in work behavior*. Dissertation, Technical University of Delft.

Zijlstra, F.R.H., & Meijman, T.F. (1989). Het meten van mentale inspanning met behulp van een subjectieve methode (Measuring mental effort by means of a subjective method). In T.F. Meijman (Ed.), *Mentale belasting en werkstress: een arbeidspsychologische benadering*. Assen: van Gorcum.

Zijlstra, F.H.R., Cavalini, P., Wiethoff, M., & Meijman, T.F. (1990). Mental effort: Strategies and efficiency. In P.J.D. Drenth et al. (Eds.), *European perspectives in psychology, Vol. I*. New York: John Wiley & Sons.

3

Ergonomics

Andries F. Sanders

1 INTRODUCTION

1.1 Ergonomics and industrial psychology

Amidst the many issues of industrial psychology, which are discussed in this volume of the Handbook, a chapter on ergonomics is not self-evident. The point is that ergonomics does not automatically fit into the variety of topics which together are coined industrial psychology. Certainly, there are contacts but there are considerable differences in context as well. The result is that a combination of an ergonomist and an industrial psychologist is uncommon, at least in The Netherlands, and that, when ergonomics belongs to a chair in industrial psychology, it is usually treated as a stepchild.

This is not surprising because the two fields have different roots. The basic roots of industrial psychology are mainly the areas of motivation, individual differences and social psychology, which lead to applied issues such as personal assessment, career planning, work motivation, leadership, conflict management and analysis of organisational structures. Ergonomics does not belong to the spin-off of these areas, but, instead, it has a technical-mathematical background with

roots in experimental psychology, workphysiology, movement science and industrial design. Due to its interdisciplinary status it cannot be simply considered as a province of industrial psychology, and certainly not in Continental Europe, where many ergonomists have completed an engineering degree. In the Anglo-saxon countries the contribution of psychology to ergonomics is much larger but, as in Europe, the background is not industrial but experimental psychology. Again, this is not surprising, since most ergonomical issues are related to man as an information processing or moving system while communicating with machines. Indirectly this extends to topics such as work motivation and satisfaction but the primary objective is application of anatomical, physiological and experimental psychological principles to man-machine system design.

The emphasis on differences in context does not mean that there are no contacts with industrial psychology, since specialists of either side should be involved in questions on work-space design, task analysis, automation, safety, training, stress, and system evaluation. Unfortunately this is not common practice, since the solution of ergonomical questions is often left to engineers with little know-how about human factors, which easily leads to gross design failures. It is of interest, therefore, that ergonomists and industrial psychologists know about and appreciate each others contribution. In addition there is overlap. One example concerns the area of complex decision-making and of decision-aiding tools. More generally, a somewhat more complex organisation may easily suffer from a deficient general structure, due to problems of command, control and communication (C3), which may be related to aspects of industrial psychology as well as of ergonomics. The same may be said of questions on training and re-training which are still always underestimated in today's second industrial revolution. Moreover, the rapid developments in society and industry are accompanied by a range of new problems, both in industrial psychology and ergonomics, which may well lead to further contacts. Hence, a chapter on ergonomics is clearly relevant to this Handbook. It will present a general, and hence, superficial helicopter view, much of which is treated in much greater detail in the well-known handbooks, which are listed in the references. One chapter is obviously not enough, and therefore some issues such as work load and safety, are discussed elsewhere in greater detail.

There are no detailed references in this chapter, which should not be taken to imply that the forthcoming discussion reflects the author's contributions. Instead, much has been derived from many texts and papers, which provide much more detailed references. The author's contributions are actually minor and can be found in Sanders (1997), which is concerned with basic and applied issues of reaction processes and attention.

1.2 Development

Ergonomics may still always be described in terms of adaptation of work to human capabilities or, more colloquially, "fitting the job to the worker". This is the opposite of fitting man to the job, as aimed at by selection, classification and training. Although the early beginnings of ergonomics stem from before World War II—for example, research on environmental effects such as noise and illumination on performance—the main emphasis during the prewar period was on mental testing. Ergonomics showed a rapid growth during and following World War II, since most newly developed military systems were often difficult to

handle by a human operator, and did less well than expected, therefore. Research on the design of the cockpit of the Spitfire—the famous "Cambridge cockpit"—and on vigilance in operating sonar and radar echoes belong to the classical examples from World War II, to which the names of Bartlett, Drew, Mackworth, Fitts and McFarland are connected as pioneers.

Thus, the relevance of ergonomics was first recognised in defence research. In the postwar industrial problems the field was originally received with some hesitation, and, even now, one may maintain that ergonomics has not yet reached the status it deserves. There are of course reasons for this state of affairs. One is undoubtedly the lack of basic knowledge, so that many ergonomical problems required expensive experimental research, and could not be solved by simple recommendation or best guess about the optimal design. The lack of basic knowledge was due to the fact that psychological theorising of the prewar period—Gestalt theory and behaviorism—could not address the issues of man-machine interaction. Hence, the major ergonomical applications came initially from sensory psychophysics and from workphysiology—disciplines which, at least in Europe, were hardly seen as domains of psychology but rather of physics and engineering.

The early fifties witnessed a revolution in experimental psychology away from the above research traditions to a conception of the human as an information-processing system. For the ergonomical practice, this provided initially not much more than some theoretical background for designing "knobs and dials" in control rooms. This was still rather peripheral and remote from the ideal to take part in the total concept of system design. However, much progress was made in the course of the recent decades, which is, among others, reflected in the successive editions of McCormick's textbooks, which are now continued by Mark Sanders. This does not mean, though, that there is now sufficient knowledge about human capabilities and optimal usage in automated systems. The point is that the technological advances raise new issues, which, in turn, require other basic research. This has become evident in the increasing emphasis in experimental psychology on complex cognitive issues, relating to problem solving, knowledge acquisition and representation, and internal mental models about the environment. The counterparts in ergonomics are human-computer interaction, design of expert systems, process control and decision aiding, all issues which were fully unknown during the sixties.

1.3 Methodology

The relation between basic and applied research is faced with a methodological problem which is more serious as the involved human-machine system is more complex. The problem may be summarised by saying that human performance in real life consists of more than the sum of elementary skills. It is rather a matter of complex interactions, so that it is hazardous to predict performance in complex systems on the basis of research on elementary mental functions. The alternative is that human behaviour in complex systems is merely studied in realistic simulations with a considerable physical validity. This is not only expensive but there is also the problem that results of simulation studies cannot be generalised either. Hence, studies in simulators under realistic conditions have often rendered disappointing results, although for specific purposes, such as training, they have proven to be highly useful. Field studies suffer from even stronger constraints, in view of problems with experimental control and variation.

Thus, there remains the dilemma that, methodologically, serious objections can be raised to laboratory research on elementary functions as well as to field studies on total work situations. It would be incorrect, though, to sharpen the contrast between these two extreme options too much. Basic as well as field research may be of interest, given a specific set of conditions. In addition there are interesting mixtures, and they do not exclude each other either. Thus, it may be useful to develop a design on the basis of suggestions derived from basic research and, then, to test the adequacy in a simulation. Yet, the trend in ergonomics develops into the direction of specialisms, such as traffic, aviation, robotica etc, which expresses the need of special domain-specific knowledge. In addition there remains a need for generalists, in particular with respect to embedding new developments of a more general nature.

1.4 Human-machine systems

It is now almost trivial to mention the fact that, due to automation, much manual labour is being replaced by supervisory inspection. This is not to say that the problem of physical load has disappeared. The number of back complaints is still increasing, albeit probably due to problems with sitting rather than with carrying heavy loads. Supervisory control means that computer systems and connected equipment perform the task, while the human operator merely watches whether the processes develop satisfactorily. This may be somewhat exaggerated but still contains a great deal of truth. It has been suggested that ergonomics may outlive itself in fully automatised systems, which are fully self-supporting, including issues of trouble shooting and supervisory control. As will be argued in the section on system analysis, this suggestion is wrong. Here it is only noted that the design of total systems always raises the issue which tasks should be performed by human operators and which by machines. In view of the advances in computer technology, this question cannot be answered in any absolute way. Yet, it is interesting to repeat some traditional replies: With regard to routine actions and to remembering large amounts of statistical information the computer is clearly superior. The human is still always better in pattern recognition, although the computer is making rapid progress in this area. When flexible responses to unforeseen and new events are a characteristic of a task, the human operator is still far superior. Yet, the operator cannot be expected to do the impossible, and certainly not when a system is constructed in a way which does not correspond to natural human skills.

This has led to attempts to frame human skills in simulation programs, which, in turn, can be connected to simulations of the machine part of the system. This would enable advance probe trials on total performance of a human-machine system. Although this approach is preferred to total neglect of "the human factor"—as still happens too often—a warning against computerised human performance models should be issued as well. So far the models are too static and sometimes too optimistic about what a human can accomplish. Thus, in some, fatigue and motivation are not taken into account, while, in others, errors are not supposed to occur. Yet, the developments on performance simulators should not be underestimated either. Each new generation performance model is better than the previous one, which should be expected from a maturing field like human performance.

1.5   Outline

Any classification of ergonomics in separate fields is arbitrary, and that is also the case for the present taxonomy, which is based on the relations between ergonomical problem areas and chapters from experimental psychology. A first category is hardware ergonomics, which contains many traditional ergonomical problems and derives from research on perception and motor behavior. Second, there are human factors related to work load and stress, which addresses energetical aspects of work, and is of particular concern to psychophysiology. A third theme is software ergonomics, which relates to memory, learning and knowledge representation as background for studying human-computer interaction. System analysis is a fourth category. It derives in particular from process control with special reference to engineering models on optimal control. Gradually, this area is widening to include decision heuristics and mental models in decision making and diagnosis, as well as techniques of task analysis.

There is the obvious objection to this classification that human factors issues usually run through all four categories, although there are differences in emphasis. Following a schematic sketch of some more detailed ergonomical issues which have their main emphasis within one of the four categories, a somewhat larger prototypical applied area will be briefly discussed. Thus road traffic research is largely related to hardware ergonomics. In the context of work load and stress some remarks will be made on shift work, while software ergonomics will be illustrated with the example of search in data storage systems. Finally, safety issues are prototypical to system analysis.

As mentioned the sketch will be very global, without any reference to the underlying scientific background. More detailed information and references to the detailed literature are found in the extensive literature on human factors. The jour-

nals *Ergonomics* and *Human Factors* play a key role in the dissemination of new results. In addition there are some very important texts, among which the Sanders and McCormick (1993) book is undoubtedly used most frequently. Furthermore there is the extensive *Handbook of Human Factors*, edited by Salvendy (1987), and various other texts like Oborne (1985, 1987) and Wickens (1992). Following a discussion of a category, a short list will be presented of some relevant and more specific references to the literature.

2   HARDWARE ERGONOMICS

Hardware ergonomics is primarily engaged with perceptual-motor performance in man-machine interaction. Older texts (e.g. McCormick, 1970; Morgan et al., 1963), but also some more recent ones (Oborne, 1987) are largely restricted to hardware issues, based upon a trichotomy of input processing, central processing and output processing. Input processing is primarily engaged with information presentation in the visual and auditory domains. Central processing refers mainly to the translation from perception to action, whereas output processing deals with motor aspects of operating machines. In designing workspace, functional anatomy (anthropometry) is of prime importance.

2.1   Presentation of alpha-numerical information

This refers to a large diversity of questions, varying from the optimal design of printed text, to designing text on screens and on traffic signs. Much is known about the optimal design and presentation of verbal material, in which questions of visibility, legibility and readability are distinguished. The first two refer to the design of single symbols, such as digits and letters, while readability is concerned with comprehension in reading continuous text. It is of interest that there is no unique prescription about shape and size of letters and digits, which is optimal for all conditions. In particular, continuous text, such as in a book, and single words, such as in name plates or traffic signs, appear to have different require- ments. In the last case reading distance is of major importance, while reading speed plays the major part in reading continuous text.

As an illustration of the type of factors which should be taken into account, some major guide- lines will be discussed for designing road signs. Besides by form and size of the letters, reading distance is obviously affected by illumination, whereas the type of contrast between symbol and background is of interest as well, i.e. black-on- white (negative contrast) or white-on-black (posi- tive contrast). A sharp contrast leads to the phenomenon of irradiation. In the case of positive contrast the white symbol irradiates which leads to better legibility than in the case of negative contrast, where a white background blurs the symbol. In the case of traffic signs a negative effect of irradiation can be avoided by using, say, green-on-black or white-on-blue, which is often used in road signs. Thus, strongly illuminated white-on-black symbols should be thinner; in contrast, symbols should be thicker in the case of a low level of illumination or in the case of a high level of illumination of the background. On a screen, a negative contrast leads to faster reading, presumably due to the similarity with printed text, which is black-on-white as well. A golden rule with levels of contrast is the relation 1:3:10 for negative contrast—or 10:3:1 for positive con- trast—in regard to the fixated symbols, the immediate background and the wider background, as in the case of sunlight from outside (Boyce, 1981).

With respect to symbol shape, it was not uncommon to recommend capitals, which is still found in older texts. In the case of single words, capitals are not worse but also not better than lower case letters, while lower case letters are always better in sentences. The advantage of lower case letters is that they have a larger variety in size and shape, which results in a richer feature set for identification. Capitals may be used incidentally to emphasise a single word. However a similar effect is reached by presenting a single word in bold, in italics or with reversed contrast. The letter size is of course directly related to the required reading distance. The advent of computer screens had a serious problem in regard to identifying alpha-

numericals, since the symbols used to consist of segments or rough dots, which had a pronounced negative effect on their distinguishing features. In the meantime the resolution in computer screens has improved to the extent that the problem can be considered as solved.

With respect to readability of text it is relevant to have a limited number of words with an active and positive grammar, without abbreviations and without addition of explanations or comments. There is the widely quoted example in the litera- ture of a text to minimize the use of the elevator. The text was: "Please, walk up one floor, walk down two floors, for improved elevator service". A better alternative from the perspective of read- ability would be: "To go up one floor or down two floors, please walk". Operating instructions and manuals are notoriously poor with respect to readability, which may be particularly dangerous in time limited conditions as in the case of fire alarms.

A major problem in designing properly read- able information on traffic signs, and also on computer screens, is to find the optimum between readability and amount of information. It is evident that, as more information is presented, it is less possible to comprehend the text in a single glance. Moreover, the identification of single words is impoverished by neighbouring items. The problem may be particularly urgent when the information is only partly relevant, as on traffic signs which contain information about different destinations. The problem is that simply omitting information is no solution, whereas too much information does not only affect readability but also leads to incorrect decisions. Sometimes it is best to present separate destinations on separate signs, as long as this does not lead to a multitude of successive signs in a small area. As a rule of thumb the number of propositions on a traffic sign should not exceed three items. One may use road number codes rather than destinations, which, however, requires a well established routine in map reading. Thus, the use of alpha-numerical codes is never recommended in signal systems in buildings, plants or campuses. It is not uncommon to find a frequent use of abbreviations, such as "Faculty PP", indicating "Psychology and Education" (Pae- dagogics). The main problem with abbreviations is that one cannot assume that they are understood by those who need the information most. Abbreviations, but also numbers and color codes, are only permissible when one can be sure that users know or can easily retrieve their meaning.

Abbreviations are often used on computer screens in order to save space, but the disadvantage is that, although one has acquired their meaning, reactions remain slower and error proportions higher. An example is buying KPN instead of KNP shares or vice versa. There are some general rules for presenting information on screens which are all related to optimal organisation of data with the aim of facilitating search for a relevant target. First, there are the classical Gestalt principles for grouping visual categories. Grouping may be accomplished through spatial separation but also through inserting common features such as colour or contrast. Although combinations of these rules—e.g. spatial organisation together with colour differences within each spatial category—may further facilitate search, one should avoid too many categorical distinctions, since the positive effect of organisation may easily turn into a negative effect of disorganisation. Moreover, the categorical differences should be perfectly valid: When a red colour has a certain categorical meaning, say a type of ship in a listing of all ships embarked in a harbour, an exception to this rule will be difficult to detect. A taxonomy for categorisation should obviously correspond to well-known or natural differences. This is related to the internal representation or mental model of a system which will be returned to in the context of software ergonomics.

2.2   Presentation of non-verbal visual information

The design of non-verbal displays, such as indicators, pictograms, and other icons like arrows, belongs to the classical issues of hardware ergonomics. For example, the optimal design of indicators was an early application of information theory, in which the question was raised how many alternatives could be distinguished on a continuous scale. Meanwhile, there are a number of general design principles: More categories can be distinguished in a single glance on a circular than on a horizontally or vertically shaped display.

It is obvious that the accuracy of a pointer display is determined by the threshold for absolute perceptual discrimination. In line with the Gestalt principles, it is wise to group scale markings by using variation in marker length. A moving pointer usually leads to better accuracy than a moving scale. If quantitative accuracy is the only thing that matters, a digital scale is unsurpassed.

It is not recommended, though, to apply these principles rigidly, since the optimal shape is determined by the total context in which the display is positioned. In the case of a display panel, in which rough deviations of an optimal reading have to be detected, circular moving pointer displays are optimal, provided that the optimal position of all pointers is the same. For detecting direction circular displays are also optimal. As said, a digital indicator is best for a precise quantitative reading, but for estimating aircraft altitude, and in particular for changes in altitude, a vertically moving pointer display is superior due to the spatial correspondence between display and distance from the ground.

This last principle is usually coined "display compatibility", since it refers to the experienced location in space, with regard to body posture. Application of the same principle in representing the attitude of an aircraft with respect to the horizon leads to a peculiar paradox. Thus, one may display the horizon straight and the aircraft oblique—which is the real situation or, alternatively, one may display the aircraft display straight and the horizon oblique—which is the perceived situation, with the exception of rapid changes in attitude. Research (see Wickens, 1992) suggests that neither display is optimal. The best solution is something in between, in which rapid changes in attitude are reflected by an oblique display of the aircraft, whereas slower and smaller changes are expressed by an oblique horizon. In fact, this mixture corresponds best with the combination of experienced proprioceptive and visual information and, hence, is most "display compatible".

The concept of "display compatibility is also applied to comprehension of pictograms or icons, which have the advantage that they do not require specific language skills and that they are better legible, which makes them particularly attractive as information signs in traffic or in buildings. It is evident, though, that their meaning should be self-explanatory. A standard for international acceptance of an icon is that the proposed symbol should be studied in at least six different countries, with at least 66% correct interpretation in any test. An excellent set of icons is presently used in Dutch railway stations (Zwaga & Boersma, 1983).

Recent years have witnessed an increasing interest in so-called integrated or diagnostic displays. The point is that, for many years, an indicator, like a pointer display, provided only information about a single parameter of a system, whereas usually a diagnosis is needed about the state of the total system, which requires an integrated evaluation of all indicators. This raises serious problems in diagnosing complex and rapidly changing processes, which will be returned to in the section on system analysis. Integrated displays aim at summarising the state of a number of indicators into a single value, so as to facilitate the diagnosis of the state of the system. In the design of integrated displays the basic research on perceiving integral dimensions (Garner, 1974) has been particularly useful. Integral dimensions have the property that the resulting perceptual pattern is more than the sum of the variations on the individual dimensions, so that a unique perceptual pattern may arise for each particular diagnosis.

Apart from indicators or icons, non-verbal information is found in warning signals, such as stroboscopic movements at railway crossings or flashing lights on police cars or ambulances, in advertisements and in codes. In the first two cases, non-verbal conspicuity is aimed at. Thus a moving advertisement attracts attention, provided it is the only moving element in the visual scene. Besides movement, one may use colour, form and size as coding principle, single or in combination with verbal information. For instance, a signposting system in a building, a hospital or a campus may encode rooms in terms of a combination of verbal and non-verbal information. Corridors, wings or even whole units, may be indicated by a colour, while the rooms which belong to the specific colour group are assigned a number. One should be careful, though, to limit the number of colors to a maximum of some three or four. Despite the fact that many colours can be distinguished in a comparative judgement, people perform poorly in absolute judgement of perceptual dimensions. An additional advantage of using a limited number of colours is that colour deficient people have no problems, in particular not when colour and brightness covary.

2.3 Visual ergonomics

The discussion of visual information presentation will be concluded with some general remarks about visual factors which should be taken into account in a design. The relevance of proper illumination and contrast was already briefly touched upon. In addition, there is the issue of reflection of shining surfaces or screens. This leads to competition between the reflected image and the text on the screen as soon as the contrast of the text is less than ten times that of the reflection, False reflections can be avoided by using mat surfaces or by positioning lightsources in a way that no reflections are caused. Frequent interaction with computer screens may cause serious visual complaints in the sense of visual fatigue, headache and irritant eyes. There are indications that these complaints may be due to problems with eye convergence, which system takes care of fusing the images from both eyes. If the distance from the eyes to the screen does not correspond with the natural convergence distance—and there are pronounced individual differences in optimal distance—the convergence system is forced to adapt all the time which would cause the above mentioned complaints.

Working on computer displays has a number of other potential problems such as angle of regard and continuous shifts of focus from the screen to a handwritten text and back, which may imply frequent shifts between light letters and a dark background and dark letters and a light background. It is obvious that such shifts should be avoided in the design of the task. Shifts in focus may also subtend a large visual angle, which creates problems of integrating information from successive percepts. Finally, older screens still suffer from flicker. Glare is still always a main problem in traffic and is caused by sunlight as well as headlights.

2.4   Presentation of auditory information

Auditory information is mainly transmitted by speech and, less so, by system specific signals and alarms. In addition, auditory effects come from noise and music, which will be returned to in the section on work load and stress. Perfect speech comprehension is obviously relevant to proper operation of systems, which is demonstrated by aircraft accidents due to failing communication between pilots and air-traffic control. Three types of problems may underlie a poor communication: Poorly pronounced speech, a lack of redundancy, and, finally, noise or echo on the communication channel. A poorly pronounced and, hence, a poorly comprehended message is mainly a matter of accent or dialect, which creates a large variability in the physical characteristics of a speech signal, which is still enhanced by the fact that the physical characteristics depend on the immediate context of a sound in a word, or of a word in a sentence. Language redundancy usually suffices to solve a potential intelligibility problem, but this may not be enough when the listener is a non-native speaker or when the communication channel filters essential frequencies (e.g. around 1700 Hz). An example is that messages on airports or on railway stations are often poorly understood.

The so-called articulation index is a common measure of the effect of noise on speech intelligibility. The range of relevant frequencies—between 200 and 7000 Hz—is divided into bands and the signal-to-noise ratio is determined for each frequency band. Next, the resulting values are weighed on the basis of their relative contribution to speech, whereupon they are added together into a final score. To test a communication channel or a space, such as a church or concert hall, there are traditional speech comprehension tests consisting of standard word lists. In addition there are now satisfactory automatic methods for evaluating speech quality, based on models of hearing and on the articulation index.

Auditory signals are often used as alarms, varying from the well-known siren to the horn and the bell. They have the advantage of a considerable attention value, but the disadvantage that they easily elicit startling or defence reactions. This is among the reasons that they are sparsely used and only applied to situations in which immediate action is required. Auditory alarms should be brief—a long auditory alarm does not make sense and may even mask other relevant auditory information. In addition an auditory alarm should only issue a general warning, whereas more detailed and specific information should be visually presented. If one really wants to distinguish among auditory alarms—as in auditory call signs—it is possible through variation of pitch and loudness to create some 12–15 properly distinguishable sound combinations. If more alternatives are needed one may extend this number by repeating brief specific sound bursts.

2.5   Control elements

Besides information presentation the choice of controls is the second traditional research topic In the design of man-machine systems. There is a wide variety of possible solutions. Next to the features of the controls as such, their mutual discriminability and their relation to the presented signals are decisive. One may choose between key presses, foot pedals, switches in various forms, a rotating knob, a steering wheel or joystick, a mouse, a rolling ball and a lightpen. The best choice depends of course on the total task. In the case of discrete responses, keys or switches are most appropriate, whereas the wheel is often used for continuous movements. Mouse, rolling ball and lightpen are relatively new and are exclusively used in operating computer screens. Much research has been devoted to the optimal shape of control elements, since one should often be able to operate controls without visual feedback about the correctness of a response. Thus, in aircraft high speed action sequences are sometimes carried out, so that immediate tactual feedback about the responses is indispensable. The shape of controls has been the major variable, but they can differ in texture and size as well, whereas variation of spatial location is a further option. Control elements have usually a visual label, often by way of an appropriate icon.

A proper choice of controls and their codes is particularly relevant when errors have the effect of serious accidents. In the case of very important controls—e.g. the control for firing a missile—one should take care to make sure that there are no similar controls with an altogether different meaning. In one task the operator had two foot pedals one for firing a missile and the other for contacting the command centre which design has a considerable risk of errors. In the case of a combination of controls, some of which are switches, meant for discrete responses and others are joysticks or thumb controls for continuous responses, the continuous elements should move to the right and to the left whereas the switches should move up and down to guarantee optimal distinction.

In regard to the dynamics of continuous controls, gain, resistance and time constant are among the major variables. Resistance refers to the force needed to initiate a movement of the control, which can be either too large or too small. In the case of a small force, there is deficient proprioceptive feedback about the extent of the movement. A high gain control means that a small movement of the control has a relatively large effect like in power steering in some cars. An advantage of power steering has never been found, and one may rather rely on the rule of thumb that the extent of the control movement and the size of the response of the total system should have a natural correspondence. This is certainly a valid rule in the case of zero-order systems which require position control. Sometimes it is profitable to have a combination of a low and a high gain control, as in the case of coarse and fine tuning of a radio. A special problem arises in the case of a control element with a large operating range and a small range of sensitivity. One may think of mixing taps which rapidly change from a cold to a hot water stream. Another problem arises when a rotating knob controlling a gas ring easily reaches a zero position—which means that the burner is turned off—while a low level of burning is hard to set. However, controlling a system becomes really problematic with large time constants, which cause a delay between command and execution of the intended action as is the case in manoeuvring super tankers. This issue will be returned to in the section on system analysis.

The above discussed issues of information presentation and operating controls are all highly relevant to a proper ergonomic design. Yet, the most important issue has only been incidentally met, i.e. the correspondence between information presentation and required responses, briefly labelled as stimulus-response compatibility. S-R compatibility can be achieved in two ways, namely by natural spatial correspondence or by highly overlearned codes. The first case may be illustrated by a four-burner gas cooker. The question is which knob corresponds to which burner. This is often unclear and leads to frequent errors. Written digits and letters are examples of codes that have acquired S-R compatibility through overlearning. In other cases S-R compatibility is less evident, as in the question whether the key in a lock should turn to the left or to the right to open, or whether a door should be pulled or pushed. This is a matter of more or less common population stereotypes, which are of utmost importance for a good design. One example is the positioning of the digits 0–9 on a telephone key board with a $3 \times 3 + 1$ matrix. An ascending arrangement (1–9) appears to be better than a descending (9–1) one.

The compatibility concept will return on several occasions in this chapter. Here, the issue of keyboard design will be briefly considered. It should be noted that, in view of the fact that people can develop a high speed typing skill, the incompatibility of the traditional QWERTY keyboard is usually not recognised. The fact that the long and cumbersome training period is a waste of time is either not considered or taken for granted. Yet, there are alternative systems, which combine an acceptable operating speed with a rapid rate of skill acquisition. This is even more attractive in an era in which virtually everybody uses keyboards. One alternative is the so-called chording system, which consists of a keyboard of only seven keys with a combination of keypresses as entry for each particular symbol. The system was first developed for the Hebrew alphabet, with a compatible spatial correspondence between letter shape and corresponding key presses. However, subsequent research with the Roman alphabet led to the same type of result: an acceptable asymptotic speed level—some 70% of the asymptote with QWERTY—was reached after some 20 hours of practice in a condition in which two keyboards were simultaneously operated, one with the left and the other with the right hand.

2.6 Workstation design

In the design of workstations the emphasis is on control panels of automatised or semi-automatised processes, but also on workstations in offices and work benches for manual labour. The present discussion will not elaborate on issues of presentation and control of individual elements, which were already touched upon in the previous sections. Rather the discussion is concerned with the total configuration which, until recently, used to be characterised by a large number of displays in a complex system, such as a cockpit of a modern aircraft or the control room of a chemical or nuclear plant. There are some intuitively appealing principles with respect to the relative positioning of individual displays or indicators. Thus, important or frequently used displays and controls deserve a central position in the visual field. Moreover, the sequence of use principle states that functionally coherent displays should be close together. Another principle is that clusters of displays should be well separated and distinguished from each other. In this context, the Gestalt rules find a natural application

What is the maximum permissible angle of regard for the information presented in a workstation? Given the prerequisite that the operator should be able to efficiently monitor all displays, the heuristic is that the total panel can be inspected without head movements, which means an angle of regard of no more than 45°. The same is true for relevant information while driving a car—note the position of side mirrors!—and for a typist who should be able to type and read text without making head movements. The heuristic can obviously not be maintained in the case of complex control panels, which, however, means a loss in efficiency. One may admit head movements, which means that the panel may subsume some 120° without turning the upper part of the body. One may resort to swivel chairs when 120° does not suffice—which is still better than to require an operator to walk around. The distance from the operator to the panel is determined by the range of the arms so as to reach controls on the panel and, of course, by the necessary space for the legs. If this leads to an unacceptably small distance between operator and panel—a striking example was the older personal computer which had a combined keyboard and screen—displays and controls might be separated, although this may mean a loss of S-R compatibility.

A horizontal distance of some 60 cm from the panel is still within the reach of the arm, although 40 cm is preferable. This last figure is also the optimal reading distance for verbal information. Another relevant aspect is the type of force that is required to operate the control: 60 cm is appropriate for pulling, while the distance from the panel should be less for an upward or downward movement. When operating a keyboard, the forearm should be perpendicular to the body so that the keys should be no more than 20 cm from the body. In the vertical dimension, the most important controls should never be farther than 50 cm above or below the horizontally stretched arm position— the actual location depending obviously on whether the operator stands or is seated. The type of control is also a relevant factor. A steering wheel should always be below the horizontal forearm position while a discrete response key may well be higher. Since it requires a push response a key may be pressed with the arm stretched, whereas a steering wheel should not be operated with a stretched arm. It is highly important that response keys have sufficient spatial separation and are functionally connected with their corresponding visual information. A separation of minimally 3 cm is needed to minimize errors.

Frequently used visual displays should be about 15° below eye level and perceived at a right angle. Desk height should be in between 65–80 cm and chair height some 40–50 cm, the optimal value depending on the length of the operator. The difference in height between desk and chair should provide the necessary space for the legs. If the task requires the operator to stand—which should be avoided whenever possible—the optimal height of the operating space does not basically differ from what is required when the operator is seated. The relevant factors are the height of the elbow and the required precision of the movements. When great precision is required the operating surface should be some 10 cm above the height of the elbow, while it may be 10 cm below elbow height in the case of less precise movements. As mentioned, one should always attempt to realise a workstation in which the operator is seated. There are of course tasks which require too much mobility to satisfy this requirement, but whether mobility is really needed or the consequence of a poor total design is another issue.

The above considerations are largely a matter of functional anatomy and biomechanics, disciplines which are of prime relevance in workstation design. This is also true for the macro aspects of workstation design, such as the distances and locations of machines, including their display and control elements, in order to guarantee that they can be reached at all. In designing engine rooms for ships this aspect is often neglected. A reasonable passage requires a width of 60 cm and a height of 195 cm but minimally 160 cm is needed. The 60 cm width means that people cannot pass each other. This would require an additional 50 cm. All these figures depend of course on individual differences. All too often workstation design has been based on "design for the average" so that smaller and larger people may experience problems. This was realised and has led to adjustable chairs, desks etc.

A discussion of the requirements for stairs, ladders or chairs is beyond the scope of this chapter, but they are obviously relevant for a proper ergonomic design. The same can be said for the "science of seating". In fact, this is a highly specialised area, among others characterised by the optimal distribution of forces on various parts of the body, which cannot be summarised in a couple of paragraphs. The same is the case for body posture during manual labour. A frequent adverse body posture—such as stooping with stretched legs, resulting in a lot of force on the lower parts of the back—asks for back complaints. However, equally adverse but less recognised body postures are met when seated in poorly designed chairs.

Besides the configuration of displays and controls and the role of human posture and movement, workstations often suffer from suboptimal illumination, which leads to unwanted reflections and unacceptable differences in contrast. False reflections from blackboards are a notorious example! This may be avoided by appropriate positions and shapes of the light sources—avoid a direct point of view of light—and by regulating outside sunlight. It is difficult when sunlight cannot be regulated—e.g. the outside view may be essential to the task. Yet it may fully block perception of task-relevant information. False reflections from blackboards are a notorious example! Another problem is that one does not want to lose "outside contact", which means that the elimination of sunlight is not accepted. A combination of perceiving outside information and reading from a computer screen—say, when controlling navigation in a harbour—often suffers from an unsurmountable problem of strong differences in contrast due to light from outside. In the case of shipping traffic one may wish to use both direct outside information and radar information, but the light intensities of either task are highly incompatible. In the other extreme, all light has to be excluded to improve contrast on a radar or sonar screen or of electronic plots in a command centre –which should be legible at a somewhat larger distance. Yet, a total dark is not acceptable either, since it excludes reading or writing notes or instructions. Local illumination cannot be recommended since it spoils dark adaptation which is essential to reading the above mentioned low contrast screens. A better solution is a diffuse low level of coloured—preferably blue—illumination, which neither affects contrast nor dark adaptation, while still permitting reading and writing.

Besides the physical properties of a workstation, there is the social element. Many tasks require formal communication among people, which should be possible without distracting those which are not involved. This means another functional requirement of the total configuration of workstations. In addition, though, informal communication plays a part, which should not be neglected either. At least, the issue should be addressed whether one wants to promote or avoid informal communication A distance of some 45 cm between people provides a perfect opportunity for informal contact. The relevance of informal contacts in particular in manual labour, follows from research showing that noise complaints may be due to the fact that informal communication is masked.

To account for all the above factors it is recommended to construct a static simulation of a proposed workstation design—or of a set of work stations—which may serve the role of a blueprint. The static simulations used to be built as full-size mock-ups. However, more recently, computer aided designs (CAD) have become popular since they permit advance programming of all physical and social constraints. The CAD should still be tested on potential shortcomings, since relevant parameters may have been overlooked, which are recognised in an experimental trial. Present-day virtual reality techniques have created new possibilities for testing workstation design without the need for building a total mock-up.

With respect to the literature on presentation of information on screens, the work of Pot, Padmos and Brouwers (1986) is a nice orientation. The booklet of Vos and Legein (1989) is relevant to visual Ergonomics, while the Zwaga and Boersma (1983) paper presents a nice study on constructing icons. For workstation design one is referred to the book by Schuffel, Ellens, and Pot (1989), while Grandjean (1981) is still highly recommended with respect to design of the physical elements of a workstation. Davies and Jones (1982) is a nice entrance on issues about auditory presentation of information.

2.7   An applied domain: Road traffic

Car driving is not a single homogeneous task but consists of a range of skills, each of which is called upon in different situations, so that a wide variety of ergonomical results can be applied which are obviously related to improving traffic safety. Driving skills may be distinguished on three levels: Control, manoeuvring and planning. The control level refers foremost to automatic adjustments, such as keeping a correct course on straight and curved roads, setting an appropriate speed, and keeping an adequate distance to a lead car. Manoeuvring refers to short-term actions, like overtaking, braking and accelerating, as well as deciding about the desired lane or direction. Finally, the planning level is concerned with the destination and the desired route. The classification corresponds to that of skill-based, rule-based and knowledge-based behaviour that will be returned to in the discussion of system analysis. In the following some problems on the control and manoeuvring level will be briefly discussed

The control level is particularly relevant to highway driving. Keeping a constant straight course on a road can be perfectly measured by a continuous record of the distance between the vehicle and the white side markings. In fact, road marking is a highly relevant cue for controlling the desired course and speed. Closer successive stripes have the effect that speed is reduced, since closer stripes create the illusion of higher velocity. There are various other visual illusions, and also intentional obstacles, that aim at achieving speed reduction. The advantage of these measures in comparison with traffic signs is that a control problem is counteracted on the control level rather than on the manoeuvring level, as would be the case with traffic signs. It has been well established that traffic signs are little effective with respect to the control level of driving. It has been proposed that drivers set a constant risk, which determines their speed. There are many traffic measures which do not appear to affect the risk level and have only the effect that speed is increased or decreased. According to the constant risk hypothesis research should aim at discovering variables which regulate the level of accepted risk. Part of the hypothesis is also that it takes time to adapt to sudden changes, which leads to dangerous driving in the case of a sudden fog, an unexpected slippery road or a traffic jam. Signalling systems appear to have a positive effect on adapting speed in unexpected dangerous conditions.

Along the same lines, a deviation between driving course and speed should be prevented, which is particularly relevant in designing curvatures at highway exits. When still adapted to highway speed, one is liable to drive too fast in exits. The effect is that one may lose control when curves are too sharp. Although keeping a constant stable course is basically an automatic process, it appears to be quite sensitive to fatigue and mild doses of psychotropic drugs. Indeed, course keeping has been used as criterion for estimating the effect of a drug on traffic skills. However, the absence of a drug effect on the control level does obviously not exclude an effect on one of higher levels.

Manoeuvring level: This level is characterised by more controlled information processing. Failures to detect recognised signals in the environment and making incorrect decisions are responsible for the majority of traffic accidents. Clear and unambiguous signposting and traffic signs are, therefore, of utmost importance. Yet, too many messages are perceptual overloading and should be avoided therefore. The same can be said with respect to road advertisements, which merely distract from the driving task. In road design it is relevant to avoid uncertainty about how to continue one's course at a crossing. So-called "black spot analysis" has shown that a crossing is dangerous when there are too many choices and when there is too little view of cross traffic. Equivalent crossings—on which traffic from the right has priority on the European continent—with relatively little traffic are particularly dangerous since they can cause negligence. Ergonomic measures on the manoeuvring level have shown to be highly valuable, with respect to road design, to signposting and to design of the inside of cars. With respect to this last category, there are traditional issues concerned with turning circle, steering wheel characteristics and dashboard design, but also new problems relating to the advent of car electronics. It has always been hard to fight hazardous driving, irrespective of the question whether this is a matter of "driving style"—too risky or too cautious in terms of the constant risk hypothesis—or of situational effects of alcohol, psychotropic drugs or sleep-loss. Application of microelectronics to the car may change this picture. One might imagine that the car issues a danger signal, or even stops when heartbeat frequency slows down too much or becomes too regular. Speeding can be electronically recorded and might be counteracted in a similar way. Yet, such measures are still quite remote, since they are at odds with consumer wishes, and, hence, with the policy of the car industry.

In the field of road traffic research, the classical books of Näätänen and Summala (1976) and of Shinar (1978) are still frequently quoted. Detailed issues on road traffic are investigated by the Traffic Research Unit of the Human Factors Research Institute TNO at Soesterberg, The Netherlands, and by the Road Research Center at Groningen University which both have excellent documentation at their disposal.

3   LOAD AND STRESS

As mentioned, questions on load and stress refer to the energetic aspects of the interaction between the human and his or her work conditions. In this context work load is relevant in two different ways, namely as physical load in cases of heavy physical labour or poor postures, and as mental load in cases of improper demands on information processing. Next to a brief sketch of the type of issues which are raised in research on load, the question of measurement of load will be addressed. Besides the nature of the task as such, there are various abnormal or unusual conditions which affect load. Examples include long-term monotonous work, lack of sleep, usage of psychotropic drugs, noise, heat or cold and vibration. Finally, the stress concept will be briefly touched upon.

3.1   Physical load

Here the first association may be energy consumption at heavy manual labour, but it was already mentioned in the discussion of workstation design that energy consumption is at best a single aspect of the physical demands. There is the clear notion that energy consumption has secondary meaning in comparison with the question whether relatively weak and sensitive spots of the human body are negatively affected by exposure to an incorrect static or dynamic posture. The most frequently used physiological measure for physical load is caloric consumption in Kcal (kilocalories) or KJ (kilojoules), measured by means of oxygen consumption. This measure is fairly complex, so that various derivative measures of oxygen consumption, like heartbeat frequency and respiration rate, are much more popular. These last measures have the problem that they require individual calibration, since they do not equally reflect oxygen consumption for all individuals. Individual calibration is achieved in the laboratory under standard conditions by means of a bicycle ergometer, in which both heart rate and oxygen consumption are recorded. Besides these general measures of physical load, the load on individual muscle groups can be determined by way of an electromyogram, (EMG) although the value of the EMG should not be overestimated, at least not in dynamic situations.

The amount of energy consumption—and, thus, physical work efficiency—depends on the way the work is actually carried out. Transport of a load by means of a backpack, which mainly and about equally loads the two shoulders, costs much less than when the same load is carried manually by way of two suitcases. When working on the surface, as in gardening or on floors, posture affects energy consumption. Bending with stretched legs takes about twice as much energy as kneeling. The same work takes less when sitting than when standing. Hence, it makes sense to find the most efficient form, and in particular when faced with a heavy load. It should be stressed again, however, that caloric consumption is certainly not the only criterion for physical load. Merely loading weak spots of the body—and in particular the lower area of the back—by unfavourable postures is gaining weight in an era in which much work is carried out in seated position.

In the case of a somewhat longer lasting heavy physical load—as when running—the demands on oxygen consumption exceed the natural supply which results in an "oxygen debt", the symptoms of which are a painful muscle fatigue and heavy panting. It makes sense, therefore, to avoid too much load. It is hard, though, to define strict criteria for what makes up a heavy load. This depends, among others on state of training, age and sex.

3.2   Mental work load

In many cases, manual demands have been replaced by operating machines or, when the task has been fully automatised, by supervisory monitoring. This development belongs to the main reasons for the interest in hardware ergonomics, in which context the issue of mental work load has been studied since the fifties. There are two main avenues: One may be too busy or too bored.

Intuitively, a work load problem arises most logically from too heavy demands on information processing. Provided one has a certain fixed capacity for information processing, it is evident that certain limits should not be exceeded, and this

has been the leading notion in developing work load measures. A first measure is the so-called timeline analysis, a modern version of time and motion study, which consists mainly of recording the time taken by any activity required by the task, both in the sense of observable actions and of thinking and deliberation. Besides an estimate of the total amount of time taken by the task, timeline analysis is interested in overlapping activities. The idea is that one may not do more than "one thing at a time", so that too much overlap implies overload. Recent applications of timeline analysis use computer programs, such as SAINT and MicroSAINT.

A second measurement technique is by way of a so-called secondary task, which equally starts from the idea that one can do only one thing at a time. The second task serves as a loading task, in that the better it can be carried out the less the load of the main task. Various second tasks have been proposed, among others production of a regular interval (tapping), generation of a random letter sequence, reacting to incidentally occurring stimuli and simple arithmetic. Although the second task is sometimes found to be a fair reflection of the demands of the main task—e.g. in car driving on different types of road—the method is only rarely used for a number of good reasons. First, one should have the guarantee that the second task has no negative effect on the main task. In particular in the case of time-critical main tasks a suspicion would render the technique unacceptable. Second, there are doubts about the sensitivity of the secondary task technique. The main problem is that the technique may not be insensitive to the nature of the main task. The point is that there is accumulating evidence in favour of so-called "multiple resources" or qualitatively different types of processing capacity, which correspond to the specific demands of main and secondary tasks. If this is the case, performance on the same loading task would be better in combination with some than with other main tasks, depending on whether or not a particular combination taps different or the same resources. The consequence would obviously be that a simple secondary task performance measure would be inappropriate as an estimate of mental load.

A third method for measuring work load aims at estimating the amount of spare capacity by increasing the usual demands of the main task until performance failures can no longer be avoided. An important restriction of this technique is that one should have a valid simulation of the main task, since committing errors in the real task is usually not permissible. One task in which this method was successfully applied was air-traffic control. Increasing the number of aircraft to be controlled within a constant period of time led to an estimate of the capacity limits of the system, as well as an estimate of the usual work load—also in terms of number of aircraft. The advantage of testing the limits over a second task is that, albeit at various levels of actual demands, subjects perform only the main task, the load of which is actually the main interest of the study.

Much research has been devoted to the feasibility of estimating work load by some psycho-physiological measure, with measures of heart rate, and in particular heart rate variability, as prime candidate. More recently, evoked brain potentials have been considered as well. Yet, there is little chance that a standard practical application will be successful. In this regard, there has been considerable progress with measurement of subjective judgements. In particular the SWAT technique—Subjective Workload Assessment Technique—has proven its merits in a variety of perceptual-motor tasks, among bus drivers and helicopter pilots. The method simply consists of the regular production of a set of three estimates, by way of the digits 0–2 (e.g. 2–0–1) to indicate respectively (a) the degree of being busy (b) the complexity of the present activity and (c) the experienced stress. Prior to the actual judgment the method demands individual calibration of the weights of the three dimensions by conjoint measurement so as to arrive at a single load score. A disadvantage of the technique is that it does not say anything about the question whether a certain level of estimated work load is acceptable from the perspective of actual performance. A fairly high load, but not high enough to lead to performance failures, is already likely to elicit a 2–2–2 estimate, so that the SWAT is insensitive to differences at the high side of the load continuum and does not indicate whether the main task can be completed

without errors. On the other hand, the SWAT has the advantage of a high sensitivity at the low side of the load continuum, where performance measures are of little value since the demands can be met anyway.

In summary, it can be said that, given the present state of the art, work load can be determined best by a combination of a subjective evaluation technique and a behavioural index. Normally, the behavioural measure will consist of some type of timeline analysis, although, if possible, a measure of spare capacity by testing the limits should be preferred.

3.3 Boredom

The above measurement techniques were all engaged with determining the upper limit, in order to determine to what extent the operator can cope with high task demands. In so-called vigilance tasks the issue is reversed since, apart from some incidental adjustments, the operator is idle. Research on vigilance has shown that underload leads equally to suboptimal performance, in that simple but somewhat faint target signals tend to be missed. Signal detection analysis has shown that the effect is not merely a matter of a decrement in perceiving signals but also due to a tendency to be passive—i.e. adopt a higher response criterion. Knowledge of one's performance—hits as well as misses—is a good method for counteracting the decrease in vigilance and, more generally, the effect of monotony. In practice this may be impractical or impossible to do, in which case one may consider presenting artificial signals and limit knowledge of results to the latter category. It should be noted that boredom and loss of motivation, to which the vigilance effect is thought to be due, has a similar effect in short cycled repetitive work.

3.4 Noise, sleep-loss and psychotropic drugs

Noise is a frequently studied adverse environmental condition which has a number of potential effects. The first effect concerns hearing impairment which is found to occur when regularly exposed to intensities beyond 90 dBA. Continuous noise is not necessary to bring about a hearing loss. Regular exposure to brief intensive bangs, as on a military shooting range, is sufficient to cause the effect. The common countermeasure is wearing protective noise attenuating ear plugs. A second effect of noise, which occurs at intensities over 60 dBA concerns masking of speech which hampers social communication. The effects were already touched upon in the discussion on auditory information processing. Furthermore, noise has psychophysiological effects, which are most easily demonstrated in the case of sudden bursts. The ensuing startle response consists of a general sympathetic reaction including muscle contraction, increase in heartbeat frequency, pupil dilatation and an increase in skin resistance. However, this pattern of reaction disappears soon after the startle response has passed, so that it is quite uncertain whether regular exposure to short-lasting noise—as in the vicinity of a busy airport—inflicts direct physiological damage. There are epidemiological data which suggest that living near an airport is mentally unhealthy but it is uncertain to what extent startle responses contribute. It may as well be due to annoyance, sleep-loss or anxiety which may all arise from aircraft noise.

Much research has been devoted to potential effects of noise on performance with mostly inconclusive results. If any, the effects are usually minor and dependent on specific task demands, such as short-term memory load and sustained attention. In either case, brief periods of distraction are damaging. It has also been found that perceptually loading tasks are more sensitive to noise than primarily motor tasks, and that noise tends to have the effect that decisions are made less carefully. This last effect has been sometimes ascribed to an overactivating effect of loud noise. According to the activation hypothesis noise has a stimulating effect when a person's activation level is low and a disintegrating effect when it is already high. Indeed, there are results suggesting that in a state of low activation, due to, say, sleep-loss or monotonous work, noise has a positive effect on performance and in particular when the task demands are sensitive to activation as in predominant motor activity. From this perspective it is not surprising that accompanying music is particularly appreciated when the task demands are mainly motor and much less when they have a

strong perceptual or cognitive component. In these last cases, the distractive effect of noise may be dominant.

Of all adverse environmental conditions, sleep-loss has by far the strongest effects on performance. Both perceptual and motor activity appears to slow down. It should be noted that the decrement is not gradual, but that brief periods of inefficiency and normal functioning alternate. In the case of monotonous work, such as in quality inspection, targets are liable to be missed, whereas reaction time increases when targets are clear but unexpected. Lack of sleep induces passive behavior in the sense that one tends to react rather than to anticipate on forthcoming events, which is particularly dangerous in dynamic tasks as driving, where sleepiness may well account for a considerable proportion of accidents.

Yet, the effects of sleep-loss are less general than might be suspected. Thus, central cognitive functions of reasoning and decision making seem to be less affected than perceptual-motor functions. For instance "interesting" work is still done quite well after a night of sleep loss. It has been suggested that interesting work activates, thus counteracting the deactivating effect of sleep-loss. The problem with this view is that variation of cognitive load—by varying S-R compatibility—in an otherwise equally monotonous task is little sensitive to sleep-loss, whereas a larger perceptual load—by degrading the visual signal quality—or a larger motor load—by introducing unprepared reactions—appear quite sensitive to sleep-loss. Obviously, this should not be taken to imply that the central functions are never affected by sleep-loss. Research on performance "round the clock" for 72 hours has revealed a sharp decline in more complex tasks as well, but performance is surprisingly little affected during the first 24 hours.

Effects of sleep-loss can be counteracted by stimulant drugs, such as amphetamine and caffeine, but also by motivational stimuli. A nice example of a motivational effect concerns knowledge of results which has the effect of eliminating most of the effect of 24 hours sleep-loss. When performing over a longer period of time—e.g. a half hour period of continuous work—there is little evidence for an effect of sleep-loss during the first five or ten minutes of work, the effect rising sharply during the remaining period. The conclusion is that one is not simply governed by deactivation but that, at least temporarily, effort investment may compensate performance impairment.

The last paragraph leads to consideration of effects of psychotropic drugs, such as stimulators, tranquillizers and sedatives. The effects of clinically prescribed doses are certainly measurable but they are minor in comparison with a night's sleep-loss. It is interesting that the size of the effect of stimulants depends on the level of activation. They have little effect on performance after a night of normal sleep, whereas the same dose may fully annihilate the performance decrement caused by a night of sleep-loss. In other words amphetamine has no absolute but a relative effect, depending on the distance to the optimal activation level. It is known that the effects of amphetamines and tranquillizers are mutually compensatory and that the thrust of the effects is on motor functions. In contrast a sedative—e.g. a barbiturate—has its main effect on perceptual processing. This type of result leads to a cognitive-energetical theory in terms of two major energetical supply systems: One (arousal) is phasic, dependent on outside stimulation and particularly relevant to perceptual processing. The second system (activation) feeds mainly motor processing, its effects are tonic, and it is only indirectly related to outside stimulation. Both systems are coordinated by a third hierarchically supraordinate system, which is under conscious control and may be coined "effort". A main task of the effort system is to guarantee an equilibrium of the lower order arousal and activation systems. Thus, it is capable of compensating for too little or too much arousal or activation. In this context, stimulants and tranquillizers affect activation, barbiturates have their prime effect on arousal, whereas sleep-loss affects both systems. Negative effects can be modulated by effort, which has the consequence that the laboratory effects—where subjects know that their performance is being monitored—are probably much smaller than those in everyday life (Sanders, 1997).

The last suggestion may also explain why effects of alcohol are much less dramatic when tested in the laboratory than may be expected on the basis of observation or epidemiological data. Many laboratory studies show only a minor performance effect, even after considerable alcohol consumption. Again, effort might compensate the negative effects, and certainly in short-term tests. One may of course compensate as well in real life conditions, but it is possible that there is not always sufficient motivation to do so. This suggests laboratory conditions in which a normal situation is approximated as much as possible. As said, little effect should be expected in short-term tests; however, effort is supposed to decline as a function of time-on-task so that the real effects of the drug should become more visible as time proceeds. One should be obviously careful to eliminate any implicit or explicit encouragement to do well and abstain from knowledge of results. Yet, the minor alcohol effect in the laboratory may as well have a different background. It could be that in real life the effect of alcohol is more pronounced due to an interaction with other deactivating stimuli. Thus, the depressant effect of alcohol when consumed in combination with a tranquillizer is considerably stronger than the effect of either drug as such. Again, the disinhibiting effect of alcohol may be much stronger when consumption is accompanied by party-like social stimulation than when consumption occurs in the quietness of the laboratory. In the same way the effects of long-term performance and vigilance on performance are minor after normal sleep in comparison with 24 hours sleep-loss. Combinations of adverse conditions—or more generally of conditions which affect energetics, as knowledge of results and motivation—strengthen or weaken the individual effects, depending on whether they activate or deactivate.

3.5 Stress reactions

The notion that the state of the basal mechanisms of arousal and activation are controlled by effort suggests a number of divergent stress reactions (see also Chapter 7 of this Volume). A stress reaction occurs whenever effort falls short of achieving the desired equilibrium in arousal and activation so that there is an obvious lack of optimal energetic supply. A first deficient state concerns situations in which arousal is overstimulated, as in the case of unexpected emotional or threatening stimuli, which cause panic. Stress arises when effort is incapable of inhibiting the arousal level, which has the effect that performance control is considerably weakened. In contrast, monotony has the effect of too low a level of arousal, in which case effort should increase arousal. If failing, the stress response reflects the perceived performance loss. A similar reasoning leads to another two stress responses when effort cannot compensate over- or under-activation, while, finally, effort may have a direct energetic effect on the central processes of reasoning and decision making, which could fall short as well.

A direct application of the model is found in the analysis of work situations with a paced or self-paced rate of work. In a paced condition the speed is prescribed by the system which has the effect that a previous unit should be completed when the next unit arrives. In other words one cannot afford brief periods of inefficiency due to fluctuations in activation. In turn this requires continuous effort investment. A range of studies has indeed shown that paced work elicits harmful physiological stress reactions. Hence, paced work should be avoided, unless the rate of pace is sufficiently low or the work spell is sufficiently brief to forgo effort investment.

3.6 Temperature and motion

Responses to heat and cold are fully described by heat exchange between the human body and its environment. In the case of a high temperature (30°) exchange occurs mainly through transpiration. The contribution of transpiration is negligible at temperatures of less than 20° in which case exchange occurs primarily by direct radiation and indirect air transmission. Heat exchange is determined by a combination of factors, namely air temperature, humidity, wind and temperature of objects in the direct environment. This is acknowledged in the definition of heat, i.e. an effective temperature (ET) of 21° implies a heat sensation of 21° at a humidity of 100%. In comparison ET is about 27° when humidity is only 10%. In addition the role of wind is taken into account in the ET definition.

From a human factors' perspective, the effects of heat on body temperature are of course most relevant. The general heuristic is that, during manual labour, the body temperature should not exceed 38° because body temperature appears to rise relatively fast once this temperature is reached. The effects of heat on physical labour have been well established: Given a reasonable humidity and a temperature of 30°, continuous physical labour should not last more than 30 minutes, not even in the case of moderate caloric demands. The effects of heat on mental tasks depend also on duration and, again, a fairly sharp performance loss should be expected when ET exceeds 30°.

The notion of a comfortable temperature has the problem that people acclimatise, so that subjective comfort may be optimal in a range between 17° and 22°. However, when ET drops below 15° most people find the environment cold, at least without protective cloths. Accurate and detailed motor tasks are negatively affected at an ET below 15° whereas there is little evidence for a negative effect on cognitive tasks. Effects of lower temperatures can be usually prevented by adequate clothing—again with the exception of fine motor movements.

The effects of motion are concerned with a range of issues among which are vibration, acceleration, deceleration and motion sickness. Vibrations can be regular or varying and vary in frequency and amplitude. The intensity is a combination of amplitude, displacement, velocity and acceleration of motion. In the case of varying vibration it is common to determine the frequency spectrum, in which intensity is plotted as a function of frequency. Thus, cars and aircraft have an about equal spectrum at the low frequencies, whereas higher frequencies (10–30 Hz) are much stronger in a car. Vibration may be a problem in truck driving and in operating equipment such as a pneumatic drill. The problem is physiologically reflected in an increased muscle tonus, which has the effect that manual tracking is less precise. The continuous displacement of the body as a result of vibration has the effect of a degraded visual perception. Yet, the effects on cognitive and perceptual-motor tasks are minor so that the above effects may be fairly direct and subject to compensation. Yet, there could well be an accumulating effect as a function of time-on-task, and much depends on the actual characteristics of vibration:

When in the range from 4–8 Hz, they are particularly hard to endure, even when they are low intensity, since the body tends to follow the movements. Higher frequencies are easier to bear and as frequency increases, intensity may increase as well.

Effects of acceleration and deceleration (g-forces) are mainly a problem for professions such as military pilots and astronauts. They have serious effects on a wide range of performance tasks. Moreover, there are illusions in regard to movement direction, in particular in the case of a combination of acceleration and movement of the head into the opposite direction (Coriolis illusion). Motion sickness refers to a general feeling of depression and nausea, and is found to occur in the case of regular motion with a frequency of less than 1 Hz. It is a common problem on ships, but may occur as well in cars or airplanes The effects are usually ascribed to incongruity of information from different senses, and in particular vision, kinaesthesia and equilibrium. Motion sickness can lead to severe disfunctioning on a ship.

3.7 Domain of application: Shift work

When discussing energetic factors, the notion of biological rhythms was not yet raised, notwithstanding the fact that they strongly contribute to work efficiency. Normally, the level of activation increases during the morning, decreases somewhat in the early afternoon—the so-called post-lunch dip, although actual food intake appears to have little effect on the dip –increases again in the course of the afternoon, reaches its highest level in the early evening, decreases strongly late at night and reaches a low in the early morning. The level of activation has a clear relation with performance in high speed tasks. It should be noted, though, that this picture applies in particular to extraverts. It is much less pronounced with introverts, who are typically more activated during the morning and less during the afternoon. The effects of rhythm increase after sleep-loss, in that, following a night sleep-loss, a poor performance in the early morning improves considerably during the late morning, which is followed by a much more pronounced post-lunch dip and a much stronger decrement during the evening.

The above results are relevant to shift work, which is characterised by working at unusual hours of the day or of the night (see also Chapter 5 of this Volume). In the case of three shifts, a usual scheme is 7.00–15.00 (the day shift), 15.00–23.00 (the evening shift) and 23.00–7.00 (the night shift). One may conceive of a wide variety of schemes—including one in which a person is always working in the same shift—but it is common practice to rotate, so that a changing rhythm is asked for. The rotation can be slow, in which case a change in working hours occurs after a week, interrupted by a few days off, or fast, in which case the shifts follow each other in rapid succession, albeit usually a fixed one. An important element is whether the shifts continue during the weekends. It is evident that the problems aggravate in air traffic where a shift implies a shift in time zones as well.

From the perspective of biological rhythms, it is not surprising that most problems arise with the night shift, since one is supposed to work at the low point of activation and is expected to retire when activation is rising again. This is among the reasons that the night shift people sleep less than those of the other shifts, which results in an accumulation of sleep-loss. The prime question is of course whether and to which extent a rhythm may adapt to the change in conditions. There are indications that, even when a person always works at night, the rhythms do never adapt completely. One reason could be that, when a couple of days off duty, most people return to their common day scheme. Both night shift and shift rotation are harmful, the extent of which depends on personal characteristics and on type of work. If night shift as such is viewed as the main problem one may decide to introduce a shorter cycle—i.e. less consecutive nights. Alternatively, if rotation is seen as more adverse one may wish to rotate less frequently. Although there are preferences for either a short or a longer cycle, there is no convincing evidence in favour of either one, although, when viewed merely from the perspective of biological rhythm, a show cycle is less disadvantageous. A slow cycle is also preferable for older employees (>40 years), who have gradually more problems in adapting to change and suffer more from sleep disturbance. One may also hold that older employees should be completely exempted from night shift. However, biological rhythms are not all important. For instance, is it possible to sleep well in a society which is mainly active during the day? If sleep-loss accumulates a long period of night work is obviously hard. How well may one maintain social contacts, when involved in evening and night shifts? Social events are primarily during the evening so that both the evening and the night shift are at a disadvantage. Which cycle permits optimal arrangement of spare time? This requires the possibility of planning ahead and of trading shifts. These arguments favour a short cycle. Yet, studies on employee's preference show a slight trend in favour of a somewhat longer shift. It should be admitted, though, that the results are not fully consistent, and are likely to be dominated by personal habits.

In regard to the literature, there is the somewhat older but still very useful book of Edholm (1967). The work of Tichauer (1978) is also recommended. There is an extensive literature on effects of environmental conditions, which might be entered by reading the papers in Hockey, Gaillard and Coles (1986) and, on psychotropic drugs, in O'Hanlon and De Gier (1985). With respect to shift work one is referred to Folkard and Monk (1985), and with respect to noise, to Davies and Jones (1982).

4 SOFTWARE ERGONOMICS

Software ergonomics is concerned with the dialogue between the human and a computer-controlled system. Each system has a set of operating rules which operators should have at their disposal in order to control the system. It is a matter of software when the operating rules do not directly follow from the system components as such but from system programs. The basic issue of software ergonomics is the extent to which these rules are adapted to the characteristics of the operator with special reference to memory, learning, knowledge representation and reasoning. It is evident that this type of dialogue is not exclusively found in human-computer interaction. Hence, the notion of

software ergonomics is often extended to include any ergonomical question related to processes of memory and thought. In this wider sense it includes computer simulation of mental processes—the so-called expert system—as well as the areas of system analysis and decision making, which will be discussed separately in this chapter.

4.1 Short-term memory

It is common in theories of memory to distinguish between short- and long-term memory. Short-term memory is always concerned with memorising a limited number of cognitive elements, which should be available for a brief period of time. In contrast, long-term memory refers to issues of meaning, knowledge and established action procedures. Short-term memory is sometimes conceived of as an interaction between perception, attention and memory, since aspects of all three of these mental functions play a part. Thus, the capacity of short-term memory depends on the availability of acquired codes, on relations among these codes, but also on the degree to which the codes are phonologically similar, and on the readiness to keep the codes under cognitive control. Short-term memory is of prime relevance for any mental process. It retains the surface structure of what has been perceived most recently, thus enabling extraction of essentials and integration with earlier encoded contents. When short-term memory is deficient—usually a clear sign of dementia—it is hard to keep track of a line of thought. Short-term memory is often connected to the "magical number seven"—the size of the memory span—which is actually a fairly arbitrary number. It has been known long since that a much longer sentence can be perfectly reproduced, whereas retaining three or four items may raise a problem. A typical everyday example concerned the introduction of the secret code for bank passes. Initially, many people proved to have problems in reproducing their four-digits code, despite the fact that this number is much less than the magical number seven. The problem is that, irrespective of their number, items are rapidly forgotten when they are not continuously rehearsed or intentionally learned by heart, in which case the four-digits code is added to the database of knowledge. It is evident, though, that retention is increasingly poor as the number of items is larger. Most people do not know their bank account or car registration number. Moreover, due to their sheer length, many errors are committed when copying an account or dialling a telephone number. Error rates are reduced when different cognitive categories are involved: A series of letters should be preferred above a series of digits, in particular when the letters permit recoding of the series into a meaningful or even into a pseudo word. A combination of letters and digits—e.g. KGS385—is superior to a digit combination, such as 217385, whereas a list of three digits followed by three letters is retained better than a combination like KG28SL. Application of these principles in assigning alpha-numerical codes is obviously useful.

As mentioned, when forgetting has to be avoided, codes should be added to the database or remain under continuous attentional control. The problem is that learning alpha-numerical codes belongs to the most unfavourable ways of knowledge acquisition, namely paired associate or simply rote learning. This is relevant to the design of programming languages and text processing systems which employ a lot of alpha-numerical codes. Linking these codes to natural language or to other compatible representation modes prevents a lot of artificial and cumbersome learning. For efficiency reasons, designers of programming languages tend to use meaningless codes such as "i" and "x" rather than, say, Next and Max, despite the fact that these last codes correspond more closely to the existing knowledge of the user. This is only a simple example, which will be further elaborated in the discussion of using meaningful codes in text processing.

4.2 Navigation in programming

Programming languages may be classified as navigational versus non-navigational. In the first category, the user should not only describe the actions but also the relations between actions by using the syntactic elements of the programming language. In this way, the user instructs the system how to solve the problem which obviously requires a great deal of skill in handling the syntactics of the programming language. In the non-navigational approach the program has more control; it presents the user a menu of questions among which a choice should be made; the choice, then, leads to a new and more detailed set of questions, and so forth. The menu approach makes full use of the natural language, which has the effect that the user does no longer program the solution himself but merely follows the path as recommended by the system. This may be achieved by a menu but equally well by a sequence of questions which all require a simple answer.

Navigational and non-navigational methods have both their own merits. The advantage of the non-navigational method is that the user finds solutions without actual demands on programming knowledge. The disadvantage is obviously that the possible solutions are strictly limited to the domain of the menus. Another problem concerns the degree of detail in the sequence of menus. A slow build-up, each small step of which has to be completed, is annoying when a user is capable of taking larger steps. Moreover there is the objection that the user does not gain real understanding of the system and its potential, although one may doubt whether this is really needed for solving the problem at hand. Yet, a navigational language is more suited as the users are more skilled, since it creates the operating space which a skilled user wants to have. In the case of a navigational procedure one is required to issue a sequence of verbal instructions; alternatively there is the option of a combination of verbal instructions preceded by a flow diagram. The benefit of a flow diagram may depend on the degree of detail: In general a flow diagram is made up of somewhat larger steps, so that each step requires its own program. This is usually better than a very much detailed flow diagram in which each element corresponds to a single instruction. In the case of an experienced programmer, it is unnecessary to structure the problem by means of a flow diagram, but for the less experienced one it is a perfect aid. In addition it is very useful as a demonstration of the logic of a program. Another valuable aid concerns specified computer comments following each instruction. The computer informs about the consequences of the instruction, so that the programmer can evaluate whether it actually contributes towards achieving the desired aims. Thus, it plays the role of immediate feedback. Direct indication of errors—instructions which violate the rules of the programming language—serves a similar aim.

It is evident that similar principles are applied in computer-aided instruction, in which the computer plays the role of a teacher. There are rapid developments in this area that will strongly affect the didactics of all kinds of subjects. A particular point is that the programs require precise specification of which types of didactic aids are most beneficial to learning and skill acquisition. Among the examples of didactic principles are various kinds of feedback of results, error analysis, nonverbal illustrations, and return to earlier covered material that has been insufficiently understood or assimilated. Besides the expectation that pupils will learn faster, since they are immediately informed about errors and their nature, it has been well established that feedback is motivating. The evidence that faster learning is achieved notwithstanding, there are still serious problems with respect to the quality and scope of the programs, which rapidly gain complexity as the issue is more complex. For example, the program must be aware of all types of errors and potential misunderstandings of a problem. Besides application to teaching in schools, computer-aided instruction has a promising future in retraining courses in industry.

4.3 GOMS

Experience is a decisive element in human-computer interaction. Experience refers to the degree of knowledge that a user has about the system, which determines the scope of the aims that can be achieved and which is part of the well-known GOMS model. GOMS is shorthand for Goals, Operators, Methods and Selection rules. Aims are determined by the task and vary in complexity; operations refer to the control potential of the system; methods are production systems which lead to a specific result; finally, given the aims of the task, the selection rules determine which methods are optimal. Experience is mainly a matter of availability of elaborate methods and selection rules.

The advantage of GOMS as an abstract conceptual model is that it emphasises the potential gap between a user and a specialist who actually has the task of developing a programming language. The specialist tends to overestimate the user's level of experience, which problem is, for that matter, not uniquely connected to human-computer interaction but plays a role as well in composing users' manuals for controlling and operating equipment, such as an oven or a video-recorder. The indications are almost invariably technical and declarative-explanatory and fail to provide the appropriate procedural "methods" so as to accomplish the desired aims. There are poignant examples of incomprehensible manuals, which has the effect that many options of technically excellent equipment remain unused. The best strategy for constructing a manual is to carry out a micro task analysis of the actions required for achieving a certain goal, followed by definition of the production rules for each separate action. It is of prime importance that the manual aims at transferring procedural rather than declarative knowledge. Moreover, the texts should be as brief as possible and be supplemented by illustrations and videotapes. This is particularly relevant for instructing emergency procedures, such as in the case of a hotel fire or of problems during a flight. It is highly doubtful whether the present practice suffices in cases of stress and panic.

4.4 Search in external memories

An important aspect of human-computer interaction is concerned with a search for files, which becomes an urgent problem when files are poorly defined or when their number exceeds manageable limits. Searching for a limited set of papers on a specific subject in a library is a good example. In that case, detailed search should be preceded by a retrieval specification of the category features to which the desired file belongs. Human memory may not be the appropriate metaphor for optimal construction of data file systems. The problem is that, at least thus far, external memories are serially searched, whereas search in human memory has strong parallel components as well. When searching for a poorly specified file, one may use a list of key concepts, some of which contain features of the desired file. A proper combination of relevant key concepts, then, may either directly lead to the desired item or to more detailed key concepts, which contain more concrete features of the item and, thus, limit the number of alternatives. In this way the model for data file search has the following steps: (1) determine the features of any desired file; select a list with key concepts which together determine the area in which the file should be; (3) specify further features—and hence new key concepts—whenever the earlier ones proved too general or incomplete; (4) determine a list of possible files which obey a particular subset of key concepts. If this list turns out to be too large, step 3 should be repeated, until the number of alternatives has become manageable.

This may sound simple but, in fact, constructing a well functioning system is highly complex. It depends heavily on the quality of the key concepts, which, in turn, depend on whether they are prototypical for the corresponding items. Suppose the question is to retrieve which diplomats took part in undersigning the Camp David agreement. One may decide to consult a key concept such as "diplomatic agreements". On itself, this keyword would produce a multitude of agreements so that it should be accompanied by a number of additional key concepts which together permit retrieval of the Camp David one. The Camp David file may tell that the agreement was between Israel, Egypt and the USA and the date it was signed, but not mention the names of those taking part. Yet, the newly available information may deliver new features, such as the nations involved and the date on which the agreement was signed, so that in combination with a further key concept such as "diplomats", the names of the actual undersigners can be retrieved. Thus, the accessibility of data depends very much on how well key concepts cue the data. This means that redundancy in the system is quite relevant. When designing a data search system it is recommended to decide on the set of features by logical analysis as well as by empirical checks.

4.5 Expert systems

In an expert system the computer takes over intelligent tasks, and assists in analysing problems, reaching a diagnosis and recommendations for subsequent action. Thus, in the area of medical diagnosis a computer may ask routine questions, analyse the answers, transmit the data from laboratory tests and generate hypotheses for the ultimate diagnosis. In the case of deciding whether a client is creditworthy, a bank has to arrive at a

diagnosis as well, in which case the computer may state a number of questions and arrive at a recommendation. An important task for software ergonomics in building expert systems is the so-called knowledge elicitation, i.e. determining the way in which experienced experts arrive at their final judgement and translating expert knowledge into elements which are manageable for the computer.

4.6 Domain of application: Text processing

Text processing is probably the most widespread application of the computer. There are various systems available, which are all in continuous development so that ergonomical evaluation is always dated soon afterwards. Various factors play a part in the evaluation of text processing systems. One is the way in which a system can be mastered by the average user. A satisfactory system must be easy to comprehend, which has the additional advantage that the usual fear for computers is eased. Rapid mastering and user friendliness are of course related but should be separately mentioned. Does the text as it appears on the screen correspond with the ultimately printed text? This should be expected from a user friendly system. What is the potential of the system? This is of course a relevant aspect, but a system with more options is not necessarily superior. The question is rather what is needed by the user, which has to be determined by task analysis. Thus far, the potential of a system has been too much a matter of the personal taste of computer scientists, who design systems but have little feeling for what the average user can manage and needs to do. Unfortunately, this is not only the case for text processing!

In the following two—now dated—systems will be compared since they had fully different starting points, i.e. the traditional WordPerfect system under MS-DOS 2.11 and a traditional Apple text processing system, such as MacWrite. Either system has now new versions, which tend to become more and more similar—but the initial principles of the Apple text processing philosophy remain unchallenged. The typical feature of the Apple programs is that all procedures can be carried out with spatially organised movements through controlling a mouse, so that the keyboard is completely available to typing verbal text. Hence, function keys are not found on a typical Apple keyboard. In contrast, WordPerfect required keypress responses for any action; the connections between responses and actions are listed and should be acquired by mere rote learning. In regard to procedures general ones—such as choosing, arranging, copying, starting, stopping and deleting—can be distinguished from direct procedures—such as saving, choosing of letter font and formatting. In regard to general procedures MacIntosh has the so-called desktop metaphor; there are files with documents on the desktop and there is a waste paper basket. The advantage is that the organisation of data files corresponds to what the operator is used to do when writing and filing papers on the desk. With respect to direct procedures there are menus with clear texts, such as "cut" and "paste", which can be operated by simple aiming movements of the mouse. Again, the text appears on the screen in the same format as it is ultimately printed.

Thus, the Apple programs have a large correspondence between action and effect, which avoids paired associate learning of meaningless codes. Moreover, the correspondence between text on the screen and in print prevents errors from occurring. The result is that the basics of the program can be mastered in a couple of hours, and—perhaps more importantly—are resistant against disuse. This is also due to the separation between verbal and spatial actions, which utilises a larger variety of human cognitive potential. In contrast, at least in its original forms, WordPerfect was highly incompatible; even verbal codes were inconsistent. One could maintain that pressing a "P" for "print" is a fair option, but how about "E" for "renaming", "O" for "copy" and "Y" for "delete"? Moreover, there was a lack of consistency for the various levels of the menu: In the main menu "Del" meant that a character was removed, whereas Ctrl-T implied that a word was removed. Once on the submenu, removal of a character was now achieved by Ctrl-S! This is the more serious, because the human internal representation of the processing system does not correspond to the potentials on the level of the menu but on the structure of a coherent set of actions, which together achieve a goal. This means

action sequences which run through all levels of the menu.

It is hard to understand why, the ergonomical inferiority notwithstanding, the MS-DOS systems have managed to survive throughout the years. It is correct that the MacWrite program had less options, but, as said, it is doubtful whether a wide variety of options is really utilised by the average user. It has been shown that, when keyboard commands have been mastered, the execution time is less than for mouse commands, so that skilled operators might prefer key press commands for procedures. Yet, the time needed for mastering the commands is excessive and largely a waste. The argument that carrying out mouse commands leads to "less knowledge of the system" does not convince either. It may well be that the preference for MS-DOS operated systems was due to commercial interests, which did not take ergonomical aspects into account. In this regard, the trend is rapidly changing since user friendliness is becoming a prime issue in getting a wide public ready for the computer era.

A wide variety of applications of memory research can be found in Baddeley (1990). In regard to human-computer interaction there is, among others, the classical work of Card, Moran and Newell (1983) and the edited volume of Van der Veer and Mulder (1988).

5   SYSTEM ANALYSIS

5.1   Supervisory control

This section is closely connected to the previous one. The main difference is that, whereas software ergonomics is foremost concerned with the individual interaction between man and computer, system analysis refers to process control in computer operated complex systems. Examples include nuclear and chemical plants but also more and more tasks like flying aircraft. The operator has the task of error detection and correction and one may correctly wonder whether this may not be automatised as well, so that the human operator is fully excluded. There remains the problem, though, of potentially unknown or unexpected failures, which the computer is unable to solve. In fact, the task of a process controller is unattractive since (1) (s)he has the left-overs which are hard to automatise, (2) (s)he has a boring task in which nothing happens as long as the system functions properly and (3) (s)he is expected to find the correct solution in case of emergency. Besides the potential of reacting creatively and flexibly, this type of task is not very well suited to the human operator. One problem is that the operator has excellent knowledge of the processes and possible error sources, while the usual supervision task does not involve any practice.

What does it mean to know an automatised process? The operator receives data about the flow of events by means of values of process variables, on the basis of which (s)he should construct a judgement about what is going on. In order to evaluate the data, one should have a correct internal model of the total process. The first question then is whether the operators have this at their disposal. Engineering models on process control sometimes assume that a correct internal model consists of a set of mathematical formulas with parameter values which should not exceed a certain safety margin. In everyday reality, people appear to have a more functional model, consisting of a set of heuristics which cover the normal functioning of the processes. The problem is of course that the functional model may fail in unusual conditions, in which case no adequate solution can be found. The most common procedure for counteracting the lack of experience with a malfunctioning system is to practise simulated emergency procedures; among others this is a normal routine for civilian aircraft pilots. There remains the problem, though, that unknown conditions may arise but the hope is that simulator training leads to a sufficiently differentiated internal model, which enables creative solutions for unknown situations. It is evident that this implies the implicit but unproven hypothesis that the trained scenarios provide prototypic procedural knowledge, which can be generalised to new situations. However, the available evidence suggests that neither declarative nor explanatory knowledge leads to procedural knowledge; again, experience in process control does not lead to skill in manual control.

One of the main problems in the study on mental models is a lack of tools for analysis. It is not surprising that attempts towards solving this issue have given a new impetus to classical techniques, such as introspective reports and protocol analysis. The attempts have not been completely unsuccessful, although they have shown that non-verbally represented components of internal representations are hard to mould into a verbal description. Thus, the proper methodologies are still a matter of research and debate, so that, its impact on the adequate form of simulator training programmes notwithstanding, a reliable analysis of the structure of a mental model remains problematic. There are presentation techniques, though, which promote obtaining an optimal model of a process. One is presentation of a composite flow diagram of the main process components and their interactions in a single dynamic scheme. The issue is always how detailed the diagram should be and according to which principles it should be constructed. One option is direct correspondence with the real flow of processes, whereas, alternatively, one may decide in favour of a diagram depicting the functional effects of process components and their mutual interaction. A flow diagram is already an example of a diagnostic or integrated display, which has the characteristic that it summarises the combined status of a set of parameters, which together, suggest an essential property of the system. Another option is construction of tests about the status of the system, which have the additional advantage that the operator is more active. One should be warned, though: The Chernobyl nuclear disaster was, among others, due to the fact that a planned test was carried out, while the system was already malfunctioning! This suggests a highly relevant problem in process control, namely that malfunctioning is so rare that one tends to neglect indications about errors.

Even when operators have a good internal model, the data on the displays may be ambiguous and lead to an incorrect interpretation. One example was the display about the safety valve of the cooling system of the Three Mile Island nuclear plant, which indicated the command—open! close!—rather than the actual status. This meant that a situation could arise in which the display suggested that the valve had closed—i.e.

the command was issued—while in fact, due to malfunctioning, it was still open. The problem with this type of design error is that they can remain unnoticed for a long time, because differences between commands and actual status are rare.

5.2 Accidents and human error

The analysis of human error in controlling complex systems has been an important issue, ever since a number of dramatic accidents in process control (see also Chapter 4 of this Volume). It is common to divide human activity in process control into skill-based, rule-based and knowledge-based activity. The first category refers to well practised skills which are largely beyond cognitive control. Stumbling is a good example of a skill-based error: Attempts towards regaining equilibrium are cognitively noticed but not under cognitive control. In rule-based activity, actions are cognitively controlled but they are bound to strict "if ... then" rules. To light the incorrect burner of a stove is a standard example of an error on the rule-based level. In knowledge-based activities—as in solving problems and in deciding, the actions have no strict relation to stimuli, which has the effect that a strict distinction between correct and incorrect tends to blur.

It is often assumed that human skill and rule-based activity has a 1% error probability. Fortunately most errors can be corrected in time or have no serious consequence. The error proportions are foremost determined by the degree of compatibility between stimuli and responses. In order to reduce error proportions, strict application is required of all ergonomical rules, as was previously discussed and as can be found in much greater detail in the extensive literature. This is even relevant to errors which can be easily corrected. In fact correction may occur too slowly in time-critical conditions. Any task should be subjected to a micro task analysis, in which all actions are specified in great detail. For each component it should be indicated how errors may arise and how their probability may be minimised. The issue is that, in particular on the rule- and knowledge-based levels, an accident is not caused by a single error, but by a number of errors. As such, a single error will usually not cause an accident, but contribute to the flow of actions as a latent error. In section 5.5 an illustrative example will be presented.

5.3 Deciding

Many errors on the knowledge-based level are due to an incorrect diagnosis and hence to a false decision in a situation with uncertain outcomes. Research in this area suggests that a decision maker uses heuristics, which, as such are certainly efficient but may as well be suboptimal. An important heuristic is a failure to consider all available options for action, but, instead, a limitation to a few evident ones. Moreover, diagnosticity and reliability of data on which a decision is based are insufficiently assessed but the decision maker tends to start from the assumption that all data are equally reliable and diagnostic. Furthermore, options are often eliminated on the basis of arbitrary criteria. More seriously, once an option has been eliminated, it is not easily reconsidered, even not when it perfectly fits all other criteria. Once committed to a certain option, the decision-maker tends to have a confirmation-bias, in that additional evidence is reconciled with the chosen option, or, is neglected when it is really incompatible. Another point is that a decision maker is often poorly calibrated, in that one has an unjustified confidence in one's own good judgement and decision. Finally there is a tendency of reconstructing the problem space according to momentary attitudes, so that the problem is incorrectly redefined and incorrectly solved.

Within the above framework and other heuristics, the decision maker utilises the traditional statistical decision components of probability and utility of the various alternative options, in that some type of subjectively expected utility is maximised. Yet, the heuristics impose limits on the optimal solution. In addition there is the problem of evaluation of decisions, since the actual result is not normative. It is simple to condemn a decision in hindsight. A good example is the decision of the Pearl Harbor radar station to consider the approaching aircraft on December, 7, 1941 as friend rather than foe. In the light of the outcome, this decision has been obviously condemned. However, consider the alternative that the aircraft had actually been friendly, but had been reported as foe. The effect would have been an attack by anti-aircraft guns on friendly aircraft.

Such decision problems arising in all conditions of "Command and Control", which have been best researched in military command situations. Yet, they are met in all cases of important political and industrial decisions. The common scenario consists of a multitude of messages of varying diagnosticity and reliability, which together point into the direction of a certain decision rather than of some alternative. A first question is whether all messages should actually reach the decision maker or that the messages should be subjected to advance selection. The flow of information can be so heavy that preselection is mandatory which has the effect that there are some assistant decision makers who have the task of determining the importance of each message. One may imagine that certain messages are grouped in that they indicate a common trend, which trend is passed on to the decision maker. This is a matter of cognitive-ergonomical design, which can profitably use modern means of computer graphics. It is obviously relevant that the assistant decision makers do not mutilate messages and limit themselves to transmitting relevant information. In other words the assistant decision makers should have the same mental model as the decision maker, which is not easy to establish and requires special tuning techniques. It should be noted that a similar mental model does not necessarily imply a correct mental model, and, in addition poor decisions may result from applying the above heuristics.

One possible solution for some of the issues is application of so-called decision-aiding techniques. Most of these techniques serve two aims: First, an exhaustive listing of the set of potential options for action or diagnoses. This is less relevant in the case of a simple "yes–no" decision, but many decisions have the characteristic of a choice from a large number of alternatives, which should be carefully outlined. Second, the available data should be weighed in regard to all alternatives, so that each alternative gets a set of ratings pro and con. The final outcome is a utility analysis for each alternative which should lead to the final decision in favour of the winning alternative. In some cases—such as medical diagnosis—the alternatives—diseases –should be assigned an a

priori probability, whereas the data—symptoms—are connected with a certain probability to each alternative. Utility plays a part with regard to the consequences of a faulty diagnosis. It should be noted that decision-aiding means to structure a decision problem and not to solve the problem for the decision maker.

5.4 Models for system design

When designing a predominantly automatic system there is the common problem which components should be assigned to the machines and which to the operator. In this regard, some general principles have gradually emerged: the human operator does poorly in memorising and accounting for more than a few data, whereas the computer has no problems in this respect and can simply evaluate and calculate larger numerical data sets. The human is rapidly bored and demotivated by long-term short-cyclic labour, whereas a computer is not bothered at all, and, equally relevant, does not commit errors as long as the task is fully based on rule-based knowledge. A computer, however, still has problems recognising a pattern in noise, whereas the human is perfectly capable of distinguishing signal and noise; this has been among the reasons to assign monotonous inspection work, such as quality control to the human operator and not to the computer. Finally, the human is capable of developing creative solutions for unknown problematic events, which explains why automatised processes are still always supervised by the human operator.

The above type of principle is commonly used in system design, but, in addition, there is a clear need for more detailed and task-specific statements. This is done by computer simulation. It is evident that the performance of technical system components can be satisfactorily simulated by a computer model. This has led to the wish of designing computer models of the human operator as well, so as to evaluate total system performance, dependent on which components are taken care off by machines and which by the human operator. Among others this is the goal of engineering control models, albeit with special reference to process control. There are also mathematical models—e.g. on visual inspection and on error detection of instruments—for determining the maximal number of instruments which can be visually supervised without missing critical targets. There is the problem that the experimental evidence in favour of these models is far from impressive, and that they cannot be considered as adequate models on human behaviour in visual monitoring. This is *a fortiori* the case for general simulation models on human performance, which usually have far too simple starting points and may therefore lead to bizarre outcomes. For the time being it may be better to refrain from general simulation models and to start from a set of simple heuristics for determining the load of a particular system on the human controller. Thus it may be held that one should usually avoid simultaneous actions from occurring. This is the main heuristic of the frequently applied SAINT program for calculating the acceptability of a technical system to its user.

5.5   Domain of application: Accident analysis

Accidents in situations with at least some knowledge-based components are rarely caused by a single error but rather by coincidence of a large number of errors. The main problem in analysing accidents is that their frequency is very small, which means that *post-hoc* analysis of existing accidents is the only option. It was already mentioned that a *post-hoc* analysis usually discloses a considerable number of latent errors. Two examples will be briefly elaborated, namely the Three-Mile Island near-accident and the destruction of the *Herald of Free Enterprise* on its voyage from Zeebrugge to Dover, both of which are largely derived from Reason's (1990) book.

In the case of the Three-Mile Island nuclear plant, the problem started with a clog in the main cooling water system, as such, this is an innocent incident, which asks for a shift to the reserve feedwater system. However, this reserve system had been disconnected and serviced the day before while the maintenance crew had forgotten to reconnect the system when going off duty. The result was a rise in temperature, which was counteracted by automatic measures, aimed at slowing down the nuclear processes, and by opening a safety valve to prevent undue pressure. The next problem was that, due to technical malfunctioning, the safety valve remained open, while the corresponding display suggested that it had closed, since that display indicated the command rather than the actual status of the safety valve. The operators saw a decrease in pressure due to the fact that the valve was still open—and concluded that the processes had resumed their normal functioning. Due to a lack of cooling the temperature was still rising, which initiated the last automatic defence, namely an emergency pump. This pump was manually closed *by* the operators whereupon the situation became extremely dangerous.

The example shows a structure of at least three human and two technical errors, i.e. forgetting, a design error, an incorrect conclusion, a clog and a malfunctioning safety valve. As such each error was trivial, but in combination they were extremely dangerous.

A similar conclusion follows from the case of the *Herald of Free Enterprise*. At the start of the voyage the large back doors of the lower car deck had not been closed since the assistant boatswain, whose task it was to close the doors, had fallen asleep. The boatswain had seen that the doors were still open but did not consider it as his duty to intervene. The responsible officer could not see the open doors since he had to be on the bridge at the moment of departure, and because there was no proper control display on the bridge. Moreover, certain water tanks had been filled to make the lower deck of the ferry suitable for loading cars at Zeebrugge. Due to an earlier delay there was great pressure to start the voyage, so that one had forgotten to empty the tanks. The effect was that the ferry had a larger draught than usual. This combination of failures meant that, once on open sea, the water could easily enter the ship which had a disastrous effect. In this example there are only human errors—falling asleep, task attitude, no control display, the use of a ferry which did not fit the quay of the harbour, forgetting.

Latent error analysis refers to a thorough check of a system on such "trivial" shortcomings, and to recommendations for improvement. Forgetting and falling asleep are a frequent source, which cannot be eliminated by procedures. One may decide to prevent the system from operating—i.e. no departure of a ferry—as long as essential actions have not yet been carried out. Design errors can be traced but this requires detailed task analysis. However, the most urgent problem in latent error analysis concerns the fact that they are not recognised as errors by the management—trivial as they usually are—so that they are not repaired. What would have happened if, prior to the accident, an ergonomist had pointed out the need of installing a display of the back doors on the bridge? Most likely, the commanding officers had decided that this would be fully unnecessary. Relevant literature on system analysis may be found in Rasmussen and Rouse (1981), McMillan (1989) and Reason (1990).

6 CONCLUSION

The trip through the various ergonomical chapters showed a highly variable landscape in which borders to neighbouring fields were repeatedly met. Borderlines were perhaps most obvious in the discussion of load and stress, subjects to be met again in other chapters of this Handbook from a wider and broader angle of regard. The issue of decision theory borders social psychology. There are still other borders with technical and physiological domains which might have been less obvious from the present discussion. The question whether one wants to summarise the wide variety of problems as "ergonomics" is a matter of taste, and depends on the width of the scope one is willing to permit the domain. It is broadly defined when defined in terms of any form of interaction between the human and a technical environment, and that has been the starting point of the chapter. It is of course possible to use a more narrow definition and include certain areas in industrial medicine or industrial psychology. However, the borders may as well be fuzzy; this may be the more interesting when the overlapping areas are studied by scientists from different disciplines. It is evident that ergonomics is an applied discipline, the basic theory of which is always part of related disciplines.

When reading the different parts of this chapter it is striking that they differ in regard to concrete recommendations for design. Sometimes the text consisted of fairly specific suggestions, whereas on other occasions problems were listed and backgrounds were depicted. This is obviously a matter of the relative advances of the underlying basic sciences. The more technical and physiological areas—like thermophysiology, anthropometrics, and illumination engineering—have clearly more advanced than some psychological areas such as knowledge acquisition and decision theory. Within the domain of psychology, performance theory may have developed most, so that hardware ergonomics could *be* the most concrete part of the chapter, certainly more so than human-computer interaction and system analysis. Yet, at present, these latter fields are more in the focus of interest and demand considerable research effort therefore.

REFERENCES

Baddeley, A. (1990). *Human memory*. Hove, UK: Lawrence Erlbaum Associates Ltd.

Boyce, P. (1981). *Human factors in lighting*. New York: MacMillan.

Card, S.K., Moran, T.P., & Newell, A. (1983). *The psychology of human-computer interaction*. Hillsdale, NJ: Erlbaum.

Davies, D., & Jones, D. (1982). Hearing and noise. In W. Singleton (Ed.), *The body at work*. New York: Cambridge University Press.

Edholm, O.G. (1967). *The biology of work*. New York: McGraw-Hill.

Folkard, S., & Monk, T.H. (1985). *Hours of work: Temporal factors in work scheduling*. New York: Wiley.

Garner, W.R. (1974). *The processing of information and structure*. Hillsdale, NJ: Erlbaum.

Grandjean, E. (1981). *Fitting the task to the man*. New York: IPS.

Hockey, G.R.J., Gaillard, A.W.K., & Coles, M.G.H. (1986). *Energetics and human information processing*. Dordrecht: Nijhoff.

McCormick, E.J. (1970). *Human factors engineering*. New York: McGraw-Hill.

McMillan, G.R. (1989). *Applications of human performance models to system design*. New York: Plenum.

Morgan, C.T., Cook, J.S., Chapanis, A., & Lund, M.W. (1963). *Human engineering guide to equipment design*. New York: McGraw-Hill.

Näätänen, R., & Summala, H. (1976). *Road-user behavior and traffic accidents*. Amsterdam: North-Holland.

Oborne, D.J. (1985). *Computers at work*. New York: Wiley.

Oborne, D.J. (1987). *Ergonomics at work*. New York: Wiley.

O'Hanlon, J.F., & Gier, X. de (1985). *Drugs and driving*. London: Taylor & Francis.

Pot, F., Padmos, P., & Brouwers, A. (1986). *Achter de schermen*. Den Haag: Ministerie van Sociale Zaken.

Rasmussen, J., & Rouse, W.B. (1981). *Human detection and diagnosis of system failures*. New York: Plenum.

Reason, J. (1990). *Human error*. Cambridge, UK: Cambridge University Press.

Salvendy, G. (Ed.) (1987). *Handbook of human factors*. New York: Wiley.

Sanders, A.F. (1997). *Elements of human performance*. Hillsdale, NY: Erlbaum.

Sanders, M.S., & McCormick, E.J. (1993). *Human factors in engineering and design*. New York: McGraw-Hill.

Schuffel, H., Ellens, E., & Pot, F. (1989). *Richtlijnen voor de Ergonomie van werkplekken*. Voorburg: Ministerie van Sociale Zaken.

Shinar, D. (1978). *Psychology on the road: The human factor in traffic safety*. New York: Wiley.

Tichauer, E.R. (1978). *The biomechanical basis of ergonomics*. New York: Wiley.

Veer, G.C. van der, & Mulder, G. (1988). *The human-computer interaction: psychonomic aspects*. Heidelberg: Springer.

Vos, J.J., & Legein, Ch. P. (1989). *Oog en werk*. Den Haag: SDU.

Wickens, C.D. (1992). *Engineering psychology and human performance* (2nd ed.). Columbus: Merrill.

Zwaga, H.J. & Boersma, T. (1983). Evaluation of a set of graphic symbols. *Applied Ergonomics, 14*, 43–54.

4

Industrial Safety

Willem A. Wagenaar and Patrick T.W. Hudson

1   DEFINITION

Defining safety immediately leads to a problem. While for some safety can be defined as the absence of accidents, it is clear that everyone appreciates that chance plays a considerable role in accidents. It is perfectly possible not to have had any accidents for a long time, but nevertheless to have been skating continuously on thin ice. Accidents form a very "noisy" measure of safety. This is why it is difficult to state that a company without accidents is, therefore, a safe company. Even the accident statistics of an organisation with several thousand employees still show the typical swings that indicate a considerable effect of chance. This variability grows relatively larger as an organisation becomes safer, so that just one or two accidents can result in a major change in the overall accident statistics. There are other aspects of a company or organisation that can provide as good or even a better measure for safety. For instance, criteria might include using equipment that breaks down only infrequently, selecting and promoting personnel on the basis of technical competence, and giving safety priority when taking strategic decisions. Safety is seen as determined by the extent to which such criteria are satisfied, not by more or less random accident statistics. This is the theme that will be elaborated in the rest of this chapter. As a result the chapter will be less of a review of what has been thought about industrial safety and more a reasoned argument in favour of one particular approach to safety in companies and other organisations.

2   "IN SEARCH OF MISERY"

The search for useful safety criteria can take place in two ways. One can systematically investigate safe companies in a search for common factors capable of explaining their success. We call this the "in search of safety" strategy, after Peters and Waterman's well-known book *In Search of Excellence* (1982), in which the typical features of excellent companies are investigated without spending too much time on what struggling companies are doing wrong. As an approach to safety this strategy has the important shortcoming that it is quite original, that is to say, no one has done it systematically yet; reporting the results of such an approach would make for a very short chapter. The general tradition can, rather, be characterised as "in search of misery"; one searches out accidents, or organisations with poor safety records, in order to identify what went wrong. Practically all research into safety criteria is of this second type. A third strategy is the most logical, comparing safe and unsafe companies in order to see where and why they differ. We know, unfortunately, of no such study. As a result it is on purely practical grounds that we start by following the "in search of misery" tradition, studying accidents as a way of understanding safety. As our argument develops, however, we will move towards an "in search of safety" approach, in which accidents play a minor role in determining how safety is to be assessed and managed.

3   WHAT IS AN ACCIDENT?

To study accidents one must first define what an accident is. Definitions may involve the requirement for medical treatment, the undesired release of energy or hazardous substances or even just the creation of unwanted situations. An accident may involve a cut finger, but could also involve losing in excess of a billion dollars without the loss of life or limb. One can philosophise deeply over the issue, but such discussions are of little value in practice. This is not to say that there are no definitional problems in the real world. On the contrary, the practical definition of what constitutes an accident is a major determinant of the accident statistics, so much so that without a deep insight into the definitions used the statistics are almost absolutely meaningless. Comparing different companies, whether in the same or different branches, in the same or different countries, the same or different sizes etc., is impossible in practice, because it is obvious that different definitions will have been applied.

Often accident statistics distinguish between fatal accidents and those that lead to at least one day off work (lost time incidents or LTIs). One can also register smaller accidents (restricted work cases or RWCs) and near misses where no one gets hurt. Most organisations still do not do the latter, at least not systematically. At first sight fatal and LTI accidents appear to be clear categories, but even applying those criteria creates difficulties. Someone just avoids being hit by a falling piece of

concrete, but dies shortly thereafter of a heart attack that *might* not have happened without the shock of the falling block. Is this a fatal accident to be registered by the safety department, or a case of illness to be registered by the medical department? A child, despite all warnings, plays on a construction site, is run over by a truck and dies. The child wasn't even on the payroll of the construction company! A typist traps several fingers in a drawer, and, as a result, cannot type for three days. The typist can, however, still work as a receptionist. Is this an LTI or an RWC? In our own field studies we have seen how a victim was unceremoniously deposited outside the "fence", because accidents "outside" don't count; we have seen people after they have had an accident being redeployed for two weeks as a "guard" on a location where there was nothing to guard, just because this ensured that the accident was recorded as a less serious RWC rather than an LTI! This latter redefinition was important because a significant bonus was promised for each group that reached a million man-hours worked without an LTI.

Definitions can be extremely important in determining what happens in the workplace. It is even possible for victims to be withheld medical assistance because calling in a doctor automatically leads to registration of an incident as an accident. Problems of definition are less important when accidents are not the principal measure of safety, but only provide one of a number of measures. This is the reason why, in our own research, we have used a simple rule of thumb: an incident is treated as an accident when the company provides it to us defined as such. In this case it is at least being defined as an event the organisation would rather avoid and researchers who place themselves at the service of industry have no reason to disagree with such a clear wish. Furthermore, it will become clear in what follows that ordinary observations also provide vital insights into the criteria for safe work.

4   THE GENERAL CAUSAL CHAIN

When studying accidents it proves worth while to develop a general conceptual framework, so that more general facts can be obtained from individual and highly variable events. Discovering such a general framework requires a cyclical process. Before one starts one has no idea what analytic structure might prove effective. Initial hypotheses about what is important need to be proposed, refined and rejected. After a number of accidents one begins to develop a vague notion of what might prove effective, by the thousandth one has acquired the necessary insights. But, this approach requires regularly revisiting the first accidents to see if the latest proposal actually works. The structure proposed in this chapter was developed using such an iterative approach. There are many other structures; researchers tend to follow their own tastes and preferences. There is nothing wrong with that, so long as their structures meet a number of requirements. A more detailed description of the general causal chain we use is described in Wagenaar, Hudson and Reason (1990) and Wagenaar (1991).

Figure 4.1 represents the general accident causal chain. By *general* we mean that it is applicable to every accident; by *causal* we mean that it describes the necessary conditions for the occurrence of accidents. Eliminating any one of the links in the chain breaks the chain, so that the accident no longer happens. We treat the diagram in reverse, from right to left, backtracking from the accident to the original decisions that led to it.

5   THE ACCIDENT ITSELF

An accident is the final result of the causal chain. It is, nevertheless, not always clear exactly which event one should choose to regard as the accident. Is it the fall or the injury? Is it the explosion or the ensuing deaths? Often people think of prevention in terms of the placing of some barrier between the physical event (the explosion) and the consequence (the fatality). Examples of such last-ditch preventative measures are safety helmets, seat belts, lifeboats, ejection seats, escape routes etc. The absence of such a final line of defence may be the result of a structural shortcoming in the safety policy or its implementation. This is why for our definition the accident is the fatality, not the explosion that led to someone dying, the injury rather than the fall. This definition, framed in terms of the general pathway, allows us to analyse accidents, near misses and, even, situations in which nothing has yet gone wrong in a consistent and systematic way.

6   DEFENCES

This approach makes it immediately clear what we mean by the second element, the defences, represented in Figure 4.1 as a shaded barrier interpolated between unsafe acts and the actual accident. Defence mechanisms are there to ensure that explosions do not result in accidents. Nuclear power plants are usually constructed with a so-called containment, a very strong concrete construction capable of withstanding an explosion, in order to prevent the release of radioactive material. Of course, there is no intention that the reactor be allowed to explode in the first place, but *should* it happen, such a containment represents a good defence. Where people work and hazards are involved, defences are always necessary. If and when people do fail, that should not lead inevitably to a disaster. This consideration is so important just because people most certainly will fail. Relatively simple actions, such as pushing a button on a control panel, reading a meter, opening the right valve or performing a sequence of five actions in the correct order, are performed incorrectly at least once every thousand times (Swain & Guttmann, 1983). When work is so organised that such errors lead inevitably to accidents, the necessary defences must be missing. It is not for nothing that the computer asks, before you delete everything in a directory, "Are you sure?".

There is one form of defence that we know really does not work, that is the use of specific instructions and procedures in which errors are not allowed, but no further preventative measures are taken other than telling people not to do it. When an error can result in disaster, there is little to be gained from simply forbidding that error. People do not, on the whole, make errors willingly, so forbidding unintentional errors is of little effect. See section 7.

FIGURE 4.1

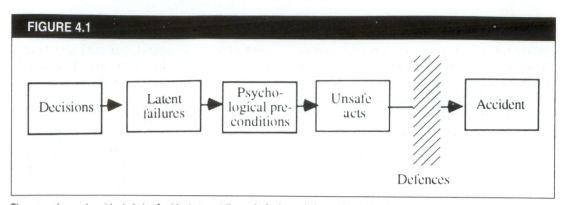

The general causal accident chain. Accidents are at the end of a long chain starting with a fallible decision.

6.1 Inherent weaknesses in defences

The major problem with defences is that no one defence system is completely safe. Alarm systems can be turned off and, sometimes, must be disabled. The Chernobyl nuclear accident is a good example as performing the safety test, which is what they were doing when things went wrong, required negating the normal alarms. People take pride in beating the system; in such cases defences can increase rather than decrease the dangers. For instance, in a certain location, work may only be carried out when the fire brigade is present. Therefore there are two locks on the door, the key to one is held by the firemen, the other is held by the maintenance department. The intended effect is that the door should only be opened when the fire brigade is present. In practice the door forms a challenge to the maintenance men to prove that, with their technical ability, they are not to be held back by a simple lock. Winning means opening the door, *without* the firemen.

Even so-called inherently safe systems are never completely safe. Here we are talking about systems that, with any disturbance, fall into a safe state as a result of the application of the laws of nature. A simple example is an "automatic level crossing half-barrier". The boom is held open by the application of a voltage on an electrical circuit. Should the electricity fail for any reason, the barrier will automatically fall into place as a result of gravity. But, this requires that the hinge is not rusted solid, that saboteurs have not propped the boom open, that, just as the boom is falling, no large vehicle is passing underneath which is subsequently trapped. Guaranteed safe is not even a characteristic of inherently safe systems; the only pure guarantee is provided by not undertaking the activity.

The design of defences requires that one has sufficient insight into the kinds of errors people make. The problem is that some errors are hard to envisage in advance. Who would have thought that a qualified electrician would have touched a 10 kV switch gear without first checking to see if it was live (cf. Wagenaar et al., 1990)? Who would have imagined that construction fitters would remove so many bolts from a steel bridge that it would fall down on its own (cf. Bignell, Peters & Pym, 1977, ch. 5)? Who would have predicted that the operators at Chernobyl would withdraw all the control rods in the reactor so that the process became uncontrollable (cf. Report of the USSR State Committee, 1986)? One cannot expect to design and construct defences such that the effects of human error will be totally eliminated.

6.2 Defences may induce errors

Defence strategies can lead to extremely fundamental discussions within organisations. The best example is the Automatic Train Control System. In principle that is a system that allows the driver to perform all the control functions of the train, but which intervenes whenever the driver makes an error. Drivers could get the feeling that they are being observed by such a system. There is also an anxiety that drivers might be sloppier because they know the system will always correct their errors. A driver could, as it were, consider passing through a red signal at full speed, because the system will still stop the train. This discussion has led to the situation that in The Netherlands the automatic system now only checks whether drivers brake for amber warning signals, not whether they stop for red. Driving through red has, as a result, become a daily occurrence. The error, once made, is not corrected by the defence that should have been there.

There is even the chance that a defensive system actually reduces overall safety. For example, an operator does not attend closely when warming a liquid in a pressure vessel. The automatic pressure protection fails to work and the vessel explodes. As a result it is decided to make the vessels much stronger. The result now is that the next time there is an explosion it will be considerably larger than the first one. The safer method, surprisingly, is to make the vessel *weaker*, so that in case of failure there will be a smaller explosion. Many defences have this counter-intuitive consequence, of making smaller accidents less likely, but when they *do* occur, the accidents are now more devastating. Train crossings are no longer manned, but shut automatically, resulting in fewer open crossings that should have shut. Because the safety margin is no longer seen as necessary, the delay between closing the crossing and the train arriving can be significantly reduced; this reduction can be so much that a train cannot stop once the track is blocked (cf. Bignell et al., 1977, ch. 8).

In summary, we can state that while defences against error are necessary, at the same time we cannot expect that they provide sufficient protection against all errors. An effective safety policy needs to encompass both defences and measures intended to make those defences unnecessary, in practice.

7 UNSAFE ACTS

Practically all accidents are preceded by unsafe acts that we identify with human errors. That does not mean that the acts will have been recognised as unsafe, let alone dangerous. In the majority of cases that is just what happens. Unsafe acts may be regarded as those acts that, with hindsight, we would regret had things turned out badly. In order to understand this we have to go in depth into the sort of errors we can distinguish.

7.1 Reason's GEMS model

Reason's (1990) model of operator behaviour (GEMS = generic error-modelling system) synthesises the theories of Norman (1981) and Rasmussen (1982, 1983). The diagram in Figure 4.2 summarises the theory. In the first instance behaviour is seen as being determined at three levels. At the lowest level, the *skill-based* or automatic level, actions are performed as reflexes. Here we have sequences of actions organised hierarchically in schemas. An example is going home after a day's work. I pack up my briefcase, leave the room, exit the building, find my car and then drive home. Each piece of the "mother" schema consists of a "daughter" schema. Leaving my room involves a sequence of putting on my jacket, picking up the briefcase, turning off the light, opening the door, stepping through the door, locking the door. The daughter schemas themselves consist of "granddaughter" schemas, so locking the door requires finding my keys (mostly in the right-hand jacket pocket), finding the correct key, the one with the two separated holes on top, inserting it into the keyhole, turning (clockwise), removing the key, replacing the keys in the jacket, checking if the door is really locked. Inserting the key, in its turn, requires moving the key towards the keyhole, minimising the distance until contact is made, pushing until resistance is felt etc. GEMS proposes that each of these actions is performed automatically and then automatically calls up the next in the sequence once there is satisfaction that the step has been completed successfully, according to the expectations carried in the schema. At this basic automatic level extremely complex sequences of actions can be performed, punctuated by control checks on success.

The transition to a higher level, the *rule-based* level, occurs when the control check reveals that not all has gone to plan. For instance, when the key fails to fit the hole, the sequence cannot proceed. A solution to this problem must be found. At the

FIGURE 4.2

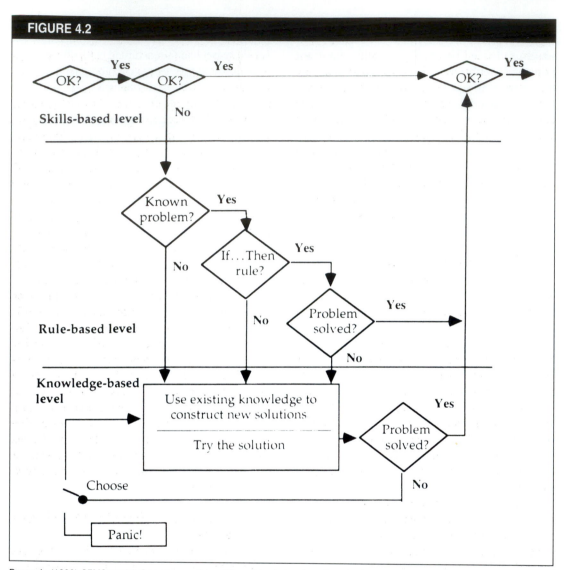

Reason's (1990) GEMS model. Operation on three different levels involves dropping from the skills-based to the rule-based level in case of an identified failure, while dropping to the knowledge-based level is caused by inability to solve at the rule-based level.

rule-based level, solutions are found to be appealing to *if... then* rules. *If* the key does not fit, *then* try another. A study of solutions to everyday problems (Wagenaar, 1992) revealed that people have the same rules in their heads. In the case that the key fails to fit, people have the following rules:

1. use a bit more force;
2. check to see if you have the correct key;
3. check to see if the key is damaged;

4. look to see what is wrong with the lock.

The rules are based upon what previously helped in similar situations, rather on any fundamental insight into the nature of the problem. The most frequently successful is tried first (using more force) even when it might have negative consequences (the lock on my car is now broken).

When the situation is not recognised as belonging to a known type, or the rules fail to solve the problem, then behaviour is shifted to the *knowledge-based* level. At this level a new solution is sought for based upon insights, often from first principles. Therefore it is necessary to diagnose the nature of the problem, discover the cause and finally think of a way to remove that cause or circumvent the problem. If I find the wrong bunch of keys in my pocket, I still have to work out how to get the door locked. This may involve working out where my keys really are, how and whether I can get them and, if not, knowing who has a copy key (we share room keys within the department so this problem now becomes, who is left in the building?).

7.2   The GEMS error taxonomy

The most important advantage of the hierarchical organisation of actions, as is used in GEMS, is that the majority can be performed without directing any attention to them. There is no alternative possible, because the majority of actions have to occur in parallel. This parallel character ensures that most of our actions can be carried out highly successfully and rapidly. With a parallel architecture, however, overt attention can only be directed to one process, rather than be directed simultaneously over all the processes, which means that the others are not attended to, which in turn can lead to problems. The parallel architecture provides the system with enormous capacity, but the downside is that errors can occur in those processes that run without attention. The system is designed to detect and correct error, by predicting what is expected to happen in a purely feed-forward manner and checking progress against those expectations. But, such checks will not always happen or will themselves be erroneous and an error may be the result.

7.2.1   Skill-based errors: slips and lapses

Errors at the skill-based level are distinguished into *slips* and *lapses*. Slips are errors of commission, failures in the performance of a plan that is itself good. They arise for all sorts of reasons. The best known type is the double-attention slip. The situations in which this occurs are when one is following a plan where at first a known scheme is followed, but which is meant to diverge at a certain point in the sequence. At the point of choice the

attention is diverted (thus "double-attention") and the execution follows the old scheme. A clear example of a "double-attention" slip is : "We now have two refrigerators in the kitchen and yesterday we moved all the food to the new one. This morning I kept opening the old one" (Reason, 1990, p. 48). A second type of error at the skills level is the "lapse after an interruption". Whenever a scheme is interrupted ("someone called me on the phone") it is difficult to pick up the task execution at the same point. A third type of error at the skills level is loss of intention: "I was going upstairs to get the stapler, but when I got up there I could not remember why I had come upstairs".

Lapses form a crucial type of unsafe act, because they are much harder to detect and, therefore, to counter. Controlled "flight into terrain", more obviously the result of mistaken behaviour of pilots and, occasionally, air traffic controllers, remains the prime direct cause of air crashes. Analyses of the causes of aircraft crashes show that the second major cause is maintenance-related. In an analysis of 276 in-flight engine shut-downs, Boeing found that 34% were due to incomplete installation after maintenance and a further 11% were due to equipment not having been installed, or left out. While the omitted items seem trivial, such as fastenings left undone or washers missing, these may be more than enough to cause a crash.

7.2.2   Mistakes: rule-based and knowledge-based errors

At the rules level completely different errors occur, which are mostly called "mistakes". It is typical of mistakes that the plan is wrong, not the execution of it. The best explanation of mistakes is therefore wrong planning. When the plan is executed, at the skills level, then it is impossible to detect the error at that level; all that is being checked for is deviation from the expectations built into the plan. At the rules level mistakes always have something to do with the applied rule. This is true when the situation is classified incorrectly. For example, the situation during the accident at Three Mile Island (Rogovin, 1979) was incorrectly identified as a less important problem which had been ongoing for several weeks. The rule applied led to a worsening of the situation instead of to a solution. It is often the case that before the signals which indicate what is actually happening are received the problem has been explained away. Rules are ordered in a certain hierarchy: rules that are often applied success-fully, become more powerful and win the "race" more easily for application in a concrete case. General rules are usually stronger than special rules, for example: *use water to extinguish fire*. However, when there is a fire in a pan with oil, water only makes it worse; *do not use water but cover the pan*. This special rule is difficult to apply, because the general rule is applied almost impulsively. This is an example of errors of the sort *strong* but *wrong*, in which what are usually the best solutions turn out to be the wrong ones. Another problem in the application of rules is that the use of "bad rules" is often systematically rewarded. The life threatening procedure that the crew of the *Herald of Free Enterprise* used for loading vehicles is a good example of a bad rule. The use of that rule, however, formed the only possible way for the ship to keep to its timetable

and it was therefore systematically rewarded. The application of such a bad rule leads in the course of time to accidents, but whilst being used that can remain hidden for a long time.

At the knowledge level once again completely different errors arise. Unlike rule-based process-ing, knowledge-based reasoning involves starting from scratch and working things out from first principles. We often call failures to find the right solution at this level "mistakes" as well, but here the origin is entirely different. Mistakes at the knowledge-based level arise because a reasoned solution to a problem is incorrect, because too little of the problem space has been considered in the solution (Evans, 1983), because the quality of the solution was not critically investigated (Nisbett & Ross, 1980), or because of too much self-confidence (Wagenaar & Keren, 1986).

A complete review of the various types of errors at the different levels can be found in Reason (1990). The brief overview given in Figure 4.3 will have to suffice here. The most important point in the figure is the clear distinction into four

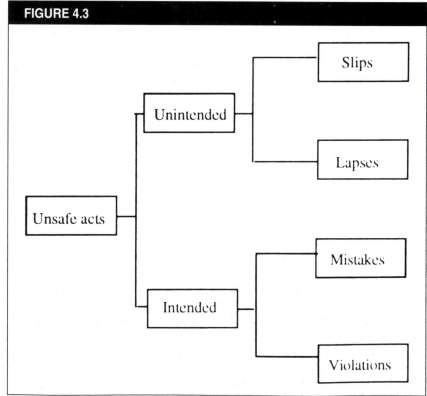

FIGURE 4.3

Four sorts of unsafe acts. The four sorts of human error each constitute different types of unsafe acts.

4. INDUSTRIAL SAFETY 73

categories of human error: slips, lapses, mistakes and violations. The first three of these cannot be avoided by instruction, or persuasion, by making personnel aware of the importance of safety nor by motivating them in special courses.

7.3 Violations

Only the last category, violations, consists of errors which people make consciously. Violations are deliberate, and therefore intentional, actions. Programmes intended to increase safety consciousness are mostly expected to have an influence on violations, but that influence is limited. The best known example is the wearing of seat belts in the car. Approximately 25% of car drivers/passengers do so voluntarily. Following the introduction of legislation making it compulsory the percentage of wearers rises to 50–60% (according to Slovic, 1985). Through checks and punishment this percentage can become even higher. Ninety per cent is certainly obtainable, but the investment in control is then considerable and has to be maintained. The reason is that some people find the seat belt uncomfortable, unnecessary and ineffective. This attitude is difficult to change and obedience of the law must therefore be enforced.

Contrary attitudes form an important problem in the compliance with rules, but not the only problem. It is a common occurrence that rules are simply not known or are wrongly interpreted. The minimum condition for the use of rules and regulations is that there should be regular checks to see whether the rules are known and understood. This precaution is no more than the regular check carried out on fire extinguishers, but is in practice little used. One of the most important causes of the fatal disaster on the Piper Alpha oil and gas production platform (Cullen, 1990) was that an employer of a maintenance company did not know the work permit rules. The fire on the Dutch submarine, *Walrus*, whilst it was under construction is mostly likely to have been caused by a foreign welder who, through his lack of knowledge of Dutch, did not know what precautions had to be taken when welding on board (*Report on Cause of Fire on Walrus*, 1987).

Another important reason why rules and regulations are not followed is that following them is impossible. Occidental, the owner of *Piper Alpha*, had prescribed that the head of a platform is in command of combating accidents. As a result of the explosion however the necessary equipment was knocked out so quickly that command within the *Piper Alpha* platform was impossible. Noone took over command, because the regulations had not foreseen this possibility.

Deliberate failures to follow procedures within the industrial setting are, unlike more everyday situations such as road traffic, not necessarily the result of poor attitudes to safety and bad intentions. Studies of offshore workers (Hudson & Verschuur, 1996) found that the intentions are not the problem, but expectations derived from previous experience are. If "impossible" procedures have not been improved and the quality of the planning makes corner cutting necessary to meet deadlines, violation is to be expected. Violators are also characterised by feelings of special competence, of being capable of bending the rules safely. This approach to the following of rules is seen as the exercise of initiative, when it is successful, and a violation only when things go wrong.

Violations, being deliberate, are not regarded as errors. Nevertheless they are not necessarily malicious and can be regarded more as mistakes by people who do not oversee the bad consequences or who sincerely believe that those consequences will not happen when they are in charge. Because of such beliefs violations form the most dangerous category of human error. In particular violators assume that everyone else is doing the right thing, carrying out the necessary checks and inspections. The fact is that while the intentions of others may be good, unintended errors can interact with violations and lead to disaster (Free, 1995).

7.4 The prevention of unsafe acts

From what has been stated above it will be clear that unsafe acts cannot always be prevented by forbidding them or by convincing people that they should, above all, work safely. Even violations are performed by well-meaning employees who are trying to get the job done. In a modern adult company, lack of commitment, motivation and even knowledge are seldom the cause of unsafe behaviour. An analysis of behaviours which lie at the foundation of hundreds of accidents on ships is shown in Table 4.1 (drawn from Wagenaar & Groeneweg, 1987). The table shows the successive steps in the decision process that lead to unsafe acts. In the first phase information must be received about the threatening danger; in 21% of the cases this information is missing, so that a decision cannot be consciously taken. In the second phase the information that is available must be understood to be an indication of danger; that is not the case in 27% of cases. In the third phase, when the danger has been recognised, a list of possible alternative plans of action must be drawn up; in 15% of all cases only one possibility is seen as plausible. In the fourth phase the alternative plans of action have to be evaluated for their possible risks; in 36% of cases the risk attached to the action plan that is finally opted for has not been recognised. Only in the remaining 1% of cases is there a consciously accepted risk. This analysis illustrates that accidents are seldom the consequence of deliberate violations, caused by lack of motivation or suchlike. In the majority of accidents the unsafe acts are slips and mistakes. The conditions in which slips and mistakes are, so to speak, provoked, follow directly from the description which is given above. Unsafe acts can, in particular, be prevented by taking away such conditions.

Example: double-attention slips occur when a task must be carried out in which the initial sequence is identical to that of a known task, but where the remainder is different. At the point at which there is divergence from the routine extra attention must be paid otherwise the known routine will be followed automatically. But at the skills level the routines unfold without any accompanying attention. A new task like this creates a working condition which provokes accidents. Whenever it is not possible to address the task in another way, then in order to actually carry it out correctly, at the point of choice extra precautions have to be taken, for instance a written checklist, extra supervision or an extra control afterwards.

7.5 Taking risks

When we look at the unsafe acts which people carry out, the illusion that easily arises is that people takes certain risks knowingly. It is then assumed that the possibility of a wrong outcome is appreciated beforehand, but that the chance is underestimated, or that it is assumed that operators incorrectly underestimate the importance of unsafe acts (according to Hofstee, 1987; Wagenaar, 1987). This conclusion has led to the introduction of programmes in which they attempt to alter the behaviour of the employees by persuasion. The premise is however incorrect; it is only seldom that the person committing the unsafe act realises what the possible consequences are. The impossibility of foreseeing the consequences of unsafe acts is based on the complex nature of accident scenarios (according to Wagenaar, 1986; Wagenaar & Groeneweg, 1987). Accident scenarios are in general very complex, even when the accident is a simple fall. The actors in the drama do not know the whole scenario; at the moment that the relevant events occur simultaneously to form

TABLE 4.1		
Decision phase	*Number of accident scenarios in which the decision went wrong*	
	Absolute number	*(%)*
1. Receipt of information	17	21
2. Detection of problem	21	27
3. Finding options	12	15
4. Evaluation of consequences	19	36
5. Conscious acceptance of risk	1	1

Where decisions about risky actions go wrong in 57 accidents at sea, reported by the Raad voor de Scheepvaart (Shipping Council) in 1984 and 1985 (some accidents are represented on more than 1 line: from Wagenaar, 1991).

the necessary coincidence, the concurrence comes as a complete surprise. Up until the last moment the accident, which happens in a very short period of time, is considered to be impossible. As soon as those involved realise that there is a real chance of an accident, they then take action. This means that "possible" accidents do not take place, and "impossible" accidents do (see also Jørgensen, 1988; Östberg, 1984).

In the previously mentioned analysis of ship accidents (Wagenaar & Groeneweg, 1987) it appeared that in 51% of the cases the necessary knowledge was divided between two actors in the drama, who did not know of each other's actions. In an analysis of 21 fatal accidents in oil production the comparable number was 86%. The number of unsafe acts that were necessary to cause an accident in both studies is shown in Table 4.2.

In the analysis of shipping accidents there were four more instances in which no clearly unsafe act was taken. In oil production this "act of God" situation did not occur at all. In the shipping industry on average 3.4 unsafe acts were needed, in oil production that was 8.0. These numbers do not mean that workers in the oil industry make more errors: on the contrary, in the oil industry there are far fewer accidents than in the shipping industry. The numbers mean only that through better organised safeguards errors in oil production do not lead so quickly to an accident: on average you need eight to create an accident. On the other hand it will, however, be clear that the limit has just about been reached in the oil industry: it is not likely that scenarios in which eight unsafe acts concur can be overseen by those present. Refraining from such acts cannot be expected in the basis of insight into the consequences. Reading the extremely complex scenarios of accidents such as the disaster in Bhopal, the fire in King's Cross Underground Station, the running aground of the *Exxon Valdez*, the explosion on *Piper Alpha*, the reader will realise that the actors in these dramas were not able to recognise their unsafe acts as such. On the contrary, they did what they usually did. Their actions were performed on the skills level or, at most, on the rule level. At both these levels the risks entailed in actions are not considered. A conscious analysis which leads to a choice for or against unsafe actions, as described in Table 4.1, can only be performed at the knowledge level. That is to say, the problem must first of all have led to a shift of control from the skills level to the rule level. There the insight has to have been that the situation does not fit into an existing category and that consequently no rule is available for the solution of the problem. This transition to the highest level generally only occurs after the accident is inevitable or has even occurred. For a more extensive discussion about risk estimation and the committal of unsafe acts we would refer you to Wagenaar (1990a, b, 1991).

7.6 Unsafe act auditing

The American process industry company Dupont has developed a safety strategy which is based on the prevention of unsafe acts. The basic idea behind it is that unsafe acts are recognisable as such and that employees can protect themselves and others against them. The technique consists of learning to recognise a number of sorts of unsafe acts. Thereafter at all levels within the organisation people have, as part of their task, to walk around and identify and report the unsafe acts they have observed. The technique has been introduced into many companies and has even become an important sales product of Dupont. It is always difficult to establish whether a strategy "works" without studies being performed with carefully chosen control groups. Dupont claims without

TABLE 4.2		
How many unsafe acts are necessary to cause an accident?		
Number of Unsafe Acts	100 Shipping Accidents	21 Accidents in Oil Production
0	4	0
1	3	0
2	22	1
	26	0
3	22	2
4	14	2
5	5	1
6	2	1
7	2	1
>7	2	14

much evidence that "unsafe act auditing" can bring about a dramatic improvement in the safety of a company. The only evidence to this effect is from Dupont's own accident statistics but, as stated, without having an insight into the precise definition of accidents a statistic can be difficult to interpret. In any case it can be said that the principle, according to which unsafe acts are always recognisable in advance, is not very plausible. The technique will be particularly effective where the personnel are committing many violations; that is to say, in companies which have a rather poorly developed safety policy. Slips, lapses and mistakes cannot however be prevented in this manner, because they are not committed consciously. They are caused by the manner in which the work is organised and unsafe act auditing cannot affect them. Unsafe act auditing is at its most effective when the *reasons* for the unsafe acts are analysed and attention is paid to the more underlying causes. The success of companies that have implemented unsafe act auditing may be attributed to their raised level of management commitment to safety, that led to implementing the behavioural technique. As the factors have never been partialled out, no firm positive conclusions can be drawn about the success of such an approach in the absence of other, deeper-seated, approaches.

8   PSYCHOLOGICAL PRECURSORS

Unsafe acts are difficult to combat when the conditions under which they take place are not known. These conditions demonstrate a clear system, which are directly linked to the three levels of Reason's GEMS model. The conditions under which errors arise in the execution of skills programmes are not the same as those in which the wrong rules are applied, in which analysis at knowledge level leads to incorrect solutions. In general we can state that performing tasks under conditions of haste, with insufficient communication and lack of necessary knowledge, are conditions that can be almost guaranteed to lead to error, despite the best of intentions.

In addition there are also conditions which force

the transition from lower to higher levels. For example: the execution of a complex task which is rarely performed. The low frequency means that factors which induce errors at knowledge level are now offered their opportunity. Such an observation leads to the reasoning that such infrequent tasks should be avoided. It is better to set up specialist teams which, wherever they are needed, come in to carry out such tasks. An example of this approach is the setting up of police arrest teams who take over the dangerous job, for arresting officers and the arrested alike, of making arrests. Completely in line with this is the increasing tendency of large companies to subcontract work to contractors; these are companies whose daily business is carrying out jobs that the parent company cannot specialise in. The disadvantage of such a working method is that naturally more actors are introduced who, not knowing about each other, can contribute to the elements of an accident scenario. On *Piper Alpha* 188 of the 226 on board were working for a contractor; employees of a maintenance contractor had removed the pressure safety valve from a compressor system, which was then started up by the operators working for the parent company. If the maintenance had been left solely to the operators, that almost certainly would not have happened.

8.1   Precursors of errors at skills-based level

The conditions that lead to errors at the skills-based levels cannot be exhaustively listed. But a few are important enough to be mentioned here.

- The execution of a new action which hides a highly automated scheme of action. For example: changing to go out to the theatre, but instead pulling on one's pyjamas.
- The execution of new action which in part is very similar to a highly automated scheme of action. For example: driving in a new car, in which the controls for the indicators and the windscreen wipers are reversed.
- The lack of a scheme of action that runs automatically. For example: being disturbed by the telephone when making coffee.
- The presentation of very similar stimuli, whereby an incorrect but highly automated scheme of action is started. For example:

walking towards the telephone when the kitchen timer rings.

- Executing two schemes of action simultaneously. For example: drinking a cup of coffee when eating chips, whereby the sugar is sprinkled onto the chips and ketchup is put into the coffee.
- Over-attention, whereby a highly automated scheme of action has to be performed at the rule or knowledge level. In section 9 we will indicate further when these precursors occur.

8.2 Precursors of errors at rule-based level

At the rule-based level errors occur when what are in fact good rules are applied in incorrect situations. Here are a number of examples.

- A situation occurs for the first time, so that the correct rule is not yet known.
- The situation is difficult to classify because there are many misleading signals.
- The situation is difficult to classify because there are too many signals.
- The situation strongly resembles another situation for which a "strong" rule exists.

Errors at rule level also occur when bad rules are applied. In this event we recognise the following situations.

- In some situations the *if* part of the *if . . . then* rule is too general or not sufficiently specific. An example: the crew of *Piper Alpha* had been taught that under no circumstances were they to jump from the platform. In the circumstances of the disaster it appeared to be the only way of saving life. All those who survived had, in the end, jumped from the platform into the sea.
- The *then* part of the *if . . . then* rule is incorrect. An example: *if* you suddenly see a car appear in front of you in the mist, *then* you have to brake strongly. *If* you want to keep the company running, *then* you have to economise on personnel costs.

The rule-based level may produce mistakes by being driven by the situation, represented by the *if* part. This is a feed-forward or forward-chaining mode of thought, as emulated by some expert systems. Alternatively, incorrect *then* parts may be applied in attempts to diagnose situations in a backward-chaining mode, such as used by MYCIN-type expert systems (Buchanan & Shortliffe, 1984). Rule-based mistakes of action or diagnosis are characterised by inappropriate rule selection followed by performance based upon the belief that the choices have all been made correctly.

8.3 Precursors of errors at knowledge level

At the knowledge-based level errors principally occur for two reasons: firstly because only a part of the problem is overseen; and secondly because incorrect knowledge is the basis on which action is taken. Here are several examples of typical errors at the knowledge-based level.

- *Selectivity* Attention is only given to part of the problem. The best known example is that in which a rule is thought up without asking oneself what kind of reaction this will produce in those involved. Example: A general prohibition on alcohol is introduced in a company without considering what the risk is of the various tricks that the personnel will use to get round that rule.
- *Out of sight, out of mind* Parts of a problem, which are not clearly presented, are easily missed. A risk analysis of a new industrial activity does not usually demonstrate how people contribute to accidents; those who take a decision on the basis of this analysis do not fill this deficiency in.
- *Preference for confirmation* People have the tendency to seek and select information which supports their own solution. Arguments to the contrary are ignored.
- *Unmotivated self-confidence* This occurs in particular when a lot of energy has been invested in looking for solutions (*sunk-cost effect*); when the solution is a compromise between various parties; when the solution is the product of a hidden agenda.
- *Halo effects* There is a tendency to rank solutions on only one dimension; for instance, in order to find the simplest (or the cheapest) solutions it is assumed that these are also the best.

- *Underestimation of complexity* Attention is only given to a simplified description of the problem, without being consciously aware of doing so. The devil lies in the details.
- *Diagnosis problems* Often solutions are based on an incorrect diagnosis of the problem. Such solutions can have a strongly counterproductive reaction, as in the near disaster in the nuclear power station at Harrisburg. There it was believed that the radioactive material that was leaking away was caused by a defect that had existed for some time. The actions which were subsequently taken made that problem greater rather than smaller. Even when the solution has been proven to be wrong there is a tendency not to review the diagnosis.

9 LATENT FAILURES

While psychological precursors provide the conditions under which unsafe acts are committed, it is questionable whether a safety management system should be based upon the identification of such precursors. Psychological preconditions are "mental states" that are not directly accessible to external inspection. While some precursors may be extant for some time, many often come and go almost as rapidly as the unsafe acts they permit or generate. Precursors, such as haste or ignorance, are also notoriously difficult to quantify. The specialised experience of a contractor and the almost inevitable blind spots that go with that experience may be guessed at, but are not to be measured. This is probably the reason why there are no safety systems that, while attempting to go beyond the unsafe act, concentrate upon the immediate precursors. The next stage, that of latent failures, is where attention falls, because they are capable of being made visible and can be defined objectively. The thought behind this is that psychological precursors are, in their turn, created by latent failures and can be best prevented by removing those latent failures.

This thought process mirrors that of the old stimulus-response psychology. To alter behaviour it is necessary to change the stimuli that generate

that behaviour; a direct influence from intervening variables is not possible. While the last word has yet to be spoken about the theoretical differences between stimulus-response and more cognitively oriented models in terms of what happens between stimulus and response in the brain, in practice this difference is less important than is often assumed. It is almost always more effective to influence behaviour by altering the context within which it is generated. In the case of unsafe acts within an industrial environment this means removing the latent failures that lie at their root.

Latent failures are weaknesses in the organisation that exist not only at the time of an accident, but are there for some time in advance. Such failures are traceable before any accidents happen and, therefore, form the most important target for preventative action. The trick is to know what sorts of failures lead to accidents and how they can be uncovered. In general these failures are to be looked for at the level of management. Examples of such approaches are MORT analysis (Johnson, 1980) and the ILCI system (ILCI, 1978). The disadvantage attached to these systems is that there is no scientific basis, while at the same time there have been no attempts to validate these systems using data gathered in the field. The only theory, and preventative approach, that is both theoretically based as well as practically validated is the Tripod method developed in co-operation by the universities of Leiden and Manchester with financial support from Shell International Petroleum Ltd (cf. Wagenaar, Hudson, & Reason, 1990).

9.1 Short description of the tripod approach

On the basis of analyses of many hundred accidents, in which the causes of all accidents, in agreement with the model in Figure 4.1, are broken down into unsafe acts, psychological precursors, latent failures and fallible decisions, it has been found that it is possible to describe the latent failures comprehensively using eleven categories of latent failure. These are called "general failure types" (Wagenaar, Hudson, & Reason, 1992). Systematic observation within a company can serve to measure the relative frequency of these underlying problem areas. This can be represented as a Failure State Profile, such as Figure 4.4, that can serve to define priorities for remediation (Hudson, Reason, Wagenaar, Bentley, Primrose, & Visser, 1994). Next one can trace the most threatening categories of latent failures back to the higher level decisions that were taken earlier, or failed to be taken. These decisions can be reviewed and such decisions can, in the future, be taken with greater weight attached to safety issues.

One case can serve as an example (Wagenaar, Souverijn, & Hudson, 1992). The intensive care departments of two hospitals were concerned about a number of small but potentially dangerous failures. The "failure state profile" of one of those wards showed that equipment failures, a hardware problem, contributed a disproportionate number of causes. The reason is that this department was perceived to be ultra-modern ten years previously, but has not been refurbished since then. The recommendation is to assign greater priority, within the financial constraints, to renewal of the equipment. The Tripod method is characterised by a dissociation from the many small errors at the workplace and a concentration of information in the direction of common factors at a managerial level.

9.2 Eleven types of latent failure

The Tripod philosophy recognises the following eleven general failure types (GFTs):

1. *Design (DE)*
Failures in the design of equipment and work areas; the design fails to take any or sufficient notice of the human factor. The probable cause is that feedback between the shop floor and the design departments is lacking, which would have prevented or removed such problems.

2. *Hardware (HW)*
Even with adequate design, the materials and availability of tools and equipment can lead to breakage or *ad hoc* substitution. There is too little attention paid to optimising the relationship between work and apparatus.

3. *Defences (DF)*
Even obvious defences can be found to be missing or inadequate for the hazards; simple alarms, protective clothing, rescue plans, holding of exercises as well as specialised containment measures and automatic shut-down equipment.

4. *Error-enforcing conditions (EC)*
The working conditions can be sub-optimal for those who work in them, such as shift work,

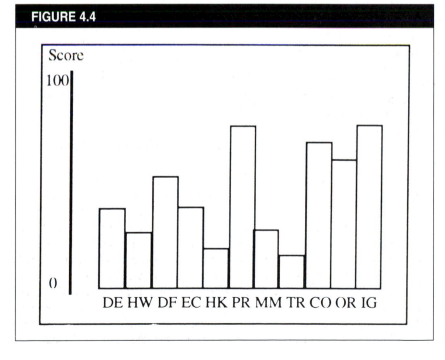

FIGURE 4.4

Failure State Profile of a hypothetical unit, such as an oil production platform or an intensive care ward of a hospital.

working under extreme heat, cold or time pressure or without sufficient knowledge to perform the task. While such conditions may always arise, when these are chronic the chances that errors will be made rise alarmingly.

5. *Housekeeping (HK)*

Often we find situations in conflict with the requirements and good practice. Housekeeping problems signal that management has little grip on affairs, or does not wish to know.

6. *Procedures (PR)*

Here we mean the existence of good procedures, accurate, comprehensible and available as well as actually being followed. Recognising problems in this area leads to the analysis of work practices to reduce the number of situations requiring administrative controls such as procedures, the introduction of procedures that can help reduce risks and extra attention being paid to compliance with the procedures that exist. Often there are too many procedures.

7. *Maintenance management (MM)*

Here we mean not just the failure to perform maintenance, but the pursuance of the appropriate management strategy for the machinery and operation in question. Maintenance is a major source of errors, especially omissions, and allows failures to be introduced where previously there was no problem. The *Piper Alpha* disaster was set off by maintenance activity.

8. *Training (TR)*

This can involve both under- and over-qualified workers performing the work. Training refers to the competence of the workforce rather than just safety training. Training and procedures can be used as substitutes for good design. All too often management does not know or try to assess whether the training has any effect.

9. *Communication (CO)*

Communication systems that break down, or people who fail to understand one another, result in people not knowing what is going on and acting mistakenly. On *Piper Alpha* the satellite platforms mistakenly thought that everything was under control so they continued to pump oil and gas into the burning platform.

10. *Organisation (OR)*

Is the organisational structure fit for the task that needs to be done? Are the managers aware of what goes on or are they believed by the workforce? Bureaucratic organisations may be just right for some critical and long-term operations, while empowerment may be the only way to get things done in other fields. In poor organisations no one knows who to tell, even when they see a danger.

11. *Incompatible goals (IG)*

Trying to do several things at once is always difficult, like juggling. The balance between production and safety has to be maintained and over-eagerness to cut costs may result in increased danger. Making deadlines and furthering one's career are goals that, just this once, may take priority over safety.

The Tripod approach is bottom-up, beginning with the information available on and from the work floor. This is where the reality of the venture is to be assessed and represented as a "failure state profile". This becomes a message sent to the management who need to see if their beliefs and the operational reality are in synchrony. The management's response to this message is the diagnosis they make of why they have the profile they do and, most importantly, what they are going to do about it to make things better. An example of a "failure state profile" is shown in Figure 4.3.

9.3 Validating tripod

The pretension that Tripod makes is that it enables one to predict the causes of an accident *before* an accident takes place. Tripod makes the prediction in terms of the organisational problems that exist before anything has actually gone wrong, proactively, rather than just waiting for an accident and analysing the causes reactively (cf. Figure 4.5). The latter approach is also perfectly possible, and even necessary, but a proactive approach is always to be preferred. The reactive approach is driven by the discovery of what clearly is wrong, because it led to an accident or at least an unsafe act. The proactive approach allows a manager to get ahead of events and solve problems applying cost-benefit analyses rather than being forced by events. In order to justify using such a proactive tool it is, nevertheless, essential that such a tool be

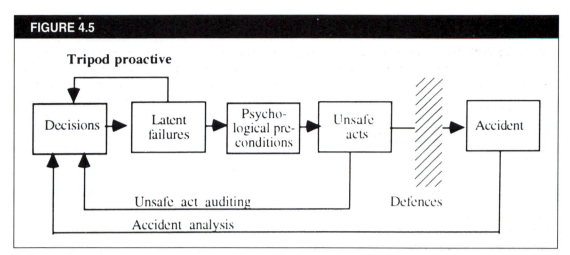

FIGURE 4.5

Tripod proactive

Decisions → Latent failures → Psycho-logical pre-conditions → Unsafe acts → Accident

Unsafe act auditing

Accident analysis

Defences

The General Causal model with the different sources of information that can be delivered to decision makers. The reactive approaches measure what has happened, such as unsafe acts and accidents, the proactive approach measures what can happen, based upon the identification of the latent failures.

validated with existing accidents. The general causal model presented in section 4 allows for both the proactive analysis of existing conditions in terms of latent failures and the reactive analysis of accidents and incidents in terms of the conditions and latent failures that caused them. The Tripod model, then, is consistent for both the proactive and reactive approaches to safety management.

First it is necessary to understand how a failure state profile can be developed without the use of accident data. In order to do this we introduce the notion of an "indicator", a small but objectively observable pointer to success or failure in the area of a specific GFT. For instance, frequent failure of a specific machine despite adequate maintenance can point to design problems, finding too many irrelevant memos in one's in-tray reflects communication problems. For each GFT a database of indicators can be constructed, typically 100 to 150 indicators. This is not to say that the problems phrased as indicators will themselves be anything more than trivial, but if one answered 20 or 30 such indicator questions for training, and found that more than the half were being answered in the "wrong" way, then it is possible to draw the conclusion that the training is a source of serious problems and may need to be looked at in some

detail. Indicators are symptoms of a disease, the latent failures form the disease.

Initially indicators were collected by having a researcher observe the activity in considerable detail. The specificity of the indicators in the Appendix shows how a detailed knowledge of the work involved is necessary to make good indicators. Currently techniques have been developed to allow the workforce to generate their own indicators and construct a database (Hudson et al., 1994). However a list of indicators is not, of itself, enough. The test, as a whole, needs to be calibrated (Hudson, Zieverink, Groeneweg, Akerboom, Wagenaar, & Reason, 1995) in order to be sufficiently accurate and useful in the industrial setting. In order to do this GFTs can be considered as different scales in a psychological test. Indicator items can then be considered as scale items and treated accordingly. Validation becomes the analysis of test–retest reliability, construct validity, content validity and, most important of all, predictive validity.

Construct validity is provided by reference to the theory, especially as it is represented by the fact that the model is based upon the GEMS model of human error and its extension to the reasons why unsafe acts are committed (Reason, 1990) distributed over the eleven GFTs. Content validity is provided by the use of the workforce as the source of the indicator items used in the test. Predictive validity has to be provided by the ability to predict which accidents will happen. The way to assess predictive validity is to measure the correlation between the failure state profiles that can be generated using the proactive test technique and equivalent accident profiles. Accident profiles can be made by analysing a sufficiently large number of incidents into the same format, a profile representing the numbers of latent failures identified as causing the accidents. Finally test–retest reliability, which is a necessary but not a sufficient validity requirement, can be guaranteed by the application of standard scale construction techniques (Cronbach, 1990).

After item analysis and selection in terms of the GFT scales, the test is now capable of achieving a test–retest reliability, without the use of parallel items, in excess of 0.7 (Hudson et al., 1995). Predictive validity had originally been assessed by comparing predicted failure state profiles against the results of analyses of accidents, giving a predictive validity of 0.72 (Hudson, Groeneweg, Reason, Wagenaar, van der Meeren & Visser, 1991) and test–retest reliabilities about 0.80 with many parallel items (Hudson, Wagenaar, Reason, Groeneweg, van der Meeren, & Visser, 1991). Recently a predictive validity in excess of 0.9 has been obtained, using the Spearman–Rank correlation between the indicator-based state profile and a profile based upon reactive analysis of incidents for a shipping operation (A.J. Pearce, personal communication, April 1997).

In its current form, after calibration has been performed, the Tripod proactive approach allows for the accurate prediction of the causes of future accidents in terms of organisational factors. In short it is possible, with considerable accuracy, to predict why an accident will happen. Given a knowledge of the hazards and exposure to those hazards, it is possible to predict where an accident will take place, but with considerably less accuracy. Unfortunately it is not possible to predict when, or to whom, an accident will occur. We have to content ourselves with why and where.

9.4 The ISRS system

The International Standard Rating System (ISRS) of the International Loss Control Institute (ILCI,

1978) is a rating scale, with points assigned to the way in which safety is organised within an organisation. The maximum number of points is 10,800 based upon 20 elements or sub-scales. The sub-scales and the items within them are weighted in accordance to the averaged subjective value of a number of American industries. The most important sub-scale is "leadership" and "administration" (contributing 1170 points); points here are assigned, for instance, with items such as having a good library (175 points), having safety in senior managers' staff reporting system, and by defining a standard by which one wishes to be measured (e.g. LTIs). Items that generate few points are: development of a procedure for refusing work when the conditions are dangerous (35 points) or co-ordination between safety and health workers. Items are similar to the Tripod indicators, but have not been subjected to any more than a test of face validity.

The disadvantage of ILCI's ISRS is that it proposes the same remedy for every disease. The same checklist is applied to very different types of organisation and the resulting remedial proposals are determined by the structure of the test. As the system works with stars (up to five, like restaurants) being handed out for reaching certain overall points levels, the danger is that the stars rather than the safety become the goal. With a limited list of items it is possible to concentrate upon just those that increase the points score rather than to treat the approach as measuring the underlying safety of the organisation. Furthermore the fact that the weights are set by reference to American industry means that locally important factors may be significantly under- or overweighted. In a Tripod analysis of a North Sea platform a major problem of management of contractor personnel was identified, but within the ILCI system this would have only generated an item worth 35 points.

The ISRS is, nevertheless, very good for organisations at an early stage in their safety evolution. An assessment can be made that tests a great many relevant factors and improvement, no matter how cynically driven, will result in the right things being done. Once, however, the safety levels have reached the point where measurement in terms of crude measures becomes difficult, the Tripod approach is intended to take a location and operation specific approach which is harder to fool.

10 FALLIBLE DECISIONS

Latent failures, weaknesses within an organisation that can lead to unsafe behaviour, themselves also have a cause. For instance, poor quality equipment was selected and purchased and has yet to be replaced. The maintenance schedule may be inappropriate for the equipment but have been determined by cost-cutting exercises or a rigid and mistaken fixation on standardised approaches to work, whether they are the best or not. Error enforcing conditions may be known about and the risk consciously "taken" to operate in ways that will generate unsafe acts.

Most latent failures are not the result of work floor errors, but flow from managerial decisions taken earlier and, often, elsewhere. The exception is maintenance-induced errors such as missing parts that may be hidden from view, waiting to create a failure when it is least wanted. The remaining decisions of managers are not, however, themselves necessarily bad decisions. They are hard decisions that have had both good and bad consequences. The latent failures are the bad consequences; the advantages were what the decision makers saw when the decisions were made, maybe as many as 20 or 30 years previously. Likewise many decisions are taken at a physical distance which precludes anything more than a superficial understanding of what the real problems might be.

Fallible decisions are themselves a form of human error, mistakes that are characterised by the belief or the hope that the good consequences will occur and the bad will not happen. As the life span of many systems is longer than the manager's own career, most people do not see just how their well-intentioned decisions can turn out to be a major source of problems for future generations. Table 4.3 lists the different types of problems that can be encountered.

Fallible decisions need to be identified, if only to see what other negative consequences may be expected. They also need to be handled with care and sensitivity, because the person who made the decision may be the one whose help is needed to

---

TABLE 4.3

The main classes of problems that manifest themselves as fallible decision making.

Habits
- *Bad habits:* people do what they know they should not do, but continue to do nevertheless (tomorrow we'll do better)
- *The organisational culture:* the unfortunate side-effects of the working practices people feel defines their organisation (e.g. can-do cultures)

Resources
- *Time shortages:* failure to allocate sufficient time to perform work
- *People shortages:* failure to allocate sufficient or sufficiently competent people
- *Money shortages:* insufficient funds to cover what needs to be accomplished

Decision making
- *Absence:* not making any decisions at all, decisions are taken by default
- *Inadequate decisions:* making decisions on the basis of incorrect or insufficient information
- *Asynchrony:* making decisions too far removed in time or space from the work floor

Accountability
- *None:* no individuals made specifically accountable for critical tasks
- *Distance:* accountability held too far from the work floor
- *Powerlessness:* people made accountable without the ability to influence events

cure the problem. What is clear is that many decisions that seemed reasonable when they were made have failed to pass the test of time; situations may have changed, new knowledge may have become available, insights may have been won. One of the lessons learned from an intensive study of accidents is that the concept of blame is not merely to be transferred from the immediate actor to the manager. The impossibility of predicting situations with many variables, which explains why the oil workers could not foresee the consequences of their actions, is equally applicable to the managers whose unsafe acts are someone else's fallible decisions.

11 CONCLUSION

It is an essential part of any effective safety strategy that the relationship between decisions and possible accidents be brought clearly out into the open. Studying safety statistics is of little help, especially when the frequency is low. As chance factors play an increasingly large role, contributing noise, and the signal becomes increasingly intermittent, it becomes progressively harder for decision makers to filter out the useful information and not be misled by immediate but irrelevant factors. Good accident investigations help, but the level of analysis needs to be reached at which the latent failures and the failures of decision making are exposed. A reactive approach to safety management needs to be served by the provision of information about the problems, the diseases, rather than the symptoms. We often hear that an accident was caused by "human error", without any description of the conditions that led to that error. With fewer accidents there appears to be less to learn about the reasons for those accidents. This is why there has to be a change when the accident frequency drops past the point that the information is reliable. It is more important to take a proactive stance in areas that we know, in advance, are those where accidents will come from if nothing is done.

The proactive stance means that it is better to improve the quality of procedures and ensure that they are followable, and followed, before there is an accident rather than waiting for an accident to

happen before any action is taken. It is better to assess how well information flows within the organisation rather than discover, after the event, that the warning messages from the safety manager were disappearing into the managing director's wastepaper basket and that the management team's intentions were being systematically reinterpreted by middle managers before they reached the shop floor. As all these are in fact nothing more than good practice, and not just restricted to safety, we can now see how our argument has developed from the "in search of misery", based upon accidents as the source of information. Now we propose that the safe way to operate is to operate well and that there need be no incompatibility between production and safety.

What we have learned from studying many different organisations is that those that are safest take safety most seriously. Ideally safety should be considered integrally with all the top-level decisions that are taken and the safety manager should be a full member of the management team. Certainly safety should be a fixed item, ideally first, on the agenda of management and board meetings. Dupont, a company with an exemplary record, has the Chief Executive Officer as the chief safety manager, thereby ensuring that commitment is maintained from the top. The common practice is still, unfortunately, that the safety manager hears of decisions taken, after the event, with the requirement of ensuring that all is safe. In small organisations or divisions of larger ones, there may not be room for the safety manager.

One way of ensuring an adequate understanding of industrial safety is to have "high fliers" spend time in the safety department, preferably carrying real responsibility. In practice safety has all too often been a place where people have been shunted, often because they are too nice to let go. The safety department is, however, an ideal location for a young manager to learn the whole of the business and acquire an overall view that can stand in good stead elsewhere. Furthermore such a young manager can see, often at first hand, just what the consequences of failures in safety policy are. If, added to this, there is a good understanding of the relationship between fallible decisions and accidents, this is knowledge that can serve to prevent accidents when that manager joins the management team and gets to make fallible decisions.

The basic philosophy of this chapter is that safety problems are primarily caused by the working conditions to which people may respond by making errors. When we started our studies of safety, we met people who explained their dangerous working practices by claiming: "These are the conditions under which we work". At first sight it looks as if workers cause their own accidents and, therefore, have all the control over their actions and, therefore, their safety. Managers feel divorced from the actual work and that the people who cause accidents are out of their control. The conditions, however, are set by managers, rather than workers. Workers have a responsibility to look after themselves, but will always work within the conditions, managers allow the conditions to exist. Workers have the responsibility of telling their managers what the conditions are, possibly by using a system such as Tripod, managers bear the responsibility of listening and acting accordingly. In this way safety management is the responsibility of everybody in a company, from top to bottom.

APPENDIX

Provisional checklist for the construction of a failure state profile of intensive care wards.

Hardware failures
1. Is there vital but old equipment of which safer designs are now on the market?
2. Are there cases of breakdown of vital equipment?
3. Do technicians spend more time at incidental repairs than on scheduled maintenance?
4. Are there any incidents based on unnoticed breakdowns?

Design failures
1. Is there sufficient space around each bed?
2. Are there alarms for all malfunctions?
3. Are there cases in which alarms were noticed too late?
4. Has "forgetting to do something" caused any incidents?

5. Are alarms being switched off because of too many false alarms?

Error enforcing conditions
1. Are there fixed protocols for receiving new patients?
2. Are checklists used for the start-up of new equipment?
3. Have incidents been caused by being interrupted during routine tasks?
4. Can stand-by staff be summoned at short notice?
5. Are non-routine tasks discussed in special meetings?

Poor housekeeping
1. Are supplies used and not replenished?
2. Does equipment get lost?
3. Can you tell how many medicine pumps there are, and where they are now?
4. Has anyone asked you in the last week "Where is the . . . ?"
5. Is there a habit of finishing all menial chores before the end of the shift?

Poor operating procedures
1. Has there been any incident in which a violation of procedure was defended as "the thing that is usually done"?
2. Are critical procedures protected by the use of checklists?
3. Are critical procedures checked for routine control at each bed?
4. Is there a checklist for routine control at each bed?
5. Have there been any incidents due to improvisations?

Poor maintenance procedures
1. Is there a regular overhaul schedule?
2. Is the overhaul schedule lagging because of acute repairs?
3. Is maintenance made impossible due to the lack of parts?
4. Is equipment controlled with checklists, after maintenance?
5. Is any technician specially dedicated to the IC ward?

Inadequate training
1. Are all staff assigned exclusively to the IC ward?

2. Are novices supervised systematically?
3. Is there a training programme for novices at all levels, before they start work in the IC ward?
4. Is there a safety training programme for all staff?
5. Are there regular safety meetings in which all incidents are discussed with staff at all levels?

Incompatible goals

1. Is the budget obstructing necessary renewal of equipment?
2. Have tasks been extended without an extension of staff; or staff reduced without a corresponding reduction of tasks?
3. Is there systematic overtime work?
4. Is equipment used while it is known to be inadequate?
5. Are there any differences of opinion between medical and nursing staff on professional matters?

Organisational failures

1. Does the hospital management pay unexpected site visits?
2. Does the hospital management receive reports on accidents and incidents, and act upon them?
3. Is a safety recording system used to compare the ward to other units inside and outside the hospital?
4. Is sticking to written procedures systematically checked?
5. Is there a planning of work in which tasks are allocated on the basis of capacity?

Communication failures

1. Are there regular meetings with related departments in the hospital in which safety issues are discussed?
2. Are there fixed protocols for shift changes?
3. Are there incidents due to services rendered by other departments being too late?
4. Have there been any incidents in which a person who was urgently needed could not be reached?
5. Are there positive checks for the flow of vital information between departments?

REFERENCES

Bignell, V., Peters, G., & Pym, C. (1977). *Catastrophic failures.* Milton Keynes: Open University.

Buchanan, B.G., & Shortliffe, E.H. (1984). *Rule-based expert systems: The MYCIN experiments of the Stanford heuristic programming project.* Reading, MA: Addison-Wesley.

Commissie 'oorzaak Brand Walrus' (COBRAW) (1987). *Rapport oorzaak brand walrus [Report into the cause of the fire on board the submarine Walrus].* Ministerie Van Defensie, 1987.

Cronbach, L.J. (1990). *Essentials of psychological testing.* New York: Harper & Row.

Cullen, the Hon. Lord (1990). *The public inquiry into the Piper Alpha disaster.* London: HMSO.

Evans, J.St.B.T. (1983). *Thinking and reasoning: Psychological approaches.* London: Routledge & Kegan Paul.

Free, R.J. (1995). Unpublished PhD. Thesis. Manchester University.

Hofstee, W.K.B. (1987). Wiens risico's lopen wij? [Whose risks are we running?] *Nederlands Tijdschrift voor de Psychologie, 42,* 47–53.

Hudson, P.T.W., & Verschuur, W.L.G. (1996). *Why people offshore bend the rules.* Report for Shell International Petroleum, The Hague.

Hudson, P.T.W., Reason, J.T., Wagenaar, W.A., Bentley, P.D., Primrose, M., & Visser, J.P. (1994). Tripod Delta: Proactive approach to enhanced safety. *Journal of Petroleum Technology, 46,* 58–62.

Hudson, P.T.W., Groeneweg, J., Reason, J.T., Wagenaar, W.A., Meeren, R.J.W. van der, & Visser, J.P. (1991). Application of Tripod to measure latent errors in North Sea gas platforms: Validity of failure state profiles. In *Proceedings of the First International Conference on Health, Safety and Environment.* Richardson, Texas: Society of Petroleum Engineers, pp. 429–435.

Hudson, P.T.W., Wagenaar, W.A., Reason, J.T., Groeneweg, J., Meeren, R.J.W. van der, & Visser, J.P. (1991). Enhancing safety in drilling: Implementing TRIPOD in a desert drilling operation. In *Proceedings of the First International Conference on Health, Safety and Environment.* Richardson, TX: Society of Petroleum Engineers, pp. 725–730.

Hudson, P.T.W., Zieverink, H.J.A., Groeneweg, J., Akerboom, S.P., Wagenaar, W.A., & Reason, J.T. (1995). *Fixing Tripod-Delta.* Report for Shell International Petroleum, The Hague.

International Loss Control Institute (1978). *International oil and petrochemical safety rating.* Loganville, GA: ILCI.

Johnson, W.G. (1980). *MORT Safety assurance systems.* New York: Dekker.

Jorgensen, N.O. (1988). Risky behaviour at traffic signals: A traffic engineer's view. *Ergonomics, 31,* 657–661.

Nisbett, R., & Ross, L. (1980). *Human inference: Strategies and shortcomings of social judgement.* Englewood Cliffs, NJ: Prentice-Hall.

Norman, D.A. (1981). Categorization of action slips. *Psychological Review, 88,* 1–15.

Östberg, G. (1984). Evaluation of a design for inconceivable event occurrence. *Materials and Designs, 5,* 88–93.

Peters, T.J., & Waterman, R.H. (1982). *In search of excellence.* New York: Harper & Row.

Rasmussen, J. (1982). Human errors: A taxonomy for describing human malfunction in industrial installations. *Journal of Occupational Accidents, 4,* 11–355.

Rasmussen, J. (1983). Skills, rules and knowledge: Signals, signs and symbols, and other distinctions in human performance models. *IEEE Transactions and Systems, Man and Cybernatics, 3,* 257–268.

Reason, J.T. (1990). *Human error.* New York: Cambridge University Press.

Rogovin, M. (1979). *Report of the President's Commission of the accident at Three Mile Island.* Washington, DC: Government Printing Office.

Slovic, P. (1985). Only new laws will spur seat-belt use. *Wall Street Journal,* 30 January.

Swain, A.D., & Guttman, H.E. (1983). *Handbook of human reliability analysis with emphasis on nuclear power plant applications.* NUREG/CR 1278. Albuquerque, NM: Sandia National Laboratories.

USSR State Committee on the Utilization of Atomic Energy (1986). *The accident at the Chernobyl nuclear power plant and its consequences.* Information compiled for the IAEA Experts' Meeting, 25–29 August, 1986. Vienna: IAEA.

Wagenaar, W.A. (1986). *De oorzaak van mogelijke ongelukken* [The causes of impossible accidents]. Duijkerlezing, Deventer: Van Loghum Slaterus.

Wagenaar, W.A. (1987). De constructie van risico. [The construction of risk]. *Nederlands Tijdschrift voor de Psychologie, 42,* 53–54.

Wagenaar, W.A. (1990a). Risk evaluation and the causes of accidents. In K. Borcherding, O.I. Larichev, & D. Messick (Eds.), *Contemporary issues in decision making.* Amsterdam: Elsevier Science Publishers, pp. 245–260.

Wagenaar, W.A. (1990b). Risk taking and accident causation. In J.F. Yates (Ed.), *Risk taking behaviour.* New York: John Wiley & Sons.

Wagenaar, W.A. (1991). *Influencing human behaviour: Toward a practical approach for exploration and production.* Report of Department of Psychology, Leiden University.

Wagenaar, W.A. (1992). Common sense problem solving in conditions of underspecification. In J. Siegfried (Ed.), *The status of common sense in psychology.* New York: Ablex.

Wagenaar, W.A., & Groeneweg, J. (1987). Accidents at sea: Multiple causes and impossible consequences. *Journal of Man-Machine Studies, 27,* 587–598.

Wagenaar, W.A., Hudson, P.T.W., & Reason, J.T. (1990). Cognitive failures and accidents. *Applied Cognitive Psychology, 4,* 273–294.

Wagenaar, W.A., & Keren, G.R. (1986). Does the expert know? In E. Hollnagel, G. Mancini, & D.D. Woods (Eds.), *Proceedings of ASI on intelligent decision support in process environments.* Berlin: Springer, pp. 87–103.

Wagenaar, W.A., Souverijn, A.M., & Hudson, P.T.W. (1992). Safety management in intensive care wards. In B. Wilpert, & Th. Qvale (Eds.), *Reliability and safety in hazardous work systems: Approaches to analysis and design.* Hove: Lawrence Erlbaum Associates Ltd.

5

Work Time and Behaviour at Work

Henk Thierry and Ben Jansen

1 INTRODUCTION

Until the second half of the twentieth century, work time arrangements and operating time arrangements that are applied in work organizations can be characterized by a dichotomy: *daytime work* and *irregular work and shift work*. By far most employees living in the industrialized countries work in the daytime only. This not only means that they do their work from early in the morning until late in the afternoon, but also that they are off at the weekend. To many, a working day amounts to something like eight working hours. Many employed have the impression that this arrangement of work time (four hours in the morning, four hours in the afternoon, off work at the weekend) forms a "natural" or "normal" pattern. One glance at the history of work time arrangements (henceforth WTAs) in Western countries, however, shows that all kinds of variations have existed throughout the centuries and that the number of working hours per day and the number of working days per week have often been (much) larger (see e.g. Ruppert, 1953; Harmsen &

Reinalda, 1975; Levitan & Belous, 1979; Scherrer, 1981). The five-day working week of around eight hours per day was not introduced on a large scale in most countries until the sixties.

It is typical of *shift work* that groups of employees take over each other's work during the 24-hour period. As a result, work is also done in the evenings and possibly also at night. When work is done during the whole 24-hour period, *semi*-continuous working means that no work is done at the weekend; *continuous* working means that work is done in seven 24-hour days. For many shift workers, a "shift"—the number of hours that work is done successively per 24-hour period—has a duration of about eight hours. Many changes have occurred in this field in the course of time (see e.g. Scherrer, 1981; Boissonnade, 1987), for instance with the advent of the guilds, and after the Renaissance, when artificial light was used on a much larger scale. The term *irregular work* is meant to refer to those WTAs in which the work organization may be "operational" throughout (a large part of) the 24-hour period, but in which no "regular" shifts of employees take over work from each other. For example, in the case of public transport, more employees are needed during peak hours only. In hospitals, a large share of the work can be done only during particular parts of the 24-hour period, whereas there is a variety of work time arrangements for employees, etc.

Gradually, however, during the fifties we saw the first signs of change. Initially these changes were WTAs that were applied on an extremely modest scale. For instance, in the fifties, some companies in Germany and Switzerland experimented with "flexitime", probably for the first time (see Robison, 1976; Maric, 1977; Ronen, 1981), allowing employees to choose for each period at what times they started work in the morning and stopped work in the afternoon. Around that time, the "compressed working week" was applied for the first time in one company in the United States (Wheeler, Gurman, & Tarnowieski, 1972; Cohen & Gadon, 1978; Nollen, 1979; Tepas, 1985). The arrangement implied that work was done on fewer days of the week, but during more hours per working day (for example, four 10-hour days instead of five eight-hour days). In addition, "part-time work" started developing: all kinds of arrangements developed in which work time was shorter than in a "full-time" arrangement.

These WTAs have been applied on an increasingly large scale ever since, though fairly gradually. They can be ranged in the "daytime work" category without much difficulty, though the "time limits of the day" (often 7.00am–6.00pm) are exceeded regularly, both in the morning and in the evening. In Europe, however, particularly since the early nineties, there has been an increase of variations of such WTAs that cannot be classed so unambiguously in either of the two categories mentioned at the outset (in the United States that increase had taken place a little earlier). Those WTAs are often referred to by the unfortunately opaque term *flexible* arrangements. These arrangements involve all kinds of variations in the number of working hours per day, in the part of the 24-hour period in which work is done, in the number of working days per week, in the average number of working hours per week, per month or per season, etc. We will mention merely a few examples:

- A standby contract may stipulate that there is

no work in one period, whereas work is done in the daytime, or in the evenings, or at night and/or at the weekend, in another period.
- A "compressed" working week may stipulate that work is done every three or four 24-hour periods in a series consisting of three consecutive 12-hour shifts: in one series from 7.00am–7.00pm, in the other from 7.00pm–7.00am. From time to time it also includes a weekend.
- Groups of employees decide to negotiate with principals over schedules containing both work time and leisure time, for instance in the context of a project. Such a schedule may contain, for instance, six weeks of work (of seven 14-hour working days each), followed by two and a half successive weeks of holidays.
- Certain occupational groups have to "work overtime" for a long time during part of the year—such as chartered accountants who have to audit the annual accounts of companies—after which the overtime hours are allowed to be taken off as days off in a later part of the year.
- Shops are allowed to (or have to) also be open in the evening. "Part timers" and "full timers" who were used to working during the daytime (save for the odd late evening shopping day) are called in for other parts of the 24-hour period, possibly by introducing "minishifts".

Several WTAs mentioned here briefly have been introduced in connection with developments towards a 24-hour economy. This is something that shiftworkers—especially those in semi-continuous shifts—have been dealing with a great deal longer. A characteristic feature of the changes in the last few years is nonetheless that a growing number of companies and institutions expect from their employees (in daytime work) and temps that work is normally also done in the evenings and in parts of the weekend. These changes may also entail that the "weekend" will no longer continue to fall on a Saturday and Sunday for large groups of the employed. As has been noted earlier, the distinction between daytime work and irregular work and/or shift work will consequently become less manageable.

Of course, the introduction of flexible WTAs does not take place in isolation. Instead, it is part of the easing of restrictions for organizations covering many more areas. The "easing of restrictions" is, in essence, present-day "jargon" for organization change (see also Chapter 8, Volume 4 of this Handbook). This means that generally there are radical changes in technology, in markets and in classes of customers, in designing the production process or the process of service, in coordination and management of employees, in job requirements, and in training and retraining employees. Concerning the behaviour of individuals and groups, these changes will lead to consequences in, for example, the "lifespan" of abilities and skills acquired, the role of previous experience in performance, the possibility of no more than one career, the meaning of "commitment" for motivation, etc. This automatically raises the important question as to what extent it is possible for a person's work to have a sufficient amount of routine and "rhythm", aspects that are very important for health.

Most of the topics mentioned just now will be paid special attention to, as independent topics in other chapters of this Handbook. In this chapter, we will specifically concentrate on the meaning and the consequences of various work time arrangements for behaviour at work. The first section contains a discussion of various psychological perspectives that may be important in investigating (and designing) WTAs. This discussion leads to a model to which we will return in the next sections. Next, in section 3, some flexible WTAs are discussed: we limit these to three that have been topics of research at least more than once before. Finally, section 4 contains a presentation of the main features of research into irregular work and shift work. Attention is also paid to various kinds of intervention in this context.

2 PSYCHOLOGICAL PERSPECTIVES

Does someone's work time, however, actually have any effect on his/her behaviour at (and possibly outside) work? And does this imply that different WTAs in turn also have a differentiating meaning? Of course, time does have a certain regulating effect, e.g. at the individual level. This is shown by research into a person's temporal orientation, for example (cf. Nuttin & Lens, 1985; Lens, 1986): it may be focused on one's own past (achievements in the past determine one's self-image), but also on the future which is expected (the person attempts to achieve challenging goals). In addition, references to time in human intercourse reveal the dominant cultural pattern of a society (cf. Durkheim, 1912; Elchardus, 1988; Van den Berg, 1995). An "endogenous" reference is story-like, episodic, "narrative", such as in the phrase: "that summer's day, when we came across her at the corner". Whereas an endogenous use is typical of a rural society with stable social relationships, "exogenous" references are found in a highly differentiated, if not segmented, urban society. An example is: "yesterday at 3.30". This usage of time is general, abstract, "chronological". It is this cultural pattern to which the phrase "I haven't got any time" belongs, with which not only the mutual relations among two or more people can be structured, but in which also time is expressed as a (scarce) resource. But again: does the distinction of *work* time (in relation to other forms or types) really contribute so much importance? The slight scepticism emergent in this question is recognizable in the perspective to be discussed next.

2.1 WTA as an additional factor

In a strict sense, this is not a typically psychological perspective. What is characteristic is precisely the lack of a theory or a model. The train of thought is that any consequences of a WTA can be demonstrated by a description of those features and effects of the WTA that *deviate* from the regular pattern of daytime work (i.e. Monday to Friday, eight-hour working day). And so attention is focused on the effect of "deviations" as frequent evening work, work at very early hours, work during the weekend, working longer than eight hours, etc., on the attitudes and preferences of employees, on their health and possibly their performance, on the productivity of the enterprise, on the coordination of work, etc. It cannot be ruled out that research on the topic of flexible WTAs that has taken place, mostly exploratory and descriptive (see also section 3), is caused to an important extent by taking this point of view.

The view that the arrangement of work time can be seen as an "addition" to the "work" (in normal circumstances) already existent has had repercussions in, for example, specific legislation and regulation, in particular concerning shift work. Both as a result of the International Labour Organization (ILO) and a large number of industrialized countries, more detailed stipulations have been formulated and ratified concerning work conditions, e.g. on the length of a working day, the frequency and the duration of breaks and rest periods, etc. (see also Thierry & Meijman, 1994). Stipulations concerning financial compensation (the shift work bonus), meals at unusual times, commuter traffic, etc., have been included in a collective labour agreement fairly often.

One of the great difficulties associated with the approach of a WTA as an additional factor, at least for scientific research, is the assumption that it is possible to identify "normal" or "usual" circumstances, conditions and consequences. This is expected primarily from the dependent variables in which a researcher is usually interested in the analysis of a WTA, such as motivation, commitment, fatigue, stress, performance, absenteeism, etc. However (as is also apparent from every relevant chapter in this Handbook), there is no such thing as "normal" motivation, usual stress, and the like. Consequently, it is neither possible to locate the "inherent" effects of a specific time arrangement. Researchers have attempted to solve this difficulty by analysing the consequences of (the introduction of) a WTA in longitudinal research, which may or may not be in comparison with the application of another WTA to one or more samples.

Yet this strategy, however useful when considered in isolation, involves the problem that, usually, the *ceteris paribus* assumption cannot be upheld. Various "remaining variables" have generally not remained constant precisely because another time arrangement causes, for example, the job content to change, or its load and the mutual relations (in this respect, and secondly, it is not strictly correct to speak of expected "normal" conditions). The application of continuous work-

ing, for example for nurses in a hospital, demonstrates what may be the case. During the night only a few nurses are present (compared to the daytime situation); various care tasks are carried out during the shifts before and after night-time if possible; only a few doctors can be paged; quiet and hectic periods alternate, etc. In business, much fewer differences occur during the shifts in a 24-hour period, but here it has also been demonstrated that variations arise in work, in supervision, in work climate, etc. The question to what extent the *ceteris paribus* clause is plausible has been hardly ever posed at all in research into flexible WTAs (see also Barling & Gallagher, 1996).

A related problem is caused by the selection effect. Various studies have shown that, in time, a smaller or larger number of shift workers tend to leave of their own accord (see e.g. Aanonsen, 1964; Thiis-Evensen, 1969; Frese & Okonek, 1984; Frese & Semmer, 1986; Jansen, Thierry, & Van Hirtum, 1986). The cause can be found in health complaints, dissatisfaction with the working hours and/or the work, etc. If workers doing shift work are now compared in a study to those in daytime working, for example in terms of aspects of health, level of performance, attitudes and satisfaction, the results will probably be slightly distorted. The possibility of a selection effect cannot be ruled out if flexible WTAs are applied for a longer period, either.

2.2   Adjustment

The second perspective draws attention to the way in which employees—individually or in groups— and the work organization try to adjust to the changes that are necessarily involved in the application of a changed WTA. All kinds of habits, both in work and in private life, have to be changed. As a result, emotions (such as uncertainty), tension and resistance often develop (see for example Bandura, 1986). In many cases, the sequence of work activities has to be arranged differently because of the new schedules, in view of the availability of groups of employees. Also, altered performance standards have to be met regularly.

At the individual level, abandoning shift work as discussed above in connection with the selection effect, can also be interpreted as a "coping" strategy, even if a drastic one. If the new WTA should require that performance is done at night from time to time, the instruction to those involved to prevent variations in the level of performance can have effect under certain conditions (see for example Chiles et al., 1968). The same can also be achieved for some time by greater dedication and effort among staff members; the disadvantage in the long term is, of course, that more fatigue develops. If the new WTA frequently results in a lack of sleep, adjustments to be considered are, for example, work schedules with fewer successive (or shorter) shifts, a noiseless bedroom, having a nap, relaxation techniques, etc. It is also highly important to what extent any members of the family are able and willing to adjust to the new WTA in terms of eating habits, spending leisure time, shopping, etc.

Yet also the company or institution, or important parts thereof will have to adjust. This not only relates to internal changes such as other forms of consultation and coordination, differently organized canteens, altered transport facilities, etc. At least as important is the way in which the work organization regulates its transactions with the environment. In quite some organization theories this topic is approached in terms of "contingency" (see also Chapters 2 and 3, Volume 4). In this approach, the emphasis may be on organic versus mechanical forms of adjustment (cf. Burns & Stalker, 1961), on differentiation and integration of sections of the organization (cf. Lawrence & Lorsch, 1967), on managerial choice (see Child, 1972), or on the environment that has a selective effect on organizations (cf. population ecology; Morgan, 1997). This topic—the mutual adjustment of organization and environment—is also important in the choice that a company makes for a flexible WTA. In terms of extremes: there are companies that translate variations in the demand for workers (depending on the supply of work) as directly as possible into attracting and then, if required, dismissing staff (consider standby workers for zero to forty hours or more). But there are also companies that try meeting such variations by a contingent, flexible organization of activities, combined for example with the application of the compressed working week and flexitime. The type of company—organic or rather mechanical—

therefore plays a major role in introducing a WTA (see Thierry & Tham, 1994; De Lange, Van Eijk, & Tham, 1995; Chapter 8, Volume 4).

2.3 Regulation of non-work time
The third perspective relates to the influence that a WTA has on the time outside work. One of its first aspects is highly obvious: every arrangement of work time marks the amount of time that can be spent in other ways. This observation acquires more meaning when non-work time—sometimes incorrectly termed "leisure" in a broad sense—is classified in categories. There are many ways of doing this. We will follow the classification according to Parker and Smith (1976) who after mentioning work time subsequently distinguish:

- "work-related time": the time for commuter traffic, for preparing or finishing work at home, etc.;
- "existence time": time for meals, sleep, personal care;
- "semi-leisure": time for activities with a somewhat committing nature such as walking the dog, visiting other people, etc.;
- "leisure": time spent entirely at one's own choice.

In the word "leisure", the Latin verb "licēre" can be recognized: "to be permitted to . . .", meaning: to be able to choose, to have options.

This aspect will be brought out in a little more relief when the "location" of the work time during the 24-hour period and during the week is added to the equation. An example will make this point clear: an average weekly work time consisting of 36 hours may produce a WTA of four nine-hour working days in the daytime (for example from 5.00am–2.00pm or from 9.00am–6.00pm), but also an arrangement of four nine-hour nights. Or one with three twelve-hour days (or nights), or even six six-hour days, etc. This should make clear that features of a WTA—apart from the average weekly work time—may affect the spending of non-work time drastically and hence also various facets of individual behaviour at work.

A second regulation aspect concerns the extent to which *meanings of work* and *leisure* interrelate. The "Central Life Interest" scale (CLI) developed by Dubin (1956) has been used rather often in research on this matter. By means of the CLI, respondents indicate the extent to which generally important values—such as autonomy, responsibility, social support—characterize their work, their leisure or both domains (see also the instrument used by Coetsier & Claes (n.d.): "Importance of life roles and values" in this connection). Research results relate primarily to the validity of two hypotheses:

1. "*Compensatory*" (sometimes referred to in terms such as opposition or contrast): characteristics that are thought to be highly/ hardly important in work are hardly/very much so in leisure. Two forms of "compensatory" relation link up to this:
   (a) "Supplemental compensation": it is characteristic that work scores low on the CLI values (such as autonomy, use of various skills), whereas leisure shows a high score on those values. What is meant by the concept of "supplemental" is that a person chooses to "compensate" in leisure whatever work does not offer.
   (b) "Reactive compensation": now work is scored highly on the CLI values and leisure is scored low on them. The person spends leisure so that he/she can relax from work.
2. "*Spillover*" (also known as: extension, generalization, congruence): work and leisure score in the same direction on the CLI values. Both areas may show either low or high values:
   (a) "Passive spillover": work and leisure both have a low value.
   (b) "Active spillover": work and leisure are given high scores on the CLI values.

Research has shown that both hypotheses are confirmed at some times and that they are not at other times. Firstly, it makes a large difference what kind of work the respondents do in fact have. Secondly, it is important whether the researcher asks for statements concerning "leisure" as a global category or concerning various domains

within it. Thirdly, a considerable number of conditioning variables are shown to have influence, for instance personal dimensions. Partly for this reason, it is possible to explain why certain CLI values are supportive of the pattern of the first hypothesis and other values support the second hypothesis, for one and the same person (see for more on this for example Wilensky, 1969; Wippler, 1968; Dubin & Champoux, 1977; Champoux, 1980; Kabanoff, 1980; Kabanoff & O'Brien, 1980; Brook & Brook, 1989; Lambert, 1980; Kirchmeyer, 1972).

Originally another, third, hypothesis was formulated: the domains of work and leisure are not linked according to the *segmentation hypothesis* (that is, at least not in terms of the CLI values). The domains have been alienated from one another, in other words. In empirical respect, there is hardly any support for this; a study conducted by Elizur (1991) is one of the exceptions.

A third aspect of the regulating relation between work time and non-work time focuses on the *preferences* of respondents for (higher) income, or for (more) leisure, respectively (see for example Shank, 1986). These can be in a mutual exchange relation. Usually two types of exchange are distinguished:

1. *Substitution effect*: the higher the salary someone earns, the more he/she will prefer *fewer* non-work hours and *more* hours of work, because more "leisure" would lead to a further loss of wages.
2. *Income effect*: the higher the earned income, the stronger one's preference will be for *more* non-work hours and *fewer* hours of work, because more can be purchased, given a higher salary (for example expenditure in leisure).

Data from an American census show that substitution takes place when the number of working hours is smaller: there is a preference for more working hours (and therefore a higher compensation) and for less leisure. But above a certain income (a certain number of working hours, respectively), the income effect holds. There is also some evidence that the preferences of women tend to show the income effect and those of men the substitution effect (Langedijk, 1995).

Thus far we have assumed that work and leisure have a regulative effect on the size, nature and meaning of non-work time. The relation may also however be the reverse: the amount, the expenditure and the meaning of non-work time may have a regulative effect on work and work time. WTAs geared to individual employees (flexible ones)— for example in the case of partial parental leave— are a case in point. The two types of causal correlation may also occur simultaneously and interactively. From this background, for example, the consequences of radical role transitions can then be investigated, both within the field of work and the non-work field and also between both areas.

2.4 Rhythmic processes

Who passes various time zones by aeroplane— and therefore travels east or west—often suffers the so-called "jet lag" syndrome on his destination for several days. This is generally expressed by fatigue at daytime, some loss of concentration, and some trouble sleeping at night. The body gradually adjusts itself to the "new" time arrangement.

This fourth perspective directs attention to the meaning of *biological* processes for the regulation of individual human existence (just as for that of animals and, in physiological respect, that of plants). Many processes have a 24-hour rhythm that is referred to by the notion of "circadian" (from "circa" approximate, and "dies" day, 24-hour period). One might consider e.g. body temperature, heart beat, internal discharge of hormones, activity of the brains, etc. These rhythms are adjusted to each other ("synchronized") due to two different factors. On the one hand, every human being has a so-called "internal clock" that is localized in the lower frontal hypothalamus (cf. Schmidt & Thews, 1983). On the other hand, all kinds of societal and social events contain signals (so-called "Zeitgebers") which convey to humans in which part of the 24-hour period they are living (for example Aschoff, 1978). One might consider the moment when someone awakes and sees that it is half-dark outside: will it be evening or is morning breaking? All kinds of sounds make it instantly clear to him or her "what time it is":

traffic noise fading out or fading in, the newspaper falling down the letterbox, children going to school, or coming home, etc.

The transatlantic traveller mentioned earlier is confronted with another "set" time in another country: the organism adjusts accordingly. The case is quite different for the person who, in continuous working for example, has to work at night repeatedly and wants to sleep in the daytime. It is not that the environment and the set time have changed, but the shift worker is the deviation: not only the pattern of night and day, but also all kinds of social signals of society working in the "daytime" make this clear. As a consequence, the rhythms of the biological processes become disordered, ("out of phase") after a short while and their mutual gearing also becomes disturbed, if only because work at night requires an active and alert organism. This process is reversed gradually again when the shift worker gets some 24-hour periods off and then works in the daytime for a while.

In research on circadian processes particular attention is due to the possibility of a "masking" effect (Aschoff, 1978). This means that a variable X affects a variable Y, but also a variable Z, in which Z also affects X. For example: the light–dark cycle has, as a Zeitgeber, an influence on body temperature; the same cycle also affects physical activity, which in turn affects body temperature. "Masking" effects may often lie at the root of apparently (seemingly) conflicting results.

This fourth point of view is characteristic of a large part of the research on irregular work and shift work. A central theme, for example, is to what extent health suffers in the short or relatively long term, respectively. Another important question is to what extent work performance, individual well-being and leisure behaviour are influenced by it (see e.g. Colquhoun & Rutenfranz, 1980; Reinberg, Vieux, & Andlauer, 1980; Folkard & Monk, 1985; Jansen, 1987; Thierry & Meijman, 1994). The results from this type of research have also led to experiments with other shift work schedules (for example Knauth & Rutenfranz, 1982; Jansen, Thierry, & Van Hirtum, 1986). As work in flexible WTAs takes place outside the "normal" working hours in the daytime more often, it is advisable also to incorporate problems on possible disturbances of rhythm in research on the topic.

2.5   Selection

From the last-mentioned point of view, a WTA—in particular one covering irregular work and shift work—may especially be conceived as a more or less risky characteristic of work (see for example Jansen, 1987). It is therefore obvious that a separate perspective is formed by the question to what extent employees can be *selected on risky dispositions*.

In many countries, it is customary that (potential) workers doing shift work are given a medical examination. Of course, it is wise that (also other) employees receive a periodic "check up". There is however little clarity on the specific criteria to which special attention ought to be paid in the case of continuous working in particular. This is because on the one hand much research is cross-sectional by nature, and on the other hand it is because of the role played by individual differences in the degree of adjustment. All the same, there is a certain consensus on the view that workers with certain chronic disorders should not be allowed to be selected for shift work (see Rutenfranz et al., 1981). These are especially people who are regularly troubled by their stomach and intestines, or have heart and vascular complaints, respectively, and people with diabetes or epilepsy. It also holds as a rule of thumb that one should no longer *start* working in shifts from the approximate age of thirty-five.

In the psychological field, the harvest is even scantier. There are indications that outspoken "morning types" are troubled more by the adjustment to repeatedly changing times than regular "evening types". A similar difference has been observed between highly introvert and highly extrovert people. The problem however is that very few people belong to the "extreme" types (morning versus evening) and that someone's score on these orientation scales is also determined by his/her pattern of living (for example Meijman et al., 1989). This point of view produces interesting questions all the same; it is also advisable to incorporate the relative risk of some flexible WTAs in this type of research.

2.6   A model

In the preceding sections five points of view were reviewed according to which work time arrangements may be analysed and studied. Every point of view leads to the formulation of certain research questions and, although indirectly sometimes, recommendations for the design of a WTA in practice. The first point of view ("additional factor") can be recognized in most research that has been conducted on flexible WTAs. The fourth ("rhythmic processes") characterizes an important part of the extensive research on shift work. But research on WTAs of course does not take place in such a stylized fashion as the points of view may have suggested. Also, we have only treated the more well known points of view; some have been left out of consideration. An even more important issue is that in nearly every study moderating variables play a role that has not been discussed in the preceding section.

For this reason we present a model in this section that incorporates the most important variables for the research on WTAs. With the use of this model the research on flexible WTAs, and on irregular work and shift work, respectively, will be discussed in the next sections. It will become clear that the model is not merely descriptive, but that it also has some normative features (as a reflection of the desires of both authors).

Figure 5.1 contains a cognitive motivational model for the explanation of an individual's behaviour at work (see for example Campbell & Pritchard, 1976; Kanfer, 1990; Ford, 1992; see also Chapter 11, Volume 4). Its main theme consists of boxes 1 to 4. We assume that the person wants to realize motives, by setting goals, for example (cf. Locke & Latham, 1990), or by coming up to the standards (cf. Thierry, Koopman, & Van der Flier, 1992), and that he expects to be able to do this by performing tasks. These tasks involve routines (scripts, schemata) (box 1). Therefore the person spends effort and performs acts that are necessary to carry out the tasks (box 2). This causes a particular performance result. Consequences can also be described as "states", as more or less exhausted resources (fatigue; quality of sleep, etc.). Such consequences lead to outcomes: part of these can be related to the goals set

FIGURE 5.1

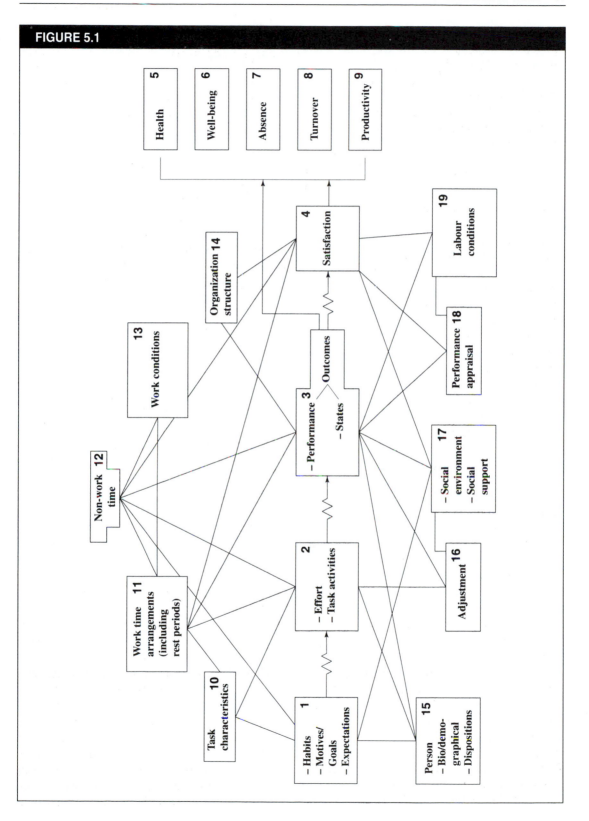

from box 1, such as recognition, reward, etc. Another part results from change of state, and implies for example a greater need for recovery time (box 3). Many outcomes are also dependent on the appraisal of performances achieved (box 18) and of applying individual or collective labour conditions (box 19). These variables impact upon the degree of satisfaction (box 4). Not only satisfaction, but also the results from box 3 have effect on consequences such as health (5), well-being (6), absence from work (7), turnover (8), and productivity (9). Obviously, there are all kinds of feedback-relations: we have omitted them for the sake of clarity.

In this chapter, most attention is devoted to the consequences of WTAs, including the arrangements of rest times during work (box 11), for example on non-work time (box 12). An important aspect of these consequences of WTAs is what work tasks (box 10) are involved, for example, in terms of identity, variety, autonomy (see Chapter 6, Volume 3 of this Handbook). Physical work conditions (box 13)—consider the degree of noise—can affect the consequences of a WTA greatly. Characteristics of the organization structure (box 14)—such as degree of centralization, type of control executed—have effect on the tasks and performance, for example. Personal variables are mentioned in box 15; both biographical/demographic data and dispositions (for example the degree of "internal control") are relevant here. By adjustment (box 16) a measure such as e.g. a noiseless bedroom is meant, but also the changing of the composition of the meal (in nightwork). The social environment (box 17) partially determines how "deviant" a particular WTA is, which also relates to the degree of social support available, for example in the case of higher levels of occupational stress.

3 FLEXIBLE WORK TIME ARRANGEMENTS

In this section we will discuss three WTAs successively: flexitime, the compressed working week, and part-time work. In addition, we will go into some other arrangements briefly. Each of these three WTAs is first given a short characterization, after which the motives or goals considered in applying the WTA are discussed very briefly. Next we will deal more extensively with the results from previous studies. Every discussion is concluded by mentioning several research problems that might be interesting in future investigations.

3.1 Flexitime

Flexitime relates to the moment when an employee starts work and the moment when he stops work. In various cases it also relates to the period in which lunch break falls. In Schema 5.1 two examples are presented.

In schedule A (Schema 1), employees may choose at what time they start work between 7.00am and 10.00am and stop work between 4.30pm and 7.00pm. We assume in this example that they have an eight-hour working day (given an operating time of twelve hours per day), whereas the regular lunch break lasts at least half an hour. Every employee is supposed to be present between 10.00am and 4.30pm: this is the so-called "core time". This type of schedule can occur in commercial service, at departments in which the work of various experts or professionals has to be properly adjusted, etc. It may imply that the choice of starting time and finishing time cannot be made by each individual employee, but only in groups,

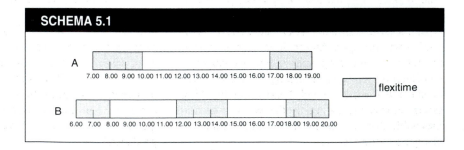

SCHEMA 5.1

by those who depend on one another in their work. In schedule B employees may also choose when, and for how long, they have a break between noon and 2.30pm. The obligatory time of attendance is from 8.00am until noon and from 2.30am until 5.30pm. In this example, the operating time amounts to fourteen hours. Such a schedule can be useful, for example, in organizations that provide services to clients who come up with a question or a problem in the morning for which an explanation is provided in the afternoon.

Flexitime arrangements can also be applied to part-time workers (see section 3.3). For instance, Perret (1980) has described an experiment with cashiers in a large French supermarket. The number of cashiers required varies per hour in the day and the day in the week. The manager indicated for every fortnight's period how many checkouts were to be open per hour. Starting from the number of working hours agreed with each cashier, groups of cashiers, supervised by a chosen coordinator, worked out their own schedules.

What happens when an employee having an eight-hour working day works longer or shorter on one or several days? There are organizations in which this should be an exception: the rule is that the working day contains the agreed number of working hours. In many other organizations, however, only a minimum and/or a maximum number of working hours is fixed per day or per week. Within these restrictions, employees have options. In this case, credit or debit hours should be settled within a week, a month, a quarter, a year, or an even longer period (see for example Fleuter, 1975; Robison, 1976; Cohen & Gadon, 1978; Hutchinson & Brewster, 1994). The last-mentioned authors point to the Hewlett-Packard business, for example, in which employees (given a standard working week of thirty-seven hours) are able to work three extra working hours per week. The leisure time saved in this way can be taken off at one's own discretion after consultation with one's own manager. An employee can influence his/her work time to a greater extent by means of a credit/debit system than if merely given the choice of starting (possibly lunch break) and finishing times, unless the nature of the work makes it inevitable that in certain weeks or months there is always overtime work.

This account shows that a great variety of flexitime arrangements may be distinguished (see also Hutchinson & Brewster, 1994). A rough estimate points out that such an arrangement applies to 10 percent to 40 percent of the employees in the countries belonging to the European Union. In the United States about five million employees were accustomed to a flexitime arrangement by the end of the eighties (Ralston, 1989). A study conducted by Tepas (1985) has shown that particularly the United States government applies flexitime. Tepas also points out that most figures are probably underestimated, because certain categories in the labour force—e.g. farmers, independent tradesmen, professors—have always been able to determine their working hours and, to a certain extent, the beginning and ending of their working hours. On the basis of a 1985 national survey in the United States, Mellor (1986) notes that these WTAs vary according to type of activity, client, legislation, (collective) employment contract and the views held by managers.

This brings us to the *motives and goals* considered in the application of flexitime WTAs. Particularly in the slightly older literature, the perspective of the employee is emphasized: more say in one's own time, less tension between the various work-related and family-related roles (notably for employed females making careers for themselves), less time wasted in commuter traffic, being late at work less often, etc. More recently, the importance of the work organization is put forward more forcefully: market fluctuations that are hard to predict create a need for variable staffing (see for example Sloane, 1975; Robison, 1976; ILO, 1978; Ronen, 1981; Tepas, 1985; Ralston, 1989, 1990; Lendfers & Nijhuis, 1989; Dalton & Mesch, 1990; Hutchinson & Brewster, 1994). In general, the literature is well-disposed to the consequences of a flexitime WTA. But at the time, Cohen & Gadon (1978) and Ronen (1981) expressed some doubt about the usefulness and the effectiveness of these arrangements. In addition, Dunham et al. (1987) state that if flexitime has produced advantages, these have still been concealed well in the scientific literature. Hence the question: what results have the studies really produced?

Not much, say Ralston et al. (1985), at least in the period between 1965 and 1985. They evaluated one hundred studies in the field of flexitime using four criteria. In order to qualify, a study was required to have used direct measures for productivity, to contain a pre-test and a post-test, to have an experimental and a control group, and to have applied correct techniques for data analysis. Only two studies met these requirements.

But what characteristics of individual behaviour (and that of groups of employees) would mainly be expected to be affected by a flexitime WTA? And what aspects of the working of an organization are considered in this connection? Moreover, are these expectations based on hypotheses of some kind or on founded assumptions at the very least? Very few authors appear to have gone into this question. Ralston et al. (1985) employ a sociotechnical point of view: in their opinion, the individual's "self control" is enhanced due to flexitime, particularly when he/she is able to determine how long work is done per day. If various departments have to contend with scarce resources (for example: the access to a "mainframe"), then this WTA will also lead to less competition. Employees can also concentrate on their work better in the case of a flexitime WTA. Hence, Ralston et al. expect flexitime to result in higher levels of employees' productivity if they have to contend with scarce resources. Their expectation was confirmed in a field experiment, in which the experimental and the control condition were formed by natural (thus not "randomized") groups. Particularly in the longer term (twelve to eighteen months after introduction of the flexitime arrangement) productivity had increased. Dunham, Pierce & Castaneda (1987) monitored the introduction of flexitime in a section of a utility company, while using a field experimental design. Respondents were randomly assigned to either the experimental or the control condition by department. No significant changes of performance occurred however. What the introduction of this WTA was associated with was a higher degree of commitment, more satisfaction, etc.

Dalton & Mesch (1990) raise the question on the basis of what considerations a relation may be expected between a flexitime WTA and a lower

turnover or a lower level of absenteeism, respectively. Three arguments concerning turnover are mentioned:

1. Due to flexitime both the "extrinsic" motivation (for example less travelling time) and the "intrinsic" motivation (for example more autonomy) increase. If the level of motivation is higher, the turnover is lower.
2. In this WTA, mutual adjustment of work time and time for private activities is better, the attitudes (towards work time and leisure) are more positive and commitment to the organization is greater. This increased "work adjustment" leads to a lower level of turnover.
3. A flexitime WTA leads to a new transaction between the organization and the employee: more stability in the individual adjustment between work and non-work is combined with greater commitment to the organization.

Dalton and Mesch also claim that absenteeism can become lower in a flexitime arrangement. There are two types of explanation:

(a) Motivation becomes higher (see 1), hence one is at work more often.
(b) It is possible to organize private circumstances better. Employees ascribe the causes of the resulting higher rate of attendance to the WTA.

Data from previous studies and data from their own study show that turnover is not affected. With regard to absenteeism, the results are not identical, i.e. sometimes they are higher, sometimes they are lower, and regularly no change occurs.

Nearly all the remaining research on flexitime WTAs is basically descriptive. The following results are shown (a more extensive treatment is provided in Orpen, 1981; Lendfers & Nijhuis, 1989; Ralston, 1989, 1990; Krausz & Hermann, 1991; Åberg, Cocke, & Söderberg, 1983) for example by:

- performance/productivity: equal or higher (rather often according to employees' or managers' *impressions*);

- absenteeism: equal, lower or higher;
- satisfaction: higher (regarding work, the time arrangement, respectively), particularly short term);
- commuter traffic: with more ease.

The result of a study conducted by Krausz & Hermann (1991) is interesting: employees with a preference for flexitime have a stronger "growth need". Clearly these people are not concerned with solving existing problems, but with gaining more outcomes, according to the authors.

Now, does the foregoing mean that this WTA is not harmful and possibly not so very important either? We tend towards this view to the extent that it only involves the choice of the moments at which work is started and stopped. Even so, it is an interesting question to what extent flexitime is viewed by employees as an expansion of the possibilities of influencing the work situation, also in the longer term. Remarkably, very few data have been collected on this. Another interesting issue is to what extent the choice of very early starting times is linked to the incidence of (near) accidents.

This WTA is probably much less "harmless" if it also involves a *debit–credit* system. In this case, very long work times may occur per 24-hour period, possibly occurring during a longer period (weeks, months). We will return to this subject more extensively in the following section.

3.2 Compressed working week

In the "compressed", (henceforth COM) working week, work is done in a smaller number of working days and a greater number of hours per day. Given a forty-hour working week, this does not involve five working days of eight hours each, but for example four days of ten hours, or three days of each twelve or thirteen hours (with an extra working day once every period). Precisely as in other time arrangements, its introduction may be combined with a reduction or an extension of the average weekly work time. What is indeed typical of COM is that the operating time of a company is almost always extended to a considerable degree. This is why COM arrangements regularly occur in combination with the application of shift work. They can also apply to part-time workers. In the United Kingdom, COM is sometimes applied in connection with two-shift working: after a shift of, say, ten hours in the daytime, a second shift of ten hours in the night-time follows after an interruption, (so-called "alternating day and night shift system; see e.g. Sloane, 1975; Walker, 1985). In addition, the EOWO schedule has received some fame in Canada and the United States (Northrup, Wilson, & Rose, 1979). In this "every other weekend off" system (which occurs mainly in the chemical and the petrochemical industry) work is done in such an order of twelve-hour shifts that every employee has every other weekend off. There are also combination arrangements in which work is done in eight hours per day during the week and twelve hours in the weekend. Although we shall not make a sharp distinction between "daytime arrangements" and "shift work arrangements", our attention in this section will focus mainly on COM arrangements in the daytime.

With what *objectives* do work organizations introduce this type of WTA? Their objectives are nearly always to improve the service provided to customers and to make better use of the means of production, by way of extending the operating time (see Maric, 1977; Tepas, 1985; Colligan & Tepas, 1986; Loontechnische Dienst, 1991b, 1992). In this sense, the intended flexible character of COM relates mainly to adjusting the composition of the workforce better to fluctuations in the demand for labour in the market. Another cause for the introduction of COM is that employees can make better use of their nonwork time, such as resting more, training and development, hobbies, etc. (for example, Meijman, 1992). Flexibility therefore involves the utility of leisure. A third consideration is that less time needs to be spent on commuter traffic (and waiting in traffic jams).

COM has been recommended as a "managerial" innovation, particularly in the early seventies. According to Maric (1977), it is really a European WTA introduced to (West) Germany and the United Kingdom in the sixties. Tepas (1985) however states that this WTA was applied in the United States in the early forties, although in another name. Around 1990, COM arrangements were found in The Netherlands in about 1 percent of the companies (especially in more operative jobs), the Loontechnische Dienst (1991b) states, whereas some expansion of it was predicted. In the United States the percentage appears a little higher (approximately 2 percent). These are predominantly organizations associated with the state, public utility, services, construction, petrochemical industry (for example oil rigs) and health care. Schema 5.2 contains an example of COM.

COM arrangements can be fairly simple and can involve for example two groups of staff members each working four ten-hour days. A slightly more complicated design however is presented in Schema 5.2. Consider a supermarket whose operating time amounts to six days of twelve and a half hours each (closed on Sundays), and the average weekly work time ("full time") is thirty-seven and a half hours. Groups 1 to 3 all work on three consecutive days, followed by four days off (including the Sunday). But groups 4 and 5 have a shorter compressed work and days off period. Apparently, Wednesday, Friday and Saturday are the days with much activity.

Compared to other flexible WTAs, COM has been a topic of research a little more often. To the extent that research is hypothesis-testing by nature, attention has been paid particularly to the extent to which COM *interferes* with the behaviour and the preferences of employees. For instance, Dunham et al. (1987) assume that a COM arrangement has a positive effect on the use of leisure, for instance at the weekend, but that it has a negative effect on the activities, for example with children, in the evening after a (long) day's work. Is this hypothesis indeed confirmed in general?

Most attention has been paid to consequences for performance or productivity. One of the first experiments is from Ivancevich (1974; Ivancevich & Lyon, 1977). Two groups of equal size were compared in a food company. The experimental group changed over to a system based on four ten-hour days, whereas the control group maintained a schedule of five eight-hour days. Repeated measurements covering a period of thirteen months showed that the experimental group attained better performance and was also more satisfied. A "follow-up" study however showed that these effects had deteriorated after well over two years. A second experimental group which had been set up during the follow-up, furthermore showed the same short-term effects. Foster, Latack, & Reindl (1979) carried out a study among computer operators. Some of them worked for thirty-eight hours in three days' time; another section worked forty hours in five days' time. The first group exhibited a higher level of productivity and was more satisfied about their own schedule than the second group. The design of the experiment does however not legitimize ascribing the results to the COM arrangement unambiguously. This is possible, however, in the study conducted by Dunham, Pierce, & Castaneda (1987): for a group of nurses, lab assistants and clerical staff, the schedule of five eight-hour days changed into four ten-hour days. After a four months' period the old schedule was reintroduced. In comparison with a control group (that continued to work in the 5×8 schedule), improvement after transition to the COM schedule occurred in one of the seven indices for effectiveness (viz. "service to the client"); in five indices only a positive trend could be observed. After returning to the old schedule six indices showed a decline. In two carefully designed experiments, Rosa and collaborators found no deteriorated performance because of the introduction of COM.

SCHEMA 5.2						
Example of a compressed working week						
	Mon	*Tue*	*Wed*	*Thu*	*Fri*	*Sat*
Group 1	X	X	X	—	—	—
Group 2	—	—	X	X	X	—
Group 3	—	—	—	X	X	X
Group 4	X	—	X	—	—	X
Group 5	—	X	—	—	X	X

What they did show was that the response time in some experimental tasks slowed down (Rosa, Wheeler, Warm & Colligan, 1985; Rosa & Colligan, 1988). It should of course be borne in mind in evaluating all stated results that not always the same COM type is introduced and, what is more, that various work tasks (and work conditions) are at issue.

The same mixed evidence incidentally emerges from survey studies and literature reviews (see for example Latack & Foster, 1985; Rosa, 1995). Northrup (1989) carried out a "follow-up" survey among managers of Human Resource Management departments on their experiences with the twelve-hour shift. Out of twenty companies, four had abolished COM for various reasons. In nine companies it was believed that productivity had increased because of COM. In three, it was believed that it had declined. Remarkably, COM had mostly been introduced at the request of the employees. According to a survey carried out by the Dutch Labour Inspectorate (Loontechnische Dienst, 1992), most companies report that productivity has risen as a result of the introduction of the four-day working week.

In several experiments the question has been examined to what extent COM shows effects in (psycho)physiological respect and in terms of health. Volle et al. (1979) compared two groups of employees in a factory manufacturing household appliances. The experimental group worked for 4 ten-hour days and the control group did for 5 eight-hour days. Many data were collected, including heart frequency, body temperature, blood pressure, volume of exhaled air, etc. The results show few differences, but this is possibly due to the fact that other periods of measurement have been used for one group than for the other. The authors conclude nonetheless that the observed increase in fatigue in the case of COM remains within acceptable limits. Peacock et al. (1983) report that police officers who changed over from an eight-hour shift (in a twelve-day cycle) to a twelve-hour shift (in an eight-day cycle) exhibited lower blood pressure, better sleep (both as to length and quality) and increased alertness. Comparable results have been found in computer operators by Williamson et al. (1994). Hale et al. (1980) observed, also in a study in the

police force, that ten-hour shifts produced less fatigue than eight-hour and twelve-hour shifts. Chen (quoted in De Carufel & Schaan, 1990) on the other hand believes that shifts lasting ten hours lead to more fatigue, more stress and, for elderly people, to a somewhat poorer health condition. De Carufel & Schaan (1990) observed in their own study in three medium-sized police forces that more complaints about fatigue are expressed in twelve-hour shifts, particularly about the last four working hours. Similar results have been found by Stafford et al. (1988), notably for twelve-hour shifts at night (see also Rosa et al., 1985). Rosa & Colligan (1988) also demonstrate—in an experiment with volunteers each performing a simulation task every five days for twelve-hours—that after approximately eight hours the number of errors increased to a considerable degree. The more days on which work was done successively, the higher the body temperature and the slower the response time became (see also the overview by Alluisi & Morgan, 1982). Rosa and Colligan draw the interesting conclusion that increasing fatigue affects behaviour more than the diurnal period in which work is done. Moors (1990) studied consequences of the introduction, for a period of three months, of a five-day working week with a nine-hour (instead of an eight-hour) working day in a Belgian glass factory. Well over half of the employees complained about fatigue, not only because of the extra hour of work, but also because there was less sleep owing to the early start.

De Feyter, Tham, & Roozemond (1993) give an account of an experiment with a four-day working week (of nine hours) for volunteers in a Dutch public organization. Those who stopped early were more tired and complained about their workload and their health more often. Martens et al. (1995) analysed data recorded by Belgian doctors concerning patients who informed them of their complaints. Those who had had a COM arrangement in their work, had worse health (VOEG questionnaire), compared to patients who had always worked in the daytime, worse well-being and a lower quality of sleep. The design of the study does not however permit drawing cause and effect conclusions. In an extensive overview of the literature on effects of fatigue at work, Rosa

(1995) arrives at the conclusion that there are no consistent effects.

As has already been shown in the preceding overview, COM (and a long watch in shift work) can be associated with positive, negative or unchanged scores on various variables. Nonetheless, concern about the application of an extended period of work of more than eight hours continues to be fairly widespread. This is also due to the fact that fatigue may not only arise from a WTA, but also from all kinds of other aspects such as the content of the tasks, the working environment, the situation at home, etc. For example, some studies show that workers who stay at and near their work for a longer period (consider oil rigs, sometimes also mines), do not appear to meet negative effects of twelve-hour shifts. Should those workers also be in traffic every day, have social duties, take care of the household and children, according to Rosa (1995), their fatigue would probably be (too) much, the safety of their behaviour decreased, etc. Research into such *combined effects* has hardly been carried out.

Now do the above results suggest that employees in a COM arrangement are generally not satisfied either? Quite the contrary, at least as regards COM: practically every study shows that the majority of especially junior employees are content with their compressed working week, particularly when they have gained experience with it for some time (cf. Hale et al. 1980; Breaugh, 1983; Latack & Foster, 1985; Dunham et al., 1987; Lendfers & Nijhuis, 1989; Northrup, 1989; De Carufel & Schaan, 1990; Van Velzen, 1994; Rosa, 1995). According to Latack & Foster (1985) two kinds of explanation might be considered. The first one concerns the possibility of "escape": because the content of the work is considered boring or monotonous, the attraction of COM is that one is working for fewer days. Indeed, in some studies a lower level of job satisfaction is found. The second explanation emphasizes "job enrichment": superiors often have another (COM) WTA than their employees. Consequently, employees have to solve more problems by themselves: this leads to the experience of autonomy and responsibility and the ability to utilize more varied skills (as often happens in nightwork). This explanation is

indirectly supported by some findings that, in addition to COM, the degree of commitment to work has also increased (Latack & Foster, 1985; De Carufel & Schaan, 1990). The research data regarding turnover and absenteeism are not unambiguous.

To what extent do the reported results from research indicate that the objectives on which the introduction of COM was based have been realized? It is surprising to observe that not one study relates directly to a better adjustment of supply of labour and demand for labour, and to the improvement of service. Insofar as improved performance or higher productivity would be viewed as the operational measure of this objective (yet, this is possible to a limited extent only), the conclusion is evidently not unequivocal. According to some studies, the second objective—better use of non-work time—is achieved. On the other hand, rather many studies suggest that more time is required to recover from fatigue building up during consecutive working days. In some studies, it is also brought forward by female employers that COM may interfere with activities at home. And the remark is heard among those working for twelve hours at a stretch that work and non-work become strictly separated domains (De Carufel & Schaan, 1990).

In continuation of what was stated at the conclusion of section 3.1, we hold the view that decision making about possible expansion of the work time per day should take place with great caution. In upcoming research, attention should be paid to the question whether "chronic" buildup of fatigue produces negative effects in the longer term. Hardly any pertinent data are available. Another important research question concerns the best possible arrangements of rest times at work (see e.g. Alluisi & Morgan, 1982; Meijman, 1992). What is optimum also depends on the nature of the tasks to be performed and the corresponding circumstances. When a COM arrangement pertains to late night, very early morning and/or later evening, attention in research should also be paid to possible disturbance of biological rhythms. In this way COM research might benefit from an important part of the research on shift work. We expect the research at issue to demonstrate that certain tasks could be carried out without too much trouble in an eleven-hour or twelve-hour working day, but also that there are all kinds of other activities for which an eight-hour working day is too long, really.

3.3 Part-time work

It remains a somewhat odd term: part-time work. What is meant is those WTAs in which employees work less than full time. But how much less? Considerably less, an often cited definition provided by the International Labour Organization states. This definition bears upon voluntarily accepted, regularly performed work during a number of working hours significantly lower than normal. A survey in companies (with ten or more employees) in eight countries belonging to the European Union (Bielenski, 1994) shows that "extreme" forms of part-time work—such as less than ten hours and more than thirty hours per week—are fairly rare. In the majority of the companies, the average weekly work time for people with part-time work (henceforth PTW) is between fifteen and twenty-five hours.

In the last few decades the application of PTW has increased strongly (Barling & Gallagher, 1996). Around 1990, one in seven employees in Western Europe worked in PTW (Hutchinson & Brewster, 1994). Among the countries there are large differences however: in the South European countries the percentage of PTWs is well below ten. In the northern countries the percentage is a great deal higher: Holland ranks highest with well over 30 percent in PTW. In the United States, one in five staff members worked part time around 1990. (Feldman, 1990). There are not only large differences among countries, though, also among branches of industry. Traditionally PTW is very rare in the building industry, and fairly rare in industry. PTW is being applied much more often in the (commercial) services in particular, such as in retail business, in banks, insurance companies and in the government. These cases usually involve less qualified jobs, held largely by females.

PTW is a general term: it covers many types. The European Survey (Bielenski, 1994) mentioned earlier shows that a fixed number of working hours per half day (in the morning or in the afternoon, or for example from 11.00am until 3.00pm) on each working day is most common by far. A form applied much less often is the one in which work is done for several full days per week and the remaining days are days off (the so-called "part-week", Barling & Gallagher, 1996). And "flexible" forms—in which the hours during which work is to be done are set only a few days ahead—belong to a small minority. Furthermore, PTW arrangements may apply for an indefinite period, but they may also be temporary.

This overview shows that the most frequently applied PTW types assume an arrangement of working hours per day and per week. A perfectly possible alternative may be: an arrangement based on a longer period (such as a quarter or a year) which allows to compensate for highs and lows (for example by season) in the demand for labour. An arrangement involving a person's entire working life has sometimes been argued for from the perspective of "education permanente" (for example, Maric, 1977; Emmerij & Clobus, 1978). This would promote employees to return to their "school" very frequently for further training and development, being able to work less when they grow older.

PTW types may also differ in organizational respect (De Koning, 1980; Driehuis & De Vrije, 1981; Hutchinson & Brewster, 1994), such as:

- *job sharing*: one job is occupied by two PTW workers. They are jointly responsible for its execution. It also occurs that a group of PTW people takes care of the fulfilment of several jobs together;
- *joint job*: every worker in PTW by himself/herself is responsible for his/her "own" share of the job;
- *split jobs*: a job is split into components, after which new jobs are created that are all performed part-time.

This brings us to the *objectives* in view of which PTW has been introduced. A first important aspect concerns the ability to compensate for highs and lows in the amount of work to be performed. This form of flexibility is sometimes termed "numerical" (cf. Konle-Seidl, Ullmann, & Walwei, 1990). An important factor for the choice of the appropriate PTW arrangements is the degree to which changes in the supply of work are predictable. A second objective relates to flexibility for the individual employee: the possibility of getting work time (more) adjusted to personal circumstances and desires, such as for example for working mothers (see for example Kogi, 1991). A third objective is the creation of more jobs, and a fourth—slightly older—objective is the promotion of emancipation of women (about which for example Demenint-de Jong, 1989 has already expressed some doubts). Fifthly, the bringing in of partly disabled employees is mentioned. The European survey (Bielenski, 1994) shows that the two considerations mentioned first are named most often, but also that there are differences among countries in emphasis (flexibility for "the entrepreneur", for "the employee", respectively).

What experiences have been gained with PTW? Fairly much has been published concerning various branches of industry in most European Union countries, even if the designs of most studies leave rather much to be desired. Bielenski (1994) asked managers and representatives of employees about their experiences in eight European Union countries. *Managers* mention the following advantages, for example:

- compensating for variations in supply of work;
- not enough work for "full timers";
- better quality of products or services.

In their view, disadvantages are mainly related to the organization of work and communication. Representatives of *employees* reported e.g. the following as advantages:

- combination of work with care tasks;
- health;
- more leisure;
- lack of a job in full work time.

The last-mentioned "advantage" is also reported by Konle-Seidl et al. (1990): they point to a survey study from 1987 from the then European Community, which shows that this theme applies especially in countries with a high unemployment rate. Disadvantages are, e.g.:

- no career prospects;

- no certainty of work;
- worse labour conditions (in some countries).

But is it possible at all to speak about "the" results of PTW in such general terms? Feldman (1990) does not think so, because there are not only all kinds of different PTW, but especially because other people are attracted by one PTW arrangement than by another. For instance, performance, satisfaction, turnover and absenteeism figures of PTWs who have a permanent contract of employment, have work all year, do so of their own free will and do not have a second job, will differ considerably from PTWs whose job is temporary, who work a part of the year, who have been hired by an external agency and have a second job elsewhere (see also Barling & Gallagher, 1996).

Insofar as there is *research* into PTW, Feldman's argument has gone almost unheard. One of the questions investigated is whether PTW workers differ from full-time workers in the degree of satisfaction. Older studies produce mixed results: Miller & Terborg (1979) observed that PTWs are less satisfied, Eberhardt & Shani (1984) that they are more satisfied, and for example Logan, O'Reilly, & Roberts (1973) and Dijkstra (1984) that both groups did not differ very much. Steffy & Jones (1990) compared "role strain" and job satisfaction among nurses in PTW at sixty-five hospitals with those working full time. They found that the differences are not large: PTWs encounter a little more workload and ambiguity in their work and are a little less content with their reward and with their colleagues (no difference in satisfaction in other areas). The authors suggest that PTWs may have lower expectations with regard to their work. Lendfers and Nijhuis (1989) state that this is perhaps reflected in several studies showing that the structure of job satisfaction of full timers is different—that is: is composed of more variables—from that of PTWs. But a field experiment among clerical employees of a utility company (Fields & Thacher, 1991) does not show this: those who went to work in PTW exhibited furthermore a significant increase in job satisfaction and commitment. Barling & Gallagher (1996) argue that PTW workers and full-time workers often differ in demographic respect, in job content, in work conditions, etc. If such differences are considered in comparative research, then the two categories do not differ in job satisfaction.

The results concerning absenteeism and turnover, particularly from older research, are contradictory (cf. Cohen & Gadon, 1978; Levitan & Belous, 1979). It has been brought forward fairly often in companies that higher management and staff jobs in particular cannot really be performed part time. Research into such jobs has shown that this, at least in principle, is usually possible indeed (Schoemaker et al., 1981; Demenint-de Jong, 1989). The latter does not mean incidentally that PTW is always desirable.

Steinberg & Dornbusch (1991) among others have asked attention for the phenomenon that many schoolgoing "teenagers" in the United States work part time. They report that when over twenty hours per week are spent on a job, there is considerably less sleep, difficulty concentrating at school and lower academic achievements. Barling, Rogers, & Kelloway (1995) however—using data from a Canadian "high school"—make a reasonable case for the claim that the quality of such a job is an important moderator variable. If this quality is high (for example relatively much autonomy, role clarity and variety in required skills), not only do the negative consequences fail to show up, but the degree of "self esteem" is also higher.

We think the objectives of PTW form an important topic for future research. Since an increasing number of conditions and expectations concerning flexible "behaviour" are specified for the company and the institution on the one hand and the employees on the other hand, more insight into the working of "flexible" WTAs cannot really be missed. In this connection—or as a separate theme—we also argue for research into PTW as a second or possibly third job. Besides the question that might be posed about its societal acceptability, it concerns the consequences for the buildup of fatigue, for safety at work (and in traffic) and for the quality of the achievements.

And thirdly, we would like to see more research into possible differences in the structure of job satisfaction between PTWs and full timers. A related question is whether such differences would cause differential effects (in terms of our cognitive model, see Figure 5.1).

3.4 Other flexible time arrangements

Besides the WTAs discussed in the three previous sections there are of course various other more or less flexible time arrangements. In most of these, flexibility means that the working hours of (a section of) the employees are affected to a great extent by variations in the demand for labour. There are also arrangements among them in which the working hours are also co-determined by preferences and circumstances of individual employees. Because research into these WTAs has been conducted only rarely, we suffice to provide a brief characterization in most of the cases (see for more details: Bielenski, 1994; Hutchinson & Brewster, 1994).

We have come across *annual hours* indirectly in the context of flexitime, compressed working week and part-time work. The number of annual hours of work to be done is predetermined in these cases. The actual arrangement may vary per day, per week, per month, etc. It also occurs that an agreement is made about the number of spare hours (being "on call") above a fixed number of working hours (say per week), for example for peak times, standing in, training and development, etc. This last form is sometimes called *flexible hours per week*.

Term-time: employees are given unpaid leave during the school holidays.

Flexible hours per day: the working days per week and the number of daily working hours vary in this type of standby contract. Employees are rewarded exclusively for the actual hours of work.

Overtime: the number of working hours is higher than management and labour agreed upon; overtime may therefore occur in part-time workers. In fact, this WTA forms one of the classical reactions of a work organization to an (excessively) high demand for goods and services. A study carried out by the Dutch Labour Inspectorate (Loontechnische Dienst, 1991) shows that in Holland, this WTA is also applied most often in companies in these circumstances.

But overtime is also introduced, according to a study conducted by Baird & Becchia (1980), when an organization has a low level of productivity. They analysed data taken from forty-two American public services. The analysis showed for example that there was a considerably strong negative correlation between the amount of work done and the average number of hours overtime per employee. Another theme is whether overtime means causing or having an accident sooner. Schuster & Rhodes (1985) observed such a connection in some organizations. But Rosa (1995), after an overview of various studies, arrives at the conclusion that besides fatigue due to working for a long time, many other variables may offer an explanation for less safe behaviour (and poorer health, respectively).

Temporary work: this is a collective term. In the case of work for a "fixed term", the date of termination is agreed upon beforehand. Konle-Seidl et al. (1990) point out that, in countries of the European Union, a positive association exists between this WTA and the percentage of unemployment. Another form is temp work: its extent, for example in Holland, grew tremendously within the past few decades. It enabled work organizations to have a relatively small core of employees. In addition, often for a somewhat longer period, consultants and possibly also interim-managers are taken on as well as technical and clerical temps or people from a labour pool. Additionally, often for a shorter length of time, workers are hired in for operational or supportive tasks. It is to this very phenomenon that the theory of the segmented labour market relates: for highly skilled jobs "core" employees are suitable, temporary but properly skilled employees are for jobs below, whereas semi- and unskilled (usually temporary) jobs are performed by hired in workers. There is usually little exchange of people between these segments. An important question is what the degree of commitment, involvement and motivation of temporary staff is like when a company or institution "invests" mainly in permanent employees (see for example Lendfers & Nijhuis, 1989). Yet another form of temp work is home employment (such as for example in workshops). Little insight has been gained into its extent.

Tele-work: several forms of this exist also. We distinguish:

- *Tele-nomads:* this refers to categories of employees who visit clients regularly, such as for example maintenance mechanics and service mechanics. They keep in touch with

their company by means of car telephone, modem, fax, E-mail, etc.
- *Home workers*: work is done at home for shorter or longer periods and regular contact with one's own work organization is maintained by means of tele-equipment.
- *Shopworkers*: employees from totally different companies communicate with their own companies in a workspace furnished for the purpose with equipment.

Particularly in the last two forms, employees have fairly much influence on the moments they work. It is also possible to consider the requirements made by special groups of people: the woman combining the care of a child with work; the partially disabled individual, etc.

In the past few years, quite a few pilot practices with tele-work have been in progress, especially in Holland. Still, it is not very clear how many tele-workers there are, also because the definition of teleworkers continues to be an issue of much debate (Van der Wielen, 1995). Experiences show a varying impression, as some exploratory studies attest (Taillieu & Van der Wielen, 1995). In some cases tele-workers claim to be able to concentrate better and to combine private and work roles better. On the other hand, there are drawbacks such as less frequent social contact with colleagues and the management team, work coordination, etc.

By using our model (Figure 5.1), various relevant research questions can be formulated concerning these flexible WTAs. One of these questions is how it comes about, as Van Praag (1996) reports on the basis from research in two thousand companies, that the application of flexible WTAs is associated with a somewhat higher level of absenteeism. Another important problem concerns the extent to which a WTA proves to meet in practice the stated objectives.

4 IRREGULAR WORK AND SHIFT WORK

As has been stated in the Introduction, this separate section is devoted to the theme of irregular work and shift work. The increasingly differentiated nature of work time arrangements however renders the borderlines between all kinds of manifestations of irregular work and shift work (and various other WTAs) less clear. This certainly applies to irregular work; we pointed out in section 1 that irregular work involves work whereby the work organization is at work during a large part of the 24-hour period, but no "scheduled" shifts of employees exchange work. An example of a WTA that can be very similar to irregular work is flexitime, in which what is understood by "daytime work" can be expanded a great deal in relation to standard daytime work. As a consequence of the easing of restrictions of work times, the nature of traditional shift work systems is changing more and more. It is becoming more customary, for instance, to let the size of the groups depend on the amount of work or the inconveniences at a certain moment. This causes the notion of "regular shifts" to become vaguer.

4.1   Nature and extent of work at uncommon hours

The daytime working culture such as the one we have known for a very long time is no longer truly typical of Holland (and of other countries), as the overview in Table 5.1 makes clear. This overview has been derived from the 1993 Labour Force Survey (EBB) carried out by the Dutch Central Statistics Office (CBS). The table shows that nearly half the workforce is (partially) employed at uncommon hours. Data from various sources indicate that this share is expanding quite rapidly, particularly in professions in which, until recently, work was rarely done at uncommon hours. Obviously there are differences between branches of industry and occupational groups in this respect. For instance, the EBB 1993 indicates that relatively much work is done at night in for example companies involved in transport, storage and communications. And out of employees with commercial jobs a substantial portion works in the evenings and weekend on a regular basis.

The "First European Survey on the Work Environment 1991—1992" presents an impression of uncommon work—applied to nightwork—in the countries of the European Union that formed the European Community at the time (see Table 5.2).

This table demonstrates that nightwork is relatively widespread in several countries, particularly in the United Kingdom, Ireland and Greece. Such data are not available for the countries outside Europe.

4.2   Effects of work at uncommon hours

Research into irregular work and shift work has a multi-disciplinary character *par excellence*. Not only in psychology, but also in physiology, economics and sociology, there is a certain research tradition. Given the scope of this Handbook, we limit ourselves to the discussion of results from psychological research, in particular concerning health, well-being, absenteeism, turnover and productivity (the "dependent" variables in Figure 5.1).

4.2.1   Health

Much research has been dedicated in particular to the relation between shift work and health (see for example Meijman et al., 1988, 1989; Thierry & Meijman, 1994). This research shows that in workers in shift work (and their house-mates), shift work:

- causes many subjective complaints concerning sleep, fatigue and workload;
- leads to various nervous phenomena, such as headaches, depression, trembling hands;
- may cause problems with appetite and increase the chance of gastrointestinal complaints;
- probably contributes to the development of cardiovascular diseases;
- possibly has a detrimental effect on the working of the female reproductive system.

Naturally, not every WTA involving work at uncommon hours causes such adverse effects; the various variables in Figure 5.1 also clearly indicate this. Personal characteristics of the shift worker and his or her working past play an important role. The individual's shift work experience and the process of adaptation are central topics in the destabilization theory developed by

TABLE 5.1

Working hours of the labour force in The Netherlands (1993).

Type of work time	[× 1000]	[%]
Regular	3.028	51.5
Irregular	2.833	48.1
only at night		0.0
only in the evening	246	4.2
weekend daytime	1.020	17.3
at night and in the evening	71	1.2
at night and at the weekend	12	0.2
in the evening and at the weekend	709	12.0
at night, in the evening and at the weekend:	772	13.1
—of which in three or more shifts: 337; 5.7%		
Total	5.862	99.6
Not observed	23	0.4
Total	5.885	100.0

Haider et al. (1981). When the shift worker starts working in shifts, it is psychological patterns in particular which play an important part in the perceived health condition (for example the motives and goals with regard to shift work). Once he/she has gained more experience in shift work, the relative importance of somatic risk factors and of sleeping behaviour increases. More specifically, four stages are distinguished in aetiology:

- adaptation stage (zero to five years of experience);
- sensibilization stage (five to fifteen/twenty years of experience);
- accumulation stage (twenty to forty years of experience);
- manifestation stage (over forty years of experience).

TABLE 5.2

Nightwork in the European Union.

% of workers working at night	B	DK	WD	OD	GR	SP	F	IRL	I	L	NL	P	VK	EU
All the time or nearly all the time	3.5	1.5	4.9	4.4	5.5	6.6	4.9	5.9	2.2	4.3	2.7	3.6	7.4	4.9
At least 50% of the time	7.4	4.8	7.9	7.5	12.8	8.8	9.1	17.6	6.2	9	6.1	8.9	16.2	9.5
At least 25% of the time	14.2	9.8	15.1	17.2	24.7	15.3	17.9	32.6	11	15.8	13.3	15.9	27.6	17.6

Practice demonstrates incidentally that very few shift workers reach the manifestation stage in shift work. This is partly due to the fact that other stressful working conditions besides shift work also occur.

There are also considerable differences among inconvenient WTAs. These emerge for example in the study by Jansen (1987), in which daytime work and various shift work systems were compared (its data derived from the scheduling practice in Dutch industry).

We see that fatigue and quality of sleep are most favourable (lowest score) in daytime working and worst in semi-continuous shift work. The discontinous and continuous shift system occupy an intermediate position, while it is remarkable that the discontinuous shifts (mostly without night shifts) do much worse than is generally assumed (see also Betschart, 1989).

4.2.2   Well-being/social life

The deviating distribution of work and leisure in work at uncommon hours may not be (immediately) harmful, it does however affect the well-being of shift workers and their families. In addition, shift workers themselves often regard the disturbances of their social life as more serious than other effects (for example Wedderburn, 1967). Findings from research on which there is a considerable degree of consensus are:

- Shift work and irregular work impose heavier demands on the organization of household and family activities in comparison to daytime working, because various patterns (which may also be viewed as "rhythms") have to be geared to another:

- one's role as a partner (sexual/company). It may be restricted;
- one's role as a parent (upbringing, contact). This role may also be restricted;
- extra activities in the household (more meals; no hoovering in the daytime);
- reduced possibility of using a crèche (and work to be done by the partner?).

- Organizing informal activities outside the family presents more problems than when work is done at "common" hours. It takes more effort to visit relatives and friends, to participate in clubs and to go out at night. As a result, one is more dependent on individual leisure activities.
- As a consequence of the above, a sense of alienation from society and isolation from the family may develop.

Again, these phenomena do not occur in all people working at uncommon hours. Personal characteristics play a part, as does the degree of "social support" which the social environment has to offer (Thierry & Jansen, 1982). Also, the respective WTAs vary. We will illustrate this once again in the light of the study by Jansen (1987; see Table 5.4) mentioned previously.

The more "deviating" the type of working, the more complaints are expressed.

4.2.3   Absenteeism

In connection with the degree to which those working in shifts express complaints about their health and well-being, it may be assumed that they will be absent due to illness more frequently than

TABLE 5.3		
	*Overall fatigue**	*Quality of sleep***
Daytime working	2.1	2.3
Discontinuous	3.1	3.6
Semi-continuous	3.7	4.4
Continuous	3.5	4.0

* Minimum score = 0, maximum score (much fatigue) = 11
** Minimum score = 0, maximum score (poor quality of sleep) = 14

Average scores on two health-related variables in daytime working and three types of shift work ($p = .05$).

TABLE 5.4		
	*Complaints about time for family activities**	*Complaints about time for social activities***
Daytime working	0.3	1.0
Discontinuous	0.9	2.1
Semi-continuous	1.1	2.3
Continuous	1.2	2.5

Average scores on two social variables in daytime working and three types of shift work ($p = .05$).

* Minimum score = 0, maximum score (many complaints) = 4
** Minimum score = 0, maximum score (many complaints) = 11

day workers. Research results in which global indices are used for absenteeism (for example, average duration and frequency of absenteeism) do not however support this premise systematically (Pocock et al., 1972; Taylor et al., 1972; Smulders, 1984; Grosfeld, 1988; Schalk, 1989). Studies, in which specific patterns of absenteeism are related to a specific work schedule, give cause to suspect yet that some relationship does indeed exist (see for example Nicholson et al., 1978). Various factors are mentioned in the literature in this connection which might bias data concerning absenteeism due to illness.

Selection effect As has been mentioned in section 2.1, there is the risk that research results are based on data deriving from a select, and therefore stronger population.

Social control/pressure Absenteeism generally means that a stand-in has to be sought or that the work becomes heavier. Fellowship now may mean that work is done longer during illness or that one is ill on the days off (see for example: Taylor, 1967; Åkerstedt & Fröberg, 1976).

Underestimation/failure to report physical discomfort Andersen (1970) observed that shift workers, more so than day workers, regard complaints concerning sleep, digestion, etc. as a "natural" component of the work situation (cf. Agervold, 1976; Åkerstedt et al., 1977). The "Shift Work Committee" of the "Japanese Association of Industrial Health" (1979) demonstrated that approximately one and a half times as many shift workers as day workers nevertheless go to work, in spite of not feeling well.

One of the shortcomings in research on the relation between WTAs and absenteeism due to illness is that many studies are cross-sectional. In the early nineties a longitudinal study was conducted in Holland (Klein Hesselink et al., 1995), in which well over three thousand employees from eighty-five companies and institutions participated for five years. Seventeen forms of deviating work time arrangements were scrutinized in total. On controlling for differences in personal background data, it was shown that there are hardly any or no differences between shift work and daytime working in percentages of absenteeism. Employees in the early morning shift have a consistently lower absenteeism percentage than comparable day workers.

4.2.4 Turnover

A first perspective concerning this theme regards self-selection or "adaptation-selection" (compare the adaptation stage, Haider et al., 1981, section 4.2). What is essential there is that persons usually enter shift work unprepared and may discover in the first two years that such a WTA is entirely unsuitable for them, physically and/or socially. These persons usually abandon the shift. A second perspective regards the reward for working at uncommon hours (the bonus for unsocial working hours or shift work bonus). This bonus quite often means that those working in shifts or those in irregular working continue this shift, while experiencing an extreme amount of physical or social discomfort. There is no choice however, because the pattern of expenditure has already been based on the extra earnings (see also Jansen, 1987).

Yet little research has been carried out in which explicit attention is paid to turnover within the context of work at uncommon hours. The studies on the influx figures of the Sickness Benefits Scheme (WAO)/IP (Disablement Pension Scheme) probably come closest in terms of systematics. These studies show e.g. that forms of shift work deviating more from "common" hours are associated with lower absentee rates on the one hand, but also a larger number of WAO/IP entries on the other hand (Nijhuis & Soeters, 1983). This fact fits in with the argument that a person doing shift work will go on until he/she cannot go on anymore.

An extensive survey by Rutenfranz et al. (1981) on the incidence of sleeping problems in persons working in different WTAs gives plausibility to the assumption that such problems are among the most important factors in abandoning nightwork.

4.2.5 Productivity

It is not possible to make unambiguous claims on the relation between irregular work or shift work and productivity on the basis of the research carried out thus far. A first difficulty is that in much work in shifts, the measurability of the nature of human *interventions* is very difficult (consider for example operators in the processing industry). A second difficulty is that many circumstances surrounding the work may change in the course of the 24-hour period (see also section 2.1). This means for example that it is practically unfeasible in less structured work to separate the "WTA" aspect from other aspects that may affect productivity.

One of the few studies in which the relation between shift work and productivity is addressed directly is the one conducted by Vidacek et al. (1986). They studied assembly work in a three-shift work situation (morning, afternoon and night). In the schedule five watches were run successively. The lowest production figures were found during the first and the second night shift. Production reached the relatively highest point in the third night shift; next, production plummeted again. In general terms, production was shown to be higher during the morning and afternoon watches. During the first three of these watches the production figures were continuously high. Both

plummeted however in the fourth and fifth morning watch and in the fourth and fifth afternoon watch.

The result of the fact that productivity is influenced by so many variables has been that in this context researchers have focused mainly on performance (capacity), making errors and preventing accidents. Regarding these subjects research basically shows the following:

- In work at uncommon hours performance at night is often lower than in the daytime (Alluisi & Morgan, 1982; Carter & Corlett, 1982; Folkard & Monk, 1985). The conclusion might be drawn from this that the level of performance parallels the circadian temperature rhythm. This general observation is however too unbalanced: the observation does apply to physical work (motorial operations) in general, but not to mental work (cognitive operations; Folkard & Monk, 1985).

- Results from research regarding errors and accidents because of working at uncommon times are not consistent. This does not alter the fact that there are some important older studies which all point in the same direction: particularly at night, but also to a lesser extent around 3.00pm at day, there is an increased risk of errors in detecting warning signals. For a matter of fact, it seems to involve an interaction effect of fatigue and circadian factors (Browne, 1949; Bjerner et al., 1955; Hildebrandt et al., 1974; Folkard et al., 1978).

Given these data it should however be considered that an equal level of performance and/or equal productivity, does not necessarily imply an equal level of effort. Accomplishing a daytime standard at night may mean an extra strain for the individual worker, precisely in connection with a partial deactivation state of the body.

4.3 Research and interventions

It is typical of research on irregular work and shift work that it relates to a much larger number of subjects—and also involves more disciplinary points of view—than research on flexible time arrangements. Although the knowledge of certain subjects is certainly not sufficient yet—of which we have given examples in the previous section—and naturally new research questions keep cropping up, we can still observe that practically all the variables from Figure 5.1 (determinants and effects) have been treated in research. This means that the research results have—also in connection with all kinds of practical experience with irregular work and shift work—led to (programmes of) recommendations to reduce objectionable consequences of and negative experiences associated with working at uncommon hours. In concluding this chapter, we will pay special attention to this topic.

Several recommendations of interventions have already been treated, more or less implicitly, in section 2, though in terms of perspectives in research. For instance, viewing WTA as an "additional factor" (section 2.1) can result in special *legislation* being developed and introduced. Its purpose may be to minimize the application of unsocial working hours, but it may also be meant to avoid as much as possible that stressful "circumstances" accumulate (for example extreme temperatures in regular work at night on demanding tasks). If the emphasis is on "adjustment" (section 2.2), interventions for example involve *coping* strategies at the individual or group level, such as when relaxation techniques are used or bedrooms are made noiseless. Adjustment at the level of a department or business unit concerns, for example, the coordination of various functional groups of staff members.

From the perspective of the "regulation of non-work time" (section 2.3), the emphasis may be placed on (better) *design of schedules*. This type of intervention can also be advocated from the perspective of "rhythmic processes" (section 2.4). By way of illustration, this involves designing a schedule in which the number of consecutive night shifts is small. Not only does this short cyclic schedule produce fewer health risks, it also has a positive effect on the utility of leisure. Another type of intervention—developed by research on rhythmic processes—is periodic exposure of volunteers to *bright daylight* in view of adjusting their circadian rhythms more rapidly to another sleep/

watch pattern (Costa et al., 1993). The interventions from the perspective of *selection* (section 2.5) are generally of a medical and/or a psychological nature.

Quite some experience has also been gained by now with two other types of intervention. Both relate to features of schedules. The first, developed by Jansen (1987), is the *Rota Risk Profile Analysis* (RRPA). The RRPA is an instrument, a computer program to be exact, by means of which the psychosomatic and the psychosocial risk of schedules may be ascertained. One of the psychosomatic features is periodicity: this indicates the degree to which a consecutive period of evening and/or nightwork takes place per week. A psychosocial feature is weekend recreation: this bears upon the extent to which work is done on Saturday and/or Sunday. On the basis of the actual risk profile of a schedule, if necessary, improvements can be applied "on paper", i.e. before a schedule is actually introduced.

The second type of intervention—*counterweight versus countervalue*—was developed in the second half of the seventies (Thierry, Hoolwerf, & Drenth, 1975; Thierry, 1980). It concerns the way in which unsocial working hours are compensated for in general. Paying an allowance or a bonus implies providing counterweight: drawbacks such as trouble with sleeping, more fatigue and less club life are contrasted with the advantage of an amount of money so high that enough people prepared to work unsocial times are found. The unsocial working hours mentioned do not change as a result, though. In offering countervalue, interventions are chosen on the other hand that try to deal with the complaints involved as much as possible. Countervalue interventions therefore involve the same themes as those on which complaints occur (see for example Jansen, Thierry, & Van Hirtum, 1986). Van Limborgh (1996) has developed a method for measuring the degree of inconvenience of a work time arrangement and for its "compensability": appraisals of it by respondents from quite different companies and institutions have been shown to reside in a broad consensus. The results make it possible to award the same bonus for the same uncommon time arrangement in all kinds of branches of industry. They also offer all kinds of starting points for trying to reduce actual unsocial working hours and risks of harmful consequences.

We think more research is required on the two last-mentioned themes, both in preventive and in curative respect. Of course, a relatively great deal of knowledge is already available on irregular work and shift work; still, in the foregoing various important gaps have been observed. In addition, our argument relates to flexible working hours at least as much: about its short- and long-term effects much less is known. Precisely because this set of WTAs shows many changes and because more and more people are faced with these WTAs, this field should not be allowed to have such an underdeveloped position in research as it has at present.

NOTES

1. Prof. Dr. Henk Thierry is Professor of Human Resource Science at Tilburg University.
2. Dr. Ing. Ben Jansen is director of ATOS, Policy consultancy and research [], in Amsterdam.

REFERENCES

Aanonsen, A. (1964). *Shift work and health.* Oslo: Universitetsforlaget.

Åberg, E., Cocke, B., Söderberg, I., & Westlander, G. (1983). The outcome of experimentation with flexible working hours. In M. J. Smith & G. Salvendy (Eds.), *Human-computer interaction: Implications and case studies.* Amsterdam: Elsevier.

Agervold, M. (1976). Shift work: A critical review. *Scandinavian Journal of Psychology, 17*, 181–188.

Åkerstedt, T., & Fröberg, J.E. (1976). Shiftwork and health: Interdisciplinary perspectives. In P.Q. Rentos et al. (Eds.), *Shiftwork and Health.* Washington, DC: NIOSH.

Åkerstedt, T., Patkai, P., & Dahlgren, K. (1977). Field studies of shiftwork: II. Temporal patterns in psychophysiological activation in workers alternating between night and day work. *Ergonomics, 20*, 621–631.

Alluisi, E.A., & Morgan, B.B. (1982). Temporal factors in human performance and productivity. In E.A. Alluisi & E.A. Fleishmann (Eds.), *Stress and performance effectiveness.* Hillsdale: Lawrence Erlbaum.

Andersen, J.E. (1970). *Three shift work: A sociomedical survey.* Copenhagen: Teknisk Forlag.

Aschoff, J. (1978). Features of circadian rhythms relevant for the design of shift schedules. *Ergonomics, 21*, 739–754.

Baird, L.S., & Becchia, P.J. (1980). The potential misuse of overtime. *Personnel Psychology, 35*, 557–565.

Bandura, A. (1986). *Social foundations of thought and action.* Englewood Cliffs: Prentice-Hall.

Barling, J., Rogers, K-A., & Kelloway, E.K. (1995). Some effects of teenagers' part-time employment: The quantity and quality of work make the differences. *Journal of Organizational Behavior, 16*, 143–154.

Barling, J., & Gallagher, D.G. (1996). Part-time employment. In C.L. Cooper & I.T. Robertson (Eds.), *International Review of Industrial and Organizational Psychology 1996.* Chichester: John Wiley.

Berg, J. H. van den (1995). *Metabletica van God.* Kampen: Kok.

Betschart, H. (1989). *Zweischichtarbeid. Psychosoziale und gesundheitlichte Aspekte.* Bern: Verlag Hans Huber.

Bielenski, H. (Ed.) (1994). *New forms of work and activity.* Survey of experience at establishment level in eight European countries. Shankill: European Foundation for the Improvement of Living and Working Conditions.

Bjerner, B., Holm, A., & Swensson, A. (1955). Diurnal variation in mental performance: A study of three-shift workers. *British Journal of Industrial Medicine, 12*, 103–110.

Boissonade, P. (1987). *Life and work in medieval Europe.* New York: Dorsey Press.

Breaugh, J. (1983). The 12-hour work day: Differing employee reactions. *Personnel Psychology, 36*, 277–288.

Brook, J.A., & Brook, R.J. (1989). Exploring the meaning of work and nonwork. *Journal of Organizational Behavior, 10*, 169–178.

Browne, R.C. (1949). The day and night performance of teleprinter switchboard operators. *Journal of Occupational Psychology, 23*, 121–126.

Burns, T., & Stalker, G.M. (1961). *The management of innovation.* London: Tavistock.

Campbell, J.P., & Pritchard, R.D. (1976). Motivation theory in industrial and organizational psychology. In M.D. Dunnette (Ed.), *Handbook of Industrial and Organizational Psychology.* Chicago: Rand McNally.

Carter, F.A., & Corlett, E.N. (1982). *Overview of research on shift work in Europe.* Dublin: European Foundation for the Improvement of Living and Working Conditions.

Carufel, A. de, & Schaan, J.L. (1990). The impact of compressed work weeks on police job involvement. *Canadian Police College Journal, 14*, 81–96.

Champoux, J. E. (1980). The world of non-work: Some implications for job redesign efforts. *Personnel Psychology, 33*, 61–75.

Child, J. (1972). Organizational structure, environment and performance: The role of strategic choice. *Sociology, 6*, 2–22.

Chiles, W.D., Alluisi, E.A., & Adams, O.S. (1968). Work schedules and performance during confinement. *Human Factors, 10*, 143–196.

Coetsier, P.L., & Claes, R. (n.d.). *Belang van levensrollen en waarden*. Oostende: Infoservice. Serie Theoretische en Toegepaste Psychologie.

Cohen, A.R., & Gadon, K. (1978). *Alternative work schedules: Integrating individual and organizational needs*. Reading: Addison-Wesley.

Colligan, M.J., & Tepas, D.I. (1986). The stress of hours of work. *American Industrial Hygiene Association Journal, 47*, 686–695.

Colquhoun, W.P., & Rutenfranz, J. (Eds.) (1980). *Studies of shiftwork*. London: Taylor & Francis.

Costa, G., Ghirlanda, G., Minors, D.S., Waterhouse, J.M. (1993). Effect of bright light on tolerance to shift work. *Scandinavian Journal of Work Environment and Health, 19*, 414–420.

Dalton, D.R., & Mesch, D.J. (1990). The impact of flexible scheduling on employee attendance and turnover. *Administrative Science Quarterly, 35*, 370–387.

Demenint-de Jong, M. (1989). *Arbeidsduur, organisatie en emancipatie*. Utrecht: Lemma.

Dijkstra, A. (1984). Leeftijdspecifieke verschillen in gezondheid en ziekteverzuim tussen deeltijdwerkers, voltijdwerkers en overwerkers. In J.J. Godschalk (Ed.), *Sociale aspekten van arbeidstijdverkorting*. Amsterdam: Swets & Zeitlinger.

Driehuis, W., & Vrije, P.A. de (1981). *Vooronderzoek experiment deeltijdarbeid, Vol. 1*. The Hague: Ministerie van Sociale Zaken en Werkgelegenheid.

Dubin, R. (1956). Industrial workers' worlds: A study of the "central life interests" of industrial workers. *Social Problems, 3*, 131–142.

Dubin, R., & Champoux, J.E. (1977). Central life interests and job satisfaction. *Organizational Behavior and Human Performance, 12*, 366–377.

Dunham, R.B., Pierce, J.L., & Castaneda, M.B. (1987). Alternative work schedules: Two field quasi-experiments. *Personnel Psychology, 40*, 215–242.

Durkheim, E. (1912). *Les formes élementaires de la vie religieuse*. Paris: F. Alcan.

Eberhardt, B.J., & Shani, A.B. (1984). The effects of full time versus part time employment status on attitudes towards specific organizational characteristics and overall job participation. *Academy of Management Journal, 27*, 893–900.

Elchardus, M. (1988). The rediscovery of chronos: The new role of time in sociological theory. *International Sociology, 1*, 35–39.

Elizur, D. (1991). Work and nonwork relations: The conical structure of work and home life relationship. *Journal of Organizational Behavior, 12*, 313–322.

Emmerij, L.J., & Clobus, J.A.C. (1978). *Volledige werkgelegenheid door creatief verlof*. Deventer: Kluwer.

Feldman, D.C. (1990). Reconceptualizing the nature and consequences of part-time work. *Academy of Management Review, 15*, 103–112.

Feyter, M.G. de, Tham, J. Ng-A., & Roozemond, K. (1993). Werkweek van 4 × 9 uur: Niet geschikt voor iedereen. *Gids voor Personeelmanagement, 1*, 26–28.

Fields, M.W., & Thacher, J.W. (1991). Job-related attitudes of part-time and full-time workers. *Journal of Management Psychology, 6*, 17–20.

Fleuter, D.L. (1975). *The workweek revolution*. Reading: Addison-Wesley.

Folkard, S., Monk, T.H., & Lobban, M.C. (1978). Short and longterm adjustment of circadian rhythms in "permanent" night nurses. *Ergonomics, 21*, 785–799.

Folkard, S., & Monk, T.H. (1985). Circadian performance rhythms. In S. Folkard & T.H. Monk (Eds.), *Hours of work*. Chichester: John Wiley.

Ford, M.E. (1992). *Motivating humans*. London: Sage.

Foster, L.W., Latack, J.C., & Reindl, L.J. (1979). Effects and promises of the shortened workweek. *Academy of Management Proceedings*, 226–230.

Frese, M., & Semmer, N. (1986). Shiftwork, stress and psychosomatic complaints: A comparison between workers in different shift work schedules. *Ergonomics, 29*, 99–114.

Frese, M., Okonek, K. (1984). Reasons to leave shiftwork and psychological and psychosomatic complaints of former shiftworkers. *Journal of Applied Psychology, 69*, 509–514.

Grosfeld, J.A.M. (1988). *De voorspelbaarheid van individuele verzuimduur*. Amsterdam: Swets & Zeitlinger.

Haider, M., Kundi, M., & Koller, M. (1981). Methodological issues and problems in shift work research. In L.C. Johnson, D.I. Tepas, W.P. Colquhoun, & M.J. Colligan (Eds.), *The twenty-four hour workday: Proceedings of a symposium on variations in work–sleep schedules*. Cincinnati: NIOSH.

Hale, R., Jodonin, R., & Kingsby, F. (1980). *Police shift scheduling: A contemporary approach*. Sudbury Regional Police Force.

Harmsen, G., & Reinalda, B. (1975). *Voor de bevrijding van de arbeid*. Nijmegen: SUN.

Hildebrand, G., Rohmert, W., & Rutenfranz, J. (1974). Variations in the daily rhythm of error frequency by shift workers and the influence of it on tiredness. *International Journal of Chronobiology, 2*, 175–180.

Hutchinson, S., & Brewster, C. (1994). *Flexibility at work in Europe*. London: Institute of Personnel and Development.

International Labour Organization (1978). *Management of working time of industrial countries*. Genève: ILO.

Ivancevich, J.M. (1974). Effects of the shorter work-week on selected satisfaction and performance measures. *Journal of Applied Psychology*, 59, 717–721.

Ivancevich, J.M., & Lyon, H.L. (1977). The shortened workweek: A field experiment. *Journal of Applied Psychology*, 62, 34–37.

Jansen, B. (1987). *Dagdienst en ploegendienst in vergelijkend perspectief*. Lisse: Swets & Zeitlinger.

Jansen, B., Thierry, Hk., & Hirtum, A. van (1986). *Ploegenarbeidroosters herzien*. Deventer: Kluwer.

Japanese Association of Industrial Health (1979). Opinion on night work and shift work. *Journal of Science Laboratory*, 55(8), 1–36.

Kabanoff, B. (1980). Work and nonwork: A review of models, methods, and findings. *Psychological Bulletin*, 88, 60–77.

Kabanoff, B., & O'Brien, G.E. (1980). Work and leisure: a task attribute analysis. *Journal of Applied Psychology*, 65, 596–609.

Kanfer, R. (1990). Motivation theory in industrial and organizational psychology. In M.D. Dunnette & L.M. Hough (Eds.), *Handbook of Industrial and Organizational psychology* (Revised edn., Vol. 1). Palo Alto: Consulting Psychologists Press.

Kirchmeyer, C. (1972). Perceptions of nonwork to work spillover: Challenging the common view of conflict ridden domain relationships. *Basic and Applied Psychology*, 231–249.

Klein Hesselink, D.J., Verboon, F.C., & Berg, T.D.P.J. van den (1995). *Arbeidstijden en ziekteverzuim*. The Hague: VUGA.

Knauth, P., & Rutenfranz, J. (1982). Development of criteria for the design of shiftwork systems. *Journal of Human Ercology*, 11, 337–367.

Kogi, K. (1991). Job content and working time: The scope for joint change. *Ergonomics*, 34, 757–773.

Koning, J. de (1980). *Optimalisering van de verdeling van de werkgelegenheid*. Rotterdam: Nederlands Economisch Instituut.

Konle-Seidl, R., Ullmann, H., & Walwei, U. (1990). The European social space: Atypical forms of employment and working hours in the European Community. *International Social Security Review*, 218, 143–179.

Krausz, M., & Hermann, E. (1991). Who is afraid of Flexitime: correlates of personal choice of a flexitime schedule. *Applied Psychology: An International Review*, 40, 315–326.

Lambert, S.J. (1980). Processes linking work and family: A critical review and research agenda. *Human Relations*, 34, 239–257.

Lange, W.A.M. de (1989). *Configuratie van arbeid*, Zutphen: Thiene.

Lange, W.A.M. de, Eijk, M.H. van, & Ng-A-Tham, J.E.E. (1995). *Bij de tijd: * besluitvorming over werktijden en arbeidstijdpatronen*. The Hague: SZW/VUGA.

Langedijk, M.C. (1995). Maatwerk binnen het arbeidsvoorwaardenpakket. *Gedrag en Organisatie*, 8, 439–458.

Latack, J.C., & Foster, L.W. (1985). Implementation of compressed work schedules: Participation and job redesign as critical factors for employee acceptance. *Personnel Psychology*, 38, 75–91.

Lawrence, P.R., & Lorsch, J.W. (1967). *Organization and environment. Managing differentiation and integration*. Boston: Division of Research, GSBA, Harvard University.

Lendfers, M.L.G.H., & Nijhuis, F.J.N. (1989). *Flexibilisering van de arbeid en gezondheidseffecten*. The Hague: Organisatie voor Strategisch Arbeidsmarktonderzoek (Doc. 66).

Lens, W. (1986). Future time perspective: A cognitive-motivational concept. In D.R. Brown & J. Veroff (Eds.), *Frontiers of motivational psychology*. New York: Springer.

Levitan, S.A., & Belous, R.S. (1979). *Minder werk, meer werk*. Deventer: Kluwer.

Limborgh, C. van (1996). *Waardering van ongewone werktijden*. Deventer: Kluwer. Academic dissertation.

Locke, E.A., & Latham, G.P. (1990). *A theory of goal setting and task performance*. Englewood Cliffs: Prentice Hall.

Logan, N., O'Reilly, C., & Roberts, K.H. (1973). Job satisfaction among part time employees. *Journal of Occupational Behavior*, 3, 33–41.

Loontechnische Dienst (1991a). *Veranderende arbeidstijdpatronen*. The Hague: Ministerie van Sociale Zaken en Werkgelegenheid (Ministry of Social Affairs and Employment).

Loontechnische Dienst (1991b). *Afwisselende arbeidstijdpatronen*. The Hague: VUGA.

Loontechnische Dienst (1992). *Ervaringen met de vierdaagse werkweek*. The Hague: VUGA.

Maric, D. (1977). *Adapting working hours to modern needs*. Geneva: International Labour Office.

Martens, M.F.J., Nijhuis, F.J.N., Boxtel, M.P.J. van, & Knottnerus, J.A. (1995). Flexibele arbeidsomstandigheden en gezondheidsklachten. *Gedrag & Organisatie*, 8, 50–59.

Meijman, T.F., & de Vries-Griever, A.H.G. (1988). Gezondheids-en welzijnsaspecten van ploegendienst. *Huisarts en Wetenschap*, 33, 130–134, 144.

Meijman, T.F., de Vries-Griever, A.H.G., & Kampman, R. (1989). *Rhythm and blues: Onregelmatige werk-en rusttijden als arbeids-en leefomstandigheid*. Amsterdam: NIA.

Meijman, T.F. (1992). *Verkorten van de werkweek en verlengen van de werkdag*. Amsterdam: Studiecentrum Arbeid en Gezondheid (UvA).

Mellor, E.F. (1986). Shift work and flexitime: How prevalent are they? *Monthly Labour Review*, 109(11), 14–21.

Miller, K.E., & Terborg, J.R. (1979). Job attitudes of part time and full time employees. *Journal of Applied Psychology, 64*, 380–386.

Moors, S.H. (1990). Learning from a system of seasonally-determined flexibility: Beginning work earlier increases tiredness as much as working longer days. In G. Costa, G. Cesana, K. Kogi, & A. Wedderburn (Eds.), *Shiftwork: health, sleep and performance.* Frankfurt: Peter Lang.

Morgan, G. (1997). *Images of organizations* (2nd edn). London: Sage.

Nicholson, N., Jackson, P., & Howes, G. (1978). Shift work and absence: An analysis of temporal trends. *Journal of Occupational Psychology, 51*, 127–137.

Nijhuis, F., & Soeters, J. (1983). Ziekteverzuim, arbeidsongeschiktheid en de organisatie van de arbeid. *Tijdschrift voor Sociale Gezondheid, 61*, 686–693.

Nollen, S. (1979). *New patterns of work.* Scarsdale: Work in America Institute.

Northrup, H.R., Wilson, J.T., & Rose, K.M. (1979). The twelve-hour shift in the petroleum and chemical industries. *Labor Relations Review, 32*, 312–316.

Northrup, H.R. (1989). The twelve-hour shift in the petroleum and chemical industries revisited: An assessment by human resource management executives. *Industrial and Labor Relations Review, 32*, 312–326.

Nuttin, J., & Lens, W. (1985). *Future time perspective and motivation: Theory and research method.* Leuven: Leuven University Press.

Orpen, C. (1981). Effects of flexible working hours on employee satisfaction and performance: A field experiment. *Journal of Applied Psychology, 66*, 113–115.

Parker, S.R., & Smith, M.A. (1976). Work and leisure. In R. Dubin (Ed.), *Handbook of work, organization and society.* Chicago, Rand McNally.

Peacock, B., Glube, R., Miller, M., & Clune, P. (1983). Police officers' responses to 8 and 12 hour shift schedules. *Ergonomics, 26*, 479–493.

Perret, D. (1980). *Experiments involving productivity and "work sharing".* Paper presented at the 5th EAPM/EFPS Congress on "Rewarding Work", Amsterdam.

Pocock, S.J., Sergean, R., & Taylor, P.J. (1972). Absence from continuous three-shift workers: A comparison of traditional and rapidly rotating systems. *Occupational Psychology, 46*, 7–13.

Praag, B.M.S. van (1996). Flexibiliteit heeft een prijs. *PW, 20*(4), 16–18.

Ralston, D.A. (1989). The benefits of flexitime: Real or imagined? *Journal of Organizational Behavior, 10*, 369–373.

Ralston, D.A. (1990). How flexitime eases work/family tensions. *Personnel, 67*(8), 45–48.

Ralston, D.A., Anthony, W.P., & Gustafson, D.J. (1985). Employees may lose flexitime, but what does it to the organization's productivity? *Journal of Applied psychology, 70*, 272–279.

Reinberg, A., Vieux, N., & Andlauer, P. (Eds.) (1980). *Night and shiftwork: Biological and social aspects.* Oxford: Pergamon Press.

Robison, D. (1976). *Alternative work schedules.* Scarsdale: Work in America Institute.

Ronen, S. (1981). *Flexible working hours.* New York: McGraw-Hill.

Rosa, R.R. (1995). Extended workshifts and excessive fatigue. *Journal of Sleep Research* (in press).

Rosa, R.R., Wheeler, D.D., Warm, J.S., & Colligan, M.J. (1985). Extended workdays: Effects on performance and ratings of fatigue and alertness. *Behavior Research Methods, Instruments and Computers, 17*, 6–15.

Rosa, R.R., & Colligan, M.J. (1988). Long workdays versus restdays: Assessing fatigue and alertness with a portable performance battery. *Human Factors, 30*, 305–317.

Ruppert, M. (1953). *De Nederlandse vakbeweging. I.* Haarlem: Bohm.

Rutenfranz, J., Knauth, P., & Angersbach, D. (1981). Shiftwork research issues. In L.C. Johnson, D.I. Tepas, W.P. Colquhoun, & M.J. Colligan (Eds.), *The twenty-four hour workday.* Cincinnati: NIOSH.

Schalk, M.J.D. (1989). *Determinanten van veelvuldig kortdurend verzuim.* The Hague: Delwel.

Scherrer, J. (1981). Man's work and circadian rhythm through the ages. In A. Reinberg, N. Vieux, & P. Andlauer (Eds.), *Night and shift work: Biological and social aspects.* Oxford: Pergamon Press.

Schmidt, R.F., & Thews, G. (1983). *Human physiology.* New York: Springer Verlag.

Schoemaker, N., Gageldonk, A. van, Demenint, M., & Vianen, A. van (1981). *Deeltijdarbeid in het bedrijf.* Alphen a/d Rijn: Samsom.

Schuster, M., & Rhodes, S. (1985). The impact of overtime work on industrial accident rates. *Industrial Relations, 24*, 234–245.

Shank, S. (1986). Preferred hours of work and corresponding earnings. *Monthly Labour Review, 109*(11), 40–44.

Sloane, P. J. (1975). *Changing patterns of working hours.* London: Department of Employment, Manpower paper. No. 13, HSMO.

Smulders, P.W.G. (1984). *Balans van 30 jaar ziekteverzuimonderzoek.* Leyden: HIPG/ TNO.

Stafford, E.F., Sherman, J.D., & McCollum, J.K. (1988). Streamlining 12-hour work shifts. *Personnel Administrator*, 51–57.

Steffy, B.D., & Jones, J.W. (1990). Differences between full-time and part-time employees in perceived job strain and work satisfaction. *Journal of Organizational Behavior, 11*, 321–329.

Steinberg, L., & Dornbusch, S.M. (1991). Negative correlates of part-time employment during adolescence: Replication and elaboration. *Developmental psychology, 27*, 304–313.

Taillieu, T.C.B., & Wielen, J.M.M. van der (1995). Waardering van telewerk afhankelijk van funktie. *Telewerken, 2*(2), 36–38.

Taylor, P.J. (1967). Shift and day work: A comparison of sickness absence, lateness, and other absence behaviour at an oil refinery from 1962 to 1965. *British Journal of Industrial Medicine, 24*, 93–102.

Taylor, P.J., Pocock, S.J., & Sergean, R. (1972) Shift and day workers' absence: Relationship with some terms and conditions of service. *British Journal of Industrial Medicine, 29*, 338–340.

Tepas, D.I. (1985). Flexitime, compressed work weeks and other alternative schedules. In S. Folkard & T.H. Monk (Eds.), *Hours of work: Temporal factors in work scheduling.* Chichester: John Wiley.

Thierry, Hk. (1980). Compensation for shiftwork. In W.P. Colquhoun., & J. Rutenfranz (Eds.), *Studies of Shiftwork.* London: Taylor & Francis.

Thierry, Hk., Hoolwerf, G., & Drenth, P.J.D. (1975). Attitudes of permanent day and shift workers towards shiftwork—a field study. In W.P. Colquhoun, S. Folkard, P. Knauth, & J. Rutenfranz (Eds.), *Experimental Studies of Shiftwork.* Opladen: Westdeutscher Verlag.

Thierry, Hk., & Jansen, B. (1982). Social support for night and shiftworkers. In K. Kogi, T. Miura, & H. Saito (Eds.), *Shiftwork: its practice and improvement.* Tokyo: Center for Academic Publications Japan.

Thierry, Hk., Koopman, P.L., & Flier, H. van der (1992). *Wat houdt mensen bezig?* Utrecht: Lemma.

Thierry, Hk., & Ng-A-Tham, J.E.E. (1994). Vrijplaats en verandering. *Gedrag & Organisatie, 7*, 422–436.

Thierry, Hk., & Meijman, T.F. (1994). Time and behavior at work. In H.C. Triandis, M.D. Dunnette, & L.M. Hough (Eds.), *Handbook of Industrial and Organizational Psychology* (2nd edn., Vol.4). Palo Alto: Consulting Psychologists Press.

Thiis-Evensen, E. (1969). Shift work and health. *Studia Laboris et Salutis, 4*, 81–83.

Velzen, M. van. (1994). *De vijfde dag.* The Hague: Ministerie van Sociale Zaken en Werkgelegenheid (Ministry of Social Affairs and Employment).

Vidacek, S., Kaliterna, L., & Radoseric-Vidacek, B. (1986) Productivity on a weekly rotating shift system: Circadian adjustment and sleep deprivation effects? *Ergonomics, 29*, 1583–1590.

Volle, M., Brisson, G.R., Pérusse, M., Tanaka, M., & Doyon, Y. (1979). Compressed workweek: Psychophysiological and physiological repercussions. *Ergonomics, 22*, 1001–1010.

Walker, J. (1985). *The human aspects of shiftwork.* London: Institute of Personnel Management.

Wedderburn, A.A.I. (1967). Social factors in satisfaction with swiftly rotating shifts. *Journal of Occupational Psychology, 41*, 85–107.

Wheeler, K.E., Gurman R., & Tarnowieski, D. (1972). *The four-day week.* New York: American Management Association.

Wielen, J.M.M. van der (1995). Onduidelijkheid over telewerken verhindert representatief onderzoek. *Telewerken, 2*(1), 6–9.

Wilensky, H.L. (1969). Work, careers and social integration. *International Social Science Journal, 12*, 543–560.

Williamson, A.M., Gower, C.G.I., & Clarke, B.C. (1994). Changing the hours of shiftwork: a comparison of 8- and 12-hour shift rosters in a group of computer operators. *Ergonomics, 37*, 287–298.

Wippler, R. (1968). *Sociale determinanten van het vrijetijdsgedrag.* Assen: Van Gorcum.

6

Sickness Absence

Jacques T. Allegro and Theo J. Veerman

1 INTRODUCTION

In The Netherlands, the term "sickness absence" usually refers to absence from work as covered by the Sickness Benefit Act. This type of absence is relatively easy to measure—in many firms and institutions sickness absence is registered (if only with a view to laying claims to the Sickness Benefit Act. This is one reason why the phenomenon is relatively well accessible for research.

Besides sickness absence (which may last maximally one year according to the Dutch Sickness Benefit Act) we will in this chapter pay attention to chronic work incapacity (as covered by the Disability Insurance Act).

Sickness absence and chronic work incapacity will especially be reviewed from a social-scientific perspective. Additionally some attention will be paid to other aspects which are important with respect to this phenomenon, like medical and legal aspects. Sickness absence is, despite its seemingly uniform measurability, a complex and heterogeneous phenomenon in nature and background.

Sickness absence can be classified in many different ways. An important criterion is the extent to which it can be avoided. While certain combinations of health complaints and job requirements

inevitably lead to absence, other combinations may not. In most cases of sickness absence, according to some estimates up to 70%, the need for absence is not fully compelling, and to a certain extent it is the employee who determines whether he/she is capable of working or not.

The latter case is also referred to as "grey sickness absence". The indication "white sickness absence" does relate to clear-cut cases of medical work incapacity, and the term "black sickness absence" refers to sicklisting without any medical justification whatsoever. One estimate is that "black" absence comprises approximately 5% of all reported absence spells (Philipsen, 1969).

The label "avoidable absence" is sometimes used for black and/or (parts of) grey absence. However in our view the concept of "avoidable absence" should comprise more—for a significant part of white absence is in principle avoidable as well. We may think of work injuries and occupational diseases, which often might be prevented, but also of workplace adaptations which may make early work resumption possible for sick employees, whatever the cause of their sickness.

Important determinants of sickness absence can be found inside as well as outside the company. Factors inside the company include job content, physical working conditions, industrial relations, and terms of employment. Factors outside the company include traffic, sport and home accidents, pregnancy and confinement, personal problems more generally due to family circumstances, stressful life events, sideline jobs or evening study classes. However, macro-social factors also influence sickness absence levels, e.g. the social security system, the health care system, legislation and economic factors. Individual characteristics (e.g. personality structure) on the other hand also affect inter-individual differences in sickness absence levels.

In short, the term sickness absence appears to relate to a well measurable phenomenon but refers at the same time to countless, rather different backgrounds. In this chapter the concept of sickness absence as is used in The Netherlands will be central: absence from work while appealing to the Sickness Benefit Act.[1] According to this definition the concept can clearly be distinguished from other forms of absence from work (e.g. absence attributed to family circumstances, or being late). Although these forms of absence can lead to significant deviations of the agreed employee attendance, here we will restrict absence to *due to sickness*. We would like to point out that this Dutch definition does not completely coincide with "absence" or "absenteeism" as used in much foreign literature, as will be explained in section 3.

It will be clear, as previously discussed, that sickness absence, carefully examined, is a phenomenon in which a great number of determinants and influences take part. There is a growing interest in sickness absence, partly because of the social, organizational and economical effects.

Although sickness absence is relatively easy to register, many different measures are used to quantify it, which are not always comparable. It is therefore preferable to make use of some standard absence measures and definitions. The most important are:

- *Absence percentage* (abbreviation: A%) The total number of calendar days (counting 7 days a week) lost due to sickness, as a percentage of the total number of available calendar days over a certain period;
- *Reporting frequency* (abbreviation: RF) The total number of sickness reports during a certain period, divided by the average number of persons employed during

that period, standardized to a period of one year;

- *Average duration of absence* (abbreviation: AD) The sum of lost calendar days of terminated cases, divided by the number of terminated cases of absence during a certain period.

In this chapter we will address the following subjects.

Section 2 will discuss the size of the phenomenon, where attention is being paid to both Dutch and foreign figures. In section 3 we will illuminate the subject from a theoretical point of view.

In sections 4, 5, and 6 we will describe the determinants at the macro (societal) level, the micro level (personal characteristics and living conditions) and the meso level (industrial and organizational level) respectively. In section 7 we will review intervention strategies and aspects of planned change.

2 SIZE AND COMPOSITION OF SICKNESS ABSENCE

2.1 Sickness absence and disability in The Netherlands

According to the costs of benefits under the Sickness Benefit Act (1992: HFL 12 billion a year) and the Disability Insurance Act (HFL 23 billion a year) we can regard sickness and disability as a major problem.

As to the level and trend in absence percentages in The Netherlands (depicted in Figure 6.1), in the 1970s, this percentage ("days lost") rose from some 6% to over 8% by 1978. Since then the percentage has been decreasing somewhat to just over 7% by 1985, and has been fluctuating between 7% and 8% since.

Overall national sickness absence rates as shown in Figure 6.1 hide over important differences as to the size of the company, seasons, and industrial branches.

Concerning company size, absence percentages in the smallest companies (less than 50 employees) and in the largest companies tend to be lower than in the medium-sized.

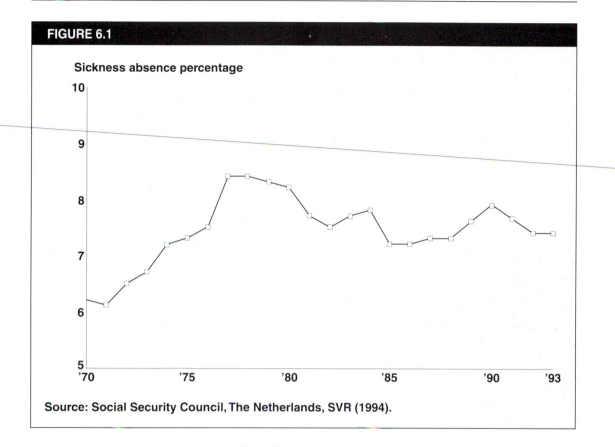

FIGURE 6.1

Sickness absence percentage

Source: Social Security Council, The Netherlands, SVR (1994).

Sickness absence percentages, The Netherlands, 1970–1993.

As to seasonal patterns, sickness absence tend to peak in January–March, and drop to lowest levels in July–August. The sickness absence percentage in the peaking months is 2.5% higher than in July–August. Reporting frequencies show an even stronger seasonal fluctuation.

Between branches of industry there are substantial differences both concerning the size of sickness absence and its development through the years. Opposite to the decrease of sickness absence in the larger industrial companies in the eighties, sickness absence increased in some services, for example education, health care and home care.

The rate of sickness absence and its development are furthermore strongly influenced by selectivity in the process of hiring and firing of employees. The least healthy employees will exit from the labour market either through the Disability Insurance Act, early retirement, old age retirement, death, voluntary or involuntary with-

drawal (dismissal), and will be (partly) replaced by a fresh inlux of younger and healthier employees. Research has shown this phenomenon to be the most important explanation of decreasing sickness absence rates since 1979. Within the groups that stayed with the same employer for a longer time there was no sign of a decrease (Kruidenier, 1981; Veerman, 1985). But the net effect of exit of less healthy workers and influx of healthier employees resulted in an overall decrease.

Information about the medical backgrounds of sickness absence might be derived from diagnoses. As diagnoses are only established and registered by a social insurance physician, who usually comes into play only in longer spells of absence, there are no statistics on medical diagnoses in more than 70% of spells of sickness absence, as most spells are relatively short. In cases of long-term sicknesses—however seldom, these concern many days and therefore include a large part of the absence percentage—the diagnosis is in most cases registered.

Of these longer-term cases with a registered diagnosis, 27% fall in the category "diseases of the musculoskeletal system and connective tissues". More than half of these concern problems with the back (low back pain especially). The category "diseases of the respiratory system" includes 18% of the longer-term sickness absences, 14% fall in the category "mental diseases" and 15% concerns the "effects of accidents". The latter group includes, besides industrial accidents, traffic accidents and accidents in sports and at home. No reliable figures on the frequency of industrial accidents are available in The Netherlands, as they are not covered by separate benefit arrangements. Comparison of available Dutch data with foreign figures give rise to the suspicion that registration in The Netherlands does not keep up with the registration abroad (Prins, 1984).

As to the Disability Insurance Act (DIA), since it was enacted in 1967 the influx into the DIA (1.4–2% of employees each year) has been higher than was ever expected. A lot of determinants known to influence DIA influx also play a role concerning long-term sickness absence: entry into the DIA is a continuation of long-term absence, after a mandatory duration of one year (the Sickness Benefit Act year). Besides this, the relatively high level of benefit payment (compared with other arrangements through which employees may exit from the labour market) and the relatively broadly defined conditions for access to a DIA benefit also are of influence.

Since 1981 the DIA influx has diminished, which probably is related with alternative "competitive" arrangements such as early retirement and redundancy schemes for older employees, and it could (for some years) also be connected with the reduction of the benefit payments (1986) and to a more restricted criterion of "incapacity for work" (1985–1987). Nevertheless, the efflux being consistently smaller than the influx, the number of persons entitled to DIA benefits has been growing further to over 900,000 in the 1990s. Various governmental measures to reduce this number, through laws and other measures to promote reintegration of the disabled, do not seem to create a satisfactory result. In order to stop the

growing of the DIA rolls the government took a number of new measures from 1992 onwards. These include intensified prevention, enlargement of the financial involvement of employers, employees, and the promotion of re-entering employment of the partially disabled. As a result, the number of DIA beneficiaries started to decrease in 1994.

Diagnoses at the intake in the DIA follow broadly the pattern we also encounter in chronic sickness absence: diseases of the musculoskeletal system and connective tissues form the major group, but it is followed in its footsteps by mental disorders. These developments can be summarized as follows:

Diagnostic main group	1974	1985	1988	1992
Diseases of the circulatory system	18%	11%	9%	7%
Mental disorders	17%	27%	31%	32%
Diseases of the musculoskeletal system	27%	32%	33%	33%

The causes of the increasing contribution of mental disorders to DIA influx over the last 20 years are not exactly known. Some researchers ascribe this to increased job demands regarding the mental and psychological emotional functions of people.

2.2 Foreign figures

To give the Dutch data some depth a comparison with foreign figures is needed. The definitions and methods of calculation, however, vary widely across countries. Therewithal, the "official" figures—if available—may only relate to part of the absence (e.g., short-term sickness absence), or only relate to a part of the working population. The consequence of this heterogeneity of figures is that the comparison between the countries in Table 6.1 falls short.

However, we can deduce from this table that The Netherlands in the available statistics—with all their shortcomings—is among the countries with the highest rate of absence.

The most striking is that—according to the different national statistics—the rate of sickness absence in Western-European countries is two or three times higher than in the United States or Japan. This has been attributed in particular to the

TABLE 6.1

Country	1978	1984	1988
Great Britain	—	—	6.5
West Germany	7.7	7.4	8.1
France	8.3	7.2	8.2
The Netherlands	12.0	7.4	8.5
Italy	10.6	9.0	6.9
Sweden	13.8	11.6	12.7
Belgium	—	4.3	6.7
USA	3.5	3.5	3.4
Japan	2.0	1.8	1.6

Sickness absence percentages in some industrialized countries 1978, 1984 and 1988, according to domestic statistics.

Various sources: taken from Prins, 1990.

lack of a developed social security system and the relatively small job protection (USA) and a high degree of loyalty to the employer, especially in Japan, where it is customary for workers to use holidays first when sick.

The limited comparability of international data stimulated further research into the differences between The Netherlands, Germany and Belgium (Prins, 1990). For this purpose sickness absence rates were uniformly calculated within four clusters of each three similar, larger companies over a period of two years. Figure 6.2 shows the sickness absence percentages, as calculated after correction for differences between the three countries in composition of the population as to gender, age and white/blue collar work. The sickness absence percentage and the reporting frequency give the lowest score in Belgium, and the highest score in the Dutch companies, Germany taking the middle position. Especially the comparatively high rate of the long-term sickness absence in The Netherlands plays an important role in the high Dutch sickness absence percentage.

To explain these differences Prins refers to differences between the three countries in respect of macro-social aspects, like social insurance and health care arrangements, job protection during sickness, legitimation procedures of sickness absence, benefit levels and the accessibility of disability insurance. On the basis of a comparative research between companies he also ascribes meaning to factors on company level, such as the firm's sickness absence policy and the selection processes at hiring and firing people. Also social

cultural differences—such as differences in the meaning and value of work—and differences in health appear to play a role in his explanation.

In a recent study, sickness absence and invalidity rates in six European countries were compared systematically, using a common definition of what is counted as sickness absence and invalidity, and standardizing for differences in gender and age structures (Einerhand et al., 1995). This standardized comparison shows that raw national statistics, as reported in Table 6.1 above, are not a sound basis for cross-national comparison of sickness absence, as the standardized figures for some countries deviate substantially from raw statistics. Still the comparison shows that The Netherlands has by far the highest sickness and invalidity rates. Figure 6.3 depicts the results, both for sickness absence ("temporary work incapacity") and for invalidity ("long-term or permanent work incapacity").

3   THEORIES ON SICKNESS ABSENCE

The phenomenon of sickness absence has been approached from different theoretical angles. When we look at foreign literature, a warning is justified. The term "absence" (or "absenteeism") does not necessarily coincide with "*sickness* absence" as it is defined in this chapter. Within "absence" as the broader concept, the distinction can be made between absence for medical reasons and non-medical reasons, or between certified and

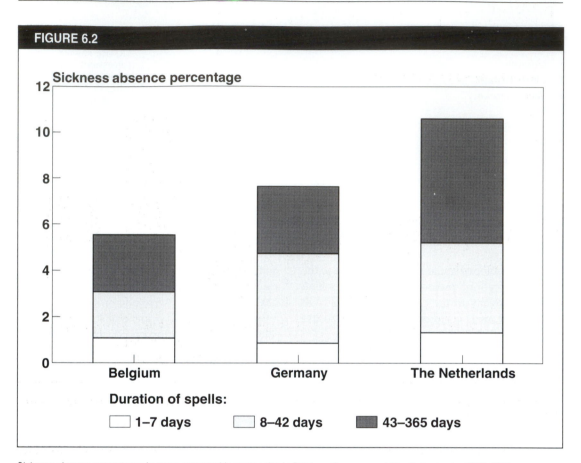

FIGURE 6.2

Sickness absence percentages in some comparable companies in Belgium, Germany and The Netherlands, 1980–1981 (standardized to age, gender and type of labour). Source: Prins (1990).

uncertified absence (with or without a medical certificate). Much of the foreign development of theories also (and sometimes exclusively) addresses non-medical absenteeism and sometimes only considers the short-term cases.

The reason for this is that in socio-psychological behavioural theories absence is not being considered as the phenomenon to be explained for its own sake, but as an easy accessible *indicator* of subjectively determined organizational behaviour—after all, absence is a concrete, well measurable and often proper registered form of behaviour. What matters in such cases is the use of the more common or general theories, not specifically developed for the explanation of absence (let alone *sickness* absence). We will give a short survey of these general theories.

Several *organizational-psychological theories* have been used in explaining sickness absence.

Firstly, three competing process approaches are well known. These are the *exchange theory* (Chadwick-Jones et al., 1982), *equity theory* (Dittrich & Carrell, 1979) and *value-expectancy theories* (Morgan & Herman, 1976). No research results are available solving the problem which of these approaches—which in principle are mutually exclusive—is "best" in explaining absence. Besides these three theories of a more general nature, four approaches exist which focus more on one cause, or one group of causes, of absence and which thus are complementary rather than competing in explaining absence. These include *role theory* (Gupta & Beehr, 1979), *leadership theories* (Johns, 1978), *socio-technical system theory* (Allegro, 1973) and the *job characteristics model* (Hackman & Lawler, 1971). By definition, each of these four only have partial value in explaining the total phenomenon of (sickness) absence.

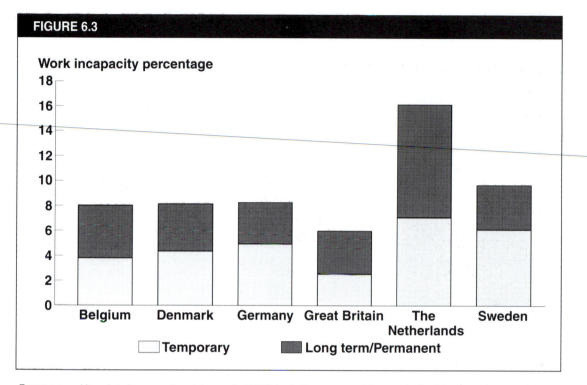

FIGURE 6.3

Work incapacity percentage

Temporary and long-term/permanent work incapacity (1990) in six European countries, standardized for age and gender. Source: Einerhand et al. (1995).

The approach cited most frequently in international literature is the socio-organizational psychological theory of Steers and Rhodes (1978) on the main influences on absence. From their literature study they developed a model of absence, highlighting the causal sequence of job situation—job satisfaction—motivation to attend—attendance or absence (see blocks 1, 4, 6, 8 in Figure 6.4).

The Steers and Rhodes model surpasses the traditional and more limited job satisfaction/absence models (see Nicholson et al., 1977, summarizing 29 studies based on such models and concluding that only weak relationships between job satisfaction and absence are to be found). This organizational-psychological one-sidedness is evaded by adding two concepts particularly relevant for sickness absence, namely:

- the *pressure to attend* (block 5 in Figure 6.4), which may involve legitimation procedures, financial (dis)incentives etc.; the concept is equivalent to the "opportunity for absence"

as used by Philipsen (1969), to be discussed later in this chapter;

- the *ability to attend* (block 7 in Figure 6.4), involving things as illness, problems at home, transportation problems; an equivalent to Philipsen's "need for absence" (discussed later).

Finally, personal characteristics and employees' values and expectations (blocks 3 and 2) are embedded in the model as well.

The Steers and Rhodes model embraces several angles relevant to absence, and its process character gives an understanding of how a spell of absence comes about. Nevertheless, three comments are in place.

1. The model hardly stresses health condition and illnesses as determinants of absence, while much empirical research—not only in The Netherlands, but for instance in the USA as well—supplies evidence that health condition explains a substantial part of an

FIGURE 6.4

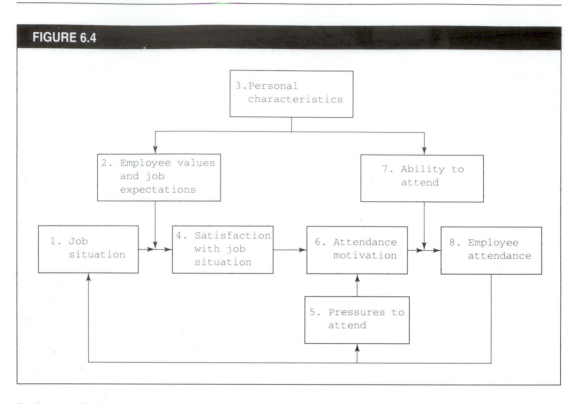

The Steers and Rhodes model of absence/attendance. Adapted from Steers and Rhodes (1978).

individual's absence (e.g., Philipsen (1969), Hackett et al. (1989), Chen & Spector (1991)). In the Steers and Rhodes model, illness is only one out of many variables constituting the ability to attend.

2. The model only focuses on the *onset* of spells of absence—just as the model proposed by Nicholson (1977)—and not on their duration/termination. Especially in the duration of absence, physical working conditions, legitimation and assessment procedures, socio-medical guidance, and the content and administration of social insurance arrangements are supposed to be of importance. The fact that in Anglo-Saxon countries long-term sickness usually falls without the financial scope of employers may have prompted this pre-occupation with the onset, rather than duration, of spells of sickness.

3. The Steers and Rhodes model focuses on task and job characteristics, and largely ignores company characteristics and organizational structure, whereas research

has provided evidence that company and organizational factors are of predominant importance in explaining sickness absence (e.g., Philipsen (1969), Nijhuis (1984), Smulders (1984a)).

Summarizing, we may conclude that "classical" organizational-psychological approaches of sickness absence, emphasizing concepts as motivation and satisfaction, fall short in explaining sickness absence fully. Nevertheless, socio-psychological theories do illuminate certain aspects of sickness absence (especially the reporting frequency) and therefore are cited regularly in literature on sickness absence. Their shortcomings are compensated by integrating a few approaches developed specifically for explanation of sickness absence, partly originating from Dutch theoretical angles, as will be sketched now.

In The Netherlands two approaches of absence are often encountered: the *model of decision* and the *model of load capability*. Also models related to *stress theory* are frequently encountered. We will try to connect the three models mentioned above into a general frame of reference on sickness absence (see also Veerman, 1990).

The *model of decision* originates from sociology—the name of Philipsen is strongly connected with this model (Philipsen, 1969). Many studies with this approach have been done since the sixties.

In this model it is stressed that in many cases, if there are health complaints (to which in this model is referred to as "absence necessity"), the employee has some freedom of decision whether to report sick or not. So sickness does not necessarily imply absence: some people keep on working while having health complaints (and sometimes there are sickness reports when only minor complaints exist).

A central concept in this situation is "absence threshold". Whenever a person's absence threshold is very high, he or she will find it difficult to report sick when experiencing health complaints. A high threshold will not always lead to a low sickness absence rate. The frequency of short-term cases will be low, but as a consequence of working during sickness the health complaints may deteriorate and in the long run cause long-term cases of sickness absence.

With the absence threshold two aspects can be determined:

1. *Opportunity of absence.* Factors which determine the space a person gets to report ill or not. These are not necessarily connected with the person him/herself (such as formal or informal sanctions, social and organizational indispensability, "waiting days", deduction (of a part) of wages, absence control strategies).
2. The *need of absence.* This concerns the personal need to make use or not to make use of the opportunity of absence. Work satisfaction plays a central part in this need; so do concepts as "commitment" or "identification" with work, "job involvement", "organizational commitment" and the like. These concepts are directly connected with several of the general socio-psychological theories mentioned earlier. Because of this, these theories are often useful as parts of a more integrated approach of sickness absence.

The *model of load capability* originates from social medicine. This model emphasizes discrepancies between a person's work demands (work load) and the capacities of the person to meet those demands (load capability). When load and capability are out of balance for a prolonged period and no recovery time is available, an accumulation of adverse effects can occur which in turn can cause sickness. "Sickness" must at this point be seen in its broadest context; as an inability to meet the physical and psychological requirements of a job.

The model of load of capability does not specify which elements determine the load and capability of a work situation. It only gives the direction for further research in a concrete situation. The function is "... the stimulation of formulation of theories with concepts and their relations. It can be used in the development of more *specific models*" (Van Dijk et al., 1990).

Some comments can be made to this model—at least to the way the model often is applied. Firstly, many authors consider the aspect of the workload is being overemphasized, whereas the load capability of the employees in this model has an equal place and deserves the same attention. One possible cause of this is that load capability is (incorrectly) regarded by some as a static, personal characteristic just to be taken for granted. Van Dijk et al. correctly suggest speaking about "absorbing capacity" instead of load capability and also giving attention to possibilities of regulation, which puts a justified emphasis on the capability and on the active role the employee may play in coping with a given work load.

Secondly, it is often assumed that the only issue in this model is the possibility of *over*load, but there is a possibility of *under*load as well. Both overload and underload are a form of discrepancy which may lead to adverse consequences. This last subject is however a phenomenon which receives more attention in stress literature (see below).

The model of load capability is often considered a competitor of the model of decision in explaining sickness absence, but this is not the way we see it. The former model can illuminate the origin of certain complaints and thus give more meaning to the term "absence necessity" from the model of decision, while the latter can be an indication of the moment the complaints rise above a certain tolerance threshold and a person reports ill.

The same link of both approaches has earlier been implicitly made by Nicholson (1977, 1989) who introduces the concept "A/B-continuum": a continuum of reasons for absence, ranging from an entirely free latitude of decision to entirely compelling reasons (e.g. serious illness). Nicholson can be regarded as the exception among Anglo-Saxon authors for his explicit inclusion of involuntary absence, such as unavoidable sickness absence, in his theories.

Elements of the *stress theory* are regularly quoted for explanation of (*inter alia*) sickness absence. In The Netherlands, especially the "Michigan-model", has established itself as a leading stress model, even though critical comments can be made to this model and other approaches to stress exist (see Buunk & De Wolff in Chapter 7 of this Volume).

In this model "stressors" ("stress-causing", burdening factors) lead to "strains" ("stress-effects", including psychological and/or health complaints, possibly also sickness absence). However, between stress factors and strains some moderator variables operate: effective "coping", social support, and a "B-type personality" could according to this theory buffer the effect of stressors or at least moderate them. Apart from that, Grosfeld (1988) has developed a model to explain the *duration* of absence that shows close resemblance to this stress model.

An interesting feature of the Michigan-model is the possibility to reformulate it into the model of load capability. After all, stressors can be seen as elements of work load, and "coping", social support and personality structure can be considered as elements of load capability or absorbing capacity. The link between both models appears to be very useful when we see that research based upon the stress model can give added empirical interpretation (the importance of several stressors and coping factors is a central point in many inquiries) to the model of load capability, which often is used as an (empirically) empty, formal frame of reference.

Besides the Michigan-model we also should mention shortly the alternative stress approach as proposed by Karasek (1979). In this approach there are two central dimensions which determine stress, namely the job demands (work load) and the worker's decision latitude. Especially the interaction of high work load and little decision latitude lead to a high degree of stress. In these two dimensions one can also recognize a clear parallel with the twin concepts of "work load" and "load capability", or "absorbing capacity". We further point to the "load-recovery-model" as sketched by Meijman (1989), highlighting concepts like "absorbing strategy" and "decision latitude". In short, in more recent publications one can observe a clear mutual advance between the model of load capability and several stress models.

The approaches that we have been discussing until now (model of decision, load capability, stress) are mainly aimed at explanation of the *origin* of health complaints or of sickness absence. Besides the origin of absence, the rate of absence is strongly influenced by the *duration* of cases of absence, thus by their moment of termination. Naturally the nature of the disorder or the recovery in a medical sense play an important role (a heart infarction requires more recovery time than the flu), but the moment of a possible resumption of work turns out to be influenced by more factors. To explain the moment of termination of absence a theory is desirable, but is missing as yet. The stated models indeed explain something (when we "read them mirrorwise") about the termination of a case of absence (also the resumption of work can be seen as a "decision" which is also influenced by the opportunity to be absent (opportunity of absence) and job satisfaction; and also for the resumption of work load and capability must have had regained their equilibrium, or developed an effective "coping"), on the other hand resumption of work is more than just the mirror image of reporting ill. The fact of the matter is that once a "case of sickness absence" has started a number of new factors will come into play determining its duration and termination. Normally the person concerned will in the course of his or her illness seek medical help, something which in itself may influence the duration of absence. It is also possible that sickness absence changes the job satisfaction itself; the satisfaction with working relations could diminish considerably when it turns out that superiors and colleagues do not show any sign of interest for the sick colleague during the period of sickness (a complaint often made by long-term absentees).

In a more general sense the socio-medical guidance is an important factor with respect to work resumption. With good guidance, the duration of absence can be shortened considerably. When guidance is absent or inefficient, it may however protract the duration of absence. Aside from this it is important to what extent the company actively tries to reintegrate the long-term sick, for example by adaptations (temporarily or permanently) of the work place or working hours.

Regarding these and similar determinants of the *termination* of sickness absence there are no specific theories, but we suggest to denote these determinants collectively with the concept *work resumption threshold*. That means that, just as there is a difference between sickness and reporting ill (which are separated by the absence threshold), also recovery (in the medical sense) and resumption of work are not identical. In studies on work resumption of patients after myocardic infarction, this has been labelled the "medical paradox" by Badura (1991): whereas the majority of these patients can be regarded as completely recovered from the medical point of view, only a minority of them resumes work. This appears to be an international phenomenon.

Just as in the case of the "absence threshold", existing general theories discussed before in this section can be of value when we give meaning to the term "resumption threshold".

Summarizing, we suggest, through a combination of several theoretical approaches, the following classification of factors determining absence (both its origin, duration and termination).

The frame of reference as sketched in Figure 6.5 appears to cover individual cases of sickness absence only; however, its scope is more general, not only including individual factors, but also factors on the meso and macro level (e.g. company characteristics and common societal factors). In the next sections we will further elaborate on these factors. Wherever possible, we will refer to the model above.

4   SOCIETAL FACTORS

On the level of the common societal factors the social security system, the health care, legislation

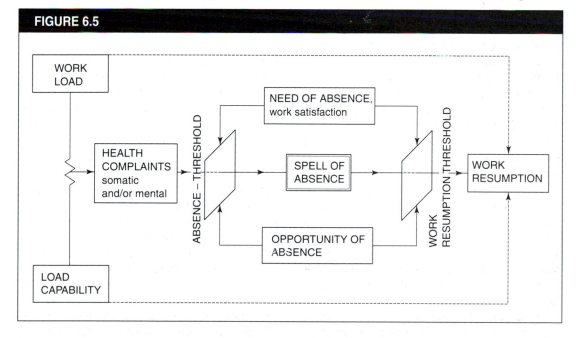

FIGURE 6.5

A theoretical frame of reference for sickness absence.

regarding labour conditions and macro-economical influences will be dealt with.

Social security arrangements influence the absence threshold and the resumption threshold especially.

The health care structure and legislation on re-employment of handicapped workers are of great importance in relation to the resumption threshold. In The Netherlands, the Labour Conditions Act aims at reducing excessive work load by improving working conditions and at an increase of capability through adequate information, education and training.

Macro-economical factors, including unemployment levels, carry many indirect influences, especially in relation to the opportunity of absence.

4.1 The social security system

In terms of the model presented in section 3 the social security system influences mainly, via the opportunity of absence, the absence threshold and the resumption threshold.

Global comparison between countries suggests a proportional relation between sickness benefit levels and sickness absence levels (Smulders, 1984a). Further research (Grosfeld, 1988; Prins, 1990) shows, however, that many intervening factors play a part, which makes direct comparison difficult. Other research also suggests that the influence of financial incentives is less predominating than is sometimes assumed. For instance, changes in benefit payments in The Netherlands in 1987 and 1988 with respect to the DIA (smaller benefits, more stringent criteria) did not lead to substantial decrease in the influx of the DIA.

German research (Dennerlein & Schneider, 1985) shows that the introduction of compulsory full wage payment during the first six weeks of sickness did not increase sickness absence rates. Also the study of Prins (1990) shows that in Germany and Belgium there is no real increase of the number of recoveries around the moment where in these countries the period of full wage payment ends and (lower) sickness benefits take over.

There seems to be a clear influence of *executing and administrative procedures* on absence, such as medical certification and control (Smulders,

1984a; Prins 1990; Prins, Veerman, & Koster, 1993a,b). The application of control of absence may have a reducing effect on sickness absence. This is however strongly contingent on the point in time: early and/or frequent sickness absence control, even though reducing frequency rates, can increase sickness absence rates because it possibly lengthens the duration of absence as a consequence of some workers continuing work while they really are sick, resulting in more serious disorders later on. The same phenomenon may occur with waiting days for sickness benefit payment ("karenz"-days, during which no wages are being paid), which do not automatically reduce sickness absence rates. An alternative explanation here is exchange theory: when workers themselves pay for their first days of sickness, they may compensate for this by late work resumption (having sickness benefits pay for the last days of sickness).

The organization and administration of social security and of health care may also influence absence, especially the duration of absence: when problems of coordination occur (for instance between the track of Sickness Benefit Act and DIA, or between the attending physician, company doctor and social insurance doctor) one can assume that this also will lengthen the duration of absence. Despite a scarcity of empirical research there are clear signs of the significance of administrative procedures. Prins (1990) remarks in his international comparative research that the administration of social security, in connection with the criteria of admission, has a clear influence on the large differences in sickness absence rates between the countries in his study. A more recent comparison of social security administration in four European countries was made by Prins, Veerman, and Koster (1993a,b).

Social security can also influence the resumption threshold and the possibilities of reintegration. The Dutch DIA also entails provisions for the promotion of reintegration (e.g. by subsidizing work place adaptations, transportation facilities). Apart from that in The Netherlands, as in many other countries, legislation exists for promoting re-employment of handicapped workers, although its effectiveness is disputed.

4.2 The health care system

Health care is of great importance concerning the resumption threshold, but also influences the influx (such as the preventive health care, which can improve the equilibrium between load and capability). One would expect extensive health care automatically to lead to a better health condition and thus to lower sickness absence rates, but there are also adverse effects of health care on absence.

The *definition of sickness* in social and medical circles has widened considerably in the course of the last decades. Many years ago, only clearly visible physical disorders were accepted as "sickness", whereas nowadays, for instance psychological disorders (including stress-related complaints) are also covered by the concept of "sickness". Besides, more and more finely tuned medical diagnostics and new treatments have arisen, which also have an absence-stimulating effect: illnesses that could not have been spotted earlier can be diagnosed today, or complaints of unclear origin now may be scrutinized in a protracted period of diagnostics. The existence of many new therapies, which can also mean a longer treatment, can possibly lengthen the duration of absence.

Dutch research shows that the organization of health care, if less than efficient, can also have absence-stimulating effects. It appears that 22% of the duration of absence of long-term cases (over 42 days) can be attributed to waiting and qualifying periods (including completely "disoriented periods"), of which 90% can be attributed to deficiencies in the organization of health care. Related to this is the earlier mentioned short-coming of social medical guidance of (employed) patients in The Netherlands, as a consequence of which the reintegration of long-term sick employees leaves much to be desired. Recent research shows that this is especially the case with mental illnesses (Schröer, 1993). In other countries, because of other forms of organization and a smaller supply of long-term sick workers, waiting periods and "disoriented periods" seem to be less of a problem (Prins, 1990).

During the last few years there seems to be a growing concern for industrial health care and industrial safety as ways to promote employee health. No empirical evidence is available however to show direct results of industrial health and safety measures in terms of sickness absence. However, partly due to European Community regulations, a general obligation was introduced in The Netherlands for employers to enlist the assistance of a professional Occupational Health Service, also with a view to reduce sickness absence.

4.3 Legislation on labour conditions

In many countries some legislation in the area of labour conditions exists. This legislation is on one hand aimed at reducing burdening factors in working conditions and on the other hand at raising the capability by means of information and education.

In the years 1981–1990, in The Netherlands, a step-by-step introduction of the Labour Conditions Act has been realized. This law compels bigger companies amongst other things to register and report their sickness absence. One of the positive effects was expected to be a lower sickness absence rate. To what extent the introduction of this law has led to a decrease of sickness absence can however not be determined. As from 1994 the Act also contains the obligation for employers to conduct an adequate absence reduction policy, based on a systematic inventory of health risks in the company, as part of the company's labour conditions policy. Here again the enlistment of independent Occupational Health Services is mandatory.

4.4 Macro-economic influences

There is a positive relationship between the level of economical activity in a country and absence. During recessions the rate of absence in a country tends to decrease. Some seek an explanation in employees' fear of dismissal (in which case the absence threshold gets higher), others believe that the primary cause is companies' more selective hiring and firing policies (made possible by a larger labour supply), creating a healthier population of employees with a higher capability— known as the "healthy worker effect". Most research material points towards the latter explanation as significant, the role of fear of dismissal as a cause of lower absenteeism is more controversial.

International comparative research (Prins, 1990) shows that the cross-national differences in exit opportunities from the labour market (especially for older workers) are of great influence on sickness absence. Where work incapacity (first sickness benefit, later disability pension) is the more attractive alternative (as in The Netherlands), this will be reflected in higher rates of sickness absence and disability benefits. Where there are more alternatives, sickness and disability benefits will not function as often as exit routes. Alternatives one could think of are arrangements for older employees like pre-retirement or functional superannuation.

5 PERSONAL AND INDIVIDUAL-LEVEL DETERMINANTS

Separate companies are barely capable of influencing the macro-societal determinants of work incapacity discussed above. This is also the case with the personal and individual-level factors to be dealt with in this section. It is however possible for a company to exert indirect influence on the individual characteristics of its workers through means of selection. Also one can think of health-improving campaigns on a company level (for instance, industrial alcohol programmes, in-company fitness facilities, health promotion campaigns) which also aim at personal habits or lifestyles.

From the perspective of our model these factors seem to have influence in different places. For one thing they are related to the capability (i.e. the coping behaviour) of workers, for another they have an effect on the absence threshold and work resumption threshold.

5.1 Individual characteristics

With respect to the origin of stress, respectively coping behaviour, individual characteristics appear to have a considerable moderating effect. In stress literature (see Buunk & De Wolff, Chapter 7 in this Volume) special attention is paid to differences between A-type persons (high ambitions, aggressive, agitated) and B-type persons (mirror image of the A-type) and to the extent

of neuroticism. A-type persons would be more prone to develop stress reactions and run a special risk of developing diseases of the circulatory system.

Further inquiry shows however that the relationship between individual characteristics, sickness absence and stress reactions appears to be very complex. It seems that certain personality types will be more prone to find themselves in stressful situations, or even bring about such situations on themselves. Aside from that there seems to be a relation of individual characteristics not only with coping behaviour, but also with individual perceptions of stress, apart from the objective situation.

5.2 Individual and demographic factors

Many sources show the importance of individual and demographic variables (Porter & Steers, 1973; Nicholson, Brown, & Chadwick-Jones, 1977; Smulders, 1984a,b; Grosfeld, 1988; Klein Hesselink et al., 1993) for sickness absence. The most important factor on the personal level is one's health status. As the general physical and mental condition declines with age, there is an almost universally found connection between *age* and sickness absence: older people are absent less frequently, but their spells are (much) longer than younger people. On balance older people have a higher absence percentage than younger people.

Concerning *gender*: in many countries women show higher rates of absence than men. Often pregnancy and maternity leave are pointed at as explanations. Indeed, even apart from the period of maternity leave (which itself sometimes is counted as "sickness absence" in statistics, the registered sickness absence of pregnant women (and with that the average sickness absence rate of women as a group) is higher. The periods just before and after maternity leave show higher rates of sickness absence, especially with physically straining jobs. Consequently, this leads to a peak in sickness absence in women of 25–30 years of age. Research also shows that some months after childbirth the rate of absence tends to decrease to usual levels. Thus the thought that female workers with children run high risks of absence as a consequence of their "double load" (work and housekeeping) is not been supported by research.

More importantly, women tend to have jobs in the "lower end of the labour market", which are connected with higher risks of sickness. When female absence rates are corrected for pregnancy and maternity, and moreover are standardized for such other job aspects in which women and men differ (part-time work, job level, nature of job) it appears that women do not show substantially higher absence percentages than men, but they seem to be absent more frequently.

Important differences in absence occur after differentiation on the basis of the *educational levels:* lowest educational levels tend to show the highest rates of absence. The interpretation of these differences is difficult because the educational level determines the functional level and with that the quality of working conditions and work load. It is generally accepted however that education, training and experience have a positive influence on the capability.

The educational level is—besides the job level and income level—one of the three characteristics of socio-economic status (SES). Research shows a strong link between the different SES-characteristics and health.

Data on sickness absence and different nationalities show that in The Netherlands foreign employees, especially "guest workers" from the Mediterranean area, have a high rate of sickness absence, mainly due to long average durations of spells. Important explanations for this fact can be found in the low or very low average of functional levels of this category of employees and in the high average age of foreign workers, and in social cultural differences or problems of assimilation which may manifest itself in the perception of sickness or feelings of illness and in the way the health care system reacts upon this. Thus, as with gender or education, it is unclear whether or not nationality is an independent determinant of sickness absence apart from its interconnection with other factors, as age or job quality.

Except for demographic factors discussed above, also personal factors can influence absenteeism in a negative way. Employees who drink too much alcohol have a higher sickness absence rate and have more accidents than moderate users of alcohol. Results of Dutch research suggest that in The Netherlands 5–6% of the working population has problematic drinking habits. In certain industrial branches and professional groups, and certain types of companies, the risk of alcohol abuse is higher than in others.

Inquiries into the influence of smoking habits show divergent results, but smoking is mainly considered as having a negative influence on sickness absence (Grosfeld, 1988) through its detrimental effect on health status.

In the context of personal factors, the broad concept of "load in leisure time" is also of importance. One can think of sports injuries (especially with young people)—a negative influence standing opposite to the health improving effects of the practise of sports—traffic accidents, holiday habits, but also the psychological strain as a consequence of domestic problems, evening studies or sideline jobs. Generally one should realize that not only factors at work—as work load—influence sickness absence, but many factors in leisure time play a part as well. Thus less exposure time to job risks may not result in lower absence, as more exposure time to leisure risks may compensate for the job risks.

6 DETERMINANTS IN WORK AND LABOUR CONDITIONS

The field discussed in this section, also denoted as the issue of the quality of work, can be characterized by four dimensions: job content, material working conditions, industrial relations, and terms of employment.

This field bears much significance for sickness absence. For instance Philipsen states in his classical research (1969) that between 50 and 80% of the differences in absence rates between organizations can be explained through means of the characteristics of the organization itself. Within this, working conditions play an important role. Other authors also put forward the importance of work and working conditions in relation to sickness absence.

For influences on sickness absence on a *company level* all elements of our frame of reference are relevant. The determinants of sickness absence in the area of quality of work are mainly related to the (work)load and the capacity (job content and working conditions) and partly to the absence threshold (working relations in terms of personal relations with supervisor and colleagues). These aspects can also be of significance for the resumption of work (e.g. job adaptations may facilitate reintegration; strong social relations will lead to earlier resumption of work).

In this process the determinants on the company level can be of direct or indirect influence on the origin of health complaints (Steensma et al., 1989).

6.1   Job content

Job content in the sense of lack of variety, autonomy and responsibility appears to be important as a determinant of sickness absence. On these job characteristics there exists an extensive tradition of research (Turner & Lawrence, 1965; Hackman & Oldham, 1976; Algera, 1981; Vogelaar, 1990). Literature shows that with inefficient tuning between person and tasks (Person-Environment fit) and lack of regulating capacity stress reactions can occur (De Sitter, 1981; Karasek & Theorell, 1990) and that these situations are especially found in industrial labour at an executive level.

The introduction of new technologies does not automatically lead to improvement of this situation. There even are some indications that the introduction of new technologies worsens the situation in the case of office work (Boonstra, 1987).

From an organizational-sociological point of view these data on underload are confirmed. Research of Conen and Huijgen (1989) shows from labour force survey data from 1971, 1977 and 1983 that within all educational levels the quality of work, measured by the level of job content, has declined. This raises the important question, what the long term health consequences will be of creating numerous new jobs if these are relatively void as to job level and content.

Also from the socio-technical tradition of action research involving the introduction of autonomous task groups we may conclude that improvements in job content are of major importance in reducing sickness absence. Recent reviews of action research conducted earlier (Terra et al.,

1988) show that through changes introduced in the structure of job division the costs of absenteeism fell by 50%, a structural trend over four consecutive years.

Moreover there are diverging developments for the different professional sectors. In a number of cases specific job demands have emerged, based on developments in micro-electronics, for which education falls short.

There is also the problem of roles in organizations with respect to job content. Stress literature (Kahn et al., 1964; Winnubst, 1984; Ekkers & Sanders, 1987; see also Chapter 7 in this Volume) shows that role conflict, role ambiguity and role overload as stressors may lead to strains such as health complaints. There are clear differences between professional groups in terms of stressor levels (Ekkers & Sanders, 1987).

6.2   Material working conditions

Surveys on literature show that worse material working conditions tend to coincide with higher rates of sickness absence.

Dependent on the definition, material working conditions include physical and chemical factors such as noise, dirt, stench, toxic substances, but also ergonomical factors such as adequacy of tools, design of work place, working methods and such, and also safety risks.

In the course of the last decades the material working conditions in The Netherlands have generally improved, even though we can find examples to the contrary, such as the increased use of chemical substances in a great number of industrial sectors, more static load on muscles for instance through the use of computer screens, and longer travelling times for commuting traffic. Also the number of employees who report working under stress has been increasing over many years. Thus, large groups in the Dutch industrial population still work under straining material conditions and increasingly report stressful socio-psychological working conditions.

6.3   Social and industrial relations

With respect to these factors we can make a distinction between direct individual support at work and more institutional factors like workers' representative structures.

The social relations with immediate superiors and colleagues clearly influence the rate of absence: the better the social relations at work, the lower the sickness absence rates (Smulders, 1984a; Grosfeld, 1988). The stress-moderating effect of social support especially seems to play an important role here. This effect is attributed by Buunk and De Wolff (Chapter 7 in this Volume) both to buffering effects—in which social support weakens or neutralizes the effect of stressors on health—and to direct effects, being the positive influence of social support on health, independent of the possible presence of stressors.

As to the more formal industrial relations, it would be plausible that a strong involvement and representation of workers in the company should enhance job involvement and organizational commitment, and thus would lead to lower absence levels. However, the relationship between institutional structures concerning industrial relations and sickness absence has not been studied empirically. Thus it is impossible to say whether the presence of representative structures, like the works council, influences absence. Anyway recent Dutch legislation on workers' representation in the formulation of labour conditions and sickness absence policies increasingly emphasizes the role of workers' representation councils in this field of company policy.

6.4 Terms of employment

From the literature on determinants of sickness absence the following factors appear to be relevant (Smulders, 1984a; Grosfeld, 1988):

- salary/wages and promotional opportunities, or the satisfaction with these;
- working and resting hours;
- job (in)security.

Satisfaction with salary and/or promotional opportunities is related with lower absence. This is partly because in higher jobs not only the basic terms of employment are better, but also other elements of quality of work. Grosfeld (1988) states that the influence of satisfaction on the duration of sickness absence diminishes after correcting for these other factors, but does not disappear entirely.

Research into the differences in absence be-

tween day work and shift work does not yield a consistent picture. This is due to methodological problems; in shiftwork there seems to be a selection (maybe self-selection) of the more healthy employees (the so-called "healthy worker-effect").

The increasing number of part-time jobs in the labour market (especially among women) is of interest, as sickness absence is related to the number of weekly working hours. Sickness absence percentages are highest in part-time personnel with relatively many working hours (over half-time but under full-time). Lower sickness absence is found in full-time employees and in part-time employees with less than half-time working weeks.

The threat of unemployment or job insecurity appears to be connected with a higher sickness absence rate (Veerman, 1985). This could be interpreted by viewing job insecurity as a stress factor. On the other hand, reduction of employment through lay-offs often is a selective process: it tends to hit the weakest personnel categories most, resulting in a healthier remaining work force and lower absence rates (another instance of the "healthy worker effect").

7 INTERVENTIONS ON COMPANY LEVEL

In this section we shall first discuss the different policies which could be pursued to reduce sickness absence rates. After that we will look at organizational context in which interventions aimed at absence reduction can be undertaken.

7.1 Styles of absence reduction policies

In accordance with the theoretical model from section 3 three policy views on interventions can be distinguished:

- *preventive policy*, aimed at adjustment of the workload and/or an increase of the load capacity, in order to create a better equilibrium between these two;
- *inhibiting policy*, aimed at heightening the absence threshold, in order to reduce the number of sickness reports;

- *curative policy*, aimed at removal (or lowering) of the work resumption threshold, with faster therapy and/or the creation of possibilities of faster work resumption after recovery.

Adequate interventions contain a mixture of elements from these three policies, sometimes differentiated into company, department and individual-level policies.

Steensma et al. (1989) also advocate the integration of a policy aimed at the individual (largely identical with what we denote as inhibiting policy) and a policy aimed at reduction of stressful working conditions, respectively at the quality of work and organization. The latter policies are understood as preventive policies. They do not explicitly discuss the curative policy.

Recent developments in The Netherlands show an increasing importance ascribed to curative policy, as witnessed by the emphasis on socio-medical guidance of sick employees. This guidance comprises individual-oriented activities aimed at restoring the equilibrium between load and capacity of workers with a view of early return to work.

In the following we will outline the most important characteristics of the absence reduction policies that we distinguish. In section 7.2 we will elaborate further on aspects of organizational change.

7.1.1 Preventive policy

This policy is aimed at adjusting the workload or quality of work (through improvements in job content, material working conditions, industrial relations and terms of employment) and/or increasing the load capability of workers, for instance through information, training and education and/or increase of the "coping capacity". In practice many absence reducing measures within this policy type will be aimed at improvements in work and working conditions, also known as "humanization of work". More specifically the following elements may be discerned:

Job content   Based on psychology of work and organization, a great number of projects have been waged aimed at the improvement of job content (often in combination with improvements in other dimensions of the quality of work). These include projects concerning job enlargement, job enrichment, and the socio-technical projects aimed at task and work organization. Most of these projects are not primarily designed to deal with absence, but in their evaluations absence is almost always one of the dependent variables. Various evaluation studies show the positive effect of an improvement in job content on absence (Smulders, 1980; Pasmore, 1982).

Material working conditions   Evaluated projects on improvement of material working conditions with the primary target of decreasing sickness absence are scarcely available (see Smulders, 1980), despite the relation between material working conditions and sickness absence found in several studies. At the same time many projects on working conditions have been carried out without any research evaluating the effects in terms of sickness absence. An exception is the Dutch so-called BEA-project (Terra et al., 1988) evaluating measures for improvement of the material working conditions introduced by companies, including effects on absence. The effects of these measures were indeed positive, resulting in consistently lower rates of sickness absence.

The same situation exists with respect to the effect of *industrial relations and terms of employment* in relation to sickness absence. There are almost no written accounts of these effects. Smulders (1980) does report among other things that possibilities of employee participation, and a more socially directed leadership are positive conditions for low sickness absence. At the same time he reports favourable effects of the introduction of variable working hours and a shortened working week.

Influencing the capability   One may assume that education and task directed training contribute to a higher capability of employees and consequently to a reduction of sickness absence, but evaluations of educational and training projects with respect to sickness absence are not available.

In this context we can point to courses and programmes concerning stress reduction, in which it is attempted to teach the individual to cope with stress at work (Ekkers & Sanders, 1987). A distinction is often made between:

1. action and problem related approaches, aimed directly at the source of stressors, and
2. emotion regulating approaches, for instance with relaxation exercises, medicine, therapy.

7.1.2   Inhibiting policy

This policy is aimed at limiting the individual latitude of decision on reporting sick or not, and consequently a limitation of the opportunity of absence, and/or an increase of work satisfaction to decrease the need of absence. As to the latter: there are hardly any projects known which tried to increase work satisfaction primarily with the aim of reducing absence; an increase of work satisfaction can however have an inhibiting side-effect on absence.

The *opportunity of absence* can be influenced by the procedure of reporting sick, absence control, activities of the insurance doctor and occupational physician, and also by loss of income or other economic incentives. The real effects of these measures on absenteeism are difficult to determine because these measures are often introduced in combination with other types of absence policies.

With regard to the *procedures on reporting sick*, it is sometimes recommended to report sick at work with one's own superior, and to ensure that some action will be taken (attention, guidance). Conversations of management with frequently absent employees also belong to this category (Steensma et al., 1989).

With regard to *the control*, a survey of studies on change (Smulders, 1980) shows that the introduction of an adequate control, where this was missing initially, has a limiting effect on sickness absence, but also that a too early and stringent control may be counterproductive (reducing absence frequency at the cost of rising duration per period).

As to the role of the (social) insurance doctor and the occupational physician, recent Dutch legislation moved several absence control and legitimation tasks from the former to the latter. The effects of giving more responsibilities to occupational physicians (and to the Occupational

Health Services generally) and less to social insurance doctors are not known yet. Some fear that the increased emphasis on absence control and legitimation, and on socio-medical guidance by occupational physicians, will limit their time available for preventive occupational health care. As to the (now limited) role of social insurance doctors, a tendency over the last years has been a more company-oriented, and less individual-oriented, way of viewing sickness absence.

As to wage loss, wage/benefit ratios and other economic incentives during the last few years new absence reduction strategies have been introduced in several Dutch companies (DSM, Volvo), including much-discussed measures with respect to (partial) loss of income and other incentives in terms of employment, directed against absence. Unfortunately there are no well-documented evaluations available. Recent Dutch research on the extent to which economic incentives are applied in reducing absence shows that employers often feel that these incentives are effective, but also that the mechanisms through which this effect comes about are quite complex (Andriessen & Reuling, 1992). In his survey of studies on change Smulders (1980) shows that it is difficult to draw conclusions on the effect of the level of insurance benefits on sickness absence. The use of waiting days ("karenz-days", first days of sickness spells not being paid) has a limiting effect on the reporting frequency, but possibly lengthens the duration of sickness absence.

This last effect points to a general risk of an inhibiting absence control policy. All measures of this type are useful only if there really is a low absence threshold to start with (which would be reflected in a high reporting frequency). If this is not the case, the inhibiting policy could be counterproductive:

1. A too high absence threshold can make workers keep on working despite real health complaints, longer than is medically desirable. The disorder can consequently deteriorate, which finally may lead to an even longer case of sickness absence.
2. Introducing a high absence threshold while the underlying causes of absence are not being tackled could have a negative effect

on the organization; for instance "internal absence from work" (attending work without being productive), lower productivity, bad atmosphere at work.

Because of this, inhibiting measures should be taken with great care and one should first check if the absence frequency rate indeed calls for such a policy.

7.1.3   Curative policy

This policy aims especially at improving socio-medical guidance and faster reintegration after sickness. There are scarcely any evaluative studies on projects aiming specifically at this. However, within the role of the insurance company doctor there normally are some aspects of a curative policy: active efforts of the insurance company doctor can accelerate the resumption of work. Besides that, the company health care can, along with its preventive possibilities, contribute to the curative policy and a flexible resumption of work after sickness.

Research by Hellinga (1989) in a big industrial company shows how specific efforts for reintegration of its own workers, who had received disability benefits, has led to a re-employment which is 50% above average in The Netherlands.

7.2   Aspects of change of absence policy

As mentioned above, there are three lines of policy as regards to content with which one can try to reduce sickness absence. To bring into practice an integrated approach—which will often have to entail a combination of these lines—changes (and knowledge about their effects) have to be well embedded in the industrial organization.

We will here outline an approach that may entail aspects both of a preventive, inhibiting and curative policy. This approach is aimed at a more fundamental change in the relation between work and health. The strategy of planned change for such an approach is derived from several projects on improvement of the quality of work, respectively work and health and the views on organizational change that they embodied (Van der Vlist, Allegro & Demenint, 1990; Boonstra, 1991).

In this approach one first tries to create a social basis within the firm for an absence policy, supported both by management and (representa-

tives of) employees. The starting point is a close cooperation between the different groups. It is therefore crucial to check beforehand the readiness for change of the groups involved. In this a useful role can be played by conferences with representatives of different levels within the firm, guided by external experts.

It is often useful for the guidance of such a project to create a temporary structure (steering committee and/or work group), consisting of members from management, employees' representatives and experts. Such a supportive structure must have clear tasks and competencies, the content of which is dependent on its assignment. We will call this the "guidance group". It is of utmost importance that a close relationship is maintained between this group and levels on and near the shop floor.

Success of such a project requires that enough time and manpower is made available; at the same time one must have enough means to be able to invest in improvements of working conditions, respectively to back up the individual guidance of absentees and the curative policy. A successful project will often have a minimum duration of two or three years.

The most important phases that can be distinguished in the cycle of the project are respectively:

7.2.1   Diagnosis

This diagnosis concerns an analysis of data on sickness absence and—in a later phase—of working conditions.

With regard to the analysis of data on sickness absence the following is indispensable: the construction of an adequate system for registration of sickness absence, adequate feedback of figures from this system to management, and discussion within the guidance group and the firm generally.

In order to diagnose working conditions, different methods may be used, including group interviews, questionnaires, inspections etc. It is of great importance to have this followed by a quick and concise report, in which attention is paid not only to bottlenecks, but to possible solutions as well. Much attention is also needed in this phase for the involvement of lower executives/middle management, because they are often pointed at (or at least feel they are) as being responsible for bottlenecks in the working conditions. Moreover, these executives will get a role in the implementation phase of change; for this reason their commitment is needed from the very beginning.

7.2.2 Action plan

Based upon the diagnosis, the guidance group will establish priorities (in subjects and/or departments) which can be started off.

Part of the priorities can be the determination of target figures for absence. Next it is possible, with regard to the socio-medical guidance of sick employees, to create a socio-medical team, consisting of experts (personnel department, company doctor, insurance doctor) and members of management (possibly circulating).

The improvement of working conditions in the short term is preferable whenever possible. It is however necessary to make it clear that a number of issues will take a longer period of time for implementation, or will need time to show effects, and that maybe some bottlenecks will never be solved completely.

7.2.3 Implementation

As far as implementation is concerned it is very difficult to formulate universal guidelines, because this has to be tailored to specific situations and is strongly dependent on the diagnosis and the action plan. It is however possible to give suggestions for the advisor/inquirer:

- The necessary integration of the (task) structural and the group dynamical approach. Management, employees and experts will indeed have to develop another way of working; just structural changes in work or paper plans are insufficient.
- The recognition of individual differences, company history and circumstances and a contrast of interests. The tackling of sickness absence in a company often has a long and sometimes fierce history. When an external adviser is hired, she certainly has to be conscious of any previous history.
- Top down but also bottom up; a combination of steering by top management on the one hand and active involvement of middle man-

agement and employees on the other hand is indispensable.
- Minimal formalization. Tackling sickness absence should be a continuous activity and therefore a project to reduce absence should lead to increasing the organization's learning ability; a detailed external report on the approach and the needed processes is not conducive to this.
- The roles of the advisers: external advisers, as well as those involved from within the company, need to play a combination of roles of guide and expert. Only through this, will the tackling of sickness absence be handed over to management and to employees.

7.2.4 Evaluation

In such an approach evaluation needs to be a continuous activity, which can lead to a new round in the cycle of the project. Because of the diversity and complexity of the backgrounds of sickness absence, it will beforehand never be sure whether a certain approach will indeed lead to the results hoped for. One should continuously bear in mind that there is always the possibility of unexpected, unwanted side-effects. Therefore one does not only need an evaluation of the course of the process, but also of the extent of realized decrease of absence.

An analysis of evaluated projects with an approach as outlined above shows a clear structural decrease of sickness absence.

In conclusion it can be said that an integrated approach offers favourable possibilities for a decrease in sickness absence. Practice has taught us that in most cases, the efficiency and productivity of the firm is also improved, because of the structural improvements in work and organization which were triggered by the absence reduction project.

8 CONCLUSION

In our introduction we mentioned that sickness absence is a complex phenomenon.

Many factors on macro-, meso- and micro-level play a role; in literature on sickness absence we find many surveys listing long series of determinants, without clarifying how each of these influence sickness absence.

In this chapter we attempted to place these determinants in an explanatory frame of reference by means of an integration of the model of load capability (elaborated further in terms of stress theories) and the model of decision. With this we attempted to gain insight into the phenomenon of sickness absence. Further we indicated how to derive three absence reduction strategies from this integrated model: a preventive policy, an inhibiting policy and a curative policy.

With the help of insights on processes of organizational change it has been indicated how, through a combination of the three approaches, absence can be tackled on an organizational level. The results of such an approach—which will need time and energy—are favourable both in terms of sickness absence reduction and of company efficiency and productivity.

NOTE

1. The Dutch Sickness Benefit Act insures workers under the age of 65 of payment of 70% of wages for a maximum of 52 weeks. The first 6 weeks (2 weeks for small employers) are paid by the employer; thereafter, collective benefit funds take over payment. After 52 weeks disabled employees may be entitled to further benefits under the Disability Insurance Act (DIA). In many collective labour agreements, compensation of 100% of wages from the first day of sickness has been negotiated.

On 1st January 1996, a revolutionary new law was passed which states that employers must continue to pay out the salary for the first year of sickness (70% of the salary or more, if so agreed under the terms of collective labour agreements; but never less than the minimum wage). The DIA will be amended on 1st January 1998.

REFERENCES

Algera, J.A. (1981). *Kenmerken van werk; de constructie van een instrument voor het meten van taakkenmerken, die van invloed zijn op de motivatie, satisfactie, en prestatie van taakuitvoerenden.* Amsterdam: Swets & Zeitlinger.

Allegro, J.T. (1973). *Socio-technische organisatieontwikkeling.* Leiden: Stenfert Kroese.

Andriessen, S., & Reuling, A.M.H. (1992). *Stimulans tot aanwezigheid? Een onderzoek naar arbeids-voorwaardelijke stimulansen gericht op het verzuimgedrag van werknemers in Nederland.* The Hague: Ministry of Social Affairs and Employment/VUGA Uitgeverij.

Badura, B. (1991). Health promotion for the chronically ill people. In B. Badura, & I. Kickbusch (Eds.), *Health promotion research: Towards a new social epidemiology* (European Series 37, pp. 365–392). WHO Regional Publications.

Boonstra, J.J. (1987). Automatisering—samenvattend overzicht van theorie en praktijk. In H.O. Steensma, & V.Chr. Vrooland (Eds.), *Automatiseren gaat niet vanzelf.* Amsterdam: Stichting CCOZ.

Boonstra, J.J. (1991). *Integrale organisatie ontwikkeling; vormgeven aan fundamentele veranderingsprocessen in organisaties.* Utrecht: Lemma.

Buijs, P.C. (1994). *Sociaal medische begeleiding—een model voor ziekteverzuimbeleid in de praktijk.* Amsterdam: AWV, Industriebond FNV, NIA.

Chadwick-Jones, J.K., Nicholson, N., & Brown, C.A. (1982). *Social psychology of absenteeism.* New York: Praeger.

Chen, P.J., & Spector, P.E. (1991). Negative affectivity as the underlying cause of correlations between stressors and strains. *Journal of Applied Psychology, 76,* 398–407.

Conen, G., & Huijgen, F. (1989). De integrale aanpak van organisatievernieuwing. Katholieke Universiteit Nijmegen.

Dennerlein, R., & Schneider, M. (1985). Untersuchung der Bestimmungsfaktoren für Schwankungen des Krankenstandes in der Bundesrepublik Deutschland. *Endbericht für den Bundesminister für Arbeit und Sozialordnung.* Augsburg: BASYS GmbH.

Dijk, F.J.H. van, Dormolen, M. van, Kompier, M.A.J., & Meijman, T.F. (1990). Herwaardering model belasting-belastbaarheid. *Tijdschrift Sociale Gezondheidszorg, 68*(1), 3–10.

Dittrich, J.E., & Carrell, M.R. (1979). Organizational equity perceptions, employee job satisfaction, and departmental absence and turnover rates. *Organizational Behaviour and Human Performance, 24,* 29–40.

Einerhand, M.G.K., Knol, G., Prins, R., & Veerman, T.J. (1995). *Sickness and invalidity arrangements: Facts and figures from six European countries.* The Hague: Ministry of Social Affairs and Employment/ VUGA Uitgeverij.

Ekkers, C.L., & Sanders, A.F. (1987). *Stress in de arbeidssituatie.* Den Haag: Ministerie van Sociale Zaken en Werkgelegenheid.

Grosfeld, J.A.M. (1988). *De voorspelbaarheid van de individuele verzuimduur.* Lisse: Swets en Zeitlinger.

Gupta, N., & Beehr, T.A. (1979). Job stress and employee behaviors. *Organizational Behavior and Human Performance, 23,* 373–387.

Hackett, R.D., Bycio, O., & Guion, R.M. (1989).

Absenteeism among hospital nurses: an ideographic-longitudinal analysis. *Academy of Management Journal, 32*, 424–453.

Hackman, J.R., & Lawler, E.E. (1971). Employee reactions to job characteristics. *Journal of Applied Psychology, 55*, 259–186.

Hackman, J.R., & Oldham, G.R. (1976). Motivation through the design of work: Test of a theory. *Organizational Behavior and Human Performance, 16*, 250–279.

Hellinga, P., Lenshoek, D.E., & Van Dijk, F. (1989). *Ziekteverzuim, WAO-toetreding en reïntegratie bij een groot industrieel bedrijf: eindrapport van het project "Verschil in WAO-toetredingsrisico".* Amsterdam: NIA.

Johns, G. (1978). Attitudinal and non-attitudinal predictors of two forms of absence from work. *Organizational Behavior and Human Performance, 22*, 431–444.

Kahn, R.L., Quinn, R.P., Snoek, J.D., & Rosenthal, R.A. (1964). *Organizational stress: Studies in role conflict and ambiguity.* New York: John Wiley.

Karasek, R.A. (1979). Job demands, job decision latitude and mental strain: Implication for job design. *Administrative Science Quarterly, 24*, 285–308.

Karasek, R., & Theorell, T. (1990). *Healthy work: Stress, productivity, and the reconstruction of working life.* New York: Basic Books.

Klein Hesselink, D. J., Kruidenier, H.J., Veerman, T.J., & Buijs, P.C. (1993). *Afwezigheid Verklaard: Literatuurstudie naar determinanten van ziekteverzuim en arbeidsongeschiktheid.* Amsterdam: NIA.

Kruidenier, H.J. (1981). *Ziekteverzuim en conjuctuur: Een beschouwing naar aanleiding van de daling van het ziekteverzuim.* Amsterdam: Stichting CCOZ.

Meijman, T.F. (1989). Belasting en herstel: Een begrippenkader voor het arbeidspsychologisch onderzoek van werkbelasting. In T.F. Meijman (Ed.), *Mentale belasting en werkstress: Een arbeidspsychologische benadering.* Assen/Maastricht: Van Gorcum.

Morgan, L.G., & Herman, J.B. (1976). Perceived consequences of absenteeism. *Journal of Applied Psychology, 51*, 738–742.

Nicholson, N. (1977). Absence behaviour and attendence motivation: A conceptual synthesis. *Journal of Management Studies, 14*(3), 231–252.

Nicholson, N., Brown, C.A., & Chadwick-Jones, J.K. (1977). Absence from work and personal characteristics. *Journal of Applied Psychology, 62*, 319–327.

Nicholson N. (1989). Absence behavior and attendance motivation: A conceptual synthesis. *Journal of Management Studies, 14*, 231–252.

Nijhuis, F.J.N. (1984). *Beoordeling van organisatiekenmerken: Een sociaal-gezondheidskundige studie naar organisatiekenmerken en ziekteverzuim.* (PhD Thesis), Maastricht: Rijksuniversiteit Limburg.

Pasmore, W. (1982). Technical systems: A North American reflection on emperical studies in the seventies. *Human Relations.*

Philipsen, H. (1969). *Afwezigheid wegens ziekte.* Groningen: Rijksuniversiteit Groningen.

Porter, L.W., & Steers, R.M. (1973). Organizational, work, and personal factors in employee turnover and absenteeism. *Psychological Bulletin, 80*, 151–176.

Prins, R. (1984). Ongevallen in het licht van officiele cijfers: Over de "onderregistratie" van arbeidsongevallen in Nederland. *Tijdschrift voor Sociale Gezondheidszorg, 62*(9), 362–368.

Prins, R. (1990). *Sickness absence in Belgium, Germany and the Netherlands: A comparative study.* Amsterdam: NIA.

Prins, R., Veerman, T.J, & Koster, M.K. (1993a). *De uitvoering van arbeidsongeschiktheidsregelingen in België, Duitsland en Zweden.* Rapport R93/10, Sociale Verzekeringsraad, Zoetermeer.

Prins, R., Veerman, T.J., & Koster, M.K. (1993b). *Work incapacity and invalidity in Belgium, Germany, Sweden and The Netherlands: Four monographs on benefit and rehabilitation arrangements.* Rapport R93/11, Sociale Verzekeringsraad, Zoetermeer.

Schröer, K. (1993). *Verzuim wegens overspanning: Een onderzoek naar de aard van overspanning, de hulpverlening en het verzuimbeloop.* Maastricht: Rijksuniversiteit Limburg.

Sitter, L. U. de)1981). *Op weg naar nieuwe fabrieken en kantoren: Productie-organisatie en arbeidsorganisatie op de tweesprong.* Deventer: Kluwer.

Smulders, P.G.W. (1980). *De effecten van maatregelen om het ziekteverzuim te beïnvloeden: Een literatuurstudie op basis van 91 Nederlandse en buitenlandse empirische onderzoekingen.* Den Haag: Ministerie van Sociale Zaken en Werkgelegenheid.

Smulders, P.G.W. (1984a). *Balans van 30 jaar ziekteverzuimonderzoek: De resultaten van 318 studies samengevat.* Leiden: NIPG/TNO.

Smulders, P.G.W. (1984b). *Bedrijfskenmerken en ziekteverzuim in de jaren zestig en tachtig: een vergelijkende studie.* Leiden: NIPG/TNO.

Steensma, H.O., Vlist, R. van der, Vrooland, V.Chr. (Eds.) (1989). *Een verantwoord ziekteverzuimbeleid; Integraal verzuimbeleid: Goed voor werkgevers en goed voor werknemers.* Amsterdam: NIA.

Steers, R.M., & Rhodes, S.N. (1978). Major influences on employee attendance: a process model. *Journal of Applied Psychology, 63*(4), 391–407.

Terra, N., Christis, J., Fortuin, R., & Meerman, M. (1988). *Op weg naar beter werk: ervaringen, modellen en instrumenten voor maatwerk in Arbo-beleid.* Amsterdam: Nederlands Instituut voor Arbeidsomstandigheden NIA.

Turner, E.L., Lawrence, P.R. (1965). *Industrial jobs and the worker: an investigation of response to task attributes.* Boston: Harvard University.

Veerman, T. J. (1985). Ziekteverzuim en bedreigde werkgelegenheid: Enige bevindingen op drie niveaus. *Gezondheid & Samenleving, 6*(3), 174–181.

Veerman, T.J. (1990). Theorieën over ziekteverzuim. In P.G.W. Smulders, & T.J. Veerman (Eds.), *Handboek*

Ziekteverzuim (pp. 55–73). Den Haag: Delwel Uitgeverij.

Vlist, R. van der, Allegro, J.T., & Demenint, M. (1990). Organisatieveranderkunde: een theoretisch overzicht. In *Organiseren en veranderen in een dynamische wereld*. Culemborg: Lemma.

Vogelaar, A.L.W. (1990). *Arbeidssatisfactie: een consequentie van werk en werksituatie en behoeftenstructuur*. Leiden: RU Leiden.

Winnubst, J.A.M. (1984). Stress in organisaties: Naar een nieuwe benadering van werk en gezondheid. In P.J.D. Drenth, e.a.(Ed.), *Handboek arbeids en organisatiepsychologie* (Aflevering 2). Deventer: Van Loghum Slaterus.

7

Psychosocial Aspects of Occupational Stress

Bram P. Buunk, Jan de Jonge, Jan F. Ybema, and Charles J. de Wolff

INTRODUCTION

Centuries ago scientists recognized that work situations may have adverse health effects. Goodell, Wolf and Rogers (1986) suggest that the involvement of medical science with work and health problems started with Hippocrates, as early as the fifth century BC. Nearly 300 years ago, the Italian physician Ramazzini published a detailed account of the diseases related to various professions. The concern for potential bad impact of work on health was particularly raised by the unhealthy and risky work environments that resulted from the industrial revolution. In the last century, the English physician Charles Turner Thackrah wrote the first systematic treatise on the occurrence and prevention of occupational diseases, and occupational medicine made its entry into industrial society. In the twentieth century, numerous government measures were taken against factors in the work environment that may constitute a threat to employee health, in particular

measures to prevent accidents, to reduce physical and chemical health risks and to reduce the number of working hours.

During the past few decades, in western society the emphasis has shifted to a particular type of health threat in the work environment: *occupational stress*, especially the psychosocial aspects of this type of stress (cf. Kahn & Byosiere, 1992). According to some authors, occupational stress has increased in recent years because more and more is demanded from workers in terms of long periods of intense time pressure and rapid changes in the nature of jobs due to, among others, introduction of new technologies, international competition, market vacillations, and governmental budget cuts (Houtman & Kompier, 1995; Johnson & Hall, 1994; Levi, 1994; Offermann & Gowing, 1990). For instance, a recent European survey of working conditions among nearly 13,000 employees showed that 20% permanently experience a high time pressure, 35 to 40% report a lack of job control and nearly a quarter of the work force is involved in repetitive tasks of short duration (Paoli, 1992). Next to musculoskeletal problems, overall job stress and depression were the problems mentioned most often in a recent Labour Force Survey in the United Kingdom (Hodgson, Jones, Elliott, & Osman, 1993). In a US nationwide study of occupational stress (Northwestern National Life, 1991), the proportion of workers who reported "having multiple stress-related illnesses" had almost doubled between 1985 and 1990. In The Netherlands, as in other European countries, there was a sharp increase in occupational disability during the 1970s and 1980s, and about a third of the cases in The Netherlands were diagnosed as due to mental factors. In 1990, no less than 58% of those leaving employment for reasons of disability were diagnosed as having "mental complaints" (Gründemann, Nijboer, & Schellart, 1991).

Already in the past century the idea that psychosocial stress at work may affect a person's *physical health* was put forward by physicians who pointed out that excessive work involvement was typical of people with cardiovascular disease (Dembrowski & MacDougall, 1985). Indeed, an increasing number of epidemiological data suggests that occupational stress may lead to a variety of physical diseases (for an overview, see Fletcher, 1988). In England, for example, mortality among unskilled labourers was found to be almost twice as high as among professionals. Mortality rates due to diseases like pneumonia and other respiratory diseases were about five times higher among unskilled labourers than among professionals. Of course, such differencs may partly be due to differences in physical working conditions. However, the fact that people with lower-level jobs were also more at risk of developing cardiovascular diseases suggests the operation of psychosocial factors as well (Cooper & Smith, 1985; Marmot, 1994). Indeed, various authors have shown that there are important differences in psychosocial features of work at different occupational levels, which may partly explain these differences in physical health. For example, the lower the occupational level, the fewer social contacts people have at work, the less control they have of their work and the more high work pressure is experienced (Johnson & Hall, 1988; Schnall, Landsbergis, & Baker, 1994; Siegrist, 1991; Theorell & Karasek, 1996).

In this chapter we focus upon the psychosocial aspects of occupational stress, and upon the way in which such stress may affect mental and physical health. We first present a brief history of the research in this area, and discuss the various definitions of stress, emphasizing that stress is primarily an emotional process. Next we deal with various models of occupational stress, describe various stressors, discuss the role of coping with stress, and pay attention to the role of social support and personality characteristics as moderators in the stress process. Furthermore, some long-term consequences of occupational stress are dealt with. Finally, we make a few comments on the prevention of and intervention in work-related stress, but we refer to Chapter 17, Volume 3 for a full treatment of this topic. It must be emphasized that there is some arbitrariness in defining what issues fall under the field of occupational stress. Nevertheless, it is safe to say that in the past decade there have appeared thousands of papers dealing with, or directly relevant for, understanding the causes, nature and consequences of occupational stress. Therefore, our review intends primarily to present a general overview of the theories, issues and findings in this area, without pretending any completeness. We focus primarily on chronic stress at work, and do not pay attention to issues such as acute stress (Kleber & Van der Velden, 1996). Moreover, we do not pay attention to stress due to work-family conflicts, because this issue is dealt with in Chapter 16, Volume 3 in the present volume.

A BRIEF HISTORY OF RESEARCH ON PSYCHOSOCIAL ASPECTS OF OCCUPATIONAL STRESS

It was not until the second half of the twentieth century that psychosocial aspects of occupational stress became a subject of empirical research. The classic work *The American Soldier* (Stouffer, Suchman, De Vinney, Star, & Williams, 1949) is considered a forerunner of this type of research. This extensive study carried out in the US army in World War II showed, among others, that feelings of threat may lead to psychosomatic complaints and reduced motivation, and that stress can to some extent be prevented by certain organizational interventions, like rotation of military units. Pioneer work from an entirely different angle was a training programme concerned with the psychological aspects of occupational health that was started at the University of Cincinnati in 1948 (Goodell et al., 1986).

However, the major impetus for research on occupational stress was provided at the end of the 1950s by an extensive research programme at the Institute for Social Research of the University of Michigan (French & Kahn, 1962). The originators of this programme had been strongly influenced by Kurt Lewin, the "father" of modern social psychology. The concept of subjective social environment—the organization as it is consciously or unconsciously perceived by the individual—which was central to this programme, was a direct derivative of Lewin's concept of *psychological life space*. The influential book *Organizational stress: Studies in role conflict and ambiguity* by Kahn, Wolfe, Quinn, Snoek and Rosenthal, which was published as part of this research programme in 1964, illuminated how all kinds of problems connected with the employee's *role* may lead to stress. The concepts that were introduced in this book, particularly role ambiguity and role conflicts, have had a profound influence on occupational stress research.

Several other, more or less isolated, developments in that period were relevant to research in this field. For instance, Kornhauser (1965) carried out his classic investigation into the mental health of assembly line workers in a car factory which showed that feelings of helplessness, powerlessness, withdrawal and pessimism were widespread and that there was a spill-over of such feelings to the workers' life outside work. Whereas Kahn et al. (1964) and Kornhauser (1965) were only concerned with mental health, French and Kaplan (1970) and several others linked occupational stress with cardiovascular disease in the early 1970s. In the late sixties, Frankenhaeuser and her colleagues (1971) started an extensive research programme into the relationship between psychological aspects of the work situation and physiological processes. Even earlier, in the mid-1950s, the cardiologists Friedman and Rosen-

man were already working on their research on Type A behaviour, a behaviour pattern characterized by e.g. a high degree of work involvement that was found to be accompanied by an increased risk of cardiovascular disease (Friedman & Rosenman, 1974). This variable has later frequently been included in research on occupational stress.

In the early 1980s, the scientific attention devoted to occupational stress increased sharply. This is apparent from *Psychological Abstracts*: during the 1970s less than 50 scientific articles appeared each year coded as dealing with occupational stress. But from 1981 onward the number of articles on this subject grew rapidly, to almost 200 in 1984. Since that time, the number of articles has stabilized around 200 a year. Not only researchers showed a growing interest in occupational stress in the 1980s, but governments and international organizations became aware of the importance of the subject as well. For example, the European Community set up a research programme entitled *Breakdown in Human Adaptation to Stress*. Since that time, occupational stress research has received regular attention from international organizations. For instance, in 1991 a joint meeting on a healthier work environment, in which many leading scholars in the area participated, was organized by the World Health Organization, the European Community, the International Labour Office, and the US National Institute for Occupational Safety and Health (World Health Organization, 1991).

WHAT IS STRESS?

It is virtually impossible to write about stress without observing that there is little agreement as to how "stress" should be defined (cf. Kahn & Byosiere, 1992), and that there is no general theory of stress (Schabracq, Cooper, & Winnubst, 1996). Van Dijkhuizen (1980), for instance, found more than 40 definitions of the concept of stress in the literature, all of them at least slightly different. One of the main reasons for this lack of agreement lies in the large number of disciplines involved in stress research, such as biology, psychology, sociology, and epidemiology. The lack of consensus on what exactly constitutes stress is also apparent from the wide variety of phenomena that are examined and lumped together as stress research. Under the heading of occupational stress research alone, many different stress reactions have been studied, e.g., physiological changes, work dissatisfaction, anxiety, sexual problems, authoritarian behaviour, strikes, smoking, absenteeism, illness, alcoholism, neuroticism, violence and accidents (Holt, 1982). For this reason, several authors consider it impossible or pointless to define stress and hold the view that the concept of stress is no more than a somewhat vague, general term denoting a certain field of research. For example, in an early review article on occupational stress, Holt (1982) even went as far as to refuse to define stress any more precisely than terming it the "dark side of work" (p. 421).

However, despite disagreement about its exact definition, most researchers seem to agree that the term stress is used in three quite different ways (e.g., Cooper & Payne, 1988; Crandall & Perrewé, 1995; Elliott & Eisendorfer, 1982; Kahn & Byosiere, 1992; Kasl, 1987; Lazarus, 1993; Semmer, 1996).

The stimulus approach

In some theories stress is primarily viewed as a *stimulus*, as an external load or demand, in other words, as an event or situation that affects the individual and is potentially harmful. This use of the term can be found at least as early as the fourteenth century (Lazarus, 1993). Kahn (1985) and Kahn and Byosiere (1992) observed that this view of stress closely resembles stress as it is defined in science and engineering: any force or pressure exerted upon an object. Similarly, according to Kahn, the term stress refers to the external forces or conditions that are supposed to have, or have been shown to have, possible negative effects on the organism. Later, Kasl (1987) drew a distinction between *objective* and *subjective* stimuli. The former are especially relevant to occupational epidemiology and refer to objective environmental conditions, while the latter can be defined as subjective perceptions or appraisals of objective environmental conditions. With this distinction, Kasl moved close to the

mediational definition of stress that we will discuss below. In general, a potentially stressful event or situation is not referred to as a stress, but as a stressor.

The response approach

In many theories and definitions, stress is regarded as a psychological or physiological response of the organism to some kind of external threat. Selye's (1978) theory is undoubtedly the best-known example of this approach. According to Selye, stress may be caused by a variety of factors, and is a non-specific reaction of the organism to an external threat. The organism tries to defend itself from the threat by means of a complex of physiological reactions, which Selye called the General Adaptation Syndrome (GAS). This syndrome consists of three stages. The first stage is the *alarm reaction*, in which the organism mobilizes itself by means of physiological and hormonal changes to protect itself against the threat. If the stressor lasts longer and there is a possibility that it can be counteracted, the *resistance stage* begins. This is the period of optimum adaptation, and the organism has activated the most appropriate systems for overcoming the specific threat posed by the stressor. After protracted, continual exposure to the same stressor, the adaptation energy of the system with which the stressor is dealt with becomes depleted, and the final stage, *exhaustion*, is reached. The more often this GAS is activated, the more negative consequences for the individual are to be expected in terms of fatigue, illness and ageing (Ivancevich & Matteson, 1980). However, the idea that the same general response pattern is triggered by different stressful events has proved untenable. Different types of physiological and hormonal reactions may occur, depending on the nature and interpretation of the stimulus and on the emotion that is experienced (e.g., Hamberger & Lohr, 1984; Lazarus, 1993).

The mediational approach

Finally, there are mediational conceptualizations of stress (Lazarus, 1985, 1993; 1995), which focus on the cognitive, evaluative and motivational processes that intervene between the stressor and the reaction. Central to this mediational approach of stress is that potentially stressful stimuli may lead to different emotional responses in different individuals, depending on their cognitive appraisals of the situation and their resources. In his early work, Lazarus (1968) found such individual differences in the response to stressors, and demonstrated that the cognitive interpretation of a stressful situation can be experimentally influenced. An important advantage of the mediational perspective is that the psychological processes which mediate the effects of stressors on well-being are highlighted, which may stimulate refined theoretical views on the stress process than solely focusing on the nature of stressors or stress reactions. However, the other side of the coin is that most studies that employ such a perspective rely only on self-reports for both the stressful events and the reactions to these events. This means that the occurrence of an event, its perception, and the emotional reaction to it are often not clearly distinguishable, which makes it very difficult to draw conclusions about the causal order in the association between situational factors and individual reactions. Nevertheless, several current definitions on occupational stress take such a mediational perspective, and view stress as caused by demanding work situations that are difficult to control for the people involved (cf. Karasek & Theorell, 1990; Landsbergis et al., 1993).

Two general stress models that employ a mediational perspective are Lazarus and Folkman's (1984) highly influential cognitive model on stress and coping, and Hobfoll's (1989) Conservation of Resources Model. According to Lazarus and Folkman (1984), psychological stress is "a relationship between the person and the environment that is appraised by the person as taxing or exceeding his or her resources and endangering his or her well-being" (p. 21). Lazarus and Folkman distinguished three types of cognitive appraisal: primary appraisal, secondary appraisal, and reappraisal. Primary appraisal refers to the judgement of whether a situation is irrelevant, benign, or stressful, and whether a stressful situation is perceived as threatening (a potential loss), as harmful (an actual loss), or as challenging (a potential gain). Secondary appraisal refers to the perception of opportunities for action, and coping with a stressful situation. Reappraisal refers to changes in appraisal, based on new

information from the environment, or based on cognitive coping processes, in which, for example, a threatening experience is reappraised as a challenge.

Hobfoll's (1989) Conservation of Resources Model is in many respects quite similar to Lazarus's model. Hobfoll (1989) stated that "People strive to retain, protect, and build resources and that what is threatening to them is the potential or actual loss of these valued resources" (p. 516). Hobfoll distinguished several kinds of resources, including objects (e.g., owning a house), personal characteristics (e.g., being high in self-esteem), conditions (e.g., being employed), and energies (e.g., time or money). A situation is regarded as stressful when a potential loss or an actual loss of resources is experienced, or when an anticipated gain in resources following an investment (of resources) is not realized. In contrast to Lazarus and Folkman's model, Hobfoll states that these threats and actual losses should not be assessed in a purely subjective way, but that these appraisals should be validated using objective and shared social standards of what constitutes a loss. This means that stressors and stress reactions may be better distinguishable in the Conservation of Resources Model than in most other mediational perspectives, which is an important advantage of this model. Moreover, the Conservation of Resources Model makes predictions about human behaviour not only in times of high stress, when the prevention of a loss of resources is pursued, but also in times of low stress, when people strive for gains and accumulation of resources.

OCCUPATIONAL STRESS AS AN EMOTIONAL PROCESS

Following the perspective of Lazarus (1993; Lazarus & Folkman, 1985), we would like to suggest that the confusion about the definition of stress can to a large extent be avoided by taking the view that, in general, psychosocial stress refers primarily to the occurrence of negative emotions that are evoked by demanding situations. Indeed, although a large variety of stress reactions can be distinguished, an increasing number of authors argue that negative emotions constitute a major feature of stress (cf. Gaillard & Wientjes, 1994). For example, Pekrun and Frese (1992) suggested that stressors at work may produce a variety of negative emotions, including anger and disappointment, and that such emotions should be regarded as the crucial dependent variables in the stress process. Warr (1987) conceptualized mental health at work primarily in terms of various affective states, i.e., anxiety, depression, and discontent. There is general agreement that negative emotions are usually elicited by the evaluation that an event is a threat to, or blocks the attainment of important needs and goals (Oatley & Jenkins, 1992). According to Spielberger (1985), stress always involves a situation or stimulus that is perceived as potentially harmful, dangerous or frustrating. Such a perception causes a certain emotional reaction in which either *anxiety* (varying from tension, nervousness and apprehension to fear and panic) or *anger* (varying from irritation to anger and rage) is central. Negative emotions are often accompanied by physiological changes like increased heart rate and blood pressure, increased secretion of certain hormones, and rapid breathing—which are often refered to as stress symptoms. There is evidence that different emotions—in particular anger, fear and depression—involve different neuro-endocrinological responses (Zillmann & Zillmann, 1996).

There are many different kinds of negative emotions that may be experienced in the context of occupational stress (see e.g., Lazarus, 1993). Although a complete typology of these conditions is beyond the scope of this chapter, we mention the most important negative emotional experiences in the occupational context:

1. *Anxiety* and *apprehension* may be evoked by threatening or ambiguous situations. Examples of such situations are ambiguous expectations on the part of others, the threat of a potential dismissal, an impending evaluation, a promotion that is questioned.
2. *Anger*, *irritation*, and *resentment* may result from frustrating situations, like work that has been done in vain, being interfered with, or failure to reach a goal.
3. *Depression*, *disappointment*, and *grief* characterize situations of loss or depri-

vation, such as a promotion that is cancelled, the loss of interesting work or control, or actual dismissal.

4. *Envy* and *jealousy* are found primarily in situations characterized by an unfavourable social comparison, for example observing similar others who have obtained a promotion that one wanted oneself, or who are perceived as being more competent in their work.
5. Feelings of *shame* and *embarrassment* are found in situations in which moral imperatives are violated or goals are not accomplished due to one's own faults or behaviours, for example displaying rudeness to someone due to an inability to control oneself.

Although anxiety is often considered to be the most typical emotion associated with stress (cf. Hamberger & Lohr, 1984), there are indications that other emotions mentioned here may occur at least as frequently in the face of occupational stress (cf. Warr, 1987). For instance, in a study among young engineers, Keenan and Newton (1985) found that respondents seldomly reported anxiety, but much more frequently reported anger and irritation, accompanied by feelings of frustration.

Although a variety of negative emotions that can be distinguished on an experiential and a physiological level, at the same time it is true that emotions can be quite malleable and plastic (Zillmann & Zillmann, 1996). People may not always be able to distinguish emotions from each other, and various emotions may merge into each other. Moreover, there may be a large gap between people's conscious awareness of their emotions, and physiological and behavioural indications of these emotions (Oatley & Jenkins, 1992, Thoits, 1984). Stress is often accompanied by nonspecific tensions and ambiguous physical sensations, which may be labelled in different ways, and such labels may change under the influence of cognitive processes and social influence (Buunk, 1994). Indeed, Schachter and Singer (1962) showed in their classical experiment that subjects who are in a state of unexplained arousal as a result of an epinephrine injection are readily influenced by the angry or euphoric behaviours of a stooge, and assimilate such emotions. In a similar vein, there is evidence that particularly when individuals are under stress, they may copy certain health complaints from others, sometimes even without communication (Hatfield, Cacioppo, & Rapson, 1994; Skelton & Pennebaker, 1982; Sullins, 1991). Moreover, even when the individual is aware of the nature of the emotions he or she experiences, these emotions may transform into one another when a different interpretation of the situation arises. For instance, through communication with colleagues individuals may attribute their stress symptoms to organizational factors and may replace their anxiety by anger (Geurts, Buunk, & Schaufeli, 1994a).

Most individuals experience negative emotions from time to time, and when such emotions are coped with adequately, they often will have no long-term negative consequences for mental and physical health. However, health damage is likely to occur when a person experiences prolonged, intense emotions that he considers undesirable, and when he is unable to remove or avoid the cause of these emotions or to reduce the negative feelings themselves. Indirect support for these assumptions was provided by, for instance, Van Dijkhuizen's (1980) in-depth study, which showed that the relationship between stressors and health were *mediated* by negative emotions. There was no direct effect of stressors at work on psychosomatic complaints and physiological variables, but only an indirect effect through negative feelings. Similarly, Barling and MacIntyre (1993) showed that the effects of role stressors on daily variations in emotional exhaustion among military instructors were largely mediated by negative mood. In the light of these findings it is hardly surprising that many surveys have found only weak associations between the presence of certain psychosocial stressors and health complaints, because stressful situations first lead to negative emotions, and only in the long run, and under certain conditions, to impaired health.

MODELS OF OCCUPATIONAL STRESS

Many different models focusing on occupational stress have been presented in the literature,

especially with respect to occupational burnout (see Schaufeli, Maslach, & Marek, 1993 for an overview). We will confine ourselves here to the most well-known general occupational stress models, i.e., the Social Environment Model (Kahn et al., 1964; Kahn, 1981), the closely related Person-Environment Fit Model (French, 1973; French, Caplan & Harrison, 1982), the Demand-Control-Support Model (Johnson & Hall, 1988; Karasek & Theorell, 1990), and finally the Vitamin Model (Warr, 1987, 1994).

Social Environment Model

The Social Environment Model, which was developed at the Institute for Social Research of the University of Michigan (hence it is sometimes designated as the "ISR Model" or "Michigan Model"), is the best-known occupational stress model. As noted before, this institute has played an important, stimulating role with regard to research on organizational stress (French & Kahn, 1962; Kahn et al., 1964; Kahn, 1981). Since the model was first devised, several different versions of it have been developed (Van Dijkhuizen, 1980; Kahn & Byosiere, 1992). We describe only the most general model here (e.g., Kahn, 1981; Winnubst, De Jong, & Schabracq, 1996). The Social Environment Model is basically a combination of a number of conceptual categories (i.e., types of variables) rather than a coherent theory, although some attempts have been made to define these categories more precisely and to determine their interrelations. The following conceptual categories are identified within this model:

1. *Objective environment.* The objective environment refers to organizational characteristics such as company size, hierarchical structure and job description. This environment is independent of the worker's perceptions of it.
2. *Subjective environment.* The subjective environment, on the other hand, is part of a worker's perceptions, and is also called the "psychological environment" (Lewin, 1951). It contains phenomena such as role conflict, role ambiguity, lack of participation and role overload. These are called "stressors", and may lead to:

3. *Stress reactions or strains*. Strains are affective, physiological, and behavioural responses of the individual, such as job dissatisfaction, high blood pressure or high heart rate, and smoking. Long-term stress reactions may include absenteeism, turnover, and early retirement from the job.

4. *Illness*. Illness refers to both mental and physical illness, including, for example, burnout, depression, cardiovascular disease and gastric ulcers. These illnesses may result from persistent stress reactions.

5. *The person*. The conception of the person includes all more or less enduring genetic, demographic or personality characteristics of the person (like Type A behaviour and rigidity) which serve as conditioning or moderating variables on stressor-strain relationships.

6. *Social support*. Social support refers to interpersonal relationships either at work (supervisor, colleagues) or at home (partner, family). Two kinds of support are particularly important in the model: (1) tangible support, and (2) emotional support. Social support is conceived as a relatively enduring variable that moderates stressor-strain relationships.

Although the Social Environment Model can be adequately operationalized (see Winnubst et al., 1996), and has stimulated a lot of research, several criticisms of the model still remain. First, it is not based on a clear theoretical perspective that leads to specific hypotheses. This means that most studies using this model examine large amounts of potentially relevant variables, which generally leads to some statistically significant, but not necessarily theoretically meaningful, relationships among these variables. This makes it hard to empirically evaluate the model. Second, all kinds of stress reactions are lumped together, whereas some of these reactions may occur immediately in a stressful situation (e.g., anxiety), others may only occur after extensive exposure to stress (e.g., high blood pressure), whereas again others may not necessarily be due to stress (e.g., turnover). Third, the model tells us little about mediating processes between different elements in the model, and it ignores various social psychological

processes that may play a role, such as social comparison of one's situation with that of colleagues (e.g., Buunk & Ybema, 1997), and cognitive interpretations of stressful events and health complaints (e.g., Peeters, Schaufeli, & Buunk, 1995a).

Person-Environment Fit Model

The theory underlying the Person-Environment Fit Model is also an example of a mediational perspective on stress. The model is based on the view that behaviour is a function of both the person and the environment (Lewin, 1935, 1951; Murray, 1938, 1959). Following Lewin, French (1973) suggested that the interaction between environmental variables and relevant characteristics of the person determines whether stress occurs. According to the P-E Fit Model, occupational stress is the result of a discrepancy ("misfit") between what the individual desires, and what the job supplies, or between the abilities of the individual and the demands in the work environment. The P-E Fit Model makes a distinction between subjective and objective misfit. The first type of misfit refers to a discrepancy between the people's view of themselves and their view of the environment (referred to as the subjective person and the subjective environment). For instance, workers may feel that they lack the abilities that they perceive the work situation demands, or they may have desires, for instance for career advancement, that cannot be realized. The second type of misfit concerns the discrepancy between how the person actually is and the objective characteristics of the work environment (referred to as the objective person and the objective environment). For instance, there may be a discrepancy between the required level of typing speed and the actual typing speed of a secretary. The correspondence between the objective person and the subjective person is labelled "accuracy of self-assessment", while the correspondence between the objective and subjective environment is labelled "contact with reality". According to the model, *defence mechanisms* are supposed to reduce the subjective misfit without any changes in objective misfit, for instance by denial. In contrast, *coping* refers in this model to strategies that may reduce objective misfit (cf.

Caplan, 1983; French et al., 1982), for instance, by learning new skills or by securing a lower workload.

An important assumption in the P-E Fit Model is that both a positive misfit (e.g., one has more capabilities than are required, or one wants less than is provided) and a negative misfit (e.g., one has less capabilities than are required, or one wants more than is provided) lead to stress. Thus, a curvilinear, U-shaped relationship between fit and strains is assumed. In a number of studies such relationships as proposed by the model have indeed been found (for a review, see Edwards, 1991). For example, in the pioneering study by Caplan, Cobb, French, Van Harrison, and Pinneau (1975) among over 2,000 workers a U-shaped relationship was found between the discrepancy of actual and desired complexity of work on the one hand and level of depression on the other. Both too little and too much complexity were related to depression. More recently, Edwards and Van Harrison (1993) found additional evidence that a perfect fit between what an employee desires and obtains is related to the lowest level of strains.

In spite of the plausible assumptions underlying the model, several problems must be mentioned. To begin with, various aspects of the model have hardly been tested empirically. In particular, defence and coping mechanisms are seldom measured, and therefore there is little evidence for such mechanisms. In addition, usually only the subjective person and environment, and not the objective person and environment, are assessed (Cox & Ferguson, 1994). Furthermore, the fit between person and environment characteristics often does not have unique effects on strains compared to the effects of person and environment characteristics assessed independently (Caplan, 1983; Semmer, 1996). Finally, the P-E Fit Model does not specify where the standards—i.e. desires and aspirations—come from. Such standards may also be adapted to reality, such that they are made consistent with the opportunities and restrictions that are found in the actual work setting. In that case, the causation may even be the other way round: People who are psychologically healthy have realistic aspirations, which leads to a good P-E Fit, whereas unadapted workers have unreal-

istically high or low standards, leading to a misfit between person and environment.

Demand-Control-Support Model

Karasek and his team originally developed a model known as the Job Demand-Control (JD-C) Model, but extended this model later to the Demand-Control-Support Model. In order to understand the basic ideas of both models, we will first discuss the Job Demand-Control Model. This model, which was first mentioned in a widely cited article by Karasek (1979), can be considered a synthesis of two well-known lines of research, viz. the job redesign tradition (e.g., Hackman & Oldham, 1980) and the Michigan stress tradition which is apparent in the Social Environment Model and the Person-Environment Fit Model (e.g., Caplan, et al., 1975; Kahn, 1981). The aim of the JD-C Model was to provide a theoretical framework for the development of guidelines for the enhancement of the quality of working life. In addition to emphasizing the necessity of reducing work-related strains, the model also emphasizes the importance of promoting work motivation, learning and growth. Therefore, the model includes as outcome variables not only the consequences of stress such as exhaustion, psychosomatic complaints, and cardiovascular disease, but also work motivation, learning and job satisfaction. In this way, the model reconciles the stress tradition with the insights of social learning theory and adult education theory (Landsbergis, 1988).

The JD-C Model postulates that the primary sources of stress lie within two basic characteristics of the job (Baker, 1985). The JD-C Model emphasizes the need to categorize these job characteristics as either *demands* or *control*, and does not simply list all job features as potential stressors (Schnall, Landsbergis, & Baker, 1994). In line with the mediational definition of stress, psychological strains are viewed as a consequence of the joint effects of the demands of a job and the range of job control available to the employee (Karasek, 1979). Accordingly, four different kinds of psychosocial work situations may result from four combinations between high and low levels of psychological job demands and job control. Karasek (1979) uses the following terms for the four kinds of work situations: (1) high strain jobs: (2)

active jobs; (3) low strain jobs; and (4) passive jobs.

The first major prediction of the JD-C Model is that the strongest aversive job-related strain reactions (e.g., exhaustion, anxiety and health complaints) will occur when job demands are high and worker's control is low (i.e., high strain jobs). High job demands produce a state of arousal which is normally accompanied by increased heart rate and adrenalin secretion. If there is also an environmentally based constraint, i.e., low control, the arousal cannot be converted into an effective coping response. Such conditions produce a more extensive reaction for a longer period, a so-called damaging, unused residual strain. The opposite situation is termed "low strain jobs", that is, jobs in which workers' control is high and job demands are low. In this situation the model predicts lower than average levels of residual strain. The second prediction of the model, which is sometimes overlooked, is that motivation, learning and personal growth will occur in situations where both job demands and workers' control are high (i.e., active jobs). The opposite of this situation is formed by passive jobs, in which skills and abilities may atrophy, a situation which resembles the "learned helplessness" phenomenon (cf. Abramson, Seligman, & Teasdale, 1978; Lennerlöf, 1988).

The expansion of the model by including social support came from the realization that job control is not the only resource available for coping with job demands (cf. Johnson & Hall, 1988; Johnson, 1989), but that *workplace social support* may also function as a moderator of job demands (Johnson, 1989). Therefore, Johnson and Hall (1988) redefined the JD-C Model by adding workplace social support. Karasek and Theorell (1990) defined workplace social support as overall levels of helpful social interaction available on the job. In the extended model, called the Demand-Control-Support Model (DCS Model), eight instead of four kinds of work situations were modelled, i.e., the four types of work situations in the JD-C Model in combination with either low or high social support. Thus, the DCS Model describes the joint, interactive, effects of the three basic characteristics of the work organization, viz. job demands, job control and workplace social support.

A large number of studies evaluating the two models failed to provide clear and unambiguous support (Jones & Fletcher, 1996). Most studies did not find the postulated interaction effects (e.g., Carayon, 1993). A number of reasons for this have been presented in the literature. First, a large number of studies was based on secondary analyses of already collected data, in which the variables often were not operationalized adequately. Second, the measures of job control usually included not only items reflecting control about various workplace conditions, but also items reflecting skill utilization and job complexity (Ganster & Fusilier, 1989). Indeed, Wall, Jackson, Mullarkey, and Parker (1996) showed that when job control was measured specifically, the hypothesized interaction was found, whereas the interaction was not found when the much broader definition of job decision latitude, including variables like skill use and task variety, was used. Third, the interaction effects between job control and job demands have been tested in at least four different ways, not all of which were appropriate (cf. Landsbergis, Schnall, Warren, Pickering, & Schwartz, 1994). Fourth, in some studies it is not clear to what extent the variables in the model are confounded with other variables (such as socioeconomic status and health behaviour). Fifth, the models were confirmed by studies using large and heterogeneous samples, while studies based on small and homogeneous samples could not confirm the predicted interaction effects. This might be due to the lack of variance in the latter samples. Finally, many studies have failed to take into account individual differences (such as locus of control, or Type A/B behaviour), emotional responses and coping strategies.

Vitamin Model

This model, that is very similar to the P-E Fit Model, was developed by Warr (1987). The central idea underlying the Vitamin Model (VM) is that mental health is affected by job characteristics in a way that is analogous to the effects that vitamins have on physical health. Generally, vitamin intake initially improves health and physical functioning, but beyond a particular intake level no further improvement is observed. Continued intake of vitamins may have two different kinds of effects. First, a so-called constant effect may occur: health does not improve any further, nor is the individual's physical health impaired. Second, an excessive intake of vitamins may lead to a toxic concentration in the body ("hypervitaminosis"), which causes poor bodily functioning and ill health. In this case, observed associations between vitamin intake and health are expected to be inversely U-shaped.

Because, according to Warr (1987), certain job characteristics may affect mental health in the same way as vitamins affect physical health, De Jonge and Schaufeli (in press) refer to these characteristics as "psychological work vitamins". Generally, the absence of certain job characteristics will impair mental health, and initially the presence of such characteristics will have a beneficial effect on employee mental health. However, beyond a certain required level, a plateau has been reached and the level of mental health remains constant. Further increase of job characteristics may either produce a constant effect or may be harmful and impair mental health. According to Warr (1987, 1994) the type of effect depends upon the particular job characteristic under consideration. After a thorough examination of the literature, Warr identified nine job features that act as "vitamins", i.e., as potential determinants of job-related mental health. Warr assumes that six of these features (i.e., job demands, job autonomy, social support, skill utilization, skill variety, and task feedback) have curvilinear effects. The lack of such features as well as an excess of such features will affect mental health negatively. The remaining three job characteristics (i.e., safety, salary, and task significance) are supposed to follow a linear pattern: the more such a characteristic is present in the work situation, the higher the level of mental health will be.

In the VM, a more specific conceptualization of affective well-being is proposed than in most other models of occupational stress. This model, therefore, comes closest to our earlier presented view of occupational stress as an emotional process. According to Warr (1987), affective well-being as an indicator of *job-related* mental health has three dimensions: (1) discontented-contented; (2) anxious-comfortable; and (3) depressed-actively

pleased. In occupational settings, the first component has usually been operationalized through measures of job satisfaction, but measures of job attachment and organizational commitment have been used as well. The second component is usually tapped through measures of job-related anxiety, job-related tension, and job-related strain. Finally, the third component has been assessed by measures of, for example, occupational burnout, job-related depression, job boredom, and fatigue.

Although the VM focuses on characteristics of the work environment rather than on the experience of the worker, individual characteristics are viewed as possible moderators of the effects of job characteristics on mental health. That is, such effects are supposed to occur more for some than for other people. Warr (1994) mentions three categories of individual characteristics: (1) *abilities*, i.e., all kinds of personal skills that can be viewed as relatively stable characteristics (e.g., intellectual and psychomotor skills); (2) *values*, i.e., all sorts of specific value orientations, such as preferences, motives and attitudes; and (3) *baseline mental health*, i.e., dispositions such as negative affectivity. Moderating effects of such characteristics are expected especially in the case of a so-called "matching" individual characteristic (Warr, 1994). Individual characteristics that match particular job characteristics will cause a stronger moderating effect than those which lack this matching property. Job autonomy may serve as an example: a matching individual characteristic might be "need for autonomy". It is assumed that the need for autonomy is a moderator for the relationship between job autonomy and, for instance, job satisfaction (cf. Warr, 1987).

In a thorough summary of the empirical evidence with respect to several aspects of the VM, Warr (1987, 1994) showed that *in isolation* his nine job characteristics act as predicted by the model. In recent years, however, a number of cross-sectional studies have investigated the patterns proposed by the VM (e.g., Fletcher & Jones, 1993; De Jonge & Schaufeli, in press; Parkes, 1991; Warr, 1990; Xie & Johns, 1995). Taken together, the results of these studies are mixed and inconclusive. Job demands and job autonomy, for instance, seem to be curvilinearly related to some aspects of employee mental health in the way that is predicted by the model, whereas the effect of workplace social support does not follow the model. Most importantly, however, all studies failed to take account of the ways in which possible combinations of the nine job characteristics affect job-related well-being.

METHODOLOGICAL PROBLEMS IN OCCUPATIONAL STRESS RESEARCH

Almost 20 years ago Kasl (1978) wrote a critical review in which he called many occupational stress studies trivial and expressed fundamental criticism of most research in this field. The field seems to have made little progress, considering similar critical comments on occupational stress research that have appeared in more recent articles (Kasl, 1986, 1987, 1989, 1996). In general, the following methodological problems with much research and many models in this field can be noted.

1. The mediational definition of stress often acts as a self-serving methodological trap, in which the measurement of the independent variable (such as perceived role ambiguity) and the dependent variables (such as feelings of insecurity) are sometimes so close that they appear to be two measures of the same construct. Several authors have argued for independent assessment of stressors and strains, using a multi-method approach, in which objective measures, peer ratings, and subjective measures are paired (cf. Cox & Ferguson, 1994; Frese & Zapf, 1988; Kasl, 1986; Semmer, Zapf, & Greif, 1996; Spector, 1992).

2. Strains may in some cases wrongly be attributed to the work situation. The influence of the work situation on strains and illness is often overestimated, not only in comparison to the home situation (Robinson & Inkson, 1994), but also relative to the influence of stable personality characteristics. The assumption in much occupational stress research is that negative emotions and psychosomatic complaints, such as dizzi-

ness, loss of appetite, palpitations, sleeplessness, loneliness and dissatisfaction, are *caused* by stressful working conditions. However, similar reactions are included in personality measures of neuroticism, and may simply reflect a stable personality disposition. Indeed, various authors have argued that many symptoms that are usually considered as strains, basically reflect the negative affectivity characteristic of neurotic individuals, and that neurotic individuals also tend to perceive more stressors in their work environment (e.g., Payne & Jones, 1987; Spector & O'Connell, 1994). This could mean that associations between stressors and strains merely reflect this personality dimension (e.g., Burke, Brief, & George, 1993). Although well-designed research (Semmer, 1996) shows that substantial associations between stressors and strains may remain even when negative affectivity is controlled for, these associations do become weaker. Therefore, it is important to control for neuroticism when examining such associations (Parkes, 1994).

3. Because most studies on occupational stress have cross-sectional designs, the causal direction of the relationships can rarely be established. It is generally assumed that the causal flow is unidirectional from stressors and social support to strains. However, not only do stressors and support affect strains, but strains can also affect people's perceptions of stressors and of social support. For example, in a longitudinal study, Marcelissen, Winnubst, Buunk, and De Wolff (1988) found that the existence of strains had a deteriorating effect on perceived support from co-workers, and a few studies have demonstrated that simultaneous reciprocal causation between stressors and strains does occur (e.g., James & Jones, 1980; James & Tetrick, 1986; De Jonge, 1995; Kohn & Schooler, 1983). Nevertheless, most evidence seems to suggest that strains tend to occur *after* stressor perceptions, rather than vice versa (De Jonge, 1995; Warr, 1987).

4. Related to the previous points, in most stress research, stressors, strains, and moderating variables such as social support are assessed *between* subjects, and these variables are usually measured through global assessments of how the respondents experience their work situation in general. We learn, for example, how many somatic complaints are experienced by people who perceive a high degree of overload in their work situation. Relatively little attention has been paid to the effects of stressful *events* at work on changes in strains on a day-to-day basis. Indeed, it is important to examine such *within* subjects' effects, and to assess events and strains at work in a much more detailed way. Buunk and Verhoeven (1991) developed a method referred to as the Daily Interaction Record in Organizations (DIRO) with which, over the course of a week, daily the number and nature of stressful events, the number and features of all social interactions, and the degree of negative affect at the end of the day are assessed. A number of studies has shown the viability of such an approach (for a review, see Buunk & Peeters, 1994).

5. By analogy to Warr's ideas (1987, 1994) there may be non-linear relationships between stressors and strains. Van Dijkhuizen (1980), for instance, found that only 32% of all causal connections examined in his study were really linear. In addition, De Jonge and Schaufeli (in press) found several curvilinear, U-shaped, relationships between job characteristics and psychological outcomes. For instance, most anxiety was found in people who experienced either low or high job demands. Nevertheless, most studies test only the linear associations between stressors and strains.

6. Differences in stress, mortality or morbidity between occupational groups are not necessarily caused by the nature of the work, but may also be due to, for instance, self-selection in occupations and positions, selection by organizations, the fact that unhealthy workers leave certain occupations earlier ("healthy worker effect"), or differences in living conditions and health behaviour.

7. In general, criterion variables are measured and analysed as if they were continuous variables, while this is not always the case. Brown (1985) points out that correlational analyses with psychological disorders like depression are inadequate. According to Brown this is rather a dichotomous variable; a person either is, or is not clinically depressed. In a similar vein, it may be the case that, for example, individuals are either experiencing burnout as a disorder or not, rather than experiencing burnout to a certain degree.

ASPECTS OF OCCUPATIONAL STRESS

Guided by the models outlined above, and cautioning against the methodological limitations of many occupational stress studies, we will now examine a number of categories of psychological variables and processes that are involved in occupational stress, and how these variables are related to the emotional stress process.

1. *Stressors.* We focus in particular on the psychosocial causes of negative emotions at work, such as role ambiguity and low status.

2. *Coping behaviour.* Coping refers to the way in which individuals try to change, reinterpret or reduce the negative emotions, either directly or through modifying the causes of these emotions, e.g., through instrumental action and cognitive effort.

3. *Moderator variables.* Some characteristics may moderate the effects of stressors on the experience of negative emotions and health. The most notable of these are personality traits and social support.

4. *Long-term stress reactions.* In the long run, occupational stress may have several adverse health consequences, such as burnout, depression, psychosomatic complaints, and impairment of physical health.

Stressors

Hamberger and Lohr (1984) have pointed out that there are many different definitions of stressors: stimuli that are unpleasant, stimuli that lead to a stress reaction, stimuli that result in a strong attempt to adapt, every problem that a person needs to solve, and every situation that requires a major adaptation. In accordance with the view of stress as an emotion, we consider here as a stressor every event, situation or cognition that may evoke a negative emotion in an individual. A first implication of this definition is that every stressor is only a stressor in a *probabilistic* sense, as Lazarus (1985) emphasizes. There are few events or situations that will lead to negative emotions in everybody under all conditions. A second implication is that the nature of stressors may strongly vary: they may be day-to-day worries, major events, but also prolonged problematic work situations (Bailey & Bhagat, 1987). A third implication is that stressors may also be certain ideas, thoughts and perceptions that evoke negative emotions. A typical example of such stressors is formed by mid-career problems, such as the idea that one may not reach the position that one aspires to, or the idea of almost belonging to the older generation in the organization (Buunk & Janssen, 1992).

This reasoning suggests that many occupations have their own characteristic stressors. This may be illustrated by a few examples. Female managers may experience typical stressors such as sexual harassment, sex discrimination, and a denial of access to challenging assignments (Burke, 1996). Keenan and Newton (1985) asked engineers which stressful incidents they had experienced. The most frequent experience was the situation that one's time or efforts were wasted, immediately followed by interpersonal conflicts and qualitative underload (having to do work that is too simple). For nurses stressful incidents are obviously of an entirely different nature. Bailey (1980) developed seven categories of work aspects that function as potential stressors for nurses, including interpersonal relationships, physical work environment and patient care. Bus drivers have been found to experience characteristic stressors as well, including irregular work-schedules, traffic pressures, responsibility for

passengers, and stressful contacts with passengers (Kompier, 1996). Among police officers typical stressors include upsetting situations such as traffic incidents and problematic and frustrating interactions with the public (Buunk & Verhoeven, 1991).

It is, of course, impossible to give an overview of all potential stressors within the scope of this chapter. It is also not possible to present a theory-based, all-embracing categorization of stressors. Most categorizations of stressors in the work situation are descriptive and pragmatic (e.g., Burke, 1988; Cooper & Marshall, 1978; Fletcher, 1991; Ivancevich & Matteson, 1980). We will therefore confine ourselves to five groups of common psychosocial stressors without claiming to be exhaustive (cf. Fletcher, 1991; Fletcher & Payne, 1980; Karasek, 1979; Karasek & Theorell, 1990; Payne, 1979).

1. *Task and work characteristics*. This refers to stressful aspects inherent in the task and in the work environment, for example high workload, high physical effort, great responsibility, shift work and time pressure. Various studies have shown that such stressors play a major role as contributors to different job strain outcomes, including dissatisfaction, coronary heart disease, high blood pressure, musculoskeletal problems, psychosomatic symptoms, anxiety, exhaustion and depression (for an overview see Bongers, De Winter, Kompier, & Hildebrandt, 1993; Crandall & Perrewé, 1995; Karasek & Theorell, 1990). It must be noted that, unlike the stressors described below, demanding task and work characteristics do not necessarily involve psychosocial stress in terms of negative emotions. Indeed, a high mental load is not by definition stressful (Gaillard & Wientjes, 1994), but negative emotions may result from an overload as well as from an underload, depending on the discrepancy of mental load and the capabilities and aspirations of the individual worker.

2. *Role problems*. Occupational stress can be due to the particular role the individual worker plays within the organization. In an

organization, there are certain, often unspecified expectations about which behaviours are and which behaviours are not acceptable in a certain position. Especially these role expectations may contain major stressors. As noted above, Kahn et al. (1964) have focused in particular on the effects of role conflict and role ambiguity. *Role conflict* occurs when expectations and demands are difficult to meet or are mutually incompatible. Four basic types of role conflicts can be distinguished: (1) the intrasender conflict (different expectations and demands from the same other person); (2) the intersender conflict (different demands from different persons); (3) the interrole conflict (expectations from different roles that are difficult to combine, such as the role of parent and that of employee); and (4) the person-role conflict (a tension between the needs and values of the person and the demands and expectations from the environment). *Role ambiguity* arises when people do not have sufficient or adequate information to fulfil their role properly. Kahn et al. (1964) point out that employees should know which rights, duties and responsibilities belong to a certain position, how the required activities should be carried out and which behaviours will be rewarded or punished. Important areas of role ambiguity are the scope of one's responsibilities, the question whose expectations should be met, and the question how one is appreciated by others.

There is considerable support for the stress-inducing properties of role conflict and ambiguity. In an early review, Van Sell, Brief and Schuler (1981) showed that role conflicts and role ambiguity in different occupations are indeed related to job dissatisfaction and feelings of job-related strain. Recent research has supported this conclusion. For example, in a study among public sector employees, Terry, Neilsen and Perchard (1993) found that, when controlling for neuroticism, role ambiguity and role conflict remain significant predictors of psychological well-being and job satisfaction. Manlove (1994) found that burnout

among child care workers was related to role ambiguity as well as role conflict. In the context of the perspective outlined above, we would expect relationships between particular stressors and particular negative emotions. There is some evidence for this. For instance, Van Dijkhuizen (1980) reported that role conflicts were particularly related to irritation, while role ambiguity showed a stronger relationship with feelings of anxiety. In a similar vein, Keenan and Newton (1984) described that role ambiguity was a better predictor of job dissatisfaction and anxiety than role conflicts were.

3. *Interpersonal conflicts*. Just like other interpersonal relationships, relationships between people at work may also be characterized by all kinds of stressful situations, including open conflict, lack of trust, poor communication, hostility, and competition. According to Van de Vliert (Chapter 15, Volume 3) a situation may be called a conflict when either of the parties feels thwarted or irritated by the other; this is characterized by some kind of subjectively experienced frustration. This means that a conflict need not be acted out openly, but that it is also possible to have a conflict with somebody without the other person being aware of it. Also, a conflict is not necessarily about another person's behaviour. For instance, somebody else's appearance or opinions may lead to interpersonal conflicts. Stokols (1992) argued that *conflict-prone* organizations exist in which the physical arrangements and social conditions predispose the members of the organization towards chronic conflict and health problems. Such organizations are characterized by, among others, an absence of shared goals, rigid ideologies, competitive coalitions, little participation in organizational decision making, an anomalous and turbulent environment, a relatively unstable role structure and membership, an ambiguous allocation of space and territory in the organization, and inadequate environmental resources for meeting organizational goals. Although the stressful consequences of

interpersonal conflicts have not been studied as extensively as those of other stressors, there is evidence that conflicts at work are in general very stressful, and are accompanied by a high level of strains (e.g., Keenan & Newton, 1984; Spector & O'Connell, 1994). For example, in a study among nurses, Tyler and Cushway (1995) found that conflicts with other nurses and medical doctors were negatively related to mental well-being. In two studies, one among police officers and the other among secretaries, Buunk and Peeters (1994) found that, over a period of five days, the number of interpersonal frustrations in the relationship with colleagues and superiors, had a higher correlation with negative affect at the end of the day than any other type of stressful event. Moreover, there is evidence from longitudinal research among bus drivers that conflicts with superiors predict absence frequency as recorded by the company (Geurts, Schaufeli, & Buunk, 1993). Finally, it must be noted that not only conflicts with co-workers and superiors may lead to stress, but also conflicts with the people to whom one's work is directed. For example, in a study among teachers, Sutton (1984) found a high correlation between a lack of job satisfaction and problems in discipline with students, and in a study among correctional officers, Buunk and Peeters (1994) found that disobedience by prisoners was correlated with negative affect.

4. *Status and career problems*. This category includes problems experienced with regard to status, recognition, prospects, and material and symbolic rewards. The low status of a profession may affect employees' well-being negatively, particularly when they feel they are entitled to more. For instance, a study among teachers in Connecticut showed that the low pay and low status of the job were considered to be the main problems (Litt & Turk, 1985). Siegrist and Peter (1994) argued that among blue collar workers, low status control (low expectations of job stability and promotion prospects) impairs self-esteem and the sense of mastery, and subsequently physical health. In line with this reasoning, Siegrist and Peter showed a relatively much higher risk of coronary disease among blue collar workers who experienced, in addition to poor rewards, a low status control. Social comparison plays a central role in matters of status, pay, and promotion, and individuals may experience stress when they perceive that similar others are in such respects better off (Buunk & Ybema, 1997). For example, in a study among blue collar workers, Geurts, Buunk & Schaufeli (1994b) found that the perception that one was in various ways less well off than one's colleagues, was accompanied by feelings of resentment. Especially people who value upward mobility continually evaluate how they are doing compared to others in similar circumstances. In mid-career the experience of career stagnation may be very painful for such people, and *relative deprivation* may occur. This concept is used to refer to the situation that a person has achieved a lot from an objective point of view (e.g., a relatively high income, many possibilities for self-actualization and clean and safe work), but is still dissatisfied because he or she has not attained the status, salary and recognition to which he or she feels entitled, compared to similar others. Research has shown that such perceptions lead in general to feelings of resentment and depression, especially in mid-career when career prospects appear bleak (Buunk & Janssen, 1992).

5. *Lack of control and influence*. As has been noted above, in many theories of stress (e.g., Lazarus, 1995) a lack of control of one's situation is considered to be an important factor that may both cause and aggravate stress. Indeed, a lack of control has been found to be a major dimension of stressful events at work (Peeters, Buunk, & Schaufeli, 1995b). Control has often been studied as a personality characteristic that acts as a moderator, i.e., as a variable that may buffer the negative effects of stressors on strains (e.g., Etzion & Westman, 1994; Fox,

Dwyer, & Ganster, 1993; Theorell & Karasek, 1996). However, a lack of control has also been studied as a stressor in the work environment. Nevertheless, control as a personality characteristic and control as a feature of the work environment are difficult to separate, especially because both types of variables are usually measured through subjective assessments. In general, the term "control" is defined as power or mastery of the environment (Fisher, 1989), and refers more specifically to a sense of having the cognitive or behavioural possibilities to bring about a desired situation, or to end an undesired situation. Early experimental social psychological research showed that the same noise level was experienced as less stressful when it was possible to switch the noise off (even though this possibility was not used!) than when no such possibility existed (Glass, Reim, & Singer, 1971; Reim, Glass, & Singer, 1971). Generally, lack of control initially leads to feelings of anxiety, anger or hostility, and to attempts at restoring control. At a later stage it may lead to depression, if failure to gain control of a situation after repeated attempts is ascribed to general stable personality factors ("I am just not much good at anything") (Abramson & Seligman, 1981; Fisher, 1989).

In the work situation, various types of control can be distinguished. Fisher (1985) made a distinction between three basic forms of control: (1) *personal competence*: the feeling that one is able to achieve and create things; such expectations may occur in work situations when a person makes more or less complete, clearly recognizable products; (2) *interpersonal control*: the idea that one is able to exert power and influence over others, an expectation that may be stimulated by, for example, a participatory leadership style; and (3) *sociopolitical control*: the expectation that one is able to reach one's goals as a group, through, for example, strikes and participation in workers' councils. It must be noted that, although this typology may have high face validity, it does not seem to be supported by psycho-

metric studies (Ingledew, Hardy, & Cooper, 1992). Moreover, control in the workplace has been conceptualized most often in a different way, i.e. terms of autonomy or freedom in scheduling one's own work and determining how to perform one's job (e.g., Hackman & Oldham, 1980). Such a lack of autonomy has been recognized as a major stressor at work (cf. Frese, 1989; Ganster & Fusilier, 1989; Sauter, Hurrell, & Cooper, 1989; Jones & Fletcher, 1996). In general, many studies have shown that a lack of control at work operationalized in a variety of ways is associated with adverse health outcomes, including cardiovascular risks, emotional exhaustion, psychosomatic complaints, anxiety and depression (e.g., Ellis & Miller, 1993; Evans & Carrere, 1991; Ganster & Fusilier, 1989; Sauter, et al., 1989; Schaufeli & Buunk, 1996).

Coping behaviour

In the literature on stress it is often assumed that the way in which people cope with stressful events and situations partly determines the eventual consequences of such events and situations for their physical and mental health. Nevertheless, there are many definitions and ways of measuring coping (for overviews, see Latack & Havlovic, 1992; O'Driscoll & Cooper, 1994; Parkes, 1994). In some of these definitions, coping is conceptualized as a stable dispositional characteristic or *coping style*, which is measured by asking individuals how they usually deal with stress, or somewhat more specifically, with stress at work (e.g., Pearlin & Schooler, 1978). However, whereas some coping strategies, such as thinking positively, seem to be more or less stable across situations, other coping responses, such as seeking social support, are not (Lazarus, 1993). Therefore, most perspectives on coping emphasize that an individual's coping responses may *vary* strongly across situations, and that coping responses should not be regarded as a stable personal style. A study by Scheier, Weintraub, and Carver (1986) demonstrated, for instance, that in controllable situations, people high in optimism mainly used problem-focused coping and positive reinterpretation of the situation, whereas in uncontrollable situations, they showed acceptance and resignation. To capture such variation in coping responses, O'Driscoll and Cooper (1994) propose a "critical incident analysis" in which individuals specify a number of stressful situations, specify their coping behaviours in these situations, and specify the consequences of these behaviours. In contrast, Latack and Havlovic (1992) suggest that middle-range specificity in coping measures may be the most fruitful way to study coping. Assessing coping responses to categories of stressful situations (e.g., role conflicts) has more predictive value for actual behaviour than assessing general coping styles, and lead to better generalizability of findings than highly specific measures.

Lazarus (1993) conceptualized coping as a *process*, as a person's "ongoing efforts in thought and action to manage specific demands appraised as taxing or overwhelming" (p. 8). To be a little more specific, we define coping behaviour as all the cognitive and behavioural attempts aimed at changing, reinterpreting or reducing the negative emotions themselves, or the factors in the environment that cause these emotions. An important implication of this definition is that coping behaviour primarily refers to *attempts*, i.e. actions that may or may not be effective, and may in the long run even be harmful, such as drinking and smoking (Folkman, 1984). Many different taxonomies of coping strategies have been developed. One type of taxonomies is based on the *goal* of the behaviour, and a frequently found distinction is the following (cf. Pearlin & Schooler, 1978; Semmer, 1996):

1. Attempts to change, remove or reduce the stressor, which is often labelled *problem-focused* coping (e.g., Lazarus, 1993). Problem-focused coping may include behaviours like seeking help or advice, increasing efforts to encounter the threat, and more cognitive responses such as thinking out a plan of action. According to Lazarus, problem-focused coping will be found especially when an individual appraises the situation as controllable.
2. Attempts to directly change, reduce or remove the negative feelings, which is generally called *emotion-focused* coping (Lazarus, 1993). This may include behavi-

ours like smoking, drinking, and physical exercise, and cognitive strategies like avoidance and relaxation techniques. According to Lazarus, this will occur particularly when people think that nothing can be done about the problem.

3. Attempts to change the perception or appraisal of the stressor, which may be labelled *appraisal-focused* coping (e.g., Billings & Moos, 1984). This may include comparing oneself with others worse off (Pearlin & Schooler, 1978; Taylor, Buunk, & Aspinwall, 1990; Wills, 1981), and engaging in selective evaluation techniques (Buunk & Ybema, 1995; Taylor, Wood, & Lichtman, 1983), such as thinking how things could have been worse, and focusing on the benefits of the stressful event. Some authors regard appraisal-focused coping as a part of emotion-focused coping (e.g., Lazarus & Folkman, 1984).

Various other typologies have been presented, and various studies have tried to develop a classification of coping responses on a more empirical basis (for overviews see Parkes, 1994; Semmer, 1996). For instance, Carver, Scheier, and Weintraub (1989) have identified four dimensions of coping responses through a second order factor analysis, i.e. (1) active coping, (2) denial and disengagement, (3) acceptance, and (4) seeking social support and venting emotions. Additionally, Cohen, Reese, Kaplan, and Riggio (1986) assessed the following coping responses (1) direct actions, (2) inhibition of action, (3) information seeking, (4) intrapsychic processes, and (5) turning to others for support. In a study among case managers, Koeske, Kirk, and Koeske (1993) distinguished only two factors, which involve "control coping" and "avoidance coping". This dichotomy is similar to the coping styles called "monitoring" and "blunting" (e.g., Miller, 1990; Muris, 1994), i.e., the tendency to seek out information about the threat versus the tendency to cognitively distract from and psychologically "blunt" threat-relevant information. However, there is no consensus about the number and kind of coping dimensions that should be employed, and about the precise definition and content of the various dimensions (Semmer, 1996).

Although quite a few studies on occupational stress included coping measures, these studies have not produced very consistent results on the *effectiveness* of coping strategies in reducing stress in work situations. In an early review article, Murphy (1985) pointed out that coping directed at the source of stress may, in fact, even lead to more stress. In a well-known study, Pearlin and Schooler (1978) found that coping strategies were effective in reducing stress in interpersonal relationships, but had little effect on stress that results from problems at work. There is some evidence from the coping literature indicating that problem-focused coping is associated with better mental health when the problem can be remedied, whereas emotion-focused coping may be beneficial when the problem is uncontrollable (Semmer, 1996). For example, Bowman and Stern (1995) found in a study among medical centre nurses that problem-focused coping was effective in reducing stress especially when the stressful episode was deemed controllable. Moreover, they found that appraisal-focused coping generally had positive effects on well-being, whereas avoidance was strongly related to negative affect for both controllable and uncontrollable stressors. This suggests that coping directed at the cognitive appraisal of one's situation may be quite effective in reducing stress in a variety of situations.

In the past decades, it has become increasingly clear that social comparison—comparing one's situation and responses to those of others—is a quite prevalent way of coping with stress (Taylor et al., 1990). Nevertheless, the coping literature has, with the exception of the early work by Pearlin and Schooler (1978), in general paid little attention to the role of social comparison. One would expect that stress would generate social comparison activity particularly in work situations, because individuals are usually surrounded by similar others. Classical social comparison theory maintains that especially when individuals are uncertain about their own emotional responses, they will be interested in comparing these responses with those of others in a similar situation in order to evaluate their own reactions (Schachter, 1959). Buunk, Schaufeli, and Ybema (1994; see also Buunk & Schaufeli, 1993) showed indeed that nurses who experienced a high degree of uncertainty were relatively more interested in learning about the way in which others in a similar situation responded, and in talking to such others. In addition, these comparison needs were elevated among nurses high in emotional exhaustion. However, these nurses high in burnout at the same time seemed to avoid comparisons with others more experienced and competent, although such comparisons might have provided information relevant for problem-focused coping. To conclude, we like to suggest that a focus on the *social* aspects of coping may be a fruitful approach for studying coping with occupational stress.

Personality characteristics

Personality characteristics play an important role in the process by which demanding work conditions affect mental and physical health (Taylor & Cooper, 1989). As noted by Parkes (1994), personality characteristics affect what kind of jobs people select, and thus to what type of stressors they are exposed. In addition, some persons may find themselves in stressful circumstances more often than others because they, often unwittingly, create their own stressors. Moreover, due to differences in personality, there are considerable differences in the way individuals respond to similar stressors. The pioneering study by Kahn et al. (1964) already showed that, for example, the presence of role conflicts did correlate with the level of experienced tension in flexible persons, but not in rigid persons. For rigid persons a slight degree of role conflict was more stressful than for flexible persons, but a high degree of role conflict evoked more tension in flexible than in rigid persons. Following this pioneering work, many other occupational stress studies have shown that the relationship between a certain stressor and a certain stress reaction mainly, or even exclusively, occurs in persons with certain personality characteristics. We will discuss three of the most studied characteristics in more detail, i.e., locus of control and self-efficacy, Type A behaviour, and hardiness.

Locus of control. The concept of locus of control refers to the extent to which individuals believe that their outcomes are determined primarily by their own efforts and ability rather than by external factors, like fate, chance, the circumstances, or powerful others (Rotter, 1966).

Various scales have been developed to assess locus of control in work settings (e.g., Ingledew et al., 1992). Feeling that one can control one's outcomes may sometimes heighten stress (Folkman, 1984), for example when exerting control involves high material or social costs, like being held responsible for a negative outcome (cf. Heider, 1958). However, there is quite consistent evidence that the impact of stressors on health and well-being is lower for those higher in internal control. For example, in a study by Koeske and Kirk (1995) among clinical social workers and intensive care managers, internal control was consistently related to higher job satisfaction, less emotional exhaustion, and lower job conflict. Among intensive care managers of severely mentally ill clients, a significant and consistent buffering effect of internal control was found. Only for workers high in external (thus low in internal control) did job strain result in diminished life satisfaction. In a study among male career officers in the Israeli armed forces, Etzion and Westman (1994) found that sense of control was negatively related to burnout, and that stress had a weaker impact upon burnout among those high in control. Various other studies have produced similar results (e.g., Cooper, Kirkcaldy, & Brown, 1994; Daniels & Guppy, 1994; Parkes, 1991; Rees & Cooper, 1992). *Self-efficacy* refers to people's judgements of their capabilities to perform certain behaviours necessary to attain a particular desired goal (Bandura, 1986). Although self-efficacy also concerns a person's control of his or her situation, it is much more specific to a certain domain than locus of control, and should not be regarded as a stable personality trait. For example, an individual may be high in self-efficacy with regard to task performance, but low in self-efficacy with regard to getting a promotion. Some studies provided evidence for the moderating role of self-efficacy in the context of occupational stress, such that those high in self-efficacy are less likely to experience strains in response to stressors at work (e.g., Matsui & Onglatco, 1992).

Type A behaviour. This behaviour pattern is characterized by (1) a sense of time urgency and impatience; (2) high work involvement; (3) excessive drive and competitiveness; and (4) reward sensitivity (Friedman & Rosenman, 1974;

Furnham, 1992). In contrast, a Type B behaviour pattern is characterized by a calmer, more patient, more contemplative and more relaxed way of functioning. Type A behaviour is often assumed to be connected with cardiovascular disease. In an extensive meta-analysis of the psychological predictors of cardiovascular disease, Booth-Kewley and Friedman (1987) concluded that in particular the competitiveness and drive aspects of Type A behaviour are associated with the occurrence of cardiovascular disease. In a sense, Type A behaviour is valued positively in our culture (Furnham, 1986), in part because it can, under certain conditions, lead to a higher productivity. Although the concept of Type A behaviour and its measurement have generated a lot of controversy (Parkes, 1994), and although the evidence is somewhat contradictory, in general, Type A persons have been found to experience more adverse health outcomes than Type B persons (Suls & Sanders, 1988). For instance, in a study among nurses, Jamal (1990) found that Type As reported more job stress, role ambiguity, and psychosomatic health problems than Type Bs. Winnubst et al. (1996) report that in a study in 13 different companies, Type A behaviour was associated with role overload and responsibility for others, and that role problems led to much stronger psychological strains among Type As than among Type Bs. In a similar vein, Henley and Williams (1986) found that Type A persons react to frustrating situations with more negative feelings than Type B persons. In general, Type As seem to have a different way of coping with stress than Type Bs. Type A persons will tackle relatively light tasks with excessive vigour, and will try to gain control of a situation even though it is insoluble. They find it hard to accept failure and blame themselves for it (Vingerhoets & Flohr, 1984). A study by Rhodewalt, Sansone, Hill, and Chemers (1991) among male school principals found indeed that Type As reported more job stress under lower levels of perceived control, and that higher job-stress levels led to greater physical and psychological impairment especially for Type As. Experimental research has shown that Type As respond with much higher blood pressure and heart rate when faced with difficult tasks than Type Bs, but respond similarly to impossible or easy tasks. When a task gets difficult, a Type A person will invest more energy in it in order to try and maintain the same level of achievement, while a Type B person will be satisfied with a lower level. (Orlebeke & Van Doornen, 1983). In general, typical of Type A behaviour is a strong hostility and a relatively enduring tendency to frequently experience anger, annoyance and irritation during day-to-day activities (Dembrowski & MacDougall, 1985). In other words, this behavioural style in itself may be accompanied by more negative emotions, independent of the challenge in the environment.

Hardiness. Kobasa (1982) introduced this concept on the basis of an existential personality theory, and suggested that hardiness may protect individuals against the health damaging effects of stress. According to Kobasa, hardiness consists of three components. The first component is *commitment*, the ability to believe in the importance of what one is doing, and deep sense of involvement in many situations in one's life. The second is *control*, the tendency to believe that one can influence the events in one's life. The importance of such control is already considered in our earlier discussion. The third component is *challenge*, flexibility in adapting to unexpected changes, and the conviction that changes are normal. There is evidence from laboratory studies that as individuals are higher in hardiness, they perceive negative feedback as less threatening, and many studies have shown that hardiness is in general positively related to mental and physical health (Wiebe & Williams, 1992). For instance, Rush, Schoel, and Barnard (1995) found in a study among public sector employees that hardiness was negatively related to stress, and Duquette, Kerouac, Sandhu, and Ducharme (1995) found that geriatric nurses high in hardiness were lower in burnout. Several early studies have shown that hardiness may also function as a buffer against the negative effects of stressful circumstances on health. For example, in a prospective study among executives Kobasa and colleagues demonstrated that people with a low level of hardiness showed much more illness under stressful circumstances than persons with a high degree of hardiness, also when the level of earlier illness was kept constant (Kobasa, Maddi, & Kahn, 1982). However, in most subsequent

research, the hypothesized buffering effect of hardiness could not be established (for a review, see Wiebe & Williams, 1992). Furthermore, there is some controversy with regard to the measurement of hardiness, and there is evidence that hardiness is highly negatively correlated with neuroticism, which evokes the question if hardiness is not simply the opposite of neuroticism (Stroebe & Stroebe, 1994).

Social support

Social support provided by colleagues, superiors and subordinates, and family and friends is generally assumed to have important stress-reducing functions. There are numerous definitions and conceptualizations of "social support", that can, according to Buunk (1990), be grouped into four different categories. (1) *Social integration.* According to this perspective, social support refers to the number and strength of the connections of the individual to others in his or her social network. Social integration may promote health by providing stable and rewarding roles, promoting healthy behaviour, deterring the person from ill-advised behaviour, and maintaining stable functioning during periods of rapid change (Rook, 1984). (2) *Satisfying relationships.* From this point of view, social support involves a good organizational climate, and pleasant, close working relationships with colleagues, superiors and subordinates. Satisfying relationships can be health-sustaining due to, among others, the gratification of affiliative needs and identity maintenance (Shumaker & Brownell, 1984). (3) *Perceived available support.* According to a number of authors, social support constitutes the appraisal that, in the case of stressful circumstances, others—in the work context in particular colleagues and supervisors—can be relied on for advice, information, empathic understanding, guidance and alliance. There is some experimental evidence that the mere perception that one can turn to someone for help, already reduces stress (Sarason & Sarason, 1986). (4) *Actually received support.* While the foregoing perspectives assume a *preventive* function of support against stress, this perspective focuses on the *curative* function of actual help when a person is under stress. Once a stressful situation has come into existence, other people may perform supportive acts to reduce the stress (Barrera, 1986; Peeters et al., 1995a,b).

With respect to the *content* of perceived and received social support, usually a distinction is made between four types of support (House, 1981): *instrumental* support (e.g., direct help provided by others, which may reduce organizational stressors like role ambiguity and role conflict, see Payne & Jones, 1987), *emotional* support (e.g., through empathy, caring, and concern helping to manage negative emotions, reducing anxiety and improving mood, cf. Rook, 1987), *informational* support (e.g., advice, suggestions, directions, which may help one to perform one's job in a more effective way, and thus may reduce stress), and *appraisal* support (e.g., feedback or social comparison relevant to a person's self-evaluation, thus enhancing self-esteem and mastery e.g. Pearlin, Liebermann, Menaghan, & Mullan, 1981). In addition, it has been suggested that not only help in itself, but particularly *rewarding companionship* (e.g., pleasant and relaxing social interaction) may alleviate stress (Rook, 1987). In three studies, Buunk and Peeters (1994) performed factor analyses of social support related social interactions at work, and found in all cases three factors, i.e., *intimate support* (including confidentiality of the contact as well as emotional and appraisal support, and sometimes including informational support), *rewarding companionship*, and *instrumental support* (sometimes including informational support). Apparently, several of the four helping exchanges distinguished by House (1981) are empirically closely related. The three dimensions found by Buunk and Peeters bear a remarkable similarity to various taxonomies of expectations and needs in relationships (e.g., Argyle & Henderson, 1985).

In general, an important effect of social support seems to constitute of coping assistance. According to Thoits (1984), social support may stimulate the employment of effective coping strategies, and may prevent inadequate coping attempts. In line with this view, Terry, Rawle, and Callan (1995) found that social support from supervisors and colleagues promoted instrumental action among employees of a retail organization, which led to higher psychological well-being and lower depersonalization of customers. Moreover, social support from colleagues reduced escapism, and this lower level of escapism resulted in higher job satisfaction, improved well-being and lowered depersonalization. A similar view on the working of social support is held by Burleson and Goldsmith (1996), who state that social support may alleviate distress when the communication between the distressed person and a counsellor facilitates cognitive coping, i.e. reappraisal of the stressful situation.

Usually a distinction is made between buffering and direct effects of social support. *Direct* effects occur when individuals who are involved in supportive and satisfying relationships have a relatively high degree of mental and physical health. Social support researchers have, however, been particularly interested in *buffer* effects, assuming that support can counteract the negative consequences of stress for health and well-being (Cohen & Wills, 1985; Buunk & Peeters, 1994). A buffer effect occurs when support functions as a buffer against the negative consequences of stress, and especially has a positive effect when strong stressors are involved. According to Cohen and Wills (1985), social support may have a buffering effect because the perception that others are prepared and able to provide the necessary support may make the situation less stressful, and because support may directly influence the negative emotions themselves and the physiological processes by which they are accompanied.

Recently, Uchino, Cacioppo, and Kiecolt-Glaser (1996) thoroughly reviewed both correlational and experimental evidence for the beneficial effects of social support on physiological processes. They concluded that social support may improve the working of the cardiovascular, the endocrine, and the immune systems. Nevertheless, the evidence for direct effects of work-related social support on well-being and health is not particularly strong and consistent. It must be noted that in many studies that include relevant measures, no correlations between support and indexes of mental or physical health are presented, sometimes because the research was primarily aimed at assessing buffer effects. A number of relevant studies have found that social support is moderately negatively related to psychological stress reactions, in particular negative affect (e.g.,

Buunk & Verhoeven, 1991; Boumans & Lande-weerd, 1992; Corrigan, Holmes, & Luchins, 1995; Dignam & West, 1988; Kirmeyer & Dougherty, 1988; Marcelissen et al., 1988; Tyler & Cushway, 1995; Winnubst, Marcelissen, & Kleber, 1982; Yang & Carayon, 1995). In one of the better designed studies, Caplan et al. (1975) found that a lack of support from the supervisor and others at work correlated higher with depression than did stressors such as role conflict, role ambiguity and lack of participation. In many studies, the majority of correlations between social support and well-being measures are significant, and on the average around 0.30 (e.g., Repetti, 1987; Reiche, 1982; Winnubst et al., 1982). Nevertheless, there are also studies in which social support is not directly related to health and well-being (e.g., Fried & Tiegs, 1993; Jayaratne & Chess, 1984), or does not make an independent contribution to health and well-being when the effects of stressors are controlled for (e.g., Constable & Russell, 1986; Dignam, Barrera, & West, 1986) or is only related to low distress for some individuals such as those high in trait anxiety (Dollard & Winefield, 1995). There is in particular limited evidence for effects of support at work upon objectively assessable indicators of health, including blood pressure, cholesterol level, heart rate, somatic diseases and absenteism, even when correlations with indexes of mental well-being are found in the same study (e.g., Kaufman & Beehr, 1986; LaRocco & Jones, 1978; Winnubst et al., 1982).

Many studies provide evidence for a *buffering role* of social support at work, but again there are quite a few studies that show inconsistent results. Among those that show a buffer effect are those of Boumans and Landeweerd (1992), Corrigan et al. (1995), Kirmeyer & Dougherty (1988), and LaRocco, House, and French (1980). However, although studies typically examined multiple stressors, stress reactions ("strains"), and social support measures, which results in large numbers of potential buffer effects, a substantial number of studies report no significant buffer effects at all (e.g., Israel, Schurman, & House, 1989; Leiter & Meechan, 1986; Parkes, Mendham, & Von Rabenau, 1994; Ross et al., 1989; Terry, Neilsen, & Perchard, 1993; Tyler & Cushway, 1995; Yang & Carayon, 1995). In other studies, not all buffer

effects that were examined were found to be statistically significant. For example, in a study of Himle, Jayaratne, and Thyness (1989) 17 out of 72 possible buffer effects were established (at a 10% level), and Winnubst et al. (1982) found 11 out of 60 effects. In many cases the number of significant effects hardly exceeds what one would expect on the basis of chance (e.g., Constable & Russell, 1986; Dignam, Barrera, & West, 1986; Haines, Hurlbert, & Zimmer, 1991; Himle et al., 1989; House, 1985; Jayaratne & Chess, 1984; Russell, Altmaier, & Van Velzen, 1987).

In some studies, social support even seemed to have detrimental effects on well-being, judging from the reversed direct or buffer effects that were reported (e.g., Kaufman & Beehr, 1986; Kobasa & Puccetti, 1983; Winnubst et al., 1982). For example, in his study of legal professionals, Burke (1982) reported that 31% of the correlates between social support and aspects of occupational stress were positive. Leiter and Meechan (1986) found indications that a more cohesive and reciprocal social network was *positively* correlated to burn-out among the staff of a residential mental health rehabilitation centre. In a similar vein, Buunk, Janssen, and VanYperen (1989) found evidence for what they called a *boomerang* effect: in some cases social support appeared to aggravate stress reactions in work units in which there was a high level of stressors, while at the same time reducing stress reactions in low stressor units. A study by De Jonge and Schaufeli (in press) among 1,437 nurses and nurses' aides showed that the highest job satisfaction and the fewest burnout symptoms were reported in persons experiencing moderate social support, but that high levels of social support were associated with lower levels of job satisfaction as well as stronger feelings of exhaustion.

Various explanations can be given for such apparently negative effects of social support. In the first place, the positive correlation between social support and strain may be spurious when exposure to stressors both heightens the strain, and triggers the enactment of supportive behaviour from others. In the second place, some studies employ structural measures for social support, such as the absence or presence of other people who are supposed to be supportive. However, the presence of these people may not only be supportive, but may also undermine well-being in the face of stress (Rook, 1984; Vinokur & Van Ryn, 1993). For instance, Vinokur, Price, and Caplan (1996) showed in a longitudinal study that financial strain increased depression among both job seekers and their spouses. The spouse's depression diminished social support and increased social undermining from spouse to job seeker, which in turn increased depression among job seekers. In the third place, social support may actually aggravate stress reactions when individuals engage in a discussion of certain work problems with sympathetic colleagues. In a group in which a negative view on these problems predominates, individuals may develop a more negative view after the discussion (e.g., Geurts et al., 1993). Social comparison processes and new arguments provided by the other group members both seem to play a role in such situations (Kaplan, 1987). Others may not only influence the perception of stressors, and thereby the stress reactions, but may also have a *direct* influence upon these reactions by acting as models showing certain symptoms that are imitated (Colligan, 1985; Schachter & Singer, 1962). For example, in a series of experiments, Pennebaker and his colleagues (Skelton & Pennebaker, 1982; Pennebaker & Brittingham, 1982) have shown that various physical symptoms, including scratching, coughing, and flu symptoms are easily adopted from others.

A last type of explanations for the negative effects of social support can be derived from experimental research on the recipients' reactions to help. Such research suggests, for example, that helping acts may backfire and trigger negative feelings when the help induces feelings of inequity, because persons are not able or willing to reciprocate the helping behaviour, or when they receive a more favourable rate of outcomes than the donor (Buunk & Hoorens, 1992; Hatfield & Sprecher, 1983; Uehara, 1995). In two studies in organizations, Buunk, Doosje, Jans, and Hopstaken (1993) showed indeed that not only feeling underbenefited in terms of support, but also feeling overbenefited, i.e., feeling one obtains more support than one provides, was accompanied by negative affect. Other negative effects of helping include the undermining of feelings of

competence and *control* (Coates, Renzaglia, & Embree, 1983) and threats to the *self-esteem*, such as when the help implies an inferiority–superiority relationship between donor and recipient and conflicts with values of self-reliance and independence (Fisher, Nadler, & Witcher-Alagna, 1982). Buunk and Schaufeli (1993) showed that, although nurses with a high degree of stress had a relatively strong desire to talk with others about their problems at work, they tended at the same time to avoid the company of their colleagues. In a study among correctional officers, Peeters, Buunk, and Schaufeli (1995c) found that instrumental support increased negative affect because this type of support induced feelings of inferiority. Lehman and Hemphill (1990) showed that many individuals under stress report unhelpful or upsetting help attempts from others, including making the stress unimportant, being overly protective, and providing unwanted information.

Long-term reactions to occupational stress

In itself, there is nothing unhealthy about experiencing negative emotions due to stress, not even when they are relatively intense, and are accompanied by distinct hormonal and physiological changes. However, if such emotions last longer or are very intense, they may upset a person's psychological or physiological balance. As illustrated on various occasions in the previous part of this chapter, in the long run this may have three kinds of consequences: (1) physical illness, (2) psychosomatic complaints, and (3) psychological problems.

1. *Physical illness*. Negative emotions may impair a person's physical health in different ways. First, stress may stimulate unhealthy habits and behaviours, like bad eating habits, smoking, and excessive consumption of alcohol (Maes, Vingerhoets, & Van Heck, 1987). Second, stress may eventually lead directly to health impairments through psychophysiological processes, such as hormonal changes, increased blood pressure, and changes in the immune system. For example, anger may lower the pumping efficiency of the heart (Goleman,

1995), and depression is accompanied by a lower activity of natural killer cells that are part of the immune system (Cohen & Herbert, 1996). A loss of status may cause various physiological changes (Buunk & Ybema, 1997). In general, negative emotions are associated with complex neuroendocrinological changes (Zillmann & Zillmann, 1996). Zegans (1982) has described numerous ways in which stress can upset a person's physiological balance. According to Zegans, if many major life changes occur, adaptation may fail, and may produce physiological impairments in a number of ways. For example, an acute physiological reaction like high blood pressure may become chronic or inhibition mechanisms may fail, and such failure may result in excessively strong physiological reactions in response to minor stressors.

As a result of such processes, occupational stress may play a role in the development of various physical dysfunctions, such as high blood pressure, high cholesterol level, asthma, stomach complaints, cardiovascular disease, colorectal cancer, and decreased resistance to infectious diseases (Goleman, 1995). In a review article, Bongers, de Winter, Kompier, and Hildebrandt (1993) found that high workload, time pressure, low control and lack of support are associated with musculoskeletal disease. In another review article, Schnall, Landsbergis, and Baker (1994) found that heart attacks occur relatively often after an increase in job-related stress. Particularly the combination of low control, high demands and lack of support in the work situation seems to increase cardiovascular risk (Theorell & Karasek, 1996). Appels (1993) has shown that occupational stress may result in "vital exhaustion", which appeared to be a strong predictor of myocardial infarction, especially in the following year. Illustrative in this context is the work on the influence of Type A behaviour on health by Dembrowski and MacDougall (1985), who showed that hostility and the suppression of anger are significantly and independently associated with various aspects of cardiovascular disease, after adjusting for other risk factors. These data again illustrate the importance of negative emotions in the stress process.

2. *Psychosomatic complaints.* Stress may play a role in the development of a variety of psychosomatic complaints, such as dizziness, fatigue, headaches, lower back pain, and palpitations. A study by Van Dijkhuizen (1980) among the middle management in a large number of businesses, showed, that especially feelings of anxiety at work led to such complaints. A large-scale investigation by De Jonge, Boumans, Landeweerd, and Nijhuis (1995) among nurses and nurses' aides in 16 hospitals in The Netherlands showed that experienced workload and physical exertion were associated with psychosomatic complaints. The higher the workload and physical exertion, the more complaints were reported. Problems of underload were apparently not experienced by these nurses. Various explanations have been given for the development of such complaints. Some explanations emphasize a disrupted physiological balance, but such explanations are unsatisfactory, because people's perceptions of their own physiological processes are highly inaccurate. People may experience bodily sensations, such as headaches and lower back complaints, even though no physiological changes can be detected. Conversely, actual physiological disorders, such as high blood pressure, or even a minor heart attack may occur without being noticed. Especially when people are under stress, numerous rather unspecific bodily changes may occur that can be interpreted in different ways. This is typically the kind of situation in which psychosomatic complaints arise. According to Pennebaker and colleagues (Pennebaker & Brittingham, 1982; Skelton & Pennebaker, 1982), for example, the following social cognitive processes may play a role in the occurrence of such complaints:

Selective perception: When the environment provides few stimuli and a person is bored, or when, on the other hand, the amount of environmental stimuli is so overwhelming that a person is unable to cope with them, it is likely that attention will be focused on bodily processes. Experimental research has confirmed the existence of such a curvilinear association (Pennebaker, 1982). From this point of view, it is quite understandable that, as was described above, all kinds of stress reactions are more frequent in persons whose work is characterized by overload as well as in persons who are faced with underload in their work (Edwards, 1991).

Social induction of hypothesis: Social information may have the result that a person adopts the hypothesis that he or she is suffering from a certain complaint or symptom; for example, when he sees someone else becoming ill, or reads or hears information about a certain disease. Experimental research has shown that persons who are casually told that there is a lot of flu about will later show more flu-like symptoms, and that symptoms like coughing can be imitated immediately, especially when a plausible reason is given for it (Pennebaker, 1982).

Looking for confirmation: People will start looking selectively for confirmation of the adopted hypothesis that they are suffering from the assumed disease. Because bodily processes are rather vague and can be interpreted in different ways, one can easily obtain at least partial support for such hypotheses. Besides, when a person pays more attention to what is taking place inside his or her body, it is more likely that he or she will actually perceive something. It has become clear from experiments that when people are told that an ultrasonic sound leads to an *in*crease in skin temperature, they interpret actual changes in skin temperature as a warming of the skin. Conversely, subjects who are told that the sound leads to a decrease in skin temperature, actually perceive changes as a drop in skin temperature (Pennebaker & Skelton, 1981).

Processes like those described above, may sometimes lead to large-scale symptom contagion within organizations. It is quite common that a variety of ambiguous and unpleasant bodily sensations occur in stressful work situations. As noted previously, when a colleague starts showing certain symptoms, and holds certain aspects of the work environment (e.g., the air conditioning or chemical substances) responsible, others may start looking for indications of the same symptoms in themselves. Such processes are fuelled by rumours and by the living proof that colleagues manifest all kinds of symptoms. Intriguing case studies have been reported in which such symptom contagion actually occurred in organizations (Colligan, 1985). In one such incident at a factory producing aluminium furniture, a woman worker one morning suddenly showed various symptoms, like headache, nausea, dizziness and a sore throat, and she complained about a strange smell. A few minutes later three other employees had the same symptoms and within half an hour another six did. Medical examination showed no physical abnormalities whatsoever, and most workers were soon discharged. Thorough investigation by independent experts on the day of the "epidemic" showed that all gases were within acceptable limits. Psychological research carried out later showed that employees with symptoms showed higher uncertainty about the future, role conflicts and lack of influence, and were further characterized by poorer health and stronger tendencies to hysteria and hypochondria. Colligan (1985) points out that the fact that most employees knew each other facilitated social influence, and that the dissatisfaction that was felt was converted into physical complaints during this process.

3. *Psychological problems.* The long-term consequences of stressful work situations may also be more psychological in nature. A consequence that has received much attention in the last few years is *burnout*, a

reaction pattern that mainly occurs in professionals with people-oriented jobs. The concept of burnout does not have a clear theoretical background, but mainly has its origins in clinical practice. Although the concept of burnout is closely related to the concept of stress, both concepts differ in a number of ways. Schaufeli and Van Dierendonck (1993) showed the discriminant validity of burnout as compared to generic mental and physical symptoms of job stress. Burnout is a multidimensional phenomenon (Maslach & Schaufeli, 1993; Schaufeli & Buunk, 1996). In addition to the central characteristic, *emotional exhaustion*, several attitudinal aspects play a role in burnout. *Depersonalization* refers to a cynical and impersonal attitude towards the recipients of one's services, and *reduced personal accomplishment* refers to a negative attitude towards one's own competence at work. Moreover, burnout can be considered as the result of chronic occupational stress which mainly occurs in occupational groups where professionals work intensively with recipients of care, for example in health settings. But also among other professional groups such as teachers (Burke & Greenglass, 1995), correctional officers (Whitehaed, 1989), social workers (Koeske & Kelly, 1995), army officers (Etzion & Westman, 1994), and psychologists (Skorupka & Agresti, 1993), symptoms of burnout have been found.

In addition to workload, a number of psychological processes and stressors may play a role in the development of burnout (Maslach & Jackson, 1982; for a review, see Schaufeli & Buunk, 1996):

Dispositional attributions. People often make the fundamental error of attribution, which refers to the tendency to attribute problems at work to personal shortcomings. Attributions of this type are especially likely when chronic stress is experienced, and when people do not talk about their problems, which results in the assumption that they are the only one experiencing such problems (cf. Buunk & Schaufeli, 1993;

Miller & McFarland, 1991). Such internal attributions of failure may enhance a negative view of one's own competence, and further burnout accordingly.

Lack of autonomy. Having little control of one's work is another factor that may lead to burnout. For example, nurses are often faced with situations in which immediate decisions are required, even though they are generally not allowed to take these decisions. Moreover, they have little influence on all kinds of aspects of their work, such as working hours, work pace and work order. De Jonge, Janssen and Van Breukelen (1996) found that nurses and nurses' aides who experienced high work pressure and, at the same time, reported little autonomy were most emotionally exhausted. This finding has recently been replicated by Le Blanc and Schaufeli (1995) in their study among over 2,000 nurses working in intensive care units.

Role problems. Occupations in which one deals with people are generally characterized by roles that are not clearly defined, and by a lack of feedback about one's work have a higher risk for burnout. Numerous studies have shown that especially role ambiguity leads to burnout (Schaufeli & Buunk, 1996). For example, Dignam, Barrera, and West (1986) found that the following variables were predictive of burnout among prison warders: role ambiguity, workload, and direct contact with prisoners that was experienced as negative. As noted previously, a study by Manlove (1994) among child care workers showed that role conflict and role ambiguity made independent contributions to burnout.

Inequity. In human service professions, the relationship with the recipients of one's care is basically unbalanced: the professional is supposed to provide care, assistance, help, advice and support, whereas the recipient is supposed to receive and give nothing in return. However, according to social exchange theory (Walster, Walster, & Berscheid, 1978), a characteristic human tendency exists to expect rewards, such as gratitude, in return for the care we provide to others. Within human service professions, such expectations are often not fulfilled, and the interaction with recipients of care typically generates more costs than rewards (cf. Maslach & Jackson, 1982). For example, patients may be worried and anxious, and interactions with such individuals is often not rewarding. Working with difficult groups, such as inmates of psychiatric hospitals, may even be less rewarding in spite of the large investments in terms of time, energy and attention. Buunk and Schaufeli (1993) suggested that in human service professions, burnout may be particularly related to the perception of having imbalanced relationships with the recipients of one's care. Indeed, this has been found in studies among nurses (VanYperen, Buunk, & Schaufeli, 1992), family physicians (Van Dierendonck, Schaufeli, & Sixma, 1994) and therapists working with inmates (Van Dierendonck, Schaufeli, & Buunk, 1996).

STRESS MANAGEMENT: PREVENTION AND INTERVENTION

One of the main objectives of occupational stress research should be to provide several forms of prevention or intervention aimed at reducing occupational stress. Numerous methods for the prevention of and intervention in occupational stress have been described (for reviews see Ivancevich & Matteson, 1988; Murphy, 1988). Many of these methods have not specifically been developed for occupational stress, but were borrowed from clinical psychology. Such individual-oriented methods teach individual employees to improve their stress-coping strategies and to prevent stress. Such programmes almost invariably contain some form of relaxation exercises, including rational emotive therapy, physical exercise, meditation or relaxation techniques, as well as social skills training. In addition, there are general workplace health promotion programmes aimed at smoking cessation, reduction of alcohol use, reducing blood pressure, stimulating physical exercise and reducing body weight.

In addition to these individual-oriented methods there are also work-oriented measures aimed at reducing or preventing employee stress (Burke, 1993). Worksite interventions which could improve the psychosocial, stress-inducing, characteristics of work have become more and more important. However, a common problem of these worksite methods is the difficulty in changing the work or task structure when the embedding organizational structure remains the same (cf. Karasek, 1992; Landsbergis, 1988). Therefore, a more integrated approach to change should not focus on one aspect within the organization, but on long-term change and development throughout the organization. Work redesign methods have long been advocated as improving work motivation and performance. More recently, attention has been paid to the potentially adverse health consequences of work redesign (Karasek & Theorell, 1990). There are a variety of worksite redesign methods that focus on work or task characteristics. Of all these methods, *job enrichment* has been the most crucial for a long time. Job enrichment involves changing a job both horizontally (i.e., adding tasks) and vertically (i.e., adding responsibility and authority). *Autonomous work groups* are another means for implementing change in the nature of work and increasing job control and social support (Gardell, 1982). Despite the enormous amount of studies on the effects of work redesign on the well-being of workers, there still remain few examples of carefully controlled evaluations of worksite interventions (Ganster, 1995). Karasek (1992), for instance, reviewed some basic trends in 19 case studies of stress prevention programmes. He found that work environment restructuring has been equally or even more effective than person-based coping enhancement programmes. From this point of view it may be desirable to redesign the job as well as to alter the worker's needs, values and abilities. Work-oriented and individual-oriented methods are dealt with in (amongst others) Chapters 2 & 6, Volume 2; Chapter 17, Volume 3; and Chapters 4 & 8, Volume 4 of this Handbook.

FINAL REMARKS

In this chapter we have emphasized that stress refers to the occurrence of negative emotions. Considering that work occupies a central place in the lives of many individuals, it is hardly surprising that situations and events at work are capable of evoking strong negative emotions. We have shown that structural characteristics of a job, role problems, interpersonal conflicts, lack of control, and lack of status may lead to occupational stress, and subsequently to all kinds of physical and mental complaints. However, individual differences in the appraisal of the situation play an important role in the stress process. A situation that constitutes a challenge for one person may be a threat for someone else. Moreover, coping strategies and personality factors, such as locus of control and hardiness, may in some situations prevent the occurrence of negative emotions. It should be noted that much occupational stress research is characterized by a lack of theoretical foundation. In this chapter we have broken a lance for more theoretical approaches from a social psychological and work psychological perspectives, with the emphasis on the psychosocial determinants of occupational stress. Although other theoretically oriented approaches to stress in work situations may be quite interesting and useful as well, we do hope we succeeded in presenting a fruitful perspective that will stimulate valuable future research on stress at work.

REFERENCES

Abramson, L.Y., & Seligman, M.E.P. (1981). Depression and the causal inference process. In J.H. Harvey, W. Ickes & R.F. Kidd (Eds.), *New directions in attribution research* (Vol. 3). Hillsdale, NJ: Erlbaum.

Abramson, L.Y., Seligman, M.E.P., & Teasdale, J.D. (1978). Learned helplessness in humans: Critique and reformulation. *Journal of Abnormal Psychology*, *87*, 49–74.

Appels, A. (1993). Exhaustion as endpoint of job stress and precursor of disease. In L. Levi & F. LaFerla (Eds.), *A healthier work environment* (pp. 258–265). Copenhagen: WHO.

Argyle, M., & Henderson, M. (1985). *The anatomy of relationships*. Harmondsworth, Middlesex, England: Penguin Books.

Bailey, J.M., & Bhagat, R.S. (1987). Meaning and measurement of stressors in the work environment: An evaluation. In S.V. Kasl & C.L. Cooper (Eds.), *Stress and health: Issues in research methodology*. Chichester: John Wiley & Sons.

Bailey, J.M. (1980). The stress audit: Identifying the stressors of ICU nursing. *Journal of Nursing Education*, *19* (6), 15–25.

Baker, D. (1985). The study of stress at work. *Annual Review of Public Health*, *6*, 367–381.

Bandura, A. (1986). *Social foundations of thought and action: A social cognitive theory*. NJ: Prentice Hall.

Barling, J., & MacIntyre, A.T. (1993). Daily work role stressors, mood and emotional exhaustion. *Work and Stress*, *7*, 315–325.

Barrera, M. (1986). Distinctions between social support concepts, measures and models. *American Journal of Community Psychology*, *14* (4), 413–445.

Billings, A.G., & Moos, R.H. (1984). Coping, stress, and social resources among adults with unipolar depression. *Journal of Personality and Social Psychology*, *46*, 877–891.

Blanc, P.M. Le, & Schaufeli, W.B. (1995). *Job demands, burnout and medical performance in intensive care units*. Paper presented at the IV ENOP Conference, Munich.

Bongers, P.M., Winter, C.R. de, Kompier, M.A.J., & Hildebrandt, V.H. (1993). Psychosocial factors at work and musculoskeletal disease. *Scandinavian Journal of Work, Environment, and Health*, *19*, 297–312.

Booth-Kewley, S., & Friedman, H.S. (1987). Psychological predictors of heart disease: A quantitative review. *Psychological Bulletin*, *101* (3), 343–362.

Boumans, N.P.G., & Landeweerd, J.A. (1992). The role of social support and coping behaviour in nursing work: Main of buffering effect? *Work and Stress*, *6*, 191–202.

Bowman, G.D., & Stern, M. (1995). Adjustment to occupational stress: The relationship of perceived control to effectiveness of coping strategies. *Journal of Counseling Psychology*, *42*, 294–303.

Brown, G.W. (1985). *Some notes on doing research on stress. A scientific debate: How to define and research stress*. National Institute of Mental Health, Center for Prevention Research. Washington, DC: US Department of Health and Human Services, Public Health Service.

Burke, R.J. (1982). Impact of occupational demands on nonwork experiences. *Journal of Psychology*, *112*, 195–211.

Burke, R.J. (1988). Sources of managerial and professional stress in large organizations. In C.L. Cooper & R.L. Payne (Eds.), *Causes, coping and consequences of stress at work* (pp. 77–114). Chichester: Wiley.

Burke, R.J. (1993). Organizational-level interventions

to reduce occupational stressors. *Work and Stress, 7,* 77–87.

Burke, R.J. (1996). Work experiences, stress and health among managerial and professional women. In M.J. Schabracq, J.A.M. Winnubst & C.L. Cooper (Eds.), *Handbook of work and health psychology* (pp. 205–230). Chichester: Wiley

Burke, R.J., Brief, A.P., & George, J.M. (1993). The role of negative affectivity in understanding relations between self-reports of stressors and strains: A comment on the applied psychology literature. *Journal of Applied Psychology, 78* (3), 402–412.

Burke, R.J., & Greenglass, E.R. (1995). A longitudinal examination of the Cherniss model of psychological burnout. *Social Science and Medicine, 40* (10), 1357–1363.

Burleson, B.R., & Goldsmith, D.J. (1996). How the comforting process works: Alleviating emotional distress through conversationally induced reappraisals. In P.A. Andersen & L.K. Guerrero (Eds.), *Communication and emotion: Theory, research, and applications.* Orlando, FL: Academic Press.

Buunk, B.P. (1990). Affiliation and helping interactions within organizations: A critical analysis of the role of social support with regard to occupational stress. In W. Stroebe & M. Hewstone (Eds.), *European review of social psychology* (Vol. 1, pp. 293–322). Chichester: John Wiley.

Buunk, B.P. (1994). Social comparison processes under stress: Towards an integration of classic and recent perspectives. In W. Stroebe & M. Hewstone (Eds.), *European review of social psychology* (Vol. 5, pp. 211–241). Chichester: Wiley.

Buunk, B.P., Doosje, B.J., Jans, L.G.J.M., & Hopstaken, L.E.M. (1993). Perceived reciprocity, social support, and stress at work: The role of exchange and communal orientation. *Journal of Personality and Social Psychology, 65,* 801–811.

Buunk, B.P., & Hoorens, V. (1992). Social support and stress: The role of social comparison and social exchange processes. *British Journal of Clinical Psychology, 31,* 445–457.

Buunk, B.P., & Janssen, P.P.M. (1992). Relative deprivation, career issues, and mental health among men in midlife. *Journal of Vocational Behavior, 40,* 338–350.

Buunk, B.P., Janssen, P.P.M., & Van Yperen, N.W. (1989). Stress and affiliation reconsidered: The effects of social support in stressful and non-stressful work units. *Social Behaviour, 4,* 155–171.

Buunk, B.P., & Peeters, M.C.W. (1994). Stress at work, social support and companionship: Towards an event-contingent recording approach. *Work and Stress, 8,* 177–190.

Buunk, B.P., & Schaufeli, W.B. (1993). Professional burnout: A perspective from social comparison theory. In W.B. Schaufeli, C. Maslach & T. Marek (Eds.), *Professional burnout: Recent developments in theory and research* (pp. 53–69). Washington: Taylor & Francis.

Buunk, B.P., Schaufeli, W.B., & Ybema, J.F. (1994). Burnout, uncertainty, and the desire for social comparison among nurses. *Journal of Applied Social Psychology, 24,* 1701–1718.

Buunk, B.P., & Verhoeven, K. (1991). Companionship and support at work: A microanalysis of the stress-reducing features of social interaction. *Basic and Applied Social Psychology, 12,* 243–258.

Buunk, B.P., & Ybema, J.F. (1995). Selective evaluation and coping with stress: Making one's situation cognitively more livable. *Journal of Applied Social Psychology, 25,* 1499–1517.

Buunk, B.P., & Ybema, J.F. (1997). Social comparisons and occupational stress: The identification-contrast model. In B.P. Buunk & F.X. Gibbons (Eds.), *Health, coping and well-being: Perspectives from social comparison theory* (pp. 359–388). Hillsdale, NJ: Erlbaum.

Caplan, R.D. (1983). Person-environment fit: Past, present, and future. In C.L. Cooper (Ed.), *Stress Research* (pp. 35–78). Chichester: John Wiley & Sons.

Caplan, R.D., Cobb, S., French, J.R.P., Harrison, R.V., & Pinneau, S.R. (1975). *Job demands and worker health, main effects and occupational differences.* Washington, DC: US Department of Health, Education and Welfare. National Institute for Occupational Safety and Health.

Carayon, P. (1993). A longitudinal test of Karasek's Job Strain Model among office workers. *Work and Stress, 7* (4), 299–314.

Carver, C.S., Scheier, M.F., & Weintraub, J.K. (1989). Assessing coping strategies: A theoretically based approach. *Journal of Personality and Social Psychology, 56,* 267–283.

Coates, D., Renzaglia, G.J., & Embree, M.C. (1983). When helping backfires: Help and helplessness. In J.D. Fisher, A. Nadler & B.M. DePaulo (Eds.), *New directions in helping behavior* (Vol. 1) (pp. 253–280). New York: Academic Press.

Cohen, F., Reese, L.B., Kaplan, G.A., & Riggio, R.E. (1986). Coping with the stresses of arthritis. In R.W. Moskowitz & M.R. Haug (Eds.), *Arthritis and the Elderly* (pp. 47–56). New York: Springer.

Cohen, S., & Wills, T.A. (1985). Stress, social support and the buffering hypothesis. *Psychological Bulletin, 98* (2), 310–357.

Cohen, S., & Herbert, T.B. (1996). Health psychology: Psychological factors and physical disease from the perspective of human psychoneuroimmunology. *Annual Review of Psychology, 47,* 113–142.

Colligan, M. (1985). An apparent case of mass psychogenic illness in an aluminium assembly plant. In C.L. Cooper & M.J. Smith (Eds.), *Job stress and blue collar work.* Chichester: Wiley.

Constable, J.F., & Russell, D.W. (1986). The effect of

social support and the work environment upon burnout among nurses. *Journal of Human Stress, 11,* 20–27.

Cooper, C.L., Kirkcaldy, B.D., & Brown, J. (1994). A model of job stress and physical health: The role of individual differences. *Personality and Individual Differences, 16* (4), 653–655.

Cooper, C.L., & Marshall, J. (1978). Sources of managerial and white collar stress. In C.L. Cooper & R. Payne (Eds.), *Stress at work.* Chichester: John Wiley & Sons.

Cooper, C.L., & Payne, R.L. (Eds.) (1988). *Causes, coping and consequences of Stress at Work.* Chichester: Wiley & Sons.

Cooper, C.L., & Smith, M.J. (Eds.) (1985). *Job stress and blue collar work.* Chichester: Wiley.

Corrigan, P.W., Holmes, E.P., & Luchins, D. (1995). Burnout and collegial support in state psychiatric hospital staff. *Journal of Clinical Psychology, 51* (5), 703–710.

Cox, T., & Ferguson, E. (1994). Measurement of the subjective work environment. *Work and Stress, 8,* 98–109.

Crandall, R., & Perrewé, P.L. (Eds.) (1995), *Occupational stress: A handbook.* Washington: Taylor & Francis.

Daniels, K., & Guppy, A. (1994). Occupational stress, social support, job control, and psychological well-being. *Human Relations, 47* (12), 1523–1544.

Dembrowski, Th.M., & MacDougall, J.M. (1985). Beyond global Type A: Relationships of paralinguistic attributes, hostility, and anger-in to coronary heart disease. In T. Field, Ph. M. McCabe & N. Schneiderman (Eds.), *Stress and coping.* Hillsdale, NJ: Erlbaum.

Dierendonck, D. van, Schaufeli, W.B., & Buunk, B.P. (1996). Inequity among human service professionals: Measurement and relation to burnout. *Basic and Applied Social Psychology, 18,* 429–451.

Dierendonck, D. van, Schaufeli, W.B., & Sixma, H.J. (1994). Burnout among general practitioners: A perspective from equity theory. *Journal of Social and Clinical Psychology, 13,* 86–100.

Dignam, J.T., & West, S.G. (1988). Social support in the workplace: Tests of six theoretical models. *American Journal of Community Psychology, 16,* 701–724.

Dignam, J.T., Barrera, M., & West, S.G. (1986). Occupational stress, social support and burnout among correctional officers. *American Journal of Community Psychology, 14,* 177–193.

Dijkhuizen, N. van (1980). *From stressors to strains.* Lisse: Swets and Zeitlinger.

Dollard, M.F., & Winefield, A.H. (1995). Trait anxiety, work demand, social support and psychological distress in correctional officers. *Anxiety, Stress and Coping: An International Journal, 8* (1), 25–35.

Duquette, A., Kerouac, S., Sandhu, B.K., & Ducharme, F. (1995). Psychosocial determinants of burnout in geriatric nursing. *International Journal of Nursing Studies, 32* (5), 443–456.

Edwards, J.R. (1991). Person-job fit: a conceptual integration, literature review, and methodological critique. In C.L. Cooper & I.T. Robertson (Eds.), *International review of industrial and organizational psychology* (Vol. 6, pp. 283–357). Chichester: Wiley.

Edwards, J.R., & Harrison, R. van (1993). Job demands and worker health: Three-dimensional reexamination of the relationship between person-environment fit and strain. *Journal of Applied Psychology, 78,* 628–648.

Elliott, G.R., & Eisendorfer, C. (Eds.) (1982). *Stress and human health: Analysis and implications of research.* New York: Springer.

Ellis, B., & Miller, K.I. (1993). The role of assertiveness, personal control, and participation in the prediction of nurse burnout. *Journal of Applied Communication Research, 21* (4), 327–342.

Etzion, D., & Westman, M. (1994). Social support and sense of control as moderators of the stress-burnout relationship in military careers. *Journal of Social Behavior and Personality, 9* (4), 639–656.

Evans, G.W., & Carrere, S. (1991). Traffic congestion, perceived control, and psychophysiological stress among urban bus drivers. *Journal of Applied Psychology, 76* (5), 658–663.

Fisher, J.D., Nadler, A., & Witcher-Alagna, S. (1982). Recipient reactions to aid. *Psychological Bulletin, 91,* 27–54.

Fisher, S. (1985). Control and blue collar work. In C. L. Cooper & M. J. Smith (Eds.), *Job stress and blue collar work.* Chichester: Wiley.

Fisher, S. (1989). Stress, control, worry prescriptions and the implications for health at work: A sychobiological model. In S.L. Sauter, J.J. Hurrell Jr. & C.L. Cooper (Eds.), *Job Control and Worker Health* (pp. 205–236). Chichester: Wiley & Sons.

Fletcher, B.(C.). (1988). The epidemiology of occupational stress. In C.L. Cooper, & R. Payne (Eds.), *Causes, coping and consequences of stress at work* (pp. 3–50). Chichester: Wiley & Sons.

Fletcher, B.(C.). (1991). *Work, stress, disease and life expectancy.* Chichester: John Wiley & Sons.

Fletcher, B.(C.), & Jones, F. (1993). A refutation of Karasek's demand-discretion model of occupational stress with a range of dependent measures. *Journal of Organizational Behavior, 14,* 319–330.

Fletcher, B.(C.), & Payne, R.L. (1980). Stress at work: A review and theoretical framework. *Personal Review, 9* (1), 19–29.

Folkman, S. (1984). Personal control and stress and coping processes: A theoretical analysis. *Journal of Personality and Social Psychology, 46* (4), 839–852.

Fox, M.L., Dwyer, D.J., & Ganster, D.C. (1993). Effects of stressful job demands and control on psychological and attitudinal outcomes in a hospital setting. *Academy of Management Journal, 36* (2), 289–318.

Frankenhaueser, M. (1971). Experimental approaches to the study of human behavior as related to neuro-endocrine functions. In L. Levi (Ed.), *Society, stress and disease*. London: Oxford University Press.

French, J.R.P., & Caplan, R.D. (1970). Psychosocial factors in coronary heart disease. *Industrial Medicine, 39* (9), 31–45.

French, J.R.P. (1973). Person role fit. *Occupational Mental Health, 3*, 15–20.

French, J.R.P., & Kahn, R.L. (1962). A programmatic approach to studying the industrial environment and mental health. *Journal of Social Issues, 18* (3), 1–47.

French, J.R.P., Caplan, R.D., & Harrison, R.V. (1982). *Mechanisms of job stress and strain*. Chichester: Wiley & Sons.

Frese, M. (1989). Theoretical models of control and health. In S.L. Sauter, J.J. Hurrell Jr. & C.L. Cooper (Eds.), *Job control and worker health* (pp. 107–128). Chichester: Wiley & Sons.

Frese, M., & Zapf, D. (1988). Methodological issues in the study of work stress: Objective vs subjective measurement of work stress and the question of longitudinal studies. In C.L. Cooper & R. Payne (Eds.), *Causes, coping and consequences of stress at work* (pp. 375–411). Chichester: Wiley & Sons.

Fried, Y., & Tiegs, R.B. (1993). The main effect model versus buffering model of shop steward social support: A study of rank-and-file auto workers in the U.S.A. Special Issue: Integrating domains of work stress and industrial relations: Evidence from five countries. *Journal of Organizational Behavior, 14* (5), 481–493.

Friedman, M., & Rosenman, R.H. (1974). *Type-A behavior pattern and your heart*. New York: Knopf.

Furnham, A. (1986). The social desirability of the Type A behaviour pattern. *Psychological Medicine, 16* (4), 805–811.

Furnham, A. (1992). *Personality at work: The role of individual differences in the workplace*. London: Routledge.

Gaillard, A.W.K., & Wientjes, C.J.E. (1994). Mental load and work stress as two types of energy mobilization. Special Issue: A healthier work environment. *Work and Stress, 8* (2), 141–152.

Ganster, D.C. (1995). Interventions for building healthy organizations: Suggestions from the stress research literature. In L.R. Murphy, J.J. Hurrell Jr., S.L. Sauter & C.P. Keita (Eds.), *Job stress interventions* (pp. 323–336). Washington: APA.

Ganster, D.C., & Fusilier, M.R. (1989). Control in the workplace. In C.L. Cooper & I.T. Robertson (Eds.), *International review of industrial and organizational psychology* (pp. 235–280). Chichester: Wiley & Sons.

Gardell, B. (1982). Worker participation and autonomy: A multilevel approach to democracy at the workplace. *International Journal of Health Services, 12* (4), 527–558.

Glass, D.C., Reim, B., & Singer, J.E. (1971). Behavioral consequences of adaptation to controllable and uncontrollable noise. *Journal of Experimental Social Psychology, 7*, 244–257.

Geurts, S.A., Schaufeli, W.B., & Buunk, B.P. (1993). Social comparison, inequity, and absenteeism among bus drivers. *European Work and Organizational Psychologist, 3*, 191–203.

Geurts, S.A., Buunk, B.P., & Schaufeli, W.B. (1994a). Health complaints, social comparisons and absenteeism. *Work and Stress, 8*, 220–234.

Geurts, S.A., Buunk, B.P., & Schaufeli, W.B. (1994b). Social comparisons and absenteeism: A structural modeling approach. *Journal of Applied Social Psychology, 24*, 1871–1890.

Goleman, D. (1995). *Emotional intelligence*. New York: Bantam Books.

Goodell, H., Wolf, S., & Rogers, F.B. (1986). Historical perspective. In S.G. Wolf Jr. & A.J. Firestone (Eds.), *Occupational stress*. Littleton, MA: PSY Publishing Company.

Gründemann, R.W.M., Nijboer, I.D., & Schellart, A.J.M. (1991). *Arbeidsgebondenheid van WAO-intrede. Deelrapport I: Resultaten van de enquête onder WAO-ers*. Den Haag: Ministerie van Sociale Zaken en Werkgelegenheid.

Hackman, J.R., & Oldham, G.R. (1980). *Work redesign*. Reading, MA: Addison-Wesley.

Haines, V.A., Hurlbert, J.S., & Zimmer, C. (1991). Occupational stress, social support and the buffer hypothesis. *Work and Occupations, 18*, 212–235.

Hamberger, L.K., & Lohr, J.M. (1984). *Stress and stress management: Research and applications*. New York: Springer.

Hatfield, E., Cacioppo, J.T., & Rapson, R.L. (1994). *Emotional contagion*. Cambridge: Cambridge University Press.

Hatfield, E., & Sprecher, S. (1983). Equity theory and recipients reactions to help. In J.D. Fisher, A. Nadler, & B.M. DePaulo (Eds.), *New directions in helping behavior* (Vol. 1, pp. 113–141). New York: Academic Press.

Heider, F. (1958). *The psychology of interpersonal relations*. New York: Wiley.

Henley, A.C., & Williams, R.L. (1986). Type A and B subjects' self reported cognitive/affective/behavioral responses to descriptions of potentially frustrating situations. *Journal of Human Stress, 12*, 168–173.

Himle, D.P. Jayaratne, S., & Thyness, A.P. (1989). The buffering effect of four types of supervisory support on work stress. *Administration in Social Work, 13*, 19–34.

Hobfoll, S.E. (1989). Conservation of resources: A new attempt at conceptualizing stress. *American Psychologist, 44*, 513–524.

Hodgson, J.T., Jones, J.R., Elliott, R.C., & Osman, J. (1993). *Self-reported work-related illness*. Sudbury, Suffolk: HSE Books.

Holt, R.R. (1982). Occupational stress. In L. Goldberger & S. Breznitz (Eds.), *Handbook of stress: Theoretical and clinical aspects*. New York: The Free Press.

House, J.S. (1981). *Work stress and social support*. Reading, MA: Addison-Wesley.

House, J.S. (1985) Barriers to work stress: I. Social support. In W.D. Gentry, H. Benson & Ch. J. De Wolff (Eds.), *Behavioral medicine: Work, stress and health*.

Houtman, I.L.D., & Kompier, M.A.J. (1995). Risk factors and occupational risk groups for work stress in The Netherlands. In S.L. Sauter & L.R. Murphy (Eds.), *Organizational risk factors for job stress* (pp. 209–225). Washington, DC: APA.

Ingledew, D.K., Hardy, L., & Cooper, C.L. (1992). On the reliability and validity of the Locus of Control scale of the Occupational Stress Indicator. *Personality and Individual Differences, 13* (11), 1183–1191.

Israel, B.A., Schurman, S.J., & House, J.S. (1989). Action research on occupational stress: Involving workers as researchers. *International Journal of Health Services, 19* (1), 135–155.

Ivancevich, J.M., & Matteson, M.T. (1980). *Stress at work: A managerial perspective*. Glenview, IL: Scott, Foresman & Co.

Ivancevich, J.M., & Matteson, M.T. (1988). Promoting the individual's health and well-being. In C.L. Cooper & R. Payne (Eds.), *Causes, coping and consequences of stress at work* (pp. 267–299). Chichester: Wiley.

Jamal, M. (1990). Relationship of job stress and Type-A behavior to employees' job satisfaction, organizational commitment, psychosomatic health problems, and turnover motivation. *Human Relations, 43* (8), 727–738.

James, L.R., & Jones, A.P. (1980). Perceived job characteristics and job satisfaction: An examination of reciprocal causation. *Personnel Psychology, 33*, 97–135.

James, L.R., & Tetrick, L.E. (1986). Confirmatory analytic tests of three causal models relating job perceptions to job satisfaction. *Journal of Applied Psychology, 71* (1), 77–82.

Jayaratne, S., & Chess, W.A. (1984). The effect of emotional support on perceived job stress and strain. *Journal of Applied Behavioral Science, 21*, 141–153.

Johnson, J.V. (1989). Control, collectivity and the psychosocial work environment. In S.L. Sauter, J.J. Hurrell Jr. & C.L. Cooper (Eds.), *Job control and worker health* (pp. 56–74). Chichester: Wiley & Sons.

Johnson, J.V., & Hall, E.M. (1988). Job strain, work place social support, and cardiovascular disease: A cross-sectional study of a random sample of the Swedish working population. *American Journal of Public Health, 78* (10), 1336–1342.

Johnson, J.V., & Hall, E.M. (1994). Social support in the work environment and cardiovascular disease. In S.A. Shumaker & S.M. Czajkowski (Eds.), *Social support and cardiovascular disease* (pp. 145–167). New York: Plenum Press.

Jones, F., & Fletcher, B.(C.) (1996). Job control and health. In M.J. Schabracq, J.A.M. Winnubst & C.L. Cooper (Eds.), *Handbook of Work and Health Psychology* (pp. 33–50). Chichester: John Wiley & Sons.

Jonge, J. de (1995). *Job autonomy, well-being, and health: A study among Dutch health care workers* (PhD thesis). Maastricht: Datawyse.

Jonge, J. de, Boumans, N.P.G., Landeweerd, J.A., & Nijhuis, F.J.N. (1995). De relatie tussen werk en werkbeleving (The relationship between job characteristics and psychological outcomes). *Tijdschrift voor Ziekenverpleging, 105* (7), 212–216.

Jonge, J. de, Janssen, P.P.M., & Breukelen, G.J.P. van (1996). Testing the Demand-Control-Support Model among health care professionals: A structural equation model. *Work and Stress, 10*, 3, 209–224.

Jonge, J. de, & Schaufeli, W.B. (in press). Job characteristics and employee well-being: A test of Warr's Vitamin Model in health care workers using structural equation modelling. *Journal of Organizational Behavior*.

Kahn, R.L. (1981). *Work and health*. New York: Wiley.

Kahn, R.L. (1985). *On the conceptualization of stress. A scientific debate: How to define and research stress*. National Institute of Mental Health, Center for Prevention Research. Washington, DC: US Department of Health and Human Services, Public Health Service.

Kahn, R.L., & Byosiere, P. (1992). Stress in organizations. In M.D. Dunette & L.M. Hough (Eds.), *Handbook of industrial and organizational psychology* (Vol. 3, pp. 571–650). Palo Alto, CA: Consulting Psychologists Press.

Kahn, R.L, Wolfe, D.M., Quinn, R.P., Snoek, J.D., & Rosenthal, R.A. (1964). *Organizational stress: Studies in role conflict and ambiguity*. New York: Wiley.

Kaplan, M.F. (1987). The influencing process in group decision making. In C. Hendrick (Ed.), *Review of personality and social psychology* (Vol. 8, pp. 189–212). Newbury Park, CA: Sage.

Karasek, R.A. (1979). Job demands, job decision latitude, and mental strain: Implications for job redesign. *Administrative Science Quarterly, 24* (2), 285–308.

Karasek, R.A. (1992). Stress prevention through work reorganization: A summary of 19 international case studies. In ILO, *Conditions of work digest on preventing stress at work, 11* (2), 23–41.

Karasek, R.A., & Theorell, T. (1990). *Healthy work: Stress, productivity and the reconstruction of working life*. New York: Basic Books.

Kasl, S.V. (1978). Epidemiological contributions to the study of work stress. In C.L. Cooper and R.L. Payne (Eds.), *Stress and work*. New York: Wiley.

Kasl, S.V. (1986). Stress and disease in the workplace: A methodological commentary on the accumulated evidence. In M.F. Cataldo & T.J. Coates (Eds.),

Health and industry: A behavioral medicine perspective (pp. 52–85). New York: Wiley.

Kasl, S.V. (1987). Methodologies in stress and health: Past difficulties, present dilemmas, future directions. In S.V. Kasl & C.L. Cooper (Eds.), *Stress and health: Issues in research methodology* (pp. 307–318). Chichester: Wiley & Sons.

Kasl, S. V. (1989). An epidemiological perspective on the role of control in health. In S.L. Sauter, J.J. Hurrell Jr. & C.L. Cooper (Eds.), *Job control and worker health* (pp. 161–189). Chichester: Wiley & Sons.

Kasl, S.V. (1996). The influence of the work environment on cardiovascular health: A historical, conceptual, and methodological perspective. *Journal of Occupational Health Psychology, 1* (1), 42–56.

Kaufman, G.M., & Beehr, T.A. (1986). Interactions between job stressors and social support: Some counterintuitive results. *Journal of Applied Psychology, 71* (3), 522–526.

Keenan, A., & Newton, T.J. (1984). Frustration in organizations: Relationships to role stress, climate, and psychological strain. *Journal of Occupational Psychology, 57,* 57–65.

Keenan, A., & Newton, T.J. (1985). Stressful events, stressors and psychological strains in young professional engineers. *Journal of Occupational Behaviour, 6,* 151–156.

Kirmeyer, S.L., & Dougherty, T.W. (1988). Workload, tension, and coping: Moderating effects of supervisor support. *Personnel Psychology, 41,* 125–139.

Kleber, R.J., & Velden, P.G. van der (1996). Acute stress at work. In M.J. Schabracq, J.A.M. Winnubst & C.L. Cooper (Eds.), *Handbook of work and health psychology* (pp. 295–310). Chichester: John Wiley & Sons.

Kobasa, S.C. (1982). Commitment and coping in stress resistance among lawyers. *Journal of Personality and Social Psychology, 42,* 707–717.

Kobasa, S.C., Maddi, S.R., & Kahn, S. (1982). Hardiness and health: A prospective study. *Journal of Personality and Social Psychology, 42,* 168–177.

Kobasa, S.C., & Puccetti, M.C. (1983). Personality and social resources in stress resistance. *Journal of Personality and Social Psychology, 45,* 839–850.

Koeske, G.F., & Kelly, T. (1995). The impact of overinvolvement on burnout and job satisfaction. *American Journal of Orthopsychiatry, 65* (2), 282–292.

Koeske, G.F., & Kirk, S.A. (1995). Direct and buffering effects of internal locus of control among mental health professionals. *Journal of Social Service Research, 20* (3–4), 1–28.

Koeske, G.F., Kirk, S.A., & Koeske, R.D. (1993). Coping with job stress: Which strategies work best? *Journal of Occupational and Organizational Psychology, 66,* 319–335.

Kohn, M.L., & Schooler, C. (1983). *Work and personality: An inquiry into the impact of social stratification.* Norwood, NJ: Ablex Publishing.

Kompier, M.A.J. (1996). *Bus drivers: Occupational stress and stress prevention* (Working paper). Geneva: International Labour Office.

Kornhauser, A. (1965). *Mental health and the industrial worker.* New York: Wiley.

Landsbergis, P.A. (1988). Occupational stress among health care workers: A test of the job demands-control model. *Journal of Organizational Behavior, 9,* 217–239.

Landsbergis, P.A., Schnall, P.L., Warren, K., Pickering, T.G., & Schwartz, J.E. (1994). Association between ambulatory blood pressure and alternative formulations of job strain. *Scandinavian Journal of Work, Environment, & Health, 20,* 349–363.

Landsbergis, P.A., Schurman, S.J., Israel, B.A., Schnall, P.L., Hugentobler, M.K., Cahill, J., & Baker, D. (1993). Job stress and heart disease: Evidence and strategies for prevention. *New Solutions,* Summer, 42–58.

LaRocco, J.M., House, J.S., & French, J.R.P. (1980). Social support, occupational stress, and health. *Journal of Health and Social Behavior, 21,* 202–218.

LaRocco, J.M., & Jones, A.P. (1978). Co-worker and leader support as moderators of stress-strain relationships in work situations. *Journal of Applied Psychology, 63,* 629–634.

Latack, J.C., & Havlovic, S.J. (1992). Coping with job stress: A conceptual evaluation framework for coping measures. *Journal of Organizational Behavior, 13,* 479–508.

Lazarus, R.S. (1968). Stress. In D.L. Sills (Ed.), *International encyclopedia of the social sciences* (Vol. 15). New York: MacMillan.

Lazarus, R.S. (1985). *Stress, appraisal and coping capacities. In a scientific debate: How to define and research stress.* National Institute of Mental Health, Center for Prevention Research. Washington, DC: US Department of Health and Human Services, Public Health Service.

Lazarus, R.S. (1993). From psychological stress to the emotions: A history of changing outlooks. *Annual Review of Psychology, 44,* 1–21.

Lazarus, R.S. (1995). Psychological stress in the workplace. In R. Crandall & P.L. Perrewé (Eds.), *Occupational stress: A handbook* (pp. 3–14). Washington: Taylor & Francis.

Lazarus, R.S., & Folkman, S. (1984). *Stress, appraisal, and coping.* New York: Springer.

Lazarus, R.S., & Folkman, S. (1985). Stress as a rubric. In *A scientific debate: How to define and research stress.* National Institute of Mental Health, Center for Prevention Research. Washington, DC: US Department of Health and Human Services, Public Health Service.

Lehman, D.R., & Hemphill, K.J. (1990). Recipients' perceptions of support attempts and attributions for support attempts that fail. *Journal of Social and Personal Relationships, 7,* 563–574.

Leiter, M.P., & Meechan, K.A. (1986). Role structure and burnout in the field of human services. *Journal of Applied Behavioral Science, 22* (1), 47–52.

Lennerlöf, L. (1988). Learned helplessness at work. *International Journal of Health Services, 18* (2), 207–222.

Levi, L. (1994). Work, worker and wellbeing: An overview. *Work and Stress, 8* (2), 79–83.

Lewin, K. (1935). *A dynamic theory of personality.* New York: McGraw-Hill.

Lewin, K. (1951). *Field theory in social science.* New York: Harper & Row.

Litt, M.D., & Turk, D.C. (1985). Sources of stress and dissatisfaction in experienced high school teachers. *Journal of Educational Research, 78,* 178–185.

Maes, S., Vingerhoets, A.J.J.M., & Heck, G. van (1987). The study of stress and disease: Some developments and requirements. *Social Science and Medicine, 25* (6), 567–578.

Manlove, E.E. (1994). Conflict and ambiguity over work roles: The impact on child care worker burnout. *Early Education and Development, 5* (1) 41–55.

Marcelissen, F.H.G., Winnubst, J.A.M., Buunk, B.P., & De Wolff, Ch. J. (1988). Social support and stress: A causal analysis. *Social Science and Medicine, 26,* 365–373.

Marmot, M. (1994). Work and other factors influencing coronary health and sickness absence. Special Issue: A healthier work environment. *Work and Stress, 8* (2), 191–201.

Maslach, C., & Jackson, S.E. (1982). Burnout in health professions: A social psychological analysis. In G.S. Sanders & J. Suls (Eds.), *Social psychology of health and illness.* Hillsdale, NJ: Lawrence Erlbaum.

Maslach, C., & Schaufeli, W.B. (1993). Historical and conceptual development of burnout. In W.B. Schaufeli, C. Maslach & T. Marek (Eds.), *Professional burnout: Recent developments in theory and research* (pp. 1–16). Washington: Taylor & Francis.

Matsui, T., & Onglatco, M.L. (1992). Career self-efficacy as a moderator of the relation between occupational stress and strain. *Journal of Vocational Behavior, 41* (1), 79–88.

Miller, S.M. (1990). To see or not to see: Cognitive informational styles in the coping process. In M. Rosenbaum (Ed.), *Learned resourcefulness: On coping skills, self-control, and adaptive behavior* (pp. 95–126). New York: Springer.

Miller, D.T., & McFarland, C. (1991). When social comparison goes awry: The case of pluralistic ignorance. In J. Suls & T. A. Wills (Eds.), *Social comparison: Contemporary theory and research* (pp. 287–313). Hillsdale, NJ: Erlbaum.

Muris, P.E.H.M. (1994). *Monitoring and blunting: Coping styles and strategies in threatening situations* (PhD thesis). Maastricht: UPM.

Murphy, L.R. (1985). Individual coping strategies. In C.L. Cooper & M.J. Smith (Eds.), *Job stress and blue collar work.* Chichester: Wiley.

Murphy, L.R. (1988). Workplace interventions for stress reduction and prevention. In C.L. Cooper & R. Payne (Eds.), *Causes, coping and consequences of stress at work* (pp. 301–339). Chichester: Wiley.

Murray, H.A. (1938). *Explorations in Personality.* New York: Oxford University Press.

Murray, H.A. (1959). Preparations for the scaffold of a comprehensive system. In S. Koch (Ed.), *Psychology: A study of a science: Formulations of the person and the social context* (Vol. 3). New York: McGraw-Hill.

Northwestern National Life (1991). *Employee burnout: America's newest epidemic.* Minneapolis, MN: Northwestern National Life Insurance Company.

Oatley, K., & Jenkins, J.M. (1992). Human emotions: Function and dysfunction. *Annual Review of Psychology, 43,* 55–86.

O'Driscoll, M.P., & Cooper, C.L. (1994). Coping with work-related stress: A critique of existing measures and proposal for an alternative methodology. *Journal of Occupational and Organizational Psychology, 67,* 343–354.

Offermann, L.R., & Gowing, M.K. (1990). Organizations of the future: Changes and challenges. *American Psychologist, 45* (2), 95–108.

Orlebeke, J.F., & Van Doornen, L.J.P. (1983). A-type gedrag: kosten en baten (Type A behavior: Costs and rewards). In E.J. Boer, F. Verhage, & Ch. J. de Wolff (Eds.), *Stress. Uitdaging en bedreiging.* Lisse: Swets and Zeitlinger.

Paoli, P. (1992). *First European Survey of the Work Environment 1991–1992.* Dublin: European Foundation for the Improvement of Living and Working Conditions.

Parkes, K.R. (1991). Locus of control as moderator: An explanation for additive versus interactive findings in the demand-discretion model of work stress? *British Journal of Psychology, 82,* 291–312.

Parkes, K.R. (1994). Personality and coping as moderators of work stress. *Work and Stress, 8,* 110–129.

Parkes, K.R., Mendham, C.A., & Rabenau, C. von (1994). Social support and the demand-discretion model of job stress: Tests of additive and interactive effects in two samples. *Journal of Vocational Behavior, 44* (1), 91–113.

Payne, R.L. (1979). Demands, supports, constraints and psychological health. In C. Mackay & T. Cox (Eds.), *Response to stress: Occupational aspects* (pp. 85–105). London: IPC.

Payne, R.L., & Jones, J.G. (1987). Measurement and methodological issues in social support. In S.V. Kasl & C.L. Cooper (Eds.), *Stress and health: Issues in research methodology* (pp. 167–205). Chichester: Wiley.

Pearlin, L.J., & Schooler, C. (1978). The structure of coping. *Journal of Health and Social Behavior, 19,* 2–21.

Pearlin, L.J., Lieberman, M.A., Menaghan, E.G., & Mullan, J.T. (1981). The stress process. *Journal of Health and Social Behavior, 22*, 337–356.

Peeters, M.C.W., Schaufeli, W.B., & Buunk, B.P. (1995a). The role of attributions in the cognitive appraisal of work-related stressful events: An event-recording approach. *Work and Stress, 9* (4), 463–474.

Peeters, M.C.W., Buunk, A.P., & Schaufeli, W.B. (1995b). A micro-analytic exploration of the cognitive appraisal of daily stressful events at work: The role of controllability. *Anxiety, Stress, and Coping, 8*, 127–139.

Peeters, M.C.W., Buunk, A.P., & Schaufeli, W.B. (1995c). Social interactions, stressful events, and negative affect at work: A micro-analytic approach. *European Journal of Social Psychology, 25*, 391–401.

Pekrun, R., & Frese, M. (1992). Emotions in work and achievement. In C.L. Cooper & I.T. Robertson (Eds.), *International review of industrial and organizational psychology* (Vol. 7, pp. 153–200). Chichester: Wiley.

Pennebaker, J.W. (1982). *The psychology of physical symptoms*. New York: Springer-Verlag.

Pennebaker, J.W., & Brittingham, G.L. (1982). Environmental and sensory cues affecting the perception of physical symptoms. In A. Baum & J.E. Singer (Eds.), *Advances in environmental psychology*. Hillsdale, NJ: Erlbaum.

Pennebaker, J.W., & Skelton, J.A. (1981). Selective monitoring of physical sensations. *Journal of Personality and Social Psychology, 41* (2), 213–223.

Rees, D.W., & Cooper, C.L. (1992). The occupational stress indicator locus of control scale: Should this be regarded as a state rather than trait measure? *Work and Stress, 6* (1), 45–48.

Reiche, H.M. (1982). *Stress aan het werk* (Stress at work). Lisse: Swets & Zeitlinger.

Reim, B., Glass, D.C., & Singer, J.E. (1971). Behavioral consequences of exposure to uncontrollable and unpredictable noise. *Journal of Applied Social Psychology, 1*, 44–56.

Repetti, R.L. (1987). Individual and common components of the social environment at work and psychological well-being. *Journal of Personality and Social Psychology, 52*, 710–721.

Rhodewalt, F., Sansone, C., Hill, C.A., & Chemers, M.M. (1991). Stress and distress as a function of Jenkins Activity Survey-defined Type A behavior and control over the work environment. *Basic and Applied Social Psychology, 12* (2), 211–226.

Robinson, P., & Inkson, K. (1994). Stress effects on the health of chief executives of business organizations. *Stress Medicine, 10* (1), 27–34.

Rook, K. (1984). Research on social support, loneliness and social isolation. In P. Shaver (Ed.), *Review of personality and social psychology* (Vol. 5, pp. 234–266). Beverly Hills: Sage.

Rook, K.S. (1987). Social support versus companionship: Effects on life stress, loneliness, and evaluations by others. *Journal of Personality and Social Psychology, 52*, 1132–1147.

Ross, R.R., Altmaier, E.M., & Russell, D.W. (1989). Job stress, social support and burnout among counseling center staff. *Journal of Counseling Psychology, 36*, 464–470.

Rotter, J.B. (1966). Generalized expectancies for internal versus external control of reinforcement. *Psychological Monographs: General and Applied, 80* (1, Whole No. 609).

Rush, M.C., Schoel, W.A., & Barnard, S.M. (1995). Psychological resiliency in the public sector: "Hardiness" and pressure for change. *Journal of Vocational Behavior, 46* (1), 17–39.

Russell, D.W., Altmaier, E., & Velzen, D. van (1987). Job related stress, social support, and burnout among classroom teachers. *Journal of Applied Psychology, 73* (2), 269–274.

Sarason, I.G., & Sarason, B.R. (1986). Experimentally provided social support. *Journal of Personality and Social Psychology, 50*, 1222–1225.

Sauter, S.L., Hurrell Jr., J. J., & Cooper, C.L. (Eds.) (1989), *Job control and worker health*. Chichester: Wiley & Sons.

Schabracq, M.J., Cooper, C.L., & Winnubst, J.A.M. (1996). Work and health psychology: Towards a theoretical model. In M.J. Schabracq, J.A.M. Winnubst & C.L. Cooper (Eds), *Handbook of Work and Health Psychology* (pp. 3–29). Chichester: John Wiley & Sons.

Schachter, S. (1959). *The psychology of affiliation*. Palo Alto, CA: Stanford University Press.

Schachter, S., & Singer, J.E. (1962). Cognitive, social and physiological determinants of emotional state. *Psychological Review, 69*, 379–399.

Schaufeli, W.B., & Buunk, B.P. (1996). Professional burnout. In M.J. Schabracq, J.A.M. Winnubst, & C.L. Cooper (Eds.), *Handbook of work and health psychology* (pp. 311–346). Chichester: Wiley & Sons.

Schaufeli, W.B., Maslach, C., & Marek, T. (Eds.) (1993), *Professional burnout: Recent developments in theory and research*. Washington DC: Taylor & Francis.

Schaufeli, W.B., & Dierendonck, D. van (1993). The construct validity of two burnout measures. *Journal of Organizational Behavior, 14*, 631–647.

Scheier, M.F., Weintraub, J.K., & Carver, C.S. (1986). Coping with stress: Divergent strategies of optimists and pessimists. *Journal of Personality and Social Psychology, 51*, 1257–1264.

Schnall, P.L., Landsbergis, P.A., & Baker, D. (1994). Job Strain and Cardiovascular Disease. *Annual Review of Public Health, 15*, 381–411.

Sell, M. van, Brief, A.P., & Schuler, R.J. (1981). Role conflict and ambiguity: Integration of the literature and directions for future research. *Human Relations, 34*, 43–72.

Selye, H. (1978). *Stress*. Utrecht: Het Spectrum.

Semmer, N. (1996). Individual differences, work stress and health. In M.J. Schabracq, J.A.M. Winnubst & C.L. Cooper (Eds.), *Handbook of work and health psychology* (pp. 51–86). Chichester: John Wiley & Sons.

Semmer, N., Zapf, D., & Greif, S. (1996). "Shared job strain": A new approach for assessing the validity of job stress measurements. *Journal of Occupational and Organizational Psychology, 69*, 293–310.

Shumaker, S.A., & Brownell, A. (1984). Towards a theory of social support: Closing conceptual gaps. *Journal of Social Issues, 40* (4), 11–36.

Siegrist, J. (1991). Contributions of sociology to the prediction of heart disease and their implications for public health. *European Journal of Public Health, 1*, 10–21.

Siegrist, J., & Peter, R. (1994). Job stressors and coping characteristics in work-related disease: Issues of validity. *Work and Stress, 8*, 130–140.

Skelton, J.A., & Pennebaker, J.W. (1982). The psychology of physical symptoms and sensations. In G.S. Sanders & J. Suls (Eds.), *Social psychology of health and illness*. Hillsdale, NJ: Lawrence Erlbaum.

Skorupka, J., & Agresti, A.A. (1993). Ethical beliefs about burnout and continued professional practice. *Professional Psychology: Research and Practice, 24*, 1–5.

Spector, P.E. (1992). A consideration of the validity and meaning of self-report measures of job conditions. In C.L. Cooper & I.T. Robertson (Eds.), *International Review of Industrial and Organizational Psychology* (pp. 123–151). New York: Wiley & Sons.

Spector, P.E., & O'Connell, B.J. (1994). The contribution of personality traits, negative affectivity, locus of control and Type A to the subsequent reports of job stressors and job strains. *Journal of Occupational and Organizational Psychology, 67* (1), 1–12.

Spielberger, C.D. (1985). *Emotional reactions to stress: Anxiety and anger. A scientific debate: How to define and research stress*. National Institute of Mental Health, Center for Prevention Research. Washington, DC: US Department of Health and Human Services, Public Health Service.

Stokols, D. (1992). Conflict-prone and conflict-resistant organizations. In H.S. Friedman (Ed.), *Hostility, coping and health* (pp. 65–76). Washington, DC: American Psychological Association.

Stouffer, S.A., Suchman, E.A., De Vinney, L.C., Star, S.A., & Williams, R.M., Jr. (1949). *The American soldier: Adjustment during army life, Vol. 1*. Princeton, NJ: Princeton University Press.

Stroebe, W.S., & Stroebe, M.S. (1994). *Social psychology and health*. Pacific Groves, CA: Brooks/Cole Publishing Company.

Sullins, E.S. (1991). Emotional contagion revisited: Effects of social comparison and expressive style on mood convergence. *Personality and Social Psychology Bulletin, 17*, 166–174.

Suls, J., & Sanders, G.S. (1988). Type A behavior as a general risk factor for physical disorder. *Journal of Behavioral Medicine, 11* (3), 201–226.

Sutton, R.J. (1984). Job stress among primary and secondary schoolteachers. *Work and occupations, 11*, 7–28.

Taylor, H., & Cooper, C.L. (1989). The stress-prone personality: A review of the research in the context of occupational stress. *Stress Medicine, 5* (1) 17–27.

Taylor, S.E., Buunk, B.P., & Aspinwall, L.G. (1990). Social comparison, stress, and coping. Special Issue: Illustrating the value of basic research. *Personality and Social Psychology Bulletin, 16* (1), 74–89.

Taylor, S.E., Wood, J.V., & Lichtman, R.R. (1983). It could be worse: Selective evaluation as a response to victimization. *Journal of Social Issues, 39*, 19–40.

Terry, D.J., Neilsen, M., & Perchard, L. (1993). Effects of work stress on psychological well-being and job satisfaction: The stress-buffering role of social support. *Australian Journal of Psychology, 45* (3), 168–175.

Terry, D.J., Rawle, R., & Callan, V.J. (1995). The effects of social support on adjustment to stress: The mediating role of coping. *Personal Relationships, 2*, 97–124.

Theorell, T., & Karasek, R.A. (1996). Current issues relating to psychosocial job strain and cardiovascular disease research. *Journal of Occupational Health Psychology, 1* (1), 9–26.

Thoits, P. (1984). Coping, social support and psychological outcomes: The central role of emotion. *Review of Personality and Social Psychology, 5*, 219–238.

Tyler, P., & Cushway, D. (1995). Stress in nurses: The effects of coping and social support. *Stress Medicine, 11* (4), 243–251.

Uchino, B.N., Cacioppo, J.T., & Kiecolt-Glaser, J.K. (1996). The relationship between social support and physiological processes: A review with emphasis on underlying mechanisms and implications for health. *Psychological Bulletin, 119*, 488–531.

Uehara, E.S. (1995). Reciprocity reconsidered: Gouldner's "moral norm of reciprocity" and social support. *Journal of Social and Personal Relationships, 12*, 483–502.

Van Yperen, N.W., Buunk, B.P., & Schaufeli, W.B. (1992). Communal orientation and the burnout syndrome among nurses. *Journal of Applied Social Psychology, 22*, 173–189.

Vingerhoets, A.J.J.M., & Flohr, P.J.M. (1984). Type A behaviour and self-reports of coping preferences. *British Journal of Medical Psychology, 57*, 15–21.

Vinokur, A.D., Price, R.H., & Caplan, R.D. (1996). Hard times and hurtful partners: How financial strain affects depression and relationship satisfaction of unemployed persons and their spouses. *Journal of Personality and Social Psychology, 71*, 166–179.

Vinokur, A.D., & Ryn, M. van (1993). Social support and undermining in close relationships: Their independent effects on the mental health of unemployed persons. *Journal of Personality and Social Psychology, 65*, 350–359.

Wall, T.D., Jackson, P.R., Mullarkey, S., & Parker, S.K. (1996). The demands-control model of job strain: A more specific test. *Journal of Occupational and Organizational Psychology, 69*, 153–166.

Walster, E., Walster, G.W., & Berscheid, E. (1978). *Equity: Theory and research.* Boston, MA: Allyn & Bacon.

Warr, P.B. (1987). *Work, unemployment, and mental health.* Oxford: Clarendon Press.

Warr, P.B. (1990). Decision latitude, job demands, and employee well-being. *Work and Stress, 4* (4), 285–294.

Warr, P. (1994). A conceptual framework for the study of work and mental health. *Work and Stress, 8* (2), 84–97.

Whitehead, J.T. (1989). *Burnout in probation and corrections.* New York: Praeger.

Wiebe, D.J., & Williams, P.G. (1992). Hardiness and health: A social psychophysiological perspective on stress and adaptation. *Journal of Social and Clinical Psychology, 11*, 238–262.

Wills, T.A. (1981). Downward comparison principles in social psychology. *Psychological Bulletin, 90*, 245–271.

Winnubst, J.A.M., Jong, R.D. de, & Schabracq, M.J. (1996). The diagnosis of role strains at work. In M.J. Schabracq, J.A.M. Winnubst & C.L. Cooper (Eds.), *Handbook of work and health psychology* (pp. 106–125). Chichester: John Wiley & Sons.

Winnubst, J.A.M., Kleber, R.J., & Marcelissen, F.G.H. (1982). Effects of social support in the stressor-strain relationship: A Dutch sample. *Social Science and Medicine, 16*, 475–482.

World Health Organization, Regional Office for Europe (1991). *A healthier work environment. Basic concepts and methods of measurement.* Copenhagen.

Xie, J.L., & Johns, G. (1995). Job scope and stress: Can job scope be too high? *Academy of Management Journal, 38* (5) 1288–1309.

Yang, C.L., & Carayon, P. (1995). Effect of job demands and social support on worker stress: A study of VDT users. *Behaviour and Information Technology, 14* (1), 32–40.

Zegans, L.S. (1982). Stress and the development of somatic disorders. In L. Goldberger & S. Breznitz (Eds.), *Handbook of stress: Theoretical and clinical aspects.* New York: The Free Press.

Zillmann, D., & Zillmann, M. (1996). Psychoneuro endocrinology of social behavior. In E.T. Higgins & A.W. Kruglanski (Eds.), *Social Psychology: Handbook of basic principles* (pp. 39–71). New York: Guilford.

8

The "Older Worker" in the Organization

Johannes Gerrit Boerlijst, Joep M.A. Munnichs and Beate I.J.M. van der Heijden

1 WHO ARE TERMED "OLDER WORKERS"?

The concepts "younger worker" and "older worker" are common in the business community. Between both these age categories, there is a fairly large middle category in most organizations, though this is seldom given an age-related label. Although it is an established fact that roughly halfway through their career, many people are faced with functioning and personality problems or with feelings of depression and psychosomatic complaints—designated by terms such as "mid-career problems" or "mid-life crisis"—(Gerrichhauzen, 1989; Hunt & Collins, 1983; Kleber, 1982; see also Chapter 12, Volume 3 of this Handbook), the middle age group seldom receives special attention in the practical implementation of personnel policy. Such attention is, however, given to the "young" and the "old" because they are viewed as potential high-risk groups. Policy in the case of younger workers aims at averting the

danger of problems of adaptation and adjustment and at reducing the risk of excessive unproductive orientation periods. In the case of older workers, policy is concerned essentially with preventing or eliminating productivity losses resulting from "aging" or "not being able to keep up". Health problems are also a major factor in this policy.

While not leaving the "middle" age group out of account, the focus in this chapter is on "older" workers. Precisely who these are cannot be specifically defined. The dividing line between the "older" and the "middle" age categories is a gradual one and varies from sector to sector and from company to company. Even within an organization there is often a certain band width. A number of reasons can be given for this. People who stop work at 65 tend to be classified as "older" later in their career than those with a lower retirement age, as for example in the case of the so-called "taxing" professions such as the army, the fire service and the police force. Where organizations have voluntary or mandatory early retirement schemes, the lower the person's retirement age, the sooner the label "older" is applied.

Another reason is the variety of views held within companies on supposed links between a person's age and certain output variables such as productivity and creativity. For example, in certain sectors such as research and development and the software industry it is argued that only employees younger than 35 or 40 have the flexibility, inventiveness and élan to keep up with the high rate of successive innovations in knowledge and technology as well as in market requirements. Considerable added value is expected from the efforts of this age group. As regards the performance of innovative, creative work, the over-40s are simply written off. In such sectors one is labelled "too old" for some tasks at a relatively young age. Other sectors reserve the term "older" for those nearing retirement. The vagueness in defining who is termed an "older worker" is reflected in literature on this subject and consequently in this chapter as well.

In the remainder of this chapter the following will be discussed:

- fluctuating interest in the subject of "the older worker" (section 2);
- decline in job opportunities and the position of older workers (section 3);
- dejuvenization, aging and the position of older workers (section 4);
- the functioning of older workers (section 5);
- the mobility and employability of older workers (section 6);
- education, training and development of the over-40s (section 7);
- motivation and well-being of older workers (section 8);
- social networks of older workers (section 9).

The chapter concludes with an epilogue (section 10) summarizing observed necessities for further research.

2 FLUCTUATING INTEREST IN THE SUBJECT OF "THE OLDER WORKER"

Interest in the older worker on the part of the business community and government fluctuates and seems to be connected with the economic climate and the situation in the labour market. In periods of increasing prosperity and full employment, such as the post-war period up to around 1965, the older skilled and unskilled worker was in demand. At that time, themes such as functional age, further training/retraining and task changes were studied against this background (Belbin & Shimmin, 1964; Griew, 1964; Munnichs, 1966; Munnichs, Dirken, Dohmen, & Thierry, 1968). In this period, schemes were even set up to offer older employees work *after* retirement on a voluntary basis (Boerlijst-Bosch, 1962).

Subsequently, with the ebbing of the period of boom, interest in the added value of older, skilled and unskilled employees declined rapidly. They were no longer in great demand or even welcome on the labour market. Increasing international competition, hectic market developments and the need for drastic organizational, economic and technological modifications and innovations forced companies and organizations to face the possibility of rapidly increasing obsolescence of knowledge on the part of management and workers (Dalton & Thompson, 1971; Dubin, 1971; Kaufman, 1974, 1975). In this period the theme of "survival, renewal and rejuvenation" of the organization came to the fore and was then never to disappear from the scene. Personnel play a crucial role in this theme. The human activities and qualities needed for survival and renewal have never been systematically studied, presumably being thought self-evident and trivial. In business and in management literature, the view is held that salvation is to be sought in "creativity", "innovative ability", "élan", "decisiveness", "flexibility" or qualities of similar purport, more often attributed to younger than to older workers. Those lacking in these qualities to any degree are not wanted. Older workers tend to be labelled "less capable", "less efficient", "slower on the uptake" and so on (Boerlijst, Van der Heijden, & Van Assen, 1993; Rosen & Jerdee, 1976a; Stagner, 1985, p. 789f). The question as to whether this is a "valid" attribution in the sense that *under all circumstances* younger people are supposedly more creative etc. than comparable older colleagues is difficult to investigate. Double-blind psychological experiments would have to be conducted to exclude the possibility of *self-*

fulfilling prophecies. However, these are scarcely feasible in everyday business practice.

Prejudices have left their mark on personnel policy for younger and older employees. They foster considerable age discrimination, which starts right from recruitment and selection (Rosen & Jerdee, 1976b, Craft, Doctors, Shkop, & Benecki, 1979). The substantial investments made by organizations in the development of younger personnel are often unforthcoming in the case of older personnel (Boerlijst, 1995). Moreover, organizations are not averse to taking measures to exclude older people from work before their official retirement in order to make room for "more capable" younger people. In certain sectors in The Netherlands there are virtually no workers over 60 and the cohorts of the over-55s are in the process of being significantly depleted. The lack of confidence in the creativeness and renewing value of older people is not the only significant factor here. Declining employment within companies and increasing concern about the relative level of labour costs have also undermined the position of older people. We will return to this in section 3.

Around 1985 a re-evaluation of "being older" and the meaning of "older workers" began. The reason for this lay more in force of circumstance than in doubt as to the prevailing prejudices pertaining to older versus younger people. These circumstances relate to the expected changes in the composition of the (working) population and are generally referred to by the terms "dejuvenization" and "aging". In most prosperous industrial countries, an absolute as well as a relative increase in the number of over-40s both on the labour market and in industry is envisaged over the coming decades. This group will attain a hitherto unparalleled size. The consequences for the aforementioned attitude towards older people will be examined in section 4.

3 DECLINE IN JOB OPPORTUNITIES AND THE POSITION OF OLDER WORKERS

In most industrial countries of Western Europe, increased prosperity and a range of other social factors have caused a sharp rise in labour costs since the end of the Second World War. In addition, companies and organizations have been obliged to make increasingly larger financial sacrifices to be able to meet international competition, ever more demanding markets and the necessity for rapid adaptability to abrupt changes in the ratio between supply and demand. In private and public sectors alike, there has been a considerable reduction in the positive margin between the costs and benefits of human labour. In the past 20–30 years, more and more companies have found themselves obliged to reduce their labour costs drastically. For this, three measures are appropriate:

- structurally eliminating work tasks by no longer carrying out certain activities or having them carried out elsewhere;
- replacing human labour by other, cheaper means of production; or
- "exporting" jobs to so-called "low-wage countries" outside Western Europe.

The last two measures in particular have resulted in a considerable growth in structural unemployment. For large numbers of employees, workplaces and work have been lost without any alternative compensatory employment. Many school leavers are no longer offered appropriate work when entering the labour market.

In theory, decisions on shedding jobs may be taken without consideration of individual personnel, in other words without taking account of the status, age and so on of those holding those jobs. This does actually happen in some cases, for example when a company or organizational unit as a whole is closed down and all the employees, young and old and from top to bottom, are made redundant.

If a more favourable cost/benefit ratio is to be achieved not by closure but by downsizing or shrinking the personnel ranks, a "blind" choice of those to be retired from the field is not the most appropriate method. In terms of productivity and expendability, employees cannot be treated as if they were all the same. Seen in the long term the expected benefits to be derived from one employee are greater than those from another and in theory it is possible to make selections on this basis. Often, however, decision makers—employers as well as trade unions—prefer to indicate at a category level rather than at an individual level those first in line to go. The selection of a personnel category has advantages in terms of industrial law. It can be regulated via a collective bargaining process or a "social plan", and requires fewer contestable "judgments of Solomon". Furthermore, it tends to make a more "objective" impression on those concerned as well as on the outside world than the designation of individuals. With the dismissal of entire categories, a process of downsizing can be accomplished quickly and the desired economizations achieved without delay. This is especially important when a company is in financial difficulties and must change course as fast as possible. Obviously, the categories to be laid off are preferably those which will generate relatively large economizations and encounter relatively little internal or external resistance. In practice the first choice often seems to fall on "older personnel". Various reasons can be found for this:

1. Older workers entail higher costs for an organization than younger ones. In our remuneration system, the sum of salary, labour costs and emoluments (extra holidays, gratuities, etc.) of older workers is on average higher than in the case of their younger colleagues (cf. Gelderblom & De Koning, 1992b, p. 15). It is plausible that older workers' productivity is therefore assessed as lower than that of younger colleagues, even when the latter achieve roughly the same productivity or less. It is therefore assumed in the business community and by the government too that if older people were to stop work or be obliged to stop work *en masse*, there would be a considerable rise in average productivity per employee. This hypothesis does not, in fact, have a sufficiently empirical basis (WRR, 1992, p. 112). In this context we refer to countries such as Japan (Boerlijst, 1986; Boerlijst, Van Dijk, & Van Helvoort, 1987) and Australia, where personnel in some companies are given the choice at the age of 55 of whether to retire or to continue at a lower salary than previously. The second

alternative avoids loss of returns in terms of economics. Of special interest are cases where employees have been given other jobs to which they, as older people, are eminently suited in view of their experience and expertise. In this way, they do not stand in the way of the careers of the young people.

2. In our present-day labour force, older workers as a group are at a considerable educational disadvantage. The need for restructuring and reorientation of a company generally implies the need for training/retraining and, respectively, changing of employees' functions, the costs of which are higher for older people and with less likelihood of adequate returns. The time remaining for recovery of training costs is, after all, shorter. This is a highly complex issue. Many kinds of technological, informational and market developments have led to the life span of functions in companies being sharply reduced in comparison with 20 or 30 years ago. Those who are entering the labour market today should take into account a number of often radical changes in their functions.

3. Our society finds redundant younger workers harder to accept than older ones. To our knowledge, no systematic research has been carried out into the social motives for this. Furthermore, older workers are accorded less "right to work". It is significant that in most countries, including The Netherlands, companies are allowed to keep their doors closed (and very often do so) to applicants above a certain age (Van Beek & Van Praag, 1992). There is no law in The Netherlands comparable to the "*Age Discrimination in Employment Act*" in the USA, which makes this illegal. Another example is the fact that in the period of high unemployment among young school-leavers round about 1985, there was public support for initiatives calling for older employees to make way for younger ones. The first voluntary early retirement schemes owe their existence to this (Van Koningsveld, 1988).

4. Personnel reorganizations are often necessitated by a sudden deterioration in economic conditions. Prompt, firm decisions are called for. Under great pressure of time, rational choices are superseded by decisions based on prejudices and stereotypes which appear to meet the set target (Bodenhausen, 1990; Gilbert & Hixon, 1991; Kaplan, Wanshula, & Zanna, 1992). Many studies have revealed that a person's age forms one of the principal bases for stereotypical characterizations of people (Brewer & Lui, 1989; Fiske, 1993). The business world is no exception to this attitude. The stereotypes relating to "older" and "younger" workers widely accepted in our culture are, to some extent, opposites. The qualities attributed to "the young" match the image of an energetic, self-renewing, creative, dynamic organization. The qualities attributed to "the old" tend largely to be associated with the reverse (Boerlijst et al., 1993, pp. 44–46; Bromley, 1988, pp. 191–192; Wiggers, Baerts, Van Rooy, 1990, p. 18). As the object of personnel cuts in general is to breathe new life into a company, it is understandable that the "new shoots" should be saved and the "dead wood" pruned (Sheppard & Rix, 1977). Incidentally, before things get to the "pruning" stage, numerous discriminatory actions take place, felt as such by older personnel (McAuley, 1977). Stagner (1985) points out that stereotyping of the young versus the old is also encouraged by some researchers, Levinson (1978), for example. They make suggestive generalizations about observed significant differences, even when these are very slight and the groups overlap to a great extent. What is more, their conclusions often cannot hide the fact that they do not doubt the correctness of such stereotypes. Stagner suggests using other methods of reporting which ensure that managers and personnel officers do not forget that older employees simply cannot be treated as if they were all in the same category. In a survey, Craft et al. (1979) and Rosen and Jerdee (1976a) have revealed the stereotypical reactions of employers on the subject of the young versus the old. Employers were presented with curricula vitae of applicants identical in every respect. The only difference was the age stated. The employers were asked to give their opinion on a number of qualities possessed by these applicants. Their negative stereotypical opinions on the older among them were only too clear. Furthermore, they defended their unwillingness to employ the over-50s on the same basis.

An additional factor is that the young and old themselves often believe in such stereotyping and match their behaviour to the qualities attributed to their age group (Kogan & Wallach, 1961).

5. Compensating loss of earnings to an acceptable level on becoming redundant is easier for older people than for younger people. The same applies to filling gaps in pension build-up. After all, for older employees, the time still remaining before retirement is comparatively short. A host of financial provisions and schemes have been put into effect by the government and the business community to make it possible and even attractive to stop work before normal retirement age. In addition, large-scale use has been made of schemes which were actually intended for other purposes. In The Netherlands the main case in point is the statutory financial incapacity benefit. Older employees have often been assessed as qualifying for this benefit by the medical boards concerned without exhibiting any obvious signs of dysfunctioning (Van't Hullenaar & Van Koningsveld, 1986). Utilization of this provision is advantageous to companies because the costs involved are met out of general government funds. Nowadays, its abuse is widely acknowledged.

This summary is not complete. Additional examples are given by Kamstra and Van der Craats (1991, p. 23).

In combination with the structural developments in the economy referred to earlier, the above-mentioned factors have contributed to a serious undermining of the position of older employees on the labour market, especially that of older men. Up to 1960 approximately 90% of the male population between 50 and 65 participated in the labour process. By 1988 this level had dropped to a mere 60%. In contrast, the participation of older women has shown an upward tendency since 1960, from 13.5% to 19.3% in 1988. Following the trends, the proportion of older women in the working population has increased, like that of younger women, though continuing to be much smaller than for men. If we consider the composition of the working population as a whole, the proportion of the younger age cohorts between 25 and 50 has shown a substantial rise (from 50.9% in 1971 to 66.2% in 1988), at the expense of the older generations (CBS, 1989, pp. 77–78).

It is striking that redundancies in "older" people are generally found acceptable by the people concerned. An important factor is undoubtedly that many redundancy and retirement schemes are financially attractive. In some companies, other factors may be that the persons in question feel freed from the stress brought about by physical discomforts (such as wear and tear in the back or knees), as well as by impending reorganizations and increasing work pressure (Durinck, 1993). In the second place it is notable that the "exodus" of older employees is not confined to the lower echelons with a relatively low educational level. Economic conditions necessitate an increase in effectiveness. Organization experts have put forward a number of methods for this, including so-called "delayering" of the organization. By this is meant the reduction of the number of hierarchical layers in an organization, both at top and middle levels (Keuning, Maas, & Ophey, 1993). In view of the fact that management levels in the organization are invariably achieved via seniority, implementation of a delayering process results mainly in the departure of older employees. Other forms of "downsizing" do not spare top and middle management either (*vide* Philips and IBM). Again it is the older rather than the younger worker who is put forward for redundancy, whether voluntary or otherwise. Financial compensation at these levels is often so attractive that it tempts many who the organization can actually ill afford to do without. This undesirable effect of a collective approach to age groups has meant that the business community and government have

begun to give consideration to possible "flexible" early retirement schemes or to "flexibility" in the official retirement age as well as to other forms of individualization of terms of employment (WRR, 1992, p. 210; Loen & Van Schilfgaarde, 1990).

What then is the psychological implication of the worsening position of older employees in the labour market and of the dismissive attitude recently adopted by the business community *vis-à-vis* older employees? We will mention two aspects:

1. With the disappearance of so many older people from the labour process, management's *interest* in the pros and cons of the over-50s in the organization has been virtually reduced to nil. Employers' and employees' organizations have not, until recently, seriously concerned themselves with potential problems of the over-50s *in employment*. This has only become a subject for policy consideration since it became apparent that the working population is starting to age and that the costs of continuing premature redundancies of older employees cannot be met in the long term. This problem was first observed—and dealt with!—in the still very young-looking but rapidly aging Japan (Boerlijst, 1986; Boerlijst et al., 1987; POA, 1983).

2. Older employees in an organization discover that the organization as well as their own immediate circle more or less expect them to leave before official retirement age. Many experience moral pressure in this direction. This gives older employees the feeling of being socially isolated within their own working environment or, as Dresens (1989) terms it: "no longer being needed by the others". Stress and frustration are the all too frequent consequences. Departure from the organization is then experienced almost as a liberation. This is probably one explanation of why so many take up the offer of a so-called "voluntary" redundancy scheme, despite the appreciable loss of income that this may entail.

4 DEJUVENIZATION, AGING AND THE POSITION OF OLDER EMPLOYEES

The labour market is in the process of aging. This is the consequence of a number of demographic factors which, for The Netherlands, have been excellently summarized and clarified in a publication by the Advisory Council on Government Policy (WRR, 1992, p. 35f). A brief summary follows:

- a substantial decrease in "fertility" (the number of children per woman) (Van Hoorn, 1989): the average number of children dropped from 3.04 to 1.51 between 1965 and 1985 (and in fact rose again to 1.62 between 1985 and 1990 (WRR, 1992, p. 38)).
- a high, and still rising, life expectancy between 1965 and 1990: this rose for men from 71 to 74 and for women from 76 to 80 (WRR, 1992, p. 38).
- a rise in the age at which people get married and a fall in the number of marriages, as well as a weaker link between marriage or other forms of cohabitation on the one hand and procreation on the other hand (WRR, 1992, p. 45).
- a substantial increase in the number of divorces (a fivefold increase percentage-wise since 1960, CBS, 1985).

Economic and demographic analyses indicate the existence of a close link between these demographic factors and economic, medical and institutional developments (Clark, 1988). Examples are the improvement of the food supply, hygiene and living conditions and the improvement and accessibility of the health care system.

The process of aging and the fall in the number of births is not unique to The Netherlands but is manifested in all OECD countries, albeit with varying duration, rate and intensity (De Jouvenel, 1989; Van de Kaa, 1987; Warr, 1994). In this development, The Netherlands lags behind compared with most other European countries. It has had a comparatively young population for a relatively long period of time, but the drastic decline in fertility means that in 2040 it will probably be one of the oldest populations in the world, along with Switzerland, Germany and Denmark (OECD, 1988). The rate at which the population of The Netherlands is aging is only surpassed by Japan and Canada (UN, 1991; Feeney, 1990). The increasing immigration of foreigners into The Netherlands may well cause this picture to change, but up to now its effects appear to be relatively slight (De Beer & Noordam, 1988).

As the great majority of those entering the labour market for the first time were born and registered 15 to 25 years earlier, the consequences of demographic developments for the composition of the working population in a particular calendar year have been more or less firmly established for a very long time. The qualification "more or less" has to be made because substantial changes in the participation in the labour process by 15 to 64-year-olds—population migrations, natural disasters and so on—may, of course, undermine such a prognosis.[1] It would now appear that with participation in the labour process assumed to be at a constant level (reference year 1990), the proportion of younger people in the working population (the 15 to 29-year-olds) will drop from 36 to 27% in the period up to 2005. This phenomenon is referred to by the term "dejuvenization of the working population". After that, it will rise again, but up to 2050 the proportion will remain smaller than it was in 1990. In the same period, the proportion of older people in the working population (the 45 to 64-year-olds) will be permanently higher than in 1990, when it was approximately 24%. In 2005 it will have risen to 31% and in 2020 it will have reached a maximum of 35%. Up to 2050 it will remain a few per cent under this maximum (WRR, 1992, p. 105). This development is an illustration of "aging".

It is highly likely that the less than rosy outlook for the position of older employees in the labour market (NFB, 1984) will undergo a change as a consequence of the change in structure of the working population. Whether this will also mean an improvement remains to be seen.

There is an increase in the pressure caused by the large proportion of the over-65s compared with the total number of 15 to 64-year-olds in the population. It is from the latter group that the active working population is recruited which will have to realize a large proportion of the costs of the older non-working population (income provisions, costs of sickness and incapacity). In view of the fact that the group of over-65s will become larger in an absolute sense as well, these costs will become greater. The present situation is that every 100 Dutch people between the ages of 15 and 65, working or not working, provide financially for roughly 19 over-65s, fully or partially. By 2030 this number will have risen to somewhere between 33 and 43, depending on the actual developments in fertility, life expectancy and migration (WRR, 1992, p. 69). The rise in costs for the working population is disproportionately large because, within the group of older people, the proportion of the elderly in need of care will also increase as a result of a higher life expectancy. At present, the costs expended on the health care of the average over-85-year-old are nine times as high as those of the 30 to 50-year-old. The average over-65-year-old necessitates significantly fewer health care costs, though this figure is still twice as high (Koopmanschap, Van Royen, Bonneux, Bonsel, Rutten, & Van der Maas, 1994). This means that the working population, diminishing in proportion, will have to produce disproportionate efforts in the next 50 years to go some way towards financing the costs of the increasing numbers of the retired and the senior citizens.

At the same time, the costs of children and young people are also borne almost entirely by the working population. Every 100 Dutch persons from the group of 15 to 64-year-olds bear the costs of 26 to 27 people from this group. As births are now going up again, the pressure caused by the large proportion of younger people is expected to increase rather than decrease both in the long and the short term (WRR, 1992, p. 67f). It is very much the question as to whether productivity per working person is still capable of being stepped up enough to be able to keep the costs of the pressure caused by both these large groups permanently at the current level. It is more likely that a structural enlargement of the base to support this burden is needed, in other words the *number* of people productively participating in economic life.

A consequence of the "dejuvenization" of the working population is that in the somewhat longer term this base must be broadened by increasing the proportion of over-40s in employment.[2] Suitable, that is adequately trained, younger people are not available in sufficient numbers. Older people not or no longer in employment are in abundance. Enlarging the base by deploying older people will not, however, be easy to accomplish (Kamstra & Van der Craats, 1991). Companies have more faith in the contribution of the young than the old. It is therefore expected that discussions on the necessity for enlarging the base will be frozen and that preference will be given to "siphoning off" younger people from the labour market for as long as possible. Besides this, many organizations are experiencing "internal aging" as a result of the fact that their expansion and growth has stagnated while the "real" older employees (over 60 or 55) have already stepped down via an early retirement scheme or on incapacity grounds. Every year the personnel ages and the number of over-40s increases both in an absolute and a relative sense. It is therefore only too obvious that in such circumstances vacancies are not going to go to jobseeking older people. In any case, companies in general have little idea of their "internal" long-term demographic development. They rarely have access to usable prognosis models or valid initial data (Boerlijst et al., 1993).

Nonetheless, it is realistic to assume that the increase in dependent older non-working people is becoming so great that the deployment or re-entry of older people can no longer be avoided. Bearing this in mind, it is important to consider what problems *older working people* do or do not cause, and how particular problems might be prevented or solved (cf. Hale, 1990; Kerkhoff & Kruidenier, 1991). In the following sections we will discuss a few aspects of these problems. We will concentrate as far as possible on findings derived from work and organization psychological research. A selection will have to be made from the multitude of subjects and results available. Anyone wishing for a broader perspective may consult the compilations of Stagner (1985) and Warr (1994), from whom some of our information has been derived.

5   THE FUNCTIONING OF OLDER WORKERS

Can any criticism be made about the *functioning* of older employees? If the answer to this question is in the affirmative, the potential for a more positive influence on this should be looked into.

One then comes up against a problem which is difficult to overcome. Normally speaking, results from present-day research cannot simply be generalized to apply to situations in the more distant future. When we compare various age cohorts with each other—a cohort comprises all those originating from the same, usually short, birth period—we are not only concerned with age differences but with generation differences as well. The over-20s, over-40s and over-60s of the year 1995 are in a different position from the corresponding age groups of 25 years ago. Neither can they simply be compared with those of the

year 2020 (Rhodes, 1983; Doering, Rhodes, & Schuster, 1983). The greater the difference in the historic contexts in which they lived or will live, the more difficult a generalization of one generation of over-40s to the next becomes. A much used example is the fact that owing to the influence of many kinds of cultural and socio-economic factors, the educational level of the young is much higher these days than 20 or 30 years ago. Education often influences functioning in a positive sense. If the older people of this day and age do not on average function as well as is desirable, this may well be attributable to their poor educational base. With this in mind, it is dangerous to draw conclusions about the older people of the future merely from research on the functioning of the older people of today. The risk of misrepresentation could be reduced by involving in the research older people (and possibly younger people) who are assumed to have the same level of education as their corresponding peers in the future.

A further problem is that employers and managers tend to approach the functioning of individuals from a business economics-related rather than a human point of view. They look for "hard" facts, for example in the matter of the productivity or

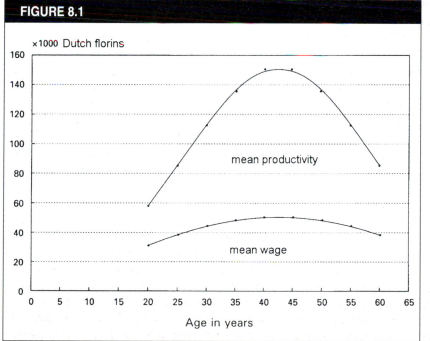

FIGURE 8.1

×1000 Dutch florins

mean productivity

mean wage

Age in years

Source: A. Gelderblom & J. de Koning. (1992c) *Meerjarig, minder-waardig? een onderzoek nar de invloid van leeftijd op produktiviteit en beloning.* [More years, less value? Investigation into the influence of age on productivity and wages.] OSA-pilot study V39, April 1992.

"added value" of older versus younger people. Research invariably shows that there is a parabolic link between measured productivity and age (Gelderblom & De Koning, 1992b,c).

Evaluating functioning on a basis of productivity measurements may prove to be complex. For instance, the top of the curve, which indicates the most productive age, differs per profession and per function (Jablonski, Rosenblum, & Kunze, 1988). However, productivity at 60 is often no less than at the age of 35. Furthermore, the differences *within* an age group are often larger than those *between* age groups. (See also section 3, point 1.)

Results based on management appraisal of functioning are as a rule more positive than those based on productivity measurements. However, a disadvantage is that appraisals of functioning are difficult to disassociate from appraisals of the person himself, as a result of which stereotyping of people, for instance based on age, has a very great influence on an appraisal of this nature. In a survey conducted for the government, Gelderblom and De Koning (1992a,b) asked personnel for an appraisal of their own functioning. The findings of the last appraisal interview with superiors were also taken into account. The most notable aspect of these interviews is that the appraisals of civil servants over the age of 45 prove in the great majority of cases to be favourable, just as positive as in the case of younger people. By and large, 48% function satisfactorily and a further 37% above the specified requirements on several points. The differences between the differentiated age groups are minimal. The researchers report that negative appraisals occur only rarely (only 1% in the case of 54-year-olds), but that older people of 45-54 display a peak of 7%. This somewhat less enthusiastic assessment of the 45 to 54-year-olds appears to occur in all kinds of functions. We would like to point out that in literature, this age category is that of the so-called "mid-life crisis" (Hunt & Collins, 1983; Munnichs, 1987; Gerrichhauzen, 1989). The "disappearance" of the peak in the oldest age group is attributed by the authors to "modified expectations" and "selectiveness": "a number of those who experience problems with functioning at this age have already ... departed via a redundancy or disability scheme".

The above findings are consistent with those of Price, Thompson, & Dalton (1975) and Mercer (1981) and are largely confirmed by findings from recent research in 10 large to medium-sized Dutch companies (Boerlijst et al., 1993, p. 75f; Boerlijst, 1995). This research related to individual over-40s at middle and higher functioning levels as assessed by their superiors. In general, they tend to rate the quality of the functioning of their over-40s satisfactory or high. The functioning of the higher functioning level is appraised somewhat more favourably than that of the middle level. Older and younger over-40s in higher functions do not differ significantly. At the middle level, older people function slightly less well than younger ones and we again encounter the above-mentioned "peak", or rather the "dip", in the group of 47 to 52-year-olds. From a comparison of these results with those of Gelderblom and De Koning we conclude that becoming older does not lead to functioning problems either in the business world or in government circles. In every age group and at every level, a relatively small contingent can be found whose work is "below standard". The researchers assume that such "underachievers" can equally well be found among the under-40s. Incidentally, for reasons yet to be clarified, less favourable opinions are held in company circles on the quality of functioning of the over-40s in the government sector.

The fact that the functioning of older people gives rise to so few complaints tallies with findings from psychogerontological studies which demonstrate that existing capacities and abilities remain virtually stable up to pensionable age. They display a far greater variation *within* age groups than *between* them (Botwinick, 1984; Birren & Schaie, 1985, 1990). Serious deterioration in most cognitive functions does not appear until after the normal retirement age of 65. Birren, Cunningham, and Yamamoto (1983) and Labouvie-Vief (1982, 1985) show that in spite of the fact that the abilities present at a younger age invariably cease to produce peak performances (during tests!), they remain more than sufficient for "everyday" work. In fact, some people appear to be capable of peak performances at work at an older age, as demonstrated in the case of R&D personnel (N = 1200) by Pelz and Andrews

(1966). Here, statistics show that peak perform- ances occur in two age groups in particular: one between the age of 40 and 45 and the other around 55. There are strong empirical indications suggest- ing that the ability to reach peaks at a later age is dependent on the pattern of acquisition of knowl- edge and experience during the career (Gerpott, Domsch, & Keller, 1988; Pelz & Andrews, op. cit.; Van Assen & Keijsers, 1993). The latter point out that the results of Pelz and Andrews' studies have scarcely been given any attention by R&D management. They attribute this to the following: "This is a correlative study, not warranting con- clusions in terms of cause-effect relationships. In specific R&D culture, the correlation between performance peaks and "variety" (being occupied in many different ways with matters within the function and transcending the career) is easily explained from the prevailing "good chap" syn- drome ("talent will out" and "you can't keep a good man down"). The talented developer has a high performance level and keeps breaking out of all kinds of organizational pigeon-holes." Another factor not to be underestimated is that many older working people have performed the same function for long periods of time on end, repeating virtually identical tasks. This enables them to rely on the daily routines and expertise kept intact by continu- ous use. As long as people can keep on doing more or less the same work their skills appear to be adequate.

In the United States the "Age Discrimination in Employment Act", amended in 1986, forbids enforced retirement on the grounds of a person's age. At that time, a number of exceptions were made on the grounds of stereotypical consider- ations relating to a decline in creativeness, alert- ness etc. in older people, namely for "tenured college faculty" and "public safety employees". By order of Congress, special studies were carried out into the appositeness of these exemptions. These results have led Hammond and Morgan (1991) and Landy and associates (1992) to be of the opinion that age is hardly a determinant in differences in achievements and that the exemp- tions must therefore be eliminated. Previous stu- dies had shown that if appraisers are trained to rate human activities and achievements at their true value, the correlation between age and appraised

achievement drops significantly. The variation in achievements, in contrast, rises with age (Meier & Kerr, 1976, p.148). The number of years of experience *in the particular working environment* is a better predictor of work achievement than age is (Giniger, Dispenzieri, & Eisenberg, 1983; McDaniel, Schmidt, & Hunter, 1988; McEnrue, 1988; Schwab & Heneman, 1977a).

Warr (1994) has compiled a veritable thesaurus of available research results on the link between age and achievements in many kinds of fields and at various levels of work. These results are not easy to summarize. The tasks that people have to perform, either in laboratory situations or in the reality of the workplace, are difficult to compare. They differ in a host of dimensions, both content- wise and in terms of complexity. The same applies to the characteristics and work behaviour of the individuals themselves. Warr has devised an interesting theoretical framework enabling the results to be classified according to type and clarified. It is a model based on task requirements, with two logically distinguishable dimensions.

The first dimension relates to the question as to whether or not the task requirements call for certain "basic capabilities" in which a decline has been established with increasing age. These cap- abilities stem from physiological processes which are inevitably subject to wear and tear during the course of a person's life. Examples are certain sensory functions, such as hearing and sight, speed of reaction or speed in information processing and certain storage and searching functions of the memory (Welford, 1976; West & Sinnott, 1992). There are also basic capabilities which do not display such a decline or may even "grow" continuously, such as certain cognitive intelli- gence aspects, and which mature through an increase in absorbed experience. They are referred to in literature by terms such as "wisdom", "plasticity of thinking" and "crystallized intelli- gence" (Baltes & Baltes, 1990; Berg & Sternberg, 1985; ; Cornelius & Caspi, 1987; Dixon, Kramer & Baltes, 1985; Labouvie-Vief, 1985).

The second dimension concerns the question as to whether a continuous accumulation of relevant knowledge and experience goes on raising the level of desired achievements. A combination of the two dimensions produces four types of activities or task categories.

		Do basic capabilities remain sufficient?	
		Yes	No
Is achievement improved	Yes	Type A tasks	Type C tasks
by cumulative experience?	No	Type B tasks	Type D tasks

Source: Warr (1994, pp. 501, 513).

Type A refers to tasks for which the basic capabilities during active life remain sufficient and for which an increase in experience acts in an achievement-enhancing manner. As an example, Warr cites knowledge-based judgements reached without pressure of time. Type B comprises tasks for which the basic capabilities remain sufficient and for which an increase in experience does not produce/no longer produces any enhancement in achievement, such as work that calls for relatively little mental or physical effort. Types C and D include tasks or activities for which the necessary basic capabilities show a decline during active life. In type C, this decline can be compensated for by increase in knowledge and experience, for instance through building up routines, skills and expertise. In type D, the increase of experience either does not help or has ceased to help. Examples are continuous rapid information processing under pressure of time, and hard physical work—tasks in which sensory and perceptual mechanisms, selective attention, working memory or speed of information processing are of the essence (Davies & Sparrow, 1985). The typology implies certain hypotheses on the relationship between age and achievements. In type A, predominantly positive relationships are to be expected, in type D, predominantly negative ones. In types B and C, there will either be no clear relationship, or else positive and negative connections will be in equilibrium. The two behaviour-related processes which decrease the most sharply with age are *speed of reaction* and *memory function* (Light, 1991). Several studies show that in the case of tasks with a time limit, older people are subject to greater stress, make more mistakes and produce fewer achievements than younger people (Arenburg, 1965; Eisdorfer, Axelrod, & Wilkie, 1963; Troyer, Eisdorfer, Bogdonoff, & Wilkie, 1967). In the case of imprinted tasks without a time limit, there are generally no differences between the achievements of older and

younger people (Taub, 1967). In the workplace the forms of decline referred to may often be compensated for by technological provisions, memory aids, and so on.

Warr's typology is methodologically enlightening but does not solve all problems of interpretation. As he himself indicates, water-tight explanations of research findings are often difficult to provide because most tasks form a complex integration of type A, B, C and D activities. People do not always go about them in the same way. One day, an employee may get down to work immediately, relying on his/her experience and routine. The next day he or she may set these to one side, as it were, and pause to reflect before taking action. Thus achievements may differ from one day to the next.

6 THE MOBILITY AND EMPLOYABILITY OF OLDER WORKERS

The mobility of older people in the labour market (external mobility via change of job or change of employer) tends to be considerably lower than that of younger people (Van Altena, Plantegna, Schippers, & Siegers, 1990). On the one hand, this is the result of the application of age criteria to the recruitment and selection of personnel (Doup, 1990.) The over-45s are at a disadvantage here. On the other hand, pension schemes are often an obstacle to job changes (WRR, 1992, p. 130f). Research by Boerlijst et al. (1993) shows that *functional* mobility, meaning the transition to another position or function, by employees at the middle or higher levels of large to medium-sized companies sharply declines from their fortieth year onwards. seven out of every eight employees over 50 have been in their present position for longer than seven years. Furthermore, in their superiors' opinion, they will no longer be employable elsewhere in the foreseeable future, either outside their own organization or within it. Amongst the younger over-40s, those between 40 and 46, the same applies to one in eight at the higher functioning level and two in eight at the middle level. This difference demonstrates the intensity and the speed at which older employees become set in their ways. In any case, it transpires that in the superiors' expectations, the perceived mobility and the employability of the over-40s studied is confined to a transition to functions "close to home". In other words: to functions within the employee's own department or organizational unit, and in the area of his own familiar expertise.

In the above-mentioned study no relation has been found between the mobility and employability of the over-40s on the one hand and the quality of their functioning, as well as the significance or the usefulness of their current function in the organization on the other. There is, however, a positive relationship with the "learning value" of this function. By this is meant the extent to which the function forms a good breeding ground for acquiring new, instructive experiences and new skills. It appears that for the over-40s at middle and higher functioning levels, the "learning value" of their function is often minimal, which is probably the result of the fact that many people have performed this function for years on end without any drastic changes in their tasks, responsibilities or working environment. More highly educated over-40s are often over-specialized in the function area which they are familiar with, but the majority fail to measure up in other areas of skills and expertise. Thijssen (1993) has also observed the same phenomenon, which he terms "concentration of experiences", at lower function levels.

Research by Boerlijst et al. (1993) has also shown that activities and interventions by management may enhance the mobility and employability of the over-40s. In everyday management practice, however, these activities are often unforthcoming, increasingly so in the older over-40-year-olds, and they have virtually ceased in the case of the over-50s. What is more, they are invariably confined to encouraging vertical mobility within a function area which for some time the over-40-year-old has been part of. Encouraging horizontal mobility and a switch to other or new task areas seldom if ever takes place. As a possible explanation of these phenomena, Boerlijst et al. mention the combined effect of at least three factors:

1. a dominant "instrumental" management attitude;
2. the comparatively brief duration of the period during which superiors bear or envisage bearing responsibility for the fortunes of individual subordinates (Boerlijst & Van der Heijden, 1997);
3. a lack of confidence on the part of management in the capability of the over-40s, particularly the older range, to develop in new, unfamiliar directions.

The hypothesis of a dominant "instrumental" management attitude (1) has previously been put forward by Van Assen (1990) and Van Assen and Keijsers (1993). The basis of this hypothesis is that managers view their subordinates primarily as a means of realizing certain objectives held by the organization or the department, but only to the extent that and for as long as they as managers bear managerial responsibility for this. Instrumental management implies attention on the part of managers to the subordinates' ability to function optimally, but confined to the period of a superior/subordinate relationship. Data from the research referred to above reveal that managers work on the premise of a comparatively brief period, viz. no longer than four to five years, in which they expect to be dealing with particular subordinates (2). They presumably consider that what happens subsequently is not *their* responsibility but that of their successors. Instrumental management does not rule out managers' attention to their subordinates' development, although this, too, will be primarily directed to what is deemed to be of importance for the duration of the manager's "own" period. Preference will be given to the "maintenance" of existing knowledge and skills rather than to the exploitation of new territories which may well be of importance at a later stage. Other data from the research by Boerlijst et al. demonstrate that management's confidence in the creativity and development potential of personnel decreases in inverse proportion to their age (3). For these reasons, the majority of managers endeavour to attain a "young" personnel structure in their departments. The fact that managers restrict their mobility-enhancing activities to the young is in line with this endeavour.

As indicated above, the over-50s are no longer

thought by their managers capable of undertaking completely new activities in their work and are also assumed to have little inclination to undergo drastic changes (Boerlijst et al., 1993). However, the dejuvenization and aging of the available potential labour force mean that one should not automatically reject the possibility of "poly-employability" of older workers as unfeasible (WRR, 1992, p. 124f). Research must be carried out into whether older employees are capable of activities and achievements of an interdisciplinary nature, meaning lying beyond their own, familiar functioning territory. If this should prove to be the case, management must be persuaded to change its attitude.

Section 5 mentioned the fact that the cognitive abilities of older employees generally continue to be adequate up to retirement age as far as "day-to-day work" goes. But would these abilities also be adequate for a switch to other areas of knowledge, skills and expertise? The aforementioned studies by Pelz and Andrews (1966) and Van Assen and Keijsers (1993) provide an answer that is relevant to this question. Their results point to the importance of a carefully planned variation in task/working environment factors for the field of expertise to be broadened, which is a necessary condition for successful switching to new areas of function and experience. Warr (1993, p. 537f) observes that up to now the business community and researchers alike have concentrated on the question as to the influence of age on behaviour and attitude in the workplace. The question concerning the influence of the work itself, the influence of the working environment and work experience on "mobility" and "employability" of older employees has hardly been addressed. Warr emphasizes the importance of research into the long-term effects of environmental components on the development of personnel (cf. Hall & Parker, 1993).

Discussion of and research into the possible growth of cognitive abilities and the part played in this by experience accumulation during adulthood are an important theme in so-called "life-span psychology" (Avolio & Waldman, 1987; Avolio, Waldman & McDaniel, 1990; Brouwer, 1990; Butler & Gleason, 1985; Cavanaugh, 1993; Green, 1972; McEvoy & Cascio, 1989; Schaie & Willis,

1986, 1991; Schmidt, Hunter, & Outerbridge, 1986; Schooler & Schaie, 1987; Sparrow & Davies, 1988). There is certain evidence that "life experience" may also be a stimulus for the development of higher forms of "transcendent reasoning"—labelled "wisdom" by some people (including Birren, 1985; Dittmann-Kohli & Baltes, 1985) and "intuition" by others—and "plasticity" in adults and older people (Baltes & Willis, 1982; Munnichs, Mussen, Olbrich, & Coleman, 1985). These higher forms can enable them to continue to sustain their position in the broad and dynamic social everyday context (for more details and references to relevant literature, see Chapter 12, Volume 3 of this Handbook). It is advisable to investigate whether, and in what way, these findings from developmental psychology may be helpful in the context of "growing older in the working environment" (Boerlijst & Van der Heijden, 1997).

Deployment of personnel in what is for them a new area requires them to be able to command sufficient relevant skills, knowledge, routine and expertise within a relatively short period of time to be able to meet the required standard. In the business world, development of new expertise or skills in older employees has hardly been addressed up to now. A great deal is known about the *dynamics* of expertise development in a wide variety of areas (cf. Anderson, 1982; Ceci, 1990; Charness, 1989; Charness & Bosman, 1990; Chi, Glaser, & Farr, 1988; Ericsson & Smith, 1991 and Salthouse, 1990). It is worth investigating to what extent general conditions for the development of new expertise are present or lacking in the work situation of (older) personnel and to what extent they could be "built in". Whether or not older people will be able to meet certain conditions of expertise development in what is for them a new area is still an open question. The fact that the possession of expertise helps older people to compensate for particular handicaps not experienced by younger people—for example reduced reaction time—has been demonstrated by Salthouse (1984) amongst others.

Our use of the term "expertise" may possibly create the misunderstanding that we consider the possibility of broadening of skills to be confined to an elite amongst older personnel. In our view, almost every employee, from top to bottom, from well-educated to less well-educated, from old to young, should either be or be able to become an "expert", at least in a number of aspects of his own work.

In terms of mobility enhancement, it is debatable what would be wiser: acquiring *more than one area of expertise* within adjacent or radically different fields, or acquiring a *strategy* to be able to master a new area of expertise in another territory as quickly as possible. The latter option would seem to offer more advantages. It is, after all, exceptionally difficult, if not impossible, to predict the progress of every individual career. Many changes and transitions (cf. Barton, 1982) take place suddenly and unpredictably. It is therefore equally difficult to divine what "subject of expertise" will be needed at a later stage. However, it should be borne in mind that actual *experience in acquiring more than one area of expertise* is also a basic condition for the efficient acquisition of and ability to master a *strategy* for developing *new areas of expertise*. It is not likely that such a strategy can be "picked up from a book". It must also be remembered that the mastery of more skills, routines and expertise in different areas is also accompanied by an increase in the opportunities for transfer to other areas.

There is a widespread assumption in the business community that the ability to acquire new competencies and skills is reduced in older people and that in some it is more a case of loss of competency and inability to continue functioning at the same level. To keep this group in the labour process, downward mobility (Hall & Isabella, 1985), usually termed "demotion" or, more euphemistically, "career shift" (Koningswijk, 1989; Dresens, 1989, p. 141) is considered. By transferring these older workers to functions categorized at a lower level and thus providing an adaptation to proved shortcomings or failings, things will become easier for them. Koningswijk (1989) summarizes a number of conditions which he considers necessary for a successful "career shift", such as a culture change, exemplary behaviour on the part of management, better terms of employment, new functions that are better suited to the employee, application of objective criteria to be satisfied by candidates, remuneration of the

employee's own initiatives and avoidance of constraint. Koningswijk's view is that the culture shift is necessary in order to prevent the career shift from automatically resulting in loss of status. We, however, believe that with labour relations as they are, loss of status on demotion cannot be avoided. For this reason, such a "career shift" will never be an attractive option for all those whose original function and income reflect and guarantee status (West, Nicholson, & Rees, 1990). The management of large and medium-sized companies views demotion as a scarcely realizable option for older personnel at middle and higher levels. We find exceptions to this in cases in which demotion appears to be the only means of avoiding the redundancy of too expensive older workers during a projected reorganization (Boerlijst et al., 1993, p. 135).

As well as cognitive abilities, motivation—and more particularly the willingness of older personnel to change—are factors in their mobility and employability. We will return to this in section 8. We will first go more deeply into a major determinant of their development, namely the combination of education, training and human resource development.

7   EDUCATION, TRAINING AND DEVELOPMENT OF THE OVER-40s

The development of various new kinds of technologies goes hand-in-hand with a growing need for a poly-employable labour force. These people must be enabled to adapt quickly to new circumstances and, without much trouble, to continue the process of qualifying themselves for different/changing kinds of work during the course of their career. As stated before, it is traditionally assumed that only young people can meet these requirements. It is a fact that older people are at a disadvantage. Their professional qualifications are generally no longer equal to the rapidly changing function requirements of modern dynamic organizations. One of the consequences is that older personnel are often only too readily inclined to make use of any opportunity handed to them to bid a premature farewell to the labour process

(Bartel & Sicherman, 1993). Comparatively little is done to bring these qualifications up to scratch either. Companies make much less provision for the over-40s in the way of education, training and human resources development than for younger people. In 1990 half of the 15 to 40-year-olds in the Dutch working population were taking part in education in some form or other compared with 30% of the 41 to 50-year-olds and 16% of the 51 to 64-year-olds (Warmerdam & Van den Berg, 1992). The lower participation percentage of the over-50s reflects the low level of primary education in the present generation of older people in comparison with that of younger people. Someone who has had little education during the earlier stages of his/her career is less likely to receive or to aspire to education at a later stage (Prevoo & Thijssen, 1992). If we examine the participation of the over-40s at the middle and higher level of large and medium-sized Dutch companies (Boerlijst, 1995), then their participation percentages are considerably higher. However, here too, there is a clear decrease in percentage with an increase in age. Of the "juniors" and "mediors" between 40 and 52, 70 to 80% go on courses at least once a year. In the case of "seniors" aged 53–64 this percentage has dropped to 50%. For juniors and mediors (40 to 52 year-olds) a participant's average course length is a little over a week and three days in the case of seniors. At these levels the majority of course and training time spent is set aside for "maintenance work" in the employee's own, already familiar, function area and is intended to give the person the opportunity to "keep up". Where these courses are in other areas, either new or unfamiliar to him/her, participation drops considerably, to below 20%. Here, the differences between age and function have vanished. It is significant that the average duration of this type of training course amounts to less than one day. The same applies to training courses or programmes geared to personal education, social intercourse, leadership and so on.

The fact that education within organizations is largely restricted to "maintenance work" as an extension of a person's current function can be seen as a consequence of "instrumental" management (see previous section). The decrease in participation and time spent by seniors can prob-ably be traced back to misgivings on the part of management, and possibly also on the part of the employees themselves, as to the profitability of the necessary investments for education and training. After all, retirement age is fast approaching, added to which is the doubt as to the learning and absorption potential of older people.

Enhancement of the employability of older employees requires an increase, at least, in effort put into training courses. Maintenance work on existing skills and expertise should not, of course, be neglected, but more money, time and attention will certainly need to be invested in broadening the horizon and in developing and consolidating knowledge and ability on a number of fronts. It will be clear from the above that the functioning of older employees cannot be brought up to scratch by education, training and development alone. Such activities must be integrated with "permanently instructive" work experience, tasks and responsibilities. Further research into this should reveal in what way the "learning value" of functions can be maintained for older employees in particular and, with this in mind, how the architecture of organization and management can be optimized (cf. Fischer & Silvern, 1985).

Current perceptions of the cognitive development potential and learning capabilities of older employees are not as yet sufficient to guarantee an effective approach to the problems of immobility and employability (Sinnott, 1994). Experience in so-called "*outplacement*" counselling (Harrick, Mansel, & Schutzius, 1982; Van der Heijden, De Jong, & Van Spengler, 1993) suggests that it is possible to teach older people how to cope with the possible loss of their job, how best to present themselves as persons in the labour market and how to find ways and means to secure a new position. The individual approach adopted in such forms of counselling does justice to the increasing heterogeneity of employees as they grow older. The history of their life course is the central issue. Use is made of so-called "narrative" biographical methods (Munnichs, 1990), in which confrontation of the employee with his own life story and system of values and norms (Hermans, 1987, 1988; Hermans & Bonarius, 1991) is at the core. In this area, Van de Loo (1992) has developed an interesting but methodologically as yet not entirely watertight tool within the framework of systematic individual guidance in problems and transitions during the career.

8   MOTIVATION AND WELL-BEING OF OLDER WORKERS

At the top of the agenda in discussions on older workers is their immobility. How can older employees without work/no longer in work rejoin the labour process once more and are older employees willing and able to abandon the old ways and tread new paths? This is, of course, not only a cognitive, but also a motivational problem. As an example we wish to cite the findings of Boerlijst et al. (1993, pp. 110 et seq.) that those at the head of the middle and higher levels of large and medium-sized companies consider 50 to 60% of their subordinates between the ages of 40 and 52 to have the potential to develop to the extent of being able to operate successfully in an entirely different field. However, according to the same sources, approximately one third of those "competent" are not prepared to do so.

The questions as to why anyone is, in fact, prepared to perform certain tasks and strive for certain achievements, and what it *actually* takes to persuade someone to make this effort, can only be properly answered at an individual level. Everyone makes personal choices in which he or she relies on insights and feelings which have been formed and coloured by his own history, and life/career experiences. Individual motivation patterns are the result of an ongoing learning process. Cultural influences (upbringing, education, social environment, etc.) are, of course, important factors, but the role of *idiosyncratic* factors (personal experiences and perceptions) should not be underestimated. General measures to enhance the motivation and well-being of employees are interpreted in widely varying ways by different people, and by no means always in the manner intended by the policymakers. This means that employees' reactions to such measures may not only vary considerably but also deviate from what is intended by these measures. Anyone who does not take account of individual differences and the

necessity for an individual-oriented approach, but who expects enhancement of motivation via collective provisions and regulations, may be in for a shock. Such an individual approach requires a thorough knowledge of a person's life history, career, as well as his/her personal and attitudinal development. Anyone ascribing a prime role as motivation-enhancer to executive management must realize that such knowledge is probably still too scantily available in these circles (Boerlijst et al., 1993).

In fact, an individual approach is, in itself, not sufficient. We are not only concerned with motivation of the employees themselves. In most cases, other important factors are the opinions and driving force of people around them with an influence on their attitude and behaviour or on the situations they find themselves in. We have seen that the mobility of older people is far less enhanced by management activities than the mobility of younger people. This is probably the consequence of rational considerations ("there's no point anyway, because …") and stereotype conceptions ("it's just too big a step, at their age").

In other words: anyone wishing to enhance the mobility of older people by motivational means will have to analyse both the *individual* side and the *relevant social system*. On the basis of such an integrated analysis, interventions and measures on both these fronts could be thought up which could well offer a perspective of the desired result.

Motivational process models such as those employed by the schools of Vroom (1964) and Adams (1965) may be helpful in an analysis of this nature (see Chapter 11, Volume 4 of this Handbook). The application of such models to the analysis of the individual life course and career is, in theory, possible. They have the advantage of not being normative. In other words, they do not postulate a fixed pattern of motivational changes which are supposedly valid for everyone (cf. Alderfer, 1972) but leave it open.

The importance of objective and instrumentality-related considerations in the understanding of the expectations, motivation and behaviour of older people has been adequately demonstrated (Baker & Hansen, 1975; Harel & Conen, 1982; Reichelt, 1974; Thierry, Koopman, & Van der Flier, 1992). Results of research by Schwab &

Heneman (1977a,b) into the effects of age and experience on productiveness suggest that the validity of Vroom's expectancy model is greater in the case of older people than it is for younger people. An obvious explanation might be that because of their head start in life experience older people are better able to estimate the various model components than younger people. This supposition of an age-related differential validity of Vroom's expectancy model in relation to work-related criteria has, however, found little support in other research conducted up to now (Van Eerde, Thierry, & De Haan, 1994).

In the context of research on older workers, Adam's "equity model" has to our knowledge not found any application. The central theme of this model (behaviour control influenced by feelings of either fairness or unfairness when weighing up the relative costs and benefits required for particular efforts) may well offer a basis for the explanation of certain observed motives and behaviour both of older workers *themselves* and of others *in relation to* older workers. For instance, approximately 20% of the over-40s at the middle or higher levels of large to medium-sized Dutch companies are, in the opinion of their own superiors, not prepared to work in an entirely different field at a later stage in their careers, although this same 20% might well have the capacity to do so (Boerlijst, 1995). They may consider the likelihood of the efforts required for such a radical change being sufficiently rewarded or valued too small. Another example is associated with the fact that considerably less time and money is spent on the training, education and development of older than of younger workers (see section 7 of this chapter). Here, too, considerations of fairness and costs/ benefits—this time on the part of management— may play a part.

The extent to which the findings of empirical research using such process models are usable for the enhancement of motivation in older personnel *in a general sense*, remains to be seen. These findings are often historically/culturally determined. They cannot simply be generalized to apply to future cohorts of older workers. Value patterns and configurations of objectives change in the course of time. Instrumentality estimates as well as feelings of satisfaction are influenced by the social circumstances within which a life takes place. It makes a great deal of difference whether older people's careers have undergone the crucial effects of war or peace, economic recessions or— in contrast—"*booms*" (Stagner, 1985, p. 808).

The work motivation of older people is often associated with their personal well-being (cf. Bourne, 1982). In the view of Palmore and Luikart (1972), the personal experience of health is the principal determinant of satisfaction or dissatisfaction amongst older people. (Incidentally, regularly conducted research in The Netherlands [cf. CBS, 1993] shows this factor to be of major importance for *all* age groups.) Analyses of indices relating to absenteeism and incapacity for work and of occupational health-related and medical benefit agency-related diagnoses provide an insight into the connection between factors of age and health (see also Chapter 6, Volume 2 of this Handbook).

The so-called absenteeism frequency (the number of occurrences of sickness-related absenteeism in a single year divided by the number of employees in a given company) decreases with age. The absenteeism percentage (the percentage of man-days lost through absenteeism) increases with age. Increase in age therefore goes hand-in-hand with reduced absenteeism frequency. This absenteeism is, however, of longer duration than in the case of younger workers. The likelihood of more permanent incapacity thus increases as one grows older. After all, entitlement to benefit is conferred only after a lengthy qualifying period of sickness.

Unfortunately it is not possible to supply reliable age-related figures relating to diagnoses of absenteeism: normally, checks on benefit claimants are not carried out until some days after they have been reported; medical officers often attend only the more serious cases; lower-level personnel are visited sooner and more frequently than those higher up the scale; statements by the claimant or by non-medical inspectors do not suffice; notice to attend a medical examination by the company medical officer or medical benefit agency doctor often produces a miraculous cure, etc. Other statistical data are available showing that the instances of older personnel attending company medical officers' surgeries are significantly higher than in the case of younger personnel. Thirty per cent of the symptoms reported by older personnel are diagnosed as "mental disorders" (sleep disorders, depression, stress reactions) and 20% in the case of younger personnel. A second major diagnosis category confronting the company medical officer is formed by "motor disorders", often in combination with "overstraining" of the physical mechanism", or its "reduced ability to cope with strain", which may manifest itself in "symptoms of fatigue". Such symptoms increase with age but are, in certain circumstances, also reversible (cf. Meijman, Chapter 2, Volume 2 of this Handbook; De Zwart & Meijman, 1995).

Statistical data (GMD, 1993) reveal that each year between 1988 and 1992 around 1.3% of the working population in The Netherlands qualified for full incapacity benefit and a further 0.3% were judged partially unfit for work. As incapacity is, for many, of long to very long duration, the percentage of those with full or partial benefit entitlement rose over the years to 11.6% in 1992. This percentage is much higher in The Netherlands than in other countries for as yet unclarified reasons (Prins, 1990). In view of the alarming rise

in incapacity benefit costs, the Dutch government recently decided to tighten up the entitlement criteria; since then the percentage of those qualifying has dropped slightly. The business community itself has also got the message that it should do its best to avoid its occurrence (Klomps, Kommers, & Kamphuis, 1991). In the context of the subject matter before us, it is significant that the annual influx to the ranks of those applying for a partial or full benefit increases with age, as can be seen in Figure 8.2. The influx of men to these ranks lags slightly behind that of women. In both groups an acceleration occurs between the ages of 40–50, followed by a slowing down in the increase. Durinck (1993, p. 206) ascribes this "saturation phenomenon" to an increase in occurrences of death, especially in older people of poor health, and to possibly having passed a risk threshold. A further cause given by him is the possibility that older people hang on when the "end of the working life" is in sight or when they are able to depart from the company with a favourable voluntary retirement scheme.

In the Netherlands the numbers of new benefit claimants every year has, up to now, not been

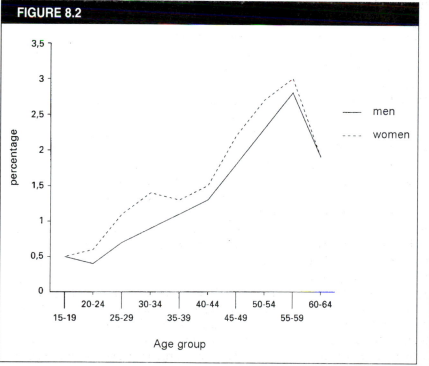

FIGURE 8.2

New full and partial incapacity benefits in 1992 in the Netherlands, per 100 insurants, by age and sex. Source: GMD (1993, p. 35).

accompanied by an equal or greater number of those leaving these ranks, having been declared either fully or partially fit for work. This means that the proportion of older people among benefit claimants has steadily increased since the relevant statutory regulations have come into force. This is illustrated in Figure 8.3. Approximately 50% of people registered for incapacity benefit are over the age of 50 (Munnichs, 1993, p. 40).

There is a considerable difference diagnosis-wise between younger and older workers declared fully or partially incapable of work (Durinck, 1993, p. 208). Such differences are not easy to interpret. The diagnosis categories used by medical advisers are very rough and inadequate and often lack validation. For example, there is a category entitled "other mental disorders", comprising the so-called "exogenous or situational reactions". These include sleep disorders, unstableness, psychosomatic symptoms, nervousness, agitation and anxieties, all of which are looked on as reactions to stress factors, such as an overload in the workplace, labour conflicts, recent or impending redundancy, or relational-, loneliness- or life-stage problems (Van Eck, 1991; Munnichs, 1993, p. 39). Statistical data would

appear to point to the conclusion that mental disorders as the diagnosed chief cause of incapacity decrease with age. However, this is countered by an increase in cardiovascular diseases (GMD, 1993). Munnichs (1993, p. 40) makes the following comments: "When we realize the size of the mental component in diseases of the cardiovascular system, we may state that this mental component is a factor of great importance for a very large number of older people and merits further study. It would seem that the nature of the workplace is such that the person either suffers from brief periods of stress and begins to display mental disorders in the form of situational or exogenous reactions, or is confronted by diseases of the cardiovascular system brought on by longer-term stress. He endeavours to cope with problems by a process of interiorization, which may then give rise to cardiovascular diseases." It is worth noting here that, based on their empirical research into the causes of incapacity for work, Van 't Hullenaar & Van Koningsveld conclude (1986, p. 160), "the cause of so many older people becoming unfit for work is not the working conditions or how they are experienced". They suggest that "this phenomenon can probably be

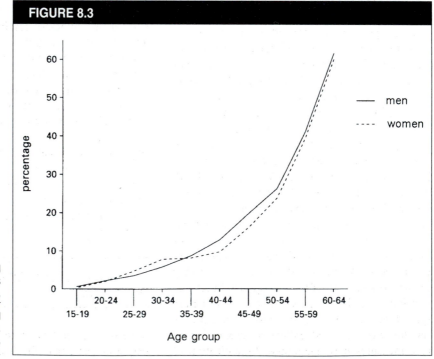

FIGURE 8.3

Total number of full and partial incapacity benefits in 1992 in the Netherlands, per 100 insurants or beneficiaries, by age and sex.
Source: GMD (1993, p. 51).

ascribed in particular to the personnel policy of the company and the manner in which the benefit agencies react to this. (...) It is highly likely that many of those pronounced "unfit for work" are not burnt out but cast aside." The explanation is sought by the authors in the socio-economically more vulnerable position of older people in comparison to that of younger people. They attribute the ready sanctioning of their "redundancy" by the medical benefit agencies to "the inability to differentiate processes of natural aging from accelerated pathological aging, with the result that age is becoming a kind of health indicator."

All in all, the likelihood of stress reactions with ongoing age appears to be increasing. The extent to which older people are more often confronted with stress factors in the workplace than younger people and the nature of these stress factors, cannot be said with any degree of certainty. It is likely that the negative image of older people and their awareness of belonging to a relatively undervalued group may play a part in this. Another factor may be the fear that sooner or later one may be pushed aside as superfluous or "out-of-date". That the old experience greater feelings of fear than the young has been demonstrated by Troyer et al. (1967) and Kuhlen (1977). It may be that older people are not treated with very much respect or they may feel neglected, powerless or abandoned by management or younger colleagues. There may also be less subjective factors at play, for example, a decline in the "quality of work" of the older person, or a diminution in individual resistance to stress or a failure in "coping" behaviour (Osipow, Doty, & Spokane, 1985; for more general reflections on this see Cooper & Payne, 1988; Fisher & Reason, 1988; Winnubst & Schabracq, 1992 as well as Chapter 7, Volume 2 of this Handbook). In many companies, categorical measures are taken within the context of the "policy on older people", to prevent or reduce an excessive workload and stress (cf. Schabracq & Winnubst, 1993). These invariably amount to an easing of tasks, responsibilities and working conditions for everyone over a certain age. Munnichs (1993) propounds the hypothesis that the character and collective application of such measures may encourage stigmatization of

older people. They label older workers without exception as people who are no longer fully able to bear the burden of their work. However, it is questionable whether this label matches reality for everyone. It is also conceivable that certain measures intended to be stress-alleviating are more likely to be stress-intensifying, for example in the case of those who feel discriminated against in consequence, or those who feel demoted to a position where further personal development is prevented.

The well-being and, more especially, the job satisfaction of the older people in employment are, of course, not solely determined on the one hand by issues of health, or on the other hand by the presence or absence of symptoms of stress and overload. Other determining factors have been described in detail in Chapter 11, Volume 4 of this Handbook, which also discusses the relation to work motivation. We will confine ourselves here to the comment that no direct and permanent relation has been found between age and job satisfaction, but that age often does play the role of moderator in the interaction between satisfaction and other variables (Hong, Bianca, Bianca, & Bollington, 1993; Lee & Wilbur, 1985; Pond & Geyer, 1987; Snyder & Mayo, 1991). For example, the future perspective held at a younger age is a clear indicator of job satisfaction. At a later age, the future perspective loses its significance and the relation to job satisfaction vanishes (cf. Dresens, 1989). There are thus more variables which, during the course of a person's life, acquire a different significance and consequently a different relation to well-being—sometimes stronger, sometimes weaker. Examples are the degree of positive and negative self-esteem in relation to others, the way in which a person appraises his own course of life or career, the perception of life and death (Munnichs, 1990), the ability to adapt to new circumstances, the way a person spends his time, and so on.

9   SOCIAL NETWORKS OF OLDER WORKERS

Research and policy in respect of older people begins at the point of the differences from younger categories or at the point of the perceived differentiations between individual older people. The importance of the *social context* in which older people have been categorized, while being acknowledged, nonetheless receives relatively little attention. One aspect has been examined fairly comprehensively in the context of studies into the so-called "mid-career phase". This relates to the *social support* from the "boss" and the partner at home, and to its possibly diminishing effect on stress reactions (Winnubst, Buunk & Marcelissen, 1988; Buunk, 1990). Social support would seem to have different effects on young and old. In the case of the young, the effect is, in the main, favourable, with support resulting in fewer mental symptoms and improved job satisfaction. In the case of older people, it may have the opposite effect. Support from superiors does not automatically result in fewer mental symptoms or increased job satisfaction. Support from a person's partner proves to reinforce rather than to diminish stress-related feelings of resentment and depression (Janssen, 1992). These findings are not easy to explain. Buunk (1990) and Janssen (1992, p. 99f) urge the necessity for more empirical research into the social processes in the workplace, in which account is taken of the age of those concerned, their specific work situation and any changes in the nature of inter-personal relations.

It is striking that a different aspect, namely the *social networks* in which the personnel in an organization do, or more likely, do not participate, has up to now been given little attention in work and organization psychological research. By "social networks" we mean not only formally instituted departments, project groups, teams, task/work groups, meetings and such like, but also informal groups, consultative groups, societies, clubs, congresses, family relationships and contacts with colleagues and friends.

Unquestionably, the composition, quality and effectiveness of these networks have an effect on the functioning, development and mobility of the participants (and possibly also of those on the outside!). It is likely that the crucial significance of social networks as a learning and experience environment also applies to older workers and that conversely the qualities and influence of the older personnel, in their turn, and maybe particularly,

achieve full recognition via their networks. The significance of social networks for older personnel has, to our knowledge, not often been studied as yet.

Empirical research suggests that superiors in large and medium-sized businesses are not in general *au courant* with the external and informal circuits in which their older personnel participate. Their awareness of this is probably restricted to their personnel's participation in "formal" networks within their own department and only to the extent that they consider these circuits to be of reasonable/great importance to the organization. Presumably they are less well informed about the social relationships of those functioning at middle level than they are about those at the higher level (Boerlijst et al., 1993, p. 86f).

An alternative hypothesis, namely that many personnel (roughly 75% at the middle level and around 40% at the higher level of functioning) work independently and confine their contacts to within their own department, seems less plausible. Of those stated by their superiors as not taking part or not known to take part in any network, there is a surprisingly high percentage on whose functioning more than 10 people depend. It is rather unlikely that personnel who carry along so many other people in their wake, as it were, do not maintain regular informal network contacts with any of them. The same applies to contacts confined to their own department. The work of many referred to by their superiors as "Einzelgänger", is said by those same superiors to have an effect or influence outside the organization. This also appears inconsistent.

The assumption that superiors are insufficiently *au courant* with their older personnel's informal contacts is further corroborated by the fact that they seem not to be in the habit of noting down the internal and external work contacts of their personnel.

The importance of informal (and of course formal) social networks as a *learning* and *influential environment*—not only for the older generation of course—cannot be underestimated. It therefore seems to us unwise not to give consideration to this in personnel management and research into functioning and mobility.

With respect to the perceived "immobility" of

older people, it should be considered to what extent this can be attributed to participation in the "old", more "closed" type of network. It seems to us a plausible hypothesis that long-standing networks, with hardly any mobility or new (in this case, young), "blood", tend to "age" sooner than open and, in terms of composition, more dynamic networks.

We would like to add a third aspect. This relates to the frequently heard view that the greater experience of older people in comparison with younger people should admirably equip them to perform the role of coach. We feel that some comments are in order here (cf. Boerlijst et al., 1993, p. 96).

- The function of coach should not be seen as a sinecure. A coach should be a good and trusted mentor. The role of mentor is a task for which one must be well-equipped and trained and is not innate. In other words, coaching calls for its own kind of expertise and skills.

- The experiential knowledge of a coach should not only *be* up to date but also *be able to remain* up to date. A "free standing" coach, who is more or less at a standstill and is no longer actively taking part in work itself, can be compared to a well that is in the process of drying up. Passing on dated knowledge is not necessarily "uninstructive" but must at least be relevant to the "pupil's" present and future.

- The social network within which the coach operates as such must "count" in the organization as valuable and useful. This also applies to the coach *mutatis mutandis*.

- Companies and organizations often vest their hope on an "influx of up-to-date knowledge" by the young. Given such an influx, it is advisable to extend just such a responsible coaching function to *younger people*, for the benefit of older people. Thus, their up-to-date knowledge and, in a more general sense, their experience as the new generation may reach the circle of the over-40-year-olds in a very direct and personal way. In this sort of two-way traffic between young and old the different generations can learn a lot from each other without age hierarchy playing a determining role.

10   REVIEW AND FUTURE PROSPECTS

From the foregoing it transpires that many older workers depart from the labour process, whether voluntarily or not, because they are no longer able to summon up the physical or mental effort required for their task, or because they are no longer capable or thought by management to be capable of adjusting successfully to certain necessary changes in function or field of work. Studies carried out in medium-sized and large organizations show that the majority of older people both in and out of work, at whatever level, have become rooted to one particular function and associated specialisms. As long as that function continues to exist and retains its values for the organization, their functioning generally gives the management no cause for complaint. However, workers over the age of 50 are considered by their superiors to be virtually no longer employable in a different post in a different function area. In practice, there is no mobility in this age group either. We must conclude that the knowledge, experience, skills or expertise built up by older people seem to be inadequate or to be considered inadequate to cope with drastic changes in their job description or workplace. Furthermore, there is considerable doubt on the part of management as to whether older people are capable of achieving competence in a new territory and are prepared to put in the extra effort to this end.

Fossilization in the function is the result of a process that begins to manifest itself in many over-40-year-olds. It is of course important to know whether this process is an unavoidable consequence of becoming older *per se* and thus happens to everyone sooner or later, or whether it is partly, or maybe even mainly, influenced by variable, and possibly controllable, factors in the person and in the environment in which a person's career evolves. There is still little detailed empirical knowledge on the potential and motivation for learning and development among older workers and the way this could be successfully activated in the everyday practice of the business world. Demographic developments within companies, entailing aging and possibly also dejuvenization of the personnel, impel greater attention to this matter. Although certain cognitive functions, in particular speed of reaction and the short-term memory, will tend to decrease with an increase in age—albeit with large individual differences—there are as yet no signs of a "natural" blockage in the capacity of older workers to learn and adapt. On the other hand, however, little is known about how wide-ranging these capacities may be and the conditions enabling them to be activated at a later age. It has, however, been firmly established that management actions targeted at promoting workers' mobility are often unforthcoming in the case of older personnel.[3] A predominantly "instrumental" attitude on the part of management, a stereotypical lack of confidence in the still remaining development potentials and motivation of their older personnel are probably the principal reasons.

The processes characterizing the aging of personnel in organizations can best be studied within the framework of longitudinal career research. After all, seen in this context, not only can the passage from "young" to "old" in its successive phases and transitions be studied, but the sequential correlation between the development of the individual and his/her relevant work and living environment will remain visible. When a study of this nature is set up, it is recommended that a career model be opted for that leaves scope for considerable *individual differences* within each age cohort. Certain of the models familiar from literature are deficient on this point. Examples of this are the so-called life-course models of Super (1957), Erikson (1968), Lievegoed (1975, 1977) and Levinson (1978, 1986). They divide up a person's life course into successive life stages corresponding to particular age bands. Each phase is differentiated from the preceding and succeeding one by, amongst other things, certain characteristic role expectations and role patterns, or by certain characteristic role transitions, by which those in the age group in question can be identified. These authors look on "older people" as a more or less invariant category conforming to

certain characteristics and expectations. They give much greater emphasis to the supposed *similarities* in the attitude and the behaviour of older people than the *differences* which are so conspicuous in everyday life. Some of these models, those of Lievegoed and Levinson for instance, have been arrived at via a compilation of clinical observations and interviews, in which existing social prejudices on the part of both young and old and also prejudices held by the authors themselves have not been identified as such and consequently eliminated. The fact that such models underline accepted social prejudices gives them a certain popularity. They are therefore not challenged any more, even though various research results point in a different direction. The existing theories and models on "burnout" problems or crises in the so-called "mid-career phase" (cf. Hunt & Collins, 1983; Nagy, 1985) are also currently enjoying popularity. Research by Gerrichhauzen (1989) and Janssen (1992) shows that such problems and crises are not characteristic of one particular age group. Many people do not exhibit them at all whereas others do, but not or not only in the mid-career phase. More may be expected from the so-called "matching models", in particular those of Hall (1975, 1976), Dalton, Thompson, and Price (1977, 1980), Schein (1978) and Super (1984). These models are based on the assumption that a person's development during his career is dependent on the availability of certain development-specific tasks, and that when selecting those tasks, there must be adaptation to the particular stage of development of the individual. Moreover, they allow for the fact that motivations and needs during a person's life course may change (Alderfer, 1972). An example of a non-age-specific individual growth model, incorporating ideas from Hall and others, is that of Sterns (Sterns & Alexander, 1987). This model, too, allows for the various stages that may be passed through during a person's career and the various events, stimulations and impediments which may influence the individual's development and mobility. However, the difference from previous phase models is that these stages and events do not have a normative content for particular age groups.

The similarities and differences between individual processes of aging within organizations may well only be thrown fully into perspective in a research form employing a longitudinal or sequential character (Schaie, 1983; Schaie & Willis, 1991; Taris, 1994; Warr, 1994; see also Chapter 2, Volume 1 of this Handbook). If it is a case of research into physical or technological processes, this form has the full approval of the business community (take for example the so-called "life test"). However, in these circles there is considerable, effective resistance to longitudinal socio-scientific research. This derives from apprehension as to its long duration and the efforts incumbent on research of this nature—not only in a financial sense, but also in an organizational and motivational respect. If one wishes to elevate opinions within organizations on the development and development potential of older workers above the level of non-validated prejudices and haphazardly collected notions of managers and other policymakers, then theory formulation on the basis of longitudinal data is indispensable. This is the message that must be spread to every corner of the business community.

NOTES

1. By "working population" we mean all 15 to 64-year-olds who are either in or seeking employment. The "gross participation in the labour process" of a particular group out of the total population is the percentage in that group of those in and seeking employment. The "net participation in the labour process" is the percentage of those actually in employment, in other words those performing paid work.
2. Including so-called women returners.
3. Relevant research on this has up to now only been carried out in medium-sized and large organizations and companies. This is not to imply that mobility, employability and development of older workers in small organizations and companies are necessarily differently structured.

REFERENCES

Adams, J.S. (1965). Inequity in social exchange. In L. Berkowitz (Ed.), *Advances in experimental social psychology*, Vol. 2. New York: Academic Press.

Alderfer, C.P. (1972). *Existence, relatedness and growth*. London: Collier-Macmillan.

Altena, A. R. van, Plantegna, J., Schippers, J.J., & Siegers, J.J. (1990). *Demografische ontwikkelingen en het functioneren van de arbeidsmarkt: Een verge-lijkende studie naar het overheidsbeleid in de Bonds-republiek Duitsland, Frankrijk, Zweden en Nederland* [Demography and the labour market: Government policy in Germany, France, Sweden and The Netherlands]. The Hague: Organization for Strategic Labour Market Research (OSA). Working document W73.

Anderson, J.R. (1982). Acquisition of cognitive skill. *Psychological Review, 89*, 369–406.

Arenburg, D. (1965). Anticipation interval and age differences in verbal learning. *Journal of Abnormal Psychology, 70*, 419–425.

Assen, A. van (1990). *Technologie en personeelbeleid* [Technology and personnel policy]. Inaugural lecture. Nijmegen: Catholic University.

Assen, A. van, & Keijsers, G. (1993). Loopbaanontwikkeling en inzetbaarheid van "kennis-werkers" [Career development and employability of "knowledge workers"]. In J.G. Boerlijst, H. van der Flier, & A.E.M. van Vianen (Eds.), *Werk maken van loopbanen: Ontwikkeling en begeleiding* [Making careers your business: Development and guidance], 107–120. Utrecht: Lemma.

Avolio, B.J., & Waldman, D.A. (1987). Personnel aptitude test scores as a function of age, education and job type. *Experimental Aging Research, 13*, 109–113.

Avolio, B.J., Waldman, D.A., & McDaniel, M.A. (1990). Age and work performance in non-managerial jobs: The effects of experience and occupational type. *Academy of Management Journal, 33*(2), 407–422.

Baker, S.H., & Hansen, R.A. (1975). Job design and worker satisfaction: A challenge to assumptions. *Journal of Occupational Psychology, 48*, 79–91.

Baltes, P.B., & Willis, S.L. (1982). Plasticity and enhancement of intellectual functioning in old age: Penn State's Adult Development and Enrichment Project (ADEPT). In F.I.M. Craik, & S.E. Trehub (Eds.), *Aging and cognitive processes*. New York: Plenum.

Baltes, P.B., & Baltes, M.M. (1990). *Successful aging*. Cambridge: Cambridge University Press.

Bartel, A.P., & Sicherman, N. (1993). Technological change and retirement decisions of older workers. *Journal of Labor Economics, 11*(1), 162–183.

Barton, P. (1982). *Worklife transitions*. New York: McGraw-Hill.

Beek, K.W.H. van, & Praag, B.M.S. van (1992). *Kiezen uit sollicitanten: concurrentie tussen werkzoekenden zonder baan* [Selecting from among applicants: Competition among job-seekers]. The Hague: Sdu [Government Printing Office].

Beer, J. de, & Noordam, R. (1988). Effect van buitenlandse migratie op ontgroening en vergrijzing [Effect of foreign migration on dejuvenization and aging]. *Maandstatistiek van de bevolking, 36*(9) [Monthly Bulletin of Population Statistics, 36*(9), 16–20.

Belbin, E., & Shimmin, S. (1964) Training the middle

aged for inspection work. *Occupational Psychology, 38*(1), 49–57.

Berg, C.A., & Sternberg, R.J. (1985). A triarchic theory of intellectual development during adulthood. *Developmental Review, 5,* 334–370.

Birren, J.E. (1985). Age, competence, creativity, and wisdom. In R.N. Butler, & H.P. Gleason (Eds.), *Productive aging: Enhancing vitality in later life.* New York: Springer.

Birren, J.E., Cunningham, W.R., & Yamamoto, M. (1983). Psychology of adult development and aging. In M.R. Rosenzweig, & L.W. Porter (Eds.), *Annual Review of Psychology, 34,* 543–575. Palo Alto, CA: Annual Reviews Inc.

Birren, J.E., & Schaie, K.W. (Eds.) (1985, 1990). *Handbook of the psychology of aging* (2nd and 3rd ed.). New York: Van Nostrand Reinhold.

Bodenhausen, G.V. (1990). Stereotypes as judgmental heuristics: Evidence of circadian variations in discrimination. *Psychological Science, 1,* 319–322.

Boerlijst, J.G. (1986). Veroudering van de beroepsbevolking in Nederland en Japan [Aging of the working population in The Netherlands and Japan]. In E. Abma, D.W. van Bekkum, M. Doorman-Degens, H.P. Gallacher, M.L. Koen, D. Nauta, M.E.F. Prins, W.J. Rietveld, E.J. Birfelder, & I. Spruit (Eds.), *Cahiers Bio-Wetenschappen en Maatschappij* [Bio-Sciences and Society], *3,* 41–47.

Boerlijst, J.G. (1995). The neglect of growth and development of employees of over-forty in organizations. In J. Cremer, & J. Snel (Eds.), *Work and aging: A European prospective* (pp. 251–271). London: Taylor & Francis.

Boerlijst, J.G., & Heijden, B.I.J.M. van der (1997). Human resource management in distress. In U. Munander, & C. Semiawan, Optimizing excellence in human resource development. *Proceedings of the Fourth Asia-Pacific Conference on Giftedness, Jakarta 1996* (pp. 473–480). Jakarta: University of Indonesia Press.

Boerlijst, J.G., Dijk, N. van, & Helvoort, E. van (1987). Japans personeelsbeleid en de oudere werknemer [Japanese personnel policy and the older worker]. *M & O, Tijdschrift voor Organisatiekunde en Sociaal Beleid* [M & O, Journal of Organizational Studies and Social Policy], *41,* 338–351.

Boerlijst, J.G., Heijden, B.I.J.M. van der, & Assen, A. van (1993). *Veertig-plussers in de onderneming* [The over-forties in organizations]. Amsterdam/Assen: Van Gorcum.

Boerlijst-Bosch, E.F. (1962) Binnenkort met pensioen. Een onderzoek onder 60 aanstaande gepensioneerden [On the brink of retirement. Research conducted among 60 employees approaching retirement]. Eindhoven: Philips, April 1962 (internal report).

Botwinick, J. (1984). *Aging and behavior: A comprehensive integration of research findings* (3rd ed.). New York: Springer.

Bourne, B. (1982). Effects of aging on work satisfac-

tion, performance and motivation. *Aging and Work, 6,* 37–47.

Brewer, M.B., & Lui, L.N. (1989). The primacy of age and sex in the structure of person categories. *Social Cognition, 7,* 262–274.

Bromley, D.B. (1988). *Human aging, an introduction to gerontology.* Harmondsworth, UK: Penguin.

Brouwer, W.H. (1990). Veroudering, cognitie en compensatie [Aging, cognition and compensation]. *Vox Hospitii, 14*(3), 6–11.

Butler, R.N., & Gleason, H.P. (Eds.) (1985). *Productive aging: Enhancing vitality in later life.* New York: Springer.

Buunk, B.P. (1990). Affiliation and helping interactions within organisations: A critical analysis of the role of social support with regard to organisational stress. *European Review Social Psychology, 1,* 293–322.

Cavanaugh, J.C. (1993). *Adult development and aging* (2nd ed.). Pacific Grove, CA: Brooks/Cole.

CBS (Centraal Bureau voor de Statistiek) [Statistics Netherlands] (1985). Groei van de gescheiden bevolking, 1950–2000 [Growth in the percentage of divorced people, 1950–2000]. *Maandstatistiek van de bevolking [Monthly Bulletin of Population Statistics], 33*(9), 9–10. The Hague: CBS [Statistics Netherlands].

CBS (Centraal Bureau voor de Statistiek) [Statistics Netherlands] (1989). *Negentig jaren statistiek in tijdreeksen; 1899–1990* [Historical Series of The Netherlands: 1899–1990]. The Hague: SDU [Government Printing Office]/CBS [Statistics Netherlands].

CBS (Centraal Bureau voor de Statistiek) [Statistics Netherlands] (1993). *De leefsituatie van de Nederlandse bevolking 1992: Kerncijfers* [Well-being of the population in The Netherlands 1922: Key figures]. The Hague: SDU [Government Printing Office]/CBS [Statistics Netherlands].

Ceci, S.J. (1990). *On intelligence ... more or less.* Englewood Cliffs: Prentice-Hall.

Charness, N. (1989). Age and expertise: Responding to Talland's challenge. In L.W. Poon, D.C. Rubin, & B.A. Wilson (Eds.), *Everyday cognition in adulthood and late life* (pp. 437–456). Cambridge: Cambridge University Press.

Charness, N., & Bosman, E.A. (1990). Expertise and aging: Life in the lab. In T.M. Hess (Ed.), *Aging and cognition: Knowledge organization and utilization.* Amsterdam: Elsevier.

Chi, M.T.H., Glaser, R., & Farr, M.J. (1988). *The nature of expertise.* Hillsdale, NJ: Erlbaum.

Clark, R.L. (1988). De economie van een vergrijzende beroepsbevolking [The economy of an aging labour force]. *Economisch Statistische Berichten* [Economical Statistical News], 1021–1025.

Cooper, C.L., & Payne, R. (1988). *Causes, coping and consequences of stress at work.* New York: Wiley.

Cornelius, S.W., & Caspi, A. (1987). Everyday problem solving in adulthood and old age. *Psychology and aging*, *2*, 144–153.

Craft, J.A., Doctors, S.I., Shkop, Y.M., & Benecki, T.J. (1979). Simulated management perceptions, hiring decisions and age. *Aging and Work*, *2*, 95–102.

Dalton, G.W., & Thompson, P.H. (1971). Accelerating obsolescence of older engineers. *Harvard Business Review*, 57–67.

Dalton, G.W., Thompson, P.H., & Price, R.L. (1977). Career stages: A model of professional careers in organizations. *Organizational Dynamics*, *6*(3), 19–42.

Dalton, G.W., Thompson, P.H., & Price, R.L. (1980). The four stages of professional careers: A new look at performance by professionals. In M.A. Morgan (Ed.), *Managing career development* (pp. 43–60). New York: Van Nostrand.

Davies, D.R., & Sparrow, P.R. (1985). Age and work behaviour. In N. Charness (Ed.), *Aging and human performance*. Chichester, UK: Wiley.

Dittmann-Kohli, F., & Baltes, P.B. (1985). Toward a neofunctionalist conception of adult intellectual development: Wisdom as a prototypical case of intellectual growth. In C. Alexander, E. Langer, & M. Oetzel (Eds.), *Higher stages of human development: Adult growth beyond formal operations*. New York: Oxford University Press.

Dixon, R.A., Kramer, D.A., & Baltes, P.B. (1985). Intelligence: A life-span developmental perspective. In B.B. Wolman (Ed.), *Handbook of intelligence* (pp. 301–350). New York: Wiley.

Doering, M., Rhodes, S.R., & Schuster, M. (1983). *The aging worker; research and recommendations*. Beverly Hills: Sage Publications.

Doup, A.C.B.W. (Ed.) (1990). *Leeftijdscriteria in het arbeidsbestel*. [Age criteria in the established system of work]. Alphen aan de Rijn: Samson Tjeenk Willink.

Dresens, C.S.H.H. (1989). *"Hebben ze mij niet meer nodig?" Een sociaal-wetenschappelijk onderzoek naar de positie van ouder wordende medewerkers bij het GAK* ["Don't they need me any more?" A socio-scientific investigation into the position of aging employees at the Joint Administration Office]. Doctoral thesis, University of Amsterdam.

Dubin, S.S. (1971). *Professional obsolescence*. Lexington, MA: Heath.

Durinck, J.R. (1993). Gezondheid, veroudering en werk [Health, aging and work]. In J.G. Boerlijst, H. van der Flier, & A.E.M. van Vianen (Eds.), *Werk maken van loopbanen: Ontwikkeling en begeleiding* [Making careers your business: Development and guidance] (pp. 203–219). Utrecht: Lemma.

Eck, M.A.A. van (1991). Diagnosestelling: Categorie V [Making a diagnosis: Category V]. In R. Bijl, & D. Bauduin (Eds.), *Categorie V: Arbeidsongeschikt heid wegens psychische stoornissen* [Category V: Incapacity for work owing to psychological disorders].

Report by the Dutch Mental Health Centre, Autumn Conference. Utrecht: Nederlands Centrum Geestelijke Volksgezondheid [Dutch Mental Health Centre].

Eerde, W. van, Thierry, H., Haan, W. de (1994). *Thirty years of research on Vroom's expectancy model and work related criteria: A meta-analysis.* Amsterdam: University of Amsterdam.

Eisdorfer, C., Axelrod, S., & Wilkie, F. (1963). Stimulus exposure time as a factor in serial learning in an aged sample. *Journal of Abnormal and Social Psychology*, *67*, 594–600.

Ericsson, K.A., & Smith, J. (1991). *Toward a general theory of expertise: Prospects and limits.* Cambridge: Cambridge University Press.

Erikson, E.H. (1968). *Identity, youth and crisis.* New York: Norton.

Feeney, G. (1990). *The demography of aging in Japan, 1950–2025.* Tokyo, NUPRI Research Paper Series No. 55.

Fischer, K.W., & Silvern, L. (1985). Stages and individual differences in cognitive development. *Annual Review of Psychology*, *36*, 613–648. Palo Alto, CA: Annual Reviews Inc.

Fisher, S., & Reason, J. (Eds.) (1988). *Handbook of life stress, cognition and health.* New York: Wiley.

Fiske, S.T. (1993). Social cognition and social perception. *Annual Review of Psychology*, *44*, 155–194.

Gelderblom, A., & Koning, J. de (1992a). *Ouder worden een probleem?* [Is aging a problem?] (Literature study). Rotterdam: Netherlands Economic Institute (NEI).

Gelderblom, A., & Koning, J. de (1992b). *Leeftijd en functioneren: Een aanzet voor een beleid bij de rijksoverheid.* [Age and functioning: A start on policy within the government] Rotterdam: Netherlands Economic Institute (NEI).

Gelderblom, A., & Koning, J. de (1992c). *Meer-jarig, minder-waardig? Een onderzoek naar de invloed van leeftijd op produktiviteit en beloning* [A study of the influence of age on productivity and remuneration]. The Hague: Netherlands Economic Institute (NEI)/ Organization for Strategic Labour Market Research (OSA)-preliminary study V39.

Gerpott, T.J., Domsch, M., & Keller, R.T. (1988). Career orientations in different countries and companies: An empirical investigation of West-German, British and US Industrial R&D professionals. *Journal of Management Studies*, *25*, 439–462.

Gerrichhauzen, J.T.G. (1989). *De middenloopbaanfase bij managers: Een wetenschappelijke proeve op het gebied van de sociale wetenschappen* [The mid-career phase in managers: A scientific test in the field of social sciences]. Doctoral thesis, Catholic University of Nijmegen.

Gilbert, D.T., & Hixon, J.G. (1991). The trouble of thinking: Activation and application of stereotypic beliefs. *Journal of Pers. Soc. Pychol.*, *60*, 509–517.

Giniger, S., Dispenzieri, A., & Eisenberg, J. (1983).

Age, experience and performance in speed and skill jobs in an applied setting. *Journal of Applied Psychology, 68,* 469–475.

GMD (1993). *Jaarverslag 1992* [Annual report 1992]. Amsterdam: Gemeenschappelijke Medische Dienst [Joint Medical Service].

Green, R.F. (1972). Age, intelligence and learning. *Industrial Gerontology, 12,* 29–41.

Griew, S. (1964). *Job re-design.* Paris: OECD.

Hale, N. (1990). *The older worker: Effective strategies for management and human resource development.* San Francisco: Jossey-Bass.

Hall, D.T. (1975). Potential for career growth. In H.G. Kaufman (Ed.), *Career management: A guide to combating obsolescence.* New York: IEEE Press.

Hall, D.T. (1976). *Careers in organizations.* Pacific Palisades, CA: Goodyear Publishing Co.

Hall, D.T., & Isabella, L.A. (1985). Downward movement and career development. *Organizational Dynamics, 14,* 23f.

Hall, D.T., & Parker, V.A. (1993). The role of workplace flexibility in managing diversity. *Organizational Dynamics, 22,* 5–18.

Hammond, P., & Morgan, H.P. (Eds.) (1991). *Ending mandatory retirement for tenured faculty: The consequence for higher education.* Commission Report for the National Research Council. Washington, DC: National Academy Press.

Harel, G.H., & Conen, L.K. (1982). Expectancy theory applied to the process of professional obsolescence. *Public Personnel Management, 11*(1), 13–21.

Harrick, E.J., Mansel, M, & Schutzius, E.E. (1982). Outplacement training, process, content and analysis. *Training and Development Journal, 36,* 78–85.

Heijden, H.Th.J. van der, Jong, R.D. de, & Spengler, E.C. van (1993). Outplacement: Ondersteuning bij verlies van werkkring; stimulans bij heroriëntatie en verdere groei [Outplacement: Support on job loss: A stimulus in reorientation and further growth]. In J.G. Boerlijst, H. van der Flier, & A.E.M. van Vianen (Eds.), *Werk maken van loopbanen: Ontwikkeling en begeleiding,* [Making careers your business: Development and guidance], *187–201.* Utrecht: Lemma.

Hermans, H.J.M. (1987). Self as an organized system of valuations: Toward a dialogue with the person. *Journal of Counseling Psychology, 34,* 10–19.

Hermans, H.J.M. (1988). On the integration of ideographic and nomothetic research methods in the study of personal meaning. *J. Personality, 56,* 785–812.

Hermans, H.J.M., & Bonarius, H. (1991). The person as co-investigator in personality research. *European Journal of Personality, 5,* 199–216.

Hong, S.M., Bianca, M.A., Bianca, M.R., & Bollington, J. (1993). Self esteem: The effects of life-satisfaction, sex and age. *Psychol. Reports,* (72), 95–101.

Hoorn, W.D. van (1989). Bevolkingssamenstelling [Population composition]. *Maandstatistiek van de Bevolking, 10* [Monthly Bulletin of population statistics, 10], 12. The Hague: CBS [Statistics Netherlands].

Hullenaar, R.H.J. van 't, & Koningsveld, D.B.J. van (1986). *Afgebrand of afgedankt: Een onderzoek naar oorzaken van arbeidsongeschiktheid* [Burnt out or discarded: Research into causes of incapacity for work]. Lisse: Swets & Zeitlinger.

Hunt, J., & Collins, R.R. (1983). *Managers in mid career crisis.* Sydney: Wellington Lane Press.

Jablonski, M.L., Rosenblum, L., & Kunze, K. (1988). Productivity, age, and labour composition changes in the US *Monthly Labour Review,* 34 38.

Janssen, P. (1992). *Relatieve deprivatie in de middenloopbaanfase bij hoger opgeleide mannen* [Relative deprivation in the mid-career phase in male graduates]. Maastricht: UPM [Maastricht University Press].

Jouvenel, H. de (1989). *Europe's ageing population: Trends and challenges to 2025.* Guildford, UK: Butterworth & Co (Publishers) Ltd.

Kaa, D.J. van de (1987). Europe's second demographic transition. *Population Bulletin,* 42. Population Reference Bureau, Washington.

Kamstra, E., & Craats, W. van der (1991). Eenrichtingsverkeer op de arbeidsmarkt [One-way traffic on the labour market: An investigation of exit and re-entrance flows of older employees]. *Organization for Strategic Labour Market Research (OSA)-working document W 91.* The Hague: NSS Beleidsonderzoek & Beleidsadvies.

Kaplan, M.F., Wanshula, L.T., & Zanna, M.P. (1992). Time pressure and information integration in social judgment: The effect of need for structure. In O. Svenson, & J. Maule (Eds.), *Time pressure and stress in human judgment and decision making.* New York: Plenum.

Kaufman, H.G. (1974) *Obsolescence and professional career development.* New York: AMACOM.

Kaufman, H.G. (Ed.) (1975). *Career management: A guide to combating obsolescence.* New York: IEEE Press.

Kerkhoff, W.H.C. (1981). *Onderzoek oudere werknemers, deel 1 (Ouder worden, verouderen en het personeelsbeleid) en deel 3: (Ouder zijn en ouder worden)* [Research on older workers, part 1 (Growing older, aging and personnel policy) and part 3: (Being older and growing older). The Hague: Dutch Joint Council for Business Development [COB]/Socio-Economic Council (SER).

Kerkhoff, W.H.C., & Kruidenier, H.J. (1991). *Bedrijfsleven en de vergrijzing: Aanzetten voor een leeftijdsbewust personeelsbeleid* [The business world and aging: A start on an age-related personnel policy]. Amsterdam: Nederlands Instituut voor Arbeidsomstandigheden [Dutch Institute for the Working Environment (NIA)].

Keuning, D., Maas, T.H., & Ophey, W. (1993). *Verplatting van organisaties* [Delayering of organizations]. Assen: Van Gorcum.

Kleber, R.J. (1982). *Stressbenaderingen in de psychologie* [Approaches to stress in psychology]. Deventer: Van Loghum Slaterus.

Klomps, A., Kommers, H., & Kamphuis, P. (1991). Wat kunnen bedrijven doen aan arbeidsongeschiktheid? [What can companies do about incapacity for work?] (Report) Tilburg: IVA, Catholic University of Brabant.

Kogan, N., & Wallach, M. (1961). The effect of anxiety on relations between subjective age and caution in an older sample. In P.H. Hoch, & J. Zubin (Eds.), *Psychopathology of aging*. New York: Grune & Stratton.

Koningsveld, D.B.J. van (1988). *Vut, nu en straks* [Early retirement, now and later]. Assen: Van Gorcum.

Koningswijk, L.A. (1989). De arbeidsorganisatie en de veroudering van de beroepsbevolking: Loopbaanombuiging, normaaltoekomstperspectief? [Organization of labour and the aging of the working population: Career shifts, normal future perspectives?] *Management en Organisatie, 1* [Management and Organization, 1], 53–64.

Koopmanschap, M.A., Royen, van L., Bonneux, L., Bonsel, H.J., Rutten, F.F.H., & Maas, P.J. van der (1994). Cost of diseases in international perspective. *European Journal of Public Health, 4*, 258–264.

Kuhlen, R.G. (1977). Developmental changes in motivation during the adult years. In B.L. Neugarten (Ed.), *Middle age and aging*. Chicago: The University of Chicago Press.

Labouvie-Vief, G. (1982). Dynamic development and mature autonomy: A theoretical prologue. *Human Development, 25*, 161–191.

Labouvie-Vief, G. (1985). Intelligence and cognition. In J.E. Birren, & K.W. Schaie (Eds.), *Handbook of the psychology of aging* (2nd ed., pp. 500–530). New York: Van Nostrand Reinhold.

Landy, F.J., and associates (1992). *Alternatives to chronological age in determining standards of suitability for public safety jobs.* Technical Report Center of Applied Behavioral Science, Pennsylvania State University.

Lee, R., & Wilbur, E.R. (1985). Age, education, job tenure, salary, job characteristics, and job-satisfaction.–A multivariate analysis. *Human Relations, 38*, 781–791.

Levinson, D.J. (1978). *The seasons of a man's life.* New York: Knopf.

Levinson, D.J. (1986). A conception of adult development. *American Psychologist, 41*(1), 3–13.

Lievegoed, B. (1975). *Organisatie in ontwikkeling* [Organization in development]. Rotterdam: Lemniscaat.

Lievegoed, B. (1977). *De levensloop van de mens* [The human life course]. Rotterdam: Lemniscaat.

Light, L.L. (1991). Memory and aging: Four hypotheses in search of data. *Ann. Rev. Psychol., 42*, 333–376. Palo Alto, CA: Annual Reviews Inc.

Loen, C.D., & Schilfgaarde, P. van (1990). *Flexibiliteit binnen stabiele arbeidsrelaties: Mogelijkheden van interne arbeidsflexibiliteit* [Flexibility within stable labour relations: Possibilities of internal flexibility in labour]. Assen: Van Gorcum.

Loo, R.P.J.M. van de (1992). *Verheldering van loopbaanperspectief* [Clarifying career perspectives]. Academic doctoral thesis, Catholic University, Nijmegen.

McAuley, W.J. (1977). Perceived age discrimination in hiring: Demographic and economic correlates. *Industrial Gerontology, 4*, 21–28.

McDaniel, M.A., Schmidt, F.L., & Hunter, J.E. (1988). Job experience correlates of performance. *Journal of Applied Psychology, 73*, 327–330.

McEnrue, M.D. (1988). Length of experience and the performance of managers in the establishment phase of their careers. *Academy of Management Journal, 31*, 175–185.

McEvoy, G.M., & Cascio, W.F. (1989). Cumulative evidence of the relationship between age and job performance. *Journal of Applied Psychology, 74*, 11–17.

Meier, E.L., & Kerr, E.A. (1976). Capabilities of middle-aged and older workers: A survey of literature. *Industrial Gerontology, 3*, 147–156.

Mercer, W.M. (1981). *Employee attitudes: Implications of an aging work force.* New York: William M. Mercer, Inc.

Munnichs, J.M.A. (1966). *Oudere werknemers, een verkennende studie* [Older workers, an exploratory study]. The Hague: Commissie Opvoering Produktivi teit/Sociaal-Economische Raad [Dutch Productivity Committee/Socio-Economic Council] (SER).

Munnichs, J.M.A. (1987). Loopbaan, levensloop en de midleven-ervaring [Career, life course and the mid-life experience]. In P.A.E. van de Bunt, & K. Nijkerk (Eds.), *Handboek Organisatie* [Organization Handbook] *Subject 25.100, Supplement 14*, 1–10. Alphen a/d Rijn: Samson, Kluwer.

Munnichs, J.M.A. (1990). *Gerontologie, levensloop en biografie* [Gerontology, life course and biography]. Deventer: Van Loghum Slaterus.

Munnichs, J.M.A. (1993). De levensloop stokt: Over werk, levensloop en ouder worden [The life course stalls: On work, life course and growing older]. In H.C.M. vam Seumeren (Ed.), *Arbeid en levensloop: Dissonant of harmonie?* [Labour and life course: Dissonant or harmony?] (pp. 31–46). Utrecht: SWP.

Munnichs, J.M.A., Dirken, J.M., Dohmen, N.J.P., & Thierry, H. (1968). Leeftijd en bedrijfsbeleid [Age and company policy], no. 52. Nederlandse Vereniging voor Bedrijfspsychologie [Dutch Association for Industrial Psychology]. Leiden: H.E. Stenfert Kroese.

Munnichs, J.M.A., Mussen, P., Olbrich, E., & Coleman, P. (Eds.), (1985). *Lifespan and change in a gerontological perspective.* New York: Academic Press.

Nagy, S. (1985). Burnout and selected variables as components of occupational stress. *Psychological Reports, 56,* 195–200.

NFB (Nederlandse Federatie voor Bejaardenbeleid) [Dutch Federation of Organizations for the Elderly] (1984). *De arbeidsmarktpositie van ouderen* [The position of the elderly on the labour market]. The Hague: NFB.

OECD (1988). *Ageing populations. The social policy implications.* Paris: OECD.

Osipow, S.H., Doty, R.E., & Spokane, A.R. (1985). Occupational stress, strain, and coping across the life span. *Journal of Vocational Behaviour, 27,* 98–108.

Palmore, E., & Luikart, C. (1972). Health and social factors related to life satisfaction. *Journal of Health and Social Behavior, 13*(1), 68–80.

Pelz, D.C., & Andrews, F.M. (1966). *Scientists in organizations.* New York: Wiley.

POA (Policy Office for the Aged) (1983). *Aging in Japan.* Tokyo: Prime Minister's Secretariat.

Pond, S.B., & Geyer, P.D. (1987). Employee age as a moderator of the relation between perceived work alternatives and job satisfaction. *Journal of Applied Psychology, 72,* 552–557.

Prevoo, E., & Thijssen, J.G.L. (1992). Bedrijfskundige setting en scholingsdeelname van 35+ personeelsleden [Setting in a managerial perspective and participation in education by personnel over the age of 35]. Utrecht: Rabobank, The Netherlands (internal report).

Price, R.L., Thompson, P.H., & Dalton, G.W. (1975). A longitudinal study of technological obsolescence. *Research Management,* 22–28.

Prins, R. (1990). *Sickness absence in Belgium (FR), Germany and The Netherlands: A comparative study.* Doctoral thesis. Limburg State University, Maastricht.

Reichelt, P.A. (1974). Moderators in expectancy theory: Influence on the relationships of motivation with effort and job performance. Unpublished doctoral dissertation, Wayne State University.

Rhodes, S.R. (1983). Age-related differences in work attitudes and behavior: A review and conceptual analysis. *Psychological Bulletin, 93*(2), 328–367.

Rosen, B., & Jerdee, T.H. (1976a). The nature of job-related stereotypes. *Journal of Applied Psychology, 61,* 180–183.

Rosen, B., & Jerdee, T.H. (1976b). The influence of age stereotypes on managerial decisions. *Journal of Applied Psychology, 61,* 428–432.

Salthouse, T.A. (1984). Effects of age and skill in typing. *Journal of Experimental Psychology: General, 113,* 345–371.

Salthouse, T.A. (1990). Cognitive competence and expertise in aging. In J.E. Birren, & K.W. Schaie (Eds.), *Handbook of the psychology of aging* (3rd ed., pp. 310–319). San Diego: Academic Press.

Schabracq, M.J., & Winnubst, J.A.M. (Eds.) (1993). *Handboek arbeid en gezondheid psychologie, Vol. 2 (Toepassingen)* [Handbook of labour and health psychology, Vol. 2 (Applications)]. Utrecht: Lemma.

Schaie, K.W. (Ed.) (1983). *Longitudinal studies of adult psychological development.* New York: The Guilford Press.

Schaie, K.W., & Willis, S.L. (1986). Can adult intellectual decline be reversed? *Developmental Psychology, 22,* 223–232.

Schaie, K.W., & Willis, S.L. (1991). *Adult development and aging* (3rd ed.). New York: Harper Collins.

Schein, E.H. (1978). *Career dynamics: Matching individual and organizational needs.* Addison-Wesley Publishing Co.

Schmidt, F.L., Hunter, J.E., & Outerbridge, A.N. (1986). Impact of job experience and ability on job knowledge, worksample performance, and supervisory ratings of performance. *Journal of Applied Psychology, 71,* 432–439.

Schooler, C. & Schaie, K.W. (Eds.) (1987). *Cognitive functioning and social structure over the life course.* Norwood, New Jersey: Ablex Publishing Corporation.

Schwab, D.P., & Heneman, H.G. (1977a). Effects of age and experience on productivity. *Industrial Gerontology, 4,* 113–117.

Schwab, D.P., & Heneman, H.G., (1977b). Age and satisfaction with dimensions of work. *Journal of Vocational Behavior, 10,* 212–222.

Sheppard, H.L., & Rix, S.E. (1977). *The graying of working America: The coming crisis of retirement age policy.* New York: The Free Press.

Sinnott, J.D. (Ed.) (1994). *Interdisciplinary handbook of adult lifespan learning.* Westport, Conn.: Greenwood Press.

Snyder, R.A., & Mayo, F. (1991). Single versus multiple causes of the age/job satisfaction relationship. *Psychological Reports, 68,* 1255–1262.

Sparrow, P.R., & Davies, D.R. (1988). Effects of age, tenure, training, and job complexity on technical performance. *Psychology and Aging Journal, 3,* 307–314.

Stagner, R. (1985). Aging in industry. In J.E. Birren, & K.W. Schaie (Eds.), *Handbook of the psychology of aging* (2nd ed.), pp. 798–817.

Sterns, H.L., & Alexander, R.A. (1987). Industrial gerontology: The aging individual and work. In C. Eisendorfer (Ed.), *Annual Review of Gerontology and Geriatrics, 7,* 243–264.

Super, D.E. (1957). *The psychology of careers.* New York: Harper & Row.

Super, D.E. (1984). Career and life development. In D. Brown, L. Brooks, and associates (Eds.), *Career choice and development.* San Francisco: Jossey-Bass.

Taris, T.W. (1994). Analysis of career data from a life-course perspective. Unpublished PhD thesis, Free University, Amsterdam.

Taub, H.A. (1967). Paired associates learning as a function of age, rate, and instruction. *The Journal of Genetic Psychology, 111*, 41–46.

Thierry, H., Koopman, A., & Flier, H. van der (1992). *Wat houdt mensen bezig? Recente ontwikkelingen rond motivatie en arbeid* [What keeps people busy? Recent developments to do with motivation and labour]. Utrecht: Lemma.

Thijssen, J.G.L. (1993). Ervaringsconcentratie: Drempel voor kwalificatievernieuwing in de tweede loopbaanhelft [Concentration of experience: Threshold for renewal of qualifications in the second half of the career]. In J.G. Boerlijst, H. van der Flier, & A.E.M. van Vianen (Eds.), *Werk maken van loopbanen: Ontwikkeling en begeleiding* [Making careers your business: Development and guidance], 121–141. Utrecht: Lemma.

Troyer, W.G., Eisdorfer, C., Bogdonoff, M.D., & Wilkie, F. (1967). Experimental stress and learning in the aged. *Journal of Abnormal Psychology, 72*, 65–70.

UN (1991). *World population prospects.* New York: United Nations.

Vroom, V.H. (1964). *Work and motivation.* New York: Wiley.

Warmerdam, J. & Berg, J. van den (1992). *Scholing van werknemers in veranderende organisaties* [Training of workers in changing organizations]. The Hague: Ministerie van Sociale Zaken en Werkgelegenheid [Ministry for Social Affairs and Employment].

Warr, P. (1994). Age and employment. In M. Dunnette, L. Hough, & H. Triandis (Eds.), *Handbook of industrial and organizational psychology* Vol. 4, pp.

485–550). Palo Alto, CA: Consulting Psychologists Press.

Welford, A.T. (1976). Motivation, capacity, learning and age. *International Journal of Aging and Human Development, 7*(3), 189–199.

West, M., Nicholson, N., & Rees, A. (1990). The outcomes of downward managerial mobility. *Journal of Organizational Behavior, 11*, 119–134.

West, R.L., & Sinnott, J.D. (Eds.) (1992). *Everyday memory and aging: Current research and methodology.* New York: Springer.

Wiggers, J.A., Baerts, J.E., & Rooy, M.J.C.C. van (1990). *Ouderen en arbeidsmarkt: Een onderzoek naar de arbeidsmarkt-participatie van ouderen* [The older employee and the labour market: A study of participation of older people in the labour market]. The Hague: Ministry of Welfare, Health and Cultural Affairs.

Winnubst, J.A.M., Buunk, B.P., & Marcelissen, F.H.G. (1988). Social support and stress: Perspectives and processes. In S. Fisher, & J. Reason (Eds.), *Handbook of life stress, cognition and health.* New York: Wiley.

Winnubst, J.A.M., & Schabracq, M.J. (Eds.) (1992). *Handboek arbeid en gezondheid psychologie, Vol. 1 (Hoofdthema's)* [Handbook of labour and health psychology, Vol. 1 (Main themes)]. Utrecht: Lemma.

WRR (Wetenschappelijke Raad voor het Regeringsbeleid [Advisory Council on Government Policy]) (1992). *Ouderen voor ouderen: Demografische ontwikkelingen en beleid* [Older people on behalf of older people: Demographic developments and policy]. The Hague: Sdu [Government Printing Office].

Zwart, B. de, & Meijman, T.F. (1995). The ageing shift-worker: Selection or adaptation. In J. Cremer, & J. Snel (Eds.), *Work and aging: A European prospective.* London: Taylor & Francis.

9

Labour Market Disadvantage, Deprivation and Mental Health

David Fryer

In this chapter I intend to pay tribute to the massive contribution to psychology of C.S. Myers but also to draw attention to a puzzling omission from his research agenda.[1] I will then attempt to present and integrate evidence relating to mental health consequences of unemployment and other adverse labour market experiences. Finally, I intend to consider the role of deprivation in these mental health consequences, emphasising the role of restrictions upon the personal agency of people experiencing adverse labour market conditions.

C.S. Myers was fascinated early on with experimental psychology, particularly psycho-physics, taught experimental psychology at both Cambridge and London and wrote two influential textbooks of experimental psychology.

However, World War I was an intellectual watershed for him. His work on, what he was amongst the first to recognise as, shell shock and on personnel selection led to Myers choosing to give his Royal Institution lectures in London in 1918 on "Present Day Applications of Psychology with Special Reference to Industry, Education and Nervous Breakdown". In that same year Myers also began a 10-year involvement with the Industrial Fatigue (later Health) Research Board and

wrote what he described as his first book on Industrial Psychology. This was entitled *Mind and Work* and was published in 1921 (Myers, 1921), the year C.S. Myers also founded the National Institute of Industrial Psychology (NIIP), of which he became Director and later Principal. C.S. Myers and the staff of his Institute published literally hundreds of other papers and books in occupational psychology (Chin & Grainger, 1971; Raphael 1971). In addition to many papers and reports Myers himself published: *Industrial Psychology in Great Britain* (Myers, 1926, republished once); *Industrial Psychology* (Myers, 1929, republished seven times over four decades); and *Ten Years of Industrial Psychology* (Welch & Myers, 1932). C.S. Myers founded the *Journal of the National Institute of Industrial Psychology* in 1921. This became subsequently retitled *Human Factor* (1932–1937) and in 1938 was again retitled *Occupational Psychology*.

Amongst nearly 300 publications of the NIIP from 1922 until 1971 (Chin & Grainger, 1971) are many publications on ability, IQ and vocational testing and on education and career guidance, on interviewing and selection and training, on movement study, job analysis and job design, on work efficiency, job satisfaction, fatigue, accidents, absence, accidents, labour turnover and many market research and industrial case studies.

However, it is what is missing from the work of C.S. Myers and the London based NIIP, in particular from 1921–1939, which is in retrospect so striking: unemployment and other labour market experiences with psychologically adverse consequences. It is true that C.S. Myers occasionally referred to unemployment but every example I have found is in passing in the context of attacks on crude scientific management which Myers detested; restriction of output; resistance to occupational psychological interventions; or industrial unrest. I have found no trace of C.S. Myers engaging directly with the relationship between recession, unemployment and mental health and only one NIIP paper addressing it.

This is surely remarkable for several reasons. Firstly, C.S. Myers and colleagues were carrying out occupational psychological research in a very wide range of industries during a major international economic slump during which unemployment peaked at record levels in 1931 and 1932.

Secondly, as a well-read scholar, C.S. Myers can hardly have been unaware of the considerable international applied psychological interest in unemployment. He might reasonably have been expected to have come across Bakke's (1933) unemployment research in London, Beales and Lambert's (1934) unemployment research for the BBC, Zawadski and Lazarsfeld's (1935) unemployment research in Poland, Marie Jahoda's unemployment research carried out in Wales in 1937 and partly published in *Occupational Psychology* in 1942 (Jahoda, 1938/1987; Jahoda, 1942), the Pilgrim Trust's (1938) research on unemployment in the north of England and Eisenberg and Lazarsfeld's (1938) seminal Psychological Bulletin review paper, which reviewed 112 international publications and concluded that the psychological consequences of unemployment were severe, widespread and negative.

Thirdly, Oakley, Director of the Scottish Division of the NIIP which was formed in January 1930, focused specifically on "psychological problems of a depressed area" in a British Association paper which was subsequently published in Myers' own *Human Factor* (Oakley, 1936). In addition to his own experience in Scotland in 1935, Oakley referred specifically to the work of Lazarsfeld-Jahoda and Zeisel (1933) in Austria, of Gatti in Italy (1935) and of the Americans Beckman (1933), Hall (1934) and Israeli (1935).

Oakley summarised his understanding, derived from close personal contact, surveys and preparation of publications, of psychological problems arising out of unemployment as including fear, frustration, irritability, declining self-respect, a sense of time losing its meaning, isolation, apparent apathy, resignation and experienced futility of activity, combined with persistently high levels of employment commitment ("I have never met an unemployed man who did not really want to work. Those persons who say otherwise have, in my opinion, failed to understand the behaviour of the unemployed men to whom they have spoken" (Oakley, 1936: 393).

After nearly 60 years of apparent massive social and cultural change, contemporary researchers have come to very much the same conclusions regarding the mental health consequences of unemployment conceptualised in terms of suboptimal mental health by Warr (1987), drawing on Jahoda (1958) and others, i.e. as concerning affective well-being, aspiration, competence, inter-related independence and integrated functioning—although more generally encountered in the unemployment literature in their negative modes as psychological distress, resigned apathy, helplessness and powerlessness, social isolation and disintegration.

This research is well confirmed across different countries including England, Wales, Scotland, Northern Ireland, the Republic of Ireland, Germany, Austria, Italy, Spain, Australia and the United States by researchers working from very different ideological assumptions, in a variety of institutional settings, on the basis of quite different funding arrangements (see Fryer, 1992).

To illustrate this point, the findings of the Austro-Marxist research group in Vienna in the 1930s associated with Jahoda and Lazarsfeld, recent findings of Research Council funded academics and of psychologists working for Government Departments are in extraordinarily close agreement.

Every respectable, and indeed some not so

respectable, social scientific method has been used by researchers in this field: depth-; semi-structured; and structured interviews; document analysis; sociography; action research; psychiatric assessment; medical/physiological and epidemiological techniques. These studies spanning time, cultures, research groups and research methods converge in their conclusions that unemployment is associated with poor mental health.

For many, however, the most impressive contemporary input has been made by researchers using quantitative psychological methods. Anxiety, depression, dissatisfaction with one's present life, experienced strain, negative self-esteem, hopelessness regarding the future and other negative emotional states, all operationalised in the form of acceptably reliable validated measures, have each been demonstrated by cross-sectional studies to be higher in groups of unemployed people than in matched groups of employed people. Compared with employed people, unemployed people are also disproportionately likely to report social isolation and relatively low levels of daily activity. There is also an emerging consensus that the physical, as well as mental, health of unemployed people is also generally poorer than that of employed people.

It is one of the major achievements of recent research to have demonstrated beyond reasonable doubt that unemployment causes, rather than merely results from, poor psychological health. Well designed, longitudinal studies have tracked large, carefully selected, samples of people in and out of paid jobs, from school or employment to unemployment, from unemployment to employment etc., using valid and reliable measures. Groups which become unemployed during the course of such studies exhibit deterioration in mean mental health compared with continuously employed groups.

Most of these studies deal with the average mental health of large groups of people. Within those groups there are wide variations in experience and health costs. Some people are affected very badly, some hardly at all and there are even some whose psychological health improves when they become unemployed. For many, probably most, the experience of unemployment is multi-faceted, composed of negative aspects,

positive aspects and aspects about which they are ambivalent—at one and the same time.

For all these reasons, whilst if a large group of people becomes unemployed one can confidently predict that the mean scores indicating mental health will decrease, one cannot infer from that fact that any particular individual has been made unemployed that that individual's mental health will actually suffer or that those whose mental health do suffer will suffer in every respect. A more useful way to think about it is that the risk of that individual's mental health deteriorating in at least some ways has increased compared with an otherwise similar person who did not become unemployed.

Many of these points can be well illustrated by research by Dooley and colleagues (Dooley, Catalano, & Hough, 1992) who interviewed over 10,000 people in three areas of the United States using a highly structured diagnostic symptom check list developed for use by trained interviewers to reliably assign respondents to specific categories of the American Psychiatric Association diagnostic system. People were categorised as suffering from an alcohol disorder if they were either using alcohol excessively with resulting impairment in work or social functioning as indicated by specified behavioural patterns or if they were physically dependent upon alcohol as indicated by specified behavioural patterns indicating tolerance or withdrawal.

Seventy nine per cent of the original sample (over 8,000 people) were reinterviewed one year later. Those people, with no prior history of alcohol disorder, who had gone from employment at first interview to unemployment a year later were nine times more likely to have become alcohol disordered in the intervening period than the consistently employed.

Interestingly, Dooley and colleagues also reanalysed data on "intemperance" which was available from Rowntree's study of York in 1910 (Rowntree & Lasker, 1910) and again found evidence for a causal link between unemployment and alcohol disorder, as well as some evidence for selection. This research, then, provides persuasive evidence for a causal relationship between unemployment and a specific serious mental health disorder over 80 years of massive social change, two continents and vastly increasing research method sophistication. Many other studies have done the same in relation to other aspects of mental health.

In January 1994 the official, unadjusted, Department of Employment figure for the number of people unemployed in the UK was 2,889,300. However, the Independent Unemployment Unit calculates the number of unemployed people on the basis used by the UK Government in 1982, i.e. ignoring the 30 or so changes made since then for administrative and/or political convenience. Calculated in that way the figure for January 1994 was 4,001,500 (14.3 per cent of the workforce in employment). By comparison, in January 1994 alongside those 4 million unemployed people were a mere 117,100 officially notified job vacancies (Unemployment Unit, 1994: 13–14).

The scale of unemployment combined with the risk to mental health of unemployment is sobering. However, I now want to go on to suggest that the psychological costs of involuntary unemployment are only a tiny fraction of the psychological costs of adverse labour market experience more generally.

Unemployment puts at risk the mental health not only of unemployed people but also their families. Oakley (1936: 400) reported that the German psychologists, Buseman and Harder (1932) had "showed in their investigation that unemployment among German parents brings about a drop in the school marks of two-thirds of their children". Where unemployment was very long term, three or four years, they reported a further decline in school work. Recent Dutch work has again found poorer school performance in children with unemployed fathers (Baarda, 1988; Te Grotenhuis & Dronkers, 1989).

More generally, Oakley (1936) reported that children with unemployed fathers were disproportionately likely to see their fathers as failures, and home discipline to weaken. McLoyd recently likewise concluded, after an extensive literature review, that children with unemployed fathers are at risk of "socio-emotional problems, deviant behaviour, and reduced aspirations and expectations. The child also may model the somatic complaints of the father" (McLoyd, 1989). McLoyd cites specific evidence regarding: mental

health problems, withdrawal from peers, depression, loneliness, emotional sensitivity, distrustfulness, decreased sociability and low self-esteem.

The effects of unemployment on younger children and babies is harder to gauge but babies' growth might be considered one suggestive indication of whether and how well they are thriving. Cross-sectionally, however, the mean birth weight of 655 babies born to unemployed fathers in Glasgow was found by researchers to be significantly less (150 grams on average) than that of babies born to employed fathers, even after controlling for sex, social class, mothers' height etc. Longitudinally, babies with unemployed fathers grew significantly less in length (1.3 per cent) during their first year than babies with employed fathers (Cole, Donnet, & Stanfield, 1983).

Research has also demonstrated that unemployment puts the mental health of spouses of unemployed people at risk. Even in the 1930s the Pilgrim Trust (1938) demonstrated that wives bore the burden of want in most unemployed families and Oakley (1936) reported unemployed fathers' status to be lowered in their families with mothers likely to take over as head of household, with family relationships likely to be disturbed and increasing friction at home as results.

Modern research broadly confirms these claims. McKee and Bell (1986) pointed to the difficulties spouses, generally female partners of unemployed men, face in trying to manage on reduced income, to cope with the spouses' intrusive presence in the household, to support distressed partners and deal with intra-family conflict. Fletcher and colleagues (e.g. Jones & Fletcher, 1993) have demonstrated in recent years that occupational stress can be transmitted to partners and it seems that unemployment distress can also be transmitted. There have also been suggestions in the literature that members of extended families may be affected by unemployment (Binns & Mars, 1984).

So far I have suggested that unemployment puts at risk the mental health not only of unemployed people but also their families. But what about unemployed people who cease to be unemployed? Some of these people go onto some form of Government quasi-employment/ training scheme—employment training, youth training, community programme etc.

Back in 1936, Oakley reported that "many investigators consider the worst aspect of unemployment ... unemployment of youths and girls ... after they leave school. Not only does inactivity and the absence of an occupational goal sometimes render them permanently unemployable, but ... they may become undesirable members of the community" (Oakley, 1936: 401).

Such fears, amongst other considerations, have prompted British Governments over the last half century periodically to set up training schemes for both young people and adults. Back in 1936, Oakley described Ministry of Labour "Instructional centres" in Scotland where "unemployed men take a three months' course of heavy outdoor work. The aim is to build up physical fitness and confidence, by work, by social life, by order and routine". For women there were centres in Scotland "where women and girls are trained for private domestic service", the service sector of the economy! He added that "these centres should not be confused with the labour camps of some other countries" (Oakley, 1936: 399).

Some research has suggested that participation in modern schemes can be psychologically benevolent in at least some respects. Stafford, for example, found that trainees in a precursor of Youth Training, the Youth Opportunities Programme (YOP), had significantly better mental health scores than members of an unemployed comparison group and their mental health (assessed by GHQ-12) was not significantly worse than an employed comparison group. Longitudinally, it was shown that this could not be accounted for by differences in their scores at school. However, the protection was temporary—when YOP trainees became unemployed, their psychological health deteriorated (Stafford, 1982).

However, other research into Youth Opportunities Programme (YOP) participation has found that YOP trainees were not, on average, significantly less depressed (as assessed by the Beck Depression Inventory) than members of an unemployed comparison group and were significantly more depressed than an employed comparison group. Interviews suggested that the trainees

perceived YOP as low status ("cheap labour"), as providing inadequate training, as lacking in meaningful purpose, as actually hindering search for a "proper" job and as unlikely to lead to adequate, secure employment (Branthwaite & Garcia, 1985). Davies (1992) more recently investigated experience of Community Programme, reporting generally positive participant evaluation of the work but generally negative perception of the context of the scheme and its temporary nature—with frequently experienced anxieties about the future. The psychological well-being of Community Programme participants was on a par with that of comparable employed people but their felt control was as low as comparable unemployed people (Davies, 1992).

So the mental health of unemployed people, their families and those in quasi-employment schemes appears to be at risk. But what about those very many unemployed people who leave the unemployment figures for employment?

The conventional wisdom is that re-employment makes everything better again and indeed a number of quantitative psychological studies have, for example, found that psychological well-being (assessed by GHQ-12) improves after re-employment (e.g. Payne & Jones, 1987).

Others suggest a more complicated picture, however. For example Shamir (1985: 77) states "the implicit assumption that the transition from unemployment to re-employment is symmetrical to the transition from employment to unemployment ... is not fully warranted since it is known that some of the effects of unemployment may persist into the period of re-employment". Kaufman (1982) found that one fifth of his sample of re-employed professionals were under-employed i.e. had to accept jobs which were inferior in terms of salary, type of work and use of skills. Only 47 per cent reported their lives had returned to normal following re-employment (Kaufman, 1982). Daniel (1974, 1990) has shown that re-employment is likely to be at a lower level and that re-employed people are more vulnerable to future redundancy due to last in, first out practices.

Detailed qualitative studies are still more informative on this point. Fineman followed up a previously unemployed sample and found "those re-employed in jobs which they felt to be inadequate were experiencing more stress, and even poorer self esteem, than they had during their period of unemployment" (Fineman, 1987a: 269). Half of Fineman's re-employed informants had what Fineman described as legacy effects, whatever the quality of the new job. This legacy took the form of feeling there was a lasting blemish or stigma on their work record, of continuing doubts about their abilities, of feelings of personal failure. Organisationally they were prepared to give less of themselves to their new jobs.

Incidentally, if the number of people unemployed at any one time is shockingly large, the number who sample unemployment and then move into jobs or schemes is vast. On average about 350,000 people cease to be unemployed each month (Unemployment Unit, 1994, p. 13)—i.e. 4,000,000 per year departures from the unemployment count, although some people no doubt feature more than once.

Mental health risks of unemployment extend, then, beyond unemployed people to their families, to those on schemes and to those unemployed who have become re-employed. However, what about those people who are left in organisations after others have been made redundant—so-called survivors. Can they breathe a sigh of relief?

Longitudinal research has found that anticipation of redundancy is at least as distressing as the experience of unemployment itself (Cobb & Kasl, 1977; Fryer & McKenna, 1987, 1988). During recession and economically unsettled times, many more people, of course, anticipate and worry about unemployment than actually become unemployed.

Powerful evidence comes from studies of job insecurity. Seasonal workers, fixed term contract employees (a growing group), new "probationary" employees are all liable to job insecurity but the largest number of job insecure employees are probably employees who make the "fundamental and involuntary change from a belief that one's position in the employing organisation is safe, to a belief that it is not" (Hartley, Jacobson, Klandermans, & Van Vuuren, with Greenhalgh & Sutton, 1991: viii).

Studies carried out in Israel, The Netherlands and the UK reported by Hartley et al. (1991) have demonstrated job insecurity to be associated with severe uncertainty, experienced powerlessness and impaired mental health, operationalised in terms of reported psychosomatic symptoms and depression, reduced job satisfaction, reduced organisational commitment, reduced trust in management, resistance to change and deteriorating industrial relations. See also Burchell (1994).

So far, I have suggested, unemployed people, their families, those on schemes, those re-employed, those anticipating unemployment or left in insecure employment after others have been made redundant, all have elevated risk of consequent mental health problems. But what about the many people who become or remain employed in economically secure organisations?

Some of the most persuasive longitudinal quantitative studies, have been done with young people. Typically these studies measure the mental health of large groups in school and follow them into the labour market over a number of years measuring the mental health of those who get jobs and those who do not and comparing group mean scores cross-sectionally and longitudinally. In study after study, groups of unemployed youngsters are demonstrated to have poorer mental health than their employed peers but if one looks at the scores of the same groups when at school there is no statistically significant difference, i.e. poor mental health is the consequence rather than the cause of the labour market transition.

Winefield and colleagues followed approximately 3,000 youngsters over eight years in South Australia in just such a design. However they also asked the employed youngsters about their job satisfaction using a widely used and well validated scale. They found that those employed youngsters who were dissatisfied with their jobs were indistinguishable in terms of mental health scores from the unemployed youngsters (Winefield, Tiggemann, & Winefield, 1993), i.e. it was as bad for mental health to make the transition into a job with which one was dissatisfied as into unemployment. Feather (e.g. 1992) has reported similar findings from his research programme.

There is also a massive literature on occupational stress, increasingly referred to as strain. Cooper has spelled this out (Cooper, 1986). A traditional way of coping with such strain has been to change jobs. However, in recessionary labour market conditions, people are increasingly likely to become trapped in psychologically distressing jobs.

Moreover, many in jobs not conventionally associated with psychological strain work with casualties of adverse labour market conditions. General practitioners have reported via their professional journals that they have been inundated with such work (Smith, 1987).

For example, following a statistical analysis of his practice records before and after the closure of the principal local employer, a physician in the west country of England reported an approximately 20 per cent increase in consultation rates and an approximately 60 per cent increase in hospital outpatient visits for job losers and their dependants as a result of the closure. This is a massive increase not only in costs to the UK National Health Service but in workload for medical and health personnel (Beale & Nethercott, 1985).

Fineman has studied the implications of unemployment not only for physicians, but also for clergy, probation officers, and police officers. He has documented not only the quantitative and qualitative work load but also role conflict and other stressors which are producing for these professionals, according to Fineman (1990), a sense of crisis in the face of unemployment.

The British Psychological Society organised a media briefing especially to highlight the negative implications of unemployment for clinical psychologists. Whilst useful this was still only to highlight the demands placed by unemployment upon high profile "High Street" helpers. We should also consider workers in myriad other formal and indeed informal, back street, organisations who are affected directly or indirectly by unemployment.

In addition to all the above, Sinfield has drawn attention to the wider impact of recession. Mass unemployment and its sequelae affect many more people even than those so far discussed: trade union influence is reduced, wages are depressed for those in jobs (minimum wages and wages councils have recently become things of the past), improvements to the working environment regarding health and safety and the "humanisation of work" are slowed down or put into reverse, employment as rehabilitation after physical injury, illness, mental breakdown and prison becomes decreasingly available and minorities may become increasingly vulnerable to exclusion from the labour market with consequent further marginalisation and impoverishment. All of these factors impinge on mental health via the labour market (Sinfield, 1992).

Finally, mass unemployment is a major factor in inequitable income distribution, i.e. relative impoverishment and there is persuasive evidence that the latter is related to mortality in populations of whole countries. Wilkinson (1990), for example, analysed data from nine Western countries on the relationship between life expectancy and income distribution (the percentage of total post tax income and benefit received by the least well off 70 per cent of families). Income distribution correlated 0.86 with life expectancy at birth. By comparison, across 23 Organisation for Economic Cooperation and Development (OECD) countries, gross national product per capita was not itself significantly associated with life expectancy. There was no relationship whatsoever (0.02) between changes in gross national product per capita and life expectancy over the 20 years from 1970 to 1990, for example (Wilkinson, 1990).

To summarise so far, I have suggested that unemployment puts the mental health of the following groups at risk: unemployed people, their families, those on employment training schemes, those re-employed, those left in insecure employment after others have been made redundant, those trapped in psychologically stressful jobs, those who work formally or informally with people suffering adverse labour market experience and those who are subject to the wider impact of recession, mediated by experience of the labour market.

I have spoken so far as if these are discrete groups of people but this is not necessarily so. Many people have careers of labour market disadvantage consisting of moving from school or insecure, psychologically dissatisfying and stressful jobs within the secondary labour market via training schemes into further unemployment or other insecure psychologically dissatisfying or mental health threatening employment or sickness and so on in a cycle of adverse labour market experience. All this takes place, for many, in the context of living in communities hard hit by unemployment, with a disproportionate likelihood of family and friends also being unemployed or in psychologically poor quality jobs, in a nation in which the real value of benefits, wages and working conditions are deteriorating and where the labour market is being increasingly casualised, part-time, short contract and insecure employment increasing and full-time, secure, employment decreasing and where the gap between the relatively poor and the relatively well-off is widening.

Many tend to be preoccupied with the problems of long-term unemployment. My suspicion is that careers of labour market disadvantage, repeated unemployment, unsatisfactory employment and scheme attendance, is not only far more common than long-term unemployment but, at least as—possibly more—psychologically corrosive.

How can one understand and explain the mental health effects of adverse labour market experience? I agree completely with Orford that the aetiology of mental health problems involves "person and social setting and systems, including the structure of social support and social power" in interaction over time (Orford, 1992: 4). As regards the mental health consequences of adverse labour market experience, two accounts of the nature of the person, social setting and system and locus of social power have been proposed. Both appeal to (rather different) notions of deprivation.

Marie Jahoda claims that employment is a social institution with objective "consequences that occur for all affected by it, overriding individual differences in feelings, thoughts, motivation and purposes" (Jahoda & Rush, 1980). Some of these, such as earning a living, are intended or manifest. Others are unintended or latent. According to Jahoda: "employment of whatever kind and at whatever level makes the following categories of experience inevitable: it imposes a time structure on the waking day; it compels contacts and shared experiences with others outside the nuclear family; it demonstrates that there are goals and purposes which are beyond the scope of an individual but require a collectivity; it imposes

status and social identity through the division of labour in modern employment; it enforces activity" (Jahoda & Rush, 1980). Crucially, unemployment is said by Jahoda to damage mental health because of the psychological deprivation of these unintended latent consequences of employment, which normally function as psychological supports (Jahoda, 1979).

This account has a number of strengths: intuitive appeal; parallels with other appeals to the notion of psychological deprivation in the discipline (bereavement, maternal, sensory); and has ready policy implications in the form of recommending by implication surrogate latent functions for unemployed people as psychological supports.

However, whilst "unemployment" and "redundancy" are frequently treated as interchangeable terms, not all unemployed people have been made redundant (some have never been employed) and not all people made redundant become unemployed—some move straight into other employment. Moreover, the term "redundancy" suggests an acute, sudden, transitional life event, dominated by what is lost—a job. "Unemployment", on the other hand, suggests a state of chronic immiseration with its own continuing stressors. Jahoda's account lends itself more to an explication of the acute trauma of redundancy rather than the chronic immiseration of unemployment.

I have argued in detail elsewhere however that Jahoda's account: is exceedingly difficult to operationalise; is unfalsifiable due to provisos; confuses cause and effect; fits uneasily with wider literature on the negative psychological impact of employment. Attempts at direct evaluation (Miles, 1983; Fryer & McKenna, 1987, 1988) have been unpersuasive. The account is overly retrospective in nature, assumes the passivity of persons and implies the psychological benevolence of contemporary, i.e. twentieth century employment. It also has policy implications which worry some—e.g. providing apparent psychological legitimacy for schemes like Workfare.

Jahoda's Latent Function Deprivation account is not really a theory in the sense of an empirically testable system but rather a meta-theoretical framework of assumptions about the nature, locus and degree of compelling force of power and support in the interaction over time of person and social context.

I have offered an alternative framework of meta-theoretical assumptions around the notion of agency restriction (e.g. Fryer, 1986, 1992, 1995).

The assumptions underlying Agency Restriction Theory are firstly that people are socially embedded agents actively striving for purposeful self-determination, attempting to make sense of, initiate, influence and cope with events in line with personal values, goals and expectations of the future in a context of cultural norms, traditions and past experience. Secondly that, whilst personal agency is sometimes empowered in interaction with labour market social settings and systems, agency is frequently undermined, restricted and frustrated by formal and informal social forces including: powerful constituting and regulating social institutions and organisations; required social relationships entailing psychological strain inducing obligations combined with minimal collective and individual rights; inadequate personal, family, social, community and material resources; and powerful, socially constructed, norms, role expectations and disentitlements.

In particular, unemployment is psychologically destructive, I believe, because it impoverishes, restricts, baffles and discourages the unemployed agent. Interestingly, Oakley emphasised that distress arose in part through "an indeterminate feeling of being thwarted" (Oakley, 1936: 396), i.e. of having one's agency restricted.

This account particularly lends itself to an explication of the chronic immiseration of unemployment rather than the acute trauma of redundancy, in the sense articulated earlier. Two factors in particular are emphasised as central in the mental health costs of unemployment for many people because they restrict personal agency. Firstly unemployment cuts the unemployed person off from any future, making looking forward and planning very difficult. Secondly unemployment generally results in psychologically corrosive experienced poverty.

Unemployed people are poor in UK society. Currently the single person's unemployment benefit in the UK, is £44.65 and that of an unemployed couple is £72.20 per week. Even with means-tested additions, this virtually ensures hardship and inadequate resources for effectively addressing every day and exceptional problems and crises. Not surprisingly, then, debt, non-repayment of hire purchase loans and power disconnections are frequently reported in the literature (Cooke, 1987) and activity involving expense declines sharply with the cuts in income which accompany unemployment (Warr & Payne, 1983).

However, it is relative poverty which I believe affects most unemployed people most negatively—material deprivation relative to self selected reference groups. Even "affluent" unemployed professional people can experience distressing relative deprivation.

Most unemployed people experience massive cuts in income: 66 per cent of one large sample of unemployed people had a total household income of between 33 per cent and 50 per cent of their previous income when employed (Warr & Jackson, 1984).

Not surprisingly, unemployed people consistently tell us—when we allow them—that their major problems revolve around money and indicators of psychological distress are associated with measures of both subjective and objective financial distress.

Whelan (1992) has reported some of the best recent work in this area. Using nationally representative multi-stage random sampling, incorporating both stratification and clustering, giving each person on the register of electors in the Republic of Ireland an equal probability of being selected, Whelan completed fully structured interviews with 3833 respondents who self-defined as unemployed. Psychological distress (as assessed by GHQ-12) was positively associated with both objectively assessed life style deprivation (lack of basic food, clothing, heating, persistent debt due to routine expenses); secondary life style deprivation; (holidays, leisure, consumer durables) and independently with subjective experience of financial strain.

Whelan concluded: "The findings presented here clearly demonstrate the role of poverty in mediating the impact of unemployment not only for the individuals involved but also for the members of their families" (Whelan, 1992: 341–342).

The very process of claiming is reported to be distressing. Kay (1984) pointed particularly at unacceptably poor physical conditions, perceived invasion of privacy, sense of being passively processed, of humiliation and degradation.

State financial support has frequently been reported as experienced as a stigmatised, illegitimate, source of income in contrast with earned income (Fryer & Fagan, 1994; Kelvin & Jarrett, 1985; Marsden & Duff, 1975; McGhee & Fryer, 1989).

There is even some evidence that income maintenance may be stressful in its own right. In 1938, the Pilgrim trust reported: "real distress ... [caused by] ... the same dead level ... with no hope of an extra at any time" (Pilgrim Trust, 1938) and Thoits and Hannan (1979) reported a small but reliable increase in divorce rate, geographical mobility and psychological distress in income maintained participants.

It is not just a matter of not having enough money and the unacceptability for many of the processes by which it is "earned", however, which restricts agency and distresses. Expectations regarding which patterns of expenditure and consumption are appropriate or inappropriate for unemployed people, can be very strongly projected towards and experienced as deeply restrictive disentitlements by unemployed people. Moreover, the performance of many roles—for example that of the breadwinner—is inhibited by poverty (Komarovsky, 1940; Fryer & Fagan, 1993) and particular forms of conspicuous and symbolic consumption and spending which are important parts of some sub-cultural roles (Engbersen, Schuyt, Timmer, & Van Waarden, 1993; Jordan, James, Kay, & Redley, 1992; Wight, 1993) may become impossible to maintain. Personal identity is increasingly experienced and expressed through spending and consumption. Dittmar (1992) wittily recast Descartes cogito, "I think therefore I am", for contemporary times, as "I shop therefore I am".

Within families, relative poverty becomes translated into tortuous budgeting strategies, painful prioritizing of differing family members' needs, conflict prone domestic division of financial responsibility and coping behaviour (McGhee & Fryer, 1989). McLoyd (1989) concluded that most of the effects of paternal job loss on children are "indirect and mediated through the changes that economic loss produces in the father's behaviour and disposition" (McLoyd, 1989: 293). Shamir (1985: 76) concluded that the "difference between men's and women's reactions to unemployment appears to hinge on varying degrees of financial hardship".

Income related factors are, then, central to the mental health costs of unemployment. However, recall that agency restriction particularly emphasises two restrictions: by relative poverty and also by future insecurity. The unemployed person is cut off from any future, making looking forward and planning very difficult if not impossible. Both of these notions coalesce in the notion of economic insecurity. It is striking, to me at least, how frequently income insecurity factors have been implicated in the mental health costs of what I have called adverse labour market experience more generally.

Economic insecurity, future income uncertainty, was at the root of the difficulties faced by the unemployed men Bakke (1940) interviewed and the psychological costs of government job scheme participation reported by Branthwaite and Garcia (1985). Fineman (1987) concluded that "the act of becoming re-employed does not in itself mean that negative consequences of unemployment are automatically reversed. There is the likelihood of increased anxiety, and susceptibility to stress, in circumstances where financial and emotional security are threatened" (Fineman, 1987a: 279). Beale, the physician, reported: "the increase in morbidity began two years before redundancy—at the time when it became apparent to the ... families that their economic futures were not secure" (Beale & Nethercott, 1985: 513). Eisenberg and Lazarsfeld (1938) even concluded that: "just having a job itself is not as important as having a feeling of economic security. Those who are economically insecure, employed or unemployed, have a low morale" (Eisenberg & Lazarsfeld, 1938: 361). Wilkinson has argued persuasively that "our environment and standard of living no longer impact on our health primarily through direct physical causes, regardless of our attitudes and perceptions, but have come to do so mainly through social and cognitively mediated processes" (Wilkinson, 1990: 405).

I believe these processes involve the restriction of agency by persistently adverse labour market experience, including the consequent experience of socially constructed, relative poverty and economic insecurity. Indeed, I am increasingly inclined to emphasise what unemployment, scheme attendance, psychologically satisfactory and unsatisfactory employment share conceptually, rather than what distinguishes them. All are social relationships between parties involving psychological contracts in which work determined by one party is done in exchange for income by another party in a context of mutual rights and obligations, constituted and regulated by powerful social, community, organisational and social institutional forces. In an interesting sense, unemployed people can be usefully regarded as essentially poorly paid, low status, insecure, public sector workers with virtually no negotiating rights whose work (persistent near hopeless job search, humiliating benefit related rituals, management of households on inadequate resources etc.) carries a high risk of occupational strain.

Myers' contribution, directly and via the organs and institutes he founded, to the field which has been variously referred to as industrial, work, organisational or occupational psychology is clearly vast. I hope it has not seemed churlish to focus on his omissions, his apparent puzzling neglect of one of the most serious and distressing occupational psychological health related problems of his—and our—time—those related to adverse labour market experience. I draw attention to it here because I fear that social scientists are again failing adequately to engage with the mental health repercussions of adverse labour market conditions, giving them neither the social scientific attention nor the high public profile they surely require. Psychologists and others must engage with the mental health costs of psychological and material deprivation which is part and parcel of the labour market careers of many people.

However, we need a research treatment of deprivation which is not merely "academic", in the pejorative sense. Feiffer wrote: "I used to think I was poor. Then they told me I wasn't poor, I was

needy. Then they told me it was self-defeating to think of myself as being needy, I was deprived. Then they told me deprived was a bad image, I was underprivileged. Then they told me under-privileged was overused, I was disadvantaged. I still don't have a cent but I have a great vocabulary" (cited in Pilger, 1989: 237). We must never lose sight of the fact that we are concerned not merely with a matter of semantics but with real misery and risk of mental health costs for very many millions of people.

NOTE

1. This chapter was first published in *The Psychologist, The Bulletin of the British Psychological Society*, 8(6), 265–272, 1995.

REFERENCES

Baarda, D.B. (1988). *School prestaties van kinderen van werkloze vaders* [School performances of children of unemployed fathers] with a summary in English. Unpublished PhD thesis, Rijks University of Utrecht.

Bakke, E.W. (1933). *The unemployed man*. London: Nisbet.

Bakke, E.W. (1940). *Citizens without work*. New Haven: Yale University Press.

Beale, N., & Nethercott, S. (1985). Job loss and family morbidity: a study of a factory closure. *Journal of the Royal College of General Practitioners*, *35*, 510–514.

Beales, H.L., & Lambert, R.S. (1934). *Memoirs of the Unemployed*. Wakefield: E.P. Publishing.

Beckman, (1933). Mental perils of unemployment. *Occupations*, *xii*, 28–35.

Binns, D., & Mars, G. (1984). Family, community and unemployment: a study in change. *Sociological Review*, *32*(4), 662–695.

Branthwaite, A., & Garcia, S. (1985). Depression in the young unemployed and those on Youth Opportunities Schemes. *British Journal of Medical Psychology*, *58*, 67–74.

Burchell, B. (1994). The effects of labour market position, job insecurity and unemployment on psychological health. In D. Gallie, C. Marsh, & C. Vogler (Eds.), *Social change and the experience of unemployment*. Oxford: Oxford University Press.

Buseman, & Harder (1932). Die Wirkung vaterlicher Erwebslosigkeit auf die Schulleistungen der Kinder.

Zsch. fur Kinderforsch, xl, 89–100. Cited in Oakley (1936).

Chin, C., & Grainger, M. (1971). Some publications of the NIIP and its staff. *Occupational Psychology, (Jubilee Volume on the NIIP), 44*, 51–62.

Cobb, S., & Kasl, S.V. (1977). *Termination: The Consequences of Job Loss*. Cincinnati: US Department of Health, Education and Welfare.

Cole, T.J., Donnet, M.L., & Stanfield, J.P. (1983). Unemployment, birth weight and growth in the first year. *Archives of Disease in Childhood, 58*, 717–722.

Cooke, K. (1987). The living standards of unemployed people. In D. Fryer & P. Ullah (Eds.), *Unemployed people: social and psychological perspectives*. Milton Keynes: Open University Press.

Cooper, C.L. (1986). Job distress: Recent research and the emerging role of the clinical occupational psychologist. *Bulletin of the British Psychological Society, 39*, 325–331.

Daniel, W.W. (1974). *A national survey of the unemployed*. London: Political and Economic Planning Institute.

Daniel, W.W. (1990). *The unemployed flow*. London: PSI.

Davies, J.B. (1992). *The experience of community programme, unemployment and employment: Mental health and individual differences*. Unpublished thesis submitted to the University of Sheffield for the degree of Doctor of Philosophy.

Dittmar, H. (1992). *The Social psychology of material possessions: To have is to be*. Hemel Hempstead: Harvester Wheatsheaf.

Dooley, D., Catalano, R., & Hough, R. (1992). Unemployment and alcohol disorder in 1910 and 1990: Drift versus social causation. *Journal of Occupational and Organizational Psychology, 65*(4), 277–290.

Eisenberg, P., & Lazarsfeld, P.F. (1938). The psychological effects of unemployment. *Psychological Bulletin, 35*, 258–390.

Engbersen, G., Schuyt, K., Timmer, J. & Waarden F. van (1993). *Cultures of unemployment: A comparative look at long-term unemployment and urban poverty*. Oxford: Westview Press.

Feather, N.T. (1992). *The psychological impact of unemployment*. New York: Springer Verlag.

Fineman, S. (1987a). Back to employment: wounds and wisdoms. In D. Fryer & P. Ullah (Eds.), *Unemployed people: Social and psychological perspectives*. Milton Keynes: Open University Press.

Fineman, S. (Ed.) (1987b). *Unemployment: Personal and social consequences*. London: Tavistock.

Fineman S. (1990). *Supporting the jobless: Doctors, clergy, police, probation officers*. London: Tavistock/Routledge.

Fryer, D. (1986). Employment deprivation and personal agency during unemployment. *Social Behaviour, 1*, 3–23.

Fryer, D. (1992). Psychological or material deprivation: why does unemployment have mental health consequences? In E. McLaughlin (Ed.), *Understanding Unemployment*. London: Routledge.

Fryer, D. (1995). Agency Restriction Theory. In N. Nicholson (Ed.), *Encyclopedic dictionary of organisational behaviour*. Oxford: Blackwell.

Fryer, D., & Fagan, R. (1993). Coping with unemployment. *International Journal of Political Economy, 23*(3), 95–120.

Fryer, D., & Fagan, R. (1994). The role of social psychological aspects of income on the mental health costs of unemployment: an action research perspective. *Community Psychologist, 27*(2), 16–17.

Fryer, D., & McKenna, S. (1987). The laying off of hands—unemployment and the experience of time. In Fineman, S. (Ed.), *Unemployment: Personal and social consequences*. London: Tavistock.

Fryer, D., & McKenna, S. (1988). Redundant skills: temporary unemployment and mental health. In M.G. Patrickson (Ed.), *Readings in organisational behaviour*. Sydney and London: Harper and Row.

Gatti, A. (1935). Prima relazione sulla efficienza lavorativa dei disoccupati. *Italian Archives of Psychology, xiii*, 67–91.

Hall, O.M. (1934). Attitudes and unemployment: A comparison of the opinions and attitudes of employed and unemployed men. *Archives of Psychology, 25*, 165.

Hartley, J.F., Jacobson, D., Klandermans, B., & Vuuren, T. van with Greenhalgh, L and Sutton, R. (1991). *Job insecurity: Coping with jobs at risk*. London: Sage.

Israeli, N. (1935). Distress in the outlook of Lancashire and Scottish unemployed. *Journal of Applied Psychology, 19*, 67–68.

Jahoda, M. (1938/1987). Unemployed men at work. In D. Fryer & P. Ullah (Eds.), *Unemployed people: Social and psychological perspectives*. Milton Keynes: Open University Press.

Jahoda, M. (1942). Incentives to work—a study of unemployed adults in a special situation. *Occupational Psychology, 16*(1), 20–30.

Jahoda, M. (1958). *Current concepts of positive mental health*. New York: Basic Books.

Jahoda, M. (1979). The impact of unemployment in the 1930s and the 1980s. *Bulletin of the British Psychological Society, 32*, 309–314.

Jahoda, M., & Rush, H. (1980). Work, employment and unemployment. *Occasional Paper Series, 12*. The University of Sussex: Science Policy Research Unit.

Jones, F., & Fletcher, B.C. (1993). An empirical study of occupational stress transmission in working couples. *Human Relations, 46*(7), 881–903.

Jordan, B., James, S., Kay, D., & Redley, M. (1992). *Trapped in poverty: Labour-market decisions in low-income households*. London: Routledge.

Kaufman, H.G. (1982). *Professionals in search of work: Coping with the stress of job loss and underemployment*. New York: Wiley.

Kay, D. (1984). Counter benefits: Making contact with the DHSS. *Working Paper 7*. Glasgow: Scottish Consumer Council.

Kelvin, P., & Jarrett, J.E. (1985). *Unemployment: Its social psychological effects*. Cambridge: Cambridge University Press.

Komarovsky, M. (1940). *The unemployed man and his family*. New York: Dryden.

Lazarsfeld-Jahoda, M., & Zeisel, H. (1933). *Die Arbeitslosen von Marienthal*. Psychologische Monographien, 1933. An English language translation appeared in 1972 as *Marienthal: The Sociography of an unemployed community*. New York: Aldine Atherton.

Marsden, D., & Duff, E. (1975). *Workless: Some unemployed men and their families*. Harmondsworth: Penguin.

McGhee, J., & Fryer, D. (1989). Unemployment, income and the family: An action research approach. *Social Behaviour, 4*, 237–252.

McKee, L., & Bell, C. (1986). His unemployment, her problem: the domestic and marital consequences of male unemployment. In S. Allen, S. Waton, K. Purcell, & S. Wood (Eds.), *The experience of unemployment*. Basingstoke: Macmillan.

McLoyd, V.C. (1989). Socialisation and development in a changing economy: The effects of paternal job and income loss on children. *American Psychologist, 44*(2), 293–302.

Miles, I. (1983). *Adaptation to unemployment*. University of Sussex: Science Policy Research Unit Technical report.

Myers, C.S. (1921). *Mind and work: The psychological factors in industry and commerce*. London: University of London Press.

Myers, C.S. (1926). *Industrial psychology in Great Britain*. London: Jonathan Cape.

Myers, C.S. (Ed.) (1929). *Industrial psychology*. London: Thornton Butterworth Ltd.

Myers, C.S. (1971). Autobiography. *Occupational Psychology*, (Jubilee Volume on the NIIP), *44*, 5–13. (Original work published 1936).

Oakley, C.A. (1936). Some psychological problems of a depressed area. *Human Factor, 10*, 393–404. Text of a paper read before section J (Psychology) of the British Association Meeting at Blackpool, September 1936.

Orford, J. (1992). *Community psychology: Theory and practice*. Chichester: Wiley.

Payne, R.L., & Jones, G. (1987). Social class and reemployment. *Journal of Occupational Behaviour, 8*, 175–184.

Pilger, J. (1989). *A secret country*. London: Jonathan Cape.

Pilgrim Trust (1938). *Men without work*. Cambridge: Cambridge University Press.

Raphael, W. (1971). NIIP and its staff 1921–1961. *Occupational Psychology*, (Jubilee Volume on the NIIP), *44*, 63–70.

Rowntree, B.S., & Lasker, B. (1910). *Unemployment: A social study*. London: Macmillan.

Shamir, B. (1985). Sex differences in psychological adjustment to unemployment and reemployment: A question of commitment, alternatives or finance? *Social Problems, 33*(1), 67–79.

Sinfield, A. (1992). The impact of unemployment upon welfare. In J-E. Kolberg & Z. Ferge (Eds.), *Social policy in a changing Europe*. Frankfurt: Campus.

Smith, R. (1987). *Unemployment and health: A disaster and a challenge*. Oxford: Oxford University Press.

Stafford, E.M. (1982). The impact of the Youth Opportunities Programme on young people's employment prospects and psychological well-being. *British Journal of Guidance and Counselling, 10*(1), 12–21.

Te Grotenhuis, H., & Dronkers, J. (1989). Unequal opportunities in a West-European Welfare State. *The Netherlands Journal of Social Sciences, 25*(1), 18–29.

Thoits, P., & Hannan, M. (1979). Income and psychological distress: The impact of an income maintenance experiment. *Journal of Health and Social Behaviour, 20*, 120–138.

Unemployment Unit (1994). *Working brief, 52*, March.

Warr, P.B. (1987). *Work, unemployment and mental health*. Oxford: Clarendon Press.

Warr, P.B., & Jackson, P.R. (1984). Men without jobs: Some correlates of age and length of unemployment. *Journal of Occupational Psychology, 57*, 77–85.

Warr, P.B., & Payne, R.L. (1983). Social class and reported changes after job loss. *Journal of Applied Social Psychology, 13*, 206–222.

Welch, H.J., & Myers, C.S. (1932). *Ten years of industrial psychology: An account of the first decade of NIIP*. London: Pitman.

Whelan, C.T. (1992). The role of income, life-style deprivation and financial strain in mediating the impact of unemployment on psychological distress: Evidence from the Republic of Ireland, *Journal of Occupational and Organisational Psychology, 65*(4), 331–344.

Wight, D. (1993). *Workers not wasters. Masculine respectability, consumption and employment in central Scotland*. Edinburgh: Edinburgh University Press.

Wilkinson, R.G. (1990). Income distribution and mortality: A natural experiment. *Sociology of Health and Illness, 12*, 391–412.

Winefield, A.H., Tiggemann, M., & Winefield, H.R. (1993). *Growing up with unemployment: A longitudinal study of its psychological impact*. London: Routledge.

Zawadski, B., & Lazarsfeld, P.F. (1935). The psychological consequences of unemployment. *Journal of Social Psychology, 6*, 224–251.

10

Ethnic Minorities on the Labour Market

Arne Evers and Henk van der Flier

1   INTRODUCTION

In this chapter the particular position of ethnic minorities on the labour market will be dealt with, although major parts of this chapter, such as the research models described, may apply to other minority groups as well. The definition of ethnic minorities may involve many aspects such as biological, socio-economical, political and cultural ones, and a balanced definition would require discussion of both the terms "ethnic" as well as "minority". Although it is recognized that a sound definition may be useful in other cases, it is not really needed from the perspective of this chapter. We prefer to deal with this definition issue pragmatically, so we will consider any group as an ethnic minority if it differs on variables such as nationality or race from the majority or autochthonous part of the population. Furthermore, this chapter concerns only those groups that are in a disadvantageous position, or which may be treated differently because of characteristics such as nationality, language, race, etc.

The particular position these groups find them-

selves in become manifest in many ways, of which high unemployment is the most striking. As an illustration, statistics about unemployment in the European Union can be used. Table 10.1 shows the registered unemployment in seven countries of the European Union at the start of 1994 (data from other EU members were not available). Except for Spain, the unemployment rate for minorities born outside one of the countries of the European Union is at least twice that for the autochthonous part of the population. The unemployment of citizens from other countries of the European Union (who in general are not formally regarded as ethnic minorities) is remarkably lower, though still higher than that of the autochthonous citizens in each of the seven countries. What cannot be seen from these statistics is the fact that unemployment is also much higher amongst children of first generation immigrants with the nationality of their new homeland (the so-called second generation immigrants).

Different explanations may be given for the higher unemployment rates. One that especially concerns the industrial and organizational (I&O) psychology is the one of discrimination at the entrance of organizations. This is what Terborg

Source: Eurostat (1996). Migration
statistics. Luxembourg: Statistical
Office of the European Union.

TABLE 10.1

Relative Unemployment by Citizenship (All Citizens per Country = 100)

	Nationals	Other EU	Non-EU
Belgium	88	176	355
Denmark	95	162	310
Finland	99	135	305
France	93	106	263
The Netherlands	91	238	503
Spain	100	100	70
United Kingdom	97	162	243

and Ilgen (1975) call *access discrimination*. In the next part of this chapter, selection models and the consequences of different selection tools and ways of selecting people will receive ample treatment to see what is true and not true about access discrimination, and how to deal with it.

However, even when the selection hurdle is taken, ethnic minorities within organizations are in a special position, because of specific cultural habits, need for further training, less acceptance by colleagues from the majority group, etc. *Treatment discrimination* (Terborg & Ilgen, 1975) may be a consequence of this. This aspect of discrimination is discussed in the latter part of this chapter.

Various actions can be taken to challenge discrimination and to counteract disadvantages. The type of measure chosen may be dependent on the view one has on the causes of the disadvantageous position of ethnic minorities. Some views and measures are discussed in the last part of this chapter.

2   DISCRIMINATION IN SELECTION

2.1   Selection instruments

In this chapter we shall pay little attention to the more general aspects of personnel selection, since elsewhere in this Handbook (Chapter 2, Volume 3) theories and techniques of personnel selection are discussed. It is assumed that one way or the other selection is necessary to employ personnel, and that for all parties concerned, i.e. applicant,

employer and society, it is desirable that non-discriminating, valid tools are used.

For selection purposes a range of instruments is used. Jansen (1979) mentions:

- application letters or forms;
- graphological analysis;
- interviews;
- psychological tests;
- competency tests;
- references;
- diplomas and credentials;
- analysis of social background;
- check on judicial antecedents;
- medical history.

In addition Muchinsky (1986) mentions self-ratings, ratings by colleagues and assessment centres. Roe (1988) classifies application letters and forms and diplomas as biodata techniques. Competency tests are often called work samples. They are closely related to so-called situational exercises. As to content different kinds of psychological tests can be distinguished, such as intelligence tests, aptitude tests, interest inventories, personality inventories, etc. Usually interviews are classified according to the degree of structure of the conversation and rating judgement.

The graphological analysis and the analysis of one's social background are methods that will not be considered here, since their use for selection purposes is at least controversial and their validity is dubious. Checking one's judicial antecedents and medical history are methods that are of minor importance for most occupations. Moreover, these tools are only used as signs of negative risk factors; their predictive value is low. So is the validity of references. Self-ratings and ratings by colleagues are seldom used: their applicability in the selection situation is low and they must be very well structured to show any validity at all.

The remaining instruments all have their own (dis)advantages. A detailed overview is given by Muchinsky (1986). Aptitude and ability tests have the highest validities for a great variety of jobs. Work samples (including situational exercises) and assessment centres show similar or slightly lower validities. The main disadvantage of these latter methods is that they are job-specific. This makes them time-consuming and expensive procedures. An advantage of these methods, compared to psychological tests, might be that the content may closely or even actually resemble the tasks to be performed in the job, which may very well make them free of discrimination.

The interview is the most popular instrument for personnel selection (Arvey, 1979). It can differ according to the degree of structure, the number of interviewers and its content (trait-oriented versus criterion-oriented). The validity coefficient is highly dependent on the degree of structure. For very highly structured interviews, in which both questions and rating procedure are predetermined, the validity coefficients may approach those of the earlier mentioned standardized testing methods. The validity of unstructured interviews stays far behind (Hunter & Hunter, 1984). Until now there has been no evidence for any systematic bias of the interview against minorities (Muchinsky, 1986). However, the interview leaves ample room for personal favours or dislikes and one should constantly be aware of this.

The validity of grade points, diplomas and application letters/forms is rather low. However, in combination with other biographical data, and used in a standardized format (the so-called biodata list), this type of biographical data may be one of the best predictors. However, this method too has its disadvantages. One of them is that validity data for this type of instruments are relatively soon outdated, which would require a regular update of the inventory. Furthermore, it can happen that questions of the biodata list that

clearly contribute to the predictive value are not the most ethical ones to ask. So far, however, research into the validity of this method has pointed out that it is not to the disadvantage of minorities (Cascio, 1976).

In conclusion we can say that differences in selection methods exist with regard to validity, fairness towards minorities and their application (expenses and/or suitability for specific selection problems). In practice, different methods will often be used in combination. This seems to be a good policy, since different methods can supplement each other so that higher validities may be obtained. Eventually, research will reveal which particular methods are (relatively) fair towards ethnic minorities. In the following paragraphs research techniques to detect selection bias will be discussed. In addition anti-discrimination action will be discussed as well as ways to compensate for existing disadvantages.

2.2 Prediction-bias research

2.2.1 Definitions and terminology

Up to this point the terms discrimination, unfairness, disadvantage, etc. have been used more or less as synonyms. As in this technical part of the chapter the word "bias" will be introduced, the different concepts need to be defined more precisely.

Statistically speaking, discrimination is distinguishing between individuals or groups in a reliable way. Thus, the literal meaning of the word discrimination has no negative connotations. In fact, tests are developed to distinguish between individuals or groups. Therefore, different test scores between two groups do not mean *per se* that the test is in favour of the group with the highest scores. The test may simply reflect the actual existing differences (nevertheless score differences may be sufficient reason to look for the possibility of selection bias; see Hofstee et al., 1990).

Although the technical meaning of discrimination is neutral, its general meaning has the negative connotation of unfair behaviour towards an individual or group. It then refers to putting behind an individual or a group on improper grounds. In this chapter both meanings of the word discrimination will be used, depending on the context. In this way artificial descriptions or synonyms of the negative meaning of discrimination can be avoided. Since negative discrimination would be a pleonasm in common language, the word negative in combination with discrimination will only be used in this chapter to differentiate between negative and positive discrimination, the latter meaning favouring one group or members of a group that is in a disadvantaged position at the cost of the other group.

Discrimination can be distinguished into direct discrimination, indirect discrimination and a so-called discriminating effect (Roe, 1983). Direct discrimination means that irrelevant elements are taken into account deliberately to influence the selection decision, e.g. individual qualities that have no clear functional relationship with the criterion performance, such as ethnicity, gender and background. It is hard to say how frequently this type of discrimination occurs, because it is generally not acknowledged as such. So the discriminating institution or person will seldom openly admit one of these irrelevant elements to be the true reason for rejecting an applicant. Nevertheless, research indicates that the existence of this type of discrimination is beyond doubt (Bovenkerk & Breuning-Van Leeuwen, 1978; Den Uyl, 1986; Veerman & Vijverberg, 1982).

Referring to indirect discrimination, the irrelevant characteristics in itself do not affect the selection decision, yet the result will be that a group of applicants sharing a particular characteristic will be at a disadvantage. This is for example the case when a test can predict the future performance of a particular group better than that of another group. This is a paradoxical situation: it means that when ethnicity is not involved in the selection decision, members of one group, or of both groups, may be discriminated. We will come back to this issue in more detail in section 2.2.2.

For all that, a selection procedure that is free of direct and indirect discrimination may nevertheless put certain groups or individuals at a disadvantage. This is what we call a discriminating effect. It occurs when the (relevant) characteristics upon which the selection is based correlate with irrelevant characteristics. When a certain bottom level of education is required for a job, and there are two groups differing in average level of education, it will be clear that one group will have more drop-outs than the other. Usually this effect turns against ethnic minorities.

Following Jensen (1980) the term bias is used in a strictly statistical sense. It is defined as "systematic errors in the criterion validity or the construct validity of test scores of individuals that are associated with the individual's group membership" (Jensen, 1980, p. 375). Although bias is often associated with culture bias, bias against any type of group membership can be involved. For instance bias towards age, gender, social class, religion, etc. can be investigated. When research shows that a test is biased against a specific group, it obviously does not mean that the test is biased for other classifications: the existence of gender bias does not imply culture bias, etc.

So the term bias is reserved for the psychometric characteristics of a test. The term (un)fairness refers to the use that is made of test scores. Unbiased tests can be used unfairly, and biased tests can be used fairly. Opinions about what is fair and what is not are determined by moral, legal or philosophical ideas. Consequently, the evaluation of the (un)fairness of a particular test use is a political issue rather than a statistical one.

In this text the words "test" and "predictor" are used interchangeably. Both words are used as a general term for the different types of selection instruments that are used and are mentioned in section 3.1: psychological tests, situational exercises, assessment centres, interviews and biodata lists. When the word test explicitly refers to (a certain kind of) psychological tests, it will be clear from the context that the word is used in this more specific way. The word criterion is specifically used for any kind of measures of individual performance in work or education. Examples are grades, statistics on absenteeism, ratings by supervisors, etc.

2.2.2 Research model

The purpose of using tests in a selection procedure is to minimize the number of incorrect decisions. Nevertheless, errors will always occur, since it is very unlikely that tests will ever reach perfect validity. The "errors" that are the result of direct discrimination are of course reprehensible. How-ever, this type of "error" is not supposed to play a role in selection tests (the exception being the deliberate use of tests that are not suited for a specific group, for example because the members of that group do not have a good command of the language used). When discrimination with tests occurs, it is generally indirect.

Research into this kind of discrimination relies heavily on the regression model (Cleary, 1968). The basic assumption is that the criterion variable is a (linear) function of the predictor variable. The graphical representation of this function, the regression line, shows that value of the criterion is most probably linked to a particular value on the predictor. The general formula for the regression line is:

$$Y = b_{yx} X + c \tag{1}$$

where

Y	= the criterion
X	= the predictor
b_{yx}	= the regression coefficient
c	= a constant

The regression coefficient shows the rate of change in Y with respect to X or the slope of the regression line. The regression coefficient must not be mixed up with the validity coefficient, that is the correlation between predictor and criterion. There is a relation between the two coefficients:

$$b_{yx} = r_{xy} \frac{\sigma_y}{\sigma_x} \tag{2}$$

where

r_{xy}	= the validity coefficient
σ_y	= the standard deviation of the criterion scores
σ_x	= the standard deviation of the predictor scores

Formula (2) shows that when both predictor scores and criterion-scores are standardized, the regression and the validity coefficient are ident-ical. The constant in formula (1) is also referred to as the intercept; it is the point where the regression line cuts the y-axis.

In fact, the regression line is the best fitting line that can be drawn through the scatterplot of all the x- and y-score combinations. There is always a certain amount of error in prediction, that is, the scatter of observed scores around the predicted score. The standard error of estimate, SE_y, is an index for this amount of error. The simplified formula (for large N's, e.g. N > 200) is:

$$SE_y = \sigma_y \sqrt{1 - r_{xy}^2} \tag{3}$$

As we can see the height of the validity coefficient is one of the determinants of the accuracy of the prediction of criterion scores. The higher the validity coefficient (and the standard deviation of the criterion scores kept equal), the lower the standard error of estimate will be, and the more accurate the prediction will be. The standard error of estimate can be described as the standard deviation of the differences between observed and predicted criterion scores. When the standard error of estimate is higher, the scatterplot will look like a circle rather than an oval.

Now that we have defined all the elements of predictive bias, we can give a definition of predictive bias itself: "A test is a biased predictor if there is a statistically significant difference between the (two) groups investigated in the slopes b_{yx}, in the intercepts c or in the standard errors of estimate SE_y of the regression lines" (Jensen, 1980). The regression parameters should be calculated by using the estimated true scores of the persons in both groups.

Thus, a test is biased when at least one of the three above mentioned conditions is met. In this definition of bias, differences in validity coeffi-cients itself are not mentioned. Accordingly a test with different validity coefficients in the two groups may even be unbiased. When a difference in validity coefficients (or a difference in any of the other parameters that affect the existence of bias) results in a difference in one of the three variables mentioned in the formulas (1), (2) and (3), a test is said to be biased. The reason why it is not efficacious to test for differences in validity coefficients itself shall not be dealt with here. They can for example be found in Linn (1978) or in Arvey and Faley (1988).

Figure 10.1 shows some examples of biased and

Examples of biases and
unbiased tests.

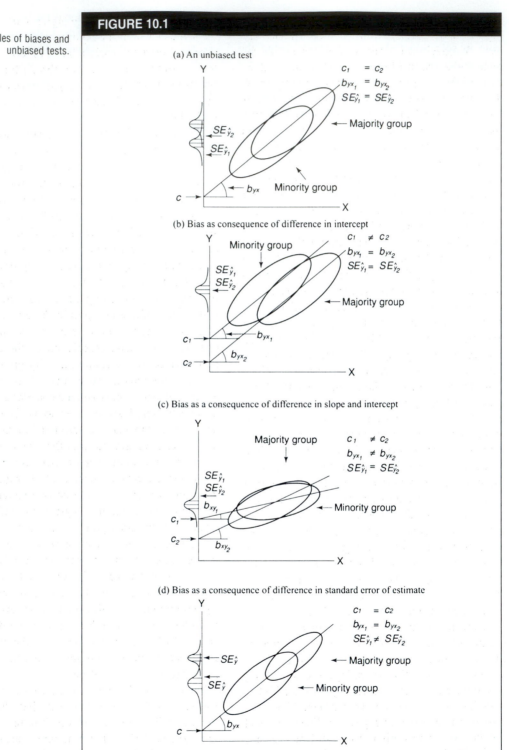

FIGURE 10.1

unbiased tests according to the regression model. Figure 10.1a is the only illustration of an unbiased test. Although on average the scores of the minority group are lower on test X, the scatterplots of the two groups are in line. Consequently, the two regression lines coincide. The test is unbiased since the two groups also have the same standard error of estimate despite the difference in mean test score for the two groups. The reason is that the difference in test score goes along with a proportional difference in criterion score. There is no question of (indirect) discrimination if this test is used for selection purposes without distinguishing between minority and majority group. Since at every critical test score there are relatively more members of the majority group, we do have a discriminating effect. This may be socially unacceptable, but it is not a matter of test bias.

In Figure 10.1b the two regression lines have different intercepts indicating bias. In the regression formulas different constants must be entered for both groups. This means that on the basis of the *same* test score a higher level of criterion performance should be predicted for a member of one group compared to a member of the other group. Assuming that the common regression line lies somewhere between the two regression lines in the figure, and not taking into account group membership, we do have a case of (indirect) discrimination. Estimates of criterion performance based on the common regression line of the group with the higher regression line will be too low and those of the group with the lower regression line will be too high. In this case this would be to the disadvantage of the ethnic minority group. This is *under*prediction of the minority group performance and *over*prediction of the majority group performance. In other words: the expected mean criterion performance of both groups is the same, but the mean test performance of the minority group is lower. The use of test scores for the selection of employees, disregarding ethnicity, would result in an unjustifiable higher rejection rate in the minority group. However, provided that different regression lines are used for the two groups this test can still be a useful predictor. There will be no discrimination and less selection errors than when using the common regression line. Consequently, members of the

majority group should have higher scores to have the same chance of being accepted. Although the use of different regression lines temporarily solves the discrimination issue, one should further analyze the test in order to investigate what caused the bias. Later in this chapter we will discuss methods to do this.

Figure 10.1c illustrates a situation where the intercept as well as the slope of the regression lines for the two groups differ (the situation that there is a difference in slope, but not in intercept—thus the intersection of the two regression lines lies exactly on the Y-axis—is somewhat artificial and will be seen as a particular instance of this general situation). Again there are more selection errors made when using one common regression line instead of two different ones. However, this would result in under- and overprediction of both groups, and not just of one group as in Figure 10.1b. The level of the test score determines the under- or overprediction. Underprediction of the criterion performance of the ethnic minority group members and overprediction of that of the majority group members occurs when the scores are below the intersection. For the scores above the intersection, it is just the other way around. The further the test scores are removed from the intersection, the higher the amount of under- or overprediction will be. When the cut-off score is at the right of the intersection there will only be overprediction of performance of the minority group and underprediction of the majority group. This amount of over- or underprediction will increase with higher test scores. In this situation a selection executive could be accused of discrimination when not taking into account group membership and using only one regression line. This may be the case, even if the mean test scores of both groups do not differ as Figure 10.1c illustrates. So even the fact that differences in mean test scores are absent does not guarantee the absence of bias.

Figure 10.1d illustrates a unique case where the test is biased despite the fact that the same regression line and regression formula apply to both groups. This is the case when accuracy of prediction in both groups differs. As can be seen in formula (3) this is either the result of a greater standard deviation in criterion performance $\sigma_{\!\!,}$, or of a smaller validity coefficient r_{xy}, or a combination of both. If the bias is caused by a smaller r_{xy} and if σ_y is equal in both groups, then, following formula (2), the standard deviation of the predictor scores σ_x must be smaller in the group with the smaller r_{xy} (because the slope of the regression line is equal in both groups). Furthermore, the smaller σ_x may result in the smaller r_{xy}. It may be worth while looking into the causes of this lower variability of test scores and into other possible determinants for the greater error of prediction in one of the groups, in order to improve prediction in that group. Another reason for investigating differences in standard error of estimate could be that these differences are to the disadvantage of qualified members in the best predicted group, since some of their positions will be taken by false positives in the other group.

In the section above a description is given of three examples of differential prediction and of one situation where no differential prediction exists. These three have been selected because they were considered as important and interesting cases. For a more extensive overview the reader is referred to Bartlett and O'Leary (1969).

Research on differential prediction, according to the model described above, should also indicate whether differences in standard error of estimate, slope and intercept between the distinct groups are significant. A short description of the test procedure is given in Jensen (1980, pp. 456 et seq.). The differences in the three parameters should be tested with a hurdle approach: First of all differences in standard error of estimate are tested, then differences in slope and finally differences in intercept. If, at a prior stage, predictor bias is found as demonstrated by significant differences, it is useless to perform further statistical tests. So, if there are differences in the amount of error in prediction, one does not need to do any further tests for differences in slope; if there are differences in slope there is no need to test for differences in intercept. The statistical reasoning behind this sequential testing can be found in Gulliksen and Wilks (1950).

A practical problem with the testing method described above is that it is rather laborious. A more fundamental drawback was pointed to by Lautenschlager and Mendoza (1986). The step-by-step procedure of Jensen can be compared with a step-up hierarchical multiple regression procedure. Typical for these procedures is that at each step all higher order effects not included in the model are pooled into the sum of squared error term, potentially decreasing the power of the sequential testing procedure. Lautenschlager and Mendoza propose a step-down procedure which begins by testing the hypothesis that a common regression line alone is sufficient to account for the relation of the predictor with the criterion. This is the so-called test of the omnibus hypothesis of prediction bias. If this hypothesis is rejected, subsequent tests for slope and for intercept differences must be performed. This method is more powerful because it deals with the error terms more adequately. Besides, it is more practical because it can be easily done with a standard statistical package. The only disadvantage is that it does not test for differences in standard error of measurement between the groups.

Overviews of research into differential prediction amongst various ethnic groups (mostly African-American and Caucasian in the USA) are given by Jensen (1980, chapter 10) and Arvey and Faley (1988, chapter 5). These studies show great variation in test purposes and in nature of the predictor and criterion measures used. Studies both in educational as well as in working situations are described, where predictors vary from traditional intelligence tests to job samples and criterion measures from school grades to ratings by supervisors. Despite this variation, the general conclusion is that most studies do *not* reveal differential prediction. In the few instances where there is differential prediction, we are mostly dealing with differences in intercept, whereby nearly always the regression line of the majority groups is found to be *above* that of the minority group. Thus, one might say that in most cases the tests proved to be unbiased predictors and that in the cases that bias was found, it was not to the disadvantage of the minority group (when using the common regression line, performance of group members with the lower intercept is *over* predicted).

A study on differential prediction of ethnic minorities in an educational situation in The Netherlands (Evers & Lucassen, 1991) can be taken as an illustration of the results typically found in bias research. In this study, school performance was predicted from the scores on the Dutch adaptation of the Differential Aptitude Tests. Twenty predictor criterion combinations were tested for differences in standard error of measurement, slope, and intercept. No differences in standard error of estimate were found, three differences in slope were found, and of the remaining 17 combinations 10 showed a significant difference in intercept. In these 10 cases the regression line in the ethnic minority group was *below* the one of the majority group. Even for two of the three cases where difference in slope was found, the intersection of the regression lines was at such a point that the regression line of the minority group was below that of the majority group in the whole effective range of the test scores. These results are consistent with the results as summarized by Jensen (1980) and Arvey and Faley (1988), and again, this study shows that if bias is found, it is hardly ever to the disadvantage of the minority group.

2.2.3 Philosophies of fair selection

For several reasons it appears to be impossible to design a foolproof selection procedure, as has been pointed out above. As long as there is a need to select people there will be people who will be treated unfairly. Irrespective of the care that is taken to develop an optimal procedure and the effort that is put into minimizing errors as much as possible, there will always be applicants rejected or accepted by mistake. In general, this is not considered discrimination, as long as it affects random individuals and not a specific group of applicants. But what about the situation when the number of selection errors differs for various subgroups in the population of applicants? According to the differential prediction model described before this is an irrelevant fact and it need not reflect discrimination. Yet it is clear that when (i) the predictor is unbiased, (ii) the cut-off point for members of both groups is the same, and (iii) the groups differ in mean predictor score, there will be differences in the number of false positives and false negatives in both groups. With this fact taken into account there will be less agreement on the non-discriminatory nature of

this predictor. Apart from the correctness of the selection decisions, and to make things a little more complex, it was stated earlier in this chapter that decisions or tools can have a discriminatory effect, although they may be fair decisions (at least from a selection point of view). Moreover, in a selection procedure indirect discrimination may occur. All in all this situation is fairly complex, and both in professional practice and in science there is no consensus on how to deal with selection errors, discriminatory effects, and indirect discrimination. All the different opinions were categorized by Hunter and Schmidt (1976) into three general philosophies of fair selection.

The first philosophy of fair selection is called *qualified individualism*. The basic idea is that only task-relevant variables, such as capacities and skills, may be part of the selection procedure and that variables such as group membership should be left out. Supporters of this philosophy argue that we are to treat everybody alike, one should disregard ethnicity, religion, gender, etc. Furthermore they believe unequal treatment to be the same as discrimination. At first sight, such a point of view is anti-discriminating. However, this policy is only correct if the predictor is unbiased. The regression lines of the subgroups will correspond and moreover this line will be the same as for the whole group. In case of a biased predictor one should use different regression lines for the subgroups to minimize prediction errors e.g. to maximize validity. Disregarding group membership means using one regression line only, even if the predictor is biased. This reduces the predictive value, and introduces indirect discrimination: the criterion performance is underpredicted for one group and overpredicted for the other (or for parts of both groups when regression lines cross each other). A solution of this problem could be to add variables to the regression formula to repair for this loss in predictive value. These should be variables that correlate both with group membership and criterion. Usually these are biographical data such as place of birth, educational background, place of residence, etc. With the addition of these variables the predictive value can be improved without considering group membership. However these variables may not be relevant for job performance either. Moreover, by way of the correlation with group membership, group membership is introduced into the prediction formula, be it indirectly. According to the philosophy of qualified individualism a biased test will result either in indirect discrimination or at best in the introduction of group membership into the prediction, which is not in agreement with the philosophy itself.

The philosophy of *unqualified individualism* like that of qualified individualism aims at maximum predictive validity, yet it justifies the use of any possible predictor, including group membership. Whenever a variable significantly contributes to the predictive validity, it should be included into the prediction formula. This not only means that different regression formulas may be used for different subgroups (introducing group membership), but even different predictors may be used in the different subgroups if prediction is improved by this. The results of both philosophies will be the same, namely one single regression line for the whole group, with an unbiased predictor. In case of a biased predictor the unqualified individualism philosophy scores better. Selection according to this philosophy will result in the highest mean criterion performance of the group of accepted applicants, it will lead to less selection errors and it will prevent indirect discrimination. Both strategies may have a discriminatory effect as its occurrence primarily depends on the relation between the predictors and group membership.

The third philosophy uses *quotas* to secure equal treatment of subgroups. The idea is that each of the demographic groups to be differentiated should be fairly represented in the working population. This implies a deviation from the selection strategies used in the two other philosophies described above. Applicants from different subgroups are deliberately treated unequally. Less capable candidates from one group can be accepted at the expense of better candidates from the other group. Ethic, social or economic arguments may justify this strategy, the goal of which is to counteract disadvantages in the labour-market situation of a specific group which may be the result of any other disadvantages (for instance less admittance to education) they have had in the past. Selection by means of tests is compatible with the quota philosophy, even when identical

tests are used in both groups. Selection will either take place within each individual group until a specific quotum is reached, or it will take place within the whole group, using some kind of compensation for the minority group.

In practice many different quotum arrangements are used. Most of them are rather straightforward and use target figures. This means that the ultimate goal of the arrangement is that a specific percentage of all jobs (or of a specific job or group of jobs) should be allocated to members of the minority group. Generally, the target figure is based on the ratio of the minority group to the whole population within a certain geographical region. When for example 30% of the population of the city of Amsterdam belongs to ethnic minorities, then ultimately 30% of the jobs in this region should be taken by ethnic minorities. The use of target figures implies a temporary increase (a higher percentage than the target figure) of people selected from minority groups, in order to eventually reach the target figure. There are several ways to implement this policy. A straightforward and popular way is to stipulate that the selection ratio in both groups should be the same, in other words the percentage of accepted people in the majority group and the minority group should be the same. At first sight this may not look like a quotum arrangement, but like a basic principle of fair selection.[1] However, it is a quotum arrangement if differences in capability between the subgroups are by no means accounted for. Figure 10.1a for example shows that with an unbiased predictor and a difference in mean test performance between two groups, one single cut-off score would just result in different selection ratios for the two groups (and for equal selection ratios one would need different cut-off scores). Apart from that, any quotum arrangement will only have the intended effect when the percentage of members of the minority group in the whole group at least equals the target figure. In order to reach the target figures, it may be useful to formulate intermediate quantitative goals, as in the Dutch so-called EMO plan (Ministerie van Binnenlandse Zaken, 1990). The EMO plan is a policy for affirmative action to employ people from ethnic minorities for governmental services. It requires that from 1987–1990 the percentage of members of ethnic minority groups in governmental services rises from 2% to 3%.

In the types of affirmative action that are mentioned before, no reference is made to the capability of the applicants. An illustration of a mild type of affirmative action is when preference will be given to an applicant of a minority group, when there are two or more applicants of equal capability. However, the effect of such an arrangement appears to be small. The city of Tilburg in The Netherlands uses a stricter method. Of the people that meet the job requirements, they do not simply select the best of the whole group, but only the best of the target group (Krosse, 1991). These target groups for example include ethnic minorities. The purpose of this policy is to fill 100% of the vacancies with applicants from target groups. This should guarantee that in the shortest possible period the target figure will be reached. There are a number of other, more complicated, models for preferential treatment, that include the capabilities of the applicants in defining the quota, and of which the effects are somewhere in between the soft and the extreme model. One of the oldest models is that of Thorndike (1971). This model holds that in a fair selection procedure the ratio of accepted and potential successful applicants in both groups should be equal. Other, partly comparable, models were proposed amongst others by Cole (1973), Linn (1973) and Bereiter (1975). The basic idea of all these models is that it is legitimate to achieve that a higher percentage of people from minority groups will get a job at the expense of a lower profit of the selection procedure in terms of a lower mean criterion performance of the total group of accepted applicants. These models may justify the selection procedure pursued or to be pursued for all parties concerned, i.e. employers (accept a lower mean criterion performance), majority group (the rejection of a higher percentage of capable candidates) and minority group (the time it takes to catch up with the majority group).

If one decides to use the quotum approach, one should justify this. Subsequently, the choice for a specific model, quotum or speed for catching up the disadvantage is a matter to be decided upon as well. Although both choices are rather a matter for politicians (or of employers) than for personnel psychologists, the latter group may contribute to the discussion by giving so-called utility models. In these models every single decision is evaluated. A predecessor of utility models is the *culture-modified criterion model* (Darlington, 1971). In this model one explicitly states the amount of criterion performance that is sacrificed in favour of affirmative action. When there is agreement on this value K, it will be subtracted from the expected criterion performance of members of the majority group, or the equivalent will be subtracted from the test scores of the majority group, which will have the same effect. Subsequently, in the whole group those candidates with the highest expected criterion performance will be accepted. By means of manipulation of K each desired quotum may be determined in advance. The use of different norm-tables for the minority and the majority group is in accordance with this. This procedure is frequently used. However, often the effects (on criterion performance and selection ratios) are not quantified and therefore remain obscure.

The *expected utility model* (Gross & Su, 1975; Petersen & Novick, 1976) is a complete utility model in that each outcome of the selection procedure is being evaluated. There are four possible outcomes:

(a) acceptance of a potentially successful applicant;
(b) rejection of a potentially successful applicant;
(c) rejection of a potentially unsuccessful applicant;
(d) acceptance of a potentially unsuccessful applicant.

In general the outcomes (a) and (c) will be given positive values and (b) and (d) negative values. There are several ways to determine these values or utilities. Roe (1983) distinguishes objective, subjective and objectified methods. In objective methods some kind of objective appraisal criterion is used to assess the values of all four outcomes (for instance a cost-benefit analysis). In subjective methods the utilities are determined by means of subjective ratings either on management level or

FIGURE 10.2

Empty utility matrix.

	Rejection	Acceptance	
Successful	U_b	U_a	$Y \geqslant Y_0$
Unsuccessful	U_c	U_d	$Y < Y_0$
	$X < X_0$	$X \geqslant X_0$	

by the people who are directly involved in selection. The use of a utility function is characteristic for objectified methods. It quantifies the relation between criterion Y and utility U. With either one of these methods the values in the empty utility matrix can be filled. These are called the *actual utilities*. Hence, the expected utilities of the alternative decisions "accept" or "reject" for each predictor score can be computed with the aid of an expectancy table. In an expectancy table the probabilities of attaining specified criterion scores are given for each predictor score. In general, the higher the test score the higher the probability that an applicant will perform well at a particular level. When the minimum satisfactory criterion level is specified, the expectancy table gives the probability of a success or failure for each predictor score. The *expected utility* is the sum of the products of these probabilities and the actual utilities that belong to the selection outcome concerned.

The importance of this approach is that different values may be attributed to the actual utilities of the minority and the majority group. It illustrates the efforts an organization puts into a policy of affirmative action. Figure 10.3 gives an example of different actual utilities for two groups.

This example shows that the rejection of an unsuccessful candidate has a positive value (U_c) and that accepting an unsuccessful candidate gets a negative value (U_d). The absolute value of U_d is greater than that of U_c: after all, an unsuccessful employee may cost the company a lot of money. In the example given above, the values for U_c and U_d are equal for the minority and the majority group. This is not the case however for U_a and U_b. Although accepting a successful candidate (U_a) has a positive value for both groups, an affirmative action policy is reflected in a higher value for the minority group. It is obvious that rejecting successful candidates should be avoided as much as possible. Therefore, a negative utility (U_b) is assigned to this outcome. The difference between these utility values of the minority and the majority group shows that rejecting a potentially successful employee from the minority group is considered an even greater loss.

The model described above is a so-called *threshold utility model*. A disadvantage of such a model is that the degree of capability is not taken into account (Petersen, 1976). Candidates with scores just above the success–failure cut-off point on the criterion are given the same utility as those who would be extremely successful. This is compensated for in a *linear utility model*, where the utility value is a monotonically increasing or decreasing function of the criterion score (Mellenbergh & Van der Linden, 1981), and different values for the minority and the majority group can be used.

In summary, caution against the use of qualified individualism is called for. In the case of a biased predictor the effect of this strategy turns out to be a quota strategy, and it stays unclear which group is favoured, which group is disfavoured, and to what extent. Unqualified individualism will give the

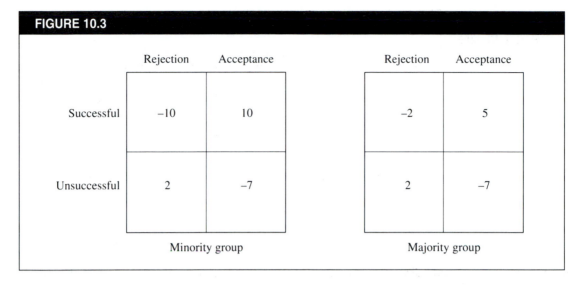

FIGURE 10.3

	Rejection	Acceptance		Rejection	Acceptance
Successful	−10	10		−2	5
Unsuccessful	2	−7		2	−7
	Minority group			Majority group	

Example of utility matrices for the same job for minority and majority group in the case of affirmative action.

best selection results. In the case of a biased predictor it provides the opportunity to use different regression formulas for different subgroups avoiding indirect discrimination. Because of the lowest error rate, this model is fairest for all candidates. It is the most profitable strategy, since the predicted mean work performance score is the highest. However, this is all technical reasoning, and from a social or ethical point of view one may argue in favour of a quotum model, which may be the only way to compensate for the lower employability rate of minority groups and to counteract the discriminating effect of selection (even when an unbiased predictor is used). This is why Drenth (1989, p. 79) concludes: "Ultimately it is a political decision which equilibrium in a given situation is preferred between 'fair chances' and 'efficiency' given the economical and political limiting conditions". However, before any decision is made, the basic assumptions and the actual choice for a strategy should be openly and explicitly discussed with all parties concerned.

2.2.4   Criterion bias

Research into prediction bias and its models all assume that criterion measures are unbiased. However, if the criterion contains some kind of bias that runs parallel to the bias in the predictor (that is to say that it equally disfavours one of the groups), then the predictor is wrongly considered unbiased. Criterion bias is defined as the discrepancy between measures for work performance (the actual criteria) and the employee's real value for the organization (the ultimate criterion) (Schmitt, 1989). It means that in a systematic or consistent way something else other than the ultimate criterion is being measured. Again, as with predictor measures, different scores on criterion measures between groups in itself are not evidence for bias, since they may reflect real differences in the ultimate criterion. However, a practical problem is that one can never have the scores on the ultimate criterion. One can work with estimates at best, which in turn need not be unbiased.

The way to solve this problem is to collect data on different criterion measures, to investigate the relations with a number of predictors and check if differences in these relations between groups are related to criterion type. Studies dealing with this issue tend to differentiate between *objective* and *subjective* criteria. Examples of objective types of criteria are turnover and absenteeism rates, measures for quantity of output (number of errors, number of units produced, etc.) and cognitive measures (training tests, job knowledge tests), etc. Subjective criteria are ratings by supervisors or colleagues. These may either be ratings of one's overall performance or judgements about specific aspects of one's performance. The idea of differentiating between objective and subjective criteria is that the first will be relatively free of bias. When differences in predictor criterion relations between both criteria types are found this may very well indicate bias in the subjective criteria.

The relation between objective and subjective criterion measures *per se* is studied both in laboratory settings as well as in experimental field settings. In the laboratory situation one typically finds high to very high correlations. Correlations from .42 to .97 are reported (Bigoness, 1976; Borman, 1978; Schmitt & Lappin, 1980). At least part of the explanation for these high values may be that in laboratory studies one is very keen to develop criterion measures that are easy to observe and to quantify. In experimental field studies the correlations usually are much weaker and often non-significant (Kirchner, 1960; Bass & Turner, 1973). Heneman (1983) did a meta-analysis and reports a mean correlation of .28 between various objective criteria and ratings for the overall performance of employees. Ford, Kraiger, and Schechtman (1986) did a meta-analysis to study the relation between objective performance measures and subjective performance indices and found a mean correlation of .43. For one part, the rather low reliability of criterion measures in practical settings may account for the low agreement between both types of criteria. Rater bias however, may also play a role here.

Although the results of studies into criterion bias are not equivocal, studies that investigate racial influence of the rater in relation to that of the subject confirm that there is at least a suspicion of bias in performance ratings. The first studies in this area show that raters tend to rate persons of their own race higher (Cox & Krumboltz, 1958; De Jung & Kaplan, 1962). In a number of more recent studies no bias was found (Bass & Turner, 1973; Schmidt & Johnson, 1973). Hamner et al. (1974), however, did find a significant racial effect again in their study with African-American and Caucasian raters. In the experiment that Hammer et al. performed, African-American and Causasian students had to judge film shots of African-American and Caucasian employees, matched on level of performance. Both African-American and Caucasian raters had higher ratings for employees that belonged to their own race. However, differ-

ences were only small and could not be replicated (Bigoness, 1976).

Kraiger and Ford (1985) did a meta-analysis on 74 studies with Caucasian raters and 14 studies with African-American raters to investigate racial ratee effects in performance ratings. They found small, yet significant mean correlations between the race of the subject and that of the rater, e.g. .18 for Caucasian raters and .22 for African-American raters, both groups giving higher ratings for members of their own race. An interesting part of this analysis was that the possible influence of five moderators was taken into account: rater training (yes/no), type of training (behaviour/trait), rating purpose (administrative/research), experimental setting (laboratory/field), and the composition of the workgroup (percentage of African-Americans in each study). The first three variables do not appear to have any influence on the size of the racial effect. The experimental setting however does. A racial effect was found in field settings, but not in laboratory settings. Moreover, racial effects tended to increase as the percentage of African-Americans in the workforce decreased.

Later research by Pulakos, White, Oppler, and Borman (1989) and Sackett and DuBois (1991) showed that the racial rater–ratee effect applies to Caucasian raters only; African-American raters do not give higher ratings to members of their own racial group. Differences with the results of Kraiger and Ford are caused by the fact that in the more recent studies only supervisors are used as raters, whereas Kraiger and Ford used ratings by colleagues as well. When studies based on ratings by colleagues are excluded from the meta-analysis, the results of Kraiger and Ford are more similar to those of Pulakos et al. and Sackett and DuBois: Caucasians rate Caucasians higher than African-Americans, but the reverse is not true for African-Americans. Kraiger and Ford conclude that the differences in ratings may be the result of true differences in performance, but that this cannot account for all of the variance. This hypothesis was studied by Oppler, Campbell, Pulakos, and Borman (1992). They controlled for the effect of differences in performance by partialling objective measures from the race-rating correlation. It appeared that the difference in ratings given by the Caucasian raters for the different groups became slightly smaller and the difference in ratings by the African-American raters slightly increased. The differences with the zero-order correlations were small however. This result may point to the existence of ethnic bias in the use of ratings as criterion measures.

More evidence about the presence of criterion bias can be found in studies in which ethnic groups are compared with respect to differences in performance level on the basis of objectively defined measures and subjective ratings. Ford, Kraiger, and Schechtman (1986) collected data of 53 studies with African-American and Caucasian employees, in which both objective and subjective criteria were used. With respect to both types of criteria significant racial effects were found. However, group differences for objective and subjective criteria were equal. The correlation between group membership and criterion score was .20, independent of criterion type, the white employees getting the higher scores. So far, these results could imply that there is no bias since the results on the objective and subjective measures run parallel. In order to further examine this, three types of criteria were classified: performance indicators, absenteeism, cognitive criteria (training and job knowledge tests). The relation with race was the lowest for absenteeism. Furthermore, these data practically showed no difference for the relation between subgroup and objective and subjective measures ($r = .11$ and $.15$ respectively). The relation with racial group was slightly higher for the performance measures; a significant difference between the correlation coefficients of the objective and subjective measures was found. The racial effect was lower for the objective indicators ($r = .16$ and $.22$ respectively). The cognitive criteria showed the highest relations. This type of measures revealed a significant difference between the relations of objective and subjective indicators with race as well, but here the objective measures showed the highest correlation ($.34$ and $.23$ respectively). Thus, the differences between African-American and Caucasian employees on objective cognitive criterion measures were even greater than on the subjective measures!

Assuming that objective criteria are unbiased performance measures, this analysis may lead one to conclude that subjective criteria show little bias.

From research on prediction bias, using subjective criteria, and not revealing any differential prediction, one could conclude that predictors for minority groups are fair even when subjective measures are used as criterion. According to Ford et al. (1986) this conclusion needs further explication. First of all, differences (in terms of standard deviations) on ability tests tend to be greater than for work performance, with the exception of job knowledge tests where the differences found tend to be the same as on ability tests. This could imply that this type of predictor and this type of criterion measure a construct that is related to ethnic group, in addition to the intended objectives of measurement (this could point to internal bias, which will be dealt with in the next part of this chapter). Alternatively, one could argue that in the actual work situation minority group members can compensate for lower skills by other characteristics like work experience, motivation, etc. Thus, the effect of compensation may be greater with work performance criteria than with cognitive criteria.

Finally, we have to bear in mind that actual work-performance measures may be biased as well. Although this subject has not been systematically investigated, it could be that differences in performance between subgroups are due to differences in working conditions between the two groups, whereby the conditions for the minority group would be worse than for the majority group, e.g. older equipment, working in less successful districts, high-risk jobs, etc. It could also be that employees from minority groups cannot fully use their abilities because of external factors in the worksituation that are beyond their control. One of these factors may be sabotage by majority group-members as is mentioned by Haefner (1977). Sikking and Brassé (1987), however, found no such discrimination effect in their study which was done in The Netherlands.

Reviewing the research on criterion bias one may conclude that the use of ratings as a measure for performance may be at the disadvantage of minority group members, the more so since raters will for the greater part belong to the majority group. Although this effect is relatively small and the ratings appear to be partly determined by actual work performance, nevertheless action is called for, in order to prevent this kind of bias as much as possible. This can be done for example by using behaviour-oriented scales and the formation of multi-ethnic rating teams. With respect to objective criteria American research on African-Americans and Caucasians rather consistently shows higher scores for the majority group. The degree of differences varies according to the type of criterion measure used. So these measures are by no means interchangeable and each individual measure by itself cannot be considered a proper indicator for the ultimate criterion. In sum, it appears that additional research into the validity of criterion measures determining the criterion construct is needed.

2.3   Internal test bias

This approach to the problem of test bias does not primarily focus on the degree to which a test over- or underpredicts with respect to a specific external criterion, but on the characteristics of the test itself and the interpretation of the test scores. The central issue here is whether the test refers to a theoretical concept or construct in the same way in different cultural groups.

The importance of this approach, which can be seen as being complementary to the study of prediction bias, lies in its explanatory character. Finding that the meaning of a test changes in a certain direction when it is administered to individuals and groups with different cultural backgrounds will more readily lead to hypotheses about biasing factors and to recommendations for adapting the instrument or the administration procedure.

Analysis of internal bias can take place at the level of the total test or at the item level. In the first case the composition of the test is not a point of discussion and bias analysis is based on the total test scores. It can be determined for instance, whether the total scores are related to other indicators of the construct and whether they differentiate from indicators of other constructs in the same way in the various groups. In addition, the (differences in) relationships of test scores with relevant background variables such as social class and educational level, and the sensitivity of test scores to experimental variations in administration conditions such as the amount of instruc-

tion and training, may also provide information about the degree to which test scores can be interpreted in the same way in the groups distinguished.

In the case of bias analysis at the item level, the individual items are seen as operationalizations of the construct represented by the test as a whole. It is investigated whether the relationships between the items or the relationships between the items and the total test satisfy the requirements of the measurement model in the same way in the various groups. Items that do not satisfy the requirements or which show deviating results are considered to be biased and may be removed from the test.

On the basis of this distinction between bias at the level of test scores and item bias, the main issues in this field of research will be discussed in the next sections.

2.3.1   Bias in measuring the construct

Test bias is not primarily a characteristic of the test as such but is linked to the test interpretation. If person 1 with cultural background x answers more test items correctly than person 2 with cultural background y, this could simply be seen as an empirical fact which (apart from possible discussions about the scoring rule) did not require any consideration about the possibility of test bias. However, a problem is created when, on the basis of this difference, one concluded that person 1 ranked higher than person 2 with respect to some general personality characteristic. A problem certainly arises if this characteristic is held to be stable and/or genetically based.

In the past, researchers have expended considerable efforts constructing so-called "culture free tests" (Cattell, 1940). It was thought to be possible to eliminate the influence of environmental factors on test performance and to draw conclusions about differences in inborn potential irrespective of the cultural background of the persons taking the test. However, for cognitive ability tests at least, these attempts have never been very successful. Cross-cultural test research has provided us with many examples of cultural groups not possessing the specific skills presupposed by standard ability tests to a sufficient degree (Hudson, 1960, 1967; Deregowski, 1979).

Of course, some tests are more widely applicable than others and less dependent on specific learning experiences. A good example of such a test is Raven's Progressive Matrices (Raven, 1960). The Raven test has been used very often in cross-cultural research and is considered to be one of the least culturally dependent cognitive ability tests. However, even for this instrument, construct validity has been shown to be partly determined by cultural factors (Irvine, 1969a; Chan, 1976). A summary of factors that may influence the meaning of test scores is presented in Table 10.2. When comparing persons with different backgrounds, factors such as these may produce unintended variation in test performances and lead to biased interpretations. The influence of these factors can be reduced in different ways. In the first place, one may think of expanding the instructions and adding more practice items for candidates who lack the necessary test-taking skills. A number of studies have shown that additional test training leads to a substantial improvement in test performance, especially for groups lacking these skills (Dyer, 1970; Feuerstein, 1972, 1979; Kroeger, 1980).

In the second place, adaptation of test items and testing procedures may also reduce the influence of culturally determined skills on the test scores. Ord's (1970) adaptation of Koh's Blocks provides an interesting example. For other examples and an overview of procedures to improve the cross-cultural equivalence of test instructions and stimulus materials, the reader is referred to Warwick and Osherson (1973), Brislin, Lonner, and Thorndike (1973), Triandis and Berry (1980) and Lonner and Berry (1988).

Finally, it is also possible to restrict the interpretation of test scores to selected parts of the population that have shown, or can be assumed to possess, the required skills and knowledge to a sufficient degree. Proposals to let a testability or acculturation test precede the administration of the real test are in line with this thought. Others (Hofstee et al., 1990) have pointed out that this means it might be an advantage to a test candidate to get a low score on the pre-test. This problem will also arise if the score on the pre-test is used as a correction factor.

From the foregoing it will be clear that in comparing the test performances of persons with varying cultural backgrounds it will generally not be possible on a priori grounds to exclude the possibility that the differences have to be ascribed to differences in test-taking skills or other unintended factors. In answering the question of whether the test has the same meaning for the various candidates (refers to the same construct in the same way), psychometric criteria will also have to be taken into account.

This question, however, is preceded by the more fundamental question of the validity of the construct or attribute for the cultural groups concerned. Does it make sense, for instance, to apply concepts like spatial ability or arithmetic reasoning outside the Western cultural system in which they originated? Inspired by ideas from cultural anthropology, a number of investigators have argued that cognitive functioning is conceived as an adaptation to specific cultural and ecological requirements and should be defined in terms of these requirements. Cross-cultural comparisons of test performances, in this view, become practically impossible. For an overview of the discussion about this topic we refer to publications by Berry (1972), Jahoda (1977, 1983) and Poortinga and Malpass (1988). We will confine

---

TABLE 10.2

- Understanding the test instructions
- Familiarity with the testing material (pictures, words, grammatical structures, letters, figures, objects), relevant concepts, problem-solving strategies and answering possibilities
- Experience with the testing task or comparable tasks
- Experience with working under time pressure
- Test attitude, motivation, concentration, fear of failure, social desirability

Sources of Unintended Variance in Test Scores.

ourselves here to a pragmatic approach in which an attempt is made to formulate psychometric criteria for the comparability of test scores, taking the "psychic unity of mankind" and the universality of constructs as a point of departure.

A good example of this last approach is the work carried out by Poortinga (1971, 1975), which draws a distinction between different levels of comparability. For total test scores the distinction is drawn between functional equivalence and score equivalence. Functional equivalence relates to the requirement that the test qualitatively measures the same attribute in the different groups. When dealing with more than one test to which this requirement applies, the testable condition follows that the relationships between the tests are the same in the groups concerned. Score equivalence implies that the test should measure the attribute on a quantitatively similar scale in the distinguished groups; when there is more than one test, the requirement of similar regression coefficients follows.

The functional equivalence of measurement instruments across different cultural groups has been studied relatively often. Comparison of factor structures is one of the most appropriate methods. An advantage to the comparison of separate correlation coefficients or correlation matrices is the possibility of starting from an appropriate theoretical framework, which makes the assumption of equal relationships between theoretical concepts a less arbitrary one and creates the possibility of interpreting changes in meaning. Among the intelligence theories based on factor analytic research, both the hierarchical model by Vernon (1950) and Cattell's (1963) theory of fluid and crystallized ability have shown their cross-cultural applicability (Irvine, 1969b; Vernon, 1969; Hakstian & Vandenberg, 1979; Vandenberg & Hakstian, 1978), while most of Thurstone's (1938) "primary mental abilities" have also been recovered in divergent cultural groups (Vandenberg & Hakstian, 1978; Irvine, 1979).

A number of methods have been applied to compare factor structures. The most simple and widely used method is one in which the factors found in the different groups are separately rotated to simple structure. Factor structures or factor patterns can then be compared by inspection (see for instance Irvine, 1969b). A formal test of the differences does not take place. There are also a number of methods in which a factor matrix is transformed in a linear way to a matrix resembling another matrix (the goal matrix) as much as possible. This is called a Procrustian transformation (Niemöller & Sprenger, 1977), though the term "Procrustes rotation" is usually used. The goal matrix may be an a priori determined hypothetical matrix or, in the instance of a comparison between different samples, one of the subgroup matrices or an overall matrix for the combined samples (see for an example Van der Flier, 1980).

Another method for the combined factor analysis of correlation matrices from different populations, developed by Jöreskog (1971) provides an indirect test of the equality of the factor matrices. This method makes no attempt to rotate independent factor structures to a common solution, but the model to be tested is specified on an a priori basis. The LISREL program (Jöreskog & Sörbom, 1984) can be used to carry out this confirmatory factor analysis.

According to Ten Berge (1986) many investigators do not find the statistically advanced LISREL program very practical. Among the reasons are technical problems such as lack of convergence, the fact that the method is particularly suited to showing that a model does *not* fit, and the problem that LISREL provides little information about the question of what has happened to the factors not found in another population. It is also often found to be difficult to specify the elements to be fixed on an a priori basis. As to the more descriptive approaches, where (on the basis of a limited number of components) rotation takes place to maximum congruence, the problem is that a number of arbitrary choices have to be made, such as the number of components to be retained and the type of rotation (orthogonal or oblique) to be used.

A new method proposed by Ten Berge is Pekon (Perfekte Kongruentie: Camstra, 1985) which implies that a second group's factor structure is rotated to perfect congruence with a first (reference) group's factor structure. This is done by applying the weight matrix of the first group to the correlation matrix of the second group. In this way the second group's factor structure has, by definition, the same meaning as the original group's factor structure. The question is then whether the same factors explain as much variance in the second group as in the first. This approach resembles the Multiple Group Method developed by Gorsuch (1983).

2.3.2 Item bias

As for the test as a whole, individual items may contain elements which create additional problems for certain subgroups. This may concern the specific knowledge or specific skills required to produce the correct answer, formal characteristics of the item to which the groups react differently, or differences in the degree to which certain response alternatives are found attractive or socially desirable. If, because of this, the items reflect differences between groups that the test does not intend to measure one may speak of item bias or, more neutrally, about differential item functioning (DIF).

In the field of statistical item bias research many methods have been developed over the last 30 years (Angoff & Ford, 1972; Van der Flier, Mellenbergh, Adèr, & Wijn, 1984b; Holland & Thayer, 1988; Lord, 1980; Mellenbergh, 1982; Scheuneman, 1980; Stricker, 1982; Wright, Mead, & Draba, 1976; see also Holland & Wainer, 1993 and Millsap & Everson, 1993). A distinction can be drawn between unconditional and conditional methods. In unconditional methods an item is considered to be biased when, in comparison with the other items of the test, it is relatively easier or more difficult for one of the groups or in other words, when there is a significant item × group interaction. One of the most widely known unconditional methods is the delta method (Angoff & Ford, 1973; see also Angoff, 1982) in which the transformed difficulty indices (p-values) of the items in the different groups are plotted against each other.

Strong deviations from the line indicating the relationship between the difficulty indices in the different groups are interpreted as an indication of item bias. Other unconditional methods based on analysis of variance, such as the one by Plake and Hoover (1979) in which item responses are analysed within an item × group factorial design and a significant interaction between the factors is taken as an indication of item bias, have also been frequently applied.

These unconditional methods lead to a number of practical and theoretical problems (Mellenbergh, 1982). In the first place, the methods are not independent of the score distributions in the various groups and are therefore sensitive to the real differences in trait level between the groups. A second objection is that the bias of the item is defined in relation to the other items in the test and is therefore dependent on the specific collection of items.

Conditional methods for the detection of item bias, however, do compare item responses at the same trait level. Items are being called unbiased if the probability of a correct answer is the same for the distinguished groups. Within the group of conditional methods a distinction can be drawn between methods based on latent trait models, and methods in which the total score on the test is used as an estimate of the trait level. Methods based on latent trait models are preferable in principle, but make higher demands with respect to the characteristics of the items and/or numbers of testees.

Latent traits are hypothetical dimensions which provide an explanation for the relationships between the test items. The complete latent space is made up of all the dimensions needed to explain these relationships. Within this space, the conditional distributions of item scores, given the latent trait positions, are by definition the same for all relevant populations (Lord & Novick, 1968). When a test consists of homogeneous items one may assume that the relationships between the items can be explained by one latent trait. The regressions of the item scores on this trait are called item characteristic curves or item ogives. If the complete latent space is indeed one-dimensional, these item characteristic curves are invariant for the various groups. When item characteristic curves in two culturally different groups appear to be different, there is obviously a second dimension, related to group membership, implying that the items involved have to be considered as being non-equivalent. Deviations between item characteristic curves can be quantified by comparing difficulty and discrimination parameters or by taking the surface between the two curves (see for instance Kok, 1988). Well-known examples are methods based on the three-parameter logistic model (Lord, 1980) and the one-parameter (Rasch) model described by Wright, Mead, and Draba (1976); see also Mellenbergh (1972).

Item bias methods in which total test scores are used as ability estimates are generally easier to apply than methods based on latent trait models. A well-known example is a procedure proposed by Scheuneman (1979, 1981) in which, on the basis of the total test scores, the groups which are to be compared are divided into a number of subgroups, each defined by a certain score range. Per item, it is checked then whether the numbers of correct answers in these subgroups deviate from the numbers that would be expected on the basis of the distribution of the groups over the score categories and the proportions of correct answers within these categories. The differences between the observed and the expected numbers are tested with a chi-square test.

Mellenbergh (1982) has proposed an improved version of this method in which the data are analysed by fitting log linear or logit methods (Fienberg, 1980). An example is given in Table 10.3 below. Respondents from two cultural groups ($j = 1,2$) are divided into five score categories on the basis of the total scores on the test ($i = 1, 2, 3, 4, 5$). For the 10 cells the proportions of correct answers (p_{ij}) are calculated. The item is taken to be unbiased if the proportions of correct answers within the same score category are the same in the two groups ($P_{i1} = P_{i2}$).

For the sake of clarity it should be noted that this condition does not imply that the proportions of correct answers in the groups as a whole have to be the same. This is only the case if the distributions over the score categories are the same in the different groups. Logit models take the natural logarithm of the ratio of (proportions of) correct and incorrect responses as a point of departure for the analysis. The logit model corresponding to an unbiased item is:

$$\ln [p_{ij}/(1 - p_{ij})] = C + S_i,$$

in which C is a parameter for the overall item difficulty and S_i stands for the main score category effect (see also Mellenbergh, 1985). The fit of the model is indicated with a G^2 value which is asymptotically chi-square distributed.

As to item bias, a difference can be made between uniform bias and nonuniform bias. Uniform bias means that the p_{i1}-values are higher or lower than the p_{i2}-values in all score categories or, in terms of the logit model, that for a good fit an additional parameter (G_j) is needed, indicating the main effect of the group membership. If the model with this additional parameter does not fit the data either, the bias is called nonuniform, meaning that the difference between p_{i1} and p_{i2} varies per score category. In this case a good fit is only achieved by adding a parameter ($SG)_{ij}$ to the model, indicating the score category × group membership interaction effect.

A serious weakness of conditional item bias models is that if the test contains a large number of biased items, the measure of the ability level used in classifying subjects into score categories will also be biased. This can mean that some biased items are not classified as such, and that some unbiased items are erroneously classified as biased. Van der Flier, Mellenbergh, Adèr, and Wijn (1984b) therefore developed an iterative logit procedure. Briefly, this method involves removing biased items from the test (or, more accurately, not counting them in determining the total score) so that the number of items removed increases by one with each successive iteration. At the end of the first iteration the most biased item is removed from the test, at the end of the second iteration the *two* most biased items, etc. Items eliminated at an early stage may be included again

TABLE 10.3

Proportions of Correct Answers per Score Category in Two Cultural Groups. Example of a Biased Item (the Item is Biased against Group 2).

Score category		Group membership	
		($j = 1$)	($j = 2$)
0–11	($i = 1$)	.34	.27
12–15	($i = 2$)	.51	.31
16–19	($i = 3$)	.71	.52
20–23	($i = 4$)	.79	.56
24–29	($i = 5$)	.94	.49

at a later stage. The algorithm is terminated if, at the end of the iteration, one of the following conditions arises: the prescribed number of iterations has been performed or the maximum chi-square of the set of unbiased items is below the critical value.

The iterative logit procedure appears to be very efficient in detecting biased items. The results of simulation studies (Van der Flier, Mellenbergh, & Adèr, 1984a) and studies in which item bias was induced experimentally (Kok, 1982; Kok, Mellenbergh, & Van der Flier, 1985) suggest that the iterative procedure is a substantial improvement on the non-iterative one and that the method is relatively insensitive to real differences in trait level between groups. The iterative logit method has been applied in cross-cultural research (Van der Flier, 1983; Poortinga & Van der Flier, 1988) and more specifically for the analysis of test data of various immigrant groups in The Netherlands (Kok, 1988; Te Nijenhuis & Van der Flier, 1994; Pieters & Zaal, 1991). Kok (1988), especially, has given attention to the problems surrounding the explanation of statistical bias. Three research strategies are distinguished:

1. *post hoc* inspection of statistically biased items, looking for striking features that can be related to well-known differences between the groups;
2. defining specific item qualities and investigating the association between bias and these qualities over the items; and
3. experimental studies in which item characteristics are varied and the consequences for the degree of bias of these items are studied.

While this combination of strategies has certainly led to a clearer picture of the causes of item bias, the conclusion has to be that it is generally not possible to indicate beforehand, on the basis of item characteristics, which items will turn out to be biased against specific groups. Kok's study on item bias in the CITO achievement test at the end of primary education with respect to Turkish and Moroccan pupils in The Netherlands provides a good illustration of this point. Kok formulated three general hypotheses to explain statistical item bias in this test. These hypotheses concerned a lower level of proficiency in the Dutch language, a lower personal working speed, and a lack of test-taking skills. Based on these hypotheses, expectations were formulated with respect to the critical features of biased items. The hypothesized critical features were: complexity of the question, numbers of difficult words and sentences in the question itself and in the response alternatives (in connection with the lower proficiency in Dutch), rank number in the order of administration (personal working speed) and deviance of chosen (wrong) alternatives (test wiseness). Next, 2×2 tables were set up of numbers of biased and unbiased items with and without a specific feature. For features chosen on the basis of the language proficiency hypothesis, the expected relationship was found in one-third of the cases. The hypothesis about differences in working speed was not supported at all. The hypothesis about differences in test wiseness was only supported for the Turkish pupils.

Another contingency table method for the detection of biased items that has been the focus of much recent research is the Mantel–Haenszel (MH) method (Mantel & Haenszel, 1959), extended by Holland and Thayer (1988). This method is used at the Educational Testing Service (ETS) as the primary DIF detection device. The basic data used in this method are in the form of s (score level) $\times 2$ (group) $\times 2$ (item score) contingency tables, and the null DIF hypothesis tested is that the odds of getting an item right at a given score level is the same in both groups across all score levels. The MH statistic provides a χ^2 test of significance. The MH statistic is efficient, conceptually simple and relatively easy to use. A disadvantage, as compared with the logit method just discussed, is that it is less suitable for detecting non-uniform bias. For a description of the MH method and the way it is used at ETS we refer the reader to Dorans and Holland (1993).

Opinions differ about the importance of item bias research. According to some investigators (Humphreys, 1986; Schmitt, 1989) the possible contribution of this kind of research to the solution of the problem of the weak position of minority groups on the labour market is relatively small and is detracting attention from the real problem, which is the cause of the differences in criterion performance between different cultural and ethnic groups. On the other hand it can be noticed that psychometrically oriented journals such as the *Journal of Educational Measurement* have paid considerable attention to this subject, both to the evaluation and improvement of detection methods and to the application of these methods to existing ability and achievement tests. Whether this attention is in proportion to the results that might be expected is difficult to say and would seem to be dependent on the progress made in the explanation and prediction of statistical item bias on the basis of the content and formal characteristics of the items. At any rate, one might legitimately conclude that item bias has become a regular topic in modern test theory and that item bias research has made a clear contribution to the development of theories in the field of psychometrics. As to the practical consequences of item bias for the use of tests, Hofstee et al. (1990) conclude that if a small number of biased items are found in a test, its applicability is decreased since it is difficult to correct for this bias. However, since corrections are possible, at least in principle, and the effect of item bias on total test scores is usually small, finding some biased items does not mean that the test cannot be used at all. If a test has not been analysed for item bias its applicability is likewise limited.

A relatively recent contribution to the discussion about the impact of item bias and measurement bias in general comes from Millsap (1995). This author has shown that if a test is unbiased in a measurement sense (defined as invariance in the relationship between the test or the test items and the latent variable to be measured) this will usually mean that the test is biased in a predictive sense, and vice versa. The implications of this duality for group differences research have not yet been fully discussed, but may require a reinterpretation of common empirical findings in this field.

2.3.3 Deviant score patterns

The bias detection approaches that have been discussed up to this point are based on groups identified in advance. This limitation may not always be justified. Minority groups may not originate from culturally homogeneous backgrounds, and for first and second generation immigrants different degrees of adaptation to the majority culture are to be expected. However, methods have been developed in which the requirement of comparability of test performances is applied at the individual level. These methods are more or less complementary to item bias methods. The same data matrix is used, but the focus is on the individual persons instead of the individual items.

The basic idea is that an analysis of score patterns on the items may help to identify the individuals and groups for which test scores have a different meaning. Measures have been developed to quantify the degree to which score patterns deviate from expected score patterns in reference groups, reflecting also the degree to which the total test scores can be compared with the scores in these reference groups. In this area, too, a distinction can be drawn between methods based on latent trait models (Drasgow, 1982; Levine & Rubin, 1979; Wright, Mead, & Draba, 1976) and methods in which total scores on the test are used as ability estimates (Van der Flier, 1980; Tatsuoka & Tatsuoka, 1982), see also Molenaar and Hoijtink (1990) and Meijer (1994). Among the terms in use are deviance scores, aberrance scores, (in) appropriateness scores and person fit scores.

As to practical applications, the detection of deviant score patterns presents the same problems as the detection of item bias and some more besides. In the first place, large reference groups and substantial numbers of items are required for the estimation of item and person parameters. In the second place, finding that a score pattern deviates from an expected score pattern does not offer a direct explanation for a difference in construct validity. Finally, a separate analysis of the score pattern is required for each individual involved. As to this last point, it can be expected that the increasing use of computers for the administration of tests will make it much easier to carry out pattern analyses as a standard routine.

3 DISCRIMINATION WITHIN ORGANIZATIONS

Insufficient information is available to answer the question of whether minorities have the same opportunities as equally qualified majority group members in work organizations in The Netherlands. While several studies have been carried out at both governmental and municipal level, only basic administrative information (distributions over jobs, job turnover percentages, etc.) have become available (Abell & Menara, 1986; Meloen & Hessels, 1985; Vriesema & Kruyt, 1986). Some qualitative information is available with respect to co-operation with Dutch colleagues.

In the US discrimination *within* organizations is also subjected to legal procedures (see for instance Latham & Wexley, 1981). If it can be shown that the career opportunities of members of minority groups within the organization deviate substantially from those of the majority, the employer has to show that the difference did not result from discriminatory practices. If promotion decisions are based on performance evaluations this means that the employer has to prove that the same promotion rules have been applied for the different groups and that the performance evaluations are valid and related to relevant work aspects. These requirements are more or less in line with the requirements applying to selection decisions.

3.1 Distribution across job levels

Information about the distribution of minority groups across job levels can be based on a publication by Ankersmit et al. (1989) in which, on the basis of a sample of 10 municipalities in The Netherlands, job level information was reported for both minorities and the majority group. It appears that the vast majority of the Turkish and Moroccan men and women in The Netherlands occupy jobs classified as simple or very simple. Only a small percentage of Dutch men and women perform work within these categories; most have jobs classified as complicated work. Surinamese and Antillian men and women occupy an in-between position, and are closer to the Dutch majority group than to the Turkish and Moroccan minority groups.

An explanation for the differences in job levels may partly be found in the differences in education between the various groups. Three-quarters of Turkish and Moroccan men and women have only been to primary school, while this is true for only

12% of the Dutch sample. At the same time, however, it can be shown that considerable differences in job level are found at the same educational level.

A second factor connected with differences in job level may be knowledge of the Dutch language. For jobs requiring more than just routine labour, knowledge of the Dutch language is an important condition. In this respect Surinamese and Antillians have an advantage over other minority groups. The educational system, the media and the situation in their home countries have provided them with information about the Dutch language and Dutch culture and society.

3.2 Turnover

Like selection and promotion, job turnover requires special attention in relation to the position of minority groups. A study carried out for the Ministry of Social Affairs and based on information from 107 organizations in The Netherlands (Verweij, Muus, & Van Eekert, 1990), shows that the proportion of minorities among workers who have left the organization is higher than would be expected on the basis of their share in the work population (16% versus 8%). This is especially true for the more problematic types of dismissal (forced dismissal, termination of temporary contracts and rejection because of unfitness for work). Clear differences can be seen between different ethnic groups. Collective dismissals have played a minor role in the last few years for both the majority and minority group members. Forced individual dismissals form a greater part for minorities (10% versus 6%). Voluntary resignations are the more frequent form for majority group members (60% versus 44%).

Further analysis of 17 of the personnel files shows that dismissals occur relatively frequently at lower job levels where minority group members are overrepresented. However, even after matching for job level, age, sex and shift work, differences are found, in the sense that minority group members more often leave the organization on the basis of forced individual dismissals, termination of temporary contracts and unfitness for work.

As to this last factor, a study by Aarts et al. (1981) showed that apart from age the physical load of the work is the most important cause in termination because of unfitness. It would seem that older Turkish and Moroccan workers suffer from the consequences of years of physical labour under less favourable work conditions (Reubsaet, 1990). Physical problems are often coupled with psychosocial problems for which Dutch physicians, pychologists and social workers do not have an adequate remedy (Meijs, 1989). Moreover, placement in other jobs is usually difficult because of the low level of schooling.

4   MEASURES

The foregoing has given an overview of the position of minorities on the labour market and within work organizations. The overall picture for minorities is not a rosy one; a relatively high number of unemployed, overrepresentation in lower level jobs, heavy physical labour and a high percentage of dismissals. Much attention has been given to the possibility of discrimination in selection, especially through the use of psychological tests. In this connection, various methods to detect test and item bias have been discussed. Of course, this kind of research is only one of the possible actions that might be taken to reduce the possibility of discriminatory practices.

In The Netherlands there is no general agreement about the question of which (combinations of) measures are required to improve the opportunities for minorities on the labour market and within organizations (Reubsaet, 1990). Points of discussion are the role of government, the responsibilities of employers and unions, and the need for further legislation in this field. Opinions also differ about the role that (organizations of) minorities should play in this discussion, at least implicitly. These different points of view have led to a large variety of recommendations for action and policy.

The diversity of positions often reflects a difference in view on the causes of the disadvantaged position of minorities. Categorization of these views may therefore lead to some order in the actions and measures recommended and provide a suitable starting point for an evaluation. Bovenkerk (1990) draws a distinction between five types of explanations, attributing the lag in

socio-economic development to (i) insufficient adaptation to Dutch society, (ii) discrimination within Dutch society, (iii) a world order founded on racism, (iv) inadequate development of the ethnic groups' own cultural potential and (v) the development of a system of ethnic stratification in which ethnic minorities constitute a "subclass". For a detailed discussion of these five theoretical perspectives we refer the reader to the publication by Bovenkerk. The distinction will be used here to structure the discussion of the various actions and policy measures.

1. Based on the idea of insufficient adaptation, it might be expected that additional training and schooling are seen as part of the solution. Both language and general knowledge courses (Bolle et al., 1988; De Haan, 1988; LCT, 1989; see also Perdue, 1987) and training in specific skills matching the requirements of the Dutch labour market can be brought to mind. Training directed at application and selection procedures (see for instance Reynaert, 1988), and programmes to create traineeships and special jobs to acquire work experience also belong to this category.

    An example of a successful project focusing on additional training is the project "Promotion and integration through re-education in The Netherlands" (PION), which aimed at the placement of minority group members in staff and middle management jobs in commercial and non-profit organizations by means of a special training course in the field of informatics (Van Leest & Bleichrodt, 1989). The course was directed at unemployed, but relatively highly educated, minority group members (preferably at college or university level). In addition to the course in informatics, the programme included training sessions in social skills, preparing the candidates for application and selection procedures and the real-life work situation. Finding traineeships and jobs for the candidates was also part of the project. One year after the completion of the project it could be concluded that 90% of the candidates had found paid work, virtually always in jobs where automation was a major element.

2. Measures intended to reduce the possibility of discrimination of minorities on the labour market and within work organizations may focus on selection and promotion decisions or on dismissals. The distinction made between direct and indirect discrimination has relevance within this context.

Direct discrimination can be reduced by (securing compliance with) fair application of rules for selection, promotion and dismissal. Formalizing the selection procedure reduces the possibility of arbitrariness in connection with the treatment of job applicants. Apart from the advantage that the validity of the selection interview is raised by this, the structuring of the interview is a good example. Training and coaching of those entrusted with the selection of job applicants may also be an effective way to prevent discrimination. Unfortunately, it appears that any change of attitude following such courses and training sessions often has a temporary character. Refresher courses seem to be needed to bring about a permanent change in attitude; in practice it will often not be possible to organize this. From a somewhat different angle, the training of selectors does not focus primarily on reducing discriminatory tendencies, but on informing those involved in the selection procedure about the cultural background of applicants from minority groups and about behavioural patterns following from this. In contrast with the approach described under (1), which tries to further the adaptation and integration of minority groups into majority culture, this kind of training tries to guarantee some degree of understanding of the minority group's culture on the part of the selector. These types of training courses do appear to be effective (Abell, 1988). In connection with this, a study carried out for the Ministry of Social Affairs and Employment in The Netherlands should be mentioned (Hooghiemstra et al., 1990). This study argues forcefully for a better tuning of the recruitment channels of employers to the

search channels of minority group members looking for jobs.

Indirect discrimination can be reduced by a careful analysis of selection procedures, selection instruments and appraisal systems, to check whether equal suitability goes with equal opportunities. The evaluation procedures that can be followed by psychologists have received ample attention in the foregoing.

A legal framework to prevent discrimination has only partly been effected in The Netherlands. The first article of Chapter 1 of the Constitution (Revision, February 1983) says that "All persons in The Netherlands must be treated equally in equal cases. Discrimination on the grounds of religion, philosophy of life, political views, ethnic background, sex or on any other grounds is not allowed". The elaboration of this in a "General Law on Equal Treatment" has not been effectuated as far as ethnic minorities are concerned.

A clear rejection of both direct and indirect discrimination has been laid down in the professional code of psychologists (NIP, 1976) and is an official part of the personnel policy employed by the government, municipal organizations and large industries in the Netherlands.

3. Racism stands for the theory of inferiority or superiority of people on the basis of their (supposed) ethnic background (Bovenkerk, 1990). Assumptions based on racism find expression in many ways, for instance in the way employees react to colleagues from minority groups (see earlier in this chapter). This chapter has given scant attention to the boundaries of, and theory around, concepts such as prejudice, stereotyping and racism. This self-imposed restriction does not only follow from its focus on the psychology of work, but also from the fact that it is not possible to treat all aspects of discrimination in a single chapter. For a more theoretical overview the reader is referred, for instance, to Dovidio and Gaertner (1986).

Information about and the exposition of racist views and behaviour are seen as ways to oppose racism. Abell (1991) has described three examples of effect studies related to these types of measures. The results were inconsistent: information (through an exposition) appeared to have a positive effect; special lessons (at primary schools) and enhancing expertise (of the police, with respect to dealing with members of minority groups), however, did not.

With respect to the diagnosis of racism the Test Screening Commission (see earlier in this chapter) deserves mention. This commission, which had the task of screening the 20 most frequently used psychological tests in The Netherlands, did not limit itself to psychometric bias, but also judged the tests on their racist or ethnocentric content. An (explicitly) racist content was defined as a content that was bound to be experienced as insulting by members of minority groups; the term "ethnocentric content" was used in cases where the test author had shown insufficient awareness of the fact that the testee might belong to a minority group. The conclusion of the study was that none of the tests contained items with an explicitly racist content. Examples of ethnocentricity, however, were found quite often, especially in verbal tests and personality questionnaires.

4. The idea that the socio-economic progress of immigrants is not primarily a matter of adaptation to the new (majority) culture, but of the realization of their own potential on the basis of their own cultural tradition, was inspired by the success of Jewish, Japanese and Chinese immigrants in the US. The degree to which this line of thought is also realistically applicable to minority groups in contemporary Dutch society is a question that we will not attempt to answer here. Information about the success of ethnic entrepreneurs within certain market sectors (Atlas Foundation, 1991) would seem to be relevant within this context. An important consequence of this perspective is that policy makers should be aware of the danger that an overly patronizing approach, directed towards adaptation to the majority culture, may have the effect of denying minority groups sufficient opportunities to develop initiatives of their own.

5. Affirmative action or positive discrimination is seen by many people as an important means by which to breach the structural social and economic inequality between minorities and majority group members. By appointing minority group members to other than low-level, blue-collar jobs the factual inequality is reduced and examples are created for others. Of course, positive discrimination also has disadvantages. The risk of failure in the better job is larger, and the reactions of colleagues who were selected ordinarily may adversely affect the work performance of candidates who were given such preferential treatment.

The policy of preferential treatment of minorities adopted by the Dutch government and a number of municipalities in The Netherlands has already been mentioned. As for industry, a common effort to create jobs for minorities was agreed on in 1987. This commitment, however, did not result in a substantial improvement in the situation. In 1990 the government therefore discussed the possibility of further measures. This resulted in a new law in 1994 that obliges companies to strive for a working force whose composition is proportionate to the composition of the labour force in The Netherlands. A register of the numbers of minority group members in the personnel has to be kept, and detailed plans have to be presented to Regional Employment Exchange Offices. The implementation of this law has so far been less than entirely successful.

It is difficult to indicate which of these different approaches to the solution of the disadvantaged position of minorities in the labour market and within work organizations can be expected to contribute the most. For the near future, affirmative action by government and industry may well produce the best results. It can also be noted that a number of instruments to enforce affirmative action remain almost unused. This is the case, for instance, in so-called contract compliance, an arrangement often applied in the US and Canada, which stipulates that in awarding contracts to private companies the government takes their efforts to employ members of minority groups into account. In The Netherlands, non-discrimination clauses in contracts, permits and subsidy agreements are seldom used (Elich & Maso, 1984). Whether such actions, which go against usual practice in the Dutch corporative economy, are justified in practice is a matter that will have to be decided by politics, in the light of the (rather meagre) results which have been achieved so far.

NOTE

1. Especially in American jurisdiction it is interpreted as such. In the USA an employer must prove that he/she is using valid selection tools (and does not discriminate) whenever it is found that the selection ratios of two groups differ. This is known as the 80% rule: the selection ratio of the group with the lowest ratio may not be less than 80% of the one of the group with the highest ratio (Equal Employment Opportunity Commission, 1978).

REFERENCES

Aarts, L., Bruinsma, H., & Emanuel, H. (1981). Determinanten van WAO-toetreding: een eerste verkenning. *Economisch Statistische Berichten, 66,* 1132–1138.

Abell, J.P., & Menara, A. (1986). *De positie van etnische minderheden aan de Universiteit van Amsterdam.* Amsterdam: Instituut voor Sociale en Bedrijfspsychologie.

Abell, J.P. (1988). *Evaluatie van de training selectievaardigheden voor de gemeente Amersfoort.* Amsterdam: Instituut voor Sociale en Bedrijfspsychologie.

Abell, J.P. (1991). *Racisme, vooroordeel en discriminatie. Bestrijding door beïnvloeding van de meerderheid met niet-juridische middelen.* Amsterdam: Universiteit van Amsterdam.

Angoff, W.H. (1982). Use of difficulty and discrimination indices for detecting item bias. In R.A. Berk (Ed.), *Handbook of methods for detecting test bias.* Baltimore: The Johns Hopkins University Press.

Angoff, W.H., & Ford, S.F. (1973). Item-race interaction on a test of scholastic aptitude. *Journal of Educational Measurement, 10,* 95–106.

Ankersmit, T., Roelandt, Th., & Veenman, J. (1989).

Mindeerheden in Nederland. Statistich Vademecum 1990. Den Haag: SDU.

Arvey, R.D. (1979). Unfair discrimination in the employment interview: Legal and psychological aspects. *Psychological Bulletin, 86,* 736–765.

Arvey, R.D., & Faley, R.H. (1988). *Fairness in selecting employees* (2nd ed.). Reading, MA: Addison-Wesley.

Bartlett, C.J., & O'Leary, B.S. (1969). A differential prediction model to moderate the effects of heterogenous groups in personnel selection and classification. *Personnel Psychology, 22,* 1–17.

Bass, A.R., & Turner, J.H. (1973). Ethnic group differences in relationships among criteria of job performance. *Journal of Applied Psychology, 57,* 101–109.

Bereiter, C. (1975). Individualization and inequality. *Contemporary Psychology, 20,* 455–456.

Berry, J.W. (1972). Radical cultural relativism and the concept of intelligence. In L.J. Cronbach & P.J.D. Drenth (Eds.), *Mental tests and cultural adaptation.* Den Haag: Mouton.

Bigoness, W.J. (1978). Effect of applicant's sex, race and performance on employer's performance ratings: Some additional findings. *Journal of Applied Psychology, 61,* 80–84.

Bolle, T., Melis, J. van, Timman, Y., & Verhallen, S. (1988). *Nederlands op de werkvloer (voortgangsrapport).* Amsterdam: Universiteit van Amsterdam, Instituut voor Algemene Taalwetenschappen.

Borman, W.C. (1978). Exploring upper limits on reliability and validity in job performance ratings. *Journal of Applied Psychology, 63,* 135–144.

Bovenkerk, F., & Breuning-van Leeuwen, E. (1978). Rasdiscriminatie en rasvooroordeel op de Amsterdamse arbeidsmarkt. In F. Bovenkerk (Ed.), *Omdat zij anders zijn. Patronen van rasdiscriminatie in Nederland.* Meppel: Boom.

Bovenkerk, F. (1990). Modellen van sociale mobiliteit. In H.B. Entzinger & P.J.J. Stijnen (Ed.), *Etnische minderheden in Nederland.* Meppel: Boom.

Brislin, R.W., Lonner, W.J., & Thorndike, R.M. (1973). *Cross-cultural research methods.* New York: Wiley.

Camstra, H. (1985). *Pekon, een Pascal-programma voor CDC-computers (Cyber).* Subfaculteit Psychologie, RU, Groningen.

Cascio, C. (1976). Turnover, biographical data, and fair employment practice. *Journal of Applied Psychology, 61,* 576–580.

Cattell, R.B. (1940). A culture-free intelligence test, Part I. *Journal of Educational Psychology, 31,* 161–179.

Cattell, R.B. (1963). Theory of fluid and crystallized intelligence: A critical experiment. *Journal of Edcuational Psychology, 54,* 1–22.

Chan, J. (1976). *Is Raven's Progressive Matrices test culture-free or culture-fair? Some research findings in Hong Kong context.* Paper presented at the Third International Conference of the International Association for Cross-Cultural Psychology, Tilburg, Netherlands.

Cleary, T.A. (1968). Test bias: Prediction of grades of negro and white students in integrated colleges. *Journal of Educational Measurement, 5,* 115–124.

Cole, N.S. (1973). Bias in selection. *Journal of Educational Measurement, 10,* 237–255.

Cox, J.A., & Krumboltz, J.D. (1958). Racial bias in ratings of basic airman. *Sociometry, 21,* 292–299.

Darlington, R.B. (1971). Another look at "culture fairness". *Journal of Educational Measurement, 8,* 71–82.

Deregowski, J.B. (1979). Lack of applied perceptual theory: The case of engineering drawings. In L. Eckensberger, W. Lonner, & Y.H. Poortinga (Eds.), *Cross-cultural contributions to psychology,* Lisse: Swets & Zeitlinger.

Dorans, N.J., & Holland, P.W. (1993). DIF detection and description: Mantel–Haenszel and standardization. In P.W. Holland & H. Wainer (Eds.), *Differential Item Functioning.* Hillsdale, NJ: Erlbaum.

Dovidio, J.F., & Gaertner, S.L. (Eds.) (1986). *Prejudice, discrimination and racism.* Orlando, FL: Academic Press.

Drasgow, F. (1982). Choice of test model for appropriateness measurement. *Applied Psychological Measurement, 6,* 297–308.

Drenth, P.J.D. (1989). Psychological testing and discrimination. In P. Herriot (Ed.), *Assessment and selection in organizations.* Chichester: Wiley.

Drenth, P.J.D., & Sijtsma, K. (1990). *Testtheorie; Inleiding in de testtheorie en zijn toepassingen.* Houten: Bohn Stafleu Van Loghum.

Dyer, P.J. (1970). *Effect of test conditions on negro-white differences in test scores.* Doctoral dissertation, Columbia University.

Elich, J.H., & Maso, B. (1984). *discriminatie, vooroordeel en racisme in Nederland.* Den Haag: Ministerie van Binnenlandse Zaken.

Equal Employment Opportunity Commission (1978). Uniform Guidelines on Employee Selection Procedures. *Federal Register, 43,* 38290–38315.

Eurostat (1996). *Migration statistics 1996.* Luxembourg: Statistical Office of the European Communities.

Evers, A., & Lucassen, W. (1991). *DAT'83. DifferentiëleAanleg Testserie. Handleiding.* Lisse: Swets & Zeitlinger.

Feuerstein, R. (1972). Cognitive assessment of the socioculturally deprived child and adolescent. In L.J. Cronbach & P.J.D. Drenth (Eds.), *Mental tests and cultural adaptation.* Den Haag: Mouton.

Feuerstein, R. (1979). *The dynamic assessment of retarded performers.* Baltimore: University Park Press.

Fienberg, S.E. (1980). *The analysis of cross-classified categorical data.* Cambridge, MA: MIT Press.

Flier, H. van der. (1980). *Vergelijkbaarheid van individuele testprestaties.* Lisse: Swets & Zeitlinger.

Flier, H. van der. (1983). Some applications of an iterative method to detect biased items. In J.B. Deregowski, S. Dziurawiec, & R.C. Annis (Eds.). *Expiscations in cross-cultural psychology.* Lisse: Swets & Zeitlinger.

Flier, H. van der, Mellenbergh, G.J., & Adèr, H.J. (1984a). Een onderzoek naar de effectiviteit van de iteratieve item bias detectie methode bij groepen met een verschillend treknivo. *Tijdschrift voor Onderwijsresearch, 9,* 61–70.

Flier, H. van der, Mellenbergh, G.J., Adèr, H.J., & Wijn, M. (1984b). An iterative item bias detection method. *Journal of Edcuational Measurement, 21,* 131–145.

Ford, J.K., Kraiger, K., & Schechtman, S.L. (1986). Study of race effects in objective indices and subjective evaluations of performance: A meta-analysis of performance criteria. *Psychological Bulletin, 99,* 330–337.

Gorsuch, R.L. (1983). *Factor analysis.* Hillsdale, NJ: Lawrence Erlbaum.

Gross, A.L., & Su, W.H. (1975). Defining a "fair" or "unbiased" selection model: A question of utilities. *Journal of Applied Psychology, 60,* 345–351.

Gulliksen, H., & Wilks, S.S. (1950). Regression tests for several samples. *Psychometrika, 15,* 91–114.

Haan, D. de (1988). Cognitive academic skills: An attempt to operationalize the concept. In G. Extra & T. Vallen (Eds.), *Ethnic minorities and the acquisition of Dutch as a second language.* Dordrecht: Foris Publications.

Haefner, J.E. (1977). Sources of discrimination among employees: A survey investigation. *Journal of Applied Psychology, 62,* 265–270.

Hakstian, A.R., & Vandenberg, S.G. (1979). The cross-cultural generalizability of a higher-order cognitive structure model. *Intelligence, 3,* 73–103.

Hamner, W.C., Kim, J.S., Baird, L., & Bigoness, W.J. (1974). Race and sex as determinants of ratings by potential employers in a simulated work-sampling task. *Journal of Applied Psychology, 59,* 705–711.

Heneman, R. (1983). *The relevance of supervisory ratings to measures of more "ultimate" criteria: A meta-analytic investigation.* Paper presented at the Fourth Annual Industrial/Organizational Psychology and Organizational Behavior Graduate Student Convention, Chicago.

Hofstee, W.K.B., Campbell, W.H., Eppink, A., Evers, A., Joe, R.C., Koppel, J.M.H. van de, Zweers, H., Choenni, C.E.S., & Zwan, T.J. van der. (1990). *Toepasbaarheid van psychologische tests bij allochtonen.* Utrecht: Landelijk Bureau Racismebestrijding. LBR-reeks nr. 11.

Holland, P.W., & Thayer, D.T. (1988). Differential item performance and the Mantel-Haenszel procedure. In H. Wainer & H.J. Braun (Eds.), *Test validity.* Hillsdale NJ: Erlbaum.

Holland, P.W., & Wainer, H. (Eds.) (1993). *Differential Item Functioning.* Hillsdale, NJ: Erlbaum.

Hooghiemstra, B.T.J., Kuipers, K.W., & Muus, Ph.J. (1990). *Gelijke kansen voor allochtonen op een baan? Werving- en selectieprocessen op de arbeidsmarkt voor on- en laag-geschoolden.* Amsterdam: Vakgroep Sociale Geografie van de Universiteit van Amsterdam.

Hudson, W. (1960). Pictorial depth perception in sub-cultural groups in Africa. *Journal of Social Psychology, 52,* 183–208.

Hudson, W. (1967). The study of the problem of pictorial perception among unacculturated groups. *International Journal of Psychology, 2,* 89–107.

Humphreys, L.G. (1986). An analysis and evaluaiton of test and item bias in the prediction context. *Journal of Applied Psychology, 71,* 327–333.

Hunter, J.E., & Hunter, R.F. (1984). Validity and utility of alternative predictors of job success. *Psychological Bulletin, 96,* 72–98.

Hunter, J.E., & Schmidt, F.L. (1976). Critical analysis of the statistical and ethical implications of various definitions of test bias. *Psychological Bulletin, 83,* 1053–1071.

Irvine, S.H. (1969a). Figural tests of reasoning in Africa. *International Journal of Psychology, 4,* 217–228.

Irvine, S.H. (1969b). Factor analyses of African abilities and attainments: Constructs across cultures. *Psychological Bulletin, 71,* 20–32.

Irvine, S.H. (1979). The place of factor analysis in cross-cultural methodology and its contribution to cognitive theory. In L. Eckensberger, W. Lonner, & Y.H. Poortinga (Eds.), *Cross-cultural contributions to psychology.* Lisse: Swets & Zeitlinger.

Jahoda, G. (1977). In pursuit of the emic-etic distinction: Can we ever capture it. In Y.H. Poortinga (Ed.), *Basic problems in cross-cultural psychology.* Amsterdam: Swets & Zeitlinger.

Jahoda, G. (1983). The cross-cultural emperor's conceptual clothes: The emic-etic issue revisited. IN J.B. Deregowski, S. Dziurawiec, & R.C. Annis (Eds.), *Expiscations in cross-cultural psychlogy.* Lisse: Swets & Zeitlinger.

Jansen, A. (1979). *Ethiek en praktijk van personeelsselektie.* Assen: van Gorcum.

Jensen, A.R. (1980). *Bias in mental testing.* London: Methuen.

Jong, J.E. de, & Kaplan, H. (1962). Some differential effects of race of raters and ratee on early peer ratings of combat aptitude. *Journal of Applied Psychology, 46,* 370–374.

Jöreskog, K.G. (1971). Simultaneous factor analysis in several populations. *Psychometrika, 36,* 409–426.

Jöreskog, K.G., & Sörbom, D. (1984). *Lisrel VI. Analysis of linear structural relationships by maximum likelihood and least squares methods. User's guide.* Uppsala: University of Uppsala, Department of Statistics.

Kirchner, W.E. (1960). Predicting ratings of sales success with objective performance information. *Journal of Applied Psychology, 44,* 398–403.

Kok, F.G. (1982). *Het partijdige item.* Masters thesis, Psychologisch Laboratorium, Universiteit van Amsterdam.

Kok, F.G. (1988). *Vraagpartijdigheid.* Doctoral dissertation, Universiteit van Amsterdam.

Kok, F.G., Mellenbergh, G.J., & Flier, H. van der. (1985). Detecting experimentally induced item bias using the iterative logit method. *Journal of Educational Measurement, 22,* 295–303.

Kraiger, K., & Ford, J.K. (1985). A meta-analysis of ratee race effects in performance ratings. *Journal of Applied Psychology, 70,* 56–65.

Kroeger, E. (1980). Cognitive development in the acculturation of migrant children: The role of training in the assessment of learning ability. *International Review of Applied Psychology, 29,* 105–118.

Krosse, H. (1991). Aanpak minderhedenbeleid in RBA-verband. Interview in: *Arbeidsmarktbeleid en personeelsbeleid voor voorkeursgroepen bij de overheid, 9,* 2–4.

Landelijk Coördinatie Team (1989). *Ontwikkelings- en ondersteuningsplan PBVE '89/90.* Utrecht: Landelijk Coördinatie Team.

Landy, F.J. (1989). *Psychology of work behavior.* Belmont, CA: Wadsworth.

Latham, G.P., & Wexley, K.N. (1981). *Increasing productivity through performance appraisal.* Reading, MA: Addison-Wesley.

Lautenschlager, G.J., & Mendoza, J.L. (1986). A step-down hierarchical multiple regression analysis for examining hypotheses about test bias in prediction. *Applied Psychological Measurement, 10,* 133–139.

Leest, P.F. van, & Bleichrodt, N. (1989). *PION-A Promotie Informatica Omscholing in Nederland voor Allochtonen, Eindverslag 1988/1989.* Amsterdam: Vrije Universiteit.

Levine, M.V., & Rubin, D.B. (1979). Measuring the appropriateness of multiple choice test scores. *Journal of Educational Statistics, 4,* 269–290.

Linn, R.L. (1973). Fair test use in selection. *Review of Educational Research, 43,* 139–161.

Linn, R.L. (1978). Single-group validity, differential validity and differential prediction. *Journal of Applied Psychology, 63,* 507–512.

Lonner, W.J., & Berry, J.W. (Eds.) (1988). *Field methods in cross-cultural research.* Beverly Hills: Sage Publications.

Lord, F.M. (1980). *Applications of item response theory to practical testing problems.* Hillsdale, NJ: Erlbaum.

Lord, F.M., & Novick, M.R. (1968). *Statistical theories of mental test scores.* Reading, MA: Addison Wesley.

Mantel, N., & Haenszel, W. (1959). Statistical aspects of the analysis of data from retrospective studies of disease. *Journal of the National Cancer Institute, 22,* 719–748.

Meijer, R.R. (1994). *Nonparametric Person Fit Analysis.* Doctoral dissertation, Free University, Amsterdam.

Meijs, J. (Red.) (1989). *De buitenlandse patiënt.* Bunnik: Bureau Voorlichting Gezondheidszorg Buitenlanders.

Mellenbergh, G.J. (1972). An investigation of the applicability of the Rasch model in different cultures. In L.J. Cronbach & P.J.D. Drenth (Eds.), *Mental tests and cultural adaptation.* Den Haag: Mouton.

Mellenbergh, G.J. (1982). Contingency table models of assessing item bias. *Journal of Educational Statistics, 7,* 105–118.

Mellenbergh, G.J. (1985). Vraag-onzuiverheid: Definitie, detectie en onderzoek. *Nederlands Tijdschrift voor de Psychologie, 40,* 425–435.

Mellenbergh, G.J., & Linden, W.J. van der. (1981). The linear utility model for optimal selection. *Psychometrika, 46,* 283–293.

Meloen, J.D., & Hessels, A.J.J. (1985). *Kleur verkennen: Een inventariserend onderzoek naar de gemeente Den Haag als werkgever van autochtonen en allochtonen.* Den Haag: Commissie Aanpak Racisme en Discriminatie.

Millsap, R.E. (1995). Measurement invariance, predictive invariance and the duality paradox. *Multivariate Behavioral Research, 30,* 577–605.

Millsap, R.E., & Everson, H.T. (1993). Methodology review: Statistical approaches for assessing measurement bias. *Applied Psychological Measurement, 17,* 297–334.

Ministerie van Binnenlandse Zaken (1990). *Overheid & arbeidsmarkt.* Den Haag: Ministerie van Binnenlandse Zaken.

Molenaar, I.W., & Hoijtink, H. (1990). The many null distributions of person fit indices. *Psychometrika, 55,* 75–106.

Muchinsky, P.M. (1986). Personnel selection methods. In Cooper, C.L. & Robertson, I. (Eds.), *International review of industrial and organizational psychology.* London: Wiley.

Niemöller, B., & Sprenger, C.J.A. (1977). *Procrustiese rotaties; subprogramma procrustus rotate.* Technisch Centrum, Universiteit van Amsterdam.

Nijenhuis, J. te, & Flier, H. van der. (1994). *Het allochtonenproject: Cross-culturele vergelijkbaarheid van de GATB 1002–B.* Utrecht: Nederlandse Spoorwegen/Amsterdam: Vrije Universiteit.

NIP (1976). *Beroepsethiek voor psychologen.* Amsterdam: Nederlands Instituut van Psychologen.

Oppler, S.H., Campbell, J.P., Pulakos, E.D., & Borman, W.C. (1992). Three approaches to the investigation of subgroup bias in performance measurement: Review, results and conclusions. *Journal of Applied Psychology, 77,* 201–217.

Ord, I.G. (1970). *Mental tests for pre-literates.* London: Ginn & Company.

Perdue, C. (Ed.) (1987). *Second language acquisition by Turkish and Moroccan adults.* Tilburg: Katholieke Universiteit Brabant, Subfakulteit Letteren.

Petersen, N.S. (1976). An expected utility model for "optimal" selection. *Journal of Educational Statistics, 1,* 333–358.

Petersen, N.S., & Novick, M.R. (1976). An evaluation of some models for culture fair selection. *Journal of Educational Measurement, 13,* 3–29.

Pieters, J.P.M., & Zaal, J.N. (1991). Culturele bias in de Nederlandse Politie Intelligentie Test: Waar psychologie eindigt en beleid begint. In H. van der Flier, P.G.W. Jansen, & J.N. Zaal (Eds.), *Selectieresearch in de praktijk.* Lisse: Swets & Zeitlinger.

Plake, B.S., & Hoover, H.D. (1979). An analytical method of identifying biased items. *Journal of Experimental Education, 48,* 153–154.

Poortinga, Y.H. (1971). Cross-cultural comparison of maximum performance tests: Some methodological aspects and some experiments with simple auditory and visual stimuli. *Psychologica Africana,* Monograph, Supplement, 6.

Poortinga, Y.H. (1975). Limitations on inter-cultural comparison of psychological data. *Nederlands Tijdschrift voor de Psychologie, 30,* 23–29.

Poortinga, Y.H., & Flier, H. van der. (1988). The meaning of item bias in ability tests. In S.H. Irvine & J.W. Berry (Eds.), *Human abilities in cultural context.* Cambridge: Cambridge University Press.

Poortinga, Y.H., & Malpass, R.S. (1988). Making inferences from cross-cultural data. In W.J. Lonner & J.W. Berry (Eds.), *Field methods in cross-cultural research.* Beverly Hills: Sage Publications.

Pulakos, E.D., White, L.A., Oppler, S.H., & Borman, W.C. (1989). Examination of race and sex effects on performance ratings. *Journal of Applied Psychology, 74,* 770–780.

Raven, J.C. (1960). *Guide to the standard progressive matrices.* London: H.K. Lewis.

Reubsaet, Th. (1990). Arbeidsmarkt en arbeidsbestel. In H.B. Entzinger & P.J.J. Stijnen (Eds.), *Etnische minderheden in Nederland.* Meppel: Boom.

Reynaert, W. (1988). *Arbeidsmarktperspektief voor allochtonen.* Assen: Van Gorcum.

Roe, R.A. (1983). *Grondslagen der personeelsselektie.* Assen: Van Gorcum.

Roe, R.A. (1988). Personeelsselektie: Modellen en instrumenten. In P.J.D. Drenth, Hk. Thierry, & Ch.J. de Wolff (Red.), *Nieuw handboek arbeids- en organisatiepsychologie.* Deventer: Van Loghum Slaterus.

Sackett, P.R., & DuBois, C.L.Z. (1991). Rater-ratee race effects on performance evaluation: Challenging meta-analytic conclusions. *Journal of Applied Psychology, 76,* 873–877.

Scheuneman, J.D. (1979). A method of assessing bias in test items. *Journal of Educational Measurement, 16,* 143–152.

Scheuneman, J.D. (1981). A response to Baker's criticism. *Journal of Educational Measurement, 18*, 63–66.

Schmidt, F.L., & Johnson, R.H. (1973). Effect of race on peer ratings in an industrial situation. *Journal of Applied Psychology, 57*, 237–241.

Schmitt, N. (1989). Fairness in employment selection. In M. Smith & I.T. Robertson (Eds.), *Advances in selection and assessment.* Chichester: John Wiley.

Schmitt, N., & Lappin, M. (1980). Race and sex as determinants of the mean and variance of performance ratings. *Journal of Applied Psychology, 65*, 428–435.

Sikking, E., & Brassé, P. (1987). *Waar liggen de grenzen? Een casestudy naar rassendiscriminatie op de werkvloer.* Utrecht: Landelijk Bureau Racismebestrijding.

Stichting Atlas (1991). *Buitenlandse restaurants en allochtone ondernemers.* Rotterdam: Stichting Atlas.

Stricker, L.J. (1982). Identifying test items that perform differentially in population subgroups: A partial correlation index. *Applied Psychological Measurement, 6*, 261–273.

Tatsuoka, K.K., & Tatsuoka, M.M. (1982). Detection of aberrant response patterns and their effect on dimensionality. *Journal of Educational Statistics, 7*, 215–231.

Ten Berge, J.H.F. (1986). Rotatie naar perfecte congruentie en de Multiple Groep Methode. *Nederlands Tijdschrift voor de Psychologie, 41*, 218–225.

Terborg, J.R., & Ilgen, D.R. (1975). A theoretical approach to sex discrimination in traditionally masculine occupations. *Organizational Behavior and Human Performance, 13*, 352–376.

Thorndike, R.L. (1971). Concepts of culture-fairness. *Journal of Educational Measurement, 8*, 63–70.

Thurstone, L.L. (1938). *Primary mental abilities.* Psychometric Monograph No. 1. Chicago: The University of Chicago Press.

Triandis, H.C., & Berry, J.S. (Eds.) (1980). *Handbook of cross-cultural psychology. Methodology, Vol. 2.* Boston: Allyn and Bacon.

Uyl, R. den. (1986). *Discriminatie bij uitzendbureaus.* Amsterdam: Subfakulteit Psychologie van de Universiteit van Amsterdam.

Vandenberg, S.G., & Hakstian, A.R. (1978). Cultural influences on cognition: A reanalysis of Vernon's data. *International Journal of Psychology, 13*, 251–279.

Veerman, J., & Vijverberg. C.H.T. (1982). *De arbeidsmarktproblematiek van Molukkers. Een verkennend onderzoek.* Rotterdam: Erasmus Universiteit, Vakgroep Sociologie.

Vernon, P.E. (1950). *The structure of human abilities.* London: Methuen.

Vernon, P.E. (1969). *Intelligence and cultural environment.* London: Methuen.

Verweij, A.O., Muus, Ph.J., & Eekert, P.M. (1990). *Uitstroom van minderheden uit arbeids-organisaties.* Rotterdam: Instituut voor Sociologisch-Evonomisch Onderzoek (ISEO), Erasmus Universiteit.

Vriesema, J.S.E., & Kruyt, G.J. (1986). *Binnenkomen—binnenblijven.* Amsterdam: Bureau voor Beleidsontwikkeling.

Warwick, D.P., & Osherson, S. (Eds.) (1973). *Comparative research methods.* Englewood Cliffs, NJ: Prentice Hall.

Wright, B.D., Mead, R., & Draba, R. (1976). *Detecting and correcting test item bias with a logistic response model.* Research Memorandum, No. 22. Chicago: Statistical Laboratory, Department of Education, University of Chicago.

11

Introducing the Field of Economic Psychology

Theo B.C. Poiesz

1   INTRODUCTION

This chapter focuses on the nature and content of economic psychology as a field of psychology related to, but not overlapping with, organizational psychology. Economic psychology is a relatively new branch of psychology, focusing upon determinants and consequences of decisions under conditions of scarcity. A distinction is often made between the different contexts in which economic decisions can be made: the general economic cultural context or economic order, the national economy, and the market. Economic decision making may be a purely individual matter, or takes place in households or in more formal organizations.

In this chapter economic behavior will be dealt with in a rather general way. Rather than focusing on economic behavior in organizations, an attempt will be made to provide a general description of the field of economic psychology, and to provide examples of research for each of its identified contexts. An inventory is made of possible areas

where economic psychology and organizational psychology may be fruitfully combined.

The title of this chapter suggests that an introduction will be presented to the psychology of individual economic behavior. There are many possible ways for doing so, and there are many economic psychological issues and findings that could and, in fact, should be included in an introductory chapter. However, obvious space limitations do not allow a very broad overview of the field, so that a selection of topics and issues will have to be made. The reader should be aware that such a selection may reflect the author's biases, interests, and personal viewpoints.

Having presented this warning, let us start by delineating the content and the structure of this chapter. First we will define the subject matter of economic psychology, and contrast an economic psychological approach with a more traditional economic approach. Then, considerable attention will be paid to how the analysis of economic behavior can be structured. Examples of empirical studies will be provided for the different structures that can be identified. Finally, some reference will be made to economic behavior in organizations. The latter discussion is intended to show when, and to what extent, economic psychology and organizational psychology can serve as complementary subdisciplines.

In order to avoid confusion it must be noted, at first, that economic psychology is a branch of psychology and not of economics. Practically speaking, this means that an economic psychologist is a psychologist, and not an economist. Sometimes, other terms are being used to designate the field like "behavioral economics", "socioeconomics", and "consumer psychology", but these terms do not adequately nor fully describe the field if we want to emphasize the psychological analysis of economic behavior in general.

If it were for historic reasons alone, economic psychologists cannot "claim" the area of economic behavior. By its very nature, the discipline of economics has dealt with economic behavior from its very beginning, even though the approach was and is quite different from that of economic psychology. Both disciplines focus upon economic behavior, but tend to employ quite different metatheoretical assumptions, theories, and analytical methods. In particular, economists tend to take economic behavior at the aggregate level. They study economic phenomena and processes "at large", that is, without being interested in the behavior of the individuals that make up these aggregate economic phenomena and processes. (There are some notable exceptions. Katona, for example, an economist to whom we will return later, did consider economic behavior at the individual level.) Generally, however, economists employ the so-called deductive approach: they deduce the explanation of behavior from the observed phenomena. For example, in microeconomics the preference for a product is deduced from its market share—the so-called "revealed preference". Psychologists work the other way around, in a more inductive way: they start their analysis at the individual level, emphasize the explanation and prediction with the help of individual socio-economic and psychological variables, and then attempt to aggregate the observed findings to a more general level. Rather than deducing "revealed preference", they make an analysis of possible determinants of the evaluation of alternative products and then conclude whether product or brand preference is based upon actual,

that is, psychological preference. Metaphorically speaking, the economist uses the telescope for studying the universe of economic behavior, while the psychologist employs the microscope. The metaphor clarifies that this is a matter of choice, not of disciplinary superiority. Both economics and economic psychology provide adequate approaches to study economic behavior, and their relationship is better qualified as complementary than as competitive.

The difference between the two disciplines boils down to a different conceptualization or model of man. Traditionally, economics employ a model that is based on rationality, assuming that individuals are perfectly informed about available behavior alternatives and their consequences, that they have perfect foresight, that they maximize utility (maximize outcomes, minimize costs), and that they engage in behavior that is ultimately most rewarding to them. Even though in economics the basic assumption of rationality has been alleviated considerably (see, for example, Simon, 1957 with his notion of "bounded rationality"), the discussion on the rationality concept is hampered by the different approaches to the concept. It is not only a description of behavior; it also describes the mechanisms that underly behavior. Additionally, the function of rationality is not clear. For example, is it only possible to speak of rationality when the maximum possible outcome is reached, or is it rational for a decision maker to be satisfied with a particular outcome that required less effort than the maximum outcome? In the literature, both alternatives are addressed by referring to "*maximizing*" and "*satisficing*" behavior. For a more elaborate discussion of the rationality issue, see Lea, Tarpy, and Webley (1987).

2 ALLOCATIONS UNDER SCARCITY

As the economic approach is not aimed at the provision of psychological explanations of economic phenomena, it does not provide a clear understanding of the reasons why economic behavior takes place. That is why we will introduce the psychological approach to economic behavior.

Economic psychology deals with individual

behavior under conditions of scarcity. Economic psychology is an applied discipline, which means that what is being studied is co-determined by issues and problems in real economic life. It also means that, if necessary, economic psychology will make use of concepts and theories that have been developed in other subdisciplines of psychology.

Scarcity can be said to be one of the most prevalent problematic aspects of the human race's interaction with the environment. In spite of the relative abundance that is a characteristic of many Western economies, there are definite limitations with regard to most—if not all—material and immaterial desiderata. Due to availability constraints, individuals are frequently required to make trade-offs and allocation decisions, given the simple fact that a choice among scarce options can often be made only once. That is, if a choice is possible at all (see Verhallen, 1984).

Trade-offs and decisions take place at different levels. Here we make the somewhat arbitrary distinction between the levels that relate to goals, instruments, and resources. For simplicity sake, let us refer to *goal allocations, instrument allocations*, and *resource allocations*. At the most general level of goal allocations, the decisions and trade-offs refer to the states or conditions an individual strives for. Here trade-offs are made among individual goals which are based upon personal values (see for example Rokeach, 1973), current needs (e.g. Maslow, 1954), and future needs or aspirations (Atkinson, 1958). These goals can be seen as the result of socialization, education, and the cumulation of an individual's idiosyncratic life experiences. Thus, for example, whether a person places a high value on social recognition and esteem may be a matter of cultural background and childhood educational practices. Different individual goals may be in conflict—in which case choices need to be made. For example, a person may place a high value on both social recognition and on personal and economic security. The avoidance of risks may not lead to high recognition, however, which requires the individual to emphasize these goals differently. Choices made at this general level have strong implications for choices made at the lower levels.

At the next level, the level of instrument allocation, trade-offs and decisions are made with regard to the instruments by which personal goals may be obtained. A person who strives for social recognition may attempt to do so, for example, by engaging in conspicuous consumption (large house, large car), by showing altruistic behavior (ostensible charitative spending), or by displaying a high level of social activity. Again, choices made at this level set the constraints for the choices at the next level down: the level of resource allocations.

At the level of resource allocation the question is how the goal instruments are acquired. Here decisions and trade-offs are made with regard to available resources, the most common of which are money, time, and energy (see Foa & Foa, 1980, for an inventory of possible resources). The individual who decided to be highly socially active (at the previous allocation level) may achieve this goal by spending some combination of money, time, and/or physical and mental energy. The same result may be obtained with different combinations of these scarce resources. A person with sufficient financial resources may be inclined to spend relatively more money than time and energy, while a person with a tight financial budget may spend more time for preparing a party and invest a lot of personal effort, including the mental energy of organizing and the physical energy of grocery shopping. The particular combination of resources allocated is not simply a budgetary matter, but is dependent upon subjective preferences as well. These preferences, in turn, depend on how the economic situation is perceived and interpreted by the person. Therefore, two persons with equal budgets of money, time, and energy, may differ with regard to trade-offs and actual spending behavior.

It is obvious that the three allocation levels are mutually related. Goals, needs, and values at the higher levels co-determine allocations at the lower levels. At the same time, limitations at the lower levels set the constraints for allocations at the higher levels.

It may be assumed that the allocation levels are mutually connected through the notion of *expectancy*. It is expected, through decisions at a lower allocation level, that personal goals at a higher level may be met.

There is an endless variety of goals, of instruments, and of resource combinations. They are all characterized by scarcity. Scarcity may be described by referring to three interrelated aspects: a scarce object is (more or less) universally valued, it is subject to availability or quantity constraints, and a particular unit of a scarce resource can be allocated or spent only once.

Parenthetically, apart from the goals, instruments, and resources just mentioned, more recently scarcity is also used in connection with the so-called "new scarcities" resulting from the high rate of industrialization: natural resources and a clean environment (soil, water, and air). Even though these "new scarcities" are undoubtedly important, they will not be the specific focus of interest in the remainder of this chapter.

There are several reasons why it is important to study people's behavior under conditions of scarcity.

The first reason is that scarcity is one of the determinants of individual well-being. Even though it is a popular claim that scarcity (especially the scarcity of money) is unrelated to happiness, there is some apparent asymmetry in the relationship: most individuals would not mind to be less constrained by scarcity (e.g. to have a higher income), but certainly would object against being more constrained (having a lower income). (See, e.g. Poiesz & Von Grumbkow, 1988; Van Praag, 1968.) Therefore, the availability of economic resources is an important basis for economic well-being and a central issue in economic-political policy making. Insight in people's reactions to scarcity may be functional in the formation of adequate economic policy measures.

The second reason why it is important to study behavior under scarcity is that almost all individuals spend a considerable part of their lives being involved in economic activities. Insight in the (lack of) effectiveness and efficiency of these activities may help improve individual and societal economic circumstances. The activities involve making trade-offs, making decisions, acquiring and spending scarce resources, consuming, using, and experiencing the outcomes of the decisions. In doing so, individual persons engage in different roles, simultaneously or consecutively, to handle different types of scarcity in different types of situations. A person may be an entrepreneur, an investor, an (industrial) buyer, a salesperson, a renter, a tax payer, and a consumer making different trade-offs among his/her scarce options.

These trade-offs materialize in several types of economic behavior: setting budgets, planning expenditures, choosing between spending and saving (which applies to money, time, and energy), generic allocations (e.g. a vacation versus a new car), modal allocations (e.g. a full size versus a compact car), and specific allocations (e.g. a Ford versus a Toyota). Of course, the specificity of allocations can be extended to include trade-offs among detailed product or brand attributes. These examples are to clarify that trade-offs relating to different levels of generality or specificity are mutually related. Trade-offs made at a general level largely co-determine the constraints of the more specific trade-offs.

3   BEHAVIOR IN DIFFERENT ECONOMIC CONTEXTS

3.1   The economic context: introduction

Economic psychology concerns the interaction between the individual and his/her economic conditions. This implies that the study of economic behavior involves two basic relationships: the effects of the economic conditions on economic behavior, and the effects of economic behavior on the economic situation. These relationships are visualized in Figure 11.1. (For a more elaborate model of economic psychology, see Van Raaij, 1981.)

Figure 11.1 shows that economic circumstances, or changes in these circumstances, may have a direct or an indirect effect on perception, evaluation, preferences, and economic well-being. The direct effects speak for themselves: a particular economic situation may be perceived as favorable or unfavorable, and changes in the economic situation may be perceived and evaluated correctly or incorrectly. For example, a slight positive or negative change in economic growth may remain unnoticed by most individual persons. This implies that the media serve an important role in

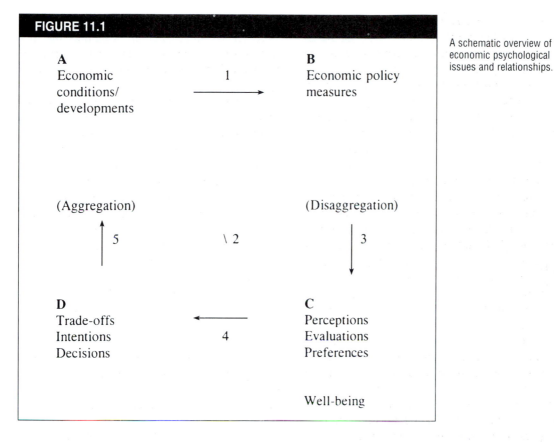

FIGURE 11.1

A schematic overview of economic psychological issues and relationships.

informing the population of economic changes (see, for example, Van Raaij & Gianotten, 1990). We may even hypothesize that the news of an economic change may even have more impact on economic well-being than the perception of the actual financial or material change taking place. For example, the mere announcement that some policy measure will decrease a person's income by 1 or 2 percent may lead to a stronger psychological effect than if the same change were not communicated; the person might not even be aware of a change in spending power.

Economic circumstances or changes therein may have an indirect effect on perception, evaluation, and economic well-being via policy measures intended to influence the economic circumstances. Also these measures may not be perceived and evaluated in the way intended by the policy makers. For example, a collective measure to compensate workers for a loss of buying power due to inflation may be perceived as an actual income increase, which might lead to

(actually unwarranted) increased spending. This is the so-called *money illusion*—the phenomenon that people tend to react to a nominal income increase *as if* it were an actual income increase (Scitovsky, 1976).

Obviously, the perception, interpretation, evaluation, and well-being consequences of economic circumstances and related policy measures will affect economic decisions and trade-offs. These, in turn, will accumulate over persons and influence the economic situation at a more aggregate level.

Even though the schema in Figure 11.1 can be seen as a basic schema of economic psychology, the field limits itself to those aspects that relate to psychological variables and behavior. Some of the phenomena and relationships displayed in Figure 1, such as A, 1, and B are the object of disciplinary approaches such as economics, and administrative and political science.

In the scheme depicted above, economic psychological analyses focus upon the phenomena indicated by C and D, and on the relationships 2, 3, 4, and 5. (Of course, to the extent that policy makers make economic trade-offs themselves, their behavior can be studied by economic psychologists, as in this case they follow the sequence 1–2–C–D–4–5.)

Of central importance to economic analyses are the individual reactions to economic phenomena and developments and to the policy measures that are based upon them, and the way the perceptions and evaluations feed into individual trade-offs and decisions. How individual behavior contributes to or boosts economic phenomena and changes is a joint issue of economics and economic psychology. Relationship 5 involves the aggregation of individual effects and behaviors to macroeconomic phenomena. How aggregated economic phenomena interact to produce economic conditions and changes lies beyond the scope of economic psychology. That is why in Figure 11.1 a boundary is placed between economic and economic psychological issues. This boundary is indicated by the aggregation—disaggregation line. Disaggregation indicates that the economic condition is relevant to the extent that it is reflected in personal economic circumstances. For example, that the general economic situation is improving may not be expressed in more spending power for the group of individuals depending upon social security benefits. For this group, only the disaggregate economic situation counts.

The scheme as presented in Figure 11.1 is limited in several ways. First, it should not be taken as a model of economic behavior. It only indicates what general types of relationships should be considered when designing a model of economic behavior. Second, it is limited in the sense that it does not distinguish between different levels of economic reality. These levels will be discussed briefly here (see also Van Veldhoven, 1981).

At the most general level we speak of the *economic order*. At this level, we refer to the way the economy is organized and institutionalized. In a way, we could refer to the economic culture, including its institutions, routines, rules, and symbols. The economic order may be viewed as transcending national economies. For example, we may speak of the economic order of the

Western industrialized countries. The economic order is so integrated in economic life that individual persons are not likely to identify its existence. For example, the availability of banks, the institute of taxation, the exchange of goods and services for money, the possibility to take out loans, the existence of a stock market are such obvious elements of the economy that their very presence remains beyond discussion. A country's particular economic-political ideology can be taken as a part of the economic order.

The second level of economic reality is the level of the *national economy*. At this level, the focus of interest is upon the relationship between the individual person and the economy. Here economic psychological questions relate to general economic well-being, economic expectations, and the perception and evaluation of, for example, the general economic condition (recession; inflation; (un)employment; economic growth), the income distribution, the tax burden, the level of social security. It is at this level that the individual person is confronted with consequences of the economic decisions made by transnational, national, regional, and local governments. Governments serve a double role here: as an important economic agent, influencing the economic circumstances at the individual or household level, and as a supplier of public goods (e.g. infrastructure) and services (administration, army, police, etc.).

The third level of economic reality is the *market* level. Here, economic psychology pays attention to the interaction between commercial and non-commercial suppliers of goods and services on the one hand and consumers or buyers on the other. Economic psychology at the market level is often referred to as *consumer psychology*, but considering the trade-offs that are made at this level, consumer psychology can be viewed as part of economic psychology.

What is important at this level is the behavior of (potential) buyers of available goods and services, the acceptance of innovations and product adaptations, the processing of market information including the different types of marketing communication, the reaction to price levels and price changes, and the acceptance of the ways in which the products and services are distributed. The trade-offs at this level are manifold and pertain to the scarcity of goods, services, and the scarcity of resources. The market supply side tends to accommodate differences in resource allocation preferences. Compare, for example, the discount stores (less money, more time and energy) and the specialty shops (more money, less time and energy).

With regard to the national economy and the market level decisions are made either individually or by collectivities (households or *decision making units* in organizations). So far, in economic psychological studies, the emphasis has been on individual behavior and not on interactions between individuals. The most likely reasons relate to the complexity inherent in studying decision making in collectivities (see Kirchler, 1988), and in the possibility to study the influences of others even when taking single individuals as the object of analysis (an individual may be asked about the influence of others).

In the following research examples will be provided for each of the three levels of economic reality, in order to give the reader an impression of the type of economic psychological studies. Of course, it will be impossible to give a complete overview of the research that has been done and that is going on. The studies that are referred to

should be viewed as selected examples. Of course, we will not discuss a random sample of studies, but will base the selection upon the amount of attention that the different issues received in the economic psychological literature.

For the sake of clarity, the schematic presentation of economic psychology as displayed in Figure 11.1 will be repeated and adapted to each of the levels of economic reality.

3.2 Economic behavior and the economic order

At the level of the economic order, economic psychology deals with the way economic principles and concepts are acquired, perceived, and evaluated. Even though the economy and most economic concepts may seem rather clear and straightforward, substantial differences among different individuals may exist with regard to their subjective meaning. For this reason, Albou (1984) refers to "naive economics", thereby suggesting a distinction between economists' and lay persons' notions of the economy. It is generally known in psychology that the knowledge of experts differs from that of novices. The former do not only know more, but also display stronger cognitive links among the phenomena (see, for example, McGraw

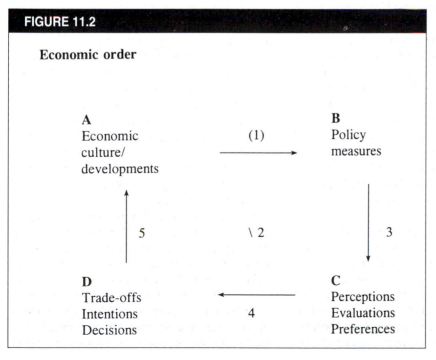

FIGURE 11.2

Economic behavior and the economic order.

& Pinney, 1992). In part, individual differences relate to the economic-cultural background. For example, Gasparski (1990) found that only a very small proportion of Poles treat banking as a form of investment to increase one's capital. Most treat banking as a means of depositing money not yet spent, or as putting aside money for some planned purpose. They do not seem to realize that banks can also be used for making investments. (We should note, however, that this is reported in 1990. Since 1990 the Polish people experienced important economic changes.) By contrast, Roland-Levy (1988) found that "(...) 67% of 14-year-old French children realize that investing money through banking is a way of increasing one's wealth" (p. 422).

Other individual differences relate to age: children progress through different stages when acquiring an understanding of the organization of economic life. The stages make up a process called *economic socialization*. It concerns "the acquisition of economic knowledge, skills, behavior, and attitudes which are relevant to the economic world" (Roland-Levy, 1990, p. 470). In several studies the knowledge and understanding of economic concepts and economic reasoning have been investigated. Age differences appear to exist with regard to the way prices and salaries are determined, with regard to trade-offs between saving, spending, and investing in the case of a financial surplus, how to make (more) money, how to react in the case of shortage (older children would consume less; younger children would work more), attitudes towards poverty and wealth, egoistic versus altruistic motives (see Kirchler & Praher, 1990: 483).

Harrah and Friedman (1990) report that between 11 and 14 years of age the child begins to understand a system of exchanges that include the various economic roles: "The hierarchical organization of work is extended to include more than simply the employer and the employee. With this extension comes an understanding of the differing degrees of wealth and poverty among people in a community. The prestige of an occupation and the classes in society are also taken into account." (p. 497).

Jahoda found some evidence that not until the age of 11 do children begin to understand the concept of profit (Jahoda, 1979). One of the conclusions of a cross-cultural study on economic socialization was that young (pre-adolescent) children conceptualize the economy from the perspective of the *social man*, whereas some older children have shifted the conceptualization to that of the *economic man* (Leiser, Sévon, & Levy, 1990).

Money is one of the concepts that received elaborate attention in studies on economic socialization: the sources of money (Kirchler & Praher, 1990), competence related to money matters (Lea et al., 1987), and different ways of paying (Wosinski & Pietras, 1990).

Let us elaborate here on the notion of money as a central instrument in the economy and as one of the most universal and generally accepted scarce resources.

According to Hanley and Wilhelm (1992): "Money itself holds little value, it is merely a means of exchange. But for a great number of people projection of the emotional psychological value of money far exceeds its relative economic value." (p. 5). Money is valued in its own right, apart from its economic function. For example, people have been found to save money even when there is no goal in saving. The permanent income theory (Friedman, 1957) assumes that people maximize lifetime levels of consumption. This theory implies that older people, after retirement, will reduce saving as, with reducing life expectancy, they need to make less provision for the future. However, retired persons show a tendency to continue adding to their savings until their death (Menchik & David, 1983).

Maital (1982) defines money by the trust people put in its exchangeability. However, money is not easily defined. Snelders, Hussein, Lea, & Webley (1992) view money as a polymorphous concept, whose cognitive status is poorly defined, and whose meaning is merely based upon family resemblance and prototypicality. Wernimont and Fitzpatrick (1972) showed that people attach a variety of symbolic meanings to money including failure and social acceptability. They also found that these symbolic meanings differ among different occupational groups. Goldberg and Lewis (1978) note that the most common of these meanings are the ability to purchase power, security, freedom, love, and personal satisfaction. Belk and Wallendorf (1990) even refer to the "sacred meanings" of money, and discuss the different non-economic functions that money may serve.

A considerable amount of research has been done on the phenomenon of perceptual accentuation in the case of money (see Bruner & Goodman, 1947), better known as the *money size illusion* (Leiser & Izak, 1987). This illusion refers to the overestimation of the size of coins—the differences in coin size estimates are assumed to co-vary with differences in subjective value. It is interesting to note, in this respect, that a currency change in Ireland led to an underestimation of the newly introduced coins (Smith, Fuller, & Forest, 1975). Other indications of the symbolic meaning of money are reflected in the acceptability/unacceptability of money as a gift (Webley, Lea & Portalska, 1983; Cameron, 1989).

Technological developments change the nature of money and the nature of monetary transactions as a distinct economic behavior. Along with these developments, the research interest shifts in the direction of the psychological meaning of (and behavior with regard to) "new" types of money, such as credit cards (see, e.g. Feinberg, 1986), and "new" types of monetary transactions—the automated teller machines (Burgoyne, Lewis, Routh, & Webley, 1992).

In the process of economic socialization, children and adults acquire what may be called economic values—more or less commonly shared ideas about what is generally right and wrong in the economic realm. Several examples may be provided of values that seem specifically economic in nature.

Materialism points at the subjective importance of possessions or wealth to the self (see Dittmar, 1992). A directly related concept is that of conspicuous consumption: the deliberate ostentative display of material wealth in a social context. Braun and Wicklund (1989) provide an interesting theoretical and empirical study on the psychological antecedents of conspicuous consumption. They conclude that there is a compensatory relation between perceived personal deficits and material symbols.

At a more general level, economic values relate to a person's individual ideas with respect to the distribution of wealth and to one's own absolute and relative position in that distribution. To the extent that stable individual differences exist with regard to the adoption of these values we may even speak of economic personality variables. Examples are greed, thrift, altruism, solidarity, the need for economic achievement (see Atkinson, 1958; Gilleard, 1989; McClelland, 1961), or more generally, work ethics (Max Weber's Protestant Work Ethic—see Furnham, 1990), the acceptance of economic risk, and the concept of internal–external locus of control (Rotter, 1966).

These variables may help explain economic behavior, more specifically, the value placed on hard work and on the accumulation of wealth (property), on the perceived relationship between wealth and social recognition, and on risk taking (including entrepreneurial behavior). They may also provide an explanation for what may be called deviant behavior (depending upon the viewpoint taken): economic fraud, theft, and "free riding" (the unjustified use of social benefits).

The issues raised in connection with this level of economic reality correspond to what has been referred to previously as goal allocation. At this level it is determined what is valued by individual persons in their personal economic context. In part, this is a purely individual matter, but partly it is determined by the cultural and social context as well.

Goal allocation determines to what extent a person is willing to invest money, time, and energy to acquire and accumulate money, material possessions, social recognition, leisure time, and the opportunity to engage in a self-determined variety of activities. The question whether a person wants to work full time, more than full time, or wants to combine a part-time job with a study on anthropology is not merely a matter of *ad hoc* personal interests but also of economic values that have been formed in the process of economic socialization. This observation is meant to show that issues at the level of economic order have an impact on the issues that play a role at the level of the national economy. Therefore, we will take it as a step towards the next level.

3.3 Economic behavior and the national economy

Again, for the sake of clarity, we will repeat the schematic presentation of economic psychology as displayed in Figure 11.1, now translated into the phenomena that are relevant at the level of the national economy. See Figure 11.3.

At the level of the national economy phenomena and processes take place that are dependent upon (inter)national economic developments, and upon national (regional/local) political decision making. Essentially, an important part of political decision making has to do with the (re)distribution of income and work, or, in other words, with the (re)distribution of money, time, and energy.

3.3.1 Income and taxation

It should be noted here that, in comparison with organizational psychology, economic psychology approaches income from a somewhat different perspective. The former subdiscipline puts a relatively stronger emphasis on the relationship between income and job characteristics and circumstances, while the latter emphasizes income as a condition for budget allocations, as an indicator of a person's social status, and as a means for satisfying needs (see Van Veldhoven,

1985). The particular way in which income is acquired has received relatively less attention in the economic psychological literature. Income evaluation has been studied by economic psychologists (Poiesz & Von Grumbkow, 1988), and by economists (see, for example, Goedhart, Halberstadt, Kapteyn, & Van Praag, 1977; Kapteyn & Wansbeek, 1985; Van Praag, 1968). The latter developed the so-called *Welfare Function of Income (WFI)*, a lognormal welfare function based upon individual evaluations of income distributions. From this function, subjective well-being associated with a particular income level can be estimated. Income evaluation is partly determined by the income level, and partly by subjective interpretations of that level. In the organizational context perceived equity (the perceived outcome of the comparison of invested and acquired resources, relative to the perceived outcome of this comparison for relevant others) has been shown to be an important determinant of income evaluation. In the broader economic realm other aspects are involved as well, including social comparison effects—one's (perceived) position in the (perceived) income distribution, and subjective evaluations of justice (see Schoormans, 1990; Tajfel, 1978).

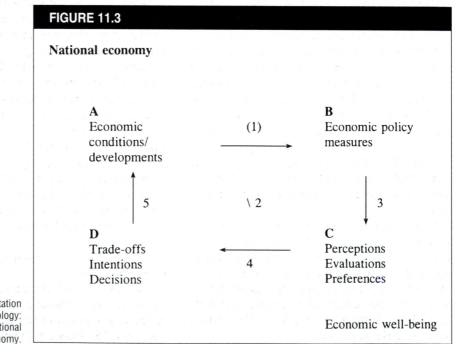

FIGURE 11.3

National economy

A Economic conditions/ developments	(1) ⟶	B Economic policy measures
↑ 5	\ 2	↓ 3
D Trade-offs Intentions Decisions	⟵ 4	C Perceptions Evaluations Preferences

Economic well-being

A schematic presentation of economic psychology: the level of the national economy.

Conceptually related to income evaluation is the evaluation of the tax system and the tax burden. Tax evasion or tax cheating has been a topic receiving considerable interest in the recent economic psychological literature.

Tax structure or schedule and the so-called *fiscal connection* have an effect on the willingness to evade taxes (Baldry, 1986). The term *fiscal connection* refers to the perceived personal share in the financing of publicly provided goods and services. It implies an evaluation of the purposes on which tax money is spent by the government. Also the *perceived* tax burden, independent of the *actual* tax burden, co-determines tax evasion (Becker, Büchner, & Sleeking, 1987). Cowell (1992) reports evidence indicating that tax evasion is influenced by various aspects of perceived inequity.

Tax evasion differs considerably between groups within society (Groenland & Van Veldhoven, 1983). Knowledge that other members of the community evade taxes exerts a strong influence on individual decisions to evade (Porcano, 1988). Cowell (1992) suggests a possible ambiguity in this finding as it may reflect a self-fulfilling prophecy.

Porcano (1988) discusses a number of correlates of tax evasion. Only three variables —honesty, opportunity to evade, and perceptions of tax evasion by others were significant contributors to the explanation of evasion. Several researchers refer to the prospect theory (Kahneman and Tversky, 1979) for an explanation of tax evasion behavior (e.g. Weigel, Hessing, & Elffers, 1987). In the reasoning of the theory, a tax refund may be viewed as a gain, while a tax bill may be viewed as a loss. Extending this argument, tax evasion is less likely in the former than in the latter case. Robben et al. (1992) report several studies supporting the notions put forward by the prospect theory.

Of special interest in this domain of economic psychology are the methodological/ethical problems involved in tax evasion research. Several approaches have been used to acquire tax evasion data without compromising the guarantee of anonymity and privacy of research respondents (see Elffers, Robben, & Hessing, 1992; Elffers, Weigel, & Hessing, 1987).

3.3.2 *Economic confidence*

Economic developments at the aggregate level affect individual economic behavior. For example, economic growth may imply the reduction of financial and material constraints, the generation of favorable employment conditions, and the reduction of economic concerns. Recession and inflation may have contrary effects and may produce considerable subjective economic uncertainty as a by-product. Uncertainty, or a lack of confidence, has been shown to explain variance in discretionary expenditures, that is, after income effects have been accounted for (see Antonides, 1991).

It may be assumed that the lack of confidence and the increasing uncertainty causes people to safeguard future expenditures. For example, Katona (1974) suggests that savings increase during a period of economic recession. A similar reaction has been noted in a period of inflation (Katona, 1975): inflation can be viewed as increasing uncertainty which is expressed in saving—even though saving in a period of a decreasing value of money is essentially irrational from a strictly economic point of view. Here we have to make a distinction, however, between "running" (high level) inflation and "creeping" (low level) inflation. It is obvious that in the case of running inflation saving will not increase as the reduction of monetary value is notable on a daily basis by incessant and substantial price increases.

Economic news that is distributed through the media affects economic expectations, which, in turn, affect economic decisions with regard to spending, saving, credit, and investments (see Van Raaij & Gianotten, 1989). As may be expected, expectations are especially important for discretionary spending, saving and borrowing—thus excluding contractual expenditures and expenditures on necessities. Expectations have a stronger effect if they relate to the evaluation of the development of the household financial situation as compared to the evaluation of the development of the general economic situation (Van Raaij & Gianotten, 1990).

The concept of economic expectations is closely related to that of economic (un)certainty, optimism/pessimism or consumer sentiment (see Katona, 1975; Katona & Mueller, 1968; Mueller,

1963), and confidence. Surveys on consumer sentiment using the *Index of Consumer Sentiment* are taking place on a regular basis in the USA and Western European countries. The Index is a summary measure of the evaluation of the present and future (12 months ahead) household economic and financial situation, and of the judgment whether the time is right to make major expenditures on durable goods. See also Vanden Abeele (1983). Consumer confidence has been found to affect the willingness to spend. Expenditures stimulate economic activity. Thus, indirectly, economic expectations have a positive effect on the economic climate.

Economic expectations have been proven relevant in other domains as well. Bartels, Murray, and Weiss (1988), for example, report on a business equivalent of the Consumer Sentiment Index. They succesfully employed the *Index of Business Sentiment*, based upon business outlooks, output, and new orders, to forecast telecommunications traffic.

Wachtel and Blatt (1990) compared people's self-reported needed and expected income levels. They found that people anticipate making less money than they will actually need. These authors suggested that "(...) in a growth-oriented economy the stimulation of needs may be such as to continuously outstrip people's capacity to fulfill them" (p. 403).

Thus, on the psychological side of the economic coin we find citizens' reactions to the economic conditions, to the changes in these conditions, and to the economic political measures by governments.

Several effects have been the object of economic psychological studies. Reactions to unemployment have been studied by a variety of discplines and, within psychology, by a variety of subdisciplines (organizational, occupational, social, health, abnormal, educational, and economic psychology). In economic psychology, unemployment has a broader meaning than the loss of work and its related benefits, and includes implications for the socio-economic status, for the position in social security, for household financial management, for spending power, and for individual economic perspectives (see, e.g. Furnham, 1988). For an elaborate comparison of employed and unemployed in terms of economic and psychological factors see Van Raaij and Antonides (1991).

3.3.3 Economic well-being

The different psychological effects at this level (income, taxation, employment and unemployment, economic development, present evaluations and future expectations) feed into the subjective evaluation of the overall economic circumstances, which may be referred to as economic well-being. Groenland (1990) defines socio-economic well-being as that part of the individual's universal well-being which is strongly related to money and material means. The concept includes a financial aspect, a material aspect (goods and services), financial security, and a financial independence dimension (Groenland, 1989). Groenland (1990) concludes that with regard to the structure of the concept, material aspects of well-being may be distinguished from immaterial aspects. Of course, well-being or happiness is a general concept that comprises more than socio-economic well-being alone, including one's evaluation of physical and mental health, and the evaluation of the quality of the (social) environment (see Veenhoven, 1984).

It is generally assumed that having more money (income) and goods leads to greater satisfaction or well-being (Wachtel & Blatt, 1990). However, there is considerable evidence suggesting that satisfaction increases by further increases in income are very small once middle-class income levels are reached (Campbell, 1981; Wachtel, 1989). Similarly, "(...) societies that have experienced considerable economic growth cannot in any simple or direct way be characterized as happier or more satisfied than their less rapidly growing confrères" (Wachtel & Blatt, 1990, referring to Boulding, 1985, and Easterlin, 1974).

3.3.4 Financial management

The present level of the individual's position relative to the national economy may be described by referring to the present and the anticipated future economic, financial, and material situation. Thus, economic behavior is described in a very general way.

Consumer behavior at the market level deals with more specific allocations. Before we can address this type of allocation, we have to consider more global allocations that may be subsumed under the heading of household financial management. Here we will treat financial management as the bridge between economic behavior at the level of the national economy and economic behavior at the market level.

In financial management, decisions are made with respect to the categories of spending, saving, debt, and investing.

The term "financial management" suggests some rational aspect to economic budgeting and planning. However, several authors have pointed to the fact that rationality is not necessarily implied. For example, financial management often takes place without a financial plan (Ferber, 1973). Olander and Seipel (1970) report that only a small percentage of people actually plans saving, or adequately plans saving (see also Olshavsky & Granbois, 1979).

Saving, as one of the activities underlying financial management, may be defined in an economic and in a more behavioral way. According to economists, saving refers to that part of income that is not spent. A more behavioral approach to saving is suggested by Wärneryd (1989): "Refraining from consumption during one period in favor of later possibilities for consumption" (p. 516).

Several economic theories have been proposed for the explanation of saving behavior. One of the most well-known theories concerns the life cycle hypothesis (Modigliani & Brumberg, 1954). This theory assumes that persons want to maximize consumption at the same level in all phases of their life. Like the permanent income theory of Friedman (1957) this theory assumes that spending and saving at a particular moment is determined by the present income, by expectations with regard to future income, and by lifetime expectation. Limitations of this theory led to an adaptation called the *behavioral life cycle hypothesis* (Thaler & Shefrin, 1981). These authors add several psychological aspects to account for deviations from a more strictly rational approach to saving. One of these aspects is self-control (in psychological terms: delay of gratification)—regarding the willingness to postpone consumption for the sake of future expenditures. A second adaptation is included in

the notion of so-called *mental accounts*. People may place money in different mental accounts (such as current income, current possessions, future income) and decide about spending and saving in reference to these particular accounts. So the likelihood that some amount of money will be spent or saved is dependent upon its association with a particular mental account. A third related adaptation refers to the framing of money (e.g. as a gain or as a loss) which determines to which account money is allocated.

In the literature a variety of saving motives has been proposed by different authors (see, for example, Lindqvist, 1981; Katona, 1975; Keynes, 1936; Strumpel, 1976; and Sturm, 1983). These include motives relating to specific future consumptive goals, saving for the benefit of others (heritage), and saving to provide for buffer income. Saving may be aimed at synchronizing short run income and expenditures, and saving may be the result of mere routine or habitual behavior. Some saving is purely residual—as the unplanned balance between income and expenditures. Residual saving is the most passive, unintended form of saving behavior and strictly, may be, should not be taken as saving behavior at all.

The financial counterpart of saving is debt and credit. Lea, Webley, & Levine (1993) conclude that "compared with many other kinds of economic behaviour, debt has been relatively little explored from a psychological viewpoint" (p. 85). These authors make a distinction between debt and credit, and simply summarize the difference as follows: "(...) credit implies a willing lender (...) and debt implies an unwilling lender". Their study shows that debt is strongly influenced by adverse economic conditions, and by social and psychological factors. Persons with a high level of debt were found to know more other people in debt, and were less likely to think that the social environment would disapprove if it would know of their debt.

It may be argued whether issues like financial management, saving, credit, and debt should be treated under the general heading of the national economy or under the general heading of market behavior. That no definite allocation to these headings is possible demonstrates that the different levels are not strictly separated and may be seen as partly overlapping. Even though the boundary line is not well-defined, let us cross this boundary anyway at this rather arbitrary point.

3.4 Economic behavior at the market level

3.4.1 Market behavior: introduction

First we will show an adaptation of the general scheme of economic psychological analyses.

When discussing behavior at the market level we refer to suppliers, marketers, consumers, buyers, and users. Individual persons in these roles have to make decisions under restrictions determined by scarcity of allocations and scarcity or resources.

Before considering some of the major behavior issues that have been presented in the literature, it is necessary to point at the fact that the processes and phenomena that take place at this level occur in close association with changes in the general context. For example, the products and services that can be offered to consumers are largely dependent upon technological progress being made. But they are also dependent upon market structures, political decision making, and international trade relations.

In part, consumer psychology can be viewed as the psychological counterpart of micro-economics and marketing. As a consequence, the attention is partly devoted to fundamental research for the development of consumer behavior theories, concepts, and methods. And part of the attention is paid to the possibilities for application in (commercial and non-profit) marketing contexts. Here the emphasis is on the development of concepts and methods specifically geared to practical market and marketing questions, including questions on consumer reactions to products, services, prices, communication, and distribution.

Of the three levels discussed so far, most attention in the literature has been paid to behavior at the market level. At this level, the number of studies on consumer behavior far exceeds the number of studies on behavior related to the other relevant roles mentioned above. Therefore, we will emphasize research issues and developments with regard to consumer psychology, thereby not

FIGURE 11.4

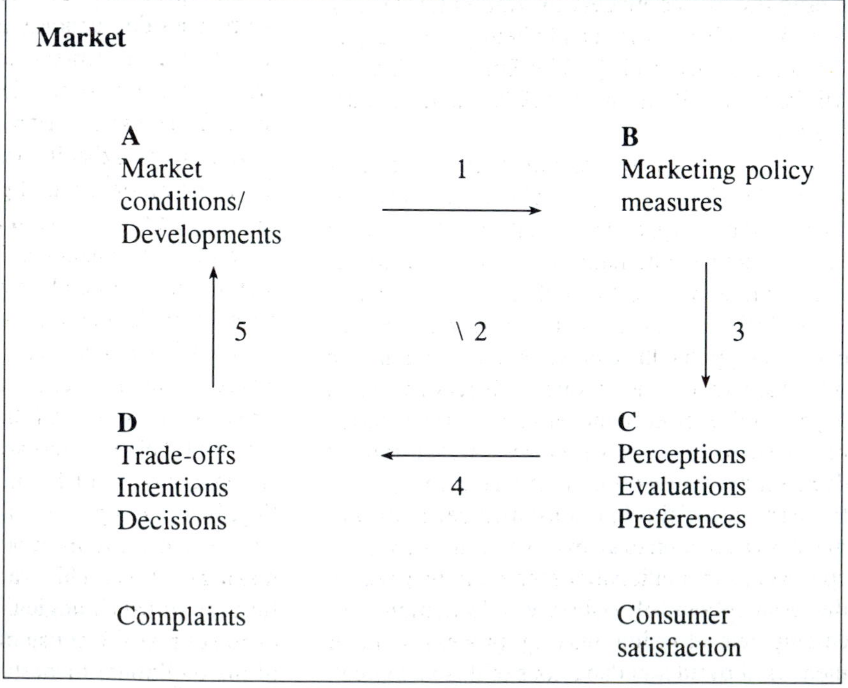

A schematic presentation of economic psychology: the market level.

meaning to suggest, however, that the other behavior areas are less relevant or interesting. Because of the considerable body of research, we will limit ourselves here to some of the general developments in the literature.

3.4.2 Consumer behavior

The earlier studies on consumer behavior focused upon the significance of individual concepts for the analysis of consumer behavior. Examples of these concepts are personality, consumer motivations, and perceived risk (as experienced with regard to product purchases). In the sixties, theory-building in consumer psychology was strongly stimulated by the introduction of so-called comprehensive consumer decision making models. These models attempted to simultaneously include a large variety of factors of potential influence for the explanation of the consumer decision making process. Often, the decision process was dissected into a number of distinct phases with labels such as problem recognition, information search and evaluation, choice, consumption, and evaluation of consumption. These models, introduced in the sixties and seventies, were very elaborate which prevented their validation and practical application. Examples are the models by Andreasen (1965), Nicosia (1966), Howard and Sheth (1969), Engel, Kollat, and Blackwell (1973); Engel, Kollat, and Miniard, (1986), Bettman (1979), and Howard (1989).

The earlier models assumed elaborate consumer decision making in which the consumer was presumed to gather information with regard to his/her purchase alternatives, to critically evaluate this information, and to combine the information to a decision. Even though research showed convincingly that the evaluation and combination of information was strongly dependent upon psychological effects, the basic conceptualization of consumer as a more or less well-informed decision maker was not questioned. Thus, while the early theorizing on consumer behavior was meant as a reaction to an overly rational economic approach, some rationality seemed to reappear in the assumptions of elaborate information processing and decision making processes. Later theories allowed for adaptations of this viewpoint:

also routine problem solving and limited problem solving were included as possible alternatives for the more extensive problem solving views.

Especially in the last two decades, there has been a strong emphasis on consumer information processing. But, as might be expected on the basis of the theoretical developments just indicated, also the extensiveness of information processing was increasingly questioned.

In the more recent literature changes can be noted that point at a departure from the more traditional information processing paradigm. In this respect, the involvement concept has played a major role, as evidenced by hundreds of publications. The concept was (re)introduced in the consumer behavior literature in the mid-sixties (Krugman, 1965), but it was not until the eighties that it started to have a strong influence on consumer behavior research. Involvement is best interpreted as "personal relevance". The initial theoretical approaches to consumer behavior relied too heavily on the (implicit) assumption of high involvement, thereby almost conceiving of the consumer as a caricatural decision maker—a person who makes careful trade-offs between alternatives even in the case of relatively unimportant products. The more recent theoretical approaches do explicitly allow for the possibility that low involvement information processing, product evaluation, and decision making may take place. The most important function of the involvement concept is that it questioned the emphasis on the quasi-rational paradigm of information processing, and that it resulted in a more realistic concept of the consumer. The concept made clear that previous research overemphasized consumer behavior under conditions of high involvement.

Part of the increasing attention for different levels of involvement may be attributed to the stronger emphasis on the external validity of consumer behavior research. The development of early theories, models, and concepts took place in (highly involving!) research conditions that deviated considerably from actual consumer decision making contexts. This was reflected in the limited function of psychological concepts for the explanation of real-life consumer behavior. Adaptation of the traditional theoretical and methodological approaches definitely improved the validity of research.

In addition, some structural market changes emerged that did affect the nature and extent of consumer information processing and decision making. Here we will make a very brief review of the most apparent changes.

For many products and services one of the major developments is the reduction of (perceived) inter-brand quality differences, which are due to technological progress and increasing marketing sophistication. Within a particular product category a variety of different brands tends to be located at the high end of the (perceived) quality continuum, where they are perceived to differ only marginally, if at all. To this we should add that their product knowledge is often insufficient, making it difficult for consumers to correctly identify and judge technical product attributes. Communication on these attributes might be functional but is frequently not fully understood. The combination of these developments increasingly reduce the perceived risk involved in purchase decisions, and reduce the consumer's willingness to carefully and elaborately compare different brands prior to purchase. The resulting consumer behavior seems to be in conflict with the more or less rational view traditionally held (see, e.g. Olshavsky & Granbois, 1979; Poiesz, 1993; Poiesz & Robben, 1993).

This general development may have strong implications for the conceptualization of the consumer decision process. The pre-purchase deliberation and information processing may be much more limited than considered possible thus far; shopping behavior may be more related to its hedonic aspects (shopping for fun) than to risk-prevention, the evaluation of the product after purchase and during consumption may not take place to the extent that actual brand loyalty may develop, and consumers may develop tactics to avoid the unpleasant aspects of decision making (e.g. by implicitly or explicitly delegating the decision to the retailer, to an intermediary agent, or to persons with product experience). More superficial brand images may become more important than brand attitudes based upon factual information on the brand's intrinsic qualities, and

the choice of a service may depend more on the person offering the service than on the actual quality of that service. Product knowledge (true or false) stored in memory may turn out to strongly dominate new incoming information from commercial sources, such as advertising.

In summary, it is argued that consumer behavior and consumer behavior theory will increasingly reflect the changes that can be observed in the market place. It is expected that the difference with the traditional rational point of view will even become larger.

3.4.3 Relationship with organizational psychology

Because this is a chapter in a book on organizational behavior, the latter expectation prompts the question to what extent buyer behavior is more rational in an organizational context. This question seems adequate as organizations tend to put a stronger emphasis on the justification of decisions, and where formalized control reduces the dependency upon psychological idiosyncrasies of individual decision makers. Let us finish this chapter, therefore, by addressing the question of the rationality of organizational economic decisions.

In market economies, organizations, as purposefully structured social entities, are usually referred to as "firms" or "enterprises" of which the most general goal is to provide benefits for its owners and members or employees on a continuous basis. Firms can be viewed as being engaged in economic behavior: they allocate scarce resources in order to obtain the desired outcomes. At a somewhat less general level the outcome often translates into profit as the difference between financial outcomes and costs. Profit expresses the organization's quality of performance, it serves as a return on investment, and it guarantees continuity. In organizations, money may be used to compensate suppliers and investors, to compensate workers, or to invest. Time must be allocated to different activities within the organization and, partly independent of time, energy or effort is divided over the various organizational tasks.

In short, like individuals in other settings, individuals in organizational contexts have to deal with scarcity of instruments and scarcity of resources. For the organization's performance and continuity, the quality of economic behavior is an important matter. Erroneous or inappropriate decisions may imply inadequate, that is, ineffective or inefficient, allocations and might even endanger the organization. Therefore, it is important to understand how allocations are made.

For the description and explanation of economic behavior different types of general theories or models may be employed. The nature of these theories or models is determined, to a large extent, by the disciplinary background from which it emerges. Here a crude distinction can be made between economic and psychological bases of existing theories and models of economic organizational behavior. It is important to briefly discuss the differences between these general disciplinary approaches. As we have described earlier, traditional economic theories have a tendency to focus on rational aspects of behavior. They adopt a rational model of the human race which involves the assumption that decision makers strive for utility maximization, have complete information on behavior alternatives, have clear and stable goals and preferences, and have perfect foresight with regard to decision consequences. An (incidental) deviation from rational behavior is assumed to be a temporary phenomenon by self-correcting tendencies based on performance feedback.

In an organizational context the rational approach would amount to the assumption of profit maximization, perfect knowledge of goal alternatives and alternative routes to these goals, and the absence of intra-organizational conflicts.

In daily life and in empirical studies, the rational model of the human race has proven to be too optimistic with regard to the human race's motivation, capacity, and opportunity to maximize utility.

The same observation can be made with regard to economic behavior in firms. March and Sévon (1988) summarized the criticism on the economic approach to the behavior in firms in two points. The first is that rational decision making is unlikely as it would imply extraordinary (= unrealistic) demands for time and information in organizations; the second point is that while

rationality assumes absence of inter-individual preference differences, intra-organizational conflicts do in fact occur—and even occur quite frequently.

Simon (1979) reports on empirical observations that do not support the strict rational approach to organizational behavior. Earlier, the same author (Simon, 1957) introduced the notion of *bounded rationality*, thereby pointing at limitations in human decision making capabilities which prevent or hamper profit or utility maximization. Cyert and March (1963) elaborate upon the notion of bounded rationality by introducing four organizational concepts suggesting a departure from strict rationality: *quasi-resolution of conflict* (e.g. the adoption of merely acceptable rather than optimal solutions, or the solution of conflict by separating the concerning organizational units with their own "local rationalities"), *uncertainty avoidance* (rather than facing actual uncertainties, the context is restructured or selected so as to guarantee perceived certainty), *problemistic search* (information search is dominated by the occurrence of problems instead of by the functionality of the information *per se*), and *organizational learning* (expressed in, for example, the adapation of organizational goals to actual performance).

Obviously, these tendencies are not limited to business organizations. However, for business organizations they imply that profit maximization or optimization may not be achieved, and that organizations and individuals within organizations do not behave in accordance with rationality principles. In short, the assumption of rationality should not be taken as the basis for a theory of organizational or individual economic behavior.

4 CONCLUSION

In this chapter, economic psychology as a relatively new branch of psychology was briefly introduced by discussing some of the major issues that have been presented in the economic psychological literature. A number of issues could not be dealt with due to space limitations, and some relevant issues could not be dealt with for the simple reason that no sufficient scientific knowledge has been accumulated.

There are a number of areas that are in need of economic psychological research, not only for academic reasons but for practical reasons as well. Economic psychology as an applied field focuses upon a domain of life that is important for many persons in different roles, to which and in which they allocate a considerable part of their resources. Economic aspects of life are strongly associated with economic well-being, both in a positive and negative sense. On the one hand, consumption experiences add to the quality of life; on the other hand, economic limitations affect well-being in more than only one respect. Economic behavior is often a positively oriented type of behavior that contributes to personal and social well-being. Sometimes, economic behavior appears in a more negative form, such as consumer debt, economic fraud, free riding (e.g. unwarranted use of social benefits), shoplifting, and compulsive buying behavior. These different areas are important and should receive more attention.

Too little is known of the economic behavior associated with some particular decision making roles. For example, there is very limited evidence only on the economic decisions made by entrepreneurs and economic political decision makers. Yet, the consequences of decisions made by persons in these roles may be very important. Organizational psychologists and economic psychologists have, to some extent, different interests. But at this point their interests seem to coincide.

REFERENCES

Albou, P. (1984). *La psychologie economique.* Paris: Presses Universitaires de France.

Andreasen, A.R. (1965). Attitudes and consumer behavior: A decision model. In L.E. Preston (Ed.), *New research in marketing.* Berkeley, CA: University of California, Institute of Business and Economic Research, 1–16.

Antonides, G. (1991). *Psychology in economics and business.* Dordrecht, The Netherlands: Kluwer Academic Publishers.

Atkinson, J.W. (1958). Towards experimental analysis of human motivation in terms of motives, expectancies, and incentives. In J.W. Atkinson (Ed.), *Motives in fantasy, action, and society.* Princeton, NJ: Van Nostrand.

Baldry, J.C. (1986). Tax evasion is not a gamble. *Economics Letters, 22,* 333–335.

Bartels, R., Murray, J., & Weiss, A.A. (1988). The role of consumer and business sentiment in forecasting telecommunications traffic. *Journal of Economic Psychology, 9,* 215–232.

Becker, W., Büchner, H-J., & Sleeking, S. (1987). The impact of public expenditures on tax evasions: An experimental approach. *Journal of Public Economics, 34,* 243–252.

Belk, R.W., & Wallendorf, M. (1990). The sacred meanings of money. *Journal of Economic Psychology, 11*(1), 35–69.

Bettman, J.R. (1979). *An information processing theory of consumer choice.* Reading, MA: Addison-Wesley.

Boulding, K. (1985). *Human betterment.* Beverly Hills, CA: Sage.

Braun, O.L., & Wicklund, R.A. (1989). Psychological antecedents of conspicuous consumption. *Journal of Economic Psychology, 10,* 161–189.

Bruner, J.S., & Goodman, C.C. (1947). Value and needs as organizing factors in perception. *Journal of Abnormal and Social Psychology, 42,* 33–44.

Burgoyne, C.B., Lewis, A., Routh, D.A., & Webley, P. (1992). Customer reactions to automated teller machines (ATMs): A field study in a UK building society. In S.E.G. Lea, P. Webley, & B.M. Young (Eds.), *New directions in economic psychology* (pp. 177–195). Brookfield, Vermont: Edward Elgar.

Cameron, S. (1989). The unacceptability of money as a gift and its status as a medium of exchange. *Journal of Economic Psychology, 10*(2), 253–257.

Campbell, A. (1981). *The sense of well-being in America.* New York: McGraw-Hill.

Cowell, F.A. (1992). Tax evasion and inequity. *Journal of Economic Psychology, 13,* 521–543.

Cyert, R.M., & March, J.G. (1963). *A behavioral theory of the firm.* Englewood Cliffs, NJ: Prentice-Hall.

Dittmar, H. (1992). *The social psychology of material possessions: To have is to be.* New York: Harvester Wheatsheaf.

Easterlin, R.A. (1974). Does economic growth improve the human lot? Some empirical evidence. In P.A. David & M. Reder (Eds.), *Nations and households in economic growth.* New York: Academic Press.

Elffers, H., Robben, H.S.J., & Hessing, D.J. (1992). On measuring tax evasion. *Journal of Economic Psychology, 13*(4), 545–569.

Elffers, H., Weigel, R.H., & Hessing, D.J. (1987). The consequences of different strategies for measuring tax evasion behavior. *Journal of Economic Psychology, 8,* 311–337.

Engel, J.F., Kollat, D.T., & Blackwell, R.D. (1973). *Consumer behavior* (2nd Edn). New York: Holt, Rinehart and Winston.

Engel, J.F., Kollat, D.T., & Miniard, P.W. (1986). *Consumer behavior* (5th Edn). Chicago, IL: The Dryden Press.

Feinberg, R.A. (1986). Credit cards as spending facilitating stimuli: A conditioning interpretation. *Journal of Consumer Research, 13,* 348–356.

Ferber, R. (1973). Family decision making and economic behavior. A review. In E.D. Sheldon (Ed.). *Family economic behavior: Problems and prospects* (pp. 29–61). Philadelphia, PA: Lippincott.

Foa, E.B., & Foa, U.G. (1980). Resource theory: Interpersonal behavior as exchange. In K.J. Gergen, M.S. Greenberg, & R.H. Willis (Eds.), *Social Exchange: Advances in theory and research.* New York: Plenum.

Friedman, M. (1957). *A theory of the consumption function.* Princeton, NJ: Princeton University Press.

Furnham, A.F. (1988). Unemployment. In W.F. van Raaij, G.M. van Veldhoven, & K.-E. Wärneryd (Eds.), *Handbook of economic psychology.* London: Kluwer Academic Publishers.

Furnham, A. (1990). The Protestant work ethic: The psychology of work-related beliefs and behaviours. London: Routledge.

Gasparski, P. (1990). Saving motives: Characteristics of saver groups. In S. Lea, P. Webley, & B. Young (Eds.), *Applied economic psychology in the 1990s* (Vol. 1), Exeter: Washington Singer Press, 476–486.

Gilleard, C.J. (1989). The achieving society revisited: A further analysis of the relation between national economic growth and need achievement. *Journal of Economic Psychology, 10,* 21–34.

Goedhart, T., Halberstadt, V., Kapteyn, A., & Praag, B.M.S. van (1977). The poverty line: Concept and measurement. *Journal of Human Resources, 12,* 503–520.

Goldberg, H., & Lewis, L. (1978). *Money madness: The psychology of saving, spending, loving and having money.* London: Springwood.

Groenland, E.A.G. (1989). *Socio-economic well-being and behavioral reactions: A panel study of people drawing benefits from the Dutch National Social Security System.* Doctoral dissertation, Tilburg University: Tilburg University Press, The Netherlands.

Groenland, E.A.G. (1990). Structural elements of material well-being: An empirical test among people on social security. *Social Indicators Research, 22,* 367–384.

Groenland, E.A.G., & Veldhoven, G.M. van (1983). Tax evasion behavior—a psychological framework. *Journal of Economic Psychology, 3,* 129–144.

Hanley, A., & Wilhelm, M.S. (1992). Compulsive buying: An exploration into self-esteem and money attitudes. *Journal of Economic Psychology, 13* (1), 5–19.

Harrah, J., & Friedman, M. (1990). Economic socialization in children in a midwestern American community. *Journal of Economic Psychology, 11* (4), 495–515.

Howard, J.A. (1989). *Consumer behavior in marketing strategy.* Englewood Cliffs, NJ: Prentice-Hall.

Howard, J.A., & Sheth, J.N. (1969). *The theory of buyer behavior.* New York: John Wiley.

Jahoda, G. (1979). The construction of economic reality by some Glaswegian children. *European Journal of Social Psychology, 9,* 115–127.

Kahneman, D., & Tversky, A. (1979). Prospect theory: An analysis of decision under risk. *Econometrica, 47,* 118–140.

Kapteyn, A., & Wansbeek, T. (1985). The individual welfare function. *Journal of Economic Psychology, 6,* 333–363.

Katona, G. (1974). Psychology and consumer economics. *Journal of Consumer Research, 1,* 1–8.

Katona, G, (1975). *Psychological economics.* New York: Elsevier.

Katona, G., & Mueller, E. (1968). *Consumer response to income increases.* Washington DC: Brookings Institution.

Keynes, J.M. (1936). *The general theory of employment, interest and money.* London: MacMillan.

Kirchler, E. (1988). Household economic decision making. In W.F. van Raaij, G.M. van Veldhoven, & K.-E. Wärneryd (Eds.), *Handbook of Economic Psychology* (pp. 258–294). London: Kluwer Academic Publishers.

Kirchler, E., & Praher, D. (1990). Austrian childrens' economic socialization: Age differences, *Journal of Economic Psychology, 11,* 483–495.

Krugman, H.E. (1965). The impact of television advertising: Learning without involvement. *Public Opinion Quarterly, 29,* 349–356.

Lea, S.E.G., Tarpy, R., & Webley, P. (1987). *The individual in the economy.* Cambridge: Cambridge University Press.

Lea, S.E.G., Webley, P., & Levine, R. (1993). The economic psychology of consumer debt. *Journal of Economic Psychology, 14,* 85–119.

Leiser, D., & Izak, G. (1987). The money size illusion as a barometer of confidence? The case of high inflation in Israel. *Journal of Economic Psychology, 8*(3), 347–357.

Leiser, D., Sévon, G., & Levy, D. (1990). Children's economic socialization: Summarizing the cross-cultural comparison of ten countries. *Journal of Economic Psychology, 11,* 591–614.

Lindqvist, A. (1981). *The saving behavior of households.* Doctoral dissertation, The Stockholm School of Economics.

Maital, S. (1982). *Minds, markets, and money: Psychological foundations of economic behavior.* New York: Basic Books.

March, J.G., & Sévon, G. (1988). Behavioral perspectives on theories of the firm. In W.F. van Raaij, G.M. van Veldhoven, & K.-E. Wärneryd (Eds.), *Handbook of Economic Psychology* (pp. 368–404). London: Kluwer Academic Publishers.

Maslow, A. (1954). *Motivation and personality.* New York: Harper and Row.

McClelland, D.C. (1961). *The achieving society.* Glencoe, IL: The Free Press.

McGraw, K.M., & Pinney, N. (1992). The effects of general and domain-specific expertise on political memory and judgment. *Social Cognition, 8,* 9–30.

Menchik, P.L., & David, M. (1983). Income distribution, life time savings, and bequests. *American Economic Review, 73,* 672–690.

Modigliani, F., & Brumberg, R. (1954). Utility analysis and the consumption function: An interpretation of the data. In K.K. Kurihura (Ed.), *Post-Keynesian Economics.* New Brunswick, NJ: Rutgers University Press.

Mueller, E. (1963). Ten years of consumer attitude surveys: Their forecasting record. *Journal of the American Statistical Association, 58,* 899–917.

Nicosia, F.M. (1966). *Consumer decision processes: Marketing and advertising implications.* Englewood Cliffs, NJ: Prentice-Hall.

Olander, F., & Seipel, C.M. (1970). *Psychological approaches to the study of saving.* Urbana-Champaign: University of Illinois.

Olshavsky, R.W., & Granbois, D.H. (1979). Consumer decision making: Fact or fiction? *Journal of Consumer Research, 6,* 93–100.

Poiesz, Th.B.C. (1993). The changing context of consumer psychology. *Journal of Economic Psychology, 14,* 495–506.

Poiesz, Th.B.C., & Grumbkow, J. von (1988). Economic well-being, job satisfaction, income evaluation, and consumer satisfaction; an integrative attempt. In W.F. van Raaij, G.M. van Veldhoven, & K.-E. Wärneryd (Eds.), *Handbook of Economic Psychology* (pp. 570–594). London: Kluwer Academic Publishers.

Poiesz, Th.B.C., & Robben, H.S.J. (1993). Individual reactions to advertising: Theoretical and methodological developments. *International Journal of Advertising, 13,* 25–55.

Porcano, T.M. (1988). Correlates of tax evasion. *Journal of Economic Psychology, 9,* 47–67.

Praag, B.M.S. van (1968). *Individual welfare functions and consumer behavior.* Amsterdam: North-Holland.

Raaij, W.F. van (1981). Economic psychology. *Journal of Economic Psychology, 1,* 1–24.

Raaij, W.F. van, & Antonides, G. (1991). Costs and benefits of unemployment and employment. *Journal of Economic Psychology, 12,* 667–687.

Raaij, W.F. van, & Gianotten, H.J. (1990). Consumer confidence, expenditure, saving and credit. *Journal of Economic Psychology, 11*(2), 269–291.

Robben, H.S.J. et al. (1990). (12 authors of different nationalities in total). Decision frame and opportunity as determinants of tax cheating: An inter-national experimental study. *Journal of Economic Psychology, 11*(3), 341–365.

Rokeach, M. (1973). *The nature of human values.* New York: The True Press.

Roland-Levy, C. (1988). Children's economic socialization: The case of France. In P. Vanden Abeelde (Ed.), Psychology in micro & macro economics. *Proceedings* of the 13th Annual Colloquium of the International Association for Research in Economic Psychology, Belgium, pp. 1–16.

Roland-Levy, C. (1990). Economic socialization: Basis for international comparisons. *Journal of Economic Psychology, 11,* 469–482.

Rotter, J. B. (1966). Generalized expectancies for internal versus external control of reinforcement. *Psychological Monographs, 80*(1), 609.

Schoormans, J.P.L. (1990). *Rechtvaardigheid van sociale zekerheidsuitkeringen.* Doctoral dissertation, Tilburg University, Sociale Zekerheidswetenschappen, nr. 12.

Scitovsky, T. (1976). *The joyless economy.* New York: Oxford University Press.

Simon, H.A. (1957). *Models of man: Social and rational.* New York: Wiley.

Simon, H.A. (1979). Rational decision making in business organizations. *American Economic Review, 69,* 493–514.

Smith, H.V., Fuller, R.G.C., & Forest, D.W. (1975). Coin value and perceived size: A longitudinal study. *Perceptual and Motor Skills, 41,* 227–232.

Snelders, H.M.J.J., Hussein, G., Lea, S.E.G., & Webley, P. (1992). The popymorphous concept of money. *Journal of Economic Psychology, 13*(1), 71–93.

Strumpel, B. (1976). Saving behavior in Western Europe and the United States. *American Economic Review, 65,* 210–216.

Sturm, P.H. (1983). Determinants of saving: Theory and evidence. *OECD Economic Studies,* 147–196.

Tajfel, H. (1978). Social categorization, social identification, and social comparison. In H. Tajfel, (Ed.), *Differentiation between social groups* (pp. 61–76). London: Academic Press.

Thaler, R.H., & Shefrin, H.M. (1981). An economic theory of self-control. *Journal of Political Economy, 89,* 392–406.

Vanden Abeele, P. (1983). The index of consumer sentiment—predictability and predictive power in the EEC. *Journal of Economic Psychology, 3,* 1–17.

Veenhoven, R. (1984). *Data-book of happiness.* Dordrecht, The Netherlands: D. Reidel Publishing Company.

Veldhoven, G.M. van (1981). Economic psychology: A new discipline? *Advances in Economic Psychology,* Heidelberg, Meyn.

Veldhoven, G.M. van (1985). Individueel financieel beheersgedrag. In van Raaij (Ed.), *Jaarboek van de Nederlandse Vereniging van Marktonderzoekers,* 175–208.

Verhallen, T.M.M. (1984). *Scarcity: Unavailability and*

behavioral costs. Unpublished doctoral dissertation, Tilburg University, The Netherlands.

Wachtel, P.L. (1989). *The poverty of affluence: A psychological portrait of the American way of life.* Philadelphia, PA: New Society Publishers.

Wachtel, P.L., & Blatt, S.J. (1990). Perceptions of economic needs and of anticipated future income. *Journal of Economic Psychology, 11,* 403–415.

Wärneryd, K-E. (1989). On the psychology of saving: An essay of economic behavior. *Journal of Economic Psychology, 10,* 515–541.

Webley, P., Lea, S.E.G., & Portalska, R. (1983). The unacceptability of money as a gift. *Journal of Economic Psychology, 4,* 223–238.

Weigel, R.H., Hessing, D.J., & Elffers, H. (1987). Tax evasion research: A critical appraisal and theoretical model. *Journal of Economic Psychology, 8,* 215–235.

Wernimont, P., & Fitzpatrick, S. (1972). The meaning of money. *Journal of Applied Psychology, 56,* 218–226.

Wosinski, M., & Pietras, M. (1990). Economic socialization of Polish children in different macro-economic conditions. *Journal of Economic Psychology, 11*(4), 515–529.

12

Social Indicators

Harry L.G. Zanders

ABSTRACT

Social indicators are a varied set of measures to describe and evaluate social trends in society. In this chapter, origins, different approaches, and leading research projects in the "social indicator movement" are discussed. Some examples of Dutch social reporting are also presented. Furthermore, the social indicator movement is confronted, for theoretical and methodological reasons, with a split between objective and subjective social indicators. As examples, the main research projects of the Organization for Economic Co-operation and Development (OECD) in Paris and the Institute for Social Research (ISR) in Michigan are outlined. Some questions about the macro- and micro-approaches, and especially about the harmonization of "social indicators", are discussed to indicate the social indicator perspective.

It is concluded that an integrated approach has not yet been achieved and that integration and harmonization have still a long way to go. However, a growing need for internationally comparable data and information is stimulating the integration of research processes and procedures.

1 INTRODUCTION

Social systems are complex systems in which many participants try to realize various ideas or objectives by various means. When the system is limited in size and when the number of objectives and means remains restricted and stable, the system can be surveyed. If the system becomes larger and more complex, however, systematic information on its development is desirable. A modern society is such a complex and dynamic system. The number of objectives pursued is particularly large as is the number of means with which persons or groups try to realize their objectives. In addition, the means and objectives are often very changeable. As a consequence, a continuous flow of information is needed to evaluate the dynamics of the social system.

What kind of information is needed to monitor the social system? Where and how can the data be found that offer us a clear and reliable picture of the conditions and processes in society? These questions have long been asked from the perspective of various scientific disciplines. Particularly in economics they have been worked out into operational models (Fox, 1974), where the development of indicators and standards for economic quantities was started. Models were constructed which allowed the mutual relations between the quantities to be studied. These models were developed in the thirties on the basis of the application of mathematics in economics. The rise of the computer after World War II made it possible to tackle and work out more sophisticated models.

Today, such economic models are generally applied at the macro-level. In The Netherlands, this is done by, for example, the Central Planning Office (Centraal Planbureau). They are, however, completely economic in nature, i.e., the factors implied in such a model all refer to economic quantities, such as wage cost, prices of raw materials, and capital costs. Because the economic models describe and analyze only a part of social reality, this approach is necessarily limited. In the sixties and seventies, in particular, the emphasis began to shift from material to more immaterial aspects of social intercourse, the demand for more than just economic information grew. With the help of economic models and, on the basis of presuppositions, the degree to which national production was going to increase, could be calculated. However, these economic models had a limited relevance for non-economic factors. Such non-economic information is needed in order to pursue a sound policy. Therefore, it was necessary to start developing standards with which general social trends could be registered. Such standards are called social indicators. These social indicators are primarily used to describe a social system. The next step is to design models based on these social indicators, in which the mutual relations between the indicators can be analyzed.

Social systems and society have been mentioned several times in this introductory text. It may be concluded that this contribution will emphasize the developments around social indicators at the macro-level. However, there is an increasing demand for indicators at the meso-level that mainly refer to the immaterial output of organizations (Dierkes & Bauer, 1973). Nowadays, questions about environmental protection and total quality management require strategic choices (Harrington, 1994; Stockbauer, 1994). To this end, systematically gathered information that relies on social indicators, about which there is at least some consensus, is necessary. This consensus is needed to guarantee the acceptance of the indicators in the models.

What is meant by social indicators? This is the key issue in the first part of this contribution in which the contents and meanings that are attributed to social indicators in the literature are reviewed. Next, the background and a historical chronology of the interest in social indicators will be considered. Finally, several large international projects will be discussed that demonstrate the activities and applications of the construction of social indicators. Several remarks on a number of discussions about the "state of the art" in the social indicator movement will conclude this chapter.

2   DESCRIPTIONS AND DEFINITIONS

Indicators are used to bridge the gap between theory and empiricism. They play a central role in the process of translating theoretical concepts into empirically observable phenomena; they are the operationalized variables of theoretical concepts (Boesjes-Hommes, 1973; Segers, 1975). A definition of social indicators is given in Bauer's standard work (1966): "Social indicators (are) statistics, statistical series, and all other forms of evidence that enable us to assess where we stand and are going with respect to our values and goals, and to evaluate specific programs and determine their impact".

Three types of indicators can be derived from this very broad description. First, social indicators can be used for the description of systems and trends. Secondly, we can relate them to certain norms or standards for the evaluation of social phenomena. Third, the information that social indicators offer may be used to predict possible future events. The question whether an indicator is descriptive, evaluative or predictive depends on the way in which the indicator concerned is applied. The following example will make this clear. If we use the figure for officially registered labour reserve as an indicator, this unemployment statistic can be looked at in different ways. We can use it neutrally to describe the situation on the labour market. We may also compare the figure with a certain standard, thus making the indicator evaluative in character. Thirdly, we can make statements about other social phenomena, for example, feelings of social exclusion or voting behaviour, using the unemployment rate. This third predictive application demands a theoretical framework that allows us to make connections between social phenomena.

Bauer's definition is only one of many found in the literature. The most important common characteristic of all the descriptions and definitions is that social indicators are considered quantitative standards relating to socially relevant aspects of society. Furthermore, there may be great variations in the demands made on the qualification as a social indicator. Land (1971), in particular, has argued that the term "social indicator" should not be equated with all the forms of statistical information in the social field. He proposes using the term when: (a) the indicators concerned are part of a social system model; (b) when they can be gathered and analyzed at different points in time and can be included in time series; and (c) when they may be aggregated and disaggregated according to levels that the model requires. Land's starting point is a model which

includes social indicators. From this, the informative value of the social indicators can be determined.

Land (1975b) presented his line of reasoning by way of a diagram, that is partly represented here (Figure 12.1). The schematic representation is based on a distinction frequently found in the literature on social indicators, based on the trilogy "input-system-output". In the left-hand column, which refers to the input of the system, two types of indicators are distinguished which refer to factors that can be manipulated by the policy and the factors that are fixed data for the policy, respectively. A corresponding division is found in the last column of the diagram, in which the implementation is indicated.

A further distinction is made between intended effects and non-intended or side-effects.

Land points to the educational process as an example. Input data to be manipulated, which can be changed through policy, may include: financial means, material supplies, manpower. Examples of data that cannot be manipulated are, according to Land, individual abilities, especially intelligence, and family situation. The result consciously selected and realized, the output, is, in that case, school

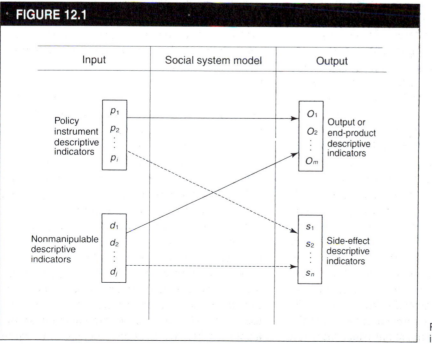

FIGURE 12.1

Relations between indicators.

achievement. As examples of side-effects, Land points to the occupational and income level that individuals may reach, also by means of that education, to a life style and cultural orientation. The information on social processes in a certain field (e.g., education) may be structured with the help of this outline. But it is also clear that the distinctions are relative and are initially determined by the particular perspective on social processes. In many cases, things like occupational level and cultural orientation will certainly not be considered side-effects of education, but rather consciously chosen and intended results.

3 BACKGROUND AND DEVELOPMENTS

The need for information on a wide range of social phenomena and processes is the root of the social indicator movement. Social indicators are the standards by which social phenomena and developments may be described and analyzed. The need to develop social indicators arose particularly in the sixties. It was acknowledged, both in political circles and scientific quarters, that too little information was available to plan and guide social developments. To meet the need for information, new standards needed to be designed, in which not only the quantity but especially the quality of social developments could be expressed. The fields of health care and education are two examples. The quality of those sectors is determined by more than just the number of medical doctors or hospitals and the number of teachers and schools. Different criteria are necessary, with which the qualitative aspects can be recorded and analyzed. The subjective assessments of persons who become involved with certain provisions are especially relevant.

The so-called "social indicator movement" originated in the sixties as a result of the increasing number of activities concerning the registration of social developments. Yet, the origin of the movement to trace and quantify social developments via indicators dates back to an earlier period. The comprehensive 1933 report *Recent Social Trends* of the Research Committee on Social Trends in the USA is generally considered the seminal work.

This committee, formed in 1929 by order of the American president Herbert Hoover, had the task of studying the social consequences of the economic crisis at that time and establishing national priorities. At the same time, an effort was made to sketch an overall picture of the situation, rather than make a series of detailed studies. The emphasis attaining an overall picture of social developments remained a main feature of the social indicator movement. Many of the themes discussed in the report of the committee, led by Mitchell and Ogburn, are still today research themes (Report of the President's Research Committee on Social Trends, 1933). Examples are: changing social attitudes and interests, the family and its functions, changing occupational patterns, women working outside the home, recreation and leisure time, consumer behaviour, welfare activities, and administration and society. This report laid the foundation for the development of social indicators. Until about 1960, however, interest was rather limited.

In the mid-sixties, the trend was resumed by Bauer (1966) with the publication of *Social Indicators*. His research, sponsored by the National Aeronautics and Space Administration (NASA), analyzed the effects of the rapid technological developments on American society, especially of the space programme. Such an approach, based on systematic and integrated research into the direct and indirect effects of the introduction of a new technology, is known nowadays as "technology assessment" or effects research. In this case, the study of possible side-effects of technological developments is emphasized. In his project, Bauer mentioned "second order consequences", i.e., the consequences of certain technological innovations, which are not especially intended or expected. The introduction of the automobile as a means of transport is an example. Only later were radical changes discovered in, for example, the field of recreation, and living environment (suburbanization).

A strong point of Bauer's project is that it was not restricted to the side-effects of technology. Together with Biderman and Gross (1966), he designed a broader programme for measuring social developments and relating them to social objectives. Illustrative of the lack of data is Biderman's contribution which proved that statistical data were available for only half of the objectives formulated by the American government, especially in the field of cultural developments. Such a lack of data makes an evaluation of social developments very difficult. There is, then, little opportunity for rational planning in the social field.

In 1966, the report of the presidential committee on Technology, Automation and Economic Progress was published in the USA. In it, a plea was made for, among other things, the development of a system of social accounts that was to give a more comprehensive and balanced impression of the meaning of social and economic progress, also on the basis of a cost-benefit analysis. Such social accounts were analogous to the usual financial accounting systems. The wish to use social indicators was strongly supported in political circles in 1967, when the so-called "Full Opportunity and Social Accounting Act" was proposed at the initiative of the then Senator Mondale and others. This required the president to present a Social Report to the Congress every year. Also in 1967, *Social Goals and Indicators for American Society* appeared, edited by Bertram Gross and containing several articles contributing to the discussion of social indicators.

In 1968, Sheldon and Moore published *Indicators of Social Change, Concepts and Measurements*, the first publication within the framework of the "Monitoring of Social Change Project" of the Russell Sage Foundation. The study emphasized structural and institutional changes in such fields as population development, leisure time, and the professional population. Next, *Toward a Social Report* was published in 1969 by the Department of Health, Education and Welfare. In this report, a limited number of figures was presented, due to the lack of essential data. This study was an important step in the development of a system of periodical social reports. Various social fields were scrutinized, and the state of knowledge on the progress towards generally accepted objectives was examined. Health, social mobility, physical environment, income and poverty, law and order, education, and participation and alienation were discussed.

We cannot dwell here on the content of these publications and projects. The survey was simply a review of the social indicator movement in the USA. The most important conclusion we can draw from these sixties' publications is that a shift in emphasis took place in the perspective from which social phenomena and changes are viewed. The primacy of economics and technical information on social developments was challenged, because social factors began to play a part in the information process.

This was initially a derivative, "second-order" role, but very soon information on social factors played a more independent role. From that perspective, the measurement and evaluation of social developments should be considered on a par with the analyses of economic and technical developments.

In the seventies, the activities around the development of measures and systems for registering and analyzing social developments were vigorously pursued in the USA. A limited selection from the literature, with a concise characterization follows.

1972: Leslie D. Wilcox and Ralph M. Brooks (Eds.), *Social indicators and social monitoring. An annotated bibliography*. Besides a historical survey and a discussion of social indicators by E. Brooks, an annotated bibliography of more than 600 titles is presented.

1972: Angus Campbell and Philip E. Converse (Eds.), *The human meaning of social change*. This publication, like that of Sheldon and Moore, appears within the framework of the Russell Sage Foundation's Monitoring of Social Change Project. This study advocates the development of subjective indicators, i.e., indicators that proceed from personal valuations and judgements.

1973: Executive Office of the President, Office of Management and Budget, *Social indicators 1973*. The first attempt to present an extensive collection of statistical data for the description of social conditions and developments in the USA. A large quantity of data is presented without comment.

1974: Karl A. Fox, *Social indicators and social theory. Elements of an operational system*. On the basis of concepts and starting points from different social sciences, such as psychology, sociology, economics, and econometrics, an attempt was made to construct operational models. For example, Tinbergen's theory on economic policy is taken as a starting point in building quantifiable systems.

1975: Nestor E. Terleckyj, *Improvement in the quality of life: Estimates of possibilities in the United States, 1974–1983*. An attempt to develop a framework to determine the possibilities for the improvement of the quality of life in the USA. The goal was to explicitly define national objectives and priorities, to determine the progress made towards the objectives, and to determine the cost of achieving those objectives.

1975: Judith Innes de Neufville, *Social indicators and public policy. Interactive processes of design and application*. Apart from an extensive survey of the development of the social indicator movement and the origins of some indicators, e.g., the unemployment figure, De Neufville outlines the political meaning of social indicators and the relation between political decision making processes and the availability of information.

1975: Kenneth C. Land and Seymour Spilerman (Eds.), *Social indicator models*. In 14 articles, various strategies and applications of social indicators are demonstrated. The emphasis is on proving the interrelations between social indicators, whereby the meaning of both replication studies and the design of longitudinal and dynamic strategies are indicated.

1976: US Department of Commerce, Office of Federal Statistical Policy and Standards, and Bureau of Census, *Social indicators 1976*. This is, since 1973, the second collection of statistical data on social conditions and social trends in the USA. No comment is added to the data.

1976: Frank M. Andrews and Stephen B. Withey, *Social indicators of well-being. Americans' perceptions of their life quality*. The starting point of this study is the subjective or perceptual indicators, used to measure the opinions and ideas of the Americans with regard to a large number of social developments.

1976: Angus Campbell, Philip Converse and Willard L. Rodgers, *The quality of American life: Perceptions, evaluations and satisfactions*. As with Andrews and Withey, the emphasis is on the development of subjective indicators. The authors build on Campbell and Converse's work of 1972.

1978: Robert Quinn and Graham Staines, *The 1977 Quality of Employment Survey*. Institute for Social Research, Ann Arbor, Michigan. The first project was in 1969 (Quinn et al., 1971); the second in 1973 (Quinn & Shepard, 1974).

1978: Conrad Taeubner (Ed.), America in the seventies: Some social indicators. In *The Annals of the American Academy of Political and Social Science*, Vol. 435, January 1978. In this publication, the text and comments lacking in *Social Indicators 1976* can be found. More than 20 authors give their opinion on the developments derived from the data of *Social Indicators 1976*.

1979: Kevin J. Gilmartin et al., *Social indicators: An annotated bibliography of current literature*. The bibliography includes 316 entries with sections on key historical works, state-of-the-art reviews, the theoretical and methodological approaches, analysis and reporting of social indicators.

1980: Robert J. Rossi and Kevin J. Gilmartin, *Handbook of social indicators: Sources, characteristics and analyses*.

1980: Alex C. Michalos, *North American social report: A comparative study of the quality of life in Canada and the U. S. A. from 1964 to 1974*, (Vols. 1 and 2).

1980: Alexander Szalai and Frank M. Andrews (Eds.), *The quality of life. Comparative studies*. This study consists largely of workshop papers presented in 1978 at the meeting of the International Sociological Association in Uppsala. The editors chaired the ISA symposium on "comparative studies of life quality" and have assembled in this reader contributions from scholars from a dozen mainly Western and East European countries.

1981: Conrad Taeubner (Ed.), *America enters the eighties: Some social indicators*. In The

Annals, Vol. 453, January 1981. Comments and interpretations are given on the data summarized in the report of the US Department of Commerce: *Social Indicators III*. It is the fourth issue of the *Annals* devoted to the subject of social indicators.

1981: Angus Campbell, *The sense of well-being in America: Recent patterns and trends*. Campbell presents a survey of the nature and distribution of well-being and comments on the significance of that knowledge.

1981: Thomas Juster and Kenneth C. Land, *Social accounting systems: Essays on the state of the art*. A publication, with the papers from a Social Accounting Workshop in 1980, on developing objectives for future work on social accounting and recommendations for achieving them through the evaluation of existing social accounting schemes.

This literature marks the beginning of the social indicator movement. Later on, a continuous stream of publications arose. An overview of these studies can be found by consulting the journal *Social Indicators Research: An International and Interdisciplinary Journal for Quality-of-Life Measurement*, published since 1974.

The increasing need for social information was, of course, not only an American affair. In other countries, many activities were being developed that made the social indicator movement an international undertaking. Since the early seventies, periodical reports have been published by the governments of most of the industrialized countries, in which voluminous quantities of data on recent social developments are summarized. These data are usually grouped around themes that are closely connected to the existing administrative and political fields, like health, education, employment, and social security. Since the beginning of the seventies, such compendiums of statistical data can be found in England (Central Statistical Office, 1970), France (Institute National de la Statistique et des Etudes Economiques, 1974), Germany (Bundesministerium für Arbeit und Sozialordnung 1974), Japan (Economic Planning Agency, 1973), Canada (Statistics Canada, 1973), and The Netherlands (Social and Cultural Report, 1974). A more detailed overview

of the trends in social reporting is presented by Franz Rothenbacher (1993). Analogical to Biderman's (1966) "sociology of societal data" Rothenbacher outlines the national and international approaches in social reporting in western Europe.

International organizations, such as the OECD in Paris and the United Nations in New York, provided the impetus for various international projects. Initiatives have been taken which have led to a number of results. In the United Nations, especially the ideas of Richard Stone—to set up a network of social demographic statistics—has been worked out (United Nations, 1975). The most famous international project was designed by the OECD. In the early seventies, they started a very ambitious programme that, in 1973, resulted in the publication of: *The list of social concerns common to most OECD countries*. We will return to this program in section five.

4 TRENDS IN THE NETHERLANDS

Broadening the concept of "prosperity" to include well-being, the acknowledgement of the one-sidedness of economic factors, the consciously or unconsciously accepted consequences of technological innovations created, in The Netherlands too, a need for new and differently arranged information that might be used for social guidance. In The Netherlands, the first publication within this framework was *Systematische maatschappij informatie* (Systematic social information: Mootz, 1974). This report, published in 1974, was the result of a task force set up in 1971 to investigate the possibilities for systematic social information. A number of objectives, starting points, and possible elaborations were presented. The central theme was the need for a clear theoretical framework that could be interpreted conceptually in only one way and which could order the flood of potential data. The emphasis, therefore, was on a theoretical-methodological discussion of the starting points of systematic social information.

The broad perspective chosen by the task force might create the expectation that a preliminary elaboration in the form of a social report on the

Dutch situation could still take several years. Yet, we see in The Netherlands a development similar to that observed everywhere else: the need for a general theoretical framework is recognized, but at the same time action is initiated.

The Dutch social indicator movement got a boost in early 1974. The government founded the Social and Cultural Planning Bureau (Sociaal en Cultureel Planbureau). As early as 1975, the Bureau published its first and voluminous *Social and cultural report* (Sociaal en cultureel rapport, 1974). The objectives of this were, as formulated in the report's introduction, to describe the state of affairs and developments in the social and cultural domains. It may be coined as a counterpart of the reports published by the Central Planning Office (Centraal Planbureau) in the field of economics.

The 1974 report was the first in a series. In the meantime, the *Social and Cultural Reports* for 1976 to 1996 have been published every two years. These reports not only offer statistical figures, like the American Social Indicators and the English Social Trends, but extensive comments are also given; these are quite descriptive in nature however (Ester & Nauta, 1989). A few Dutch non-governmental publications should also mentioned, in which attempts were made to develop social indicators. Two of these reports are *Satisfaction in prosperity* (Tevredenheid in welvaart) and *Quality of employment, 1977* (Kwaliteit van arbeid: Zanders et al., 1977). For surveys on social indicators by Dutch authors we refer the reader to Swanborn (1974), Mootz (1975), Zanders (1975), Thierry (1977), Van de Lustgraaf and Huigsloot (1979), and Kerkhoff (1988).

5 APPLICATIONS

We will use this section to discuss several large projects in the social indicator movement. First, we will present the OECD-project, which emphasized the initiation of an information system using so-called objective indicators. We will then deal with some American projects in which the development of so-called subjective or perceptual indicators was preferred.

These two entries were chosen, because they illustrate several points with regard to the construction of social indicators which play an important role in the social indicator movement. This is especially the case for the controversial points of view on the validity and reliability of objective versus subjective indicators.

The foundation for the OECD project was laid in 1970, when that organization expressed the view that economic growth was not an aim in itself, but an instrument with which to create better life conditions. In order to determine the life conditions of individuals in their social context, the qualitative aspects of prosperity growth would also have to be considered. First, however, the domain of welfare ("well-being") had to be defined. This formed the first part of a three-phase plan by the OECD's Manpower and Social Affairs Committee. The following phases were distinguished: (I) the choice of subfields and subjects that are components of the concepts of well-being; (II) the construction of measures for the indication of the relevant components; and (III) the actual measurement of the relevant social conditions and their developments.

As a product of the first phase, the now famous *List of social concerns common to most OECD countries* (OECD, 1973) was published. The main objective of the first phase of the social indicators project was to reach a consensus on the aspects and fields that are a part of the general and broad concept of "well-being" or, as it is also called, the "quality of life". Starting from a pragmatic approach, the OECD facilitated a process of consensus forming among the member states on the selection of subfields and subjects. This resulted in the identification of the following eight primary goal areas:

1. health;
2. individual development through learning;
3. employment and quality of working life;
4. time and leisure;
5. command over goods and services;
6. physical environment;
7. personal safety and the administration of justice;
8. social opportunity and inequality.

Within each of these primary goal areas distinctions have subsequently been made in which specific fields of attention ("social concerns") were designated. A "social concern" may be described as an identifiable and definable aim or field which may be of fundamental and direct importance for human well-being. Matters that are of instrumental or indirect importance for welfare do not come under this heading. In the first phase of the OECD project, 24 "social concerns" were distinguished. The following are mentioned by a way of illustration:

Health

- the probability of a healthy life in all phases of the life cycles;
- the impact of health impairments on individuals.

Employment and quality of working life

- the availability of gainful employment for those who desire it;
- the quality of working life;
- individual satisfaction with the experiences of working life.

Social opportunity and inequality

- *the degree of social inequality;*
- *the extent of opportunity for participation in community life, institutions, and decision making.*

In 15 of the 24 fields, more detailed distinctions have been made. These are defined as "subconcerns" or subfields. A more detailed discussion of the subconcerns is beyond the scope of this chapter. The interested reader can find them in the *List of social concerns.*

After defining and formulating the primary goal areas, the fields of attention and the subfields, the first phase of the OECD social indicator project was completed. The second phase aimed to develop a system of social indicators, meant to validly express the level of well-being for each field of attention and to register the changes in those levels over time. During the second phase, there appeared to be the need to revise and amplify the already defined primary goal areas on a

number of points. For example, the fifth subfield, the availability of goods and services, was reformulated as: personal economic situation, and for administration of justice (under subfield no. 7) policy on jurisdiction was substituted. Finally, a new category was added: social environment. The emphasis in this phase was on the development of indicators for the 24 fields of attention.

The accepted indicators have shortcomings and are theoretically weak on many points. Yet, it seems particularly useful that the indicators which have been pragmatically chosen are to some extent useful for policy, even though they are still of a provisional nature. Because of the approach, the right questions relevant to various fields of policy may be raised.

The indicators developed so far nearly all refer to registering factual, objective data. For example, the following indicators were chosen for registering working conditions: (a) the number of fatal accidents in industry, (b) the number of long-term industrial injuries, and (c) the number of short-term industrial injuries. Such standards may indeed say something about the quality of working conditions in industry, but it will be clear that the quality of working life covers a much wider field than what the indicators refer to. This is also discerned by the OECD. Therefore, the possibility of individuals registering the perceptions and experiences of their own situation is referred to. The most important question of the subjective or perceptual indicators comes to the fore. The perceptions and experiences of individuals and groups are a necessary and important component of the social indicator programme according to the approach of the OECD.

The result of policy processes is indeed also expressed in the degree to which persons confronted with the policy experience it as negative or positive. As long as there are no good methodologies and standards available for registering those personal experiences, insight into the effectiveness of the policy will remain limited. Subjective indicators will therefore also have to be included in the OECD programme. The OECD has not yet been able to draw up acceptable approaches for developing such subjective indicators (Barbash,1976; OECD,1974; Portigal,1976). Meanwhile, the social indicators programme of the

OECD was ended with the publication of a statistical compendium in 1986. New developments are now expected from the European Union. But an integration and harmonization in social reporting is still far away (Rothenbacher, 1993).

For a review of the developments in the area of subjective social indicators we shall have to consult other projects or institutions. We will do this by presenting some projects in the USA that aim to measure perceptions, evaluations, and satisfactions.

In nearly every publication on social indicators, the advantages and disadvantages of registering social phenomena via objective or subjective indicators are brought up as points of discussion. Subjective indicators refer to the perceptions, feelings, preferences, attitudes, etc. of individuals. Objective indicators are quantifiable entities that are not based on individual experiences, such as crime, age, and unemployment. Andrews (1974), in particular, argued for avoiding the implicit "bias" that evokes the objective–subjective contrast by using a more neutral terminology. He rightly observed that often, in defining the phenomenon to be quantified, many subjective choice elements play a part in the so-called objective standards. Furthermore, the adjective "subjective" suggests that the indicators are less valid and less useful than those described as "objective". According to Andrews, a clear alternative terminology is not immediately available. As a kind of intermediate solution he proposes replacing "subjective" by "perceptual". Perceptual indicators are therefore based on individual perceptions, feelings, attitudes, etc.

Perceptual indicators play a central role in a number of investigations into the quality of life by the Institute for Social Research (ISR) of the University of Michigan. From the early seventies, the ISR, with the support of the Russell Sage Foundation and the National Science Foundation, has been designing and carrying out research on the quality of life. Two voluminous studies have been published in the meantime in which empirical research on subjective social indicators is reported. In 1976, Campbell, Converse and Rodgers published *The quality of American life: Perceptions, evaluations and satisfactions*. Also in 1976 Andrews and Withey published *Social indicators of well-being. Americans' perceptions of life quality*.

In both projects, individuals were chosen as the unit of research. By means of detailed interviews data was gathered from the respondents who were selected in such a way that they represented a cross section of Americans 18 years of age and older. The contents of both studies are very broad in scope. Explicit attention is paid to, among other things, housing conditions, health, work experience, marriage and family life, personal life and development opportunities. and national government. Both Campbell et al. and Andrews and Withey take the measurements, made by means of perceptual indicators, of the subjective experience of well-being to be explorative. The instruments used will have to be tested in further investigations and analyzed for validity and reliability. This is certainly true when such standards are used in international comparative research.

The Andrews and Withey project (1976) offers the best starting point for an appropriate research strategy developing subjective or perceptual social indicators. That strategy is, briefly, as follows.

As a basis for their study, Andrews and Withey worked out a conceptual model, which is summarized in Figure 12.2. The argument that led to the construction of this model is the following. In every human existence, various subfields or domains can be distinguished, that can be appreciated by means of certain criteria or values. Such domains and criteria may be arranged as schematized in Figure 12.2. Domains may comprise things like: places, things, activities, people, and roles. Criteria may be values, standards, aspirations, objectives, and, put generally, judgements on the output of the domains. The fundamental point now is to capture those domains and criteria in the model that are relevant for the study of populations. Once the scheme is completely filled in, indices may be constructed via aggregation (eventually after weighting) indicating the well-being with regard to certain domains or criteria (E_i. or $E_{.j}$) as well as an index indicating general well-being ($E_{..}$).

First the scheme has to be filled in and then the mutual relations in the scheme are analyzed. The

FIGURE 12.2

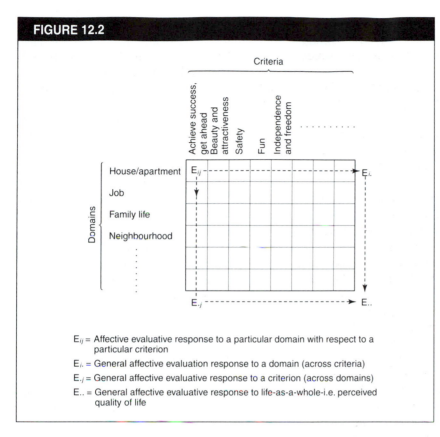

The conceptual model of Andrews and Whitney, 1976.

E_{ij} = Affective evaluative response to a particular domain with respect to a particular criterion

$E_{i.}$ = General affective evaluation response to a domain (across criteria)

$E_{.j}$ = General affective evaluative response to a criterion (across domains)

$E_{..}$ = General affective evaluative response to life-as-a-whole-i.e. perceived quality of life

strategy chosen by the investigators to fill in the scheme is inductive in nature. By means of a study of the literature and former research, and via a number of open interviews, attempts have been made to trace those domains and criteria that can be distinguished in human life. Using this practical procedure, the boundaries of the open system were traced. In this first phase, more than 800 fields ("concerns") were identified. Following a first cluster analysis, in which special attention was paid to mutual overlaps, their number was reduced to approximately 60. Next, more than 100 items were formulated in those fields which functioned as indicators for registering the state of affairs in the different fields. An important part of the study was dedicated to the development and evaluation of standards or indicators that could be used. A discussion of these standards would carry us too far afield, but we will mention a few general conclusions of the two ISR projects. They show that the nearly unlimited number of fields relevant to general well-being can, in fact, be reduced to a

limited number. This is an important conclusion to build on, from that it prevents the discussions and investigations on well-being from being diverted by factors that play a subordinate role. The wide, comprehensive field has now indeed been explored and defined. Of course, these conclusions are only valid at this point in time and only for the American situation. Longitudinal and comparative research will have to prove to what extent such conclusions will remain valid at different times and in different cultures (Cantril, 1965).

Another main conclusion concerns the research instruments developed and evaluated. From the multitude of possible approaches and procedures, a limited number of alternatives can be formulated on the basis of this research that indicate a valid and reliable course for further developments in the field of social indicators.

We have discussed the American projects because, starting at the individual or micro-level, they form a clear contrast with the projects developed by the OECD, in which representatives of national governments try to agree on the elements that make up the concepts "well-being" or "quality of life". This contrast in approach can be characterized as the *individual* versus the *institutional* approach. Both approaches have their restrictions and are one-sided.

The OECD strategy used by institutions and organizations to develop social indicators may run the risk that the indicators selected will be strongly biased. In this strategy, the process of decision making on the choice of fields of attention with regard to well-being, is for the most part, a process in which politicians, scholars and civil servants predominate. They determine the importance of certain facets of society's well-being. There is a big chance that only those aspects that are consistent with the prevailing ideology are thought to be important.

The individual approach may result in a lack of attention to structural factors that have an important influence on the functioning of social systems.

6   RECENT DEVELOPMENTS

The collection and implementation of data about social systems started in the fifties and sixties on the meso-level: specific sectoral domains like health, education, housing, labour, etc. were studied and analyzed. The work of Bauer, in the mid-sixties, introduced and promoted the macro-orientation. In the seventies we saw the development and application of general macro-models for assessing and processing social impacts. However, the strong emphasis on holistic macro-models did not continue in the eighties.

Two kinds of developments were discerned in the last decade: *stabilization* and *diversification*. These changes in orientation occurred for several reasons.

In the first place, the social indicator movement was not based on a generally accepted theoretical framework. Different theoretical perspectives were used to develop and construct societal models. Consensus on the best model was never reached.

Secondly, ideas about the "manageable" or "control" society took on more modest proportions (Beniger, 1986). The holistic and rather idealistic ideas about social planning and the steering of society, so popular and well accepted in the sixties and seventies, were reduced to more limited models and specific sectors.

The positive point of the *stabilization* trend in the social indicator movement is that the ideas of the early seventies resulted in a way of social reporting that is now widely accepted and implemented in most developed nations (Ester & Nauta, 1989; Rothenbacher, 1993). The actual social reports can be considered the children or grandchildren of the earlier efforts, according to Zapf and Glatzer (1987). Modernizing societies are concerned about developing specific sets of social indicators and socio-economic systems (Andorka & Harcsa, 1990). The work on social reporting continues in a more incremental way (Wiegand, 1988).

The *diversification* trend means that the social indicator movement seems to be returning to its starting point in the sixties. The different theoretical and pragmatic orientations of social indicators in the eighties resulted in a decline in the holistic and optimistic ideas to build generally accepted systems based on one paradigm or one grand theory. Now, middle range theories are chosen to introduce different models in specific fields and societal sectors. A review of the recent volumes of *Social indicator research* gives an impression of the selected topics. The various fields of interest and research are: environmental quality, urban renewal, measuring health, happiness, leisure, housing, education, labour market, family planning, and life feeling scales.

Another reason for the trend towards diversification and specialization is based on *economic factors*. In the seventies we saw a serious decline in the economic growth of the developed countries. Therefore, far less political attention was given to the social and welfare dimensions of society. The role of the welfare state was replaced by the market orientated society. This trend has continued since the eighties.

Special attention, finally, has to be given to the role of *new technologies*, based on the rapid developments in micro-electronics and communication systems. An intensive discussion has been initiated about the possible effects of these new technologies on society and organizations (Smits et al.,1987). Several methods and technics have been developed to trace and guide the technology. These approaches are known as: Technology Assessment (TA), Impact Assessment (IA) and Risk Assessment (RA) (Finsterbusch Llewellyn, & Wolff, 1983; Simonse, Kerkhoff, & Rip, 1989). A classification of these assessment methods was presented by Molenaar et al. (1989). According to their classification, Technology Assessment (TA) is used on the strategic level to analyze the long-term effects of the technology in a proactive way. Impact Assessment (IA) analyzes the effects at the tactical level on the middle-long term and in a preventive way. Risk Analyses (RA) analyze the short-term effects on the operational level, to correct the undesired effects. The focus of social scientists is on the social effects of different choices in societal models. They introduced "Social Impact Assessment" (SIA), defined as evaluations of policy alternatives in terms of their estimated consequences (Finsterbusch et al., 1983); environmental scientists introduced their specialty, Environmental Impact Assessment (EIA) (Armour, 1989). Even within the field of Assessment Methods specialization and diversification are common. At the same time, however, there is a push to integrate the different approaches in a more general model (Rickson, Burdge, & Armour, 1989; Berting, 1992).

Technology itself also can have an unintentionally positive effect on the integration of the different approaches, because the new information systems have the potential to store large amounts of data. These data are more and more available for scientists, planners, and politicians who have to derive meaningful information from these data. The availability of data creates the need for a frame of reference; the technology stores and distributes the data. The users of the data need theoretical models to perform optimally. The economic law of Say, explaining that supply creates demand, is also relevant for informatics and social indicators. A specification of Say's law, in our opinion, is that *data create demand for meaning*. Theories are needed to integrate the huge amount of data into meaningful models. Social scientists are being challenged to start a new social indicator movement.

In the domain of subjective indicators, some integrated trends are nowadays discernible in the work of Inglehart (1990), Halman (1991), and Ester, Halman, and De Moor (1993).

7 CONCLUDING REMARKS

Social indicators are essential for the evaluation and guidance of social developments. Since the sixties extensive research has been carried out for which social indicators have been developed. Social indicators are the result of questions raised in politics and the social sciences. As a consequence, a pragmatic approach dominated in creating information systems. The relation of the indicators to theoretical concepts often remained very limited. At first, expectations were raised that social indicators could be used to construct comprehensive social models, in which almost all sectoral domains could be taken into consideration simultaneously. Emphasis is now on the development of more limited models which use the so-called "middle-range" theories.

There are still many issues to be discussed in the social indicator movement. These include:

- The objective of social indicators. It is often argued that social indicators aim at measuring the output of social systems rather than their input. The limits are often difficult to set, however, for certain phenomena; health, for example, may function as both input and output in different models.
- The units of analysis. Social developments are ultimately evaluated by individuals. Therefore individual persons form the units of analysis in many cases. The results of research obtained in this way has to be considered in the social context to which the individuals belong. Information about this context will have to be gathered as well.
- Comparability. The cross-cultural comparability of social information is especially relevant. Identical concepts might not always

be measured identically in different social systems.

- Level of analysis. In the social indicator movement a striking distinction has grown between analyses at the macro-and micro-levels on the one hand, and at the meso-level on the other. In most of the literature on social indicators, we find discussions and data that refer to social systems or certain social sectors, like health, employment, education, etc. Moreover, many suggestions to construct social indicators refer especially to sectors or subsystems; the terms "Technology Assessment (TA), Impact Assessment(IA) and Risk Assessment (RA)" are cases in point. It seems desirable and useful to integrate the often separate developments of the various levels of analysis.

- Accessibility of data. The availability of information provides the power to guide and to control. This power should not be confined to specific groups or bodies. The access to the data that will have an impact on social developments will therefore also have to be open to all persons. Certainly in an era where the potential to manipulate data is rapidly increasing, this aspect should be given special attention.

- Data require meaning and interpretation. A variation to Say's law is applicable here. The huge amount of data, made available by information technology, creates the demand for theoretical translation of data to information. A new social indicator movement is needed. Social theory is challenged to design social frames of references for integrating the segregated assessment approaches.

REFERENCES

Andorka, R., & Harcsa, I. (1990). Modernization in Hungary in the long and short run measured by social indicators. *Social Indicators Research, 23,* Nos. 1–2 August/September, Special Issue, 1–199.

Andrews, F.M. (1974). Social indicators of perceived life quality. *Social Indicators Research, 1.*

Andrews, F.M., & Withey, S.B. (1976). *Social indicators of well-being. Americans' perceptions of their life quality.* New York: Plenum Press.

Armour, A. (1989). Integrating impact assessment in the planning process: From rhetoric to reality? International Association for Impact Assessment (IAIA): Integrating Impact Assessment into the Planning Process: International Perspectives and Experience. Special Issue: *Impact Assessment Bulletin, 8,* Nos. 1 and 2.

Barbash, J. (1976). *Job satisfaction attitudes surveys.* Paris: OECD.

Bauer, R.A. (Ed.) (1966). *Social indicators.* Cambridge, MA: MIT Press.

Beniger, J.R. (1986). *The control revolution. Technological and economic origins of the information society.* Cambridge, MA: Harvard University Press.

Berting, J. (1992). *De technologische factor* [The technological factor]. De Lier: Academisch Boeken Centrum.

Biderman, A.D., & Gross, B.M. (1966). Social indicators and goals. In R.A. Bauer (Ed.), *Social indicators.* Cambridge, MA: MIT Press.

Boesjes-Hommes, R.W. (1973). *De geldige operationalisering van begrippen.* [The valid operationalization of concepts]. Meppel: Boom.

Bundesministerium für Arbeit und Sozialordnung (1974). *Gesellschaftliche Daten,* No. 1. Bonn.

Campbell, A. (1981). *The sense of well-being in America: Recent patterns and trends.* New York: McGraw-Hill.

Campbell, A., & Converse, Ph.E. (1972). *The human meaning of social change.* New York: Russell Sage Foundation.

Campbell, A., Converse, Ph.E., & Rodgers, W.L. (1976). *The quality of American life: Perceptions, evaluations and satisfactions.* New York: Russell Sage Foundation.

Cantril, H. (1965). *The pattern of human concerns.* New Brunswick: Rutgers University Press.

Central Statistical Office (1970). *Social trends.* London: Her Majesty's Stationery Office.

Department of Health, Education and Welfare (1969). *Toward a social report.* Washington: HEW Department.

Dierkes, M., & Bauer, R.A. (Eds.) (1973). *Corporate social accounting.* New York: Praeger.

Economic Planning Agency (1973). *Whitepaper on national life 1973. The life and its quality in Japan.* Tokyo: Japanese Government.

Ester, P., & Nauta, A. (1989). Vijftien jaar sociale en culturele rapporten in Nederland [Fifteen years of social and cultural reports in The Netherlands]. *Sociale Wetenschappen, 32*(3), 176–193.

Ester, P., Halman, L., & Moor, R. de (1993) (Eds.). *The individualizing society. Value Changes in Europe and North-America.* Tilburg: Tilburg University Press.

Executive Office of the President, Office of Management and Budget (1973). *Social indicators 1973.* Washington DC: US Government Printing Office.

Finsterbusch, K., Llewellyn, L., & Wolff, C. (1983).

Social impact assessment methods. Beverly Hills: Sage.

Fox, K.A. (1974). *Social indicators and social theory. Elements of an operational system.* Chichester: John Wiley.

Gilmartin, K.J., Ross, R., Lutomski, L., & Ree, D. (1979). *Social indicators: An annotated bibliography of current literature.* New York: Garland.

Gross, B.M. (1966). Social systems accounting. In R. Bauer (Ed.), *Social indicators.* Cambridge, MA: MIT Press.

Gross, B.M. (Ed.) (1967). Social goals and indicators for American society. *Annals of the American Academy of Political and Social Science, 371* and *373.*

Halman, L. (1991). *Waarden in de Westerse Wereld. Een internationale exploratie van de waarden in de westerse samenleving* [Values in the Western World. An international exploration of values in the western society]. Tilburg: Tilburg University Press.

Harrington, H. (1994). The collapse of prevailing wisdom. In Quality: A new culture for a new Europe. *Proceedings of the 38th EOQ Annual Congress,* Lisbon, 13–17 June 1994; Vol. 2, pp. 52–58.

Inglehart, Ronald (1990). *Culture shift in advanced industrial society.* Princeton: Princeton University Press.

Institute National de la Statistique et des Etudes Economiques (INSEE) (1974). *Données Sociales 1973.* Paris.

Juster, T., & Land, K.C. (1981). *Social accounting systems: Essays on the state of the art.* New York: Academic Press.

Kerkhoff, W.H.C. (1988). "Sociale" indicatoren' ("Social" Indicators). In A.L. Knaapen (Ed.), *Methoden, technieken en analyses voor personeelsmanagement* [Methods, technics and analyses for personnel management]. afl. 5, I.6.2–1. Deventer: Kluwer.

Land, K.C. (1971). On the definition of social indicators. *American Sociologist, 6,* 322–325.

Land, K.C. (1975a). Social indicator models: An overview. In K.C. Land & S. Spilerman, *Social indicator models.* New York: Sage Foundation.

Land, K.C. (1975b). Theories, models and indicators of social change. *International Social Science Journal, 27*(1), 7–14.

Land, K.C., & Spilerman, S. (Eds.) (1975). *Social indicator models.* New York: Russell Sage Foundation.

Lustgraaf, R.E. van de, & Huigsloot, P.C.M. (1979). *Sociale indicatoren, een bewuste keuze?* [Social indicators, a conscious choice?]. Rijswijk: Social en Cultureel Planning Bureau.

Michalos, A.C. (1980). *North American social report: A comparative study of the quality of life in Canada and the U. S. A. from 1964 to 1974.* Dordrecht: Reidel.

Molenaar, J.M.A. et al. (1989). *Sociale technology assessment: Theorie en praktijk* [Social technology assessment: Theory and practice]. Universiteit van Amsterdam, Instituut voor Sociale Bedrijfs-Psychologie.

Mootz, M. (1974). Systematische maatschappij informatie in Nederland [Systematic social information in The Netherlands]. *Beleid en Maatschappij* [Policy and Society], November.

Neufville, J.I. de (1975). *Social indicators and public policy. Interactive processes of design and application.* Amsterdam/New York: Elsevier.

OECD (1973). *List of social concerns common to most OECD countries.* Paris: OECD.

OECD (1974). *Subjective elements of well-being.* Paris: OECD.

OECD (1977). *Measuring social well-being. A progress report on the development of social indicators.* Paris: OECD.

Portigal, A.H. (1976). *Toward the measurement of work satisfaction.* Paris: OECD.

Quinn, R.P. & Shepard, L.J. (1974). *The 1972–73 Quality of Employment Survey. Descriptive statistics with comparison data from the 1969–70 survey of working conditions.* Ann Arbor: Institute for Social Research.

Quinn, R.P., & Staines, G.L. (1978). *The 1977 Quality of Employment Survey: Descriptive statistics with comparison data from the 1969–70 and 1972–73 surveys.* Ann Arbor: Institute for Social Research.

Quinn, R.P., Seashore, S., Kahn, R., Mangione, T., Campbell, D., Staines, G., & McCullogh, M. (1971). *Survey of working conditions. Final report on univariate and bivariate tables.* Washington, DC: US Government Printing Office.

Report of the President's Research Committee on Social Trends (1933). *Recent social trends, Vols. I and II.* New York: McGraw-Hill.

Rickson, R., Burdge, R., & Armour, A. (1989). Future prospects for integrating impact assessment into the planning process. *Impact Assessment Bulletin, 8*(1)(2), 347–357.

Rossi, R.J., & Gilmartin, K.J. (1980). *Handbook of social indicators: Sources, characteristics and analyses.* New York: Garland STPM Press.

Rothenbacher, F. (1993). National and international approaches in social reporting. *Social Indicators Research, 29,* 1–62.

Segers. J.H.G. (1975). *Sociologische onderzoeksmethoden* [Sociological research methods]. Assen/Amsterdam: Van Gorcum.

Sheldon, E., & Moore, W. (1968). *Indicators of social change, concepts and measurements.* New York: Russell Sage Foundation.

Simonse, A., Kerkhoff, W.H.C., & Rip, A. (Eds.) (1989). *Technology assessment in ondernemingen* (Technology assessment in companies). Deventer: Kluwer.

Smits, R., Leyten, A., & Geurts, J. (1987). *The possibilities and limitations of technology assessment. In search of a useful approach.* The Hague: Dutch Ministry of Education and Science.

Sociaal en Cultureel Planbureau (1975, 1976, to 1996). *Sociaal en cultureel rapport* [Social and cultural report] 1974, 1976, to 1994). The Hague: Staatsuitgeverij.

Statistics Canada (1973). *Perspective Canada. A compendium of social statistics.* Toronto: Author.

Stockbauer, R. (1994). How to measure Total Quality Management (TQM). In Quality: A new culture for a New Europe. *Proceedings of the 38th EOQ Annual Congress*, Lisbon, 13–17 June 1994; Vol. 2, pp. 23–28.

Swanborn, P.G. (1974). Sociale indicatoren [Social indicators]. In P.G. Swanborn (Ed.), *Methoden en mensen* [Methods and people]. Rotterdam: Universitaire Pers.

Szalai, A., & Andrews, F.M. (Eds.) (1980). *The quality of life. Comparative studies.* London/Beverly Hills: Sage Publications.

Taeubner, C. (Ed.) (1978). America in the seventies: Some social indicators. *The Annals of the American Academy of Political and Social Science*, 435, January.

Taeubner, C. (Ed.) (1981). America enters the eighties: Some social indicators. *The Annals of the American Academy of Political and Social Science*, 453, January.

Terleckyj, N.E. (1975). *Improvement in the quality of life. Estimates of possibilities in the United States 1974–1983.* Washington, DC: National Planning Association.

Thierry, Hk. (1977). Sociale indicatoren: Signalen voor samenlevings-en bedrijfsbeleid [Social indicators: Signals for social and industrial policy]. In Hk. Thierry et al., *Sociale indicatoren in beweging.* [Social indicators in action]. Deventer: Kluwer.

United Nations (1975). *Toward a system of social and demographic statistics.* Department of Economic and Social Affairs, Statistical Office, Studies in Methods, Series F, No. 18. New York.

US Department of Commerce, Office of Federal Statistical Policy and Standards, and Bureau of Census (1976). *Social indicators 1976.* Washington, DC: US Government Printing Office.

Wiegand, E. (1988). Current work on the social indicators system for the Federal Republic of Germany. *Social Indicators Research*, 20, 399–416.

Wilcox, L.D., & Brooks, R.M. (Eds.) (1972). *Social indicators and social monitoring. An annotated bibliography.* Amsterdam/New York: Elsevier.

Zanders, H.L.G. (1975). Sociale indicatoren: Meetinstrumenten voor de maatschappij [Social indicators: Measuring instruments for society]. In M.R. van Gils (Ed.), *Werken en niet-werken in een veranderde samenleving* [Working and not-working in a changing society]. Amsterdam: Swets & Zeitlinger.

Zanders, H.L.G., Büchem, A.L.J. van, & Berkel, J.J.C. van (1977). *Kwaliteit van arbeid, 1977. Een onderzoek naar kenmerken van en opvattingen over arbeid en arbeidsomstandigheden* [The quality of employment in The Netherlands 1977: A survey on objective and subjective social indicators of labour and other domains], The Hague Ministry of Social Affairs/Institute for Social Research of the Tilburg University.

Zapf, W. (Ed.) (1974/5). *Soziale Indikatoren: Konzepte und Forschungsansätze, I, II, III.* Frankfurt: Herder & Herder.

Zapf, Wolfgang, & Glatzer, Wolfgang (1987). Preface to: German social report. *Social Indicator Research*, 19, 3.

Author Index

Subject Index